THE CAMBRIDGE COMPANION TO

THE ANCIENT GREEK ECONOMY

This is the most comprehensive introduction to the ancient Greek economy available in English. A team of highly distinguished specialists provides in non-technical language cutting-edge accounts of a wide range of key themes in economic history, explaining how ancient Greek economies functioned and changed, and why they were stable and successful over long periods of time. Through its wide geographical perspective, reaching from the Aegean and the Black Sea to the Near East and Egypt under Greek rule, it reflects on how economic behaviour and institutions were formed and transformed under different political, ecological, and social circumstances, and how they interacted and communicated over large distances. With chapters on climate and the environment, market development, inequality, and growth, it encourages comparisons with other periods of time and cultures, thus being of interest not just to ancient historians but also to readers concerned with economic cultures and global economic issues.

Sitta von Reden is Professor of Ancient History at the University of Freiburg. Her previous books include *Exchange in Ancient Greece* (1995), *Money in Ptolemaic Egypt* (2007), and *Money in Classical Antiquity* (2010). In 2017, she won an Advanced Grant from the European Research Council for a global economic history project entitled 'Beyond the Silk Road: Exchange, Economic Development and Inter-Imperial Relationships in the Afro-Eur~· ·ld Region (300 BCE–300 CE)'.

THE CAMBRIDGE COMPANION TO

THE ANCIENT GREEK ECONOMY

Edited by

SITTA VON REDEN

University of Freiburg

CAMBRIDGE
UNIVERSITY PRESS

CAMBRIDGE
UNIVERSITY PRESS

University Printing House, Cambridge CB2 8BS, United Kingdom

One Liberty Plaza, 20th Floor, New York, NY 10006, USA

477 Williamstown Road, Port Melbourne, VIC 3207, Australia

314–321, 3rd Floor, Plot 3, Splendor Forum, Jasola District Centre,
New Delhi – 110025, India

103 Penang Road, #05–06/07, Visioncrest Commercial, Singapore 238467

Cambridge University Press is part of the University of Cambridge.

It furthers the University's mission by disseminating knowledge in the pursuit of
education, learning, and research at the highest international levels of excellence.

www.cambridge.org
Information on this title: www.cambridge.org/9781108417266
DOI: 10.1017/9781108265249

First published 2022

A catalogue record for this publication is available from the British Library.

Library of Congress Cataloging-in-Publication Data
NAMES: Reden, Sitta von, editor.
TITLE: The Cambridge companion to the ancient Greek economy / edited by Sitta von
Reden, Albert-Ludwigs-Universität Freiburg, Germany.
DESCRIPTION: 1 Edition. | New York, NY : Cambridge University Press, [2022] | Series:
Cambridge companions to the ancient world | Includes bibliographical references and index.
IDENTIFIERS: LCCN 2022005640 (print) | LCCN 2022005641 (ebook) | ISBN 9781108417266
(hardback) | ISBN 9781108404846 (paperback) | ISBN 9781108265249 (ebook)
SUBJECTS: LCSH: Greece – Economic conditions. | Greece – History. | History, Ancient. |
BISAC: HISTORY / Ancient / General
CLASSIFICATION: LCC HC293 .C36 2022 (print) | LCC HC293 (ebook) | DDC 330.938–dc23
LC record available at https://lccn.loc.gov/2022005640
LC ebook record available at https://lccn.loc.gov/2022005641

ISBN 978-1-108-41726-6 Hardback
ISBN 978-1-108-40484-6 Paperback

CONTENTS

List of Maps	*page* viii	
Notes on the Contributors	ix	
List of Abbreviations	xiv	
Maps	xix	

1 Introduction   1
  SITTA VON REDEN

PART I DIACHRONIC PERSPECTIVES   13

2 Early Iron Age Economies   15
  IRENE S. LEMOS

3 The Archaic Period   29
  HANS VAN WEES

4 The Classical Period   49
  EMILY MACKIL

5 Hellenistic Economies   61
  SITTA VON REDEN

PART II REGIONAL PERSPECTIVES   75

6 Asia Minor   77
  ANDREAS VICTOR WALSER

7 Northern Greece and the Black Sea   94
  ZOSIA H. ARCHIBALD

8 Athens and the Aegean   106
  SYLVIAN FACHARD AND ALAIN BRESSON

9   Egypt and the Ptolemaic Empire   124
    CHRISTELLE FISCHER-BOVET

10 Hellenistic Babylonia   139
    HILMAR KLINKOTT

PART III STRUCTURES AND PROCESSES   151

11 Population   153
    BEN AKRIGG

12 Consumption, Nutrition, and the Grain Supply   172
    JOHN WILKINS

13 The Agricultural Economy   186
    DANIEL JEW

14 The Non-Agricultural Economy: Artisans, Traders,
    Women, and Slaves   202
    DANIEL JEW

15 Markets   221
    ALAIN BRESSON

16 Money, Credit, and Banking   237
    DAVID M. SCHAPS

17 Dispute Resolution   250
    KAJA HARTER-UIBOPUU

18 Taxation and Tribute   264
    ANDREW MONSON

PART IV NETWORKS   279

19 Religious Networks   281
    VÉRONIQUE CHANKOWSKI

20 Monetary Networks   298
    PETER VAN ALFEN

21 Social Networks, Associations and Trade   313
    VINCENT GABRIELSEN

PART V PERFORMANCE   329

Theoretical Approaches   331

22   Political Economy and the Growth of
Markets and Capital   331
ARMIN EICH

23   New Institutional Economics, Economic Growth,
and Institutional Change   347
SITTA VON REDEN AND BARBARA KOWALZIG

24   Regionalism, Federalism, and Mediterranean Connectivity   360
EMILY MACKIL

Empirical Approaches   373

25   Climate, Environment, and Resources   373
STURT W. MANNING

26   Technological Progress   392
SERAFINA CUOMO

27   Inequality   404
JOSIAH OBER AND WALTER SCHEIDEL

References   421
Index   478

Maps

0.1 Greece and the Aegean   *page* xix
0.2 The Black Sea   xx
0.3 Asia Minor   xxi
0.4 Egypt   xxii
0.5 Babylonia and Seleucid Iran   xxiii

Notes on the Contributors

BEN AKRIGG is Associate Professor in the Department of Classics at the University of Toronto. He is the author of *Population and Economy in Classical Athens* (2019) and the co-editor, with Rob Tordoff (York University), of *Slaves and Slavery in Ancient Greek Comic Drama* (2013).

ZOSIA H. ARCHIBALD teaches Ancient History and Classical Archaeology at the University of Liverpool. She has co-directed fieldwork at two key urban sites, Adziyska Vodenitsa (ancient Pistirus), central Bulgaria (1999–2013), and Olynthus, Chalcidice (2014–19). Her most recent book is *The Power of Individual and Community in Ancient Athens and Beyond: Essays in Honour of John K. Davies* (2019), edited with Jan Haywood.

ALAIN BRESSON is Professor at the University of Chicago. He is the author of *La cité marchande* (2001) and of *The Making of the Ancient Greek Economy* (2016), and he is preparing a new book on the role of money in ancient Greece.

VÉRONIQUE CHANKOWSKI is Director of the French School of Athens and Professor of Ancient Economy and Aegean History at the University of Lyon 2. As an epigraphist who also works with archaeological sources, she has published several studies on the ancient Greek economy. Her most recent book is *Parasites du dieu. Comptables, financiers et commerçants dans la Délos hellénistique* (2019).

SERAFINA CUOMO is Professor of Ancient History at Durham University. She has written on the history of mathematics and technology in antiquity. She is currently completing a book on numeracy in ancient Greece and Rome.

ARMIN EICH is Professor of Ancient History at the University of Wuppertal and has published a comprehensive monograph on the ancient Greek economy, *Die politische Ökonomie des antiken*

Griechenland (2006). His main interests include the history of ancient economies, especially the interdependence of fiscal, economic, political, and military structures, war and peace in antiquity, and ancient literature and epigraphy.

SYLVIAN FACHARD is Professor of Classical Archaeology at the University of Lausanne and Director of the Swiss School of Archaeology in Greece. He published *La défense du territoire* (2012) and is preparing a book on the borders of Attica while working on the publication of the Mazi Archaeological Project (Attica).

CHRISTELLE FISCHER-BOVET is Associate Professor of Classics and History at the University of Southern California. She specialises in the social and cultural history of the eastern Mediterranean from Alexander the Great to the Romans, with a special interest in Greco-Roman Egypt. Her book *Army and Society in Ptolemaic Egypt* (2014) combines documentary evidence with social theory to examine the role of the army in Hellenistic Egypt. She also co-edited with Sitta von Reden *Comparing the Ptolemaic and Seleucid Empires, Integration, Communication and Resistance* (2021).

VINCENT GABRIELSEN is Professor of Ancient History at the Saxo Institute of the University of Copenhagen and a member of the Royal Danish Academy of Sciences and Letters. His research interests include economic and maritime history and the history of private associations.

KAJA HARTER-UIBOPUU earned her PhD at the University of Graz, subsequently working at the Department of Roman Law and Legal History as well as at the Austrian Academy of Sciences in Vienna. Since 2015, she has been Professor of Ancient History at the University of Hamburg. She has published widely on Greek epigraphy and ancient legal history, especially concerning the Law of Procedure in the Greek *poleis*.

DANIEL JEW is Senior Lecturer in History and Director of Studies at the College of Alice & Peter Tan within the National University of Singapore. He is co-editor of *M. I. Finley: An Ancient Historian and His Impact* (2016) and author of a forthcoming monograph, *The Probable Past: Agriculture and Carrying Capacity in Ancient Greece*.

HILMAR KLINKOTT is Professor of Ancient History at the University of Kiel. His main fields of research are the history and administration of the Achaemenid, Ptolemaic, and Seleucid empires.

He is author of *Der Satrap, ein achaimenidischer Amtsträger* (2002) and co-edited most recently, with J. Wiesehöfer and S. Balatti, *Paleopersepolis: Environment, Landscape and Society in Ancient Fars* (2021).

BARBARA KOWALZIG is Associate Professor of Classics and History at New York University. Her particular interest is in the role of religion in the social and economic transformation of the ancient world. She is the author of *Singing for the Gods: Performances of Myth and Ritual in Archaic and Classical Greece* (2007) and is currently completing a book project entitled *Gods around the Pond: Religion, Society and the Sea in the Early Mediterranean Economy*.

IRENE S. LEMOS is Professor of Classical Archaeology and Fellow of Merton College, Oxford. She is the director of the excavations at Lefkandi in Euboea and has published on the archaeology of Late Bronze and Iron Age Greece. Recently, she has co-edited *The Companion to the Archaeology of Early Greece and the Mediterranean* (with Antonis Kotsonas, 2020) and *Beyond the Polis: Ritual, Rites and Cults in Early and Archaic Greece (12th–6th Centuries BC)* (with Athena Tsingarida, 2019).

EMILY MACKIL is Associate Professor of History at the University of California, Berkeley. She is the author of *Creating a Common Polity: Religion, Economy, and Politics in the Making of the Greek Koinon* (2013). She has written extensively on topics that explore the intersection of political and economic history throughout Greek antiquity, including federalism, monetary production, and property confiscation.

STURT W. MANNING is Distinguished Professor of Arts and Sciences in Classics, Cornell University. He is Director of the Cornell Tree Ring Laboratory. He is also a professor at the Cyprus Institute. For details of his publications, see https://cornell.academia.edu/SturtWManning.

ANDREW MONSON is Associate Professor of Classics at New York University. He is the author of *From the Ptolemies to the Romans: Political and Economic Change in Egypt* (2012) and *Agriculture and Taxation in Early Ptolemaic Egypt* (2012), and he is the co-editor with Walter Scheidel of *Fiscal Regimes and the Political Economy of Premodern States* (2015). His current projects are an edition of early Ptolemaic administrative papyri and a monograph on fiscal regimes in the ancient world.

JOSIAH OBER is Constantine Mitsotakis Professor of Political Science and Classics at Stanford University. He is the author of *Demopolis: Democracy before Liberalism in Theory and Practice* (2017), *The Rise and Fall of Classical Greece* (2015), *Democracy and Knowledge* (2008), *Political Dissent in Democratic Athens* (2008), *Mass and Elite in Democratic Athens* (1989), and other books on democracy and on political thought, ancient and modern.

DAVID M. SCHAPS, Emeritus Professor of Classical Studies at Bar-Ilan University and past president of the Israel Society for the Promotion of Classical Studies, is the author of *Economic Rights of Women in Ancient Greece* (1997), *The Invention of Coinage and the Monetization of Ancient Greece* (2004), *Handbook for Classical Research* (2010), numerous articles, and a number of mostly unpublished Greek and Latin poems.

WALTER SCHEIDEL is Dickason Professor in the Humanities at Stanford University. His research covers ancient social and economic history, premodern historical demography, and the comparative and transdisciplinary world history of labour, inequality, state formation, and human welfare. His 2017 book *The Great Leveler* surveys the history of economic inequality from the beginnings to the present.

PETER VAN ALFEN is Chief Curator at the American Numismatic Society in New York City. He has published widely on archaic, classical, and Hellenistic Greek numismatics and on ancient Mediterranean fiscal, trade, and monetary systems. In addition, he co-directs several online resources for ancient numismatics, including Hellenistic Royal Coinages (numismatics.org/hrc).

HANS VAN WEES is Grote Professor of Ancient History at University College London. He is the author of *Ships and Silver, Taxes and Tribute: A Fiscal History of Archaic Athens* (2013) and co-editor of *A Companion to Archaic Greece* (with Kurt Raaflaub, 2009) and *Archaic Greece: New Evidence and New Approaches* (with Nick Fisher, 1998).

SITTA VON REDEN is Professor of Ancient History at the University of Freiburg. She has published widely on the Greek economy, including *Money in Ptolemaic Egypt* (2007) and *Money in Classical Antiquity* (2010). She is currently running an interdisciplinary research project leading to a multi-volume *Handbook of Ancient Afro-Eurasian Economies*, of which two volumes appeared in 2019 and 2021.

ANDREAS VICTOR WALSER is Professor for the History of Ancient Cultures from the Eastern Mediterranean to the Near East at the University of Zurich. Focussing on the social, legal, and economic history of the Hellenistic world, he is author of *Bauern und Zinsnehmer. Politik, Recht und Wirtschaft im frühhellenistischen Ephesos* (2008). He is also a Greek epigraphist editing the inscriptions of Pergamum.

JOHN WILKINS is Emeritus Professor of Greek Culture at the University of Exeter. He currently works on Galen's nutrition and pharmacology.

ABBREVIATIONS

Abbreviations of ancient authors and texts follow those used by the *Oxford Classical Dictionary* (3rd edition).

ALBL	*The Arshama Letters from the Bodleian Library*, 2013.
ARV²	J. D. Beazley, *Attic Red-Figure Vase-Painters*, 1963 (2nd ed.).
ATL	*The Athenian Tribute Lists*, 1939–53.
BCHP	*Babylonian Chronographic Texts from the Hellenistic Period*, 2020.
BGU	*Ägyptische Urkunden aus den Königlichen Museen zu Berlin, Griechische Urkunden*, 1895– .
BM	*The Collection of the British Museum*
BNJ	*Brill's New Jacoby*, 2007–19.
C.Ord.Ptol.	*Corpus des ordonnances des Ptolémées*, 1964.
CAPInv.	*The Inventory of Ancient Associations*, 2011–16.
Clara Rhodos	*Clara Rhodos. Studi e materiali pubblicati a cura dell'Istituto storico-archeologico di Rodi*, 1928–41.
CT	*Cuneiform Texts from Babylonian Tablets in the British Museum*, 1896– .
Davies, *APF*	J. K. Davies, *Athenian Propertied Families 600–300 b.c*, 1971.
DGE	*Dialectorum Graecarum exempla epigraphica potiora*, 1923.

DK	H. Diels and W. Kranz, *Fragmente der Vorsokratiker*, 1952 (6th ed.).
FD iii	*Fouilles de Delphes iii. Epigraphie*, 1900– .
FGrH	F. Jacoby, *Fragmente der griechischen Historiker*, 1923– .
IACP	M. H. Hansen and T. H. Nielsen (eds.), *An Inventory of Archaic and Classical Poleis*, 2004.
IC	*Inscriptiones Creticae*, 1935–50.
IDélos	*Inscriptions de Délos*, 1923–37.
IdI	*Inschriften von den dorischen Inseln*, 1969.
IEphesos i	*Die Inschriften von Ephesos*, 1979.
IErythrai und Klazomenai	*Die Inschriften von Erythrai und Klazomenai*, 1972–3.
IG	*Inscriptiones Graecae*, 1873– .
IGBulg.	*Inscriptiones Graecae in Bulgaria repertae*, 1958–70.
IGCH	*Recueil des inscriptions grecques-chrétiennes d'Asie Mineure*, 1922.
IGerasa	C. B. Welles, 'The Inscriptions', in *Gerasa: City of the Decapolis*, ed. C. H. Kraeling, 1938: 355–494, 573–616.
IHistria	*Inscriptiones Daciae et Scythiae Minoris antiquae. Series altera: Inscriptiones Scythiae Minoris graecae et latinae. Vol. 1: Inscriptiones Histriae et vicinia*, 1983.
IIasos	*Die Inschriften von Iasos*, 1985.
IKalchedon	*Die Inschriften von Kalchedon*, 1980.
IKallatis	*Inscriptiones Daciae et Scythiae Minoris antiquae. Series altera: Inscriptiones Scythiae Minoris graecae et latinae. Vol. 3: Callatis et territorium*, 2000.
IKaunos	*Die Inschriften von Kaunos*, 2006.
ILabraunda	*Labraunda Swedish Excavations and Researches 3: The Greek Inscriptions*, 1969–72.

ILindos ii Lindos. *Fouilles et recherches, 1902–14. Vol. ii: Inscriptions, 1941.*

IMagn. *Die Inschriften von Magnesia am Maeander, 1900.*

IMylasa *Die Inschriften von Mylasa, 1987–8.*

IOropos *Hoi Epigraphes tou Oropou, 1997.*

IPaneion *Le Paneion d'El-Kanaïs. Les inscriptions grecques, 1972.*

IParion *Die Inschriften von Parion, 1983.*

IPE *Inscriptiones antiquae Orae Septentrionalis Ponti Euxini graecae et latinae, 1885.*

IPriene *Die Inschriften von Priene, 2014.*

IProse *La Prose sur pierre dans l'Égypte hellénistique et romaine, 1992.*

ISardis *Sardis, VII. Greek and Latin Inscriptions, 1932.*

ISultan dağı *The Inscriptions of the Sultan Dagi, 2002– .*

IThracAeg. *Epigraphes tes Thrakes tou Aigaiou: metaxy ton potamon Nestou kai Hevrou, 2005.*

LSCG *Lois sacrées des cités grecques, 1969.*

Maiuri, *NSER* A. Maiuri, *Nuova silloge epigrafica di Rodi e Cos, 1925.*

Meiggs, *AE* R. Meiggs, *The Athenian Empire, 1972.*

Milet *Milet: Ergebnisse der Ausgrabungen und Untersuchungen seit dem Jahre 1899, 1906–.*

ML R. Meiggs and D. Lewis, *A Selection of Greek Historical Inscriptions to the End of the Fifth Century* BC, 1988 (rev. ed.).

MMA *Cuneiform Texts in The Metropolitan Museum of Art, 1988– .*

OGIS *Orientis Graeci Inscriptiones Selectae, 1903–5.*

P.Agri. *Agriculture and Taxation in Early Ptolemaic Egypt: Demotic Land Surveys and Accounts (P. Agri), 2012.*

P.Cair.Zen.	*Zenon Papyri, Catalogue général des antiquités égyptiennes du Musée du Caire,* 1925–31.
P.Dura	*The Excavations at Dura-Europos Conducted by Yale University and the French Academy of Inscriptions and Letters Final Report 5, Part. 1: The Parchments and Papyri,* 1959.
P.Enteuxeis	*Enteuxeis: requêtes et plaintes adressées au roi d'Egypte au IIIe siècle avant J.-C.,* 1931.
P.Gurob	*Greek Papyri from Gurob,* 1921.
P.Hal.	*Dikaiomata. Auszüge aus den alexandrinischen Gesetzen und Verordnungen in einem Papyrus des Philologischen Seminars der Universität Halle,* 1913.
P.Haun.	*Papyri graecae haunienses,* 1942– .
P.Köln	*Kölner Papyri,* 1964– .
P.Lips.	*Griechische Urkunden der Papyrussammlung zu Leipzig,* 1906– .
P.Mich.	*Michigan Papyri,* 1931– .
P.Oxy.	*Oxyrhynchus Papyri,* 1898– .
P.Stras.	*Griechische Papyri der Kaiserlichen Universitäts- und Landesbibliothek zu Strassburg,* 1912– .
P.Tebt.	*Tebtunis Papyri,* 1902–76.
Page, *PMG*	D. L. Page, *Poetae Melici Graeci,* 1962.
PCG	*Poetae Comici Graeci,* 1983– .
PSI	*Papiri greci e latini della Società Italiana,* 1912– .
RC	C. B. Wells, *Royal Correspondence in the Hellenistic Period. A Study in Greek Epigraphy,* 1934.
Sarkisan, *Forschungen und Berichte*	G. K. Sarkisan, 'New Cuneiform Texts from Uruk of the Seleucid Period in the Staatliche Museen zu Berlin', *Forschungen und Berichte* 16, 1974: 15–76.

SB	*Sammelbuch griechischer Urkunden aus Ägypten,* 1915– .
SEG	*Supplementum Epigraphicum Graecum,* 1923– .
StV	*Die Staatsverträge des Altertums,* 1898– .
Syll.[3]	*Sylloge Inscriptionum Graecarum,* 1915–24 (3rd ed.).
TAM	*Tituli Asiae Minoris,* 1878– .
West, *IE*[2]	M. L. West, *Iambi et elegi Graeci ante Alexandrum cantati,* 1998.
YOS	*Yale Oriental Series,* 1915– .

Maps

MAP O.I Greece and the Aegean

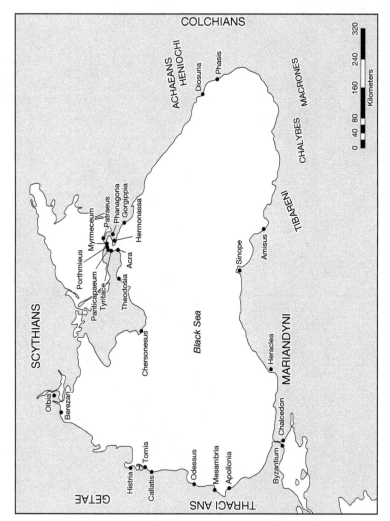

MAP 0.2 The Black Sea

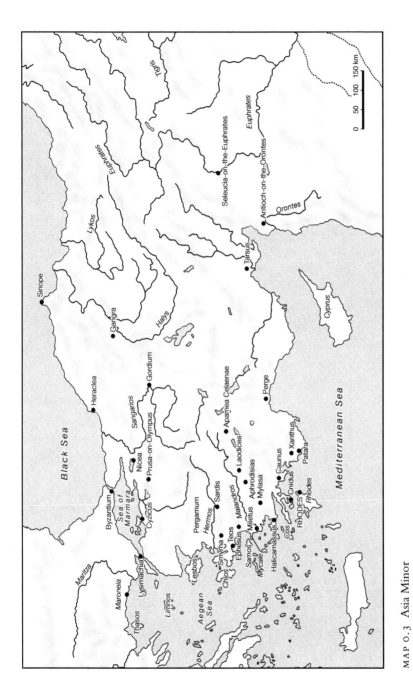

MAP O.3 Asia Minor

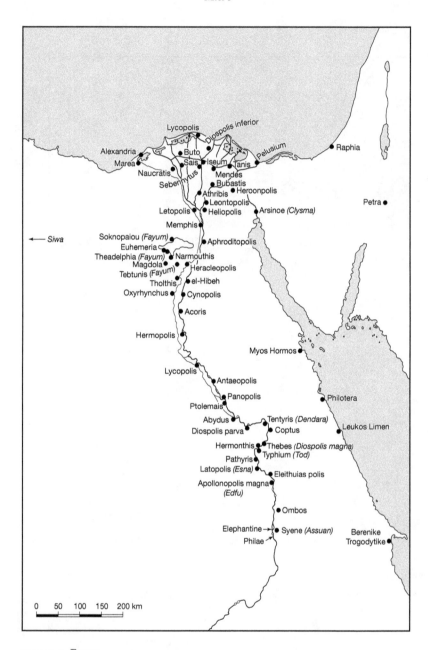

MAP O.4 Egypt

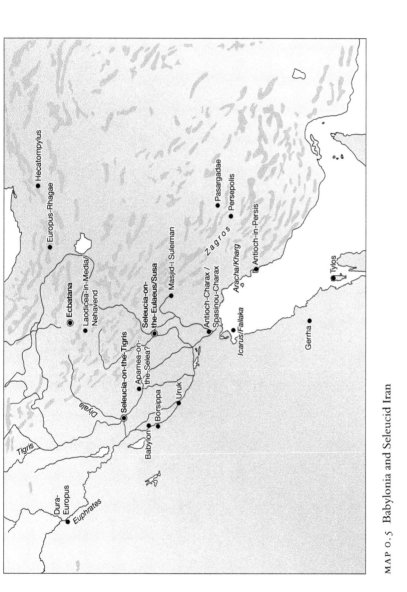

MAP 0.5 Babylonia and Seleucid Iran

1: Introduction

Sitta von Reden

The judgement of antiquity about wealth was fundamentally unequivocal and uncomplicated. Wealth was necessary and it was good; it was an absolute requisite for the good life; and on the whole that was all there was to it.

Moses Finley, *The Ancient Economy* (1999)

Archaic and classical Hellas, taken as a whole, was a wealthier place than most historians once imagined. Indeed, late classical Athens (and perhaps other advanced poleis of the fourth century BC) appears to have been among the most prosperous communities of premodernity.

Josiah Ober, *Wealthy Hellas* (2010b).

The opening quotations could not be more different in approach and content. For the Cambridge historian Moses Finley (1912–1986), wealth in the ancient economy was for kings, emperors, aristocrats, and rich landlords to hold and cherish. It was the foundation of what they would have called *eudaimonia*, a good state of mind, which was a social and moral category. In great contrast, the Stanford historian Josiah Ober describes wealth in terms of general standards of living in ancient Greece. The Greek economy produced wealth for many to share.[1] The GDP of Greek cities, had it been calculated, would have been greater than that of many other premodern states. Such a high level of prosperity would not have been achieved without a great number of people caring about profit – neither a good nor bad thing, but a natural human priority. For Finley, wealth was a matter of fact and of the status of social elites. For Ober, it was a collective achievement, and the

---

[1] In the following, Greek economy always refers to the ancient Greek economy. All dates are BCE, unless stated otherwise. Some exceptions are made for clarification, or if a date sits uneasily next to another number.

question economic historians needed to answer was how this achievement had become possible.[2]

Moses Finley argued that the ancient Greeks did not have a concept of what we call an economy. *Oikonomia* was household management, a field of knowledge for landowners rich enough to employ a bailiff, control slaves and manage the tasks of the head of a large *oikos* (household). *Oikonomia* was separated conceptually and socially from any manual labour, from monetary trade and from commercial markets. It was driven by concerns about social status and good behaviour rather than productivity and economic profit. A society that produced such a field of knowledge rather than anything comparable to Adam Smith's *Enquiry into the Wealth of Nations* was not concerned with labour as a productive activity, money as a means of exchange, or wealth creation as a collective purpose. The majority of people were small landowners who had just enough to feed themselves and their families. There was therefore not much scope, nor indeed interest, in economic development. The supply of large cities, like Athens, Alexandria, or Rome, was exceptional, based on imperialism and tribute, not on free markets and trade. The ancient economy had little in common with the economies of the modern period.[3]

Josiah Ober states the opposite. In a broad study of democracy and economic growth in ancient Greece, he contends that the difference between pre-modern and modern economies had been overstated.[4] Although probably unintentionally, Greek city states had in fact left sufficient economic data and proxy indices that revealed outstanding economic performance and development from the archaic period onwards.[5] There were good reasons for the economic success of ancient Greece. The internal organization of poleis into bodies of citizens equal before the law encouraged collective decision-making based on large amounts of information and knowledge that circulated publicly. The cooperation and competition of these small to mid-size states in the Aegean as a whole, moreover, encouraged trade and exchange. Along similar lines, Alain Bresson argued that the city-state structure of the ancient Greek world fostered local specialization and interstate exchange, leading to local capital accumulation, investment, and innovation.[6]

---

[2] See Chapter 27 below and Ober 2010b, 2015b.
[3] Finley's ideas are discussed further by Eich, Chapter 22, and Cuomo, Chapter 26, in this volume.
[4] Ober 2015a.   [5] See also Chapter 27 in this volume.   [6] Bresson 2016a.

The discrepancy between the approaches of Finley and Ober/ Bresson stands in a long intellectual tradition that has grappled with the question of how the ancient economy compared to that of the present. August Boeck, a classical philologist who pioneered ancient Greek economic history in the early nineteenth century, wrote his *Staatshaushaltung der Athener* (1817, quickly translated into English as *The Public Economy of Athens*, 1827) in light of the emerging capitalist economies of Western nation states and their theoretical reflection in Scottish Enlightenment philosophy.[7] Well into the eighteenth century, economic thought had been locked into a conceptual, social, and moral distinction between agriculture and aristocratic wealth, which were regarded as good, and commerce associated with social outsiders driven by base profit-seeking; this prevented the unbiased perception of production, consumption, and trade as connected processes.[8] It was only in the Scottish Enlightenment (to which Adam Smith belonged) that there developed a unified concept of political economy according to which production, consumption, and exchange were connected through markets. The invisible hand of the market that coordinated supply and demand was the best way of generating general prosperity within national economies.[9] This market model and the underlying principle that humans by nature act in their own, profit-oriented interest henceforth were regarded as universally valid.

However, the universalizing claims of classical economic theory did not meet with blanket approval. In the following decades and centuries, both economists and historians engaged critically with these claims and proposed different analytical frames for pre-modern and non-capitalist economies. Moreover, the increasingly mathematical methodologies that were developed in neo-classical economics from the late nineteenth century onwards raised doubts as to whether ancient societies left sufficient quantitative data to be subjected to the analyses that contemporary economic theory requires.[10]

THE SCOPE OF THIS VOLUME

The ancient Greek economy is thus a contested field, both in terms of its nature and the methodologies applied to its research. The international

---

[7] See the following: von Reden 2015; von Reden and Speidel 2019.
[8] Burkhardt, Oexle, and Spahn 1992 for an excellent survey of the intellectual history of economic thought and concepts.
[9] Eich, Chapter 22, in this volume.
[10] See, for further discussion, the chapters in Part V of this volume.

team of authors of this volume take different views on these issues, but together they represent a broad range of current approaches, methodologies and perspectives. The chapters are grouped into different sections that approach the Greek economy within different temporal, geographical and analytical dimensions. The volume starts with diachronic surveys that focus on developments within and across the periods of Greek history. The second section looks at economies in several significant sub-regions in order to showcase local variation within an economy whose unity has often been questioned. The third section establishes major structures that shaped economic processes and behaviour despite regional variation. The fourth section suggests new ways of looking at economic connectivity beyond the market principle. The chapters of the final section take up the question of development and performance again: which theoretical models are best suited to capture the economic development in ancient Greek economies, which methodologies can be applied to their analysis, and how can we assess what modern economists call economic performance?

TIME AND SPACE

The first millennium BCE can be regarded as the central period of ancient Greek economic history.[11] Yet this chronological slice is somewhat arbitrary, as it is based on disciplinary conventions that developed long before economic history became part of the academic field of ancient history. Neither the beginning of the Early Iron Age, which made its appearance in different regions of the Mediterranean from about 1200 BCE onwards, nor the victory of the Roman general Octavian over the last Hellenistic queen in 31 BCE, created abrupt economic change. While some violent disruption destroyed the palatial centres in Greece and the Aegean at the beginning of the eleventh century, the disruption did not wipe out local economic structures entirely, and some of these structures continued to influence the ways Greek economies developed after the Early Iron Age (Lemos, Chapter 2). At the other end of the period,

---

[11] There are good reasons for including the Near East in the Greek economy from the Hellenistic period onwards, if not much earlier (J. G. Manning 2018). Several chapters therefore reach far beyond what might reasonably called the Mediterranean. Chapters on the Greek economies in the western Mediterranean (as they developed in southern Italy, Sicily, North Africa, Spain, and France as a result of Greek migration) are excluded only for the sake of limiting the size of this volume. The conventional end of the Hellenistic period in 30 BCE is also disputable, as many social, cultural, and economic patterns of the Hellenistic economy extended well into the Roman imperial period; see most recently Chaniotis 2018.

Roman economic presence in the eastern Mediterranean did not start with the conquest of Egypt but reached back far into the early second century. The economies of the Greek-speaking world were transformed gradually as a result of political change, without transformation being felt to the same extent in each part of that world at the same time. Economies have their own temporal structures. They respond only gradually, and variably, to political change.

The geographical extent of the Greek economy calls equally for clarification. From the archaic period onwards, Greeks settled across the eastern and western Mediterranean as well as along the coasts of the Black Sea. At the beginning of the Hellenistic period, the Macedonian king Alexander conquered the Persian empire, which reached to the Hindu Kush in Central Asia and Egypt in Africa, and intensified links to the maritime spaces of the Red Sea, Persian Gulf, and Indian Ocean.[12] Greek soldiers and civilian immigrants settled in the conquered lands, and the new kings introduced administrative structures, legal infrastructures, and coinages that were recognizably Greek. Yet neither can the economies of the Hellenistic empires nor the economy of the ancient Mediterranean be compared to what we might call the 'British' or 'US' economies.[13] They did not form a political and economic unit comparable to that of modern nation states. Nevertheless, in the course of the archaic period, the communities that spread across the Mediterranean and the Black Sea developed some common economic patterns (van Wees, Chapter 3), and the newly founded cities and settlements in the Hellenistic period shared some of these patterns as well. The notion of the 'unity' of the ancient Greek economy raises a number of problems, but there are good reasons to regard the eastern Mediterranean, Asia Minor and the Black Sea as its central locations.[14]

The effects of the expansion of the Greek economy in the Hellenistic period are more problematic.[15] Arguably, only a thin veneer of Greekness spread across the new imperial regions, many of which broke away from Greek rule in the course of the third and second centuries BCE.[16] The degree to which Greek impact was recognizable in the political cores of the Hellenistic empires in Mesopotamia and Egypt is discussed in Chapters 9 and 10 of this volume. The Mediterranean

---

[12] J. G. Manning 2018 for the importance of these spaces in the *longue durée*.
[13] For the difference between national and imperial economies, now Haldon 2021.
[14] For the Mediterranean as a distinct ecological and economic space, Horden and Purcell 2000, which has stimulated numerous further studies; for discussion of the approach, W. V. Harris 2005.
[15] Morris, Saller, and Scheidel 2007.   [16] Fabian 2019; L. Morris 2019.

remained the cultural and symbolic homeland of the Hellenistic empires, yet economic centres moved from mainland Greece and the Aegean to the Levantine and Egyptian coasts, where Antioch and Alexandria became important crossroads between the Mediterranean and the Asian and African hinterlands. Several chapters of this volume include the economies of these spaces in the Hellenistic period, yet it should be kept in mind that many local economic structures remained in place in the Hellenistic empires despite their Greek domination.

DIACHRONIC PERSPECTIVES

The surveys of Part I of the Companion discuss major economic developments in the Greek world from the Early Iron Age to the end of the Hellenistic period. They offer the opportunity to comprehend key economic developments within their social, political, and historical contexts, and how these contexts led to particular dynamics of change. The chapters are divided along the conventional periods of ancient Greek history, which again may need some justification. Poleis, and the political relationships formed by their particular kind of connectivity, dominated Greece and the Aegean from the late eighth century onwards and remained so until the Hellenistic period when new regions and forms of social organization became part of what we may call the Greek economy. While the political organization of the polis remained a strong factor in the Hellenistic period, these poleis were now part of overarching imperial structures. The Greek economies before and after the era of the polis were thus rather different from those of the archaic and classical period and also require a different range of questions and analytical tools. While the interpretation of changing sets of archaeological data is the main challenge in writing the economic history of the Early Iron Age, as Lemos demonstrates in Chapter 2, the principal question raised by the Hellenistic economy is how and to what extent the Greek economies of the Mediterranean benefitted from their greater connection with Asia and Egypt (von Reden, Chapter 5).

The archaic period saw major economic change across the Mediterranean, such as the concentration of wealth among a predatory elite in the late eighth century, the expansion of trade and the rise of a middling class that exercised self-control over its predatory behaviour in the seventh and sixth centuries, and finally, the emergence of coined money and greater local specialization of production and trade at the end of this period (van Wees, Chapter 3). Agrarian and monetary systems remained rather unchanged in the classical period, as Mackil points out in Chapter 4. Yet significant demographic growth in the Aegean went in tandem with significant economic changes: trade and specialized local production increased, while at the same time poleis began to control the trade in vital commodities, especially grain, in order to feed their growing populations. As a result of the outstanding silver resources of Athens and the tributary structures of the Delian League, Athenian coinage became the dominant currency in the Aegean, which increased monetization and, as a result of this and increasing trade, credit finance. If we accept the scenario developed by Ober and Scheidel in the final chapter of this volume, the economy of Greek poleis reached the peak of its performance by the end of the classical period.

REGIONAL PERSPECTIVES

The Mediterranean ecology, with its numerous microclimates and local resources, created specific human responses and economic dynamics. It favoured local specialization and division of labour, yet at the same time encouraged connectivity across the relatively short distances between islands and along the benign Mediterranean coasts.[17] Most economic activity in antiquity took place at either a local or a regional level.[18] Local populations were not fully self-sufficient; nor were their demand and supply structures strong enough to coordinate production and consumption across large imperial spaces. Yet, the question of what constitutes a region – a spatial dimension between the local and imperial – has been much debated.[19] An economic region is not just a geographical entity, although geographical proximity, social neighbourhood, and ecological similarity are likely to have contributed to the formation of economic ties and networks at supra-local levels. Other factors were equally, if not more, important for the formation of economic regions. Most important were political alliances created by diplomacy and contractual agreement, as Mackil discusses in Chapter 24, frequently encouraged by sentiments of ethnic and religious commonalities, which fostered regular interaction and relationships between particular social groups.[20]

The chapters of this section therefore adopt both a geographical and political focus on regionality. The first three contributions deal with economic regions that were part of the Greek world before its expansion

---

[17] Horden and Purcell 2000; Bresson 2016a.   [18] Reger 2011, 368.
[19] Reger 2011 and 2013 on regionalism.   [20] Reger 2013.

into Asia and Egypt. Athens and the Aegean assumed some centrality in the regional interplay of local Greek economies. Asia Minor, northern Greece, and the Black Sea regions, in contrast, were more peripheral from a political (and disciplinary) point of view. Yet they were economically powerful as well. The two chapters on these regions show in what ways their economies played important roles in the Mediterranean, yet at the same time formed specifically local networks of exchange including those with non-Greek continental hinterlands. The other two chapters of this section look at regions under Graeco-Macedonian domination in the Hellenistic period. Both Egypt and Babylonia became part of the Greek fiscal-military regime after the Macedonian conquest, but their economies continued to be influenced by their specific ecological conditions and social organization. Large tracks of land were under the control of temples and kings rather than being held as private property by independent farmers. These chapters therefore have the particular purpose of showing the transformation of non-Greek economies in regional contexts, when Greek economic practices met with local social and ecological systems not typical of the Greek world.

ECONOMIC STRUCTURES AND PROCESSES

Structures are the anatomy of an economy. If we want to understand economic change, we need to understand the structures within which change unfolds. Typically, economic structures are understood in terms of the institutions and practices that shape consumption, production, and distribution.[21] Consumption, production, and distribution are constrained by demographic conditions and by fiscal extraction that takes away some of the economic surplus. Conversely, changes in population, settlement, and demographic structure are good indices of economic change. Forms of taxation influence people's economic behaviour as well as the relative power of private (non-state) and state economic activity.

Part III thus starts with a discussion of demography and ends with taxation, framing chapters on an economy's most central purposes: satisfying consumption through production and distribution. The vast majority of people in antiquity were concerned with the consumption and provision of food and other nutrients (Wilkins, Chapter 12). Grain was the most important staple, and ancient states made great efforts to

---

[21] Morris, Saller, and Scheidel 2007.

ease trade when grain was in short supply locally. In most poleis, agriculture was the dominant productive activity (Jew, Chapter 13; Athens may have been an exception, as Fachard and Bresson argue in Chapter 8). Non-agricultural activities were usually subordinate to the food sector, but this does not make the non-agrarian economy a subordinate topic of ancient economic history (Jew, Chapter 14). While it may be debatable which economic activity drove economic change in antiquity, it is uncontroversial that manufacture and the consumption of non-agricultural products were the most important stimulants of market exchange. Bresson (Chapter 15) and Schaps (Chapter 16) discuss the nature of markets and money in the Greek economy, their scope and limitations, as well as their key role for the connectivity of the Mediterranean and beyond. Harter-Uibopuu in Chapter 17 asks in what ways economic exchange could benefit from a legal infrastructure capable of effective conflict resolution.

NETWORKS

The development of regional and interregional economic relationships and exchange is dependent not just on geographical proximity and political connections but also on social and religious ties that develop quite independently of geography and politics. A socio-economic network is a web of relationships that does not require a state or any other political organization to develop. Networks emerge from regular social interaction, common religious practices, sentiments of kinship, and any other kind of interaction including regular economic exchange; they might connect social groups and populations over large distances.[22] Network approaches to interaction and exchange have been quite popular in recent research, as they bring into focus the multiple layers and interests involved in relationships of exchange.[23] In economic archaeology, they were introduced in order to describe the movement of goods and people without prejudicing the motivations and mechanism of such movements.[24] Yet as Gabrielsen shows in Chapter 21, network relationships, even if predominantly social, are likely to stimulate commercial exchange and markets, as they create social environments of trust and

---

[22] Network approaches in ancient history are discussed and explored in Malkin, Constantakopoulou, and Panagopoulou 2007a; Malkin, Constantakopoulou, and Panagopoulou 2007b; Malkin 2011; and Taylor and Vlassopoulos 2015.

[23] Malkin, Constantakopoulou, and Panagopoulou 2007b.

[24] Knappett 2013;Leidwanger and Knappett 2018; Brosseder 2015; see also Chapter 20 for various methodological directions.

fairness where formal law fails to protect the interests of the exchanging partners.[25]

The three chapters in this section adopt qualitative network approaches rather than formal network analysis. In Greek antiquity, *koinoniai* (associations of various kinds) were social and religious organizations that fulfilled important economic network functions but expressed their commonalities in very specific ways. Chankowski in Chapter 19 and Gabrielsen in Chapter 21 focus on religious and social networks that were based on presumed kinship, ethnicity, common mythical pasts, or common cults. Van Alfen (Chapter 20) reconstructs networks through numismatic evidence. He explores the scale and direction of Greek monetary networks, the agents that formed their nodes, and the range of transactions that linked the nodes. As van Alfen demonstrates, coins represent particularly complex and variable network relationships. They could be created intentionally by coin issuers that aimed to forge particular alliances. Alternatively, individual coins represent the traces that individual coin users left of their monetary transactions, that is, the links that formed in the course of various economic and social practices. Network perspectives offer new methodologies for analysing new bodies of evidence and are likely to offer great opportunities for research in the future.

PERFORMANCE

Ancient economic performance and its constraints are crucial questions for comparative historical analyses. How effectively did the institutions and structures of the ancient economy fulfil their main purpose, which may be regarded as lying in satisfying and increasing general standards of living (see Ober in the opening quotation of this chapter)? Yet establishing relevant indices and data for demonstrating economic growth in ancient societies is problematic, and the methodologies that have been offered as a substitute for the lack of data are by no means uncontroversial. In the absence of sufficient amounts of data by means of which economic growth can be assessed, arguments tend to start from the growth of particular institutions, especially markets and the circulation of coined money, that are likely to have stimulated growth. The debates over these questions go back to an important controversy that developed from Moses Finley's provocative argument about the

---

[25] See also Terpstra 2019.

absence of a market economy in antiquity. Although Finley of course did not deny the presence of marketplaces and coins in the ancient world, he argued that they did not fulfil the functions that modern economic theory attributed to them.[26] The sociologist and historian of the Roman economy Keith Hopkins, in contrast, argued that, in the Roman empire, genuine market exchange and thus the circulation of goods and money did increase significantly. Economic growth manifested itself in population growth, an increase of areas under cultivation, an increase in surplus production, and the capacity of provincial economies to pay significant amounts of monetary tribute to the imperial centre.[27] Hopkins did not only advance a new argument, and methodology, for assessing economic growth in the Roman economy, but he also argued that this economy was 'integrated' by a combination of factors. The Roman economy gradually grew into a political economy that could be compared to those of modern states. The controversy between Finley and Hopkins was dubbed quite inadequately the 'primitivism vs modernism' debate. Yet Finley did not advocate a primitive ancient economy, nor Hopkins any modernity of this economy. Rather, they debated the capacity of the ancient (and in Hopkins's version Roman) economy for real growth, that is, increase of per capita productivity. He suggested a range of factors that contributed to such growth and a quantifying methodology through which his argument could be proved.[28]

Historians of the Greek economy were more reluctant to accept the argument of growth, as the economies of the archaic and classical city states were not driven by similar military and fiscal forces to those generated by the Roman imperial regime.[29] Yet over the past twenty years, evidence and arguments that question Finley's economic stagnation model have greatly increased.[30] The chapters of Parts I to IV well reflect this change of consensus. The chapters of Part V discuss these problems from various theoretical angles. How can economic growth in Greek economies be measured and what were its driving factors? What do we mean by economic growth and performance, and are they, if

---

[26] Hopkins 1980; the Finley–Hopkins debate has frequently been described; by way of a longer bibliography, see the succinct summary in Morris, Saller, and Scheidel 2007, 3–5; and on Finley, J. G. Manning 2018, 10–16.

[27] Morris, Saller, and Scheidel 2007, 4–5 for the full list of factors.

[28] For quantifying methodology and its role in economic history, see esp. Manning and Morris 2005.

[29] See important contributions by Millett 2001, 1991; Morris 1994 for discussion.

[30] Alongside Bresson and Ober, mentioned above, see now also the contributions in Harris, Lewis, and Woolmer 2016 for recent directions.

defined in the ways modern economists do, the best standard by which the success of the ancient economy should be evaluated (Eich, Chapter 22, and von Reden and Kowalzig, Chapter 23)? The authors of these chapters differ in their answers to these questions and take different stances within the approaches they introduce, but they all agree that economic development is an important question for economic historians to address. There are no simple solutions, but the questions involved are likely to stimulate further debate and research on the ancient Greek economy in years to come. It is hoped that the chapters of this volume show the vitality of the field of research and the ways in which the ancient Greek economy can contribute to important questions of world economics through time.

PART I

DIACHRONIC PERSPECTIVES

2: EARLY IRON AGE ECONOMIES

Irene S. Lemos

INTRODUCTION

This chapter explores the economic activities of Greek communities from the twelfth to the eighth centuries.[1] It was a formative phase after the end of the Late Bronze Age (LBA) palatial administration, and there were several kinds of social and economic transformations that had an impact on the economic performance of the period. Past studies have mostly focussed on the eighth century, with brief discussions of the eleventh, tenth, and ninth centuries, but totally ignoring the twelfth.[2]

In order to comprehend Mycenaean economies, we rely on the Linear B documents and the archaeological finds. Both suggest that the quantity of resources and the number of people that were managed by the palace administration should not be underestimated, even if the palaces did not control the entire economy.[3] It has also been argued that mobilisation of goods and people characterised comparable early states whose main purpose was to support the elites in charge.[4] Indeed, Mycenaean palaces monopolised the production and consumption of a range of goods and materials – in particular, luxury goods such as high-quality textiles and perfumes. These were then exchanged for commodities (such as copper and tin) and other goods that formed part of the conspicuous consumption of palatial and regional elites. This is mostly traced in the funerary display.[5]

The fact, however, that there was no attempt to restore palatial administration after 1200 is significant, and yet the impact of its demise must have severely affected surviving communities. Indeed,

[1] I would like to thank Antonis Kotsonas and Birgitta Eder for useful comments on an earlier draft of the chapter. Antonis Kotsonas provided me with further bibliographical references of recent publications of analyses of animal bones and human skeletons.
[2] Morris 2007; 2009a with bibliography of his numerous contributions; for exceptions: Dickinson 2006; Morgan 2009; Murray 2017; Eder and Lemos 2020; Nakassis 2020.
[3] Killen 2007; Bennet 2007.
[4] Killen 2008; Halstead 2011. Both are following Earle's 1977 redistribution model in Hawaiian chiefdoms.
[5] Voutsaki 2001; Bennet 2007, 190–1; Nakassis 2020.

the post-palatial period marked profound socio-economic adaptations and changes, even if palaces did not monopolise all economic activities and the degree of centralisation differed from region to region.[6] It has been shown, for example, that the production of some goods such as pottery was not under strict palatial control.[7] Most importantly for the surviving post-palatial communities, it has been argued that agricultural products, and especially those which were not mentioned in the Linear B documents but which have been retrieved from several archaeological sites, were managed without palatial regulations.[8]

In any case, the post-palatial period is characterised by the demise of the mobilisation centres and the administrative documents that were associated with them. And as period covered by the Linear B documents comes to an end, it is archaeology that can trace the economic activities of the period until another challenging source enters the picture: the Homeric poems and Hesiod.[9]

Scholarship has long contemplated the contribution of the Homeric epics and Hesiod to the study of the Early Iron Age (EIA),[10] but priority is given here to the archaeological evidence, as the study of the period depends entirely on data provided by archaeology.[11] It is therefore appropriate to survey the archaeological evidence combined with data from bioarchaeological, palaeoclimatological, and other scientific analyses to outline some aspects of the economic activities of the period.[12]

COMMUNITIES AND POPULATION IN THE EIA

Recent palaeoenvironmental research has suggested that the climate changed from the twelfth to the eighth centuries, becoming much drier.[13] Such conditions may have challenged agricultural regimes and put pressure on economic and social structures. There has been, however, a critical response to such studies, suggesting that they lack high-resolution data and reliable chronological association between the presented proxy records, showing climate change and certain 'historical' events.[14]

---

[6] Nakassis, Parkinson, and Galaty 2011.   [7] Whitelaw 2001; Nakassis 2010.
[8] Halstead 2007; 2011.   [9] Morris 2007, 213, 231–5; Nakassis 2020.
[10] Finley 1978; Donlan 1997; Tandy 1997; Morris 2001; von Reden 2003, 13–76; van Wees 2009; Osborne 2009a, 131–52; Hall 2014, 260–6.
[11] Morris 2007, 213.
[12] For the importance of acknowledging climate variability, environmental conditions, and geographical location among other factors, see J. G. Manning 2018.
[13] Drake 2012; S. W. Manning 2013, 112–14.
[14] For a summary of the research and evaluation of the results: Knapp and Manning 2016; Weiberg et al. 2016.

Another common assumption is that after the end of palatial administration the population dropped dramatically, resulting in negative outcomes for social structures and economic growth.[15] The actual estimates of the population, however, are usually calculated by projecting backwards from the classical and later periods.[16] Though to some extent such estimates can be useful, we should take into consideration that this is a period without historical evidence and not that much explored. Alain Bresson and others have argued for a more cautious approach to estimating ancient populations.[17]

Nevertheless, since the actual area that a settlement occupied and the entire extent of a cemetery are rarely fully explored, a common concern for every period is to assess the size of a community's territory. For example, it has been estimated that during the twelfth century, some 2,000 people lived at Karphi in Crete, though only a small part of the settlement has been excavated, while on Xeropolis-Lefkandi, we assume that the whole tell (a mound formed by the debris of generations of people living at this site) was occupied, based on excavations and trial trenches. But without excavating the whole settlement, we cannot estimate accurately how densely it was occupied and how many people lived there.[18] Another way of estimating population is analysing the data from surveys. The visibility, however, of this particular period in surveys is notoriously low, while a number of sites are still to be exposed under the remains of later periods located on top of them.[19]

Despite several challenges that the first generation had to confront after the 'collapse', communities did survive. Indeed, the fact that a number of settlements experienced destruction early in the twelfth century (Lefkandi, Kynos in the Euboean Gulf, Aigeira in the Corinthian Gulf, Koukounaries on Paros, and elsewhere), while key Mycenaean regions such as Messenia were dramatically depopulated, is indicative of the volatility that characterised Greece at the time. The recovery, however, was especially swift in regions that were not closely associated with central administration and thus where palatial control was weaker, allowing more freedom in managing local economies.[20] Yet Tiryns was an exception, in having been a palatial centre that now attracted an influx of inhabitants, increasing its size and population.[21] In central Greece, a number of sites were thriving, both along the Euboean Gulf (Lefkandi, Eleon, Mitrou, Kynos) and in inland locations (Elateia,

---

[15] Morris 2007, 217–18. [16] Scheidel 2003.
[17] Bresson 2016b, 41–5, 54–63; Morgan 2009, 46–8. [18] Wallace 2010, 62; Evely 2006.
[19] Bintliff 2012, 211–20; Haggis 2015 for Crete. [20] Bennet 2007, 209–10.
[21] Maran and Papadimitriou 2006; 2016.

Agnadi, Zeli, Modi). Most of them continued to be occupied into the eleventh and the tenth centuries.[22] In Thessaly, while a number of Mycenaean sites were abandoned, others remained occupied into the post-palatial period and the EIA (Kastro in Volos, Velestino, Aerino).[23] In north-western Greece (Achaea, Elis, Kephallonia, Aetolia/Acarnania), the large number of burials in chamber and cist tombs suggests that the population increased during the twelfth and early eleventh centuries.[24] In the Aegean, the Cyclades (Chrora on Naxos, Koukounaries on Paros, Agios Andreas on Siphnos) and the Dodecanese (Rhodes, Kos) became important post-palatial centres in the twelfth century and increased their population.[25] Crete experienced relocation of population to well-chosen and defensible sites away from the coasts, such as Karphi, Monastiraki Chalasmenos, Vronda and Kastro in Kavousi, and others in the Mirabello bay.[26] At the same time, earlier palatial centres declined but were not abandoned (e.g. Knossos, Phaistos, Kydonia). Knossos, after a short decline, developed into a centre of substantial size and importance.[27]

The period from the late eleventh to the ninth century sees further developments in Athens, Argos, Corinth, Larisa, Knossos, Prinias, Gortyn, and other sites that grew into what Morgan called 'big sites'.[28] In the Euboean Gulf, the tell sites of Kynos and Mitrou and others were eventually abandoned, while Atalante and Tragana emerged in the ninth and eighth centuries as key and prosperous centres.[29] At the end of the eighth century, Xeropolis at Lefkandi and Zagora on Andros were abandoned, with the population of the former site moving to Eretria and abroad and of the latter to the nearby Palaiochora and/or to Hypsile, which were occupied into the archaic and later periods.[30] Koukounaries and Paroikia on Paros were key settlements in the eighth century, as was Minoa on Amorgos.[31] In Crete, there is another shift in settlement patterns, as some smaller post-palatial sites were abandoned and new ones were established that grew into proto-urban size during the next period.[32]

This account of selected sites occupied during the period does not do full justice to the degree of variability that characterised the transition from the LBA to the EIA and the archaic period.[33] So, although it would be wrong to argue that the population did not decline after the palatial demise, it would be similarly unwise to be too confident in any

---

[22] Lemos 2012; 2014; Livieratou 2020.   [23] Morgan 2003, 85–102; Karouzou 2020.
[24] Eder 2006.   [25] Deger-Jalkotzy 1998.
[26] Nowicki 2000, 223–47; Wallace 2010, 60–75; Gaignerot-Driessen 2016, 56–71.
[27] Hatzaki and Kotsonas 2020, 1036–42.   [28] Morgan 2003, 54–69.   [29] Livieratou 2020.
[30] Televantou 2015.   [31] Gounaris 2005.
[32] Wallace 2010, 234–53; Haggis 2013; Gaignerot-Driessen 2016, 71–9.
[33] For a regional survey, see Lemos and Kotsonas 2020, vol. 2.

guesstimates depending only on quantitative models based on later data without taking into consideration the length of the period during which significant fluctuations took place and the regional diversities of the archaeological record.[34]

HOUSEHOLD ECONOMIES

Despite uncertainties regarding the size of the population, there is consensus about the importance of household economies after the end of palatial administration.[35] While it has been argued that households were essential in maintaining palatial economies, it is after the demise of the Mycenaean administration that the archaeological landscape is characterised mostly by households of different sizes.[36] The case of Nichoria in Messenia is interesting since the houses of the palatial period were abandoned after the destruction of the palace of Pylos, suggesting that this event had an impact on the economic activities of the settlement. The picture changed in EIA Nichoria when a large household dominated the site.[37] Moreover, the size, storage capacities, and bioarchaeological remains associated with these households reveal key aspects of their economic performance, while craft production in close proximity allows us to appreciate the intricacy of their industrial activities.

Twelfth-century houses have been excavated in Tiryns, Aigeira, Lefkandi, Mitrou, Kynos, Eleon, Naxos Town, Karphi, Halasmenos, Kastro, and Vronda in Kavousi, while in the ninth and eighth centuries, edifices at Zagora, Emporio, Oropos, Lefkandi, and Eretria represent the EIA well. We mostly lack evidence from the centuries in between, but recent archaeological investigations have started to cover the gap. Actually, most of the evidence from the eleventh to the eighth centuries relies on funerary data, allowing only selective exploration of the economies of the living.

Houses were free-standing or formed agglomerated units, and they varied in size. Some had large-size rooms, as in twelfth-century Tiryns, Xeropolis-Lefkandi, and Mitrou. At Tiryns, House W and Room 8/00 outside the citadel were equipped with large central rooms divided by rows of columns.[38] On Xeropolis, the houses were large units with rooms of 5 m^2 each, while a large edifice with additional

---

[34] Morris 2007; see Murray 2017, ch. 3 for a rather negative approach based on mostly quantitative data.
[35] Stockhammer 2011, 214–36; Foxhall 2014; Day 2017.   [36] Nakassis 2020.
[37] Foxhall 2014, 418–25.   [38] Maran and Papadimitriou 2006, 108–11; 2016.

quarters had a main room of at least 61 m^2 in size.[39] Building B at Mitrou was roughly 111 m^2 and as large as its Mycenaean predecessors.[40] In Crete, the main rooms of the buildings at Vronda in Kavousi and Karphi varied in size between 30 and 56 m^2, while a large complex, A-B, at Vronda was 197.64 m^2.[41]

The monumental funerary building at Toumba, Lefkandi (nearly 500 m^2) demonstrates the potential for ambitious architectural constructions in the tenth century.[42] Also of large size was Megaron B at Thermos, now dated to the eleventh century, which occupied some 156 m^2.[43] Other free-standing edifices – mostly apsidal in plan – were smaller. In Nichoria, Unit IV-1 was 73.5 m^2 in phase 1 and 127 m^2 in phase 2; another building, Unit IV-5, is estimated to have been around 111 m^2.[44] The largest building at Asine was around 71 m^2,[45] while the building at Kephalosi in Thessaly was 52.4 m^2.[46] So the size of buildings varies depending on location, context, and function. Interestingly, houses in Late Geometric (LG) Oropos and Eretria have an average size of around 60 m^2, so they are comparable to or even smaller in size than earlier dwellings.[47] This could be because at Eretria, Lefkandi, and Oropos, walls marked compounds of buildings with both domestic and industrial activities during the ninth and eighth centuries.[48] So the buildings within these compounds should be considered as forming households comprising social and economic kin groups. An alternative spatial organisation can be seen in Zagora on Andros, where houses with courtyards fulfilled similar social and economic roles in the eighth century.[49]

Storage was clearly important in the households of the period, indicating that there was an intention to fulfil subsistence requirements. In Vronda in Kavousi, the largest building of the settlement (A-B) was provided with ample storage facilities, most probably under the control of local leaders.[50] Whether such provisions were designed for feasting or were to signify the status of elite households, they suggest that there was some sort of surplus available for display, to accommodate redistribution and to provide communal consumption on convivial occasions.[51]

---

[39] Evely 2006; Lemos 2020, 39–49. [40] Van de Moortel and Zachou 2011, 332–4.
[41] Wallace 2005, 252–3; Day 2017, 33–4; Klein and Glowacki 2016, 27–30. [42] Coulton 1993.
[43] Mazarakis Ainian 1997, 127; for the date: Papapostolou 2008.
[44] McDonald, Coulson, and Rosser 1983, 19, 33, 47–54. [45] Mazarakis Ainian 1997, 233.
[46] Karouzou 2020, 890.
[47] Oropos: Mazarakis Ainian 1998, 194–6. Eretria: Verdan 2013, 45–6; Mazarakis Ainian 1997, 58, 103–4.
[48] Mazarakis Ainian 2015. [49] Lang 2007. [50] Day 2016, 221–4.
[51] Halstead 2014, 304–19.

The importance of storage is evinced by the symbolic provision of pits to hold large pithoi (storage containers), discovered in the apse room of the Toumba funerary building at Lefkandi and in other locales in central Greece.[52] In Unit IV-1 at Nichoria, storage was clearly a priority of the household, as was the case in the even larger Unit IV-5 that accommodated considerable storage facilities in its courtyard.[53] In LG Zagora, where every house had storage facilities, the analysis of the capacity of the different types of pithoi shows that they were designed to serve special needs, including the storage of bulk goods such as olive oil and wine.[54] Provisions for storage are indicated by the discovery of circular granaries in LG Xeropolis-Lefkandi and also in the symbolic presentation of wealth in the offering of model granaries to a female elite burial in Athens and their dedication to sanctuaries.[55]

The study of faunal and archaeobotanical remains reveals an economic organisation that supported a mixed agropastoral economy engaged in the production of a diversity of resources that involved the cultivation of different species of cereal, legume crops, and fruit and the management of cattle, sheep, goats, and pigs. The prevalence of one species over others depends on regional and environmental aspects and depositional contexts, whether domestic, cultic, or funerary. In Aigeira, Xeropolis-Lefkandi, Kynos, Nichoria, Zagora, and elsewhere, barley, beans, vetches, figs, olive oil, and wine were part of the diet.[56] In Crete, and on the Aegean islands, caprine faunal remains are more numerous than those of cattle, either for micro-environmental reasons or because of the economic exploitation of certain products such as wool from the sheep and milk from the goats.[57] Cattle are more common in Nichoria and in Tiryns, suggesting that – if slaughtered young – they were kept for their meat.[58] On Xeropolis-Lefkandi, cattle were kept to an adult age, implying that they were used both for their milk and for traction in the nearby Lelantine plain.[59] Hunting deer for cult and ritual display has been attested at the sanctuary at Kalapodi, in Lefkandi, in Tiryns, and in Aigeira.[60]

---

[52] Coulton 1993, 50; on the importance of storage in central Greece: Lis and Rückl 2011. For the evidence of storage facilities in the northern Aegean: Gimatzidis 2020, 252–5.

[53] McDonald, Coulson, and Rosser 1983, 17, 28, 52–4.   [54] McLoughlin 2011.

[55] Popham, Sackett, and Themelis 1981, 15–17; Mazarakis Ainian 1997, 120–2; on storage methods that we cannot retrieve in the archaeological record: Halstead 2014, 180.

[56] Livarda and Kotzamani 2019; Margaritis 2013; Alram-Stern and Deger-Jalkotzy 2006.

[57] For Vronda: Snyder and Reese 2016 with further bibliography.

[58] Tiryns: Morgenstern 2016 with further bibliography. For Nichoria: Dibble 2017.

[59] Mulhall 2015 with comparative discussion from other sites.

[60] Mulhall 2015; for Kalapodi: Felsch 1981.

Additional information is offered by the study of human skeletal assemblages, which could serve as indicators of the health status and subsistence of ancient populations. Such data, however, is meaningful only when appropriate consideration is given to the environmental, cultural, and social contexts.[61] In addition, we should be aware that the nature of the assemblages, together with the methodology and techniques employed, can produce biased results.[62] Age, for example, is not always estimated with accuracy, while the frequent exclusion of juveniles and elderly individuals from the funerary display results in the under-representation of specific age groups.[63] Liston, for example, has noted that skeletons in Athens, assigned to adults in the 1970s by the pioneering work of Angel, were of children.[64] Hence, analyses of skeletal remains should not be taken as reflecting the structure of the living population of any past society or representing its exact size.

Bioarchaeological analyses, however, have shown that in the twelfth century in Achaia Clauss, the buried population was in general in good health.[65] In LG Argos, men and women of high status were found in equally good states of health, while evidence from their teeth revealed the consumption of food rich in carbohydrates.[66] Stature is considered a good indication of the general health of a population. It has been noticed, however, that cremated skeletons cannot provide actual calculations of stature, and thus in recent EIA studies only inhumed skeletons were employed. This restricts our data since cremation is a common rite in this period. In any case, in the EIA cemeteries in the Athenian agora, the estimated mean height of eight inhumed adults was typical for the period generally but shorter than the average individual at Torone.[67]

Stable isotope analyses (the identification of stable isotopes and chemical elements in organic and inorganic matter) conducted on the human remains from the eighth-century Agios Dimitrios cemetery in Phthiotis provided information regarding the main sources of protein in the diet of the population. The analyses show that their diet predominantly consisted of terrestrial resources with minor animal protein components. Interestingly, though the site is located near the coast, marine-derived protein did not make a substantial contribution to their diet.[68]

[61] Larsen 2015, 422–31; Liston 2017, 520; Schepartz, Fox, and Bourbou 2009.

[62] Triantaphyllou 2001, 30–2; Larsen 2015, 402–24. [63] Larsen 2015, 418–19.

[64] Liston 2017, 515–19. [65] McGeorge 2018.

[66] Pappi and Triantaphyllou 2011; for similar results in the three cemeteries examined in Macedonia: Triantaphyllou 2001, 139–41.

[67] Liston 2017, 521–2. [68] Papathanasiou et al. 2013.

Subsistence and self-sufficiency were not the only economic strategy of EIA households. Exchange of commodities and production of specialised goods are attested for even the 'darkest' parts of the period.[69] For example, textiles were an important product, as we can deduce from the discovery of loom weights in every house of the period. Two exceptional garments were given to high-status male burials at Stamna in Aetolia and Lefkandi on Euboea and display sophisticated handiwork.[70] Interesting observations of the teeth of women from the graves in Athens have revealed that spinning fibres for cloth left impressions on their teeth.[71]

Areas allocated to the manufacture of pottery and metal objects have been found near or within household compounds. Twelfth-century pottery kilns have been discovered in Kynos and Velestino on the mainland and at Kavousi in Vronda in Crete.[72] Protogeometric and Geometric potters' wasters from wells and pits in the Athenian Agora have been used to support the idea that the area was assigned as a potters' quarter, but pottery kilns have also been found in various locations around the Acropolis and in Palaia Kokkinia near Piraeus.[73] Metalworking activities at Geometric Thoricus, Oropos, and Eretria were under household control. Workshops were also found in sanctuaries later in the period.[74]

On Naxos, remains of a workshop for the production of faience objects suggest that their manufacture continued into the twelfth century, while at Argos, an installation for the refining of silver was found among the EIA levels of the site.[75] In LG Eretria, the discovery of gold globules on two sherds found in the area of the sanctuary of Apollo further evinced the operation of jewellery workshops along with those that produced copper and iron artefacts.[76]

NETWORKS OF MOBILITY AND EXCHANGE

Recent research has suggested that, during the Mycenaean period, market-based systems of exchange were in operation, alongside those of the redistribution of goods that relied on palatial organisation.[77] With the end of the palatial administration, however, the role of merchants

---

[69] Nakassis 2020; see also below, 'Networks of Mobility and Exchange'.
[70] Kolonas et al. 2017.   [71] Liston 2017, 525–6.
[72] Kynos: Dakoronia 2015; Velestino: Karouzou 2020, 891; Vronda: Day 2016, 225–6.
[73] Papadopoulos 2003; Alexandridou 2017.
[74] Morgan 2003, 149–55; Mazarakis Ainian 2015.
[75] Lambrinoudakis and Zaphiropoulou 1985, 166; Lemos 2002, 138.   [76] Verdan 2013, 148–9.
[77] Parkinson, Nakassis, and Galaty 2013.

and agents who were in charge of such tasks became even more essential in maintaining the short- and long-distance transactions that continued to operate, even if on a smaller scale.[78] It has been noted that coastal locations that were not predominantly dependent on agricultural goods became nodes of such exchanges;[79] consequently, it is not a coincidence that a number of locales during this period were on coasts and islands that controlled sea routes.[80] It is also noticeable that from the twelfth century onwards, the galley becomes popular in imagery of ships, strongly indicating that such boats continued to be maintained and facilitated faster and safer mobility across the Mediterranean.[81]

Both familiar and alternative sources for the acquisition of goods and commodities were sought, as is evinced by the rise of imported bronze objects from Italy in twelfth-century Achaea and the uninterrupted influx of Cypriot goods in Tiryns.[82]

Copper and tin were still available and not necessarily only from recycling.[83] Copper did not come only from Cyprus, as in the palatial period, but new sources were also explored. One such source might have been from Israel and/or Jordan.[84] For the earlier part of the period, the number of bronze objects found, for example, at Karphi in Crete is impressive,[85] while fresh tin has been traced in bronze objects dedicated to the sanctuary of Enodia in Thessaly, where a metal workshop engaged both imported and local copper sources.[86]

The period is also marked by the introduction of iron technology, which might have been imported as a process from Cyprus by entrepreneurs. The purpose of iron changed in less than the span of a couple of generations from a precious to a common metal for tools and weapons.[87] The introduction of iron must have advanced agricultural activities since iron ploughs and sickles could accelerate and intensify production.[88] Even with the arrival of iron, however, bronze personal items and vessels continued to be manufactured and offered to the dead and later were also dedicated to sanctuaries together with figurines.[89]

Interaction among Greek communities can be traced in the circulation of ceramics such as the octopus stirrup jars found among coastal and island communities of the twelfth century; this demonstrates sumptuous patterns of consumption, since such jars

---

[78] Broodbank 2013, 602.   [79] Sherratt 2016.   [80] Tartaron 2013, 126–30.
[81] Eder 2006; Kramer-Hajos 2016, 152–61.
[82] Eder and Jung 2005; Jung and Mehofer 2013; Tiryns: Vetters 2011, 27–30.
[83] Murray 2017, 172–3.   [84] Kiderlen et al. 2016.   [85] Wallace 2005, 259.
[86] Orfanou 2015.   [87] Sherratt 1994; 2016.   [88] Halstead 2014, 35, 113–14.
[89] Papadopoulos 2014, 181–3; Eder 2015.

were containers of desirable liquids and perfumes.[90] From the tenth century until later in the seventh, the distribution of a specific type of amphora in the northern Aegean suggests a network of consumers who benefitted from the exchange of transported commodities, probably olive oil and wine. This indicates not only that the central and southern Aegean managed redistribution of commodities but also that a busy operation ran in the north.[91]

As in the Mycenaean period, status continued to be displayed in the funerary arena with offerings either imported from within the Greek world or from abroad. The latter include bronze vessels, gold ornaments, and personal adornments made of faience, amber, glass, and ivory. It has been argued that because of the drop in population and local economic growth during this period, the number of imported goods is smaller compared to earlier and/or later periods.[92] This is indeed the case, yet the reasons might not be population decline and lesser wealth but distinctive funerary rites, social structures, and even availability of imported things ('goods') manufactured in the eastern Mediterranean. It should be noted that it was not only Greece that suffered after the events of 1200 but also most of the eastern Mediterranean, and this must have had an effect on the production of goods for export. It might also be the reason behind the circulation of antiques such as those given to the dead at Perati, Lefkandi, and elsewhere.[93]

On the other hand, the only detectable Greek artefacts found abroad are ceramics. Without a doubt, other goods were also exported, including foodstuffs, textiles, and most importantly iron and silver.[94] Luke has argued that Greek pots found in the East were the result of *xenia*, whereas Vacek interprets their presence especially in Al Mina as preliminary gifts of low material value that had a symbolic significance in initiating market exchange.[95] Interestingly, it has been suggested that production of plates by Euboean potters was targeting market demands to satisfy the requests of Levantine consumers,[96] comparable to the production of the Nikosthenic vases for the Etruscan markets in the archaic period.[97]

It has been debated for a long time whether such interactions were based on gift or market exchange. It is important, however, to note that the one does not exclude the other.[98] In any case, merchants operated in

---

[90] Deger-Jalkotzy 1998.   [91] Gimatzidis 2010, 258–69; 2020;Kotsonas 2012.
[92] Murray 2017, 199–209.   [93] Sherratt 2010, 132–3; Dickinson 2006, 72.   [94] Sherratt 2010.
[95] Luke 2003, 50–6; Vacek 2012, 19–24.   [96] Coldstream 1988.   [97] Osborne 1996, 31–9.
[98] Appadurai 1986, 11–16; Tandy 1997, 59–75; Sherratt 2016.

the eastern Mediterranean from the LBA and continued to do so in the EIA, with Cypriots and Phoenicians playing a major role but without excluding participation of Greek agents. Their role has been underestimated in recent scholarship.[99] It has been suggested that Greek communities were poor and not able to produce enough agricultural surplus to enable them to participate in any exchange. However, the case of Aegina in the archaic and classical period indicates that surplus is not a prerequisite for successful trade.[100] Indeed, it has been argued that mobility among Mediterranean communities was necessary for the subsistence of the population; thus, we cannot exclude the possibility that certain groups were engaged in the redistribution of commodities by cabotage (short-distance tramping) or by their participation in long-distance networks.[101]

Another indication of the operation of trade is provided by the discovery of balance weights that were given to a male burial at Lefkandi in the first half of the ninth century. According to Jack Kroll, their discovery indicates how Euboeans were actively engaged in trade with the eastern Mediterranean using multiple Levantine/Cypriot weight standards.[102] Equally important is the gold deposit found in one of the neighbourhoods of late eighth-century Eretria and the Tekke tomb 'hoard' in Knossos, suggesting the operation of a pre-monetary system similar to that found in the eastern Mediterranean.[103]

FROM RESILIENCE TO SUSTAINABILITY AND CHANGE

This brief survey shows that the term stagnation does not correctly characterise the period after the rejection of palatial administration.[104] Instead, it reveals similar economic indicators to those employed for studying later economies, even if we lack historical accounts and the archaeological evidence is not always visible. This lack of evidence might be the reason that economic historians often described the period as a Dark Age.[105]

Over the long term, and especially during the less visible second part of the eleventh century, climate change may have caused more arid conditions and so affected agriculture and population size in Greece.

---

[99] Monroe 2009, 237–8; Sherratt 2010.   [100] Purcell 1990, 50–2.
[101] Horden and Purcell 2000, 137–52; Bresson 2016b, 60, 100–1.   [102] Kroll 2008a.
[103] Le Rider and Verdan 2002, 141–52; Kotsonas 2006.
[104] Morris 2007, 217–19; on the theoretical framework chosen for this section, North 1991.
[105] For the use of the term: Kotsonas 2016.

However, well-explored sites such as Athens, Lefkandi, and Knossos continued to show signs of economic activity.

More recently, ancient historians have turned to the theory of New Institutional Economics, which emphasises the importance of institutions and organisations whose role is to regulate the performance of economic activities (Chapter 23, this volume).[106] It could be argued that after the palatial demise, households became the central organisations in determining economic performance. They would then have been required to be more effective in running their activities, with diversified strategies for the production, provision, and consumption of goods.

EIA households could be defined as adaptable socio-political organisations with fluid boundaries depending on the relationships and identities of their members.[107] They were kin-based but more independent than in the LBA palatial period.[108] Affluence depended on a network of relations among their own members and a network of others inside and outside their communities. Households have been ascribed to 'house societies' that, despite their regional and temporal variations, characterised the Mediterranean landscape.[109] Their continuous prominence from the Neolithic period, despite their variety in scale and breadth, was due to their ability to manage agropastoral strategies in the Mediterranean. In any case, access to land, livestock, and labour were important factors for the successful performance of household economies, and this period could not have been an exception.[110]

In order to profit and prosper, competition in 'transactions' among organisations is not only unavoidable but also necessary.[111] The archaeological evidence of communal and private feasting, burial offerings, and trade for the acquisition of necessary and desirable commodities, among other categories, records such competition among EIA communities across the Mediterranean. Indeed, it could have been one of the motives that drove Greeks and Phoenicians to set up homes away from home by the end of the eighth century, if not earlier.

So, it seems that the archaeological evidence reflects a period that is characterised by adaptive and resilient features, and which resulted in stability. Such stability becomes more visible in the archaeological data of the eighth century. The concept of resilience has been acknowledged outside the environmental science where it originates as a model to

---

[106] North 1991; Bresson 2016b, 15–27; J. G. Manning 2018, 27–32.
[107] Souvatzi 2008, 12; Huebner 2017, 6–9.   [108] Foxhall 2014.
[109] Foxhall 2014; Halstead 2014, ch. 6; González-Ruibal and Ruiz-Gálvez 2016.
[110] Horden and Purcell 2000, 270–8; Halstead 2014, 311–14; Nakassis 2020.
[111] North 1991, 107–11; Bresson 2016b, 19–20.

understand a variety of societal transformations.[112] Erica Weiberg has argued that social resilience promotes the ability of communities to recover from environmental, socio-economic, and political stress as was evinced in the Early Bronze Age Aegean. Resilience theory employs the adaptive cycle as a key concept, envisaged as a figure of eight consisting of a 'front loop' that characterises phases of exploitation and conservation and of a 'back loop' that indicates those of release and reorganisation. In this scheme, the palatial system is seen to have become unstable and vulnerable, resulting in a release/collapse point, followed by the second phase in the 'back loop' of reorganisation. As Weiberg notes, this model 'allows post-collapse processes to be viewed as dynamic rather than being dismissed as Dark Ages'.[113]

CONCLUSION

After the demise of an organisational system that collapsed – perhaps more resources were consumed than produced – the accomplishment of the EIA is in managing to adapt to institutional structures, such as those of the household economies, that could first provide stability and in the long run maximise economic performance, before new transformations evolved in response to different socio-economic constraints that emerged at the beginning of the archaic period.

Further Reading

The up-to-date contributions in Lemos and Kotsonas 2020 provide detailed accounts of the complex archaeologies surveyed in this chapter. Bintliff 2012 offers a diachronic study of the archaeology of Greece, supplemented with discussions about its economies. Dickinson 2006 presents a general survey of EIA Greece, and Halstead 2014 ethnographic material related to pre-mechanised farming in the Mediterranean. The contributions in Knapp and van Dommelen 2014 allow the tracing of developments prior to and during the period discussed here, while Bresson 2016b deals with transformations in the course of the formation of poleis during the early archaic period.

---

[112] Holling and Gunderson 2002; Weiberg 2012; McAnany and Yoffee 2010, 10–11; Faulseit 2016, 6–8, 12.

[113] Weiberg 2012, 159; Faulseit 2016, 12–14.

3: The Archaic Period

Hans van Wees

Introduction

Classical Greeks prided themselves on being a poor people whose power
was based on bravery, not money (Hdt. 7.102.1), but it is now widely
agreed that by pre-modern standards they were actually quite well off.[1]
This chapter asks how and why the economic 'efflorescence' characteristic of many parts of the classical Greek world came into being during
the archaic age, ca. 750–480. We shall see that the second half of this
period saw slowly increasing per capita productivity as a result of
regional specialisation and intensive market exchange.[2] The first half
of the archaic age, however, was characterised by a fundamentally
different system, in which growth derived from a 'predatory' economy.

Direct evidence for economic growth is lacking (Chapters 22 and
23 for further discussion). The impressive temples and sculptures of the
archaic age may at first glance seem clear evidence of growth compared to
the modest material remains of the Early Iron Age. Such changes in the
material record, however, may reflect growing inequality of wealth rather
than an overall rise in prosperity. A concentration of resources in private
or public hands could fund spectacular monumental or funerary displays
without implying that the whole community was better off. The archaeological evidence of graves, dedications, and houses almost certainly
does not represent a cross-section of society, but only the better-off
elements. An increase in the number of graves after ca. 750, and even
more steeply around 500, was due at least in part to a larger proportion of
the population receiving visible burial rather than to population growth.[3]
Moreover, a richer material record may not indicate greater wealth even
among the elite, but a shift from spending on valuable but perishable items
of wood or cloth to spending on virtually indestructible, but not necessarily more costly, stone and ceramic artefacts.

---

[1] Bresson 2016b; Ober 2015a; Osborne 2007; Scheidel, Morris, and Saller 2007; Morris 2004.
[2] Compare Chapter 15, this volume.   [3] Morris 1987; cf. Scheidel 2003, 126–31.

The textual evidence for the archaic period is equally unhelpful for analysing growth. It mostly reflects the lives of the wealthy – even Hesiod's *Works and Days* (around 700 BCE) does so, although this poem has often been taken to represent the ordinary 'peasant'[4] – and offers mainly qualitative information rather than quantifiable data. The richest sources, the *Iliad* and *Odyssey*, moreover, represent a fictional heroic past, which was no doubt in many ways modelled on the contemporary world of the poet(s) but was nevertheless an enhanced version of reality, focused on the exceptional rather than the norm. Archaeological and textual evidence thus do not provide direct evidence for measurable economic growth, but what they do provide is evidence for changing economic structures and attitudes, from which we can infer that growth very probably did occur.

ARCHAIC PREDATORY EXPANSION

Under the influence of the 'New Institutional Economics', recent scholarship has attributed growth to the creation of institutions that stimulated maximum surplus production (Chapter 23, this volume). In archaic and classical Greece, it is argued the key development was the rise of egalitarian citizen communities in which most assets were privately owned, property rights protected by law, and taxation and other impositions by central authorities minimal.[5] Such conditions would indeed help property owners prosper, but for much of the archaic period Greeks pursued maximum gains from their land and other assets *without* such institutional security. Indeed, they actively contributed to economic insecurity by resorting to violent means of enriching themselves.[6]

Works and Days laments that violence and deception even among close kin make life deeply insecure and that the ruling elite are 'gift-eaters'; yet this same poem proclaims more strongly than any other the virtue of working hard to maximise gains in a competitive pursuit of wealth. This kind of rivalry (*eris*) is 'good for mankind': 'a man wants to work when he looks at another, a rich man who earnestly ploughs and plants ... Neighbour envies neighbour as he speeds towards wealth'

---

[4] Tandy 2018; van Wees 2009, 448–50.

[5] Bresson 2016b, 106–10, 218, 222, 339–51; Ober 2015a, 11–18, 101–55; but see the comprehensive critique of this model by Rose 2019.

[6] van Wees 1999; 2000. See Mackil 2018 for the insecurity of property rights even in classical Greece.

(Hes. *Op.* 17–24; cf. 308–13, 381–2). The landowner is advised that having more than one son may produce 'prosperity beyond words', since 'more people can take care of more business, and the surplus (*epitheke*) will be greater' (376–80), and that piety will pay: sacrifice 'so that you may buy another man's plot of land' (336–41). A limitless desire for wealth and the importance of acquiring wealth honestly, rather than resorting to violence or deceit, are themes that pervade archaic Greek poetry.[7] Archaic legislation to secure private ownership of land and other assets thus did not create conditions under which landowners could begin to pursue private gain but imposed limits on an intense pursuit of surpluses and profits that was already spinning out of control.

Throughout the archaic period, we find Greeks everywhere resorting to force to seize more land and other assets and to exploit the labour of free and slave workers. Most spectacular was the occupation of territory overseas. Whether it was private enterprise or public venture, whatever its immediate goal in any given case,[8] overseas settlement from ca. 750 onwards resulted in a vast increase in the territory inhabited by Greeks as they occupied large parts of Mediterranean and Black Sea littoral. The process often involved driving native populations off their land, either from the outset – as in Sicily in the 730s (Thuc. 6.3) or Thasos in the 660s (Archilochus T4; frs. 92–8) – or after an initial period of coexistence, as in the massacres of natives reported in some foundation stories or in the war against Libyans and Egyptians sparked by the arrival of many new Greek settlers at Cyrene, ca. 570.[9]

Many Greeks also made short-term gains by raiding the coasts of the Mediterranean. Assyrian records mention 'Ionians' plundering the coast of Syria around 720. Athenian grave markers at this time were decorated with scenes of fighting around beached ships. Homeric epics treat overseas raiding as a legitimate activity, so long as it targets distant places such as Egypt, and a Solonian law likewise gives legal recognition to agreements made by raiding parties for the division of spoils. Indeed, archaic war fleets recruited their ships and captains from private owners of pentekonters, which were much like Viking longships, with limited cargo space but large crews of oarsmen, suited to raiding rather than trading.[10]

---

[7] Solon fr. 4.1–6, 11; 4b; 13.7–34, 41–2, 71–3; Alcaeus fr. 360; Theognis 27–30, 41–50, 145–6, 197–203, 227–32, 466, 596, 753, 833–6, 1141–9.

[8] See e.g. the survey in Kotsonas and Mokrišová 2020; also Osborne 2007, 283; Ellis-Evans 2019, ch. 4, for islands occupying and exploiting extensive mainland territories.

[9] Massacres: Charon *FGrH* 262 F 7ab (Lampsacus, ca. 650); Justin, *Epit.* 43.3–4 (cf. Arist. fr. 549 (Rose); Massalia, ca. 600); see *BNJ* 262. Cyrene: Hdt. 4.159.2–4.

[10] van Wees 2013, 30–6, 56–60; 'Ionian' raiders: e.g. Rollinger 2001.

Another form of acquisition that relied on violence was service in the armies of the great powers of the age, perhaps starting with the Assyrian empire, then Lydia, and above all Egypt, which from the late seventh century onwards employed tens of thousands of Greeks in campaigns and garrisons. The conquest of Egypt by the Persian empire in 525 put an end to this source of revenue, but Miletus, Samos, Chios, and Lesbos joined as 'allies' in Persian expansion, providing large fleets for Persian campaigns down to 500, and probably benefited materially from Persian funding, or a share in the spoils, or both.[11]

The major spoils from raids, warfare, and the expulsion of indigenous populations were captives, to be sold as slaves. Slaves were the main trading commodity sold by Greeks to Phoenicians (Ezekiel 27.13), and even more will have been sold by Greeks to other Greeks. Against a traditional scholarly belief that slavery did not begin to play an economically significant role in Greece until the sixth century, recent research has shown that the 'servants' (*dmoes*) in Homer's and Hesiod's poems are indeed slaves, employed in large numbers (see also Chapter 14, this volume).[12] The *Odyssey* assumes that a single herd requires four (*Il.* 18.573–8) or five (*Od.* 14.24–7, 434–6) herdsmen and thus implies that Odysseus' sixty herds (*Od.* 14.100–8) require ca. 250–300 slaves to tend them. His father's vineyard is run by a slave bailiff's family (*Od.* 24.387–90, 497) but also employs other slaves housed in a lean-to that 'runs all around the house' (24.208–10, 223–5). *Works and Days* suggests that the landowner himself will do hard physical labour (388–95), but it emerges that his main role is to make 'the slaves' do their work.[13] The advice to use the last day of the month, 'best for supervising tasks and distributing rations', to 'tell your slaves' about the next month's (in)auspicious days (*Op.* 765–7) implies a town-based landowner who visits his slave-worked estate only once a month. The notorious claim that Corinth had 460,000 slaves very probably refers to the time of Bacchiad rule ca. 750–650. The vast number is unreliable, but the idea that early Corinthians owned many slaves is reinforced by a tradition that Periander banned the acquisition of further slaves by around 600.[14]

In some new settlements abroad, the Greeks forced native populations to cultivate the land for them. At Syracuse, the Kyllyrioi or

---

[11] Mercenaries: Luraghi 2006; van Wees 2021. Relations with Persia: van Wees 2013, 33–4, 147–8; Wallinga 2005.

[12] Lewis 2018b; Harris 2012.   [13] Hes. *Op.* 459, 470, 502–3, 573, 597–9, 607–8.

[14] 460,000: Timaeus *FGrH* 566 F 5, in book 4, which probably covered the foundation of Corinth's colonies by the Bacchiads. Periander: Arist. fr. 611.20 (Rose); also Nic. Dam. *FGrH* 90 F 58.

Kallikyrioi are described as 'slaves' or 'clients' (*pelatai*) of the landowning elite; their numbers were proverbially large. Aristotle said that they were given their name when they came together at Syracuse from a variety of places (fr. 544 (Rose)), which suggests that the Syracusans, after initially expelling the indigenous Sicels, later raided or subjected the hinterland in search of a new coerced labour force. These slaves eventually rebelled in 491.[15] Heraclea on the Black Sea created a similarly large subject population, when 'they overran the territory of the Mariandynians' at or after the city's foundation ca. 550 (Paus. 5.26.7; Arist. *Pol.* 1327b12–16).[16] Our sources regularly mention these two examples, and allusions to other cases suggest that coercing indigenous labour was not unusual.[17]

The Greek homelands, too, witnessed violent expansion. Some classical and later sources suggest that warfare in the archaic age was strictly limited in scope and duration, and some modern scholars have accepted this, treating Sparta's occupation of Messenia in the course of the seventh century as a unique exception. However, while the relative scale of Spartan expansion was exceptional, the (attempted) conquest of sizeable territories was not. Later traditions suggest that at roughly the same time as Sparta, Argos, Sicyon, and Elis too were engaged in expansionist wars against their neighbours in the Peloponnese. Even if one rejects these stories as unreliable, we have contemporary evidence for Athens fighting long wars against Megara for Salamis and against Mytilene for Sigeum, sizeable territories directly exploited by Athenian settlers when they gained control. If the famous war between Chalcis and Eretria was indeed fought over the Lelantine Plain, as later sources say, it was no border war but an expansionist attempt by Eretria to seize the bulk of Chalcis' territory.[18]

Not all forms of expansion involved warfare. Starting in the late eighth century, the number of archaeological sites increased throughout the archaic period in many parts of Greece, which suggests that previously little-used areas became more intensively exploited. At the same time, settlement hierarchies developed; among a large number of very small Early Iron Age sites, a few grew into sizeable cities while the rest became dependent villages. It seems likely that local elites joined forces in the larger settlements, which thus came to control the resources from wider areas.[19] Such

---

[15] Hdt. 7.155; Timaeus *FGrH* 566 F 8a; Dion. Hal. 6.62.1; numbers: Zen. 4.54. Morakis 2015, 41–4.

[16] Cf. Pl. *Leg.* 776d; Strab. 12.3.4; Ath. 263de, with Baralis 2015.

[17] Bithynians: Phylarchus *FGrH* 81 F 8. Libyans: Hdt. 4.160–1; cf. the continued use of Libyan labour on Cyrene's royal domains to harvest silphium: Theophr. *Hist. pl.* 9.1.7.

[18] Survey of archaic wars: van Wees 2017a and 2017b. Athens: Solon frs. 1–3 (Salamis); Alcaeus fr. 428ab (Sigeion); cf. Hdt. 5.77.

[19] Bintliff 2012, 213–20, with critical assessment of the archaeological evidence; also Osborne 2007, 283–4, 287.

internal expansion is hinted at in literary references to new vineyards and orchards established by wealthy men in border areas (*eschatia*; *Od.* 18.357–9; 24.205–7). These areas will previously have been in use as common land, so that new farms here amounted to predatory 'enclosures' at the expense of the poor. Hierarchical relations between settlements, and between urban and rural populations, are reflected in Hesiod's dismissal of Ascra as 'a wretched village', Sappho's and Theognis' sneers at badly dressed 'rustics', and conversely, Xenophanes' mockery of the urban elite's luxurious lifestyle at Colophon.[20]

The territories and other resources acquired in these ways were exploited not only by means of imported slaves but also by coerced local labour forces. The Helots in Laconia and Messenia, *penestai* ('toilers') in Thessaly, and *perioikoi* ('dwellers-around') of central Cretan cities constituted the entire agricultural labour force in these regions even in the classical period, when they were regarded as in essence slaves.[21] Argos and Sicyon also had coerced rural populations in the archaic age, but Argos' *gymnetes* ('naked people') rebelled in the 490s and eventually gained their freedom. Debt-bondage is well attested in Crete and was probably widespread in archaic Greece. Athens had its *hektemoroi* ('six-parters'), whose status is disputed but who may have been sharecroppers forced to hand over a crippling five-sixths of the harvest to the landowner.[22]

Some ancient sources claim that several of these coerced labour forces had been created long ago by conquering Dorian Greeks, but such migration legends are not reliable evidence. Local labourers were probably often reduced to slave-like conditions as part of the development of settlement hierarchies and a growing separation of city and country, that is in the course of the eighth century and archaic age. This process sometimes involved military action, as at Sparta. In the archaic Greek imagination, at any rate, elite domination was often justified as derived from past conquests and current military superiority; an archaic drinking song by Hybrias of Crete boasts that a man who possesses arms, armour, and courage will be 'master of the serfs' who cower before him and supply his food and drink.[23]

Many models of Greek economic growth attribute a crucial role to a developing class of so-called middling farmers, who were independent

---

[20] Hes. *Op.* 639–40; Sappho fr. 57, 110ab; Theognis 54–6; Xenophanes fr. 3; see Crielaard 2009, 357–61; Zurbach 2017, 431.

[21] E.g. Arist. *Pol.* 1269a34–b12, 1271b41–2, 1272b17–19; modern scholars dub this category of labour 'Helotic slavery' (Lewis 2018b, chs. 6–8; Ducat 1990; 2015) or 'serfdom' (esp. de Ste Croix 1981, 133–74).

[22] Lewis 2018b, 72–6, 147–66 (debt bondage, Crete); van Wees 1999 (Solon).

[23] Skolion 909 (Page, *PMG*); the common notion that Hybrias was a mercenary overlooks the reference to the 'serfs' (*mnoia*) and the Cretan setting. Cf. Tyrtaeus fr. 6 on Messenians.

but employed only family labour. There is no good evidence for such a class before 600. Hesiod may talk about hard work and complain about the ruling elite, but as we have seen his advice assumes that the farmer's main role is to supervise slaves and hired workers. Solon's list of poor working men features, alongside craftsmen, healers, and seers, not a working landowner but a hired agricultural labourer (fr. 13.41–8). Among Solon's property classes, the name of the third class, *zeugitai* ('yoke-men'), may sound as if it refers to small farmers, but it is attached to a high property qualification that indicates leisured landowners.[24] The only other potential evidence is the emergence in the late eighth century of hoplite infantry. In classical Athens, the hoplites (heavy armed infantry) did include many middling farmers, but in classical Sparta and Crete all hoplites were leisured landowners, and we shall see that there are reasons to think that archaic hoplites generally followed the Spartan rather than the Athenian pattern until the late sixth century.

The material record reflects this polarisation between an urban elite and an impoverished rural workforce and the non-existence of a significant middling class. In archaic towns, most houses tended to be of much the same size, and the surrounding countryside seems almost empty until the late sixth century.[25] In theory, this could mean that communities were small and egalitarian, consisting of farmers who lived in town, but in the light of the textual evidence we should infer instead that the town houses represent a degree of equality within the landowning elite only and that the working population left little archaeological trace because they lived outside town in flimsy shelters, using perishable wooden tools for work (Hes. *Op.* 423–31) and wooden and wicker vessels for eating, drinking, and storage.[26]

PRODUCTION, CONSUMPTION, AND EXCHANGE, CA. 750–600

As a result of territorial expansion, more intense exploitation of local and imported labour, and the probable concentration of elites in fewer but larger settlements, the period 750–600 saw the development of estates able to produce large surpluses. The major products were grain and wine;[27] Hesiod's farmer grows nothing else, but olive cultivation

---

[24] So e.g. Foxhall 1997; van Wees 2006 (*pace* Chapter 13, this volume and e.g. Valdes Guia 2019).
[25] Houses: Lang 2005. 'Empty' countryside: e.g. Foxhall 1997; 2007; Bintliff 2012, 213–20.
[26] *Od.* 9.219–23, 246–9, 346; 14.78; 16.49–52; *Il.* 16.641–3; for wooden cups and other vessels, see e.g. Ath. 465c, 470f, 476f–77e, 494f, 495a, 496c, 498e–99a, 499e–500a, 783d.
[27] *Il.* 6.194–5, 9.577–80, 12.313–14, 14.121–4, 20.184–5; Hes. *Op.* 564–72, 609–14.

appears fleetingly in Homer, where the largest estates also have fruit trees and garden beds (*prasiai*) for vegetables, herbs, and seeds.[28] A distinctive archaic feature was large-scale livestock rearing. This was not a pastoral economy, but epic poetry often mentions herds as a sign of wealth.[29] The poems envisage islanders pasturing many animals on the mainland, using a ferry service for transport (*Od.* 14.100–2; 20.185–8) and if necessary using pasture in another city's territory, under the care of a 'guest-friend'.[30] Hesiod rears sheep and goats (*Op.* 775, 786–7, 795–7), eats the meat of a heifer 'grazed in the woods' (592), on common land, and needs a slave housekeeper 'who can follow the cows' (405–6) when they go out to graze. In his youth, the poet herded sheep in the hills near Ascra (*Theog.* 22–6), presumably looking after his father's flocks, in the manner of the sons of Homeric 'lords'.[31] Both Homer and Hesiod thus suggest livestock-rearing on a large scale, as opposed to the classical pattern of keeping a few animals on the farm to graze on the fallow land while at the same time re-fertilising it.

In Megara, large herds put so much pressure on common land that it caused popular unrest already around 640; Theagenes' *coup d'état* relied on the popularity he had won by 'slaughtering the livestock of the rich, when he caught animals illegally grazing (*epinemontas*) by the river' (Arist. *Pol.* 1305a22–5). In Attica, about thirty archaic graffiti in the hills near Vari (ancient Anagyrus) refer to shepherds, goatherds, or cowherds. Most of the 1,200 or so other graffiti here were surely also left by herdsmen, passing the time as their animals grazed.[32] As well as a range of agricultural produce, large estates thus produced much meat and leather, and wool, cheese, and milk from sheep and goats.

Epic poetry suggests, at first glance, that the bulk of these surpluses were used up in lavish feasts, by means of which the generous host created obligations among his guests and thus converted wealth into power and prestige.[33] By implication, the richest households would have produced such a variety and quantity of goods that they had little need to import and spent so much of their surplus on feasting and gift-giving that there was

---

[28] Olives: *Il.* 17.53–8; *Od.* 7.115–21; cf. Foxhall 2007, 85–95. Orchards: *Od.* 7.114–21, 11.588–90, 24.340–1; *Il.* 9.540–2; garden beds: *Od.* 7.127, 24.247; cf. *Il.* 8.306–7.

[29] E.g. *Il.* 2.705, 9.154, 9.296, 14.490; *Od.* 14.96–104; Hes. *Op.* 120, 308; see Howe 2008.

[30] *Od.* 4.634–7; 14.102; cf. Paus. 4.4.5; cf. Bresson 2016b, 136–7.

[31] *Od.* 13.221–5; *Il.* 5.313, 6.25, 6.421–4, 11.101–6, 14.443–5, 20.90–2, 20.188–91, 24.29; cf. Halstead 2014, 294–7, on the modern use of 'teenage labour' in herding.

[32] Langdon 2015; van de Moortel and Langdon 2017; Langdon, pers. comm. (12 March 2018), reports twenty texts mentioning shepherds (*poimenes*) or shepherding, six goatherds/-herding, three cowherds, and one *thyraulos*.

[33] So e.g. Finley 1978 (esp. 58, 104, 125, on retainers); Donlan 1982.

little left to export. However, we must remember epic poetry's focus on the exceptional. A closer look shows that generosity is practised on occasions that would be relatively rare in the real world and unlikely to consume the entire surplus. At the same time, the lifestyle of the elite required some resources that even rich households rarely possessed. The scope for exchange was therefore much greater than the literary sources suggest.

Feasts in Homer are usually shared by groups of social peers on a reciprocal basis. All diners bring their own contribution of food and drink to *eranos* meals (*Od.* 1.225–6; 11.415; cf. 4.621–3). Feasts are held at the expense of the host, but the participants are expected to take turns in hosting (*Od.* 1.374–5; 2.139–40), so that all contribute roughly equally in the long run. The 'wine of the elders', at which the king takes counsel with the elite, is paid for from 'public' resources (*Il.* 4.257–60; 17.248–50), and the same is likely to be true of public sacrifices and dedications. As for gift-giving, 'gifts' made within the community typically turn out to be either payments for services rendered or tributes paid to powerful men (*Il.* 9.155–6, 297–8).[34] Retainers (*therapontes*) may consume some surplus, as non-productive members of elite households. Yet only a few men in exile who take refuge in the house of a local ruler are permanent, dependent retainers.[35] The rest are economically independent and serve only on a temporary basis, above all on military campaigns (e.g. *Od.* 13.265–6; *Il.* 24.396–400); they make little if any demand on a leader's household resources. Only weddings, funerals, and hospitality to visitors from abroad entail offering feasts and gifts without material return. Such events by definition occur only rarely, remained in essence the same from the Homeric world to the classical age, and need not have absorbed much more of the surplus in early Greece than they did later.

Other forms of conspicuous consumption depicted in *Iliad* and *Odyssey* are also familiar from classical Greece: gold, silver, and bronze plate; ornate furniture; arms and armour; horses and dogs; cloth and scents. Gold and silver tableware comes as standard in the epics, and although this profusion of precious metal may seem mere fantasy, the poet did not indiscriminately imagine everything in the world of the heroes as made of silver or gold. Gold and silver are rather rare among the many prizes, gifts, and payments listed in the epics. The prevalence

---

[34] Full discussion: van Wees 2020; and already van Wees 1995 (feasts); 2002 (gifts); Osborne 2007, 295.
[35] *Il.* 9.485–91, 15.430–9, 16.570–6, 23.84–90, with Carlier 1984, 181–2; van Wees 2020.

of gold and silver tableware is thus not mere fiction but likely to reflect a pattern of contemporary elite display, which also extended to silver door handles and an array of ornate furniture with inlay of ivory, blue enamel, silver, or gold.[36] The ideal house in early Greek poetry is not a large building but one with lavish contents.[37]

Little of this wealth is archaeologically attested, but that is unsurprising. An excavated house contains only the cheapest of its movable contents such as ceramic pots and loom weights; furnishings and fittings of greater value were removed or plundered when the house was abandoned or destroyed. Dedications usually survive because they were cleared out from the sanctuary and dumped, something that would only happen to low-value objects and broken pieces. Some of the richest temples did throw out bronze artefacts such as tripods or armour, but rarely if ever gold or silver, of which they possessed large quantities.[38] Early Iron Age graves sometimes contained valuable goods (Chapter 1, this volume), but in the archaic age hardly any metal items other than dress pins and fibulae were deposited with the dead. It is therefore possible that the archaic Greek elite had modest houses and graves yet from the late eighth century competitively consumed gold, silver, bronze, iron, amber, and ivory at near-epic levels.

Other consumption needs that could not normally be met from household resources include salt, purple dye and alum, linen, natron, and scented oil. 'Holy salt' (*Il.* 9.214) was widely produced from coastal saltwater ponds, but even rich households will normally have had to acquire it by barter.[39] The extraction of purple from *murex* shellfish was a regional specialism, as was the extraction of alum, a mineral required to make the dye colourfast. Linen garments, shrouds, and sheets feature in Homer alongside woollen textiles, but flax was not widely cultivated in Greece and laborious to process. Natron was needed to bleach linen and create the 'snow-white' robes celebrated in poetry.[40] Most elite households must have acquired their linen yarn, dyes, and minerals – or indeed the finished textiles – from specialist producers or traders. The application of scented oil to body, hair, and clothes was a prominent

---

[36] E.g. *Il.* 11.628–9; *Od.* 1.441–2 (cf. 7.90), 19.55–8, 23.195–201, cf. 1.130–2, 8.372–3.

[37] See *Od.* 4.72–91, 4.125–32, 4.613–19; Bacchyl. fr. 20B.13–16. This undermines the use of house size as a proxy measure of economic growth by Morris 2004 (and e.g. Ober 2015a, 82; Bresson 2016b, 204). Buildings as such are valued in epic mainly for the quality of the woodwork of their roofs and doors, so too in Sparta (Plut. *Lyc.* 13; *Mor.* 997cd).

[38] See Kilian-Dirlmeyer 1985 for the eighth century finds from major sanctuaries.

[39] Cf. *Od.* 11.123 = 23.270, 17.455; Archil. fr. 173. Salt production: Bresson 2016b, 176, 180–1.

[40] Asios fr. 13. See Bresson 2016b, 190–4, 353–8, on dyes, alum, linen, and natron.

feature of the Greek elite lifestyle from Homer onwards.[41] Households could produce the oil base, but few could grow the quantities of flower petals or roots required to create the scent.

What is more, many commodities produced outside the Greek world were regarded as superior to their counterparts produced at home, and therefore as worth importing. An ivory cheek-piece made in Lydia or Caria is a much sought-after status symbol (*Il.* 4.141–5); silverware made in Phoenicia is the most beautiful 'in the world' (*Il.* 23.740–3); Menelaus' treasures come from Egypt and the Levant (*Od.* 4.72–91, 125–32, 613–19). This appreciation of non-Greek craftsmanship is mirrored in the eighth-century dedications from the temples of Hera at Corinth (Perachora) and on Samos, where 75 per cent of offerings were artefacts from the Levant, Egypt, or regions still further east, as well as in the imitation of eastern objects and decorative styles in orientalising Greek pottery and metalwork of the seventh century.[42]

Wine from Ismarus in Thrace plays a role in epic that suggests a special status (*Od.* 9.163–5, 204–11; cf. *Il.* 9.71–2), confirmed by Archilochus' drinking of 'Ismarian wine' (fr. 2). Hesiod drinks 'Bibline' wine, also from Thrace, rather than home-produced wine.[43] By the end of the seventh century, the list of exotic imports includes Lydian-made patterned headdresses and shoes (Alcman fr. 1.67–9; Sappho frs. 39, 98ab), Scythian shoes (Alcaeus fr. 318), and Scythian dye (Sappho fr. 210). Spartans by this time imported racehorses from both Lydia and the Black Sea region (Alcman fr. 1.45–9; cf. 172) and scented oil from Cyprus (fr. 3.71–2). Two new food seasonings, sumac and silphium, first mentioned by Solon (frs. 39, 41), were imported from Syria and Libya, respectively.[44] The frankincense, myrrh, and cassia burnt at festive and ritual occasions, first mentioned by Sappho (fr. 44.30; cf. 2.3–4), could only be found in Yemen and the Horn of Africa (Hdt. 3.107–12).[45]

By contrast, there is no sign in epic poetry of regions within the Greek world specialising in certain commodities, and only slight hints in other seventh-century poetry. Archilochus of Paros praises the wine 'like nectar' of his immediate neighbour Naxos (fr. 290). Semonides speaks of 'an amazing Tromilian cheese from Achaea' but apparently

---

[41] *Il.* 14.171–4; *Od.* 2.339 (fragrant oil); *Il.* 23.186 (rose oil); *Od.* 21.52; *Il.* 6.483 (fragrant clothes); *Il.* 18.595–6 (clothes 'gleaming' with oil; cf. *Od.* 7.107).

[42] The surviving dedications consist mainly of Phoenician and Egyptian faience scarabs, beads, and bottles, but include bronzes and ivories: Kilian-Dirlmeyer 1985; Villing 2017.

[43] Hes. *Op.* 589–92; Thracian origin: Ath. 31ab; cf. Philyllios fr. 23 K–A.   [44] Dalby 1996, 86.

[45] Detailed survey of commodities traded: van Alfen 2016.

picked this up in person as a gift for a friend back in Samos or Amorgos (fr. 23). Alcaeus praises the milk of goats from Scyros (fr. 435): milk would not keep long enough to travel far, so the animals themselves must have been exported widely enough to establish their fame. The evidence is slightly clearer for craft products: Semonides introduces 'an Argive cup' (fr. 27), while Alcaeus and his comrades play drinking games with 'cups from Teos' (fr. 322) and wield swords made at Chalcis in Euboea (fr. 140.13). The archaeological record for the archaic period clearly shows distinct regional Greek styles of metalwork and tableware.

Greek agricultural produce was nevertheless exported from an early date. Corinthian amphorae and so-called SOS-amphorae from Attica and Euboea are found all over the Mediterranean from ca. 750 onwards, and recent finds from the end of the eighth century at Methone in southern Macedonia have brought to light large numbers of amphorae from Lesbos, Chios, Samos, Miletus, and the Cyclades as well. Some of these places were later famous for their wine, but analysis so far tends to suggest that the amphorae contained oil and perhaps honey, which was a prestige food and the only form of sugar in antiquity.[46] Grain and most other agricultural or animal produce was not transported in ceramic vessels and has therefore left no trace, but we do have evidence for scented oils which were transported in ceramic *aryballoi* and other small bottle-shaped vases. These were produced in large numbers at Corinth and Rhodes and exported from the late eighth century onwards; the unguent itself, too, is likely to have been manufactured at Corinth, then packaged in orientalising *aryballoi* to enhance its appeal as an exotic luxury.[47]

By what mechanisms did the elite exchange large agricultural surpluses for a range of prestige goods? The prominence of gifts presented to visitors from abroad in Homeric epic has suggested to many scholars that in early Greece gift-giving was more important than barter as a means of exchange.[48] But a custom of creating and cementing elite networks with spectacular diplomatic gifts (*xeinia*) does not mean that most forms of exchange between communities took the form of gift-giving, and the epics illustrate a range of forms of barter as well. When the king of Lemnos sends several shiploads of wine to the Greek army at

---

[46] SOS-amphorae: Pratt 2015. Methone finds: summarised in Kotsonas et al. 2017; cf. Kotsonas 2012 (Attic and local amphorae had traces of beeswax). Honey stored in amphoras: *Il.* 23.170; *Od.* 24.68; on honey, see Bresson 2016b, 130–1; Balandier 2004.

[47] See Plin. *HN* 13.2.5–6; 21.19.42 for iris-root scent made at Corinth and its colony Leucas; Salmon 1984, 117–18; Massar and Verbanck-Piérart 2013, 277–83.

[48] For the idea of an early 'gift economy', see e.g. Tandy 1997; Osborne 2007, 301.

Troy, his agents barter the bulk of the cargo for the common soldiers' spoils (*Il.* 7.467–75). Achilles sends Patroclus abroad to sell his captives for him (*Il.* 23.741–7; cf. 24.751–3); the king of the Taphians goes abroad in person to trade a cargo of iron for copper (*Od.* 1.180–4).

Hesiod assumes that many landowners have their own ships (*Op.* 42–6, 622–32, 672–93; cf. 814–18) and may use the agricultural low season to sell their surpluses overseas (630–8, 663–94). These are not small sailing boats but oared vessels 'with many benches' (817), like the twenty-oared 'broad cargo-carrier' mentioned in the *Odyssey* (9.322–3; cf. 5.249–50), which for routine business may be crewed by 'hired labourers and slaves' (4. 634–7, 643–4). Alternatively, a landowner may put his surplus aboard another man's ship: 'praise a small ship but put your cargo in a large one' (Hes. *Op.* 643). A recently discovered poem by Sappho reveals that her (elite) family's fortunes depended on her brother returning home safely 'with a loaded ship'; later sources add that he sold wine at Naucratis in Egypt.[49] It should be noted that Hesiod prefers not to be actively involved in trade. He sees it as a risky means to escape from poverty (*Op.* 633–40, 646–7, 682–6) and accordingly is proud of never having gone to sea (649–62). It does not follow that he avoids trade altogether; he can cart his surplus to the coast (692–3) and sell it there. But he acknowledges that overseas trade can be very profitable (644–5; cf. 632), and for some landowning families the gains clearly outweighed the risk. Hesiod even has to warn farmers not to risk their 'entire livelihood' at sea (*Op.* 689–94).

Full-time traders also played a part but were looked down upon (*Od.* 8.161–4). The only professional merchants in the *Odyssey* are Phoenicians, who spend a whole year at their destination bartering 'countless trinkets' (15.416, 455–6) and are at times portrayed as greedy and deceitful (cf. 14.288–97). The appearance of Attic SOS-amphorae around 750–650 in parts of northern Africa and Spain, where Greeks did not arrive until the late seventh century, also implies Phoenicians buying Athenian produce. Significantly, the Greeks adopted versions of the Phoenicians' systems of weighing silver, weighed silver being the main measure of value and means of payment used in the Middle East. Many a Greek landowner will have been content to acquire 'eastern' prestige goods by doing business with visiting Phoenicians rather than venturing overseas himself.[50]

Prestige goods from Lydia on the other hand reached East Greek cities without Phoenician intervention, and most of these cities

---

[49] *The Brothers Poem*, 5–12 (Obbink 2016); with frs. 5, 15; Hdt. 2.135; Strab. 17.1.33. Cf. Arist. [*Ath. Pol.*]. 11.1 for the tradition that Solon made a trading trip to Egypt.
[50] SOS-amphorae: Pratt 2015, 231–2; Phoenician silver weights: van Wees 2013, 108–10.

accordingly adopted the Lydian system of weights for precious metal. The Lydian kingdom started striking electrum coins ca. 650, followed within a decade or two by many neighbouring Greek cities (Chapter 16, this volume). Coins may not have been struck in order to facilitate trade,[51] but one reason for their success was surely that in practice they were so used. Recent studies have removed the two reasons to doubt this. The coins turn out to consist not of natural electrum, with variable proportions of silver and gold and therefore fluctuating value, but of a man-made amalgam in which the proportion of gold was a precisely fixed 55 per cent and the value of the coin therefore steady. Moreover, although the main denominations had high values, the smallest subdivision was 1/192, equivalent to just over half an Athenian silver obol. It is hard to see what purpose the tiniest coins could have served other than as a means of exchange – perhaps even in retail trade, invented by Lydians along with coinage, according to Greek tradition.[52]

The introduction of coinage coincided with a wave of expansion dominated by East Greeks, from ca. 650 around the Black Sea coast and from ca. 630/20 in the western Mediterranean and at Naucratis in Egypt. Naucratis was an Egyptian town with a Greek quarter, and those who settled here clearly did so to conduct trade.[53] The same need not apply to all new Greek settlements of this period, but even if they were founded for quite different reasons, their very existence vastly increased the scope for trade. The distinctive Wild Goat-style pottery of Miletus, Samos, and other East Greek cities begins at this time to appear all over the eastern Mediterranean. The greater distance and difficulty of some routes meant that short seasonal trips by landowners were not viable, and these developments must have encouraged the emergence of more professional trade among Greeks.

Professionalisation and the scope of trade still had their limits, however. Mainland Greece played little part in this phase of expansion, except in Libya where Cyrene was founded, and did not yet adopt coinage. Even among the East Greeks, the Phocaeans, who had their own standard of electrum coinage and their own region of expansion as the first Greeks to explore the western Mediterranean, still travelled in raiding vessels rather than trading ships (Hdt. 1.163). Hired soldiers rather than merchants formed the largest influx of Greeks into Egypt.[54] Trade was thus a growing but still small part of an essentially

---

[51] The question is much debated: see e.g. van Alfen 2018a.
[52] Hdt. 1.94, 1.155. For electrum coinage, van Alfen and Wartenberg 2020; Fischer-Bossert 2018; Konuk 2012, esp. 47 and fig. 3.14 (smallest denomination).
[53] Robinson and Goddio 2015; Möller 2000.   [54] Luraghi 2006; van Wees 2021.

predatory system, and still primarily an exchange of agricultural surplus or slaves and other spoils for prestige goods.

SPECIALISATION, EXCHANGE, AND ECONOMIC GROWTH IN THE SIXTH CENTURY

It took until the late sixth century for this early predatory economy to be replaced by a system that included all essentials of the dominant classical Greek economic structure. Thucydides dated to 600 a key step towards what he regarded as a new political economy: the suppression by Corinth of maritime raiding to make life more secure for both farmers and traders, thereby generating greater public revenues from taxation, which funded the creation of greater naval power, which in turn established still greater security, and so on in a virtuous cycle (1.13; cf. 1.6–8). This change is associated by later sources specifically with the tyranny of Periander of Corinth. His father Cypselus was associated with founding colonies in western Greece (Leucas, Ambracia, and Anactorium) and levying heavy property taxes, but Periander is said to have founded only Potidaea at the end of his reign, while he built Greece's first trireme fleet and waged war continuously to 'control both seas', funded exclusively by market and harbour dues.[55]

If this is true, Corinth was well ahead of developments elsewhere in mainland Greece. Other cities continued to send settlers overseas until at least 540. Maritime raiding remained a common activity, and privately owned pentekonters were the main ship of war until the spread of public trireme fleets after 530. Almost all of 110 graffito pictures of warships drawn by the shepherds of Vari in the sixth century show pentekonters or smaller galleys; only four experimental drawings may represent triremes.[56] Sparta's wars of conquest came to an end ca. 550 with the occupation of Cynouria, and so far as we can tell the territories of most other Greek states also changed little after this time. Small-scale border conflicts continued, but larger military efforts aimed at political hegemony, achieved through military alliances and the imposition of friendly regimes, rather than conquest, and entailed no significant further extension

---

[55] Nic. Dam. *FGrH* 90 F 57.7, 58.3, 59.1 (from Ephorus); Strab. 10.2.8. Plut. *Mor.* 552e implies that Periander had to fight to retain control of these colonies. Cypselus' taxes: Arist. [*Oec.*] 1346a31–b6; Periander's taxes: Arist. fr. 611.20 (Rose). See Salmon 1984, 195–229.

[56] Vari: van de Moortel and Langdon 2017, 383–94. Navies: van Wees 2013, 30–6, 56–60.

of agricultural resources – with the exception of Athens' cleruchies (settlements abroad) and Syracuse's annexations.[57]

Extreme exploitation of labour and inequality within communities also began to be inhibited from ca. 600 onwards. Periander banned the acquisition of slaves, as noted above (p. 32). A civil conflict in Megara led to the cancellation of interest payments on debts. At Mytilene, the oligarchy of the Penthilidae, notorious for their gratuitous beatings of common men, was overthrown. A long civil conflict devastated the countryside at Miletus until ca. 570; a Hellenistic historian claimed that 'the people' had the children of fleeing property owners trampled to death by oxen on threshing floors, a distinctive atrocity confirming that the rebels were farm labourers resisting exploitation.[58] Solon at Athens banned the enslavement of debtors, cancelled debt, and enacted other measures that helped improve the lot of hired labourers and *hektemoroi*, including a ban on the export of all agricultural produce except olive oil – a major disincentive for maximisation of surpluses through labour exploitation.[59]

The exception made for oil allowed owners of plots too small to feed a family to specialise in the production of this prestige commodity for sale and export. Attic fine pottery in the sixth century included large numbers of amphorae which were presumably sold with contents, above all oil, and a striking trend in the late sixth century is that the output of amphorae is overtaken by *lekythoi*, elegant small oil bottles. Until ca. 550, *lekythoi* formed only about 2.5 per cent of surviving Attic pots, but ca. 525 they amounted to 9 per cent and ca. 500 to a staggering 34.6 per cent.[60] The numbers suggest a trend towards selling fine oil as a luxury product, in small quantities at high prices, from which in principle even a small olive farmer could make a substantial living. Similar local and regional specialisation in other high-value products such as fine wines and cloth – well attested in Attic comedy from the late fifth century onwards – may have done much to improve the economic condition of agricultural labour and improve overall productivity in the Greek world, but archaic evidence is scarce.

We can say only that the fame of some Greek regional products was established by the end of the sixth century. Milesian wool was

---

[57] See Low 2018 on 'hegemony' in (classical) Greece; van Wees 2017a and 2017b on archaic wars.
[58] Miletus: Hdt. 5.28–9; Heracleides Ponticus fr. 50 Wehrli (= Ath. 523f–24a); Plut. *Quaest. Graec.* 32. Mytilene: Arist. *Pol.* 1311b24–31; Megara: Plut. *Quaest. Graec.* 18; with Forsdyke 2012, 117–43.
[59] Ban: Solon fr. 65 L–R; other reforms, see e.g. van Wees 1999.
[60] Calculations based on data from the online Beazley Archive (20 May 2020); 'ca. 550, 525, 500' represent the archive's date ranges 575–525, 550–500, 525–475.

regarded as exceptionally fine throughout antiquity, and we are told that Sybaris in Italy imported a great deal of it before 510. In the late sixth century, Chian sculptors boasted in inscriptions that their work deserved to be as famous as Chian wine, one of antiquity's favourite drinks. At the same time, Thasos began to put official stamps on its amphorae, presumably as a guarantee of quality.[61] Another Attic example is the sought-after honey from thyme-fed bees on Mt Hymettus. Plato's comment that there used to be 'enormous pastures for livestock' on 'some mountains that now have food only for bees' (*Criti.* 111c), is vindicated by the disappearance of shepherds' graffiti at Vari near Hymettus by ca. 500[62] and suggests a real change in use of the land here towards producing honey for the market. Apiculture required little land and minimal investment, so poor smallholders could relatively easily establish a good living from producing honey.[63]

Indirect, but strong, evidence for the development of regional specialisation in the late archaic Greek world is that trade moved to new levels of scale and complexity: the first appearance of specialist merchant ships and the spread of silver coinage. The graffiti from Vari include a few drawings of vessels that still look like the twenty-oared cargo ships of Homer and Hesiod but also feature three dozen images of large merchantmen with deep hulls, powered only by sail. Earlier images from Phoenicia, Cyprus, and Etruria of merchant ships show round hulls and tall bows and sterns curving upwards. The Vari graffiti all show angular hulls and low sterns and bows, a type previously known only from a few vase-paintings of ca. 525 or later, which show traders under attack from pirates.[64] I suggest that the older images all represent Phoenician merchant ships, while the angular vessel was the first merchantman constructed and used by Greeks, in the late sixth century. Some of the ship graffiti have an inscribed caption, of which one says 'I belong to Sostratus'. If this is Sostratus of Aegina, cited by Herodotus (4.152) as the most successful trader in history,[65] his fame may have been due in part to being among the first generation of Greeks to conduct trade of a different order of magnitude, thanks to the new merchant vessels.

---

[61] Milesian wool: Timaeus *FGrH* 566 F 50. Chian wine: Hipponax test. 4 (West, *IE²*). Thasian stamps: Garlan 1999.

[62] Langdon 2015, 54–6; van de Moortel and Langdon 2017, 382–3.

[63] As noted by Balandier 2004; Bresson 2016b, 130–1.

[64] van de Moortel and Langdon 2017, 394–402. Earlier evidence: Chatzidimitriou 2010.

[65] van de Moortel and Langdon 2017, fig. 17 (but they read 'I am Sostratus', p. 400); for the other probable attestations of Sostratus (selling Attic pottery in Etruria), ca. 530–500, see Johnston 1972.

Around 550, the first silver coinages appeared, both where electrum coins were already in use and in the rest of the Greek world. With a value of about one-sixth of electrum, silver coins were suitable for lower-value transactions, with fractions as small as quarter-obols or equivalent. Few of the smallest fractions survive, but a hoard from Colophon, ca. 525, contains hundreds of small fractions struck from hundreds of different dies, which may imply original issues amounting to millions of coins. It can hardly be a coincidence that the earliest mainland Greek issues were struck at Corinth and Aegina, the two city-states with the greatest reputation as centres of trade. The spread of Aeginetan coins, especially 515–490, suggests that they had become the currency of much overseas trade. Other coinages tended to remain confined to local use, presumably in the kinds of market and retail exchange abundantly attested by classical evidence, though only barely in archaic literary texts.[66]

New opportunities created by specialisation and trade, combined with restraints on the exploitation of the free working classes, will have helped some families to establish themselves as independent farmers and begin to form a middling class. A civil war in Naxos, according to Aristotle (fr. 558 (Rose)), arose ca. 540 because a rich, town-based elite refused to pay villagers a fair price for their wares; these villagers were no longer hired or coerced labourers, but economically independent. Naxos produced one of the earliest and largest archaic silver coin issues[67] and our first clear evidence for a non-elite hoplite army: in 500 'the people' of Naxos, who had recently once again driven out the 'fat cats' (*pacheis*), 'had a shield-bearing force (*aspis*) of 8,000' (Hdt. 5.30.4). The vast number, for a modest territory, as well as their opposition to the elite, implies middling-class participation. After this, large numbers of hoplites are fairly common: 4,000 picked hoplite marines in the fleet of Chios in 494, for instance, or 8,000 Athenian, 5,000 Corinthian, and 3,000 Sicyonian hoplites in 479.[68] Aristotle's famous claim that the growing number and importance of hoplite infantry had in the past led to 'the middle' (*to meson*) replacing oligarchies of horsemen (*Pol.* 1297b16–28) also points to a late date for the rise of a hoplite class; such oligarchies were still common in the late sixth century.[69]

---

[66] Colophon hoard: Kim and Kroll 2008. Development of silver currencies: Metcalf 2012; cf. Osborne 2007, 294. Classical markets: Harris and Lewis 2016. Archaic evidence: Homeric epigram 14.2–6 = Hes. fr. 302 M–W (pottery sold in *agora* and streets); Hipponax fr. 76.18 (a place 'where the scoundrel retails cheap wine'). Hdt. 1.153 assumes that already by 545 a permanent market-place was a feature of most Greek cities.

[67] Sheedy 2006; 2012, 111.   [68] Hdt. 6.15.1, 9.28.3. Cf. Strab. 10.1.10.

[69] E.g. the Hippeis of Eretria, 546 (Arist. [*Ath. Pol.*] 15.3), Hippobotai of Chalcis until 506 (Hdt. 5.77), regime of horse-owners at Cyme, post 545 (Heracleides Lembos frs. 38–9 (Dilts)).

Archaeological evidence may reflect the development of a class of independent farmers insofar as the once archaeologically empty countryside fills up with an increasingly dense scatter of pottery sherds from the late sixth century onwards.[70] The reason is perhaps an improved standard of living for those who worked on farms – a change from home-made wooden, wicker, or leather vessels to professionally made black-glazed or painted ceramics. At Athens, marble monuments on the Acropolis dedicated between 550 and 475 by Smicythe the 'washerwoman', two fullers, a carpenter, and three potters as tithes from their earnings is direct testimony that town-based enterprises were also prospering.[71] A steep increase in the number of graves, combined with the simplicity of most grave monuments, again around 500, may be interpreted as a sign that a new social stratum was able to afford the sort of archaeologically visible burial previously confined to the elite.[72]

As newly independent farmers asserted their status by also adopting other forms of elite consumption as much as possible, they created a new demand for high-quality goods, which in turn created still more scope for specialisation in agriculture and craft production. The result was a high degree of division of labour and economic growth. Regions, towns, villages, and families were able to concentrate on selling whatever commodities or services they could most efficiently and profitably produce with their particular skills and resources and buy in markets and shops what others were better equipped to produce.

CONCLUSION

For most of the archaic period, a predatory economic system prevailed. The Greek world from ca. 750 onwards saw the establishment of wealthy elites, the widespread use of slaves, and the occupation of new territories across the Mediterranean, all of which laid the groundwork for later developments. Early archaic elite households aimed to provide directly for all their main needs by farming, herding, and raiding, while exchanging their large surpluses for rare exotic prestige goods, either as passive participants in trade or venturing out themselves as part-time traders. Elite property owners severely exploited the labour of the free poor, thereby adding to their own surpluses while keeping

---

[70] Bintliff 2012, 213–20; Foxhall 2013; Forsdyke 2006; cf. Scheidel 2003, 124–6.
[71] Potters: *IG* I³ 620 (ca. 525), 633 (ca. 510), 824 (ca. 475); carpenter: *IG* I³ 606 (ca. 530); fullers and Smicythe: *IG* I³ 554, 616, 794 (ca. 550–490).
[72] Morris 1987.

levels of consumption in the wider community minimal and archaeo-logically invisible. Only when and where social unrest or outright civil war led to restrictions on exploitation, and when new trading oppor-tunities emerged around 600, did a middling class begin to establish itself and to create demand for a range of staples that they could not produce themselves, as well as for a wider range of prestige goods. In the late sixth century, the economic and social structure of the classical Greek world took shape, as regional and local specialisation and trade networks reached a level that enabled significant – if unquantifiable – per capita growth. Not all parts of the Greek world shared equally in these developments. Sparta, Crete, and Thessaly famously retained the highly polarised social structure of leisured elite and slave workers and con-tinued to aim at agricultural self-sufficiency, institutionalising key fea-tures of the old predatory regimes that other Greek cities and regions were leaving behind.

Further Reading

The archaic age is not usually considered in much detail in major studies of the ancient Greek economy, but chapter-length discussions of the economy of the period include Osborne 2007; Descoeudres 2008; van Wees 2009. Older studies of archaic Greece tend to be rather too modernising or primitivising, but there is much of value in Starr 1977; Snodgrass 1981; and, on archaic Corinth, Salmon 1984. The major study of coerced labour is Lewis 2018b.

4: The Classical Period

Emily Mackil

Introduction

At the turn of the fifth century, the economy of the Greek world was changing rapidly in several respects. The human population was still on a trajectory of growth that had begun in the Iron Age. And despite our certainty that casualty rates in the increasingly high-stakes and frequent warfare of the fifth and fourth centuries will have slowed the rate of growth, the population nevertheless continued to increase.[1] The expansion of the Achaemenid empire to the eastern edge of the Greek world and its deployment of Phoenician and Levantine navies in the Aegean had prompted Greek states in the late sixth century to adopt triremes in place of pentekonters. These were altogether bigger ships, requiring more timber and a crew of two hundred men rather than fifty. Demand for these expensive warships only increased during the conflicts of the fifth century, prompting the need to acquire more timber and silver than ever before.[2] These needs were felt most acutely, of course, by states invested in acquiring and asserting naval power – above all Athens but also Corcyra, Syracuse, and others – but they were broadly shared in the maritime Aegean world. These basic conditions at the start of the fifth century – one endogenous and one exogenous – had far-reaching implications for the economy of the entire classical period. There were more mouths to feed, but labor was also more plentiful. The need for timber and silver influenced the strategies and policies of naval states, creating new trading opportunities and prompting a significant increase in the minting of coinage and, secondarily, in the overall monetization of the economy, a condition that dramatically facilitated trade at every level.

[1] Scheidel 2003; Hansen 2006b; Akrigg 2007.   [2] Davies 2013.

Agriculture

Agricultural production responded most immediately to the demographic growth of the classical period. As the population expanded, those engaged in agriculture moved increasingly away from subsistence strategies and toward crop specialization with an eye to selling produce in the market (see Chapters 12 and 13, this volume). While the slave population was certainly increasing, technological innovation was slow.[3] These may well be related facts: the existence of cheap slave labor would, a priori, have suppressed technological innovation, but the causal relationship is impossible to prove. The availability of slave labor was not enough, on its own, to make agricultural intensification an economically rational strategy for any but the wealthiest landowners. This is a function not only of the relatively low fertility of much agricultural land in the Greek world but also of the costs associated with the employment of slaves year-round in what was in practice a highly uneven annual cycle, with intense periods associated with plowing, sowing, and harvesting, and slack periods throughout the rest of the year.[4] Instead, subsistence and mid-range farmers relied on cattle as well as hired help for the labor crises.[5]

Extensification was more widely pursued. Some wealthy individuals were acquiring large estates on which cereal production was accompanied, on smaller scales, by the production of pulses, vegetables, and even kindling that was sold as firewood, sometimes for a significant profit.[6] Literary sources suggest, at least in Athens, that these large estates, which could encompass the production of multiple commodities, were worked by significant numbers of slaves. But extensification as a strategy was also available to less wealthy individuals prepared to cultivate lands that had previously been regarded as marginal, the produce of which complemented that of the core agricultural areas.[7] More agricultural land was made available to producers as sanctuaries began in the classical period to lease their sacred land as a means of generating revenue for their activities from the increased demand for cultivable land within a polis.[8]

Some poleis that were exceptionally well situated for growing particular commodities began in the classical period to organize the export of their surplus. Thus in the fifth century, the Thasians began to

---

[3] Lewis 2018b.   [4] Osborne 1995, 33–5.   [5] Jameson 1977–8; Halstead 2014, 60–1, 121.

[6] Predominance of cereals: Amouretti 1986, 51–2; Isager and Skydsgaard 1995, 24. Firewood: [Dem.] 42.7.

[7] Forbes 1996; Horden and Purcell 2000, 178–90.

[8] Papazarkadas 2011. Especially informative examples include *IG* I[3] 84 (= Osborne and Rhodes 2017, no. 167) and *IG* XII 7, 62 (= Rhodes and Osborne 2003, no. 59).

export their wine in significant quantities, and the inhabitants of Sicilian Akragas "accumulated fortunes of unbelievable size" by selling their olive oil to the Carthaginians.[9] Communities around the Black Sea appear to have intensified their engagement in the production of grain for export to the Aegean, evidently glad to meet the nutritional demands of an expanding population that outstripped its own growing capacity. The Greek settlers at Cyrene, possessing a territory with exceptionally fertile agricultural land, probably engaged in cerealiculture from the time they arrived in the second quarter of the sixth century, but the scale of the community's capacity for export is illuminated only by an unusual document of the late fourth century listing quantities of grain exported from Cyrene to different states in the Greek world during a widespread grain shortage.[10]

CONSTRUCTION AND INDUSTRY

The population growth of the period also resulted directly in increased construction activity, particularly visible to us in monumental projects (Chapter 11, this volume). In Athens, these projects are further associated with the fifth-century imperial experiment. This involved the monumentalization of the city on an unprecedented scale and at a rapid pace over the second half of the century, from the Parthenon (begun in 447) to the Erechtheion (completed in 407). These projects were tremendously costly but like all infrastructure projects, they spurred a great deal of economic activity, including the quarrying of limestone and marble, the acquisition of timber, the employment of architects, masons, carpenters, and sculptors, and the acquisition by mining or import of both base and precious metals.[11] The thalassocratic project to which the Athenians committed themselves in both the fifth and fourth centuries also meant constant purchases of high-value shipbuilding timber and associated goods such as hemp for sails and ropes, and pitch and ocher for waterproofing and drying hulls.[12] Timber was

---

[9] Thasos: Osborne and Rhodes 2017, no. 103. Akragas: Diod. Sic. 13.81.4–5.

[10] Rhodes and Osborne 2003, no. 96 with Bresson 2011. Horden and Purcell 2000, 65–74 describe the ecology of the Cyrenaica and explain its high agricultural capacity, while warning that the overall prosperity of the region throughout history depended on its connections with other microregions.

[11] Accounts of various stages of construction survive and are highly informative: Osborne and Rhodes 2017, no. 135 (Pheidias' statue of Athena Parthenos, 447–438), Osborne and Rhodes 2017, no. 145 (Parthenon, 434/3), and Osborne and Rhodes 2017, no. 181 (Erechtheion, 409–407) offer a representative sample with recent commentary and references.

[12] Ocher: Rhodes and Osborne 2003, no. 40. The understudied Athenian naval inventories of the fourth century (*IG* II² 1604–32) contain valuable information on the precise nature and quantity of the equipment associated with the fleet in that period.

imported primarily from the northern Greek world, and documentary evidence reveals that the Athenians cultivated relationships with the rulers of timber-exporting regions in order, presumably, to ensure a regular supply as well as to secure attractive prices.[13]

This was not a strictly Athenian phenomenon: large-scale construction and ship-building activities are attested throughout the fifth and fourth centuries. Large temples were built, for example, at Delphi, Delos, Epidaurus, and Bassai.[14] In the late fifth century, the Spartans finally built a substantial fleet; the fact that it was financed primarily by the Persians in no way diminishes the level of extraction, exchange, and labor that the effort must have stimulated. The *koinon* of the Chalcideis in northern Greece concluded an alliance with Amyntas III of Macedon in the early fourth century that granted them generous terms for the export of precious Macedonian ship-building timber.[15] And in the 360s, the Boeotian *koinon* set out to build a fleet of 100 triremes.[16] We can only infer that all of this construction generated a great deal of associated economic activity, from the acquisition of raw materials to a heightened demand for both skilled and unskilled labor.

MONETIZATION

In the previous two sections, allusion has been made to exports and imports, market exchange, the leasing of land, and wage labor. In the classical period, all of these transactions were carried out by means of precious-metal coins, overwhelmingly of silver but occasionally of electrum and even gold. If the introduction of coinage was a hallmark of the sixth century (Chapter 3, this volume), the rapid and widespread expansion of the money supply was a prominent feature of the fifth, and a development tightly bound up with other changes of the period.

Athens lay at the heart of this development. After discovering particularly rich silver deposits at Laurium in southeast Attica ca. 520–515, they began to mint their signature "owls" – tetradrachms with the head of Athena on the obverse and an owl on the reverse – on a truly massive scale. One major series minted ca. 490–480 has been estimated, on the basis of the number of dies indicated by surviving specimens, to

---

[13] Meiggs 1982, 120–32, 433–40. Athenian alliance with Perdikkas of Macedon: *IG* I³ 89, l. 31; Athenian honors for Archelaos of Macedon: Osborne and Rhodes 2017, no. 188.
[14] Delphic building accounts: Rhodes and Osborne 2003, no. 45, no. 66. Epidaurus building accounts: *IG* IV² 1, 102–20. For timber in these accounts, see Meiggs 1982, 422–33, 441–57.
[15] Rhodes and Osborne 2003, no. 12.   [16] Mackil 2013, 78–81.

have produced more than five million tetradrachms.[17] This was not an exceptional episode; the rate of coin production at Athens did not lag until the last third of the fifth century, when they began to really feel the economic effects of the Peloponnesian War. But to fully appreciate the implications of minting activity on this scale, one needs to consider not so much the labor involved in striking coins at the mint, but that required to extract the silver of which they were composed. It has been estimated that sixteen kilograms of ore had to be extracted in order to produce a single Attic drachma of Laurium silver.[18] We can thus estimate that some 320 million kilograms of ore were extracted to produce the Athenian tetradrachms issued over just two decades in the early fifth century. This was hard labor performed exclusively, as far as we can tell, by slaves. When viewed from this perspective, it is difficult to conclude that the Athenians began to mint coins on this scale simply because they discovered that they had the silver to do so. It is more plausible to connect this remarkably large-scale production of silver coinage with the Athenians' commitment to two things. The first was to build and maintain a large fleet of triremes to combat Persian power in the Aegean and western Asia Minor, the importance of which was clarified by the outcome of both the Ionian Revolt of 499–494 and the first Persian invasion of Greece in 490.[19] The second was to import enough grain to feed the growing population of Attica, which outstripped the agricultural carrying capacity of its territory at some point in the classical period.[20]

The Persian Wars certainly interrupted trade in the Aegean, and this, together with the sudden increase in production at Athens, caused a significant diminution in production of the Aeginetan silver coinage that had been dominant as a mechanism for exchange from around 515 onward.[21] After 479, Athenian coin production appears to have supplanted that of Aegina, and by the mid-fifth century, the Athenian tetradrachms, widely desirable for their consistent weight and relatively high degree of purity, had flooded the Aegean and become a widely accepted trade currency in the region.[22] Riding on the back of this

---

[17] Price and Waggoner 1975, 61–4, Group IV, produced from at least 250 dies. Cf. Kroll 2009, 196; Osborne and Rhodes 2017, 336.

[18] Rihll 2001, 115.   [19] Davies 2013.

[20] When and by how much this happened is a matter of fierce debate; for an overview of past approaches and a new model, see Moreno 2007.

[21] Aeginetan coins traveled far (including Persepolis: *IGCH* 1789) and inspired many Cycladic poleis (Sheedy 2006) as well as regions of central Greece like Boeotia and Phocis to adopt the Aeginetan weight standard when they began to strike their own coins. The result was a kind of monetary consolidation that must have facilitated trade (von Reden 2010, 71–2).

[22] Figueira 1998; Kroll 2009, 195–9.

success, the Athenians attempted to impose on all their allies the use of Athenian coins, weights, and measures, but this decree left no impact whatsoever in the numismatic record, and it was evidently not effective.[23]

The Peloponnesian War eventually derailed Athenian monetary production, but this did not come until 413, when the Spartan fortification of Decelea disrupted mining in Attica.[24] There are signs of an acute monetary shortage in the following years. By 407/6, the Athenians were melting down gold dedications that had been made in the city's sanctuaries to produce an exceptional gold coinage, and in 405, they recalled all silver coinage and issued in its stead silver-plated bronze coins to be accepted as having the same value as the equivalent pure silver coin.[25]

Elsewhere in the fifth century, states began to issue bronze coinage with a fiduciary value for exchange in perfectly normal nonemergency circumstances. This major development, which became an integral part of Greek monetary systems for the rest of antiquity, appears to have originated in the mid-fifth century in both the western and eastern peripheries of the Greek world. It appeared first in western Sicily and southern Italy in the mid-fifth century, probably under the influence of the bronze-based weight standard, the *litra*, that was prevalent throughout Italy and Sicily.[26] Bronze coinage was also produced from the mid-fifth century in some Greek settlements on the Black Sea, most notably Byzantium, Istros, and Olbia, which were probably likewise influenced by the monetary practices of the non-Greek, indigenous peoples with whom they were trading.[27] By the second quarter of the fourth century the use of Olbia's own bronze coins in local transactions had become routine and was enforced by a decree of the city.[28] The use of bronze coinage, which met the need for practical, low-value coins for local use in small-scale transactions, infiltrated the center from its peripheral origins. In mainland Greece, bronze coinage began to be produced in the first half of the fourth century. It is well attested in Peloponnesian states, central Greece, Macedonia, and the Cyclades.[29] The silver-producing Athenians,

---

[23] Osborne and Rhodes 2017, no. 155 with Kallet 2001, 205–25.   [24] Thuc. 6.91.7, 7.18–19.

[25] Gold coinage: Hellanikos *FGrH* 4 F 172; Philokhoros *FGrH* 328 F 141. Silver-plated bronze: Ar. *Ran.* 718–26; *Eccl.* 815–22 with Kroll 1996 for their appearance in hoards.

[26] Rutter 1997, 65–8, 141–3.

[27] Psoma 2001, 121. Here the innovation appears to have originated in the production of arrowhead-shaped objects in bronze, which were used as instruments of exchange with the Thracian population along the western and northwestern shores of the Black Sea in the seventh and sixth centuries: Wells 1978.

[28] Dubois 1996, 28–39 no. 14; C. Müller 2010, 387–9.

[29] Peloponnese: Grandjean 1990; 1998. Macedonia: Psoma 2001, 135–6. Cyclades: Sheedy 2012, 114. For an overview, see Picard 1989.

however, only began to produce bronze coins in the mid-fourth century in the context of a broader series of fiscal reforms.[30]

Athenian silver tetradrachms remained popular as a currency for interpolis trade throughout the Aegean world. Yet their own rate of production in the first half of the fourth century was markedly lower than what it had been at its peak in the mid-fifth century. It may have been partly in response to this reduced output that states in the eastern Aegean, Levant, and Egypt began in this period to produce what are usually called imitation owls. These are tetradrachms on the Athenian standard of generally good weight and silver purity; they bear obverse and reverse types that imitate the Athenian ones (obverse, helmeted head of Athena facing right; reverse, owl) but were not products of the Athenian mint.[31] Some of these coins found their way to Athens, where users and officials alike must have struggled over what to do with them; a well-known law of 375/4 resolved the issue by allowing foreign coins "having the same type as the Athenian" to circulate in Athenian markets, provided they were tested and found neither to have a bronze core nor to be counterfeit.[32] The plentiful supply of high-quality silver tetradrachms by the Athenians in the fifth century had clearly accustomed traders across the Aegean to their ready availability; when production levels dropped near the end of the Peloponnesian War, other Aegean users sought to fill the gap, and the Athenians themselves had to reckon with the new monetary reality that this response had created.

It is important to note one additional monetary development of the classical period, namely the appearance of "cooperative coinages," characterized by the coordinated production of coins by more than one polis on a shared weight standard and usually with at least one common type; a shared legend sometimes enhanced the unity of the issues.[33] Some of these were coinages produced within the context of a *koinon* while others were evidently minted by polis partners with no political obligations to one another.[34] Although the motivations and circumstances differed somewhat from case to case, in broad terms this phenomenon suggests that poleis sought ways to facilitate exchange with neighbors, to produce money in support of shared ventures, and to boost revenues across political boundaries. These cooperative arrangements are a subset of the broader phenomenon of monetary networks, only one aspect of which is the use of a shared weight standard

---

[30] Kroll 1979.   [31] van Alfen 2005 with references to detailed numismatic studies.
[32] Rhodes and Osborne 2003, no. 25.   [33] Mackil and van Alfen 2006.
[34] For the economic implications of *koinon* coinages, see Chapter 24 in this volume; Psoma and Tsangari 2003 provide a numismatic survey.

(Chapter 20, this volume). One of the most striking examples of such a cooperative coinage is that between Mytilene, the largest and easternmost of the Lesbian poleis, and its mainland Ionian neighbor Phocaea. An inscription of the late fifth or early fourth century documents the agreement to mint an electrum coinage, with the two cities taking responsibility for production in alternating years.[35] The basic agreement probably goes back to around 500, when the series of electrum coins minted by both cities begins. The general abandonment of electrum as a material for Greek coinage in the sixth century was probably due to the difficulty of ensuring a stable alloy and therefore an inherent value, but it persisted in northwest Asia Minor, above all at Cyzicus, and appears to have been utilized primarily in the Black Sea trade.[36] The cooperative arrangement, which also involved an agreement about the alloy, probably reflects a shared commitment to produce these coins as a commodity for export and therefore also as a source of revenue for the producers.

The mid-fourth century saw yet another major monetary change of the classical period, namely the production of a very large gold coinage by Philip II of Macedon following his conquest of the region around Mt. Pangaion, rich in both gold and silver. The gold coinage immediately saw wide circulation and set a precedent that was closely followed by his son Alexander III and the early Hellenistic rulers who claimed to succeed him. While Philip's silver coins were minted on the standard adopted by the *koinon* of the Chalcideis, Alexander quickly adopted the Attic weight standard. The mineral wealth of the Pangaion region, which had been so vital for Philip (Diod. Sic. 16.8.6–7), was but a drop in the ocean of gold and silver to which Alexander had access when his conquest of the Achaemenid empire was complete. Alexander produced silver tetradrachms on the Attic weight standard in such high volume, and with such a stable metal content, that they quickly became at least as desirable as the old Attic tetradrachms and became the international trade coinage of choice at the close of the classical period.[37]

The varying arrangements for monetary supply and circulation that have been surveyed, designed to meet every need from daily transactions in the marketplace to large state payments, attest to

---

[35] *IG* XII 2, 1; Osborne and Rhodes 2017, no. 195, with up-to-date discussion of the difficulty of dating the inscription.

[36] C. Müller 2010, 226–33 provides a helpful overview, with reference to the most important and recent hoard evidence.

[37] Le Rider 1977 is a comprehensive study of the coinage of Philip II; for that of Alexander, see Price 1991, and for a brief but recent overview with an emphasis on quantities of coins produced, see de Callataÿ 2012, 176–9.

a thoroughly monetized economy by the end of the classical period. Private lenders also began to extend credit to individuals and small groups of borrowers, which had the effect of supplementing the money supply without minting additional coins. The activities of these lenders quickly became organized and formal enough to have earned them the modern description of bankers (Chapter 16, this volume). The loans they extended provided in many cases the capital that was vital for long-distance trade; but the meager evidence for loans made without an actual transference of cash have led some historians to question the extent to which credit in this period in any meaningful way affected the money supply as a whole.[38]

TRADE

The massive increase in the monetization of the Greek world during the classical period was driven by the needs arising from market exchange and long-distance trade, while also facilitating the expansion and increasingly detailed state regulation of those processes (Chapter 15, this volume). Athenian literary sources give the distinct impression that, in the fifth century, Aegean trade was entirely dominated by Athens, with its large urban population and imperial power.[39] But archaeological and documentary evidence combine to suggest that while Athens was indeed a vital commercial hub in this period, Aegean trade was heavily dominated by cabotage, small ships carrying mixed cargoes and stopping at a variety of ports.[40] The traditional picture of Athenian domination is therefore illusory.

The investigation of ancient shipwrecks has transformed our understanding of maritime trade; they reveal not only that small and medium-sized boats were more numerous than large ships but also that the cargoes of these vessels were remarkably heterogeneous. While transport amphoras indicate a high volume of trade in wine, olive oil, pitch, and salted fish, the remains of cargoes surviving on the sea floor show that timber, metals, and both fine- and coarse-ware ceramics of all types and from a wide variety of producers were also conveyed around the Mediterranean by caboteurs in this period.[41] But this still represents

[38] Competing views are presented by Millett 1991 and Cohen 1992. For an overview, see Bresson 2016b, 278–85.
[39] E.g. Xen. [Ath. Pol.] 11–12; Hermippus frag. 61; Thuc. 1.67, 2.38, 3.86; Ar. Ach. 513–38.
[40] Athenian trade policy: Woolmer 2016.
[41] Cabotage: Horden and Purcell 2000, 342–400. For a recent survey of fifth-century shipwrecks in the Aegean, see Carlson 2013 and for the evidence of transport amphoras, Lawall 2011; 2013.

only a tiny fraction of the wide variety of goods being exchanged. A recent study of both Greek and Semitic textual references as well as archaeological evidence for Aegean–Levantine trade in the classical period reveals a vast array of goods in trade, including precious stones, glass, jewelry, herbs and spices for both medicinal and culinary purposes, dried fruit, minerals, furniture, and exotic animals.[42]

Documentary evidence reveals some additional details about commodities traded, but it is most important for the light it sheds on the strategies that states developed to derive revenue from trade. The lengthy surviving account of a customs station at Elephantine, an island in the Nile just north of the first cataract in Upper Egypt, recording duties collected over a ten-month period in 475, tells us that the Achaemenid administration in Egypt collected 20 percent of the value of incoming cargo from Ionian ships, and 10 percent from Phoenician ships. Imported goods include gold, silver, copper, tin, iron, wine, oil, wood, wool, and clay. The only commodity recorded in this list for export was natron, a soda used for dyeing and preserving.[43] In the late fifth century, the Athenians attempted a variety of measures to extract revenue from Aegean trade as their ability to collect tribute from subjects weakened.[44] More typical was their own 2 percent tax on goods imported to and exported from Athens itself, a practice widely adopted throughout the Greek east.[45] But customs duties were not restricted to maritime trade: a fourth-century inscription from Pistiros, an inland *emporion* in central Thrace, reveals the routine collection of overland transit taxes by a Thracian ruler from merchants trading in the area.[46]

Documents also reveal an interest among some states in regulating both the production and the trade of commodities in which they had a special interest. Thus in the early fifth century, the Thasians, whose wine was widely appreciated, sought to protect its quality and thereby ensure its continued value as an export commodity.[47] And when the Athenians were in a position of strength in the 360s, they claimed the right to control the export of ocher, a mineral used for the maintenance of ships as well as a pigment and medicine, from the island of Keos, one of the principal Aegean producers of this valuable commodity.[48]

---

[42] van Alfen 2016.   [43] Yardeni 1994.

[44] The *eikoste*, a 5 percent tax on maritime trade throughout the Athenian *arche* (Thuc. 7.28.4), was implemented in 413 but was certainly short-lived as a result of the Ionian War. From 410 until the defeat at Aigospotamoi in 405, they collected a 10 percent tax on merchant ships passing through the Bosporos (Xen. *Hell.* 1.2.22; Diod. Sic. 13.64.2).

[45] Andoc. 1.133–4. Typicality of customs duties as a strategy to tax on mobility: Purcell 2005.

[46] *SEG* 43.486 with *SEG* 49.911 and *SEG* 63.492.   [47] Osborne and Rhodes 2017, no. 103.

[48] Rhodes and Osborne 2003, no. 40 with Lytle 2013.

But the most heavily regulated commodity in the classical period must have been grain, with which we come full circle. The growing population of the Greek world depended increasingly on imported grain; this was routinely true for large cities like Athens, and true during periods of shortage for virtually all of them. In the second quarter of the fifth century, the Teans uttered imprecations against anyone who prevented the import of grain to the island.[49] In the later fifth century, the Athenians appear to have stockpiled grain that had been exported from the Black Sea at Byzantium, doling out to a strategically chosen few the right to draw on these reserves, which were otherwise certainly destined for Athens.[50] The renewed (if lightly reformed) imperial strength of Athens in the second quarter of the fourth century made it possible for them to promote the cultivation of grain in their cleruchies and to direct its import to Athens itself in the form of a tax.[51] After the Social War, softer tactics were also employed, including the cultivation of good relations with the rulers of grain-producing regions like the Kimmerian Bosporos and legislation to prohibit Athenian citizens from engaging in the sale of grain to any city other than Athens.[52] Officials in charge of the purchase of grain, *sitonai*, are ubiquitous from the fourth century onward, and they showed up in large numbers at Cyrene in early 320s, struggling to deal with a widespread shortage (again Chapter 15, this volume).[53] It must have been against this background that the Athenians resolved in 325/4 to send a colony to the Adriatic "in order that the people might for all time have their own trading posts and conveyance of grain."[54] Although nothing is known of the fate of this expedition, which was likely fruitless, it attests nevertheless to the constant search by states in the classical period for new strategies to secure grain for their growing populations.

CONCLUSION

In certain respects, the economy of the classical Greek world changed little from the early fifth to the late fourth century. Agricultural methods

---

[49] Teos: Osborne and Rhodes 2017, no. 102 A, ll. 6–12.

[50] Garnsey 1988, 121–3. Access granted to Methone (Osborne and Rhodes 2017, no. 150, ll. 34–40) and Aphytis, just south of Potidaia (*IG* I^3 62, ll. 2–6).

[51] Rhodes and Osborne 2003, no. 26 for taxes in kind collected from the Athenian cleruchs at Lembros, Imbros, and Skyros. A cleruchy was also imposed at Samos in 365 (Diod. Sic. 18.18), suggesting that there was a desire to expand this strategy.

[52] Rhodes and Osborne 2003, no. 64; Dem. 34.37, 35.51; Arist. [*Ath. Pol.*] 51.3–4.

[53] Rhodes and Osborne 2003, no. 96.

[54] Rhodes and Osborne 2003, no. 100 (*IG* II^3 1, 370) col. 1, 217–20.

continued largely unchanged, with a mixture of slave and free labor and limited technological innovations encouraging extensification rather than intensification. Yet in most respects, the economy of the classical Greek world underwent significant changes. Where access to land was restricted by the political fragmentation of the Greek world in this period, the volume of cabotage as well as long-distance trade increased to meet the needs of a growing population. Related to this was the marked increase of trade regulations, governing the participation of citizens in interpolis trade, the production of local goods, and the production and use of particular coinages, to name only the most prominent. Undergirding the market exchange of the classical period was a currency system that developed to accommodate changing needs and circumstances. In the early classical period, Attic tetradrachms were widely used in interpolis trade, valued for their good weight and metallic purity; by the end of our period, these had been largely replaced by the tetradrachms minted on the Attic standard by Alexander III. At the same time, bronze coinage, a peripheral phenomenon at the start of the fifth century, was widely adopted in the mainland Greek world during the fourth century to facilitate low-value, local trade, thus extending the practical monetization of the marketplace. Yet the risk of carrying high-value currency on trading expeditions and the need to acquire cargoes for import appear to have prompted a significant increase in the availability of credit through the services of private bankers, who appear in our sources for the first time in the late fifth century.

Further Reading

Bresson 2016b is an indispensable and detailed overview of the workings of the Greek economy, from the archaic to the late Hellenistic period. Halstead 2014 offers an excellent account of ancient agriculture, informed by a deep knowledge of the practices of modern rural Greece, largely untouched by industrialization. Lewis 2018b provides important correctives to many widely held beliefs about slavery in this period.

5: HELLENISTIC ECONOMIES

Sitta von Reden

INTRODUCTION

In 259, a seven-year-old girl was sold in a small town in Transjordan by a certain Nicanor to Zenon, the agent of the top finance officer serving under the second Macedonian king of Egypt, Ptolemy II. Nicanor from Cnidus was Greek, but now in the employ of Toubias, a Transjordan dynast with a Jewish background.[1] Zenon, a native of Caunus, was also Greek, but now lived in Egypt after its conquest by Alexander the Great in 332. The contract which sealed the girl's fate serves well as an introduction to the complexities of the Hellenistic economy:

[In the reign of Ptolemy] son of Ptolemy and of his son Ptolemy, year 27, [the priest] of Alexander and of the Brother and Sister Gods and the *canephore* of Arsinoe Philadelphus being those in office in Alexandria, in the month of Xandikos, at Birta in the Ammanitis: Nikanor son of Xenokles, Cnidian, in the service of Toubias, sold to Zenon son of Agreophon, Caunian, in the service of Apollonius the *dioiketes* a [Babyl]onian (or [Sid]onian?) named Sphragis, about seven years of age, for 50 drachms. [Guarantor . . .] son of Ananias, Persian, *cleruch* of the troop of Toubias. Witnesses [. . .] *dikastes*; Polemon son of Straton, Macedonian, *cleruch* of the cavalrymen of Toubias, Timopolis son of Botes, Milesian, Herakleitus son of Philippus, Athenian, Zenon son of Timarchus, Colophonian, Demostratus son of Dionysius, Aspendian, all four in the service of Apollonius the *dioiketes*.[2]

---

[1] Durand 1997, 45–55 for Toubias and his dealings with Zenon in Palestine; Pfeiffer 2010 for Toubias' background.
[2] *P. Cair. Zen.* I, 59003 (May 259) = Durand 1997, no. 3; transl. R. Bagnall in Bagnall and Derow 2004, no. 143, with minor adaptations.

What is Greek about this transaction apart from its language? Alexander had conquered an empire that had reached from Asia Minor to modern southern Russia, into central Asia as far as modern Afghanistan and Pakistan, along the Levantine coast into Syria and Iran, and into Egypt from the Red Sea to eastern Libya. Including the poleis of Greece and the Aegean, this was an immensely heterogeneous space that included not only the household economies of city states (see Chapters 2–4) but also the large estates of Mesopotamia and the Nile valley that even before the Bronze Age had developed very advanced socio-political systems based on riverine artificial irrigation. The empire also included the mountainous regions of eastern Iran, eastern Anatolia, and central Asia, as well as large stretches of hyper-arid deserts inhabited by mobile populations never easily subjected to political rule or economic exploitation.

We can take from the contract that, in the course of a couple of generations, there developed a veneer of Greekness in some of the regions conquered by the Macedonians: there were Greek military settlers (cleruchs) and civilian immigrants who served the monarchies and engaged with each other. They also dealt with local populations and elites who were willing to cooperate with the conquerors. Kings and immigrants used the Greek language, Greek contracts, and Greek currency and brought with them Greek cultures of consumption and institutions including chattel slavery, which had not been widespread in Egypt before the Greeks arrived.[3] This veneer influenced local economies and behaviour, just as the tribute extraction of the kings affected local economic behaviour in the long run (Chapters 9, 10, and 18, this volume). But can we therefore call these economies Greek? How far did such Greekness extend geographically and socially? And in what ways did the economies of the new world affect the economies of the Greek mainland so well described by Mackil in the previous chapter?

There is something distinctly Hellenistic (that is post-classically Greek) about the social situation represented in the contract. The contractual partners, guarantor, and witnesses all come from different places in the Greek world and show the great mobility that is characteristic of the early Hellenistic period.[4] Moreover, Nicanor, Zenon, and the witnesses identify themselves as subordinates (*hoi peri ton*) or 'belonging to' the troops of individuals high up in the socio-military hierarchy. This not only shows the role of elites and kings in the economies of these regions; it also suggests different

---

[3] Davies 1984.   [4] For immigrants, see Chapter 9, this volume.

structures of economic agency from those we know from Greek poleis where traders were usually independent (Chapters 14 and 15, this volume). Long-distance trade had also changed. In the classical period, directions had been shaped by market relationships between Greek poleis that spread around the Mediterranean and by political ties that created favourable conditions for traders in markets and harbours. In the Hellenistic world, the power of kings, the extent of their empires, and local power brokers influenced the directions of trade and economic opportunities. This created new geographies of trade as well as new social contexts in which it took place. The family of Toubias is well known to us. His ancestors had cooperated with the Assyrian and then the Achaemenid kings, just as he now did with the Ptolemies.[5]

The Hellenistic period was thus an evolving phase of new power relationships, new directions of trade, new fiscal patterns, new settlements, larger cities, new agrarian practices, and fundamental institutional change. Not all places were affected by all these changes to the same extent, and it is our task to understand regional economic change against the background of long-term processes in the Near Eastern-Mediterranean macro-region.[6] New archaeological, epigraphic, numismatic, and environmental data and data analyses constantly improve our evidence, so that increasingly granular analyses can be expected in the future.

URBAN CHANGE, GEOGRAPHY AND TRADE IN THE HELLENISTIC ECONOMY

The Macedonian conquest of the Achaemenid empire initiated a new phase of connectivity between the Mediterranean, the Near East, and Egypt. Alexander founded Alexandria (alongside many other cities in the course of his campaigns) as a coastal city that soon replaced inland Memphis as the royal capital and the harbour of Heracleion-Thonis on the Canopic mouth of the Nile that had been the main gateway to the Mediterranean in previous times.[7] Alexandria developed into a commercial hub, while Rhodes, closer to the western Asian coast than the Piraeus of Athens, became the major port of transit and exchange in the Aegean.[8] Ptolemy II built several ports along the western coast of the Red Sea, reaching out into

---

[5] Terpstra 2019, 125–67 for the importance of personal network relationships in the Hellenistic economies; see also Chapter 23, this volume.
[6] J. G. Manning 2018, 53–71.
[7] Fabre and Goddio 2010 for the former importance of Heracleion-Thonis for Greek trade with Egypt.
[8] Gabrielsen 2013.

the kingdoms further south in Africa and the Arabian peninsula. He also reopened a canal that connected the Red Sea with the Nile Delta between Arsione and Bubastis (see Map o. 4). From the Hellenistic period onwards, the Mediterranean economy expanded towards a 'two-ocean system' connecting the Mediterranean with the Red Sea and Indian Ocean.[9]

Seleucus shifted one of the main royal residences from Persepolis in the Persis to Babylonia, where he founded Seleucia-on-the-Tigris as a new royal centre (Chapter 10, this volume). Benefitting from the existing continental road network, smaller and larger urban foundations in Syria, one of them Antioch, connected the Babylonian core more closely to the Mediterranean and vice versa.[10] The Seleucid urbanisation policy in Asia Minor created larger urban units by synoikism (amalgamation of urban spaces), concentrated resources, and integrated smaller poleis into more powerful economic actors in a crucial region between eastern Anatolia and the Mediterranean (Chapter 24, this volume, on the economic effects of such confederations).[11]

From the late third century onwards, the growing city of Rome became a new factor that cannot be neglected in the Hellenistic economy. The links between Rome and the eastern Mediterranean became stronger when Rome asserted its control over the Greek cities of southern Italy and Sicily, which, to judge from their coinages, had maintained close economic ties with the Hellenistic east. Rome started to dominate the Aegean and Asia Minor politically from the early second century onwards. Among the many indices of Rome's increasing economic role in the eastern Mediterranean are the presence of Italian merchants in Alexandria, the eastward movement of Italian amphorae, and the settlement of Romans and Italians on Delos.[12] By 166, Rome had gained so much power over the Hellenistic world that it could grant the status of free port to Delos, which was more conveniently connected to Italy and Rome than Rhodes.

The Macedonian conquests mobilised people, resources, and goods in the Mediterranean and the Near East more than in previous centuries and linked them across a larger space.[13] With the growth of Rome and the transformation of Italy in the west, the Hellenistic economy reached a 'global' scale, even though the effects of this scale

---

[9] J. G. Manning 2018, 89; Sidebotham 2011 for the Red Sea ports; von Reden 2019c, 28 for the Pithom Canal first constructed under Darius I.
[10] Kosmin 2014, 183–211; Boehm 2018, 29–88.   [11] Boehm 2018, 99–127; Aperghis 2004.
[12] von Reden 2019c.
[13] The five-fold increase in the volume of trade that passed through Piraeus at the end of the fifth century and Rhodes in the early second, the spread of signed amphora handles, the distribution of shipwrecks, and coin hoards are clear indicators of the changing directions and volumes of trade; Davies 1984, 270–85; Davies 2006, 84–5 (for discussion of shipwreck evidence).

need to be assessed in detail at a regional level rather than in terms of global market development. What stimulated the economy, who profited from it, and how did the global imperial framework affect local economies?

WAR, FINANCE, AND INSTITUTIONAL RESPONSE

The Hellenistic empires were military monarchies. Their power and legitimacy were based on conquest, and their access to resources and people was justified ideologically by all land being 'spear-won' (*doriktetos*; e.g. Diod. Sic. 18.43.1).[14] Most first-generation immigrants were mercenaries or members of the Macedonian military elite. They settled as cleruchs (see above, p. 44), and their social status and networks were circumscribed by their military status. The successors of Alexander were constantly at war with each other, and there were areas (most notably Syria, but also Thrace, Anatolia and the Aegean) that remained arenas of never-ending warfare. Antiochus III, moreover, launched a large campaign into Asia Minor and central Asia to regain Alexander's empire, but the conquered regions were soon lost again to his rivals. From the late third century onwards, the powerful Roman military state entered the eastern Mediterranean, with armies and financial capacities of a new size, creating more destruction and economic loss than in previous centuries.[15]

The Hellenistic period was not only one of almost incessant warfare but also one of larger numbers of troops and ships and increased size of crews, as well as changing military technology, including catapults, siege engines, and war elephants. Alexander started with an army of 40,000 to 50,000 men (Diod. Sic. 17.3–5) that may be compared to the 13,000 soldiers (plus 16,000 reserve) that Thucydides says the Athenian alliance led into the war against the Peloponnesians (Thuc. 2.13.5). Ptolemy IV's army in the battle of Raphia is reported to have numbered around 75,000, while Antiochus III mobilised 62,000 infantrymen and 6,000 cavalrymen for the same encounter.[16] Kings also experimented with larger and heavier ships. The first 'hexareme' (warship with six banks of oars) is attributed to Dionysius II of Sicily. The

---

[14] Davies 1984, 295; von Reden 2019c; Fischer-Bovet 2014, and Chapter 9 below, for the ideology of spear-won country; Austin 1986 for the centrality of warfare in Hellenistic economy and society.

[15] From 200 onwards, Rome rarely mobilised armies of less than 100,000 men; for the consequences: Sekunda in Sekunda and de Souza 2007, 336.

[16] For the Ptolemaic army, Polyb. 5.65 with Fischer-Bovet 2014, 77–81. For the Seleucid figures, Sekunda in Sekunda and de Souza 2007, 347; for Roman mobilisation, ibid., 336.

fleet of Ptolemy II is said to have had two 'thirties', one 'twenty', four 'thirteens', two 'twelves', fourteen 'elevens', thirty 'nines', thirty-seven 'sevens', five hexaremes, and 224 'fours', plus triremes and smaller ships. Possibly the largest of these ships were built just for representative purposes (e.g. Plut. *Dem.* 34).[17] Elephants also became part of the shock effects of Hellenistic armies. Much of the growing maritime infrastructure along the Red Sea can be explained by the Ptolemies' demand for elephants from Nubia and Aithiopia.[18]

Military costs rose accordingly.[19] Apart from the costs of larger armies and new technologies, there was a competition for the highest honoraria to be paid to soldiers on the occasion of victory. Many of these occasions were so emblematic that new coinages were minted in the name of the glorious king.[20] After the battle of Raphia, 300,000 gold coins, equivalent to 6,000,000 Ptolemaic drachms were distributed to the troops.[21] It is no surprise that the best offers made to mercenary soldiers became a hallmark of royal power in the Hellenistic period (e.g. Theoc. *Id.* 14; see also Chapter 9, this volume).

Most heavily affected by the changing scale of warfare were the treasuries of Greek poleis. On the mainland and in the Aegean, poleis did not impose regular taxes on their citizenry but relied on harbour tolls and indirect taxes.[22] New urban infrastructure, harbours, and defensive walls to protect against heavy artillery had to be financed from special funds and the pooling of federal income.[23] Elite donations for protecting the city, repairing walls, or supporting allied cities increased in importance. A new scale of financial hardship caused by the heavy warfare of the Romans (Chapter 6, this volume) is exemplified by the correspondence between Cytinium, a small town in central Greece, and Xanthus in Asia Minor. After the walls and houses of the Cytinians had been badly damaged by the Romans, they asked for help. But the Xanthians, too, could procure no more than a mere 500 drachms:

> Not only have we spent the entire public money and taken
> out many loans, but because of a decree regulating the

---

[17] De Souza in Sekunda and de Souza 2007, 357–67.

[18] Bugh 2006a; Sekunda and de Souza 2007 for changing military technology; Sidebotham 2011, 39–53 for Red Sea development and elephant imports; Kosmin 2014, 31–58 for the gift of elephants from the Indian king to Seleucus I.

[19] Several comparative discussions in Burrer and Müller 2008.   [20] Thonemann 2015b, 24–42.

[21] Raphia Decree Gr. Text A, ll. 1–20 (Thissen); with von Reden 2007b, 50, 76.

[22] Chaniotis 2005, 115–42; Boehm 2018, 93–7; Bresson 2016b, 345–50 for the division of labour as a stimulant to market development and, by implication, the income derived from tolls and market fees.

[23] Chaniotis 2005; ibid., for the expenses for repairing walls.

financial administration, it is also impossible to impose upon the citizens any additional requisitions for a period of nine years. And the wealthiest citizens have recently made great extraordinary contributions due to the calamities that have occurred.[24]

The reply reveals not only the detrimental effect of warfare on local finances but also the administrative response the disaster evoked: long-term restrictions on public borrowing and heavier reliance on the financial capacity of a few wealthy donors. Yet despite their lament, the cities did not go bankrupt. Quite on the contrary, the need to finance warfare, diplomacy, and defence systems spurred the inventiveness of Greek cities and led to much institutional innovation.[25]

AGRARIAN DEVELOPMENT AND INNOVATION

Greek presence in the occupied territories gradually transformed agricultural practices and organisation.[26] Conversely, royal support of agricultural experiments and research on plants, animals, and hydraulic engineering in the imperial centres affected agriculture and agricultural knowledge in the wider Greek world.[27] Already in the Aristotelian school at Athens, but more so under royal patronage in the Hellenistic capitals, a body of theoretical literature developed that encouraged an interest in cultivation methods and soil improvement among an educated elite. The Roman agronomist Varro (first century) lists fifty agronomic writings that were either written or translated into Greek under the Hellenistic kings. Manuals influenced not so much the smallholders in their daily routines as estate managers, kings, and administrators that had a fiscal interest in agrarian surplus. Yet even if the impact remained socially limited, the dissemination of theoretical literature gradually spread agricultural knowledge.

There was also direct royal intervention into agricultural practice. Such intervention, however, was not motivated by mercantile policies, but by fiscal and urban demand. As is best documented in, but not exclusive to, Egypt, soldiers and military personnel were rewarded with

---

[24] SEG 38.1476, 49–57, 93–104 (206 BCE) with Chaniotis 2005, 117–18; see also IMylasa 602 (40 BCE) with Reger 2003, 351–2 for the devastation that the Romans caused.
[25] Reger 2007; Bresson 2016b passim.
[26] See Chapters 8 and 9; Vandorpe 2015 for an excellent microanalysis of the transformation processes.
[27] Thompson 1999; Reger 2007.

parcels of land (*kleroi*), which provided them and their families with an agrarian income and social status in the areas they settled.[28] The newly founded cities and military forts also required a hinterland from which garrisons and populations were fed. One of the best examples of agricultural development is the land reclamation project of the Fayum under Ptolemy II, which not only served the settlement of cleruchs but also the agrarian supply of Alexandria (Chapter 9, this volume).[29] The papyrological archive related to this project shows the intense interest the king devoted to the region and the degree of collaboration that was expected from the beneficiaries of the land-donation scheme.

The Tigris valley, too, experienced agrarian development at the beginning of the Seleucid period, probably as a result of the growth of Seleucia.[30] Arrian reports that Alexander had already improved the irrigation system around Babylon by laying a new arm to the Pallacotas Canal derived from the river Euphrates north of Babylon (*Anab.* 7.21.6). Other initiatives ascribed to Alexander include the regulation of Lake Copais in Boeotia (Strab. 9.2.18) and the reclamation of land around Lake Ptechai in Eretria.[31] Similar to the Fayum project, although on a much smaller scale, were the provisions for the use of newly reclaimed temple land at Uruk under Antiochus III (Chapter 10, this volume).[32] The Attalid king Philetaerus of Pergamum showed a special interest in cattle breeding and pasture land in his realm (*OGIS* 748).

Of broader significance for the Mediterranean economy was the shift in Egypt from emmer to naked wheat as the main crop for production, tax payment, and marketing.[33] Although more sensitive to weather conditions and more difficult to process into bread, durum (naked) wheat had long become the preferred cereal in the Mediterranean. It was therefore in greater demand in Alexandria, Syria, and other Mediterranean markets than Egyptian emmer. The Ptolemaic policy, together with the shift of the capital to the Mediterranean coast and the introduction of Greek-style coinage, shows the energy with which the kings pushed towards integration into the Mediterranean exchange networks.

---

[28] Sekunda in Sekunda and De Souza 2007, 334; Fischer-Bovet 2014, 199–220.

[29] Von Reden 2011, 429–30.

[30] J. G. Manning 2018, 116 ; chapter 10, this volume, for discussion.

[31] Bresson 2016b, 164–6 for this and other projects not all going back to royal initiative. The emphasis of our sources on royal rather than local initiative is likely to have followed royal self-representation; J. G. Manning 2018, esp. 102.

[32] Sarkisan, *Forschungen und Berichte* 16 (1974), no. 1; transl. van der Spek 2000, 31–2; and further examples.

[33] Von Reden 2011, 429–30; J. G. Manning 2018, 121.

COINAGE AND MONETISATION

Alexander had paid for his campaigns and soldiers with Macedonian gold and silver coins, thus contributing to a considerable expansion of coin use and minting along the routes of his campaigns.[34] He also captured the treasuries of the Achaemenid kings and turned them into coinage.[35] After his death, the high demand for coins continued. Mints were installed in large cities such as Alexandria, the Syrian coastal towns, Antioch, Seleucia-on-the-Tigris, and wherever kings or local administrations needed money.[36] A major source of spending was the military, but the rituals to celebrate the kings, the expansion of the courts, the festival culture, and above all payments of cash subsidies to other states also increased the demand for coins.[37] The monetisation of private exchange and of contractual relationships (tenancies, loans, labour contracts, etc.) followed. An absolute increase in the demand for coinage across the Hellenistic empires can be measured not only on the basis of mint volumes, but by the evidence of hoards. Almost 80 per cent of all hoards containing Greek coins date from the period between 330 and 30.[38] Moreover, the Meydancikkale in Rough Cilicia, uniquely in the history of numismatics, brought to light more than 5,200 coins from six different currencies.[39] It shows intense minting, especially in Alexandria, from the first half of the third century onwards.

The early Hellenistic kings introduced coinage into local administrations, paid soldiers in Greek currency, and paid in cash for the construction of the new capitals and cities. Banks were established to collect monetary taxes, pay out money to armies, and extend loans. Trade activities not only overseas but also along the caravan routes involved coinage. Under Antiochus III, finds of Seleucid coins the Persian Gulf increase significantly, suggesting that trade with the Arabian kingdoms and India involved coinage. Increasing monetisation not only increased monetary exchange among the Greeks and Hellenised parts of the population but also affected local economies. It has been shown, for example, that in Egypt there was a gradual increase in the frequency with which tenancies of temple land were based on fixed-term contracts, as typical of monetised economies, and on wage

---

[34] Holt 2016 for a recent discussion of Alexander's finances.
[35] de Callataÿ 1989; ancient references in Diod. Sic. 17.66.1–2, 71.1, 80.3; Just. *Epit.* 12.1.1.
[36] Thonemann 2015b for an excellent discussion of Hellenistic minting activity.
[37] Davies 1984 emphasises the role of the latter.   [38] Davies 1984, 277.
[39] De Callataÿ 2005b.

labour remunerated in cash. Private sales of land also became more frequent.[40]

The importance of coinage continued to differ by region. In the cities and on the islands of the Greek heartland, northern Greece, and Macedonia, little changed at first. Local governments retained their right to mint, and a number of currencies circulated together.[41] However, posthumous Alexander-type coins dominated because of their widespread acceptance. From the late fourth century onwards, moreover, there was a significant increase in the number of bronze coinages, suggesting an increase in local demand for small change, as well as a scarcity of silver to supply the ever-growing monetary needs of the royal economies.[42]

In Seleucid Asia, local coins continued to circulate; civic bronze coinages, Aramaic shekels, and Persian gold darics (Chapter 16, this volume) circulated with Seleucid coinage and the coinages of independent kings. The Macedonian kings minted special coinages locally to celebrate victories or other events. There is also evidence of Arab imitations of Alexander coins, which was another way of integrating oneself into the imperial monetary network.[43] Pressure on the population to pay with imperial coinage was exerted only to the extent that some taxes and duties were explicitly demanded in Seleucid coins. Yet they could be paid in other forms and be exchanged by tax farmers or banks before they reached the treasury.

The Ptolemies pursued a different policy. Neither the pharaohs nor the Persians had used coins in Egypt for more than limited purposes. Yet the Macedonians immediately after the conquest began to mint coinage in Egypt and to use it as an all-purpose money.[44] Ptolemy I, moreover, gradually reduced its current weight standard and stipulated that all heavy foreign coins had to be exchanged into lighter Ptolemaic currency at a ratio of 1:1. This not only created considerable income to the Alexandrian mint but also the largest closed-currency system yet established in the Greek world (see further Chapters 6, 9, and 18, this volume). The Ptolemies also pursued the monetisation of the countryside more aggressively than the Seleucids. Many taxes, tolls, and royal rents except those on grain land (and vineyards in the early Ptolemaic period) were levied in cash. In order to lubricate the cash flow, Alexandria minted a token bronze coinage that was nominally equivalent to silver coins. In the last two decades of the third

---

[40] J. G. Manning 2018, 117–25 with further discussion.   [41] Ashton 2012.
[42] De Callataÿ 2005a; Thonemann 2015b, 268.   [43] Salles 1987.
[44] von Reden 2007b for this and the following.

century, the bronze coinage became the main currency in Egypt. The different monetary policies of the Seleucid and Ptolemaic kings suggest not so much different economic policies as responses to different local constraints.[45]

Although there was clearly a significant increase in the volume of coins in circulation, the overall level of monetisation is extremely difficult to gauge. The close interdependence of payments in cash and in kind in many regions of the Hellenistic world makes it impossible to disentangle the two in the history of monetisation.[46] Although coins and monetary payments are inevitably more visible in our sources than exchanges in kind, the bias of the evidence must not mislead us. Despite the widespread use of coinage, the limits of monetisation can be seen from the fact that antiquity's largest economic resource, grain land, continued to be taxed in kind. Moreover, in view of the complex and regionally different landholding and labour patterns, no monetised markets in land and labour are likely to have developed, and thus put another limit on monetisation.[47]

DEMOGRAPHIC CHANGE AND STANDARDS OF LIVING

Population size and standards of living are generally regarded as inter-related indices of economic performance.[48] There is some evidence to suggest that, during the Hellenistic period, there was some population growth in certain areas and some increase in living standards among some parts of the population. Not everybody enjoyed better living conditions, but those who did so above all were the Greek elites who benefitted from the tributary economy, greater opportunities for trade, and improved institutional infrastructures.

There had been continuous urban and population growth dur-ing the classical period (Chapter 11, this volume). During the Hellenistic period, this growth ebbed away on the Greek mainland, while in the Near East, Egypt, peripheral areas, and also highland regions, settlement and urbanisation increased.[49] Some of these shifts

---

[45] Iossif and Lorber 2021.   [46] von Reden 2007b *passim*.

[47] Vandorpe 2015 for a very clear exposition of the complexities of landholding in Upper Egypt. She and other scholars emphasise the degree of private landholding and land conveyance in Egypt and Mesopotamia, without suggesting there was a market in land; see also Monson 2012, 82; J. G. Manning 2018, 117–25.

[48] Scheidel 2007.

[49] Reger 2003, 334–6 for the discussion of a complex picture; Scheidel 2007 with Alcock 1994, 171–90 for the settlement of marginal regions.

can be explained by migration, resettlement, and urban restructuring. Yet the size and population density of the royal capitals reached dimensions that cannot be explained by population shifts alone. The population of Alexandria is estimated at up to half a million inhabitants by the later Hellenistic period, compared to the population of fourth-century Athens, which is estimated to have numbered about 120,000 citizens plus about the same amount of foreigners and slaves.[50] The possibility of greater urban concentration in the new centres of power suggests that the urban food supply and standards of living must have improved.

What happened in the Greek poleis? Demographically, they do not seem to have increased in size. Yet already by the second half of the fourth century, magnificent and lavishly furnished private houses and tower farmsteads appear in the archaeology of Athens and Attica.[51] More so in the Hellenistic period, wealthy citizens showed off their spending power by means of impressive funerary monuments, golden statues, and generous spending on public buildings, contributions to the grain supply, festivals, city walls, and porticos surrounding Hellenistic agoras. *Euergesia* (elite benefaction) and the public display of honour and status which elite benefactors gained in return for their generosity became a structural pattern of Hellenistic poleis.[52]

Private palaces and funerary pomp were long regarded as signs of 'oriental' influence on Greek lifestyles and the corrosion of Greek egalitarian politics and ethics (for which Chapter 12, this volume). The funerary displays exhibited by Hellenistic mausolea, for example, were thought to have been inspired by Persian practices, namely that of the Carian satrap Mausolus who gave his name to these free-standing houses for the deceased. In Egypt, the residences of Greek officials resembled those of their Persian predecessors, equipped with parks, zoos, and houses furnished with elaborate decorations, silver plate, and equipment, the maintenance of which alone required an administrative apparatus. Even on rural estates, a royal lifestyle was emulated that no longer had anything to do with the moderation of respectable citizens in classical poleis.[53] Officials' behaviour, according to these views, affected Greece and became the tangible sign of increasing inequality and the concentration of wealth in the Hellenistic period.[54]

---

[50] Rathbone 1990 suggests 500,000 inhabitants for Alexandria in the Hellenistic period; J. G. Manning 2018, 222 with further literature for lower figures.
[51] Lohmann 1995.   [52] Reger 2007, 472–4.   [53] Rostovtzeff 1941, 419.
[54] Rostovtzeff 1941, 617–23; 1126–34 and *passim*; de Ste Croix 1981, 300–27.

A recent analysis of the floor plans of Hellenistic houses as a proxy for standards of living has qualified this picture. On the basis of samples from Hellenistic Delos and Olynthus, Geoffrey Kron has argued that, although there was a certain trend towards greater social inequality (as median house sizes slightly declined with an increase in the size and luxury of some elite and sub-elite houses), this trend was modest. More significantly, the evidence reflects continued widespread prosperity, and greater poverty for only a small segment of the population (see also Chapter 27, this volume).[55] More analyses of this kind are needed, but they help to put the greater luxury of elite displays into a broader social and economic perspective. Considering the economic losses caused by the destruction of resources and money as a result of warfare and tribute, the greater spending capacity of elites combined with the relative stability of the living standards of a wider range of people suggest a robust, if not growing, economy in the Greek cities during the Hellenistic period.[56]

CONCLUSION

The conquest of Egypt and Asia, leading to new urban and fiscal infrastructure and new forms and levels of elite consumption, increased the scale of trade and exchange in the Hellenistic economy. Complex institutional changes that were spurred both by fiscal-military demand and by local responses to this demand changed agrarian and commercial patterns with likely positive effects on local markets. With all due caution, given the lack of sufficient data, it can be assumed that the Hellenistic period was one of moderate economic growth both in the Greek poleis of the Aegean and in the core regions of Hellenistic Asia and Egypt. The greater presence of Roman traders in the Hellenistic East from the second century onwards is also likely to have had positive effects on market exchange and monetary circulation. Yet there is also reason to assume that in the final decades of the Hellenistic period, all regions to some extent, but particularly the Aegean and Asia Minor, suffered from the destructive forces of the Roman military presence and subsequent tributary exploitation. Only after the Roman civil wars

[55] Kron forthcoming. For the continuous prosperity of the cities in Asia Minor, Chapter 4, this volume; for cities in the Peloponnese, Shipley 2018, 160–72; for the cities in the eastern Mediterranean generally, Alcock 2007; for increased prosperity in Hellenistic Babylonia, van der Spek 2000; for Egypt, J. G. Manning 2018.

[56] Thus also Bresson 2016b, without specific consideration of change in the Hellenistic period.

came to an end and fiscal practices were better regulated did the economies of the East begin to recover and to expand along the pathways that had developed in the Hellenistic period.[57]

Further Reading

Reger 2003, Davies 2006, and the chapters in part IV of Scheidel, Morris, and Saller 2007 provide succinct overviews of the Hellenistic economies, each with different regional emphases. Davies 1984 and Austin 1986 can still be read with great profit. Thonemann 2015b is an excellent account of the multiple uses and consequences of Hellenistic coinage. Bresson 2016b covers the economy of Hellenistic poleis as part of the history of economic growth in the Mediterranean. J. G. Manning 2018 is essential for understanding the long-term economic connections of the Near Eastern/Egyptian and Mediterranean regions from the Iron Age onwards.

---

[57] Alcock 2007, 679–81, emphasising regional differences in recovery; Monson 2012, esp. 10–16; von Reden 2019d.

PART II

REGIONAL PERSPECTIVES

6: ASIA MINOR

Andreas Victor Walser

INTRODUCTION

Comprising around 750,000 square kilometers, Asia Minor is larger than Spain or Gaul and forms the largest landmass in the northern Mediterranean.[1] From the Aegean coast in the west to Mount Ararat in the east, it extends roughly 1,500 kilometers, 500 to 600 kilometers from the Black Sea in the north to the Mediterranean in the south. The mountainous peninsula is part of the Alpide belt and can be subdivided into several main regions. The fertile coastal region of western Asia Minor is highly fragmented, both by mountain ranges and by the sea cutting deeply into the land, but it is also characterized by several large, fertile alluvial plains. The climate here is typically Mediterranean, with hot, dry summers and mild, wet winters. Along the northern as well as the southern shores, long mountain ranges traverse the peninsula. In general, these mountains fall steeply to the sea, especially in the north, and do not provide easy access to the interior. Apart from the vast expanses of Pamphylia and Cilicia in the south, alluvial plains are sparse. The climate is Mediterranean on the southern shore, subtropical with heavy precipitation in the north of Asia Minor. Between the mountain ranges in the north and south lies the Central Anatolian Massif. Plateau-like, semiarid high plains and basins are the defining characteristics of this area. The climate, while still Mediterranean in the west, becomes continental toward the east, when the central massif rises up to the East Anatolian High Plateau with its deep river valleys and high volcanic mountains. Summers are still hot, but winter temperatures can fall well under freezing point. Overall, Asia Minor is characterized by sharp contrasts even on a regional scale, in both its topography and climate. Differences in precipitation in adjacent areas can be large, and variations over the years are significant (Chapter 25, this volume).

---

[1] For a history of ancient Asia Minor in all of its aspects, see now Marek 2016; ibid., 7–14 for the geography. In what follows, the literature references are limited to recent titles and those that are most essential.

Geography alone might explain why ancient Asia Minor never formed a unified economic space in any meaningful sense of the term. The coastal areas were always connected more closely by the sea with other areas of the Greek world than by land with central Anatolia or more remote regions of the peninsula. This is especially true for western Asia Minor, which throughout its history has been an integral part of the Aegean world, closely intertwined with the Aegean islands and mainland Greece even when political constellations made such connections unfavorable, as at the time when Asia Minor was part of the Persian empire.

This chapter surveys the economy of Asia Minor from the late archaic and classical periods to the end of the Hellenistic period. It looks at Asia Minor as part of the Greek world and focuses on the economy in those parts of Asia Minor that were settled by Greeks. In many ways, the economy of Greek Asia Minor was not fundamentally different from the economy on the mainland or in other regions of the Greek world: it was a Mediterranean agrarian economy with a limited, though significant, role for trade, services, and commerce. Ecological conditions in western Asia Minor were very similar to those on the mainland, the technologies applied in economic production more or less the same. Greek culture defined two basic elements of the economic setting: (1) the *oikos* (household) as the basic social unit of production and consumption and (2) the polis (city-state) as the principal institutional framework (see, by contrast, Chapter 2, this volume). These fundamental structures of the economy are discussed in depth in other parts of this book. The purpose of this chapter is, therefore, not primarily to give a comprehensive and rounded picture of the economy of Asia Minor, but to focus on its specifics.

POPULATION

Estimates of population figures for the ancient world are notoriously difficult, but those for Asia Minor are vague even by the standards of ancient demography. In his pioneering study on the population of the Graeco-Roman world, J. Beloch estimated the size of the population of Asia Minor as around 11 to 13 million in the later Hellenistic period, with 4 to 4.5 million populating the west, two million in the regions south of the Taurus, and 5 to 6.5 million in Anatolia north of the Taurus. More recent estimates, often based on Beloch's, lead to similar figures.[2]

---

[2] Beloch 1886, 223–42, with total numbers on 242; cf. Broughton 1938, 812–16; Aperghis 2004, 46–8, 56–8 (3–5 million in western Asia Minor, 0.5–1.75 million in Cilicia under Seleucid rule); Scheidel 2007, 48 (9–10 million around 165 CE).

As vague as they are, comparisons with census data from the late nineteenth and early twentieth centuries suggest that they may well be in the right order, but they convey little beyond a very general sense of magnitude. Considering the manifest regional differences between almost desert-like areas in central Anatolia and fertile alluvial plains at the coasts, an estimated average population density of fourteen to fifteen persons per square kilometer is of limited significance, and obviously the numbers say nothing about demographic development in Asia Minor. It seems reasonable to assume that it corresponds to the general long-term demographic trends in the first millennium;[3] an increase of the population is certainly to be expected, but it does not seem likely that it was in the same magnitude during the archaic and classical periods. However, archaeological surveys do not show a significant break between the classical and the Hellenistic period but rather suggest continuous economic development and growth.

All this does not take us very far when we are interested in the economy of Greek Asia Minor. At least as significant as the development of population size are changes within its structures, and they are of utmost importance when we focus on Asia Minor in the periods under discussion and more specifically on *Greek* Asia Minor. Migrants from different parts of the Greek mainland first arrived there probably in the eleventh century. Successive phases of migration over the following centuries led to the creation of a still comparatively small number of Greek communities in the coastal areas,[4] first in the west, later in the south and north.

Asia Minor was, of course, not an untouched continent when the Greeks arrived – it was inhabited by local populations. We can only speculate about the first interactions between settlers and indigenous people, immigrants and residents, processes of mixture, absorption, and displacement. The result was in any case not simply an ever-growing area of Asia Minor that was "Greek," but rather a "hybrid Greek/non-Greek cultural mixture."[5] The local populations that inhabited Asia Minor when the Greeks arrived did not form a homogenous group but rather a complex patchwork of diverse cultures with various languages.[6]

Up until the end of the fifth century and even beyond, Greek influences on these indigenous cultures remained limited. Only then did Greek acculturation intensify in Caria and Lycia in southwestern Asia Minor, and by the middle of the third century, the local cultures of these

---

[3] Cf. Chapter 11.
[4] Many questions regarding the Greek "colonization" of Asia Minor remain controversial; recent summaries are provided by Mitchell 2017; Marek 2016, 117–38; Graves 2011; Harl 2011.
[5] Mitchell 2017, 14.
[6] The literature is vast. Cf. Marek 2016, 397–400 and, for a bibliography, 713–15.

areas were deeply "Hellenized." Nevertheless, the role of indigenous traditions, in religion and beyond, remained strong and influential. Much the same is true for other regions and populations, and also in those areas of central and eastern Asia Minor where Greek culture only became dominant in the course of the Hellenistic period. The Hellenization of Asia Minor did not lead to a uniform "Greek" cultural landscape, and some indigenous communities remained largely separated from Greek culture, even though they were in close contact with it.

The Greeks were not the only foreigners that settled in Asia Minor. A significant Iranian diaspora that at least in part went back to the time of the Achaemenid empire (550–330) becomes visible through the textual material. According to Philo, Jews lived in every city of Asia, and they are indeed well represented in the literary, documentary, and architectural evidence.[7] Several groups of Celtic Galatians were brought to Asia Minor as soldiers and settled in central Anatolia, where they continued to live in their tribal structures. Italians started to immigrate in the second century and were soon present in large numbers.[8]

URBANIZATION AND COLONIZATION

From the archaic period onward, "Greekness" is inseparably connected with the polis as the defining form of social and political organization. At the beginning of the Hellenistic period, still only a small part of Asia Minor was organized as city-states with urban centers and a surrounding territory.[9] The amount of land organized in polis territories and administered by, and through, communities of citizens then grew gradually. Following the great king's example, Alexander's successors founded new cities in Asia Minor, at first primarily in the coastal regions; but new poleis also were already appearing deep in the Anatolian hinterland in the early third century.[10] In many cases, the foundations were as much rearrangements and resettlements of preexisting communities as they were genuinely new settlements. The inhabitants of these poleis created by *synoikismos* (the process whereby dispersed settlements joined into one polis) were often a varied mixture of "Greek" soldiers in the service of the kings, often of Macedonian or Thracian origins, and

---

[7] Philo *Leg.* 33 (= 245).
[8] Cf. Weiskopf 1987 (Iranian diaspora); van der Horst 2014 (Jews and Judaism); Mitchell 1993, 11–58 (Celts); Ferrary 2002 (Italians).
[9] Mitchell 2017, 22–8.
[10] Cohen 1995 provides an inventory of the Hellenistic settlements in Asia Minor.

indigenous people, who were integrated into the poleis either as full citizens or as dependent communities with lesser rights. Many of the new settlements, especially those established by the Seleucid and Attalid kings in the third and second centuries, were not self-governing poleis, but colonies of Greek or non-Greek settlers with a more or less distinct military character.[11] Over time, such *katoikiai* could nevertheless develop into cities with a more civic character and receive polis status.[12]

While the Hellenistic period saw the appearance of more than a hundred new cities in Asia Minor, older poleis also disappeared, especially in the regions first settled by Greeks in western Asia Minor. Existing poleis were merged and then formed so-called *sympoliteiai*, either by constituting a new polis or by the integration of the citizens of smaller poleis into a larger one.[13] This often happened on the initiative of a higher authority – a king or his local governor – and against the resistance of the locals.[14] These new foundations, re-foundations, or mergers of cities had profound economic consequences.[15] As political unifications in the first place, they did not necessarily imply large movements of populations in the beginning, but they nevertheless caused fundamental changes in the economic landscape and shifted the movement of people and goods. The urban centers, chosen deliberately for their favorable positions, could attract more and more people and – as centers of production, demand, and distribution – draw and concentrate resources. Only this made possible the rise of large Hellenistic cities like Ephesus or Miletus, with their theaters and gymnasia, temples and *stoai*, and led to the emergence of urban centers on a rather different scale than the small towns in mountainous regions.

These processes of intensive urbanization notwithstanding, large parts of Asia Minor preserved a decidedly rural character throughout the Hellenistic period, and poleis emerged, if at all, only under Roman rule, as in Pontus or Galatia.

AGRARIAN PRODUCTION FOR LOCAL MARKETS AND CONSUMPTION

Even in the more densely urbanized regions of western Asia Minor, agriculture was always the most important economic activity that

---

[11] The epigraphic evidence for these kinds of settlements has increased considerably in recent years: cf., e.g. Thonemann 2011; 2015a. The earlier evidence is reviewed by Daubner 2011.

[12] Famously illustrated by Toriaion: *SEG* 47, 1745; *ISultan dağı* 393.

[13] On the *sympoliteia* in general: Schuler and Walser 2015; Walser 2009; in Asia Minor: Reger 2004.

[14] Teos and Lebedus (*RC* 3–4) or Latmus and Pidasa (Wörrle 2003) are well-known examples.

[15] Cf. Scheidel 2007, 80–5.

occupied by far the most people and made the largest contribution to total production. As stated above (p. 78), agriculture in Asia Minor was very similar to that in mainland Greece or on the islands (Chapter 8, this volume). Here and there, we find a Mediterranean polyculture, with a rain-fed production primarily oriented toward the famous triad of grain, wine, and olives. Other agrarian activities, like animal husbandry, usually played a much smaller role. By far the largest part of the production was consumed by the producers themselves or was distributed locally through markets in the cities and villages, providing for the nutritional needs of the local communities. This form of agriculture should not be mistaken for subsistence farming, but still only a few, specialized agricultural products reached markets beyond the local level.

What we know specifically about agriculture in Asia Minor in the classical period is essentially based on a few literary sources. They show that the Achaemenid kings claimed ownership of all land in Asia Minor.[16] In the eyes of the kings, the *chora basileos*, the king's land, self-evidently also included the Greek poleis and their territory. Accordingly, the kings felt free to provide members of their family or friends with large stretches of land that could include indigenous villages or even Greek poleis.[17] There also existed large fortified rural estates, like that of a Persian nobleman raided by Xenophon's soldiers in the vicinity of Pergamum.[18]

The picture becomes much fuller in the Hellenistic period, when epigraphical sources provide more detailed information. With few exceptions, the inscriptions come from the coastal areas in the west and south. Archaeological surveys that provide important supplementary information usually cover small areas within these same regions. These are marked by similar environmental conditions, normally allowing rain-fed agriculture and the cultivation of olives. In consequence, we still know little about agriculture in inner Anatolia, where the evidence becomes more abundant only in the Roman imperial period.

In contrast to the situation under Achaemenid rule, in the Hellenistic kingdoms there existed a sharp division between the territories of the Greek city-states and land that was not under their control. As recent studies have shown, however, the differences between these two basic categories of land were less clear than previously thought. On

---

[16] On land tenure in Achaemenid Asia Minor: Schuler 1998, 137–57, with references to earlier literature.
[17] Themistocles was famously rewarded with the cities of Magnesia on the Maeander, Lampsacus, and Myus: Thuc. 1.138; Plut. *Vit. Them.* 29.7.
[18] Xen. *An.* 7.8.8–23.

the one hand, the status of poleis varied considerably. While some were formally recognized as free and autonomous by the kings, others were in varying degrees subject to royal command and had to negotiate their rights and obligations toward the crown. On the other hand, nor was the land beyond the borders of the cities' territories simply the property of the king. The king's land – the *chora basilike* – that was directly administered by royal functionaries only represented one part of the total. Other land belonged to settlements with a more-or-less Greek character without polis status, like the military colonies mentioned earlier. Rural communities of mainly indigenous people managed their land and affairs with a certain degree of autonomy as well and were only indirectly governed by the royal authorities. The kings also granted large estates to private individuals, usually subordinates or supporters, who held them frequently as de facto property even if the royal grant may have been under retention of title.[19]

We are not very well informed about the settlement and land-holding structures within these different categories of land, and it is not to be expected that they were uniform. The Greek poleis were already complex entities that rarely correspond to a simple model of an urbanized center, where the inhabitants lived, and a surrounding agrarian hinterland, where they were tilling the soil and harvesting the crops.[20] The territory of many cities comprised *demoi* or *komai*, small villages on the periphery that sometimes developed around a rural sanctuary or fortification or had been independent communities in earlier times. As subdivisions of the polis, they could enjoy considerable political and administrative autonomy. Some city-states also housed larger groups of people without full citizenship, whose legal status is often very difficult to define. Some of them were of indigenous origin and worked land owned by the city and paid tribute to it.[21]

Furthermore, archaeological surveys have called attention to the significance of dispersed and isolated residential farmsteads. In general, these farmsteads were not small subsistence farms, but rather larger, sometimes fortified building complexes that must have been the center

---

[19] I follow the views developed in Schuler 1998, 159–94, summarized and confronted with diverging views, e.g. Boffo 2001, in Schuler 2004, 514–19. Cf. also Thonemann 2009, with a penetrating analysis of the status of "private" estates and the famous Mnesimachus inscription *ISardis* 1.

[20] The topic has been intensively discussed in recent years. For short summaries: Walser 2015, 415–16; Schuler 2004, 519–21; Chandezon 2003b, 202–4, all with further literature; Schuler 1998, 195–215 remains fundamental.

[21] The literature on this topic is controversial. Beyond the titles already cited, cf. Papazoglou 1997, with critical remarks by Ph. Gauthier, *Bulletin épigraphique* 1998, 107.

of at least medium-sized estates. This dispersed settlement structure is of considerable economic significance. It allowed intensified agrarian exploitation of land that was not easily reachable from the main urban center of the polis. The inherent interpretative difficulties of the archaeological evidence make it difficult to trace the development of the settlement structure over time. Both in Cyaneai in Lycia and in the territory of Miletus in southern Ionia – two of the best-explored areas – the number of isolated farmsteads seems to have increased considerably in the Hellenistic period. In the hinterland of Miletus, the cultivation of less-fertile and marginal areas also intensified in the Hellenistic period. Since this required considerable investment, it seems to have been driven by larger estate-holders and could have led to a concentration of rural possessions at the expense of small peasant landholders. There are, however, no clear signs that this was a general trend in western Asia Minor.[22]

Overall, we lack evidence to assess the average size of landholdings and the distribution of possessions. Comparison with mainland Greece suggests, however, that small and medium estates owned by citizens were of considerable importance.[23] Illuminating insights into the inner structure of agricultural domains are provided by an exceptional group of land-lease records from the city of Mylasa in Caria.[24] The descriptions of the plots and estates clearly reflect the mixed character of agriculture in this region: the plots of land, sold to the city and immediately leased back by the previous owners, must have been primarily used for the cultivation of cereals, but regularly contained areas that were reserved for viticulture. On some plots stood olive, or rarely fig, trees; olive presses are mentioned as part of the inventory as well as, in rare cases, stables or beehives.

Villages of various sizes and legal statuses were clearly the dominant form of settlement in the *chora*. Their inhabitants were of Greek or indigenous origin, and they worked, sometimes side by side, farms owned by themselves, their landlords, or the kings to whom they paid tribute. These communities did not look much different from the villages and farmsteads within the territories of the poleis. Large estates that were directly managed by royal functionaries or the administrators of a private owner and worked by slaves, dependent workers, or

---

[22] Cyaneai: Hailer 2008 and more generally Kolb 2008, *passim*; Miletus: Lohmann 2004, 346–9; on the question of concentration of landed property, ibid., 348.

[23] Cf. my tentative considerations on Ephesus in Walser 2008, 169–71.

[24] The richness of these documents, now collected in Pernin 2014, is demonstrated by Chandezon 1998.

leaseholders certainly existed, but how they functioned and what their significance was is, again, hard to assess.[25]

Little can be said on the animal husbandry that was an integral, if rather marginal, aspect of Greek mixed agriculture.[26] Small stocks of sheep and goats were probably regularly raised on many farms and grazed on marginal land unsuited for the cultivation of crops or on fallow. Larger animals, like donkeys, mules, and especially cattle, were bred primarily as work animals. Oxen were indispensable as draft animals and particularly well suited for heavy labor such as plowing and transport.[27]

Animal husbandry was especially important in mountainous or dry regions and areas not well suited for mixed agriculture. According to Strabo, Bithynia and Pontus, as well as the Anatolian interior, provided especially fine grazing grounds. Already in the Achaemenid period, these regions were known for breeding horses, mules, and sheep on a larger scale.[28]

AGRARIAN PRODUCTION FOR INTRAREGIONAL MARKETS AND TRADE

A small range of agrarian products from Asia Minor met demands beyond the needs of local consumers and were exported. Wine from southwestern Asia Minor, including the adjacent islands of Cos and Rhodes, became popular in the Aegean and beyond from the third century onward. It must have been produced on a large scale and its cultivation seems to have been considerably expanded especially in the Rhodian *peraia,* the large area opposite the island on the mainland that was controlled by the Rhodian state.[29]

Wool from Asia Minor and especially Ionia was held in high esteem throughout antiquity. The "Milesian sheep," a race bred specifically for its wool, allowed the production of textiles of the highest quality. Its significance is shown not only by frequent mentions in

[25] On large-estate management: Chandezon 2011, particularly 104–8.
[26] Chandezon 2003a, 183–258 collects and comments on the epigraphic evidence from Asia Minor. Isager and Skydsgaard 1995, 83–107 provide a general overview.
[27] Cf., e.g. an inscription from Teos in the fourth century mentioning cattle as work animals, donkeys, sheep: Robert and Robert 1976, 320–32, with extensive commentary.
[28] Strab. 12.3.13, 15, 30, 38–9; 4.7; 6.1; 8.16. Strab. 11.13.8 on large numbers of animals as tribute to the Achaemenid kings. Cf. Broughton 1938, 617.
[29] On wine production in the *peraia*: Salviat 1993; Lund 2000 on exports to the eastern Mediterranean; for a summary: Chandezon 2003b, 198–9. Badoud 2018 provides a recent study on Rhodian exports to Sicily and Italy.

ancient texts but also by the fact that already in the fourth century, the taxation and commerce of wool is a prominent subject of legal regulations and contracts between poleis.[30] Other agrarian products, like honey from the southwest or figs from Caria and the Maeander valley, were exported as well. Yet they were niche products with limited economic significance outside of the local context.[31]

NONAGRARIAN PRODUCTION

By comparison with agriculture, nonagrarian production was of minor importance, as elsewhere in the ancient world. As a necessary supplement to agriculture, it played a role everywhere, but it was only in certain areas and under specific environmental conditions that it gained larger significance. The evidence is comparably rich for the Roman period, but highly limited and dispersed for earlier periods. The sources were collected and categorized more than ninety years ago by T. S. Broughton.[32] More recent epigraphical discoveries have added to this material but have not changed the general picture. A new synthesis, making full use of archaeological finds, is still missing, and I will confine myself to a few select observations.

Mining of metals in Asia Minor goes back well beyond the arrival of the Greeks.[33] Strabo mentions the occurrence of precious and semi-precious metals in many areas of the peninsula, but most mining activities had ceased before his own time, most likely because they had become unprofitable. Gold and silver deposits existed in western Asia Minor – as in the Aiolis, on Mount Tmolus, and Mount Sipylus – but they seem to have been exhausted during the Hellenistic period. The Attalids extracted silver on Mount Ida, but these deposits were of minor importance, as were those in the Pontic region. Iron existed in the Pontic mountains and was of considerable importance at least in the classical period. Deposits of copper, tin, lead, zinc, and iron all occurred in Asia Minor, but we know very little about their exploitation before the Roman imperial period. At least for now, it is unclear to what

---

[30] The sources are collected in Broughton 1938, 817–23; regulations and contracts are known from Aigai (*StV* III 456), Teos (Robert and Robert 1976, 320–1), and Erythrai (*IErythrai und Klazomenai* 15).

[31] For these and other agrarian products, see the extensive collection of sources by Broughton 1938, 607–20.

[32] Broughton 1938, 817–39.

[33] Recent research on metals in Asia Minor has focused on the Bronze and the Early Iron Age. Cf., e.g. Yalçın, Özbal, and Paşamehmetoğlu 2008 and "Antolian Metal," the series of conference proceedings published by Yalçın as supplements to the journal *Der Anschnitt* since 2000.

degree metal production in Asia Minor covered the needs of its population and what quantities of the different metals had to be imported. Metalworkers must have been active in virtually all cities and larger villages. They are well represented in inscriptions from the Roman period.

Asia Minor was rich in fine marbles.[34] Only easy access to this material, as well as other building stones of high quality, made the splendid development of the Greek cities of Asia Minor in the Hellenistic and Roman periods possible. Many larger cities quarried marbles in their own territory, and these marbles were mostly of local importance. Not so the famous marble from the Proconnesus, the small island of Marmara, which in the Hellenistic period belonged to the territory of Cyzicus: at least from the fourth century onward, its white marble was widely exported to the cities of Asia Minor and well beyond. In the Roman period, the Phrygian city of Docimeium was another important exporter of marble, but its marbles were certainly already known before.

Most regions outside of the central plateau of Asia Minor were rich in wood, which was used as firewood, charcoal, and for products like resin and pitch.[35] Especially important was the wood of large trees, like pines and cedars, suitable for shipbuilding. It was easily available in the Troad, the Pontic region, and in the mountainous areas along the southern coast. Several cities, like Cyzicus, Amastris, or Side were also renowned for their wharfs and shipbuilding.

Salt was produced in various forms: from seawater, at the great salt lakes in the interior, and by mining. Beyond its everyday use in cooking, salt was indispensable for the preservation of fish. Fishing was certainly practiced on a small scale all along the coasts of Asia Minor, as well as in some lakes and streams.[36] A few cities, like Byzantium, Cyzicus, or Parium, however, could profit from the seasonal runs of migrating fish, especially tuna and mackerel that crossed between the Aegean and the Black Sea. Several late Hellenistic and early Roman inscriptions from Cyzicus and Parium on the Hellespont provide rare insights into the fishing industries in this area.[37] They show that in this period these cities had leased out the exclusive right to catch fish in certain sectors of the coast to associations of fishermen. They also manned watchtowers that

---

[34] The papers in Ismaelli and Scardozzi 2016 provide a recent overview.
[35] On wood, see Rousset 2010, 47–50 with copious references.
[36] On fishing in general, now Bresson 2016b, 175–87; Marzano 2013, with a focus on the Roman period.
[37] *IParion* 4–5; Robert 1960, 94–5. The inscriptions are explained by Robert, ibid., 80–97.

were built along the coast for the observation of the passing schools of fish. The importance of the fishing industry even for a city like Cyzicus with a large territory is demonstrated by the fact that a tuna fish was depicted not only on the coins of the city but also on its official emblem.[38]

The artisanal trades as well as any professional services rarely enter our sources during the period under discussion. Metalworkers, potters, stonemasons, builders, as well as butchers, bakers, bankers, teachers, and many others must have been active in virtually all cities and larger villages, and in epigraphical sources from the Roman period they are very well represented, in funerary texts as well as in inscriptions set up by professional associations. While the latter become frequent in the Roman imperial period, the evidence for them is poor in earlier periods. A late-fourth-century inscription from Ephesus provides a rare glimpse into the organization of trades, listing several persons with their profession: a cattle butcher, an oil seller, a shoe seller, a seller of sandals, and a goldsmith. The specificity of these professions points to the high technical specialization of trades and crafts. This great "horizontal division of labor" is best attested in classical Athens, but the situation in one of the larger cities of Asia Minor was probably comparable.[39]

TRADE

Our knowledge about trade networks within Asia Minor and between Asia Minor and the rest of the Greek world is once again limited. The high degree of urbanization as well as the diversity of microregions in Asia Minor implies an intense retail trade over short and medium distances. The surpluses from agricultural production, both from peasant farmers and larger estates, were distributed through local markets, both within cities and in the countryside, and exchanged against goods from the nonagrarian sector.[40] This kind of everyday trade, however, rarely left traces in our sources.

Wholesale commerce over longer distances in the Greek world was dominated by the grain trade that was essential for the food supply in certain areas, especially Athens. In contrast to mainland Greece, however, Asia Minor did not seem to have reached its carrying capacity and was, under normal circumstances, able to feed its population with the

[38] Killen 2017, 224–7.
[39] For the situation in Athens, see Harris 2002b and Chapter 14, this volume.
[40] Chapter 14, this volume.

foodstuff produced locally and regionally. Even the largest cities, like Ephesus, which might have reached a population of up to 200,000 inhabitants in the Hellenistic period, seem to have been largely self-sufficient. This does not mean, however, that these cities were not dependent on imports of grain by ship over longer distances under tenuous circumstances and in times of crisis. In the early Hellenistic period, Ephesus was highly worried about the provision of grain and took various measure to promote imports. Similar concerns in other cities are also well documented.[41]

We know little about other imports into Asia Minor, but they were undoubtedly common and surely did not only include luxury items, but also slaves and raw materials. The imports were certainly mainly exchanged against the agricultural and nonagricultural products already mentioned, with wine, wool, and textiles being the primary exports.

COINAGE

Coinage was famously invented in western Asia Minor, either by the Lydian kings or the Greeks in the second half of the seventh century.[42] Over the next centuries, Asia Minor saw the circulation of a plethora of different coinages in various standards that mirror the complex and ever-changing political landscape.[43]

The first coins were minted in electrum, an alloy of gold and silver,[44] both by the Lydian kings and by the cities of Sardis, Cyzicus, Phocaea, Ephesus, and Miletus, as well as Samos. They were soon followed and gradually displaced by coins in pure gold and silver. When the Persians conquered western Asia Minor soon after 550, they seem to have continued to strike Lydian coinage in considerable quantities.[45] Darius I (521–486), however, changed the system by the introduction of two new types of coinage: a gold coin, the *daric*, and a silver coin, the *siglos*, both depicting the Achaemenid king. With minor adjustments, this system remained in place until the end of the Persian empire. Since the Greeks rarely struck coins in gold, the *daric*

---

[41] Walser 2008, 302–9 on Ephesus and other cities in Asia Minor; further Davies 2011, 187–8; in general: Migeotte 1991.
[42] Chapter 16, this volume.
[43] Metcalf 2012 offers accessible surveys on the coinage of Asia Minor in different periods.
[44] Recent research suggests that the alloy used for the minting of coins was not naturally occurring, as hitherto assumed, but rather artificially produced: cf. Wartenberg 2016.
[45] Alram 2012.

was popular and circulated widely all over the Greek world. The *sigloi*, on the other hand, had to compete with Greek silver coins and were rarely in use outside of Asia Minor; even here they played a marginal role. The Greek poleis under Achaemenid rule, as well as local dynasts, were free to coin their own money, and many of the more important cities did so.[46] As a result, the Achaemenid coins formed only a small part of the monetary supply in Asia Minor and circulated side by side with the more numerous local and imported Greek issues.

The parallel circulation of coins issued by central authorities and those struck by the civic mints of the poleis remained a defining feature of coinage in Asia Minor after the end of Persian rule. In the Hellenistic period, it was not so much the monetary system but the quantity of money that changed.[47] Its main sources were the Achaemenid treasuries from Susa and Persepolis, which provided Alexander the Great with precious metal of an equivalent value of no less than roughly 450 tons of gold. Alexander started to bring these enormous amounts of gold and silver into circulation, and throughout the following centuries the Hellenistic kings continued to issue royal coins in somewhat smaller, but significant, quantities.

In spite of the gigantic influx of royal coins, the cities in Asia Minor continued to issue more or less sporadically their own coins to satisfy their needs.[48] At least in the third century, their ability to do so was not restricted by the imperial authorities. In considerable number, they issued both their own posthumous Alexander-type and civic coins. In general, they seem to have concentrated on the production of small silver denominations and bronze coins. The situation in Asia Minor changed fundamentally, when, shortly after the peace of Apamea in 188, the Pergamene king Eumenes II created a closed-currency system (see also Chapters 5 and 20, this volume).[49] Even though his *cistophoroi*, named for the *cista mystica* depicted on its obverse, weighed only three-quarters of Attic-standard tetradrachms, they had to be exchanged and accepted by royal fiat at the same value (compare Chapter 5, this volume). The *cistophoroi* were produced in large numbers in different cities of the Attalid kingdom. Several cities, however, continued to strike civic tetradrachms in full weight, probably destined to be used in transactions with the Greek world outside the Attalid kingdom.

There is little doubt that by the end of the Hellenistic period, the economy of Asia Minor was highly and thoroughly monetarized. The fact

---

[46] Konuk 2012 for Greek coinage up to the Ionian Revolt.
[47] For a survey: de Callataÿ 2012; more technically: de Callataÿ 2005a.   [48] Ashton 2012.
[49] Meadows 2013 for detailed discussion of the nature of this currency system. On the monetary history of Pergamum in general, Marcellesi 2012.

that civic mints brought large quantities of bronze coins into circulation was of particular importance; even small denominations of silver were unsuited to everyday retail transactions in local markets, but the bronze coinage provided a medium of payment that could be used even for these purposes and simplified, and therefore, promoted retail trade.

THE STATE(S) AND THE ECONOMY

The interweaving of different strata of political authority did not only shape the monetary landscape, but public finances in Asia Minor in general.[50] Contrary to the Greeks in the mainland and the Aegean, the Greek communities in Asia Minor had to pay tribute to outside powers.[51] According to Herodotus, the Lydian king was the first among the barbarian kings to exact tribute (*phoroi*) from the Greek poleis.[52] When the Persians conquered the Lydian kingdom of Croesus, they too asked the Greeks to contribute their share to the needs of the empire. After the Ionian Revolt, Darius I had the tribute reassessed to a system based on the size of the cities' territories, and the land not controlled by the poleis was certainly taxed as well.[53] Not necessarily all revenues flowed into the king's coffer, but those from estates, villages, and even cities could be ceded to loyal noblemen. We know little about how tributes were levied, but early Hellenistic inscriptions suggest that they had to be paid partly in money and partly in kind.

When Alexander the Great "freed" Asia Minor from Persian rule, the tribute system changed, if only gradually, over the course of time. While the Greek poleis were exempt from tribute, the non-Greek communities continued to pay regular *phoroi*, now to the Macedonian king.[54] Still, Greek cities were asked to support the king's military endeavors with irregular financial contributions.

With his policy in Asia Minor, Alexander set the tone for the following three centuries. It became a commonplace to promise that the Greek poleis should remain exempt from tribute or taxes, but in practice, all monarchs controlling parts of Asia Minor sought to assert tributary claims vis-à-vis the Greek poleis, even in those cities declared "free and autonomous." Opinions differ as to the total size of the tax burden, and it certainly varied from community to community. In any

---

[50] On public finances: Migeotte 2014; for the specific situation in Asia Minor also: Walser 2015.
[51] Schuler 2007 offers a succinct overview of tributes and taxation both in the Achaemenid and Hellenistic periods.
[52] Hdt. 1.6.2–3.   [53] Hdt. 6.42.2.
[54] Thonemann 2012, reinterpreting the crucial piece of evidence, *IPriene* 1.

case, recent evidence suggests that the kings and their administration interfered deeply with the finances of the cities and thereby had a significant impact on the economy.[55]

The Greek cities and communities without polis status were not only an important source of income for the kings but often were the recipients of their benefactions. Only poleis and communities under the kings' direct control could expect ongoing transfer payments. Others could still receive one-time benefits under specific circumstances and in times of special need, but other public revenues were obviously of much larger significance. One important source of income was public property in various forms: rents from land, both public and sacred (belonging to a god, but managed by the cities), from public buildings, revenues from mines, quarries, and so on. Revenue from local tolls and taxes was equally important. Virtually all cities levied customs duties, both on imports and exports, but also various other indirect taxes on commerce and services within the communities. It has often been assumed that the poleis did not directly tax private property and private production of citizens, even if they did levy such taxes from inhabitants without citizenship. Yet at least in the case of the poleis in Asia, considerable evidence militates against this view.[56] The cities had various other revenues, and as far as they were not claimed by royal authorities, the communities of Asia Minor used their financial resources for the same main purposes as those in the rest of the Greek world. What exactly the revenues and expenditures of a community were varied from community to community and constantly changed over time.

The economic significance of the royal administration and the poleis was naturally not limited to their economic activities alone. They also provided and guaranteed the institutional framework for individual agents. However, in this respect the situation in Asia Minor seems not to be fundamentally different from other regions of the Greek world and does not need to be addressed here in detail.

CONCLUSION

From the late archaic to the early Roman imperial period, war was an almost ubiquitous phenomenon in the history of Asia Minor (Chapter 5, this volume). The constant threat of war tied up a large amount of

---

[55] Walser 2015, 419–21.
[56] The agreement of *sympoliteia* that Miletus and Pidasa decided upon in 187 illustrates the variety of direct taxes on agriculture strikingly, when it defines the taxes that the new citizens from Pidasa shall pay; see *Milet* 6.3, 149, ll. 18–35. Cf. Migeotte 2001.

resources: the training and supply of armies and navies or the construction and maintenance of walls and fortifications was costly; looming conflicts impeded trade and caused instability that furthered phenomena like piracy. The direct and indirect costs of war are impossible to assess, but they were undoubtedly considerable. When military conflicts broke out, pillages and devastations caused serious local and regional crises that often lasted for years.[57]

In general, however, the cities and communities demonstrated considerable resilience and recovered quickly. The Hellenistic period often appears as an age of war, but, paradoxically, during the same period many Greek cities in Asia Minor as well as the rural countryside seem to have flourished. It is impossible to say what this efflorescence could mean in terms of economic growth, and any long-term estimate would blur the differences in a fractured economic landscape over a fractured period of time. We must be content with the very general impression of prosperity we get when we look at splendid cities like Miletus, Ephesus, or Pergamum, or at densely populated countrysides such as in Lycia. The situation changed in the first century, when the Greeks in Asia Minor paid a heavy price for their resistance against Rome, not only during the First Mithridatic War (89–85), but also during the following years. Only the victory of Octavian over Mark Antony, ending the Roman civil war, brought stability to the eastern Mediterranean and a new golden era for Greek Asia Minor.

Further Reading

While recent studies, including Bresson 2016b, rely heavily on sources from Asia Minor, no general survey of its economy from the archaic to the Hellenistic period exists. Marek 2016 provides an excellent overview for the Roman period, relevant to earlier periods as well. Broughton 1938 remains an invaluable collection of source material. Schuler 1998, as well as the studies by Chandezon, are essential for understanding agrarian structures and conditions of production. Several contributions in Metcalf 2012 survey the development of coinage in Asia Minor. Based on Migeotte 2014, Walser 2015 surveys the finances of the cities in Asia Minor.

---

[57] Generally, Chandezon 2000b. Walser 2008 for the economic crises caused by war.

7: NORTHERN GREECE
AND THE BLACK SEA

Zosia H. Archibald

INTRODUCTION

In an unusual digression, Thucydides describes how a man, travelling light, could reach the Danube from Abdera in eleven days, by the shortest route (Thuc. 2.97.1). The historian compares this with the circumnavigation of the north Aegean coastline, from Abdera to the estuary of the Danube, which, even with a following wind, might take four days and four nights. His third parameter is a journey from Byzantium to the lands of the Laiaioi, whom Thucydides considers the most distant of the subjects ruled by the Odrysian kings. This third route is given as taking thirteen days. These extraordinary details about overland travel, which encompass many hundreds of kilometres in modern terms, have rarely been remarked on; and when they have, they are thought to yield rather more information than most students need.[1] Simon Hornblower's comments reflect the prevailing preoccupations of modern international classical scholarship, which does not dwell at all closely on areas of the Balkan region beyond Apollo's sanctuary at Delphi and eschews more distant parts of the Balkans, except when considering broad ethnographic comparisons. This chapter invites readers to consider a region often regarded as 'peripheral' to Greek history as a far more significant player in economic, but perhaps too in cultural, terms than it is often given credit for.

The landmass encompassed by this chapter is potentially vast, intruding on the territory of a dozen or so modern nation states, from the Pindus mountains to the Ukrainian steppe regions, and from the Hellespontine Straits to the Caucasus. Our understanding of ancient relations between different cultural groupings and between producers and traders in these regions during the course of classical antiquity is still limited, both by our own imaginative capacity and by the kind of

---

[1] Hornblower 1991, 371; for broad ethnic comparisons, see e.g. Vlassopoulos 2013.

evidence that we can use. Even today, and notwithstanding the ways in which digital technology has helped to telescope distances, much of the area explored here is comparatively remote at the conceptual and at the experiential levels. This remoteness dramatically affects the ways in which scholars study and analyse the region.

JOURNEYS NORTHWARDS FROM THE AEGEAN AND SOUTHWARDS FROM THE BLACK SEA

Most students of ancient history have a good familiarity with the principal coastal locations in the northern Aegean and the Straits (Thessalonike, Thasos, Amphipolis, Abdera, Byzantium, Chalcedon) and a dozen place names in the Black Sea; they are less familiar with sites inland of the coastline. Inland sites rarely appear on maps. Whereas modern visitors are actively encouraged to visit ancient urban centres in northern Greece and a good range of Black Sea ports, popular access to other ancient sites is still challenging (and, to an increasing degree, as one travels into the Black Sea). Nor can the various kinds of material evidence be used without serious qualifications. In a recent review of prosopographic data from the Black Sea area, Alexandru Avram noted that there are some 2,000 names documented in epigraphic texts that also have patronymics and can therefore be used with some confidence as markers of historical individuals.[2] Most of the data come from the Hellenistic period and onwards, into the early Roman empire; other periods are less well represented. The total data covers ca. eighty people per generation, a tiny number of travellers of Pontic origins, who were commemorated in a permanent way in other civic environments. Even if we assume a very modest level of maritime travel between the Black Sea and the Aegean at any time between the seventh century and the early Roman imperial age, we should calculate at least five times, perhaps even ten times such a number of ships, to say nothing of sailors, merchants, and other travellers, making this voyage in the space of only one year.[3]

The majority of travellers documented by Avram went to Athens. Another significant group represents names that occur within the Black Sea only. Other target locations of commemoration were the principal

[2] Avram 2014.
[3] The best numerical and qualitative evidence of a commercial fleet is that of the 320 ships stopped by Philip II of Macedon in 340 at Hieron, the northern end of the Bosporan Straits, in order to seize the 180 Athenian grain ships (Theop. *FGrH* 115 F292; Philoch. *FGrH* 392 F162; Just. *Epit.* 9.1.1–6; Front. *Str.* 1.4.13); Gabrielsen 2007, esp. 295–7: Bresson 2007; Moreno 2008, 668–89; Archibald 2013a, 205, 237–45; Russell 2017, 65–9 on ship and crew numbers.

sanctuaries of the Aegean: Amphiaraus at Oropus and Apollo at Delos. Statistically speaking, the main originating centres were also the principal cities of the Straits and Propontis (particularly Byzantium and Chalcedon), but also the big cities of the southern Pontic coast, notably Heraclea and Sinope. It is likely that the great civic focus of the Bosporan kingdom at Panticapaeum (*IACP* no. 705; p. 72: >3,000 km² in resource area) is represented by many of those designated Bospor(e)anoi, not least because of the strong presence, at sites like Delphi, of individuals from the Tauric Chersonese.[4] Callatis is, epigraphically speaking, the most prominent city from the west coast.

Commemorative inscriptions form the single most numerous and the most informative source of information about the northern part of the Balkans and Black Sea areas, and this is what forms the substance of Avram's statistics. These documents have also attracted the greatest amount of scholarly attention, alongside fourth-century Athenian forensic speeches, particularly the Demosthenic corpus, and extracts from the great narrative historians, Herodotus, Thucydides, and Xenophon, which relate directly to this region.[5] There is no doubt that such documents offer fundamental evidence about commercial relations between individual cities and other cities, or between cities and rulers in the hinterland, as well as context-specific information about the key roles often played by wealthy individuals. Nevertheless, if we are considering economic relations within this vast region, and between it and the Aegean, then we must take account of the broader framework within which economic relations operated. Commemorative inscriptions give some indications, but they cast an indirect light on commerce, since the content focuses attention on the individual who was being memorialized, not on other persons or circumstances. We need to gauge such individuals in the light of what can be established for gross patterns of exchange, rather than extrapolating general propositions from the inscribed data.

Maritime journeys that lasted no more than a few hours took local fishermen to ports or islanders (such as Thasians, Parians, Lesbians, Chians) to the mainland of Thrace, shipping ceramic containers and their edible contents to consuming communities, whether coastal or inland;[6] pilgrims to sanctuaries, such as the Great Gods on Samothrace;[7]

---

[4] Avram 2014, 100, 108–9.
[5] See e.g. Bresson 2007; Braund 2007; Engen 2010, 104–18, 233–325; Müller 2011, on Protogenes of Olbia: *IPE* I² 32; Chaniotis 2017, 157–8.
[6] Tzochev 2016a; Archibald 2013a; 2013b.   [7] Dimitrova 2008.

bulk commodities, such as marble or timber, to mainland sites;[8] or they ferried mercenaries on service (Xenophon and the remainder of the "Ten Thousand" come to mind).[9] All such journeys maintained regular economic links between established partners; provided work for sailors and ships' captains; and reinforced predictable commercial patterns, which are often described by ancient authors, as well as by modern scholars, in terms of coastal cabotage.[10]

Longer-distance traffic involved risk at least an order of magnitude greater than such local journeys and was therefore irregular. Journeys between the Aegean and the Black Sea are most likely to have been annual forays, and for a limited number of ships from the seventh and sixth centuries onwards, perhaps already sailing in groups. The combination of winds and currents made it easier to concentrate on seasonal journeys into and out of the Straits. A round trip would have taken at least several months. Ships travelling northwards, into the Black Sea, needed to wait for south-westerly winds (often at the island of Tenedos)[11] to help vessels sail successfully against the strong currents flowing into the Aegean; and, conversely, ships leaving the Black Sea made the most of north-easterly winds in order to transport grain, in particular, but also other bulk loads, including live animals, hides, slaves, and textiles (Polyb. 4.38.4–5), successfully back in the direction of Aegean ports. There were technical as well as organizational and conceptual challenges to these trips. Knowledge of the currents in the Hellespontine Straits, and the channel of the Bosporus itself, could not be mastered without local assistance or had to be acquired gradually by ships' captains travelling north. Travel also required boats that could manage these currents.[12]

The practical challenges of travelling north, into the Black Sea, and the tendency of ships to wait in convoy for suitable winds, encouraged the development of specialist pilots and escort craft, on the one hand, and of financial exactions on the other, as a justification for escort services.[13] The infrastructure of tolls and taxes underlying the exactions removed from merchants and ships' captains at the bottleneck of the Bosporus were probably an unintended consequence of the successful and generally efficient pattern of taxation levied by the Athenians from their allies

---

[8] Thasian marble: Herrmann 1999; Macedonian timber: Feyel 2006, 358–68; Athenian decree honouring King Archelaus of Macedon, which refers to the favourable import of wood and oars: IG I^3 117; Bresson 2016b, 91; Bresson 2016a, 56–7.
[9] Archibald 2013a, 105, 114–17.   [10] Horden and Purcell 2000, 123–72.
[11] Ps.-Dem. 17–19; Gabrielsen 2007, 299 and n. 38; cf. Hdt. 9.114.
[12] Russell 2017, 19–51, 236; Ivantchik 2017.   [13] Gabrielsen 2007.

after the Persian Wars, a model of operation that provided the people of Byzantium with a recipe for the successful maximization of economic advantage from their position of control, both as the principal political agent in the region of the Straits (after 403) and its chief entrepôt.[14] The combination of these long-term assets with the availability of large, seasonal shoals of tunny made Byzantium the pre-eminent maritime economic agent of the Straits prior to Roman expansion and the natural end-point of the Via Egnatia, whose completion ca. 120 greatly enhanced the developing indigenous pattern of overland traffic across the Balkans to match the maritime network.[15]

THE NORTH: MYTHS OF CULTURAL DIFFERENCE, OF COLONIAL ORIGINS, AND THE RAISON D'ÊTRE OF SAILING ON THE BLACK SEA

Byzantium may have been a very significant agent in the north, but it was by no means the principal player. There were land powers with much greater economic and political clout until the second century. The kingdoms of Macedon and of Odrysian Thrace, on the European side of the north Aegean and the Straits, the Spartocid realm in the northern Black Sea, and the Achaemenid empire (with its Hellenistic successor states) dominating the southern and eastern Pontic shores, were the significant territorial powers of the north, polities with considerable economic capacity and resources.[16] These states deserve greater recognition than they have often received in discussions of pre-Roman economies, not just of the Black Sea area but of the eastern Mediterranean as a whole. The conscious intellectual separation of the northernmost part of the Balkan peninsula and territories beyond it from the rest of the Balkan mainland is a modern way of thinking. It was heavily shaped by twentieth-century experiences, which happened in a series of stages. The beginnings of systematic archaeological survey and documentation began in the first decades of the twentieth century and constituted one of the positive scholarly outcomes of World War I. At the same time, the heritage of ancient Macedonia formed a key cultural tool in the extension of the northern borders of the Greek state.[17] The

---

[14] Gabrielsen 2007, 290–1; Russell 2017.
[15] Fasolo 2005, 103–5; Archibald 2013a, 9–10, 223–7; Archibald 2016, on inland roads.
[16] Archibald 2000; 2006; 2013a; 2013b; Avram, Hind, and Tsetskhladze 2004.
[17] Stefani 2017; see also other contributions to Shapland and Stefani 2017; cf. Archibald 2013a, 1–17.

break-up of the Ottoman empire and the emergence of Soviet Russia profoundly affected the populations of southern Europe and the countries around the Black Sea. In scholarly terms, the ideological divergences between those countries that became members of the Warsaw Pact or joined the Soviet Union, on the one hand, and those, like Greece and Turkey, that did not, exerted a deeper, long-term influence on the kind of research that has been conducted and the kinds of ideas that have been applied to these regions. These various strands of twentieth-century history explain how it has come about that Macedonia has often been seen as a 'bulwark' against unknown aggressors from the north beyond it.[18]

The ideological divide that dominated the studies of southern Europe in the period after World War II was accompanied by divergent research interests. Where they attended to economic matters, academic preoccupations in western countries focused primarily on the social divide between rich and poor in Greek cities[19] and the narrative framework of 'colonization', which often presupposed a pattern of transactions between mother and daughter cities, an assumption that was, at first, partly borne out by ceramic finds at a range of coastal (daughter) locations. However, developing investigations show that the kinds of evidence found are only partly, if at all, related to the assumed 'colonial' founding cities.[20] There are, to be sure, institutional and cultural manifestations that underscore preferred traditions, which map over certain characteristics from some founding progenitors; but there are equally strong components that indicate other links, cultural and economic, at various stages of local history.[21] Much of the surviving evidence of economic transactions is ceramic, and pottery data points to a more complex set of cultural and economic partners.[22] Even in cases where we think we understand the historic relationship between founding communities and colonial settlements, as in the case of the mainland enclaves established by the Thasians, the ceramic data shows a far greater range than simply products of Paros and Thasos.[23] The material is much more diverse than the straightforward founder–colony relationship suggests. Comparative evidence between different sites within the sub-regions of the north suggests a degree of regional coalescence,

---

[18] See e.g. Edson 1970, 44 (echoing Polyb. 9.35.3, where the context is the Gallic attack on Delphi in 279); cf. Polyb. 18.37.8–9; Hammond 1972, 19–58; Hornblower 2011, 98–9; Stefani 2017, 20–34; Kotsakis 2017, 58–63.

[19] Notably Finley [1973] 1999.   [20] Dupont 2007, esp. 31.

[21] Bresson 2007, 49–54; Russell 2017, 187.

[22] See e.g. Dupont 2007; Tiverios 2012; Misaïlidou-Despotidou 2012; Manakidou 2012.

[23] See Manakidou 2012, on Oesyme; Malama 2012, on Galepsus.

with local imitations quickly following the arrival of Ionian, Attic, and Corinthian wares.[24] This harmonizes with the assumptions we now make about coastal cabotage, where local boats, carrying mixed cargoes, redistributed commodities shipped to larger harbours.[25]

The kinds of colonial narratives that dominated Greek history for much of the twentieth century have begun to break down for a variety of reasons. Valid criticisms have been made about prevailing narratives that focus exclusively on identifiably 'Greek' phenomena, at the expense of less easily identifiable or manifestly non-Greek elements in local culture.[26] Recent scholarship has illuminated the indigenous context that enables a more culturally nuanced understanding not only of what actually took place when Greek traders and hoplites landed on distant shores but also once interactions had taken on a much more intense and creative appearance as a result.[27] At the same time, the literary narratives that were used as the basis for foundation stories have been analysed closely and identified as complex palimpsests, which were, in many cases, embroidered in Hellenistic or Roman imperial times and do not necessarily reflect the nature of early contacts.[28]

In the Soviet Bloc, historical materialism placed more emphasis on indigenous peoples and on the differences between them and ancient Greek cities, whose slave mode of production detracted from the latter's value as subjects of study. There was also a desire to counteract the ideas of Michael Rostovtzeff and his thesis that a process of 'Hellenization' emanating from Greek communities brought high culture to barbarian peoples of the north Pontic area.[29] Scholars were encouraged to publish in their own languages or in Russian; and there was very little interchange with western scholarship until well into the 1990s.[30] Beginning in the 1970s, international exhibitions of artefacts started to bring the material culture from northern regions to the attention of western audiences, alongside new discoveries from Greek Macedonia. Exhibition catalogues and associated publications and events catalysed wider interest in these societies and helped to reinforce the pioneering work of specialist local and international projects.[31] The contents of

---

[24] Dupont 2007; Tiverios 2012; Allamani-Souri 2012. [25] Lawall 2016, 267–73.

[26] Owen 2005; Rollinger 2006. [27] A. Muller 2010 and Archibald 2013a, 258–69, on Thasos.

[28] Mac Sweeney 2013; 2014; Russell 2017, 197, 203–4; ibid., 205–41, on Byzantium; cf. also Avram, Hind, and Tsetskhladze 2004, 924–8.

[29] Mordvintseva 2017.

[30] C. Müller 2010, 15–21, for a brief overview of theory; cf. also Archibald 2013a, 21–35, 211–17; Archibald 2015.

[31] See e.g. Bresson, Ivantchik, and Ferrary 2007; Descamps-Lequimes 2011; Martinez et al. 2015.

these catalogues project some of the 'dark matter' that still remains to be explored about the ancient economies of this region.

TASTE AND DESIRE: NEGOTIATING ASSETS

If there is one example of material discoveries that have changed the way in which scholars think about economies of 'the north', then it is surely the underground deposit at Methone in Pieria, which has yielded almost 200 graffiti, principally non-alphabetic marks on transport amphorae but also twenty-five owner's marks and two verse fragments.[32] The *lingua franca* of some potters identified by these marks, and some of the traders, seems to have been a Euboean Greek dialect. Nevertheless, the bulk of the commodities shipped to Methone came in amphorae manufactured in Athens, Chios, Lesbos, Samos, and Miletus, as well as Corinth and Laconia.[33] The main reason for scholarly excitement about Methone has been the early date of the inscribed marks and words (the majority have been dated ca. 725–680). John Papadopoulos has even advanced the view that Greek and Phrygian writing may have been developed at Methone, where Phoenician amphorae have also been identified.[34] From an economic point of view, it is not surprising to find systematic marks and letters applied to identify batches or separate consignments of commodities. The Phoenician amphorae may have been shipped by Euboean traders from Lefkandi or Chalcis rather than delivered by Phoenician traders, although there is historical and archaeological evidence of Phoenician or Levantine material elsewhere in the north Aegean.[35] It is worth pointing out two Carian inscriptions from Karabournaki, another key trading centre, this time on the north-east side of the Thermaic Gulf, dating from the late sixth or early fifth century.[36]

Effective communication was critical to traders and to consumers. This is one reason why letters written on lead sheets, many of which resemble contracts, or letters of intent, or invoices, are among the earliest kinds of texts written on non-perishable matter. A fair number of these have been discovered in northern locations, including Chalcidice; most of the known examples have been found in Olbia on

---

[32] Besios, Tzifopoulos, and Kotsonas 2012; Clay, Malkin, and Tzifopoulos 2017.
[33] Besios and Noulas 2012, 404.   [34] Kasseri 2012, 300–3; Papadopoulos 2016, 1246, fig. 07.
[35] Hdt. 2.44, 6.47 (Phoenicians on Thasos); 5.58 (Cadmus at Thebes); Papadopoulos 2016, 1251 with references to the archaeological material.
[36] Adiego et al. 2012.

the northern Black Sea island of Berezan or in the principal commercial ports in and around Crimea.[37] Such letters were written predominantly, but not exclusively, in Greek. The example from Pech Maho, close to the French border with Spain, was first inscribed with an Etruscan text, followed by a second, Greek one.[38] Graffiti are another source of information about traders and the agents, or consumers, with whom they did business. At Adziyska Vodenitsa, near Vetren, west of Plovdiv (Bulgaria), Thracian, Macedonian, and Greek names occur together.[39]

Greek certainly became the language of commerce in the Aegean and Black Sea areas from the fifth century onwards, and Greek was used for contracts involving parties whose first language may not have been Greek. The Pistirus inscription, setting out commercial relations in the Thracian interior, is written in an Ionian dialect, like many inscriptions in the Balkan region.[40] This remarkable document offers unique information about the provisions made for enabling commodities originating in different harbour towns of the north Aegean (Apollonia, Thasos, and Maroneia) to travel inland, as well as guaranteeing protection for merchants from these cities who stayed temporarily at Pistirus. There are other, equally unusual texts from the north, which cast a light on market sales and monopolies.[41]

THE SCALE AND FLUCTUATION OF COMMODITY TRADE

Recent analyses of different series of ceramic containers offer a broad-brush picture of the scale of commodity trade in the north. Ceramic containers and storage vessels offer proxy data for other commodity exchanges, including those in perishable form, which have not survived. The earliest kinds of ceramic imports into the northern Black Sea, including painted table and storage wares, are not found near the coast, but deep inland in the forest steppe of Ukraine and the region of Kyiv. Many of the documented fragments come from large settlements in the steppe zone, such as Bel'skoe,

---

[37] Dana 2007; Demetriou 2012, 41–4 (Emporion, Spain); Harris 2013b; Archibald 2019.
[38] Demetriou 2012, 43–4. [39] Domaradzka 2005.
[40] *IGBulg.* 5557(3); *SEG* 43.486, 46.872, 49.911; Archibald 2000–1; Demetriou 2012, 153–87; Hatzopoulos 2012; Archibald 2013b, 120–8, 226, 231–7; Archibald 2016.
[41] Archibald 2013a, 121 (on *IThracAeg.* E3, 186–90 = *SEG* 47.1026, from Abdera), 267–8 (on the Thasian law protecting Thasian wines: Osborne and Rhodes 2017, no. 103; on rules about currency exchange at Olbia: *IPE* I² 24 and *IPE* IV, 264–5; Bresson 2016b, 271, 300–1.

Trachtemirov, and Nemirovo, and date from the final quarter of the seventh into the middle of the sixth century.[42] This was also the area that attracted large quantities of wine amphorae in succeeding centuries, a trend that continued into the fifth century CE.[43] East Ionian products were dominant from the second half of the seventh century until the final quarter of the sixth (Clazomenian, Samian, Chiot, Milesian, Lesbian, Thasian, and Corinthian), evolving into a similar, if somewhat narrower range, with Thasos and Mende, together with some other north Aegean centres, taking a more dominant role in the fourth century. Pontic producers, notably Sinope and Heraclea (later Chersonesus), began to compete seriously with more-distant producers from the early decades of the fourth century. Rhodian, Cnidian, and Coan amphorae emerged in northern markets from the final quarter of the fourth century, alongside Thasian, Rhodian, and Coan containers.[44]

Within these broad trends, there are different patterns of consumption represented by the quantitative profiles at Pontic entrepôts, which represent either different stable trading partners; or different preferences, leading to particular partner contracts; or a combination of these. Demosthenes' speech *Against Lakritos* offers the case study of a triangular journey from Athens to Crimea via Chalcidice (Dem. 35.10–11), which would have conveyed Mendean wine, paid for with Athenian silver, to recipients at the mouth of the River Dnieper (Borysthenes: whether at Olbia or a neighbouring site), taking back to Athens a return cargo of wheat or wheat and other commodities.[45] Over time, those who were the real drivers were also the most successful partners. In any contractual relationship, it was important for both parties to feel that they were benefiting from the arrangement. The growing economic and political importance of states like Byzantium and Rhodes, at the expense of smaller states in the region such as the cities on the west and later the north coast of the Black Sea, had an impact on the bargaining power of states that depended on their cooperation for shipping commodities in their direction.[46]

---

[42] Vachtina 2007, 25–35.
[43] Monakhov and Kuznetsova 2017, 62–6; Vnukov 2017, 110 and fig. 5.3.
[44] Monakhov and Kuznetsova 2017, 76–8, 96–9.   [45] Bresson 2016b, 370–1.
[46] See esp. Bresson 2016a, 51–61, on contractual partners; Tzochev 2016a, 246–51, for the role of cities such as Byzantium and Rhodes.

CONCLUSION AND FUTURE RESEARCH

In cultural terms, the study of contiguous languages and of their associated prosopography, which in the Balkans include 'Thracian', perhaps a
linguistic group rather than a single language,[47] and Phrygian, as well as
'Macedonian' and various other and better-known Greek dialects, offers
an opportunity to make coherent connections that link the development of language and vocabulary with commercial and other cultural
encounters. Linguists are keen to see connections, as we have seen in the
case of scripts at Methone. In the past, the tendency to separate economic partners according to cultural groupings, in a rather anachronistic
and quasi-national fashion, has hindered effective understanding of how
communities in the north made good the deficiencies in their resource
base.

The 'hinterlands' of the Black Sea have received far less attention
than the coastal communities, which effectively acted as entrepôts for
goods passing into and out of the interior, despite good historical
evidence that underscores this relationship.[48] Ceramic containers demonstrate the active penetration of wines, oil, and other Aegean and
eastern Mediterranean products and act as proxy data for less visible,
particularly organic, commodities and specialist items, including metal
ores.[49] Nevertheless, it is silver and copper alloy coins from a wide range
of cities that flag the presence of merchants, not only at coastal entrepôts
but also far inland. Civic coins from Cyzicus, the Thracian Chersonese,
and several Black Sea ports, as well as north Aegean ones, are well
represented along the major rivers and at several key inland market
centres of Thrace, illustrating the contractual activities of their sponsor-
ing cities.[50] Coins from the Chalcidian-Bottiaian city of Olynthus
represent a particularly wide range of partners from across the Aegean,
as well as from neighbouring areas; perhaps a reflection of the many
states that sought or needed timber.[51] Crucial to this kind of analysis are
full publications of coin lists from archaeological sites. Until recently,
there have been very few such catalogues for scholars to draw on.[52] The
coins from Pella offer some evidence of the close economic relationship

---

[47] Dana 2014; 2015.   [48] Archibald 2013a, 193–248; Bresson 2016a, 57–60.
[49] Kostoglou forthcoming; Archibald 2019.
[50] Domaradzki 1987; Picard 2011; 2015; Psoma 2011a; Archibald 2013a, 233–7; Archibald 2016,
   51; cf. Höghammer 2016, 134–44, 157–9, 161, on coin circulation and networks involving Cos
   (and the northern Aegean).
[51] Gatzolis and Psoma 2016, 81–6; see now Nevett et al. 2017.
[52] de Callataÿ 2006b for a general survey and discussion; see now the contributions to Duyrat and
   Grandjean 2016, and Höghammer 2016, 134–43, on Coan bronze coins and copper alloy coins
   on Cos.

between the Macedonians and Thessalians, from at least the fourth century onwards.[53] The quantity of institutional evidence alone that has accumulated from Thessalian cities is impressive indeed,[54] and the matching material data has yet to be analysed. It is only by studying the networks of exchange across continental zones within the regions of the north that the complex nature of economic transactions can be fully understood. The analogy with 'dark matter' in physics is a valid and serious challenge to traditional approaches within the region.

[53] Kremydi and Chryssanthanki-Nagle 2016, 164–5.
[54] Decourt, Nielsen, and Helly 2004, 688–727.

8: ATHENS AND THE AEGEAN

Sylvian Fachard and Alain Bresson

INTRODUCTION

Classical Athens was a major Mediterranean power and a driving force in the Aegean economy. But by many standards, Athens was exceptional. It stood among the largest poleis of the Greek world in terms of size of territory and population; and thanks to the exploitation of its silver mines and the control of long-distance trading networks, as well as its craft industry, the city was able to import vast amounts of grain to sustain a large and diversified population, for whom agriculture did not play a dominant role. But despite these peculiarities, Athens also shared many features and realities with Aegean poleis in terms of climate, agricultural exploitation, production, laws, labor, institutions, and trade regulations.

EXPLOITING THE RESOURCES OF THE CHORA

The economic base of any polis was defined by the resources of its territory (*chora*). Agriculture was the primary creator of wealth in the ancient world,[1] and Xenophon reminds us in the *Oeconomicus* (6.1) that even the wealthiest individuals could not do without it. However, agricultural surfaces in Attica and the Aegean were limited, typically averaging 20–40 percent of a landscape essentially dominated by mountains and rocky hills often covered with maquis. Agricultural production was concentrated in a few valleys, plains, and dolines. Cultivated areas could be increased by erecting terrace walls on slopes and by draining marshy areas, yet these operations required a significant investment in labor.

Attica and the Aegean currently get 360–700 mm of rain per year on average, and droughts appear at regular intervals. The classical climate was slightly wetter and cooler than today, yet not different enough to picture significant changes in terms of crops and vegetational

---

[1] Bresson 2016b, 118.

landscape. Barley was the most common cereal, while wheat was risky due to limited rainfall. Because of biennial fallow, widely attested in the epigraphical record, the cycle of grain production was two years. Manuring was limited, and yields per hectare varied depending on soils and microregional variations: in Attica and central Euboea, production might have averaged 650–800 kg, but some privileged niches could achieve yields of 1,000 kg in good years. Grain cultivation was compromised with less than 250 mm of rain, a situation that might have happened four to five times in a century for Attica, or even twice in a row under terrible circumstances. Viticulture produced wine in abundance, as well as vinegar and grapes, and could generate cash. Low-quality wine was made almost everywhere and consumed mostly locally. However, some Aegean *grands crus* were exported to foreign markets, such as the wines from Thasos, Lesbos and Chios.[2] Olive oil and olives provided lipids, as well as fuel for lighting and fine oils for perfumes. Complementary products such as figs, legumes, almonds, lentils, and fruit were grown on farms in the countryside and in suburban gardens and often made their way to local markets. Honey was mostly produced on marginal lands, but beehives are also found in urban contexts. Attica, Euboea, Rhodes, and the Cyclades produced renowned honey that could reach foreign markets. Moreover, the rocky and hilly landscapes of Attica and the Cyclades provided extended surfaces for pasture. The latter was dominated by goats and sheep, which produced milk, cheese, and meat, as well as leather and wool. Small herds could be owned by average farmers and were, therefore, complementary with agriculture. Larger herds, however, required specialized labor and extended marginal areas to support them. A city like Athens would have required large amounts of cheese, milk, and meat on a daily basis and thus provided an important market for specialized pastoralism.

Attic Agriculture

Estimating the agricultural output of Attica has long been on the agenda of scholars, yet with contrasting methods and results. Classical Athens had a territory of ca. 2,400 km², of which at least 875 km² would have been cultivable (36 percent).[3] It is impossible to estimate the various

---

[2] Carlson 2013 for the amphorae and exports from Erythrai and Chios.
[3] This new assessment is based on a GIS-based model cautiously selecting agricultural land with a slope comprised between zero to seven percent. Overall, it seems reasonable to assume that between 700 and 950 km² could have been cultivated in Attica without terracing.

percentages of land dedicated to a particular crop, yet even if the entire agricultural area of Attica had been solely dedicated to grain, it could probably have never fed more than 120,000–140,000 people – well below the needs of its total population (citizens, resident foreigners, and slaves), which fluctuated between 200,000–300,000 in the fifth and fourth centuries. Therefore, by the sixth century onward, Athens had to import grain from overseas markets.[4]

But what amount could be grown locally? An inscription for the year 329/8 establishes that Attic grain production amounted to 367,000 *medimnoi* in that year.[5] Some 170 km² would have been needed to produce this quantity of grain, suggesting that, with biennial fallow, 340 km² were dedicated to grain cultivation in Attica.[6] This is strikingly similar to the 1911 data, a period when the population of Attica was 338,000, and preindustrial farming conditions were similar to those of antiquity.[7] Grain production could have been increased, but not dramatically. Vital crops such as olives and vines had to be grown in the remaining 300–500 km² available, but, to a certain extent, mixed cropping offered alternative solutions. Table 8.1 reconstructs a tentative distribution of land dedicated to the main crops grown in Attica, while Table 8.2 offers alternatives for mixed cropping.

Table 8.1 *Attica: estimate of areas dedicated to specific crops*

Crop	Area (km²)
Grain	340–400
Olives	210–300
Vines	100–140
Hay	60–80
Legumes	10–20
Gardens	4–10
Figs	2–5
Total	**726–955 km²**

[4] And as much as perhaps 70–80 percent in the classical period (Bresson 2016b, 409–14).

[5] *IG* II² 1672; see Bresson 2016b, 405–9.

[6] Based on an average yield of 725 kg/ha. A lower yield of 650 kg/ha would have produced 329,452 *medimnoi* (after keeping 20 percent of seeds for the following year); a yield of 800 kg/ha some 405,456 *medimnoi*.

[7] The total area under cultivation was then 652 km² (27 percent of Attica), of which 174 km² were dedicated to grain (another 171 km² were left fallow).

Table 8.2 *Scenarios for mixed cropping in Attica (per year)*[a]

Agricultural surface	Oil	Barley (in *medimnoi*)
500 km²	4,500,000 l	375 km²: 356,000–438,000
700 km²	6,300,000 l	525 km²: 498,000–613,000

[a] Implying that a field of 1 ha has 60 trees and 0.75 ha dedicated to grain (Foxhall 2007, 79). Oil production: 3 l per tree every 2 years. Barley production: biennial, yields of 650–800 kg/ha, minus 20 percent for seeds needed the following year. Weight of a *medimnos* of barley: 27.4 kg.

Table 8.3 *Estimating olive production in Attica (per year)*

Land dedicated to olive cultivation	Number of trees (100/ha)[a]	Olive-oil production[b]	Number of households supported (90 l per household of 6)[c]
210 km²	2,100,000 trees	3,150,000 l.	35,000 households (210,000 people)
300 km²	3,000,000 trees	4,500,000 l.	50,000 households (300,000 people)

[a] Max. of 100 trees per ha (Foxhall 2007, 79); 80 trees per ha (Amouretti 1986, 196).
[b] Amouretti 1986, 196. Oil production: 3 l per tree per biennium, 2 l for yearly production.
[c] Ninety liters of oil for a modest family of four with two slaves (Amouretti 1986, 195–6).

Such dependence on imported grain was not peculiar to Athens. Aegean cities also relied more or less heavily on foreign grain. Nor did this dependence necessarily create a "negative balance": foreign grain was relatively affordable, and it was less profitable in the Aegean to devote large areas of agricultural land to barley when they could be dedicated to the production of more profitable "cash crops" such as olive oil and wine.[8]

Considering Athens' needs in olive oil, a minimum of 210–300 km² of agricultural land would have been needed (Table 8.3). The production could have been increased by planting trees at the edges of fields dedicated to grain (see Table 8.2), a practice well attested in the Mediterranean.[9] Small farmers might have preferred it, growing enough trees within their

[8] Bresson 2016b, 413–14.   [9] Foxhall 2007, 114–16; Halstead 2014, 210–11.

fields for their subsistence, while large landowners could afford to dedicate larger plots in specific regions to focus on olive-oil production for the internal market.[10] Pollen evidence for Brauron and part of the Mesogaia shows limited cereal cultivation and a marked intensification of *Olea* exploitation in the archaic and classical periods, perhaps resulting from a deliberate economic strategy.[11] Overall, however, Attica was barely self-sufficient in oil, and shortages did occur.[12] Attica did not export its oil, except that contained in the Panathenaic amphorae received by the victors at the Panathenaic games.[13] Regarding viticulture, some 100 km² of vineyards would have produced 300,000 hectoliters of wine, arguably enough to cover local demand.[14] Additional land was dedicated to hay (to feed cattle and horses in the winter), legumes, and gardens for fresh vegetables, figs, and other fruit, but fresh vegetables and other products were regularly imported from Megara, Boeotia, and Euboea to satisfy demand. Overall, the situation in Attica is well summarized by Herakleides (1.2): "The products of the earth are incomparable, but there are too few of them."

Land Ownership, Sizes of Estates, and Labor

Literary sources describe various patterns of land ownership and cultivation. Based on the estimates of Table 8.1, it appears that between 13,000 and 17,000 Athenian citizens could have, in theory, owned a plot of five hectares (approx. sixty *plethra*), considered large enough to sustain a family (Chapter 13, this volume). Therefore, there was not enough land to provide a sustainable plot for each of its 30,000 adult male citizens at the end of the fourth century. Written evidence for this period suggests that 12,000 citizens owned at least thirty *plethra* (2.7 ha) and 9,000 owned more,[15] which means that some 10,000 citizens were landless and that many more did not own enough land to sustain a family.[16] Overall, one-third of the citizen population might have owned 85 percent of the land.[17] Small landowners in a rural Attic deme might have opted to live off their land. Some might have specialized in olive oil for the Attic market, while

---

[10] See Amouretti 1986, 196. [11] Kouli 2012. [12] *IG* II³, 1 1315. [13] Bresson 2016b, 405.

[14] One hectare would produce thirty hectoliters per year on average (Bresson 2016b, 147). The 1911 proxy of 95 km² would thus provide 0.75 liters a day for 104,000 individuals in one year, or 0.375 liters for 208,000 people.

[15] Bresson 2016b, 143.

[16] For an estimate of the population of Athens in 320–300 at 200,000–250,000, see Hansen 2006a, 45.

[17] Bresson 2016b, 143.

others lived in the city and managed an agricultural estate from afar, relying on slaves (Chapter 13, this volume).

The number of farmers required to farm the land is difficult to extrapolate. Working one hectare of land for grain required some forty-eight days of work for a man working 175–200 days a year.[18] In order to farm the surfaces recorded in Table 8.1, 4,300–5,500 farmers would have been needed to cultivate grain each year, while another 6,700–7,000 could cultivate 300 km^2 of olives and 140 km^2 of vineyards. However, agriculture was mainly organized according to households, which planted different crops and had different labor forces at their disposal, including slaves. Amouretti estimated that a standard plot of some five hectares required two male workers in the fields and a third for milling and other processing tasks (often assumed by women).[19] If we divide the agricultural land of Attica between 17,000 theoretical domains of sixty *plethra*, then Attic agriculture might have occupied as much as 51,000 persons, including women and slaves. Yet, due to biennial fallow and a production cycle of two years for olive, roughly half of this workforce was needed each year (25,500). Large estates with a strong labor force would be more effective, but as a whole, Attic agriculture might have directly employed a labor force of 12,000–25000 individuals. On the other hand, it has been estimated that some 10,000 citizens were occupied in the nonagricultural sector, 19,000 metics worked as crafts-men, and 10,000 slaves were employed in the Laurium mines alone.[20] All considered, if we estimate an active male population of some 62,000–73,000 aged 20–49 or 20–59 in the fifth century (and 47,000–55,000 for a population of 225,000 at the end of the fourth century),[21] it appears that, in Athens, there was not enough agricultural land to make agriculture the largest sector of the economy.[22]

Strategies of Agricultural Exploitation and Settlement Patterns

Climate variations, local conditions, and the fragmentation of cultivable land limited the options of farmers and landowners as much as they

---

[18] Oliver 2007, 75–6, following T. W. Gallant.   [19] Amouretti 1986, 206–7.

[20] Harris 2002b, 70 (with ref.).

[21] Based on Hansen (1986, 12), individuals aged 20–49 and 20–59 would represent 41.77 percent and 48.62 percent of the total male population, which we estimate at 150,000 from a total population of 300,000 in the fifth century (Hansen 1988, 12).

[22] Similar conclusions have been reached by Harris 2002b and Bresson 2016b, 143; Jew, Chapter 13 in this volume, is more skeptical, but in the periods when the mines were in full production this is beyond doubt.

influenced their choices. Consequently, strategies of agricultural exploitation must be studied along with rural settlement patterns, which varied greatly throughout the Aegean and over time, as demonstrated by the results of archaeological field surveys. In Attica, some demes privileged centralized habitation in the classical period, characterized by a nucleated hub of settlement surrounded by small hamlets. Other microregions, like in the southern deme of Atene, seem to have preferred a dispersed pattern of habitation, dominated by wealthier farmsteads exploiting seemingly large estates.[23] Differences between models depend on a variety of geographical, social, and economic factors. At the microregional level, it is clear that each Attic deme had unequal agricultural resources at its disposal.[24] Ownership of a unified estate of several hectares would justify the building of a farmstead within it, while the possession of smaller dispersed fields in the same plain and within a radius of one to three kilometers might have privileged habitation in, and exploitation from, a central nucleus. Landforms, climate, sizes of estates, distribution of land property, agricultural economic strategies, individual wealth,[25] and patterns of inheritance varied considerably within regions and through time, and there is no ubiquitous model for studying the agricultural economy of the Aegean.

Nonagricultural Resources

Although agriculture was dominant, Aegean poleis enjoyed other types of resources within their *chora*. Various types of stone (limestone, conglomerate, sandstone, and marble) were widely used in private and public construction. Local provenance was always privileged to reduce transportation costs, and low-scale exploitation was ubiquitous. In Attica, some quarries belonged to demes and were rented off to individuals.[26] Specific marbles and limestones (Pentelic, Hymettian, Eleusinian, Steirian) used for prestigious buildings were transported over dozens of kilometers, at considerable cost. Exceptional marbles (Parian) were used for sculpture and exported over long distances to foreign markets. Metals were rare in the Aegean, except for some notable exceptions. The island of Siphnos struck gold and silver in the archaic period, but this exploitation was short-lived. The silver from Laurium in Attica represented an exceptional case. Production reached

[23] Lohmann 1993.   [24] Fachard 2016.
[25] For the distribution of wealth in Attica, see Kierstead and Klapaukh 2018.
[26] Papazarkadas 2011, 229–30.

its peak in the classical period. The mines were farmed out by the state and exploited by private workshops, which relied on large contingents of slaves operated by specialists.[27] Mining operations required large quantities of food, wine, and olive oil to support the working force, as well as wood, charcoal, and tools. This large demand supported farmsteads in the broader region of the mining district, whose operations were market-oriented, and created an important volume of trade via the agoras of the surrounding demes. The collapse of the Laurium mines after 300 modified the economy of southern Attica, prompting the abandonment of many farmsteads in the region.[28]

The Aegean was noticeably poor in timber. Attica could rely on its pine forests of the Parnes massif for small wood and fuel but relied on imports for shipbuilding and prestigious architectural projects. The Attic forests of the borderlands and the ubiquitous maquis found on the slopes of hills were used to produce charcoal, large quantities of which were transported daily to Athens by pack animals using an elaborate and state-funded road network.[29] The demand for charcoal – used for cooking, heating, and industry (pottery and metals) – was enormous, and production was combined with resin-gathering and pitch. The price of wood and charcoal was very high and probably prohibitive for many Athenians living in the city, while the rural population could rely on local sources. The region of Acharnae, in northern Attica, was famous for its charcoal production, but the majority of the charcoal produced in Athens was inevitably imported. Charcoal yields 1.65 times as much energy per unit weight as dry wood, burns at a slower rate, and produces less smoke and ash. It could be used by (wealthier) individual consumers for cooking and heating. Above all, if wood was an adequate fuel for ceramic production, charcoal was of indispensable use for metallurgy. Charcoal alone makes it possible to reach temperatures higher than the melting point of silver (962°C), the metal the production of which was vital for the Athenians. On average, the Laurium mines produced perhaps 1,000 talents of silver or twenty-six tons (more in the peak periods of production), which implied massive imports of wood and above all charcoal.[30] If indeed 10,000 tons of wood for charcoal were necessary to produce 1 ton of silver, the production of the Laurium mines was based on the annual production of 260,000 tons of wood for charcoal in the neighboring regions of Attica, especially Euboea. Securing

---

[27] Osborne 1985, 111–26.   [28] Lohmann 1995, 531–2.   [29] Fachard and Pirisino 2015.
[30] See n. 59 for the debate on the production of the mines.

access to woodlands was paramount for Athens, and the state repeatedly tried to implement patterns of exploitation and control of the forests situated in the borderlands.[31] In Delos, the sale of wood and charcoal was controlled by the local authorities,[32] and comparable monitoring measures might have been implemented in other markets of the Aegean.

The sea provided abundant resources as well.[33] Fish constituted a vital part of the Aegean diet. People fished with lines, as attested by the discovery of many fishing hooks, and professional fishermen used fishing nets (with lead weights). If the Athenians consumed imported salt fish, locally produced fish was mainly consumed fresh. Collecting murex shells on the seashores for purple dye production and diving for sponges were significant on many shores of the Aegean. Tuna fishing was widely practiced, and some catches became the stuff of legend, celebrated with dedications at Delphi and Olympia.[34] Fish could be preserved with salt, whose production in evaporation ponds was lucrative and often subject to state control. Aegean poleis exploited their coastal waters intensively. The sea also allowed communications between the islands of the Aegean, which was an exceptionally fragmented landscape. It made it easier for communities living on poorer islands, such as the charcoal burners of Icaria, to sell their produce for profit on some regional market.

Finally, it is worth stressing that the environment of the cities of the Aegean was not exempt from pollution. Everywhere in the ancient world, domestic burning of wood and charcoal for cooking and heating was a factor in lung infection, especially for women who were in charge of domestic tasks.[35] Besides, pollution linked to industrial activities, like charcoal production in northern Attica or in the islands, or, in urban or rural contexts, ceramic production or tanning and fulling, must have badly impacted the health of the population. Xenophon insisted that the Laurium mining district was an unhealthy place (*Mem.* 3.6.12). Even if the details remain unknown to us, the health condition of the miners must have been very poor. But the ubiquity of lead objects in a city that was a massive producer of this metal (because silver mines like those of the Laurium were first of all lead mines) certainly explains the high and dangerous level of pollution by lead (125 ppm) revealed by bone analysis of bodies from the Kerameikos necropolis in the Hellenistic period.[36]

---

[31] Fachard 2017.   [32] Descat 2001; Bresson 2016b, 315, 327–31.   [33] Bresson 2016b, 175–87.
[34] Paus. 10.9.3–4.   [35] Bresson 2017a.   [36] Ibid.

CRAFTS, PRICES, AND WAGES

Specialization and Professions

It is increasingly clear from the literary evidence that the many commodities consumed in Athens were produced and sold by numerous small craftsmen, sellers, and other professionals. Over 200 occupations have been recorded by Harris, ranging from cheesemongers, grain-dealers, sardine-sellers, butchers, lamp-makers, and rope-makers to cobblers and incense-sellers.[37] To this list should be added "civil servants" providing services to the polis, such as public and religious officials, and various civil corps (road supervisors, forest rangers), as well as army and navy officers.

The potters were concentrated in their own "industrial zone," the Kerameikos, while the metalworkers' quarter was situated below the Kolonos Agoraios hill (Andoc. 1.40). Small-scale production and manufacturing could take place in households, but we also have evidence for larger workshops. Demosthenes' father owned a knife factory and a furniture factory, employing thirty-two to thirty-three workers and twenty slaves respectively (27.9–11). Industrial activities were not confined to the city and its suburbs, and many workshops were strategically distributed within the *chora*, in proximity to raw materials and regional markets.

Harris has shown that the more sophisticated products, such as shields or weapons, required "vertical specialization" (the requisite sum of operations for manufacturing one final product) and employed various artisans assuming different skills simultaneously; however, the vast majority of goods and services required very limited operations and a short production line ("horizontal specialization").[38] Athens was unusual in that it had a large artisan population, but the great diversity of occupations is not necessarily exceptional, as most occupations recorded for Athens would have been required in places like Rhodes, Delos, Eretria, and Samos. As a whole, Aegean manufacturing and production was characterized by a high degree of horizontal specialization, which created conditions for a large-scale market exchange (Chapter 15, this volume).[39]

Prices and Wages

For prices, wages, and land-lease rents, we do not have for Greece or Rome bodies of archives similar to those that are provided by the

---

[37] Harris 2002b; Harris and Lewis 2016, 24; Lewis 2016.
[38] Harris 2002b; Harris and Lewis 2016, 24–5.   [39] Harris 2002b, 80–5.

cuneiform tablets of Babylonia, where for some periods we can even trace the daily evolution of prices on the market. Both public and private archives were written on papyrus or wooden tablets, and they are irrevocably lost to us. For Athens, however, we have the disparate data provided both by the literary sources and by various inscriptions on stone recording public contracts and accounts for public building construction. At Delos, the inscriptions of the accounts of the sanctuary of Apollo, especially at the period of the independence of the city between 314 and 167, are one of the rare sources that provide information that in quality and density may parallel or even surpass the dossiers of the Babylonian sources.[40]

Both the Athenian and Delian dossiers reveal a business world organized into a multitude of very small enterprises rather than "firms." We thus have information on wages corresponding to a certain task, rather than on salaries *proprio sensu*. In Athens from the sixth century onward, prices and wages are always expressed in monetary terms, that is, in units of the silver drachm of 4.33 g. The information on prices must be gauged in relation to the money supply, which varied considerably over time. In this sense, our data can be exploited in two main directions. On the one hand, the homothetic (consumer-independent) variations of prices in the *longue durée* are indicative of the variations in the money supply, which itself was based on the production of the gold and silver mines. On the other, analyzed synchronically they reveal the structure of the values of various factors of production (land, labor, and capital) as well as the local or regional institutional frameworks, even if the defective character of our information frustrates us from calculating the impact of the factors in detail.[41]

The variation of price levels over time was observed by Plutarch in his *Life of Solon* (23.3–4), who notes that prices in the time of the legislator (early sixth century) were much lower than in his own time (first/second century CE). Commenting on the seemingly low amounts of fines for the rapes of free women, he rightly comments (ibid., 23.1–2) that the law does not make sense unless money was then scarce in the city, which proves that the idea that prices fluctuated according to the money supply was perfectly familiar to him. Public wages increased by 50 percent before 432 and the outbreak of the Peloponnesian War,

---

[40] Loomis 1998 for Athens and Reger 1994 and Chankowski 2008 and 2019 for Delos, with the methodological remarks of Rathbone and von Reden 2015, 149–62. For the Babylonian evidence in the pre-Achaemenid and Achaemenid period, see Jursa 2015; for the Hellenistic period, Pirngruber 2017.

[41] Rathbone and von Reden 2015, 166–70.

which corresponds to one of the peaks of production of the Laurium mines. They then remained stable between 432 and 412, but fell sharply by 50 percent or more between 412 and 403/2, at the time when Athens had lost all its resources and when the activity of the Laurium mines temporarily came to a stop.[42] At Delos in the Hellenistic period, prices of various goods and of land rents are also directly linked to the money supply: they increased in the period of massive input of precious metal following Alexander's plundering of the Persian treasures, then decreased sharply before remaining mainly stable or only slightly decreasing until the mid-second century.[43]

INSTITUTIONS, REGULATIONS, AND STATE REVENUES

The greatest volume of economic transactions took place in the agora and the harbor. Agoras were spatially and legally well-defined locations, combining public, commercial, and religious buildings surrounding an open area. In larger cities, agoras were gradually monumentalized and embellished by the construction of porticoes. The latter could serve various functions, hosting private shops and public offices, as well as providing most-welcomed shade for shoppers. Transactions in the Athenian agora were monitored by public officials, the *agoranomoi* ("market controllers"), as well as the *metronomoi*, whose task was to make sure that official weights and measures were being used.[44] Athens also established a board of *sitophylakes* responsible for supervising the price of grain, twenty in Athens and fifteen in the Piraeus.[45] Kantharos, the commercial harbor of the Piraeus, had an *emporion* ("marketplace") delimited by *horoi* and monitored by ten *epimeletai tou emporiou* ("overseers of the *emporion*"). The Piraeus *emporion* contained several porticoes, including a massive grain warehouse known as the Makra Stoa, which supplied the sailors of the navy and where Athenians could buy their grain during difficult times.[46] Nearby stood the *deigma*, a space or building where samples of imported merchandise could be displayed before being sold.[47] A state *dokimastes* ("tester") certified the validity of coins used by shipowners and merchants.[48] Although most of

---

[42] Loomis 1998, 240–5 for the prices and Bresson 2019 for the evolution of the money supply until 450.
[43] Bresson 2016b, 422–3 and 327–8; Chankowski 2019, 244–62.
[44] Arist. *Ath. Pol.* 50.1 and 51.1.   [45] Arist. *Ath. Pol.* 51.3.
[46] Ar. *Ach.* 548; Dem. 34.7; Paus. 1.1.3.   [47] Bresson 2016b, 309–13.   [48] Stroud 1974.

our evidence comes from Athens, agora and harbor officials are attested elsewhere in the Aegean, including Delos, Rhodes, and Miletus. The Greeks knew that markets and harbors had to be legal spaces, regulated and monitored in order to secure trade, protect transactions, and attract foreign merchants. Moreover, because harbors were the main ports of entry for any polis in the Aegean, this is where customs officials were in charge of collecting import and export taxes, usually at a rate of 2 percent of the cargo's value (Chapter 18, this volume).[49]

Two statements by ancient authors seemed to suggest that the Athenians had no sense of priority in the management of their public expense and that their budget was poorly ordered. In a context dated to 352/1, Demosthenes (4.35–7) claimed that, by contrast with the care and attention they devoted to their expenses for festivals, the Athenians were very sloppy in the management of their war expenses, which explained why they were unable to oppose the threat posed by Philip II of Macedon. In the same vein, according to Plutarch (*Mor. De glor. Ath.* 349a), the Athenians even spent much more for their festivals than for their army. These views, which since August Böckh had long been taken at face value, have been reexamined by David Pritchard, who has shown that they did not correspond to reality.[50] The alleged sloppiness of Greek cities in the management of their finances is now a discredited view, as demonstrated also by the work of Léopold Migeotte.[51] As for Athens specifically, and contradicting Plutarch, it is clear that the city spent far more on its army than on the other two main items in its budget, the cost of the maintenance of the city and the cults of the gods and religious festivals. Before the Peloponnesian War, the Athenians had an income of 1,000 talents, of which 700 were devoted to the army and seemingly 250 to their festivals and to running their democracy (salaries for councillors, magistrates, judges, and public slaves), to which should be added building expense (especially for temples).[52] In the 420s, with a similar level of nonmilitary expense, Athens spent every year an average of 1,485 talents on military operations.[53] In the fourth century also, Athens spent five times more on war than on festivals and the funding of democracy (500 talents against 100 in the 370s).[54] The difference between the two periods is that, in the early fourth century,

---

[49] Bresson 2016b, 308–9. [50] Pritchard 2015, 114–20.
[51] Migeotte 2014, with conclusion 679–84: the Greek cities kept the activities of their magistrates under strict control, which limited the risks of financial drift.
[52] Pritchard 2015, 25: income of the city and 100 talents for the festivals; ibid., 88: 157 talents for the management of democracy.
[53] Pritchard 2015, 96–7. [54] Pritchard 2015, 114.

the Laurium mines produced far less than in the fifth century and that the income provided by the tribute on the allies (when Athens had an empire, between 377 and 355) never reached the level of the fifth century. Athens was now mainly dependent on the various taxes it levied on trade and other business activities, and sometimes on property (the so-called *eisphora*, Chapter 18, this volume).

From 314 to 167, independent Delos presents very different features. War was not on the agenda of this small and neutral island-state. Delos could have been only one more "goat island," but it benefitted from the reputation of its sanctuary of Apollo, which as we know especially well for the third century, was the center of a pan-Aegean and even pan-Mediterranean network.[55] The Delians managed this network very carefully, just like the finances of their sanctuary of Apollo. The accounting techniques used by the administrators of the sanctuary, the *hieropoioi*, show constant improvement over time. Citizens could also conveniently borrow from the sanctuary the monies they needed for their own private businesses.[56]

AEGEAN AND ATHENIAN TRADE: A DIACHRONIC VIEW

The determinants and characteristics of trade in the Aegean world underwent several radical transformations between the late Archaic and the Hellenistic period. At the end of the seventh century, from Phocaea in the north to Samos and Miletus in the south, the cities of the coast of western Asia Minor and the neighboring islands, in addition to Phaselis on the southern coast of Asia Minor and the island city of Aegina in the western Aegean, formed the hub of a broad network covering the whole Mediterranean, from Italy and Spain to the west, the Black Sea to the north, Cyrene and above all Egypt and the eastern Mediterranean to the south and to the east. As evidenced both by literary sources and by the distribution of their amphorae, they could sell their own products, like the wine or oil from Thasos, Chios and Samos, produced in the new farms specializing in the production of these export goods and exploiting a slave workforce bought especially for this purpose. But they also played the role of go-between for a series of states, close to them or very distant, which did not have their own traders. Thus, the cities of western Asia Minor traded goods to the benefit of the

---

[55] Constantakopoulou 2017, 156–67 and 204–24.   [56] Chankowski 2011 and 2019, 25–6.

neighbor of their immediate hinterland, the Lydian kingdom, and the Persian conquest of 547/6 did not modify this role of go-between. The Aeginetans played the role of traders for the whole Peloponnese, for the Spartans among others. Samian and Aeginetan merchants traded Laconian painted pottery to the most distant Mediterranean markets. Athenian ceramics were sold all over the Mediterranean, together with other goods produced in Athens the detail of which remains obscure to us; they were mostly not traded by the Athenians themselves but by these international traders. The profits of trade allow us to make sense of the prosperity of this group of cities, as evidenced by their prestigious building policies.[57]

The situation changed at the beginning of the fifth century. The eastern Aegean trading cities were massively and negatively affected by the repression of their failed revolt against the Persians (498–494). Until the end of the fourth century, Athens emerged as the major new economic and political actor in the Aegean. The rapid increase of its population, the exploitation of the new silver mines at Laurium, the installation of a new democratic regime and of an empire dominating the Aegean space in 477, gave this city an exceptional edge. After its defeat at the end of the Peloponnesian War, Athens could only temporarily rebuild a regional (Aegean) league between 377 and 355. The population and political influence of the city could never be restored to their previous standing. Yet, Athens remained in the fourth century the economic hub of the Aegean basin.

The city needed massive imports to feed its population and satisfy all its needs. In the fifth century, the revenue from the allies, namely 600 talents according to Thucydides 2.13.3 (the total included the revenues from the colonies and not only the tribute paid by the allies in a restrictive sense) was a source of income for the city.[58] But it is obviously the product of the silver mines (well over 1,500 talents during the peaks of production in the mid-fifth century) that allowed the Athenians to import the goods they needed.[59] Grain was the main import item. But textiles, metals, oil, wine, wood, and charcoal were also massively imported to Piraeus. Slaves were another item of massive import: they are found in many different occupations in Athens, including in various kinds of craftmanship such as furniture, weapons, or

---

[57] On the long-term evolution of the centers of power in the Greek world, see Bresson 2016b, 416–17.

[58] See Kallet-Marx 1993, 96–103.

[59] Over 1,000 talents (Flament 2007, 245–7) or over 1,500 talents (Bresson 2019) in the most productive periods.

textile production. The many slave women occupied in textiles must have worked imported wool or linen, which were in short supply (for the former) or absent (for the latter) in Athens. There should be no doubt that Athens was a major manufacturing city.[60] The presence of the Athenian market drove the prosperity of the whole Aegean area and beyond. Thus, the island of Peparethus, the cities of the Chalcidice like Mende and Scione, or the island of Thasos could sell their wines to the traders en route to the Black Sea, from where they would fetch the grain that Athens so badly needed.

The defeat of Athens by the Macedonians in 322 was followed by a massive reduction of its population and by the collapse of the production of its silver mines. Athens was no longer the hub it had been in the two previous centuries. In the third century, the political space of the Aegean was now disputed between the great monarchies, the Antigonids, the Ptolemies, and the Seleucids. The cities of the coast of Asia Minor, located on the major trade route that linked the Black Sea to the Levant and Egypt, began to experience a new prosperity, although they suffered from the consequences of the many wars of the third century. One of them, the island city of Rhodes, at the southwestern tip of Asia Minor, managed to create a regional state that encompassed its neighboring islands and parts of the continent (the so-called Peraea). Following the economic decline of Athens, Rhodes became the major trading center and port of transit in the early and mid-Hellenistic period until 167. As we can trace from its amphorae, it sold its wine all over the Mediterranean, but especially in the Black Sea, in the Levant, and in Egypt.[61]

The fate of Delos was different. Thanks to the sacred character procured by the presence of its sanctuary of Apollo and its new independence recovered from the Athenians in 314, the minuscule city of Delos, at the center of the Aegean, was until 167 the hub of a regional market where cities of the Aegean could acquire various goods, especially grain, which could come from distant suppliers.[62] But the volume of activity of the port remained far below that of the Piraeus in the classical period or of Rhodes in the Hellenistic period. In the second and first century, Rome was the new power dominating the Mediterranean. To punish the Rhodians, the senate in 167 gave Delos to the Athenians, who expelled the Delians. Being in fact only a nominal property of the Athenians, Delos, now declared a free port, became the transit hub of all the traffic between the eastern

---

[60] See Acton 2014.   [61] Gabrielsen 1997, 64–84.
[62] Reger 1994, 83–126; Chankowski-Sablé 1997.

Mediterranean and western Mediterranean. Until the island was twice destroyed by war and pirates in 88 and 69, traders from the whole Mediterranean met there. Among the main items traded in Delos were slaves, coming from the eastern Mediterranean and sold in great numbers to the western markets. A "circle" (*kyklos*) where the slaves were sold at auction has been discovered near the "Agora of Theophrastus," close to the port.[63] New systems of storage – in a domestic framework, in storage rooms, or in large warehouses aligned along the seashore – testifying to these new developments have also been found along the shore.[64] Athens temporarily benefitted from the prosperity of Delos, until it made the fatal choice of opposing Rome, which caused a new economic setback and an economic depression that lasted until the end of the first century.

CONCLUSION AND FUTURE RESEARCH

Classical Aegean cities were directly connected to Athens, and together they sustained one of the wealthiest cycles of economic prosperity in the history of the Mediterranean. Yet, Athens was not able to maintain its leading position beyond the classical period, as other Aegean players eventually took over until Rome asserted its dominance over the entire Mediterranean. There is still much work to be done on the Athenian and Aegean economies. More fieldwork is necessary to deepen our understanding of the Greek rural economy: additional surveys should provide more in-depth case studies of rural occupation and exploitation, while it becomes imperative to excavate more farmsteads or agricultural estates using the latest techniques in micromorphology, paleobotany, and zooarchaeology. Additionally, more projects on the archaeology of harbors and marketplaces are needed in order to increase the amount and range of our evidence. Future research will only confirm that the study of the ancient economy represents one of the most dynamic fields in the study of the ancient world.

Further Reading

Bresson 2016b covers in much greater detail the diverse and complex economy of the region discussed in this chapter. Amouretti 1986,

---

[63] Moretti, Fincker, and Chankowski 2012.

[64] Zarmakoupi 2018 and Karvonis and Malmary 2018, with Zarmakoupi 2015a for an overview of the transformation of Delos in this period.

Foxhall 2007, and Halstead 2014 cover the main issues related to Aegean agriculture. Pritchard 2015 is the best and up-to-date account of Athenian public finance. Reger 1994 and the monumental work of Chankowski 2008, 2011 and 2019 are essential for understanding the economy of Hellenistic Delos, an economy particularly well documented in its rich epigraphic record. Gabrielsen 1997 is the authoritative study of the economy of Hellenistic Rhodes.

9: EGYPT AND THE PTOLEMAIC EMPIRE

Christelle Fischer-Bovet

INTRODUCTION

This chapter discusses the economic developments occurring within the Ptolemaic empire, of which Egypt was the core province, focusing on military expenditure and benefits from conquest, international trade, and political economy. The framework within which these questions were discussed in the twentieth century has changed dramatically since the pioneering works of the Russian émigré Michael Rostovtzeff and the Belgian scholar Claire Préaux in the 1920s and 1930s, thanks to new sources and to the recent work of ancient historians engaging with social theory, especially the New Institutional Economics (Chapter 23, this volume). The first section provides an overview of past and current approaches to the economy of the Ptolemaic empire (323–30), the longest-lasting polity emerging from Alexander's conquests and also the second largest after the Seleucid empire. The second section sets the stage with a brief overview of the geography of the empire, its population size, and total imperial revenues, paying attention to environmental and climatic constraints. The third section focuses on the cost and benefits of military conquests, as well as the related management of migration patterns and new settlements. The fourth section offers a survey of the current understanding of the Ptolemaic political economy and its consequences on the monetization of the Egyptian economy and on society and political stability. Finally, the fifth section looks at a few examples of the synergistic relationship between empire, warfare, and trade and between the public and private spheres of the economy and sketches the purchasing power of different economic groups in Egypt.

APPROACHES AND SOURCES

Current research on the economy of Hellenistic Egypt and of the Ptolemaic empire builds on and challenges the pioneering works of

Rostovtzeff and Préaux, who almost a century ago had started exploiting the rich papyrological material (including *ostraka*) unique to Egypt. Rostovtzeff held a positive view on the development and control of agricultural production and taxation under the new Graeco-Macedonian power, which he interpreted as nascent capitalism, and on the extensive land-reclamation project in the Fayyum, as revealed by hundreds of papyri preserved in the archive of Zenon, the agent of the finance minister (*dioiketes*) on his large estate.[1] Later, Préaux offered the first thorough analysis of what she coined *L'économie Royale*, insisting on the level of control achieved by the Ptolemies and on their "planned" royal economy.[2] Préaux and the next generation of scholars in the 1970s and 1980s, such as Bingen and Will, critical of the European colonial past, read the Ptolemaic material within a similar framework of colonial exploitation of Egyptian society.[3]

The main debates still locate themselves in the degree of innovation, exploitation, and monetization, on the ruler's intentions, and on the impact of economic changes on Egyptian multicultural society, but the theoretical framework has changed. On the one hand, discussions have moved beyond the primitivist versus modernist dichotomy (Chapter 1, this volume). On the other hand, the model of oriental despotism has been rejected, while the tendency is to acknowledge that the *dirigiste* model assumes far too much control and knowledge on the part of the king over administration and population and that the colonial model "captures some, but not all, of the social dynamics of the periods" and misleadingly blends premodern and modern (nation-state) colonialisms.[4] However, discussion of the Ptolemaic economy still focuses on Egypt and partly neglects to take into consideration the other provinces because of a source imbalance, which may be partially compensated by the recent growth in Ptolemaic numismatic studies, Hellenistic archaeology across the eastern Mediterranean, and even environmental studies.

IMPERIAL SPACE, REVENUES, AND POPULATION SIZE

Under the reigns of Ptolemy III (246–222/1) and Ptolemy IV (222/1–204), the empire had reached its maximum extension, with the core province of Egypt surrounded by the province of Cyrenaica in the west, Lower Nubia in the south, Syria and Phoenicia in the east, as well as

---

[1] Rostovtzeff 1922.   [2] Préaux 1939.   [3] Préaux 1939; Bingen 1978; Will 1985.
[4] Quote from J. G. Manning 2010, 53.

Cyprus, Cilicia, Pamphylia, Lycia, and a part of Caria, some cities along the Ionian coast (intermittently), Thrace, the Aegean islands, and outposts in central Greece and Crete.[5] It is sometimes conceived as a maritime empire, but the Ptolemies, like the other Hellenistic kings, aimed at securing material and human resources not only on the coast but also – as much as possible – inland.

This vast empire was ecologically varied. Egypt, with its unique geography, was the most fertile province but relied on irrigation agriculture and thus depended on favorable annual Nile floods, while each province had specific resources.[6] For instance, Nubia and the Eastern Desert provided minerals and access to elephants and ivory; Cyprus, the Levant, and part of Anatolia supplied construction material – especially cedars – for the fleet, skilled sailors, and minerals. All the provinces taken together almost doubled the pool of human resources available in Egypt, with about 4,000,000 inhabitants in Egypt and 3,500,000 in the rest of the empire, while the annual revenue in silver (calculated here in Attic standard) from Egypt amounted to 12,000 talents according to Jerome (*Comm. to Daniel* 11.5), to which the rest of the provinces added approximately 3,600–7,000 talents.[7] For comparison, the Seleucid annual revenue in Attic silver amounted to ca. 14,000–19,000 talents, quite similar to the total revenue of the Roman empire at the time of Pompey of 14,000 talents (Plut. *Vit. Pomp.* 45.4). In addition, grain revenues for Egypt alone may have reached eight million *artabas*, which were redistributed within Egypt to the temples, as seeds to royal farmers, and as the wage portion paid in kind to soldiers, state officials, and other workers, while grain surpluses could be marketed.[8]

Documentary sources from Egypt, most notably the trilingual Canopus decree (238), show how insufficient Nile floods could threaten economic and political stability. Recent analyses conducted by J. G. Manning and historical climatologists have established a causal relationship between a certain type of volcanic eruption (causing changes in atmospheric chemistry) and low Nile levels.[9] Their frequency was high in the Hellenistic period (but no longer in the Roman period), and they largely coincided with the abrupt end of

---

[5] Bagnall 1976.   [6] J. G. Manning 2007, 438–40.

[7] For Egypt, see J. G. Manning 2003, 47–9, n. 129; for the provinces, extrapolating from Judea a rate of 1.2–2 talents per 1,000 inhabitants, see Fischer-Bovet 2014, esp. 66–70, 75.

[8] Justinian, *Edict* XIII §7; Jer. *Comm. to Daniel* 11.5 suggests only 1,500,000 *artabas*, but this is too low in view of the 20,000 km^2 (= 7,260,000 *arouras*) under cultivation, which at a low tax rate of one *artaba* per *aroura* would amount to 7,260,000 *artabas* as tax revenue, see Fischer-Bovet 2014, 68; on redistribution networks, see the survey in Muhs 2016, 233–45.

[9] Manning et al. 2017.

military episodes and periods of social unrest. Joseph Manning argues that control of regions outside of Egypt relying on rain-fed agriculture was therefore more pressing, offering a complementary and independent set of evidence for explaining the prominence of warfare in the Hellenistic world.

MILITARY EXPENSES, SOLDIERS' ECONOMIC OPPORTUNITIES, AND NEW SETTLEMENTS

The Hellenistic polities and economies that grew out of Alexander's conquests of the Persian empire cannot be dissociated from intense warfare (Chapter 5, this volume). Hellenistic kingship relied strongly on military victories, and each king was in competition for human and material resources, especially within the eastern Mediterranean but at times also beyond. War-making put pressure on the Ptolemies, as it did on their main rivals the Seleucids and the Antigonids, so that they developed steady ways to seize revenues and resources. It shaped Ptolemaic immigration and settlement patterns, especially of military families, within their provinces and above all within Egypt. Financial constraints also triggered series of adjustments to the composition of the army, soldiers' wages, and land allotments.[10]

Recent evaluations of the cost of third-century Hellenistic armies offer a quantitative basis to compare them with each other and also to show that the proportion of state income spent on the army was similar to that invested by many other expansionist premodern states. In the third century, the Ptolemies and the Seleucids could each gather about 70,000 soldiers on a single battlefield and still have troops garrisoned throughout their empires, while the Ptolemies also built the largest fleet. At a daily average wage of about one drachm for an infantryman, two drachms for a cavalryman, and four drachms and up for officers, the annual cost of the Ptolemaic army in wartime amounted to 10,200–13,400 and that of the Seleucid army to 9,000–10,000 (Attic) silver talents, the difference being mostly induced by the high cost of the fleet.[11] While the Seleucid military cost hardly went down in peacetime (7,000–8,000 Attic silver talents), the Ptolemies decreased it to 4,500–5,700 Attic silver talents thanks to the extensive use of land allotments (*kleroi*) granted to soldiers (cleruchs) in exchange for military service. When crudely compared with the total revenues in Attic silver evaluated

---

[10] Fischer-Bovet 2014, 123–55, 212–21.   [11] Fischer-Bovet 2014, 71–7.

above, Ptolemaic military costs accounted for 78 percent of the imperial budget in wartime and 34 percent in peace time (respectively 57 percent and 45 percent in the Seleucid case).[12] Of course, the high cost could partly be compensated in case of victories by plunder – goods and slaves for soldiers and quick cash flow – but quantitative data are missing, except for occasional events. For instance, Ptolemy III seized 1,500 talents from the Cilician treasury in 246, at the beginning of the Third Syrian War, which represents an extra 10 percent on the annual revenue in cash.[13]

Warfare and conquests also offered a variety of economic opportunities for the state – by expanding the pool of goods and people subject to diverse sorts of taxes and by opening new avenues for trade – as well as for individuals, in particular elite groups and soldiers. This has recently led Muhs to consider military campaigns as "entrepreneurial."[14] The statement of the court poet Theocritus, "Ptolemy is the best paymaster a free man could have" (*Id.* 14.59), cannot be quantitatively verified, but Egypt's legendary wealth and the Ptolemies' generous land grants in exchange for military service encouraged immigrants to settle in Egypt.[15] They constituted about 5 percent of the population in the first century of Ptolemaic rule, slightly more than half of them belonging to the military.[16] In the third century, officers and cavalrymen most commonly received 100 *arouras* while infantrymen could be allotted up to thirty *arouras*, mainly in the Arsinoite, Herakleopolite, and Oxyrhynchite nomes, greatly helping with the cultivation of newly reclaimed land. Calculations based on later tax documents suggest that cleruchic land amounted to between 5 and 7 percent of the 20,000 square kilometers of cultivable land in Egypt, giving to these soldiers excellent economic opportunities, not only in producing diverse types of cereals and wine but also in breeding livestock and trading.[17]

The Ptolemies invested a lot of their revenues in land-reclamation projects, developing infrastructures such as dykes and canals, building new settlements and expanding others, in turn increasing their revenues and reducing the cost of their army. By doing so, they also avoided seizing land from temples and individuals. The expenditure for founding a polis varied, but the locals probably shared in the cost: in the case of

---

[12] In the third century, the Ptolemies were on average at war once every three years.

[13] *P. Gurob* = *BNJ* 160: English translation in Bagnall and Derow 2004, no. 27; list in Austin 1986, 451, nn. 8–9; 40,000 talents reported by Jer. *Comm. to Daniel* 11.6–9 has to be rejected, *contra* Le Rider and de Callataÿ 2006, 193.

[14] Muhs 2016, 249. [15] Scheuble-Reiter 2012. [16] Fischer-Bovet 2011.

[17] Fischer-Bovet 2014, 202–10; Monson 2012, 88–93 and the third-century Demotic land survey *P. Agri.*; Scheuble-Reiter 2012, 251–87 on economic activities ; for a larger estimate of third-century cleruchic land, see Johstono (2020).

the foundation of Arsinoe in Cilicia, the land was taken from the neighboring city of Nagidus, but the whole operation was run locally, unless there were disputes.[18] Craftsmen, such as carpenters, were sent with soldiers to build settlements, from forts to larger agglomerations, even far south along the Red Sea shore.[19] In Egypt, land reclamation in the third-century Fayyum seems to have been largely organized by the state, which could gather large pools of workers; in one case up to 15,000 men were to be paid from the revenues of the emmer tax.[20] The well-known archive of the architect Kleon, one of Zenon's correspondents, recently fully published, provides unique information on irrigation, dyke works, and stone-cutting.[21] The organization of the settlement and cultivation was also partially entrusted to high officials and officers. They received, in the third century, gift estates (*doreai*) of 10,000 *arouras* (27 km²), such as that of Ptolemy II's finance minister Apollonius, managed by Zenon. Even Egyptian families received *doreai*, most likely to confirm the landholding of their family estates.[22] The estate of Apollonius is sometimes characterized as an "experimental farm," since new sorts of cultivation were tried out, such as poppy, but were not always successful.[23]

Such large reclamation projects and gift-estates no longer existed in the second century. As less land was becoming available, the size of the land allotments to cleruchs diminished, though more Graeco-Egyptian and Egyptian soldiers (*machimoi*) received land, many as foot soldiers with five, seven or ten *arouras*, or twenty as cavalry-*machimoi* (*machimoi hippeis*).[24] By 195, the Ptolemaic empire was reduced to Egypt, Cyrenaica and Cyprus, and a few strongholds in the Aegean, leading to the decrease of state income and of economic opportunities for elite groups.[25] During this period, the fleet was smaller, and soldiers were apparently paid less than in the third century to reduce the military cost, with plausible exceptions during Syrian wars or dynastic conflicts. Immigration to Egypt had also stopped, except for a small-scale influx of soldiers, many of them from the lost territories (southern Anatolia, Syria-Phoenicia-Judea).[26]

---

[18] *SEG* 39, 1426.
[19] E.g. Dorion the carpenter belonged to Eumedes' expedition that founded Ptolemais-of-the-Hunt, see *IPaneion* 9 bis and Strab. 16.4.7.
[20] *P.Hal.* 1, ll. 5–6 with Thompson 1999, 112–13, yet we do not know if it actually happened; on Ptolemaic settlements, see Mueller 2006.
[21] van Beek 2017.   [22] Clarysse 1979.   [23] Crawford 1973.
[24] Scheuble-Reiter 2012, 199–206; Fischer-Bovet 2014, 212–21.
[25] Fischer-Bovet 2014, 81 no. 112.
[26] On the comparison of military immigration in the third and second century, see Sänger 2015.

PTOLEMAIC POLITICAL ECONOMY AND ITS EFFECT ON SOCIETY

War-making and securing strongholds and provinces necessitated regular state income, both in cash and kind, to pay soldiers and keep the loyalty of rent-seeking elites, and thus stimulated the elaboration of fiscal and monetary policies. The Ptolemies adapted their ruling strategies to different political traditions and ecologies in order to strengthen their networks of communication and secure revenues. This is visible in the shape of the administration and in their monetary policies, the latter being innovative but also unusual.

Administration of the Empire

The Ptolemaic administration of the empire cannot be reconstructed in detail, but patterns emerge. In Egypt, the administrative and fiscal organization of the province relied on three branches represented in each nome.[27] The first one was headed by the *strategos*, who was in charge of law and order and reported directly to the king. The second branch served to manage economic activities and was led by the *oikonomos* (financial magistrate in the nome), who reported to the central *dioiketes* (top financial magistrate) in Alexandria. The *basilikos grammateus* (royal scribe), supervising the third branch, also reported to the *dioiketes* and documented economic activities, helped by *topogrammateis* at the district level (toparchy) and *komogrammateis* (village scribes). Land surveys recorded the type of land, whether royal, temple, cleruchic, or private land, since it impacted tax rates.[28] Greek was the main language in the administration, while the use of Demotic at the lower levels decreased over time. Individuals with occupations associated with the Greek cultural sphere (e.g. teachers, athletes) were exempted from the poll tax (called salt tax) and the fiscal status of *hellen* (Greek), which could also be given to non-Greek individuals who served the state in some capacity, brought at least symbolic advantages such as the exemption from the obol tax.[29] The lower levels of the administration remained the responsibility of locals, initially supervised by Macedonians and Greeks, while poleis in Egypt and throughout the empire had their own civic administration but were subject to

---

[27] Armoni 2012 for a detailed papyrological analysis, and Muhs 2016, 211–52 for a survey; J. G. Manning 2010 for a model-based approach and Monson 2012 for a comparative approach.
[28] Monson 2012, esp. 76–9.   [29] Clarysse and Thompson 2006.

the decisions of the king and/or of the governor, and a Ptolemaic garrison was usually stationed there.[30]

Outside of Egypt, governors generally called *strategoi* administered the province, while two *oikonomoi* oversaw financial matters in Lycia, on the model of the two *archontes* who previously managed the region for the Carian Hecatomnid dynasts.[31] Letters to the *oikonomoi* in Lycia and in the districts (*topoi*) in Lesbos and Thrace point to a centralized taxation of the provinces (*P. Tebt.* I 8) and, combined with other documents (e.g. *PSI* iv 324), remind us that important state revenues came from marketing grain surpluses from the provinces.[32] Normally, the poleis paid a form of tribute (*syntaxis*) or a tithe (*dekate*) to the king, collected by tax farmers, but certain taxes raised by the poleis could also be seized by the king, such as taxes over their harbors; depending on the result of negotiations, the king could decide to cede control over such taxes to the polis, as in Iasus.[33] The construction of an administrative network was reinforced by one or a few dynastic (re)foundations in each province.[34] In Syria-Phoenicia, which was the most akin to Egypt, land continued to be partly owned by the king as in pre-Hellenistic times, but novelties were introduced such as tax farming and the regulation and rather high taxation imposed on all commercial exchange. Royal ordinances about the registration of live-stock and slaves in Syria-Phoenicia (*SB* v 8008, 260 BCE) and tax collection reflect the practices established in Egypt as recorded in the so-called Papyrus "Revenue Laws" (259).[35]

The "Revenue Laws" are an unsystematic compilation of fiscal regulations concerning tax farming and special rules on orchards and vineyards. In Egypt, the state also interfered in the production and distribution of the so-called state monopolies (concessionary industries) affecting more than thirty products such as oil, beer, and papyrus.[36] The document was first interpreted by Rostovtzeff and Préaux as evidence of a highly controlled royal economy, but following the work of Bingen, scholars now stress the absence of a systematic plan and call into question the level of control actually achieved.[37] They point, rather, to its strategies for minimizing risks for the state by securing stable revenue,

---

[30] Bagnall 1976.   [31] Bagnall 1976; Domingo Gygax 2005 on Lycia.
[32] Austin 2006, no. 278; Bagnall and Derow 2004, no. 66.
[33] Kaye and Amitay 2015, 146–51 with bibliography on *Ilasos* 2–3 and on *TAM* ii 1 (decree of Telmessos); Schuler 2007.
[34] List in Mueller 2006, 200–21.
[35] English translations in Bagnall and Derow 2004, no. 64 and no. 114; Bingen 1978.
[36] Full list with sources in Huss 2012, 50–67; see Dogaer 2021 on monopolies.
[37] Bingen 2007, 157–88; J. G. Manning 2010, esp. 150–7; for a balanced view on corruption, see Monson 2012, 227–34.

but note that it remained difficult to limit abuses on the part of tax collectors or officials, despite regular attempts in royal and amnesty decrees (e.g. *P.Tebt.* 1 5). Yet from a model-based standpoint, the Papyrus "Revenue Laws" indicate a shift from a roving bandit state toward a stationary bandit state.

Monetary Policies

Part of the state revenues were collected in grain, but the use of coins increased dramatically in Egypt through the payments to soldiers and officials and the collection of some taxes in cash (e.g. salt tax). The monetization of Egypt was also facilitated by the creation of state banks in nome metropoles and villages and, for currency exchange, private banks as well as monopoly banks, the latter being leased out by the state.[38] As stressed by von Reden, the monetization of Egypt increased the level of uniformity of the empire.[39] A slow path towards uniformity is also supported by the establishment of royal banks outside Egypt, at least in Syria-Phoenicia (probably in Ptolemais) and in Caria (Halicarnassus).[40] Yet the level of monetization in Egypt remains difficult to establish because of regional variety.[41] The economy in kind and in cash remained closely interrelated, and money could simply play the role of a unit of account.[42]

The monetary policies of the Ptolemies distinguished them from their rivals. First, as early as 305, Ptolemy I created a closed-currency system based on a lower weight standard than the Attic standard, which applied in Egypt, Cyprus, and Syria-Phoenicia (see also Chapter 5, this volume).[43] The Ptolemies made profit on precious metal when merchants exchanged their currency by gaining about 3 g from each 17 g Attic silver tetradrachm. A second particularity was the regular minting of gold coins, perhaps because of existing gold mines in the eastern desert, whose use was intensified from the beginning of the dynasty onward.[44] Gold was mainly used for donatives and projected royal propaganda for courtiers and officers, yet it contrasted with the very

---

[38] On types of banks, see Bogaert 1998 and von Reden 2007b, 253–95; Maresch 2012 for documents from a royal bank.

[39] von Reden 2007b, 301.   [40] Bogaert 1998, 201–2.

[41] Taxation in kind limited the monetization of the economy; see J. G. Manning 2010, 164.

[42] von Reden 2007b, 79–150; Criscuolo 2011.

[43] de Callataÿ 2005b; Lorber 2012, 214–15. Cyrenaica had its own different closed system, see Lorber 2018, ch. on Ptolemy I Soter, 19 no. 199.

[44] Faucher 2018 for the recent excavations at Bir-Samut.

limited use of gold coins in the Seleucid open-currency system. A third distinctive mark was the abundant use of bronze coinage, which increased with the monetary reforms of Ptolemy II in 261/0 and even more under Ptolemy III, who largely removed the circulation of silver coins within Egypt, probably because silver supply had always been challenging in Egypt.[45]

The reforms that took place around 210 under Ptolemy IV introduced a bronze standard using a decimal system in which a theoretical bronze unit was converted into silver at a 1:60 ratio.[46] Though the purchasing power of the bronze currency diminished in the second century, one must be cautious with past models based on scattered prices and wages that reconstruct successive periods of the dropping of the ratio between the bronze and silver drachms, whereas the process was more gradual and prices could fluctuate according to contingencies.[47] Based on the supply of new coins, the wealth of the Ptolemies and of the Seleucids appears about equivalent despite the different monetary policies, with the Ptolemies producing annually about 475 talents of new coins and the Seleucid about 555 talents.[48] These sums represented only a small part of their respective annual revenue.

ECONOMIC DEVELOPMENT AND PTOLEMAIC SOCIETY

The effect of the Ptolemaic political economy on society outside of Egypt still deserves a more systematic assessment for which there is no place here.[49] The scholarly approach has focused on Egypt and on the exploitative character of Ptolemaic rule illustrated by the high number of taxes, the new poll tax as a mark of domination, and the abusive behavior of royal officials and tax collectors, which all could explain, at least partly, the outbreak of several domestic revolts.[50] Along these lines, Bingen emphasized the entrepreneurial activities of the Greeks in Egypt at the expense of the Egyptians, but current research draws a more-balanced picture of interaction between Egyptian and Greek social networks.[51] For instance, the views that Greeks were commonly

---

[45] Lorber 2012, 216.　[46] Lorber 2013, 135–6.　[47] Fischer-Bovet and Lorber 2020.
[48] Iossif 2015.
[49] For negative and positive impact, see respectively Cherry and Davis 1991 and Viviers 2011.
[50] Véïsse 2004; Crawford 1978, 199 with sources on abuses.
[51] Translated into English in Bingen 2007, esp. 203–4, 248–9.

absentee landlords, disconnected from the Egyptian countryside, or that Egyptians were less inclined to use coins, have been challenged.[52] Even among bankers, 13 percent had an Egyptian name and among those bearing a Greek name, individuals with names derived from Hermes and Heracles may have come from the Egyptian milieu.[53] Moreover, means to limit abuses by officials or tax farmers were developed – with uneven success – such as statements in royal decrees (see above, p. 132), memoranda to officials, opportunities to petition the king or high officers, and the production of tax receipts.[54] Similarly, the registration of contracts of property transfers at the local *grapheion* (record office) also made private property more secure, and a wide range of contract forms, with penalty fees in case of nonreimbursement, lowered transaction costs.[55] Justice was provided by the king in exchange for revenues.[56] Political and social stability relied on such an equilibrium, but unfavorable socioeconomic circumstances could trigger riots or revolts, the most serious episode being the Great Revolt, that is the secession of Upper Egypt (206–186). Its causes are still debated but were likely a combination of economic and political factors fueled by arguments based on religion or ethnicity.[57] The cumulation of destabilizing economic factors within a short period explains its magnitude: fiscal and monetary reforms occurring around that time coupled with insufficient Nile floods resulting from volcanic eruptions.

TRADE, THE PRIVATE SECTOR OF THE ECONOMY, AND STANDARDS OF LIVING

Despite the challenges faced by the Ptolemies, their resilience over three centuries suggests that elite groups and the military – not limited to the descendants of earlier migrants – benefited enough from the opportunities offered by the empire, even after it shrank in the second century. This section offers a few examples of the entanglement between empire, warfare, and trade and between the public and private spheres of the economy. It also sketches the purchasing power of different economic groups in Egypt.

---

[52] Scheuble-Reiter 2012, 33–6 and Fischer-Bovet 2014, 240–2; on Egyptian use of coins, see Criscuolo 2011.
[53] Bogaert 1998, 168.
[54] E.g. *P. Tebt.* 1 703 (memorandum); *P.Enteuxeis* (petitions to the king); e.g. Muhs 2005 for tax receipts; on the ideology of the good official, see Crawford 1978; Wyns 2016.
[55] Greek and Demotic contracts analyzed by type in Keenan, Manning, and Yiftach-Firanko 2014.
[56] J. G. Manning 2010, 165–206.   [57] Véïsse 2004, 11–26.

Long-Distance Trade and Empire

While textiles from Samos and Miletus were displayed at the Alexandrian court of Ptolemy II with other goods and luxury products as symbols of the empire, the Egyptian weaving industry was encouraged by the king, not only for producing wool from local sheep but also, for instance, from Milesian sheep imported to Apollonius' estate to make high-quality fabric.[58] Imports of oil came from Samos, possibly too from Anatolia (oil and wine), while ships would sail back with Egyptian grain on board.[59] Custom duties and harbor fees (e.g. *P.Cair.Zen.* I 59012) on goods transported within and outside the Ptolemaic empire, like later within the Roman empire, do not seem to have limited trade significantly. Foreign merchants who came to buy goods in the Egyptian countryside had sometimes to wait for the reminting of their coins according to the Ptolemaic weight standard, as vividly recorded in a letter to Apollonius by an Alexandrian mint official about gold coins, yet the constraints caused by the closed-currency system do not seem to have had a negative impact.[60] Trade networks within the Mediterranean, Black Sea, and Red Sea (via the eastern desert) intensified within the Ptolemaic imperial space, strengthening the networks of communication that define empires. The close link between warfare, empire, and trade is best encapsulated by the organization of elephant hunts for war-making and for trading ivory, as well as the commerce of slaves.

The slave trade was indeed one of the most lucrative. The coastal cities of Syria-Phoenicia formed a commercial hub, with slaves from Arabia and Syria, though the Ptolemies tried to limit enslavement of individuals within their provinces.[61] A letter with a list of slaves sent to the finance minister Apollonius by Toubias, a member of the local Transjordan elite who oversaw this region for the Ptolemies (Chapter 5, this volume), records what seems to be a private business agreement between these two high Ptolemaic officials rather than gifts on the part of a dynast.[62] The agents of the king did not have to keep private and public affairs separate. Conquest helped the Ptolemies and their elites to secure trade networks between Egypt and other regions, as the documentation concerning Syria-Phoenicia makes clear. Archaeological material attests that trade between this region and Egypt did not diminish after the

---

[58] See *P.Cair.Zen.* III 59430 (mid-third century).
[59] *P.Cair.Zen.* I 59015 r (after 258); for Anatolia, Sartre 1995, 77–8.
[60] *P.Cair.Zen.* I 59021 (259/8).
[61] E.g. *P.Cair.Zen.* I 59015 v, *P.Cair.Zen.* IV 59537, *P.Cair.Zen.* V 59804, *P.Cair.Zen.* I 59093.
[62] Pfeiffer 2011, 194–202, 210–14, with *P.Cair.Zen.* I 59075.

Ptolemies lost political control over it.[63] Moreover, the Ptolemaic weight system was maintained by the Seleucids, who used new methods of managing currency supply influenced by the Ptolemies, and Ptolemy V may have continued to receive some share of the tax revenues following his marriage with the Seleucid Cleopatra I.[64] Once strong trade networks were established within an imperial space, it seems that they were difficult to undo. Similarly, trade routes of the Roman empire trace back to the Hellenistic period.[65]

Wages and Purchasing Power in Egypt

The written record of private transactions increased during the Hellenistic period, and particularly rich data were preserved in the Egyptian sand. As in the public sphere of the economy, transactions within the private sphere were still partly dealt with in kind but also increasingly in cash, the level of monetization fluctuating according to time, space, and professional milieu. The implementation of banks allowed the making of transactions without having to be present, which was particularly convenient to wealthy land-lords, but money-lending never seems to have offered the same financial advantages as landholding.[66] Private loans, credits, and orders for payment could be made in private and public banks.[67] Small scale craftsmen's businesses and middlemen's trade were common, especially as part-time activities that provided an extra income, as for Ptolemaios, who served Astarte in the Serapeum of Memphis and interpreted dreams but also dealt in textiles.[68] Goods could be sold in markets that were permanent in many towns and villages and on riverbanks, where receipts for freight charges confirm that private goods were traded.[69]

It remains challenging to establish the living standards of different population groups. A glimpse into individuals' purchasing power in Egypt may serve as a first step and can be achieved by comparing workers' wages (*opsonia* or *misthoi*), often complemented by food allowances (*sitometria*), and by approximating incomes of craftsmen and professionals; it uses as a proxy measure incomes converted into wheat equivalent, while the results can be refined by better-documented cases,

---

[63] Berlin 1997.
[64] On sharing revenues, see Kaye and Amitay 2015 on Joseph. *AJ* 12.154–5 with previous bibliography.
[65] J. G. Manning 2015a.   [66] von Reden 2007b, 280–2.   [67] Muhs 2016, 234–5.
[68] On Ptolemaios, see Thompson 2012, 209–14 (mid-second century).
[69] Thompson 2012, 29–75 on Memphis based on the archives of Zenon and Ptolemaios; Muhs 2016, 246.

where overdue pay or complementary ways to make extra income offer a fuller picture of individuals' living standards.[70] There were enormous discrepancies between wages: in third-century Egypt, at the subsistence level, workers performing unskilled labor averaged one obol a day, a middle category of workers that included most soldiers and many craftsmen earned three to twelve times more, and finally high officials made at least sixty times more, yet part of their wages could serve to pay their staff. In the second century, unskilled workers' wages remain similar, equivalent to two to five *artabas* a month (i.e. 2.5 to 5.3 liters of wheat per day), thus within the lower end of the core range calculated by Scheidel for premodern societies.[71] Overall, the economic hierarchy and pay differentials remained the same in the second century, even if soldiers' wages in peacetime may have slightly decreased.[72] The rather privileged economic position of scribes was maintained, with payments sometimes still calculated on the silver standard or even paid in sliver. Finally, the price for accessing some services such as entrance to the public bath, one-fourth obol in the third century, remained stable throughout the period in relationship to wages and commodity prices, even suggesting some democratization in the use of baths.[73] While prices could be volatile during short periods of crises, this survey argues against the old view of economic decline in second-century Egypt.

CONCLUSION AND FUTURE RESEARCH

This chapter has offered a perspective on past and current approaches to and understanding of the Ptolemaic economy and has tried to avoid an Egyptocentric view by including examples from other Ptolemaic provinces and assessing the effects of imperialism on the economy. This study provides some order of magnitudes for specific processes, such as the maintenance of large professional armies or investigating individuals' purchasing power, so that it may help to tackle further questions in economic history that intersect with political, social, and even cultural history.[74] Current studies of the Ptolemaic economy play with such intersections and point in (at least) four directions. First, anthropological approaches to the economy allow us to connect politics, economics, and

---

[70] For the methodological problems and the overview proposed below, see Lorber and Fischer-Bovet 2020.
[71] Scheidel 2010, esp. 453, table 4.
[72] The extremely low wage of Ptolemaios' brother Apollonios has been reinterpreted by Lorber and Fischer-Bovet (2020).
[73] Faucher and Redon 2014.   [74] It also responds to desiderata raised by Davies 2001a, 45–7.

the symbolism of money, a perspective taken by von Reden in her work on third-century Egypt.[75] Second, sociological perspectives, coupled for instance with psychology, spark the investigation of the economics of happiness (or well-being). Despite the many challenges posed by our ancient material, including how to measure living standards, a preliminary study by Vandorpe lays the basis for developing a methodology applicable to the premodern world, starting from how many taxes one individual may pay, at what rate, and in which circumstances, rather than looking at the total number of existing taxes.[76] Third, interdisciplinary collaboration with natural sciences is a growing field, supplying environmental and quantitative data on, for instance, Nile failure, soil quality, flora, and fauna.[77] Future work needs to integrate more thoroughly this new evidence within a historical framework. Fourth, comparisons with the economies of other ancient empires, may they be entangled or not, should shed a different light on the commonalities and singularities of the Ptolemaic political economy, on monetization, trade, and living standards.

Further Reading

The works of J. G. Manning 2003, 2010 on land tenure and law and Monson 2012, 2015 on taxation offer a new theoretical framework for the study of the Ptolemaic economy, drawing on the New Institutional Economics, while also including Demotic sources. The most recent surveys of the Ptolemaic economy are Huss 2012, with a thorough bibliography, and the last chapter of Muhs 2016. The legal aspects of economic transactions are discussed in Keenan, Manning, and Yiftach-Firanko 2014. The relationship between Hellenistic warfare and the economy has been problematized by Austin 1986. The monetization of the economy and the development of banks in Egypt has been extensively discussed from different perspectives: by papyrologists such as Maresch 1996, 2012, and Bogaert 1994, by ancient historians such as von Reden 2007b, and by numismatists such as Le Rider and de Callataÿ 2006, who compared the monetary and financial policies of the Ptolemies and Seleucids. The study of Ptolemaic coinage has advanced thanks to Lorber's work, especially her 2018 updated catalogue and analysis, and Faucher 2020.

---

[75] von Reden 2007b.   [76] Vandorpe 2013.
[77] See 'Imperial Space, Revenues, and Population Size' in this chapter and Chapter 25, this volume.

10: HELLENISTIC BABYLONIA

Hilmar Klinkott

INTRODUCTION

When Alexander conquered Babylonia in 331, he took over one of the wealthiest satrapies of the Achaemenid empire.[1] The region in central and southern Mesopotamia was named after the old former capital Babylon at the Euphrates river. While Babylonia is an administrative designation of the Hellenistic period, Mesopotamia, nearly equivalent to modern Iraq, is a geographic designation for the region around and between the Rivers Euphrates and Tigris. Northern Mesopotamia, nowadays Jazirah, and the northern crescent are mentioned as Assyria in ancient sources, not clearly differentiated from Babylonia's northern border. The southern parts of Babylonia, as distinguished from the original heartland with the new capital Seleucia-on-the-Tigris and old cities like Babylon, Borsippa, and Uruk, are sometimes described as Chaldaea, bordering in the south at the gateway of the Euphrates and Tigris rivers with the regions of Characene, Mesene, and to the east at Susiane/Elymais, modern Khuzistan.[2]

Babylonia was an urbanized landscape with a developed network of infrastructure, both by water and by roads.[3] Large private estates of noble Babylonians and Persians, Babylonian family companies, and a complex system of manufacture and *kurtaš* (semifree, often foreign workers) are well known.[4] Although less is known of late-Achaemenid Babylonia, its economic importance was still unbroken. After the great Babylonian revolts, first against Darius I (522) and then Xerxes I (485), the economic and administrative situation of Babylonia changed dynamically.[5] A clearer division between "private" entrepreneurship and official ("state") institutions seems to be characteristic of this new

---

[1] Kuhrt 1990, 121–30.
[2] Monerie 2018, 47–51 for a succinct summary of the Babylonian landscapes.
[3] Graslin-Thomé 2016a, 167–86; Jursa 2010, 140–52.   [4] Stolper 1985; Jursa 2010.
[5] Briant 2002, 70–6; Waerzeggers and Seire 2018.

phase of the Achaemenid economy.[6] The traditional temple-centered Mesopotamian economy changed into a much more commercialized system under satrapal and royal control.[7] Local specialization in cash-crop production, transport, banking, acquisition of real estate, and the expansion of tenancy relationships stimulated commercialization, mon-etization, and the development of market networks, strengthened by the satrapal and royal system of taxation (Chapter 18, this volume).[8] The dynamics of this development reached far into the late-Achaemenid period and stimulated social change. In the reign of Darius II (423–404), the Murašu archive illustrates the financial influence of local elites, which they successfully translated into political power.[9] Babylonians started to hold high administrative offices, even as satraps (local gover-nors), and became members of the imperial elite.[10] On the other hand, landed property was accumulated in the hands of the Persian aristocracy.[11] Yet, it has also been suggested that there was "a weakening of the market as mode of exchange regarding the factors of production (i.e. land, labour, and capital)."[12] The military campaigns in the reign of Artaxerxes III (359–338), the takeover of Darius III (336–330), and, finally, his gathering of troops against Alexander were heavy economic burdens for this particular satrapy.[13]

FROM ALEXANDER TO THE EARLY SELEUCIDS

After Alexander's victory at Gaugamela (Arbela, 331), the attempt to preserve the city of Babylon and to stabilize its administrative situation allowed the satrapy to recover.[14] Babylon became a major center and capital of Alexander's short-lived empire, supported by the king with a great temple-restoration program.[15] Alexander's specific interest in the temple of Bel can be seen, programmatically, as a religious act of the new

---

[6] Beaulieu 2000, 43–72; Bongenaar 2000; for the character of such entrepreneurs: Joannès 2000, 36–9.

[7] Pirngruber 2017, 27–8; for the economic changes generally: Jursa 2010.

[8] Jursa 2010. On transport and the banking industry: Abraham 2004; on monetization and commercialization: Pirngruber 2017, 29–30; on the development of markets: Jursa 2014, 173–202; on taxation: van Driel 2002, 153–328.

[9] Stolper 1985. [10] Klinkott 2005, 453–8. [11] Pirngruber 2017, 36; Wiesehöfer 1999, 175.

[12] Pirngruber 2017, 36.

[13] For the wars of Artaxerxes III: Briant 2002, 681–90; for the accession of Darius III: ibid., 769–80; for war preparations against Alexander: ibid., 823–32.

[14] Heller 2010; Monerie 2018, 126 emphasizes initial continuity during Alexander's lifetime, but profound rupture in the time of the Successors.

[15] Temple restoration under Alexander in Babylon: Arr. Anab. 3.16.4, 7 and 16.5–17.4; Astronomical Diaries (AD) 330 (Berktold 2005, 117–19); under Philip III in Babylon and Borsippa: BCHP 10, 33 (Berktold 2005, 120); under Antiochus I in Babylon: BCHP 11, 2

king in accordance with traditional local habits in order to be accepted as Babylonian king.[16] Arrian (second century CE) seems to indicate that during Alexander's absence in the east, the city restored its municipal finances through local income.[17]

When Alexander returned from India, Babylon went through another phase of economic strain. From 323 to 308, various military operations and the struggle for the administrative control of the satrapy troubled the city: in 323, Babylon was besieged by Perdiccas; in 320, when Perdiccas appointed Docimus as satrap, he reconquered Babylonia; in 318/17, Eumenes fought against Antigonus Monophthalmus. Antigonus captured the satrapy in 315 and routed the ruling satrap Seleucus in 312. Seleucus reconquered the satrapy for himself and defended it against the attacks of Antigonus and his son Demetrius.[18] Only from 307 was Seleucus able to reestablish peace in his new satrapy, and from 304 made it the center of his new "Seleucid" empire. Of course, this agitated phase in the early Hellenistic period affected the economic conditions of Babylonia.

There is much evidence that suggests economic decline in Babylonia in the wake of Alexander's conquests and during the period of the Wars of the Successors (322–281). The Astronomical Diaries illustrate the development of quantities of production and prices for barley, dates, mustard, cress, and sesame, for this particular time.[19] The transition of rule from Darius III to Alexander the Great is characterized by a collapse of production (more than 50 percent in regular years during the reign of Alexander), with continued decline after Alexander's death and in the reigns of Philip III and Alexander IV (his infant son). In tandem with the decline in production, the prices of products rapidly rose with Alexander's invasion and the time of political uncertainty after his death. However, it is not evident why this happened in this situation and why some products, well-known by the Babylonian archives of the Achaemenid empire, disappeared from the Astronomical Diaries of the Hellenistic period. Cress is the only example that indicates an increase in production when Seleucus stabilized the satrapy and established the political structures of his monarchy in 307. Thus, despite offering valuable evidence for the rise and decline in production and prices of some products, this evidence brings its own problems.

(van der Spek 1987, 64); in Borsippa: Stevens 2014, 66–88; in Uruk YOS 1 52 (Kuhrt and Sherwin-White 1993, 150).

[16] Boiy 2004, 111, following Kuhrt 1990, 127.   [17] Arr. Anab. 7.17.1–4.

[18] For the war in Babylonia according to the so-called Chronicle of the Successors: Boiy 2007, 65–6; Boiy 2004, 117–37; for the reconquest of Babylon by Seleucus and the beginning of the Seleucid empire: Boiy 2004, 117–49; Schäfer 2015.

[19] Hackl and Pirngruber 2015.

Arguably, the period of economic decline after Alexander's conquest of Babylonia led to a change of perception in Greek literature. As has recently been pointed out, the topos of "wealthy Babylonia" nearly turned into its opposite in the descriptions of Strabo (writing in the first century) and Plutarch (first/second century CE).[20] Herodotus, in the fifth century, had told of a 300-fold income of barley and the multifunctional usage of the date palm.[21] Yet already Berossus (a third-century Babylonian priest), despite his panegyric description of Babylonia, no longer seems to have deployed the motif of Babylonia's outstanding fertility. In Plutarch's *Life of Alexander*, comments on Babylonia's wealth are limited to the examples of bitumen and barley.[22] Arrian does not mention any natural wealth in Babylonia at all.[23] High crop yields, assumed to have been as high as 1:14 for barley, are known from documents of the Achaemenid period only.

CONTINUITY AND CHANGE IN HELLENISTIC BABYLONIA

The economy of Babylonia in the Hellenistic period was a combination of Achaemenid continuity and Hellenistic innovation.[24] Although we lack archival evidence and documents to trace this change, it would be unreasonable to assume unbroken continuity from the Achaemenid to the Hellenistic period. Not by accident, economic histories of Babylonia in the first millennium often end with the conquest of Alexander, thus omitting the conditions of Hellenistic Babylonia as if nothing changed, or as if Babylonia became part of Greek history from then on.[25]

Administration

The satrapal administration, however, seems to have remained largely unchanged in the early Hellenistic period. The city of Babylon remained a royal residence as well as a military, political, and economic hub of the Seleucid empire.[26] Babylonian kingship remained crucial for the rulers over "Asia" under the early Seleucid kings. Fiscal continuity can be taken from the Babylonian legal and administrative documents of Borsippa, but

---

[20] Ruffing 2014, 641–2.   [21] Strab. 16.1.5 and 14 with Ruffing 2014, 641–2.
[22] Plut. *Alex.* 35.1–13.   [23] Ruffing 2014, 642.   [24] Monerie 2018, 108.
[25] Thus the fundamental work by Jursa 2010.   [26] Pirngruber 2017, 37.

above all from the so-called Esagila archive from Babylon.[27] A text dated to the time of Seleucus II (*MMA* 86.11.299 = *CT* 49, 115) shows that members of the three great temples of Babylon, Borsippa, and Cutha had to give the "tithe of harvest from these fields" directly to the temple. The majority of texts belong to treatises and bills of tithe in the context of private credit, in which the temples as third parties delegated their rights to transact money and tithes to some creditor. A group of texts, dealing with the activities of a certain Muranu and his son Ea-tab-tani-bullit, are of particular importance here.[28] The texts show Murānu and his son as addressees of orders from the temple to pay rations to the temple staff, and as creditors (deponents) in obligatory notes and contracts of deposits. Apparently, Muranu gained the right (maybe by purchase) to use the property and income of the temple in connection with his private transactions. He is an example for the continuity of private tax farmers and bankers involved in the financial administration of the temples.[29]

The use of coined money in the administration of Babylonia seems to have been an area of Hellenistic innovation, although its precise impact is difficult to gauge.[30] Silver bullion continued to be used as money especially in the temple economy, but local and imperial coins gained in importance and stimulated change in the Babylonian market economy.[31] The status of Babylon was enhanced when Alexander and Philip III Arrhidaeus (his purportedly mentally disabled brother and dynastic successor) minted lion staters in the city and made it a center of imperial coinage.[32] When the Seleucid monarchy was established, Seleucus I moved the royal mint to the newly founded residence of Seleucia-on-the-Tigris. From 300 onward, only local coins were produced in Babylon. The character of administrative recording must have changed in tandem with the increasing use of coinage. Beyond the well-documented traditional form of recording incomings and outgoings in kind on clay tablets, registration of income in terms of coin values can be assumed. Unfortunately, no evidence of such change on Seleucid ostraca, papyri, or parchment is extant. *Asylia* decrees from various Babylonian cities, freeing respectable members of the local urban elite

---

[27] Jursa 1998, 73–83; Monerie 2018, 129–132; for the interrelation between private entrepreneurs and temple administration in Achaemenid times: Joannès 2000, 25–41.

[28] Muranu and his son were not members of the temple household: Jursa 1998, 80.

[29] Jursa 1998, 78–81.

[30] Monerie 2018, 144–72 for a sustained attempt to argue for several significant changes.

[31] Jursa 2018, 116–21; for continuity of silver bullion: Bongenaar 1999, 159–74; for payments in *shekel*: Kuhrt and Sherwin-White 1993, 64.

[32] Boiy 2004, 44–5 for this and the following.

from the payment of specific taxes, might be an indirect confirmation of the transformative impact of Seleucid monetary policy, as it reflects a distinctly Greek practice of tax management in Babylonia.[33]

City Foundations

The new foundation of Seleucia-on-the-Tigris as a royal residence in Babylonia is one of the best illustrations of Babylonia's key political, administrative, and economic position in the Seleucid imperial landscape.[34] The new central city was supported by an integrated system of second-rank foundations.[35] The new urban network is likely to have stimulated the growth of existing Babylonian cities as centers of consumption, as well as encouraging local and regional production and market activities.[36] But beyond this hypothetical assumption, detailed evidence that allows us to trace the ways these cities functioned as local, regional, and transregional markets and places of consumption is lacking. Archaeological surveys in the Diyala and central Euphrates floodplain regions indicate agricultural extensification and canal constructions in the environment of the growing cities in this region.[37] Nevertheless, one has to bear in mind that agricultural melioration and the development of irrigation activities by the king's initiative was a traditional element of royal policy since the late Babylonian empire.[38] To what extent such efforts were part of a deliberate Seleucid policy and innovation therefore remains questionable.[39]

Babylonian harbor cities along the Euphrates and on the Gulf were part of this new economic network.[40] They are part of the urbanization program in Mesopotamia, especially under the early Seleucid kings, creating an urban network that integrated the older indigenous settlements, or rather integrated new Greek poleis into the urban landscape of Babylonia. The existing overland routes were connected with a new naval infrastructure through the initiative of Seleucus I to develop an urban network around Seleucia-on-the-Tigris; a network of capitals

---

[33] Sherwin-White 1987, 26–7.
[34] van der Spek 2007, 412–13; for the royal court and society: Musti 1984, 175–81; Weber 1997; Strootman 2014.
[35] Kosmin 2014, 187.   [36] von Reden 2007c, 185–8.   [37] van der Spek 2007, 413.
[38] van der Spek 2000, 28–30; Kuhrt and Sherwin-White 1993, 70.
[39] van der Spek 2007, 413.
[40] Kosmin 2014, 187–90 with maps 7, 8, and 9. For the Hellenistic foundations in Mesopotamia: Cohen 2013, 55–200 with maps on pp. 430–2. For the royal intervention and control of city foundations and supplies: van der Spek 2007, 423, 426–8. For Seleucid city policy in Babylonia: van der Spek 1987, 58–74.

with coastal harbors in northern Syria (the so-called Tetrapolis consisting of the four cities of Seleucia-in-Pieria and Laodicea-by-the-Sea linked by river to the inland cities of Antioch-by-Daphne and Apamea-on-the-Axios), again supported by secondary settlements in proximity; and finally the riverine and maritime harbors in southern Mesopotamia.[41] The nature and intensity of mutual effects on the development of harbor cities and other settlements in Mesopotamia is still unclear. However, the development of an urban network in Babylonia allows us to extrapolate economic consequences: first of all, the increase in exploiting the local hinterland for the supply of the cities and their markets; secondly, the growth of communication, trade, and transport with the related professions.[42] The archaeological surveys in the Diyala and Middle Euphrates region show a significant increase in the number of settlements and the expansion of canals, most likely developed under royal control.[43] Moreover, it seems to be as a result of the expanded urban network, connecting regions and coasts hitherto unconnected, that European and Indian plants appear on the cultivation schedule of Seleucid kings in Babylonia. Wine and rice are mentioned by Strabo as new crops of the region, while the Seleucid kings were acclaimed for acclimatizing European and Indian plants.[44] Dates and barley (plus wool) remained the core production of Babylonia, and it is noteworthy that the Astronomical Diaries do not mention any new crops. Moreover, we cannot be sure whether imported goods and agrarian surplus were used above all for the supply of the local city population, the local temples, royal or satrapal troops (either in military action or in garrisons), or for further export and other royal interests.[45] However, it is important to consider that such production zones filled important roles in the supply of Hellenistic cities in war, or in the process of overcoming the damages of war.[46]

The foundation of new colonies implied the movement and settlement of new people and populations. Examples from Lydia and Phrygia in Asia Minor or from the Dasht-i Qala plain in Bactria illustrate their economic consequences: intensification of cultivation and agricultural production, which consolidated into what has been called new productive topographies.[47] Unfortunately, precise evidence once again is missing.

[41] Kosmin 2014, 190.   [42] von Reden 2007c, 188.
[43] van der Spek 2007, 413, 427–8; Adams 1981, 179.
[44] On wine and rice in Babylonia: Strab. 15.1.18, 3, 11; Diod. Sic. 19.13.6; van der Spek 2007, 414; Rostovtzeff 1941, 1166; generally for Indian products in the Seleucid empire: Kuhrt and Sherwin-White 1993, 65.
[45] van der Spek 2007, 414; Boiy 2010b, 1–13 for discussion.
[46] Chaniotis 2011, 136–7 in the context of Hellenistic poleis.   [47] Kosmin 2014, 195.

Such processes may be deduced from parallel examples in other parts of the Hellenistic world.[48] The Achaemenid institution of *hatru* ("bow fiefs" or military colonies) and *kurtas* (semifree workers in the service of royal or elite households) continued to exist,[49] but their relationship to the Greek institution of *kleroi* (donations of land to soldiers) and *doreiai* (estates gifted to higher officials and other beneficiaries) is unclear.[50] On the one hand, Babylonian tablets show instances of the distribution of arable land to various beneficiaries by the king and his satrap.[51] On the other hand, we hear of arable land and urban estates declared explicitly as property of the temples, which seems to imply that these donations were no longer integrated into a state-sponsored socioeconomic superstructure.[52]

Trade and Exchange

Despite evidence of foreign products and cultivation methods in Babylonia, the documents of Hellenistic Babylonia indicate that the satrapy was affected little by the economic orientation of Babylonia to the Mediterranean by long-distance trade. The papyri from Ptolemaic Egypt, for example, do not mention Babylon as a trade destination, or any other regular economic exchange with Babylonia.[53] Moreover, although the road system of the Seleucid empire facilitated contact and exchange with the cities of western Asia Minor, trade relations and the export of goods from Babylonia to the Mediterranean are largely unattested. Graslin-Thomé has suggested that the import of linen to Babylonia from Egypt increased in Hellenistic times.[54] Yet such contacts were equally regular under Achaemenid rule, even though evidence is not sufficient for detailed reconstruction.[55] The commercial contacts of Babylonia with the west seem to have extended as far as Phoenicia, an important intermediary with the Aegean.[56] Yet the western orientation of Babylonian export toward the Mediterranean, attested already in Achaemenid times, cannot be confirmed to have increased significantly during the Hellenistic period.

In contrast, Babylon remained an important interregional market place oriented toward the east, as Palmyrenian inscription

---

[48] J. G. Manning 2011, 296–323; see also Rostovtzeff 1941, 490–502.
[49] van der Spek 2007, 412; Stolper 1993–7, 205–7.
[50] Pirngruber 2017, 69. For *kleroi* in Dura Europos: *P.Dura* 1: 190; Musti 1984, 200; Rostovtzeff 1941, 487–9.
[51] See *BM* 33020 = 78–10–15,1 + *BM* 33028 = 78–10–15,9.   [52] Pirngruber 2017, 69.
[53] Boiy 2004, 53.   [54] Graslin-Thomé 2016b, 63, 70–1.   [55] Jursa 2004, 129–32.
[56] van der Spek 2007, 419–20. Trade relations between the Levant and Mesopotamia: Sartre 2001, 259–61; mediating function of the Levantine cities: ibid., 262–5.

from first-century Palmyra seem to confirm.[57] Its long-distance overland and naval routes stretched towards the Persian Gulf, Arabia, India, and Central Asian Bactria.[58] Seleucid settlements on the coastline of the Persian-Arabian gulf and beyond the Strait of Hormuz, as well as Seleucid minting activities, which substantially increased under the reign of Antiochus III (223–187) – as the coin finds indicate – suggest the development of regular, monetized trade from Babylonia to Arabia and India.[59] There are some indications that some trade relations from Babylonia to the east involved cashless transactions in addition.[60]

KINGS AND TEMPLES

Alexander and the early Seleucid rulers donated money for the restoration of the ancient Babylonian temples, as was already mentioned above.[61] However, the support of Babylonian temples for restoration work was a typical form of royal legitimization under late Babylonian and Achaemenid rule and may not have been motivated by a royal interest in the usufruct of temple property in the first instance.[62] Moreover, a Babylonian cuneiform tablet from the time of Seleucus II (236) shows that royal donations, and land transactions in particular, were still linked to the legitimization of the royal family by the Babylonian priests.[63] However, we also have evidence for the Seleucids collecting tithes from the temples and showing an interest in their production.[64] A cuneiform lease contract dated to 221 shows that Antiochus III increased the agricultural production of the temple of Uruk by royal decree (*diagramma*), requiring the planting of dates on specific parts of the temple's arable land.[65] The lessee of the land was bound to the sowing schedule by royal decree and controlled by the lessor. Interestingly, however, he is called "commissioner (*paqdu*) of the temple," thus being a member of the temple administration appointed by the king.[66] On the other hand, texts like the Babylonian chronicle *BCHP*

[57] Boiy 2004, 188, 263.
[58] Connections to Persia: Wiesehöfer 2017, 250–2; Seleucid diplomacy at the Indian border: Kosmin 2014, 31–58; Seleucid economic relations to India and Graeco-Bactria: Musti 1984, 213–15.
[59] Salles 1987, 75–109; von Reden 2007c, 193.   [60] Henkelman and Folmer 2016, 133–239.
[61] N. 15; Kuhrt and Sherwin-White 1993, 154–5; Boiy 2010a, 211–20.
[62] Boiy and Mittag 2011, 111; Kuhrt 1987, 56.
[63] Kuhrt and Sherwin-White 1993, 128–9; compare for a parallel under Antiochus II: Sarkisjan 1997, 248; for religious legitimization: Schäfer 2015, 631–3.
[64] On tithes collected from the temples: van der Spek 2000, 31–2; on the general policy of the Seleucid kings toward the temples: Kuhrt and Sherwin-White 1993, 59–61; Monerie 2018, 349–82.
[65] van der Spek 2000, 31–3.   [66] van der Spek 2000, 31.

16 (173/2) show the continuous interdependence of royal, satrapal, and temple administration in Babylon.[67] The fragmentary text regulates the assignment of arable land by the *šatammu* of Esagila to a person with the Greek name Theomeles "in accordance with a letter of the satrap" (*BCHP* 16, rev. 2 and 3'). According to the obverse of the same entry, however, the king donated the property to the temple in order to secure its regular offerings of tithes (*BCHP* obv. 2'–3'). Thus, rather than increasing royal income, royal supplies and melioration initiatives may have guaranteed the economic self-sufficiency of the temples under royal protection. The need for economic protection of the temples' productive assets may be demonstrated by some examples of embezzlement of royal donations. Both Greek and Babylonian sources report that, at the time of Alexander and Antiochus I, the priesthood of Babylon misappropriated money that kings had donated to the temples for the restoration of their buildings and the running of their cultic affairs.[68] Arrian gives the explanation: "The god Bel had much land consecrated by the Assyrian kings, and much treasure too. From this, the temple was originally repaired, and the sacrifices offered to the god. But at that time the Chaldaeans enjoyed the revenues of the god, there being no cause for expenditure of the surplus income."[69] Of course, the priests themselves had no interest in preventing the restoration of the temples in their charge. More likely is the possibility that the temple economies were weakened to such an extent that cult and offerings could no longer be guaranteed by the income of the temple administration. The long list of professions in charge of the Babylonian temples documents the complexity of their administrative and economic system, in which much income may have been lost in the process.[70] Under such conditions, it is no wonder that the sale of temple prebends, intended for the maintenance of the cult, to citizens of the Babylonian cities flourished in Hellenistic Babylonia.

CONCLUSION

Mesopotamia and Persia remained politically and economically import-ant core regions in the Seleucid empire.[71] Nevertheless, our knowledge

---

[67] Edition and commentary: Finkel, van der Spek, and Pirngruber forthcoming.
[68] Under Alexander: Arr. *Anab.* 7.17.1–4; under Antiochus I: *BCHP* 6 (the so-called Ruin of Esagila Chronicle).
[69] Arr. *Anab.* 7.17.3–4.
[70] van der Spek 2007, 432; Boiy 2004, 241–61; comparison of the economic, financial, and professional structures in Achaemenid Babylonia: Jursa 2010.
[71] Wiesehöfer 2017, 250–2.

of the economy of these regions remains fragmentary.[72] As the previous discussion has demonstrated, we are missing detailed sources: while the cuneiform tablets offer spotlights on very specific aspects, the Greek texts touch the economic conditions of Hellenistic Babylonia only marginally. Yet the economy of Babylonia is not a blind spot. Despite their fragmentary status, these records offer us glimpses into the complex interplay of pre-Hellenistic continuities and Seleucid innovation that shaped the so-called Hellenizing development.

Babylonia held a crucial position in a network of overland and naval routes, connecting Arabia, India, and the Graeco-Bactrian empire in the east with the Levant, Syria, and Anatolia via the Fertile Crescent in the west. This network enabled the royal administration to combine the functions of trade and communication with settlement politics, the melioration of agriculture, and the supply of war zones. In this latter role, the Babylonian economy might have played an important part in Seleucid warfare, despite Babylonians never being involved actively in military campaigns.[73]

A new Graeco-Babylonian elite with particular kinds and levels of demand, the dynamic development of cities and settlements, the network of routes of trade, communication, and mobility connecting the western parts of the empire in the Aegean world with the east, and, last but not least, increased monetization may have provided the conditions of economic growth in Hellenistic Babylonia. Nevertheless, Babylonia had already been a very productive and economically dynamic region in the Achaemenid period. It has been questioned, moreover, whether the stimulation of the Babylonian economy led to per capita growth of productivity, or rather to aggregate growth through the mobilization and more efficient concentration of available resources.[74] There were certainly great continuities from the Persian and Seleucid empires, and one may wonder whether the efforts of the early Seleucid kings to improve lines of communication, temple economies, and monetary exchange aimed at regaining the levels of prosperity that had already been achieved before Alexander's conquests.

Further Reading

Two monographs have recently been written on the Babylonian economy (Pirngruber 2017 and Monerie 2018), offering detailed

---

[72] See van der Spek and van Leeuwen 2014, 97; Boiy 2004, 237.
[73] See also Huijs, Pirngruber, and van Leeuwen 2015, 128–48.   [74] van der Spek 2007, 432–3.

discussion of the issues raised in this chapter, especially with regard to the highly complicated evidence available for Hellenistic Babylonia. Van der Spek 2007 helps to put Babylonia into the wider perspective of the Seleucid economy. Jursa (2009, 2010, and 2014) emphasizes the profound impact of monetization, institutional change, and market development in first-millennium Babylonia.

PART III

STRUCTURES AND PROCESSES

11: POPULATION

Ben Akrigg

INTRODUCTION

It would be hard to exaggerate the importance of demography for the history of ancient Greece, and especially for its economic history. Some of the connections are obvious, such as the implications of the overall size of a population for aggregate production and consumption, but the relationships between population and economy can also be more subtle.

Demography has the potential to provide both direct indications of and proxies for economic performance and explanations for economic change. Despite this, the potential of historical demography has not been fully realised or given its due attention by historians of the ancient Greek world. There are several specific reasons for this. In the first place, it can seem inaccessible. Demography is itself a large, specialised, technical discipline. Even those who are generally comfortable with quantitative approaches may therefore find it off-putting. On the other hand, those who are familiar with that discipline as it is applied to the modern world will find it hard to relate its insights to antiquity, just because the data are so poor for the latter.

This poverty of data presents a second reason for the relative neglect of historical demography: there just is not very much raw material to work with for ancient Greece, even compared to the Roman world. From a certain point of view this might not be such a disadvantage as it appears – the more abundant Roman data have not always been useful, in practice, for historical demographers. Nonetheless, material such as reported Roman census figures and the ages at death provided on Roman tombstones have offered focuses for detailed discussion that are familiar and accessible to all Roman historians but for which there are no obvious parallels in the Greek world.

A third reason is that those, relatively few, Greek historians who have engaged with historical demography have not always been good at encouraging others to follow them. The technicalities can sometimes seem to be the ends rather than the means. Why exactly population history might matter is rarely made entirely clear. Sometimes this seems to be due to an assumption that the importance of demography is self-evident. More often that importance is acknowledged explicitly, but in practice the subject is treated as the background to more specific, and implicitly more interesting, questions, and exactly how and why population numbers and structures affect societies generally is left for the reader to work out themselves.

Finally, demography itself is a large and sprawling subject which has at least as much inherent tendency to inter- or at least multi-disciplinarity as Classics does, and this can make it resistant to accessible summaries. Providing such a summary in full is beyond the scope of this chapter; the following can only provide some starting points.[1]

POPULATION AND ECONOMY

Demography is relevant to most of the important questions in the economic history of ancient Greece. Greece is not unique in this, however, as population is important for the economic history of all societies. It is worth considering some general points before looking at our specific case.

Economics is interested in assessing economic performance. Measuring performance requires quantification, and it is also intrinsically comparative. Demography provides a range of quantitative measures that provide useful direct indications of and proxies for economic perform-ance. History is fundamentally about explaining change in the past; a key goal of economic historians then is to explain changes in economic performance in the past. Historical demography has a clear role to play here. While population sizes and structures, and changes to them, often demand explanation themselves, they also have their own explanatory power, a power that is especially clear in the economic realm.

The most basic aspect of demography is population size. The historical demography of ancient Greece has sometimes seemed to involve little else. The focus on size is due in part to that lack of much evidence to consider other issues, and partly because of the kinds of questions that ancient historians have asked, which, especially when it comes to Athens, have often been ones about the extent of political participation and food supply (Chapter 8, this volume) – and even the

---

[1] Scheidel 2007 provides a broader perspective at greater length.

food supply has usually been addressed from a political perspective.[2] Nonetheless, the relevance to economics is apparent. The size of a community's population is clearly related to the overall size of that community's economy. The more people there are, the more they will be able to produce, the more they will need to consume, and the more possibilities there are for exchanges. So even if we only have snapshots of the size of a population, they will tell us something useful, and so the simplest measures of population can be, and have been, taken as measures of performance. Such measures have the advantage of being both easy to grasp and easy to compare.

It is only a small step beyond this to consider changes and trends in population size. Again, these have obvious utility as proxies for economic performance more generally. Where a population can be seen to be growing, it is reasonable to infer that the economy is producing enough to support that larger population. This will be true whether the population increase is being caused by an excess of births over deaths (what is sometimes called "natural" growth, rather unhelpfully and misleadingly as it implies that there is something unnatural about human mobility when the very opposite is the case) or by net immigration. Conversely, a decline in population is in most circumstances at least consistent with an economy that is performing less than optimally, whether the cause is increased mortality, suppressed fertility, emigration, interruptions to immigration, or some combination of all of these.

Population change will also not just reflect but affect economic performance in some way. Exactly how, and whether the impact will be positive or negative, and for whom, will depend on a range of factors. There is a central, and familiar debate here. The consequences of population growth for economic performance might be negative, as limited resources have to be stretched ever more thinly; or they might be positive, by providing a greater stock of physical and mental resources for overcoming existing limitations. Thomas Malthus is the figurehead for the pessimistic view, Ester Boserup for the optimistic view.[3] The debate has so far resisted a final resolution, because both views can be supported by reference to the historical record, and because they are not wholly incompatible. The key point that emerges from these discussions is that population is not independent of the other variables we are concerned with in economic history.

---

[2] Politics is to the fore in Gomme 1933 and Hansen 1986 and is the reason for investigating the food supply in Moreno 2007.
[3] Malthus 1803 and Boserup 1965.

Population size is important in itself, but it is also inextricable from other direct measures of and proxies for economic performance. The distinction between extensive, aggregate growth and intensive, per capita growth can only make sense when we understand the population.[4] Assessments of living standards depend on information about the size of a population that is producing and consuming goods. Although there has been growing interest in pursuing alternative measures of performance, and dissatisfaction with the usefulness of GDP measures for contemporary economies, let alone ancient ones, growth remains the central indicator for most economic historians.[5] It is possible to have population growth without per capita growth, where each additional person produces the same output as before, but the total output goes up (which might be extractable by a minority of the population); it is also possible to have per capita growth without population growth, if the number of people stays the same, but for some reason at least some people in the community are able to improve their level of output (because they are better organised, or are motivated to do more useful work, or have access to new techniques or tools). An increasing number of people might actually lead to lower per capita output, as existing resources have to be stretched further, even if total production goes up. Finally, an increasing number of people might also help to drive more output, as more people might result in more new ideas and new incentives for improving productivity. In this last case, the extra output might lead to the possibility of even more people, who produce yet more in a positive feedback loop. This combination of increasing population *and* per capita production is at the core of what Goldstone called 'efflorescences', a term which has been adopted with enthusiasm by some ancient historians.[6] The extent to which such efflorescences can be identified in the ancient world, and how they compare with similar phenomena at other times and in other places, is an important focus of debate.

When we turn from population size to population structures, the implications for economic history multiply.[7] Under structure, we might include age and sex distribution, but also the structures of families and households. Aside from the unusual contexts of classical Athens and Ptolemaic Egypt, we are usually very short of direct information on specific structures of any kind for ancient Greece (and even these are

---

[4] Saller 2002, esp. 257–67   [5] Scheidel 2019; Ober 2015a; Bresson 2016b.
[6] Goldstone 2002; Ober 2015a.
[7] Saller 2007 on family structures. Thompson 2006 for Ptolemaic Egypt.

only very partial exceptions), but that does not mean that we should not be alert to the possible range of variation and the difference that such variations would have made across time and space.

Discussion of human populations is inseparable from that of the mobility of humans. Mobility has been particularly prominent in ancient economic and environmental history since the publication of Horden and Purcell's *The Corrupting Sea* in 2000. As with demography, mobility and migration studies represent a large technical area with which ancient historians have begun to engage more fully in recent years.[8] Archaeological science – and especially the investigation of DNA and isotopic analysis of human remains – is revolutionising our understanding too, although not yet for the Greek world with the same intensity as, for example, with Roman Britain.

Again, it is difficult to summarise, but two points are worth emphasising here. First, humans never move entirely alone. We usually move in groups or along routes that others have laid out for us. Furthermore, we take other species along with us – visible and invisible, and deliberately and otherwise.[9] The second is that the motivations for movements are rarely straightforward. While it is still often convenient to talk in terms of 'push' and 'pull' factors, such a stark dichotomy rarely captures the complexity of the motivations and constraints that operate on migrants in reality.

Constants and Variables

The usual chronological frame for Greek history is very roughly the first millennium: starting with the Early Iron Age in the Aegean and ending with the fall of the last major Hellenistic kingdom to Rome. A thousand years is a very short span of time indeed at geological scales, but it is still long enough that the physical environment for human endeavours was subject to significant alteration; long enough, for the swells of the *longue durée* to represent a scale on which changes took place, not just a static backdrop. There are, then, more variables than constants for us to deal with. It may not be going too far to suggest that change itself is the most important constant. Ancient historians are familiar with this in geographical terms (often adopting Horden and Purcell's terminology of micro-regions) and

---

[8] Garland 2014. Tacoma 2016, 1–74 provides a discussion of pre-modern migration which is useful beyond its Roman context.

[9] Cardete 2019 provides one example of combined human and non-human mobility with clear economic implications.

are used to emphasising a high degree of inter-annual variability in levels of precipitation as a feature of 'Mediterranean' climate regimes, but change in the climate itself is a factor that needs to be taken into account over the course of Greek antiquity.[10]

One practical constant that should be acknowledged lies in the constraints of human biology. There is no reason to think that the mechanisms of reproduction, possible causes of death, and the limits of dietary energy requirements changed significantly over this period. This is not to say that there was physical uniformity across the populations we want to study, only that the parameters within which choices could be made and agency exercised were similar.

The basic determinants of population size and structure were always the same: fertility, mortality, and migration. Mortality would have been high by modern standards everywhere, with the details determined by the disease regime, and infectious diseases the most important causes of death. The details of mortality and fertility rates would however have been highly variable across time and space. The disease regime in turn would have been determined primarily by a range of environmental factors. Fertility and migration were subject to a higher though still-incomplete degree of human agency. Expected ages at marriage for both men and women, the degree of tolerance or encouragement for same-sex relationships, practices of birth spacing and breastfeeding, and the acceptability of infanticide (which in demographic terms is effectively a constraint on fertility), all have direct fertility consequences and can be altered to reflect changing circumstances.[11] Immigration in the ancient world could be increased by the capture or purchase of slaves; it was also at least possible to think about ways to incentivise more voluntary migrants, even if the success of deliberate policy in this area is difficult to assess. Emigration could likewise be enforced sometimes (as with the Spartans' notorious *xenelasia* or by the despatch of a colony), although the demographic effects of such actions were limited.[12] Restricting unwanted emigration would again have been rather hard; archaic colonisation seems to have reflected the absence of community or elite control over populations rather than their strength.[13]

In communities that survived or even thrived, high mortality had to be countered by high fertility. Locally of course immigration would have

---

[10] Horden and Purcell 2000; J. G. Manning 2018, 135–72. Harper and McCormick 2018 is a useful summary, albeit focused on Roman history.

[11] Bresson 2016b, 54–70. [12] Scheidel 2003. [13] Osborne 1998; Shepherd 2009.

played a part in sustaining the growth of some communities, but even that ultimately meant taking advantage of higher fertility somewhere else, as one region's immigrants are another's emigrants. Populations with high mortality and high fertility have different kinds of structures from those with low mortality and fertility, with the most obvious difference being that the former will contain many more young people than the latter, with this being particularly marked if the population is increasing through reproduction. There are also immediate consequences for women in high-fertility demographic regimes, including elevated mortality, as they are exposed to greater risks from repeated pregnancies and child-birth. High mortality has economic consequences beyond constraining the options for women's economic activity within and outside the household, important as that undoubtedly is – and if anything its signifi-cance in distinguishing the classical Greek experience from the efflores-cences of early modern northern Europe has been underappreciated by ancient historians.[14] The obvious one is that investment in training and education is made less rewarding when its beneficiaries may not live to repay the investment. A further, slightly less obvious example, well illustrated by Richard Saller, is that the number of orphaned children would have been high, and this in turn would surely also have had a significant impact on investment practices.[15]

That the climate during the Holocene, although generally condu-cive to agriculture and the expansion of human populations in many parts of the world, has not been entirely stable, has become increasingly clear in recent years. Historians of the classical period have been able to avoid an intensive engagement with this issue because of the coinci-dence that the climate of the Aegean seems to have been broadly similar in the fifth and fourth centuries and in the twentieth. This issue has however received much more attention from historians working on other periods, including much of Roman history.[16] One key lesson of this scholarship is that the relationships between climate variables and human populations – especially where complex societies have been formed – are not straightforward.

The degree of stability in the climate was itself subject to change over our period. Of the very many factors that influence climate, perhaps the most easily grasped in this respect is global geological activity. Claims about the Roman Climate Optimum rely not just on average levels of rainfall or temperatures, but on a degree of stability in climate conditions in the Mediterranean and adjacent regions, which

[14] Scheidel 1995; 1996.   [15] Saller 2007.   [16] Harper and McCormick 2018.

seems to be connected to relatively low levels of volcanic activity in the last two centuries BCE and first two centuries CE – the familiar and spectacular eruption of Vesuvius in 79 CE notwithstanding. The fifth century BCE by contrast seems to have been a period of unusually high activity globally.[17]

While climate and other environmental factors impose important constraints on human actions, humans have also always acted, both consciously and unconsciously, to modify their environments. Our ability to do so has obviously increased enormously since the industrial revolution, but it is important not to underestimate the potential scale of alterations that are made possible just by the use of fire and enthusiastically wielded felling axes. The more humans there are, the larger their cumulative impact will be, especially on their local surroundings.

The degree, nature, and consequences of ancient Greek and Roman exploitation of forestry resources remains a central question in environmental history. A full discussion is beyond the scope of this chapter, but clearly the demand for timber and fuel would have been closely related to population levels (see also Chapter 8, this volume). The supply of these resources would also have acted as a constraint on the growth of urban centres; in turn, the attempts to secure those supplies meant that the economic impact of towns and cities extended well beyond their immediate hinterlands.

ARCHAIC GREECE

The archaic period in Greece was one which saw rapid changes in societies and economies, almost all of which were connected in some way to demography, and especially to population growth. The most familiar features of this period are the urbanisation associated with the emergence of the polis and the mobility that has usually been discussed under the heading of 'colonisation'. These are linked, both because it was a larger population that allowed the possibility of sending part of that population abroad and because the increases in mobility and connectedness themselves encouraged the creation of urban sites in new locations.

Urbanisation is a complex phenomenon and one that can be hard to define, but at some level it must depend on population size and, especially, density.[18] It is itself taken to be a proxy for economic

---

[17] J. G. Manning 2018, 164.   [18] Scheidel 2007, 74–85.

development, and for good reasons. Colonisation was not necessarily driven by increasing population, nor could emigration have had a particularly significant impact on population growth in the areas of origin, but again it is a phenomenon which cannot be explained without reference to demography.

From the archaic period onwards, we do tend to think of the Greek world as one of cities, although it is also common now to bring up the caveats that many communities were not dominated by urban centres, and that most of the urban centres that did exist did not deserve the title city and would barely qualify as towns in other times and places (Chapter 13, this volume). There is not much point getting bogged down here in definitional squabbles. Questions of size and density are, however, worth bearing in mind for the purposes of comparison across cultures.

Towns and cities are both symptoms and causes of mobility. Urbanisation can drive trade, but trade can also drive urbanisation, and it is not always easy to work out which comes first, or perhaps more accurately, what can start a feedback loop. Scheidel has suggested that the appearance of many new urban centres might be due first to the emergence of a new class of landlords and the strengthening of local government in their hands. There is nothing implausible about this, but it might prompt us to ask what caused that strengthening of government institutions, and whether it might not have been the 'colonisation' movement itself. The traditional narrative of colonisation was that emerging and maturing poleis sent out children (as classical poleis effectively did; it is worth noting that the biological model of reproduction is explicit) as organised foundations. An obvious problem with this story is that there is little contemporary sign (as opposed to later stories) of such organisation, and instead the mobility of Greek colonists may well represent a lack of control over populations and manpower in a world which was a long way from full. Increasing contact with a wider world via trade may also have weakened traditional social relationships between elites and non-elites and incentivised the creation of formal institutions and laws – mobility could have driven institutions rather than the emergence of institutions driving increased mobility.

Scheidel also suggested that the emergence of urban centres led to elevated mortality in those areas, providing a brake on (but not altogether stopping) further population growth, which delayed the negative impacts of declining marginal productivity, and which in turn is part of the explanation for the relatively long duration of the growth phases of Greek (and Roman) civilisation. Again, this suggestion is entirely plausible, but two possible responses might still nuance it. In the first place, the urban focus of the Greek world (and to a large degree the Roman world too) really makes most sense when we prioritise the institutional definitions of urbanism rather than those definitions that emphasise quantitative measures or criteria for what counts as urban. Prioritising the institutional is appropriate for many purposes but might also have consequences when we are thinking about disease regimes and mortality. In the second place, it seems now that pre-industrial cities, even those that deserve the title by any definition, might not have been such aggressive population sinks as we used to assume.[19] On the other hand again, the trade routes by which cities were supplied (and which, as noted above help to explain their existence and location in the first place) were also going to be routes that facilitated the spread of diseases by which their populations might well not otherwise have been troubled (the obvious example of this being the 'plague' that afflicted classical Athens).

For explaining change in this period, it is the timing, scale, and pace of those population increases that is perhaps the most important factor of all.[20] Providing such an explanation is beyond the scope of this chapter, not least because, even to the extent that this is acknowledged as an issue, there is no consensus yet about what was happening. This will be a key area for new contributions in the next few years. It is important in this context to recognise that this phenomenon is not limited to the Greek world, and explanations therefore have to account for population trends across a wide swathe of Eurasia at similar latitudes to Greece, from Spain to China.

When the possible causes of this increase are discussed directly, there tend to be essentially two lines of approach (usually only pursued briefly before the discussion moves on to more immediately interesting issues). One is to point out that a recovery was only to be expected after the collapse in the late Bronze Age, which seems, whatever its ultimate cause, to have brought the population of Greece well below the level that could be easily sustained by the available resources at the prevailing level of agricultural technology.[21] On this view, the interesting point is not the start of the recovery, but that it was so strong and prolonged that it actually overshot, with the result that even higher levels of population than at the previous peak could be attained and then sustained for an extended period. There is merit in this view: it was not so surprising that

---

[19] Hin 2016.   [20] Ober 2015a; Bresson 2016b.
[21] Scheidel 2003, 122; see also Chapter 2, this volume.

there was a recovery from the collapse that ended the Bronze Age, and that, once the mechanisms that allowed for expansion were in full flow, it may be more important to pay attention to what they were and how they interacted than to look at the initial ignition. But still it seems a little unsatisfying to say that 'population was likely to rebound', as later contractions of the population in Greece were not always followed so swiftly by such rapid recoveries.

The main alternative is to suggest that changes in climate were connected in some way to the recovery.[22] As we have noted, climate is an important variable for the history of human populations, although most obviously because it has consequences for disease regimes and for the productivity of agriculture. It is likely that climate change early in the first millennium had an impact on the human population of Greece and will have to be part of the story. Establishing the details of that impact is more complicated, and there is a great deal of work still to be done here.

Whatever the explanations, and whatever the quantitative details, it is undeniable that the population did increase. The evidence for this period does not really allow for detailed quantifications either of the absolute levels of population or of the rate of increase in any area, but it leaves no room for doubt that there were many more Greeks at the end of the sixth century than there were at the start of the eighth, let alone the tenth, century. At a very basic level, the growth in population was what made the invention of new institutions necessary. While the political consequences of this tend to get the most attention, there were economic ones too. We are familiar with narratives about monarchs mobilising community resources and the increasingly manpower-intensive institutions of warfare both on land (hoplites) and especially at sea (galleys, and from the sixth century, triremes). Larger populations, sometimes living in denser settlements, were clearly going to pose new challenges for stability and dispute resolution. In this sense, population growth is part of the background to the emergence of written law codes. From an economic perspective, the important point here is that as populations grew, and as land became increasingly scarce compared to labour, the ability of members of the elite to maintain their positions on the basis of close personal relationships would have weakened. This would have led them to prefer more formal mechanisms to protect their status and properties. At the same time, good will and respect from their neighbours would have been becoming less important as means of

---

[22] E.g. Sallares 2009, 166–7; Bresson 2016b, 101.

asserting status than the purchase of goods imported from abroad. Population growth, mobility, the development of markets, and new legal and political institutions are all therefore intimately connected, and potentially at least mutually reinforcing. Given that some of the most enthusiastic early adopters of coinage, such as Aegina, were those whose population exceeded their local agricultural base, it is not too far-fetched to claim a role for population in the development of this key technology and institution of exchange in the ancient world.

Another facet of changing social relations is represented by the reconfigurations of slavery in the Greek world, as illustrated recently by David M. Lewis.[23] Slavery is not something that is new in the archaic period, but its nature and structures do seem to undergo changes at this time. By the end of the period, the fact that large numbers of slaves were coming from outside the Greek world affected every aspect of demography in those cities that were acquiring them: obviously Athens but presumably also Chios and Aegina and many other poleis. Slaves were acquired in sufficient numbers to be significant in population totals, even if precise quantification remains very difficult.[24] Slavery was probably the biggest single driver of long-distance, long-term human mobility in the ancient world. As with population issues in general, slavery provides some clear indications of economic activity: slaves were routinely bought (not just captured or born into slavery), indicating the generation and distribution of economic surpluses; that people were being imported into areas that were already densely settled must be telling us something about labour markets and economic institutions more generally in those areas.[25] The possibility of acquiring slaves would also have had consequences for fertility decisions at the level of individual households.

ATHENS AND CLASSICAL GREECE

The trend of population growth that started during the archaic period did not end with the sixth century or with the defeat of Xerxes' invasion. Much of the Greek world, including southern and central Greece and the Aegean islands, seems to have been more densely populated during the fifth century than it would be at any time before the nineteenth century. The headline political and military stories of the classical period are dominated by a small number of poleis that were

---

[23] Lewis 2018b.   [24] Fisher 2001 is still worth consulting on this subject.   [25] Lewis 2018b.

powerful because they had exceptionally large populations, especially Sparta, Athens, and Syracuse. These large poleis, and Athens in particular, have a prominent place in economic history too, and this place is not entirely undeserved. That they receive the bulk of the attention from writers both ancient and modern is partly because they really were important. The economic flourishing of the classical poleis (and the kingdom of Macedon under Philip II and Alexander III) is inextricably tied up with densely settled and intensively worked hinterlands, and trade networks that were able to pull in resources from more extensive, and more extensively worked, territories, just as their military resilience, ambitions, and successes are linked to, if not inexhaustible then certainly abundant, manpower resources for filling the ranks of phalanxes and the rowing benches of triremes.

Genuinely urban environments like those of classical Athens have consequences in their turn for demographic profiles and structures. This is obviously the case for mortality patterns, as dense human populations can sustain diseases that more scattered ones cannot, as well as providing additional challenges for sanitation. Dense residential districts tend to be in low-lying areas that are vulnerable to malaria. It is possible though that the extent to which ancient cities acted as 'population sinks' has been exaggerated in the past.[26] It is sometimes suggested that Greek town planning and medical knowledge may have helped in this regard, although the evidence and the scope for such optimism is limited.[27] However, the speed with which some of these cities –Athens and Syracuse in particular – grew must have been partly due to migration. Depending on how that migration took place and what marriage opportunities there were for migrants, there will have been fertility consequences too. Different kinds of jobs and work would have altered the logic of decisions about household structure and marriage patterns. Urban craftsmen and traders have different needs and opportunities from those of rural farmers – and the cost of housing is likely to be higher in cities than in rural areas, and so fertility calculations will be different. This means that cities can act as brakes on population growth even without being high-mortality black holes. It has plausibly been suggested that this braking effect would have been a contributing factor to the sustainability of the population growth that started in the archaic period.[28]

---

[26] Hin 2013 and 2016.
[27] Bresson 2016b, 43–9 makes a very optimistic case, but the grounds for such a degree of optimism seem flimsy.
[28] Scheidel 2003.

This was the period of Athens' dominance: the very notion of a 'classical' period of Greek history that spans the fifth and fourth centuries makes the most sense from the perspective of this city. 'Atheno-centrism' can be a problem if we assume that other cities were just like Athens. But while Athens was quite untypical in many ways, the large concentration of people in a relatively restricted urban area that it represented did have economic implications which extended beyond its own immediate territories and the Aegean. The sheer scale of the demand generated by classical Athens for imports (especially for food, but there must have been a voracious demand for fuel and other raw materials too), and the mechanisms by which that demand was satisfied, have had an important part to play in the economic history of ancient Greece. Simply by existing it created novel (at least for the Greek world) demands, opportunities, and incentives. This was as visible in traditional sectors of the economy (including obviously farming) as well as creating whole new ones such as banking.[29] Urban development incentivised changes in agricultural strategies, and particularly those which involved the pursuit of investment, improvement, and specialisation. The agricultural worlds of Hesiod and Xenophon were different largely because of the demographic changes that had taken place between the seventh and the fourth centuries.

Classical Athens is one of the few places where headline population numbers can be tracked with some limited degree of precision and confidence.[30] One point worth noting here is that, even though the population was probably much the same at the end of the fourth century as it had been at the beginning of the fifth, the size of the population had fluctuated significantly between those dates. In the middle of the fifth century, at the height of the empire and the start of the Peloponnesian War, there must have been very large numbers of people: at least 60,000 citizens, before taking into account their wives and children; tens of thousands of metic families too and many slaves – the total must have been approaching 400,000 at its peak. The speed with which that population grew in the fifth century could be explained to some degree by the slackening of constraints on fertility as Athens was able to take material advantage of its growing empire, but again much of it must have been due to immigration.

The economic history of Athens itself was vitally shaped by its historical demography in ways that go beyond the quantification of its demand for resources. Athens in the fifty years or so between the defeat

[29] Cohen 1992.   [30] Akrigg 2019.

of Xerxes' invasion and the outbreak of the Peloponnesian War was a place of rapidly expanding population and one experiencing vast influxes of wealth from the empire, largely successful warfare, and (presumably) expanded opportunities for trade (these factors would to an extent have been mutually reinforcing). While 'ordinary' citizens would have benefitted from some of these opportunities, some of them would have been rather double-edged: there were also opportunities to die a long way from home; the benefits of trade and the expanding urban centre would have been far from evenly distributed, with those with property in or near the city itself best placed to take advantage (which might seem trivial but it is worth recalling that sixth-century Athens at least seems to have been big enough for regional resentments to build up), and the wealthy again surely best placed of all. These would have been circumstances where we would expect inequalities of wealth to be becoming increasingly stark, even if we restrict our view to the citizen body in Attica alone and ignore the fact that the numbers of slaves and resident non-citizens would also have been increasing. Some metics (such as Cephalus, the father of Lysias, whose house provides the setting for Plato's *Republic*) were extremely wealthy, but the same cannot be assumed of all of them. To the extent that they were voluntary migrants (as opposed to manumitted slaves), it is worth noting that the Florentine *catasto*, which provides an appealing set of comparative data for classical Athens, reveals that the metropolis attracted migrants at the extremes – the destitute poor and some of the truly rich – whereas immigration to the other, smaller, towns was more homogeneous.[31] This may not have been conducive to continuing economic flourishing. To the extent that post-war Athens was performing well in economic terms, experiencing growth but with tolerably egalitarian distribution of wealth (as it is common to claim), this may have had as much to do with the purgative and disruptive effects of war, plague, and civil strife in the last third of the fifth century as with democracy or its institutions (Chapter 27, this volume).[32]

THE HELLENISTIC WORLD

As with the transition from the archaic to the classical period, the dramatically new political and military environment of the Hellenistic

---

[31] Kron 2011 for the comparison with Florence; Herlihy and Klapisch-Zuber 1985, 114 for the status of rural–urban migrants.
[32] Cf. Scheidel 2017, 188–99.

period did not cause a complete rupture in every aspect of Greek societies and economies, and there were many continuities from the previous period. In very general terms, the key features of the Hellenistic period are also reminiscent of the earlier, pre-classical, archaic world: the horizons of the Greek world broadened, large numbers of people moved around within those expanded horizons, and new urban centres were founded. As a direct result of the conquests of Alexander of Macedon, the Greek world became very much bigger, in both its geographic extent and the number of people that it contained. Questions of identity, and who counted as Greek, became even more complicated. Most of these questions lie beyond the scope of this chapter, but it is worth noting that if the total number of Greeks is a figure of interest, it gets even harder to estimate now.[33] What is clear is that the overall size of anything that might be called a Greek economy was very much larger than it had been previously. This geographical expansion, much of it into new kinds of environment for the Greeks, makes generalisation even harder than it was for the earlier periods.

One undeniably important feature of this period was the enthusiasm of Hellenistic rulers for encouraging even more urbanisation. New cities were founded, and some of those foundations, such as Seleucia-on-the-Tigris and Alexandria in Egypt, became very large indeed by any pre-industrial standards, let alone those of the archaic and classical worlds. Those super-cities are symptoms of the novel forms of economic organisation that were required to permit their development and which were driven by unprecedented levels of aggregate demand. They also represented exceptionally dense concentrations of wealth and its expenditure. It is not surprising that it is in this period easiest to find clear evidence of technological innovation in the Greek world, even if its economic impact is not always obvious or easy to assess. As in the archaic period, urbanisation is inextricably linked with migration and mobility. While the movement of Greeks eastwards into the new kingdoms is evidently a major and consequential source of mobility, the movement was not all in one direction.[34]

In a period defined by military conquests and their consequences, it is particularly appropriate to note the consequences of the movements of large armies and fleets. Military movements constitute a rather singular form of organised human mobility, and one which is disproportionately prominent in our literary sources. The movement of armies, and

---

[33] Osborne 2004 and Hansen 2006b for this question.
[34] As illustrated neatly by Davies 1984, 264–9; Günther 2012 collects a number of useful papers.

even more so the establishment of new garrison cities and other settlements of soldiers, especially in the early Hellenistic period, was nonetheless a phenomenon with major demographic and economic consequences. Perhaps the most mobile forces were fleets, whose construction, crewing, and maintenance must have had particularly serious economic implications now just as they had in the classical period.

So far in our story, we have mainly seen how population growth is connected to improvements in economic performance. In this period, away from the glittering royal capitals and thriving cities of the east (and the intensively reclaimed and settled Fayyum region in Egypt), we seem to encounter the reverse phenomenon of narratives of decline.[35] The exact extent and the precise timing of the downturn in the fortunes of the poleis of mainland Greece remains controversial, but it does seem clear that this region was no longer at the centre of population growth. Geographical explanations are important here. The conquests and foundations of Macedonian rulers created new political landscapes and new opportunities. But the climate also continued to change, with the last two centuries BCE seeing the arrival of what is conventionally but not altogether helpfully named the 'Roman Climate Optimum', whose consequences, as with all climate changes, were not equitably distributed and may have been rather less optimal for Greece. The new political geographies created by the Hellenistic kingdoms and, later, by the rise of Rome and its intrusion into the eastern Mediterranean, are relevant here, as they resulted in new economic networks.[36]

Although the evidence remains poor outside Ptolemaic Egypt, there are some indications that there were changes in family and household structures in the Hellenistic period. The pressures for change here may have come both from above and from below. At the top of the social and economic hierarchies, the range of roles and statuses for women may have been influenced by the dominance of monarchy in ruling families and the increasing importance of dynasties. One consequence was that at least some wealthy women were able to assert themselves more visibly within their communities. How far this affected the life choices of women outside the elite is less clear. But the combination of increased urbanisation in many regions with the high degree of mobility that followed the conquest of Alexander would have created new pressures and incentives for decision-making within households. The safe assumption is that there was still a high degree of variability in family structures across the Greek world, and that these would have had

[35] Alcock 1993; Bresson 2016b, 58–64.   [36] Boehm 2018, 89–139.

some economic consequences in turn. What is less clear however is exactly what actually changed in this period, as opposed to our focus and available evidence moving away from those poleis which had dominated the classical world, but which were also always exceptional, again including Athens above all.

CONCLUSION

I hope that this chapter has demonstrated both the importance of historical demography and illustrated some of the ways it matters for economic history. Because I have been mostly positive to this point, I want to conclude this chapter with a pair of cautionary notes. First, I want to repeat that the evidence we have for ancient Greek populations is very poor. We can often be reasonably certain about the directions of trends, and we can have useful discussions about the limits of the possible and of the plausible. Continuing developments in environmental archaeology will, as Manning (Chapter 25, this volume) demonstrates, continue to provide us with more information about disease regimes, climatic conditions, and the health status of people in the past. The fundamental issue of explaining the population expansion of the early first millennium is gaining more attention. Having said all that, quantification will continue to be a challenge. Precise figures for population size or rates of increase should always be treated with caution. In the case of the latter in particular, it is important to pay attention to the time period in question and to distinguish between what might be due to reproduction and what to migration. It is also often difficult to assess the full significance of population sizes and trends in the absence of further data. The paucity of wage and price series data for the Greek world is a particular handicap.[37]

Second, we need to be careful about exactly how we use the demography of Greece for comparison. I started by observing that part of the appeal of looking at population is that it can provide us with material that seems well-suited for doing comparison. But in practice the difficulty of obtaining precise quantitative data makes comparison harder. This seems particularly important when it is claimed that the economic performance of Greece was very good by pre-industrial standards. Identifying what, if anything, was really distinctive or unique about the demography of Greece in this period, and perhaps especially at

---

[37] Rathbone and von Reden 2015 summarises what there is.

the start of the archaic period, remains a key question, but one that is beyond the scope of this chapter and is difficult to answer at present. This in turn should probably caution us against making over-optimistic arguments about its economic history. There seems to be little real basis at present to warrant for Bresson's claim (2016b, 42) that 'the demography of Greece was truly unique' beyond the obvious point that to some degree the demography of any society is unique.

Finally, demography is important, but it has to be seen in a wider context. The Brenner debate in medieval history demonstrated the poverty of arguing that only demography, or only class, was the explanatory factor that matters.[38] It is in the interaction of demography with institutions that explanations need to be sought.[39]

Further Reading

Scheidel 2003 and 2007 remain fundamental starting points. The chapter on 'People in Their Environment' (31–70) in Bresson 2016b is learned and engaging and makes a number of important arguments, although (as noted above) I think that his arguments about Greek exceptionalism should be treated with caution. Hansen 2006b is a useful introduction to the pursuit of population numbers for Greece (especially in the classical period) generally. I attempt to pursue some of these issues in more detail for classical Athens in Akrigg 2019. On the mobility of Greek populations in the archaic and classical periods, Garland 2014 provides an interesting and wide-ranging survey, informed partly by migration studies.

---

[38] Hatcher and Bailey 2001; Turchin and Nefedov 2009, 6–21.
[39] Goldstone's demographic-structural theory (Goldstone 1991) provides a potentially useful model for ancient historians here.

12: CONSUMPTION, NUTRITION, AND THE GRAIN SUPPLY

John Wilkins

INTRODUCTION

In Greek thought, the consumer lived in demanding circumstances. First, the land and environment were harsh and mountainous, barely able to support the population. Unlike the rich lands of Asia Minor ruled by the Persians, or the fertile valley of the Nile, Greece demanded of its inhabitants unrelenting toil to wrest sustenance from the soil.[1] Those Greeks forced abroad to find new lands generally found greater riches than in Greece itself – on the shores of western Anatolia, on the Black Sea coast, on the coasts of Sicily and southern Italy, and in Cyrene in Libya and Marseilles in France. Hesiod's agricultural poem *Works and Days*, composed in Boeotia at around 700, describes the life of the arable farmer as unremitting toil, the diligent countryman struggling to get a decent living from the hostile earth. This harsh life, Hesiod tells us, was imposed by the hostility of the gods who controlled the natural order and the growth of animals and plants. Hesiod uses the myth of Prometheus to explain both the resentment of the gods and the conse-quent development of human culture.[2] Agriculture was encoded within a sacrificial system that established men within their cosmic place between immortal gods and mortal animals and gave them their role within a culture of farming and technology.[3]

The second and more fundamental challenge was human need, which gave rise to agriculture in the first place. Like all animals, human beings need nutrition, which is required to replace lost energy and body heat and maintain vital functions.[4] Along with warmth and shelter, these three are the basic drivers of human activity,[5] and throughout the thought of the ancient world, these are the basic essentials on which

---

[1] Herodotus compares Persia and Egypt with Greece in books 1 and 2; Hippocr. *Aer.* 14–19 contrasts Greece with Asia Minor and the Black Sea area.
[2] Hes. *Op.* 27–105; compare also *Theog.* 535–616.   [3] Vernant 1989.   [4] Gal. *san. tu.* 1.3.
[5] Pl. *Prt.* 320c8–323a4.

societies are built and on the elaboration of which wealth and distinction might be displayed. Such elaborations embrace social hierarchies, commensality, religious and mythological thought, medical science, and the seductions – for the well-off – of luxury. For the majority, however, too little food was the challenge in many parts of the Eastern Roman empire.

DIET

A scientific account of this insistent need for food experienced by human beings appears in the Hippocratic *Ancient Medicine* in the fifth century[6] and in Galen nearly a millennium later. The former offers an anthropology of human development, showing how human life improved from the 'raw and brutish' life of eating wild plants as animals do to growing, processing, and cooking cereals. In medical theory, the human body 'cooked' food in the digestive process: with normal body heat, food was converted into blood and other bodily fluids. The body mainly required cooked food since raw foods were thought to contain juices that would overpower the body heat. Cooked food, consumed by the heat of the body, produced health and flourishing. Conversely, imbalances and excesses produced ill health and brought disease. This model of consumption and cooking draws on deep cultural norms (related to the cooking of meat in sacrifice mentioned above, p. 172), that kept the citizen in balance and resistant to antisocial excess. Cooking and eating should meet bodily needs and not become so elaborate that the body might be tempted into luxurious excess. Doctors urged patients to listen to medical advice on what was good to eat and resist the tempting dishes of chefs for hire. Few hired cooks in antiquity, but the principle was strong, as we shall see: consumption always required regulation, whether medical, religious, or social. But for most people, again, too little food was the challenge, not too much.

The Greeks had a different understanding of nutrition from ours, with striking consequences. Nutrition dominated medical science, to which pharmacology and surgery also contributed. The emphasis was on maintaining health with a balanced diet and lifestyle. Dietary balance was as important as balance in Aristotle's political systems or in the principles of architecture. Indeed, an early medical text (Alcmaeon fr. 24) compares balance in the fluids of the body with balance in the city.

---

[6] *Ancient Medicine* 3.

Nutrition was built into the cultural norm of balance just as excess is built into patterns of eating within capitalism. Doctors from the Hippocratic authors of the fifth century to Galen in the second century CE give us the best lists of foodstuffs commonly consumed,[7] starting from barley and wheat providing energy. Galen explained how the products of agriculture gave energy and nutrition to the human body in a study of the impact of foods on the body entitled *On the Properties of Foodstuffs*. In some 150 chapters, Galen describes a wide range of food plants, meats, and fish; he offers, for example, a great variety of cereal plants according to soil and climate. Galen cannot to be said to confine his attention to the diet of the wealthy since his survey includes acorns, bitter vetch, and nettles.

It has been observed that there is little in ancient nutrition that would trouble a modern nutritionist,[8] despite a very different model of human physiology. Garnsey criticises 'errors' made by ancient doctors in this field, but his criticism is based on modern biochemistry, which itself has not achieved a healthy diet in Western populations.[9] Biomedicine does not place nutrition at the heart of medical science, as it was in antiquity, leaving modern populations to fend for themselves against the cultural power of advertisements for sugary drinks and 'ultra-processed' foods. Garnsey's case is at its strongest in respect of pregnant women, who were thought to need a reduced diet in ancient medicine while they experienced the excessive demands of the foetus. This, combined with high levels of perinatal mortality, increased the hazards of childbirth in the pre-modern world. Garnsey's impatience with the 'ignorance' of ancient doctors is understandable but fails to consider medical science as a cultural product and not as eternal truths to be discovered. Ancient doctors had centuries of experience to draw on and knew to a large extent what 'worked', as did agricultural populations across the ancient world. Doctors built medical theories on that experience – the most important guide in all of Galen's works – and on what brought health and what brought sickness. The study of nutrition in antiquity depends on Hippocratic authors, Galen, and the other medical systems who followed different physiological models.

Subsistence and the basic diet can be thought of in many ways. The diet was a 'Mediterranean' diet, with a large emphasis on a varied diet and on indigenous plants supplying energy, with low consumption of meat and fish.[10] Meat depended on religious and civic festivals, fish on

---

[7] Hippocr. *Reg.* 2.39–56.   [8] Nutton 2013, 247.   [9] Garnsey 1999.
[10] Horden and Purcell 2000.

periodic arrivals of shoaling species. It is the diet now recommended by the World Health Organization, though it was often in antiquity in less than adequate volume at the end of winter. So strong was this pattern, and so closely linked with Greek identity, that apparently strongly contrasting political identities and ideologies, such as those between the Spartans and Athenians, seem to have made few differences to the food consumed or the strength of commensality.

There is scope for studies into food more broadly within the ancient economy, based on production estimates, agricultural practice, and the possibilities of trade and distribution. Trade in foods was always important, as far as the cities were concerned. At the super-regional and imperial level, grain stores and grain shipments dominate; at the local level, mills and technologies for processing grain were widespread. Studies of techniques and distribution are complemented with studies of cereal plants and legumes, of agricultural production and the potential of farming.[11]

SURVIVAL

In his influential study of the ancient food supply, Garnsey sets out the challenges.[12] Wheat failed one year in four, barley one year in seven. Diversification was the important strategy for small farmers, often using primitive wheats rather than bread wheat, and millet in damper climates.[13] Beans and pulses provided vital protein. Cities had the economic muscle to command grain imports and normally managed to avoid bread shortages (Chapter 8, this volume).[14] Athenian imports from Egypt and the Black Sea are well documented, while Rome added to these Libya and other productive wheat fields in North Africa. In the Greek world, wheat seems to have been the less dominant grain, with much barley consumed as porridges and flatbreads. Garnsey shows that while famine rarely struck the Mediterranean world, food shortages were endemic.[15]

The Greeks were well aware that they had stronger and better-resourced neighbours in the Middle East, but their responses to a harsh landscape created their distinctive tough identity. Some overseas Greeks such as the Ionians of western Anatolia and the Sicilian cities lived in plenty, the latter supporting monarchies; but the prevailing Greek pattern was oligarchies and (a few) democracies based on city states

---

[11] See e.g. Garnsey 1988; Sallares 1991; Gallant 1991; Amouretti 1986.   [12] Garnsey 1988.
[13] Forbes and Foxhall 1982.   [14] See also Moreno 2007.   [15] Garnsey 1988.

and their hinterland. At all times, the history of food in this culture was based on survival, commensality, and foods to mark distinction. For almost everyone, too, the social and communal context of consumption was key: these modes expressed status, gender, and identity. Early patterns of consumption based on the city state and its hinterland later followed wider influences, especially within the Graeco-Roman synthesis of the Roman period. There was variety between cities, whether inland or coastal, and within political systems, but all followed broadly the same pattern.

In a second nutritional treatise, *On Good and Bad Juices*,[16] used by Garnsey, Galen reports that country people suffered malnutrition in late spring as their winter supplies ran out: they had sent their best grains to cities to get the best prices, as well as the best beans and pulses. The country people were forced down the food chain to eat animal fodder unsuitable for human consumption. Galen is an excellent reporter, and the quality of his analysis has recently been corroborated by archaeobotanical studies, one of which has shown that the diet detailed by Galen matches fairly closely the evidence of a sewer unearthed at Herculaneum.[17] The large sewer runs beneath a row of shops, with flats above – the homes of working people and not members of a wealthy elite, who had sufficient resources to meet their needs from the market and were far less subject to the challenges of the natural order. The natural order prescribed the basic diet, based on the triad of cereal products, olive oil, and wine, while the human order worked and shaped the farmed versions of those plants to sustain and give shape to the great variety of cities and communities in which they lived. Meat and fish products were added to these basics and provided far more symbolic than nutritional value to the ancient diet.[18]

COMMENSALITY, SACRIFICE, AND THE SYMPOSIUM

One of the key markers of civic identity was participation in communal animal sacrifice. The communal aspect was by far its most important function and was marked by being the main occasion on which the Greeks ate meat. Culturally troubled by the killing of animals, the Greeks imagined that animals might consent to their death, with the moment of throat-cutting partly disguised by ritual cries from the women participating. The agricultural basis of the sacrifice was reaffirmed by the use of

---

[16] Gal. *Bon. Mal. Suc.* 1.   [17] Robinson and Rowan 2015.
[18] Dalby 2003 lists the full range of foods most often found.

barley grains and wine, and the animals chosen depended on the civic or private context. Wealthy cities such as Athens sacrificed several hundred cattle in the major festivals to Athena and Dionysus in the fourth century; the animals were taken to the Athenian acropolis for slaughter, and the butchered meat was distributed to all participants. Inscriptions record the special portions to be given to priests and officials – male and female – and all others received an equal share of meat.[19] This share marked participation and the communal effort to keep the goddess Athena well disposed in her temple and to ensure her favour to the community. Similarly, Demeter and Dionysus were honoured in major festivals that reinforced identity, divine inclusion, and guarantees for corn and wine production. Smaller festivals had more modest offerings, and at local or deme levels, local divinities and heroes were worshipped for community benefits. Private families also sacrificed on special occasions. Sacrifice frequently extended to other agricultural products such as barley and honey cakes, as the sacrificer showed deference to a god. It was possible to buy meat in markets that had been surplus to temple requirements, but participation in the ritual was of a much higher priority. Mode of consumption depended on the rules of the particular temple. Some prescribe division of meat that might be taken home; some must be eaten within the temple precinct; sometimes by men only, by women only, or by both. This constitutes commensality with the god, and around many temples dining rooms have been found to enable this sharing of consumption with the god to take place. This dining was often contained within religious associations who met at regular intervals to celebrate their community and shared objectives within the structure of sacrifice and religious ritual. So important was meat consumption to city life that renunciation of meat was an extreme statement of separation. Socrates prescribed a vegetarian diet for Plato's ideal Republic,[20] and neo-Platonists held up a vegetarian diet as the ideal for the wealthy ascetic. The followers of Pythagoras rejected meat-eating as the consumption of fellow creatures. Pythagorean cities in southern Italy were however unable to follow such a prescription and were forced to compromise in order to be able to function as cities.[21] These exceptional philosophical declarations demonstrate the strength of the meat-eating ideology.

Meat, then, was at the centre of sacrificial ritual. While large civic sacrifice in cities such as Athens demanded the acquisition of animals from beyond the rocky fields of the Attic hinterland – from places such as Euboea and Boeotia – many sacrificial animals were supplied locally. The smaller and more common animals of sacrifice, pigs and sheep,

---

[19] Parker 2011, 124–69. [20] Pl. *Rep.* 372a5–373c6. [21] Detienne 1993, 37–59.

were particularly offered during the late spring and early summer, when breeding animals were most likely to produce young. Jameson has shown the striking correlation between the sacrificial calendar and the production of young animals.[22] This again shows the close relationship between city and hinterland in food production, though there was always a tension between the agricultural ways of the countryside and the slick new ways of the city.

Scholars have often contrasted the sacrifice in which all participated with the symposium that was private and held in the home of the wealthy. Here another agricultural practice, wine production, found its consumption closely tied into social ritual with a religious dimension, with equal shares for all participants, in a mixture of wine and water agreed in advance by all. Murray makes a strong case for sympotic drinking as an elite practice.[23] This seems to have been the case in the archaic period, when reclining at the symposium came in as a marker of belonging to an international elite. Special furniture, and poetry celebrating the great and the good, is well attested for this period, for example in the elegies of Theognis (sixth century). By the fifth century, if not earlier, this contrast between public and private is unsustainable. Davidson tried to argue that in the democratic city of Athens, the symposium with its rituals of drinking, along with eating fish bought in the unregulated marketplace, marked upper-class life.[24] The rituals of drinking showed communal responsibilities and patterns of restraint, while dancing girls and fish-eating encouraged desire: the task of the drinkers was to navigate between these two principles as they became slowly more drunk. The mass of the population, Davidson argues, had no access to ritualised drinking and got wine instead from commercial taverns in the non-ritualised marketplace.

There are strong arguments against this public–private, rich–poor contrast. First, domestic architecture in the Piraeus, in Olynthus in northern Greece, and in other cities shows that the *andron* or ceremonial drinking space in the home was present in quite modest homes. Secondly, the rituals of drinking were widespread. Wine mixed with water was drunk at festivals and in civic buildings, as is attested in the public buildings of the Athenian agora. Ritual drinking was not an upper-class preserve. Exclusive furniture, good wine, special poetry certainly were enjoyed by the rich, but not exclusive ritual that forced the mass of the population into commercial transactions. Thirdly, sympotic practice is widespread in Greek comedy and not identified as the

[22] Jameson 1988. [23] Murray 1990; see also Schmitt Pantel 1992. [24] Davidson 1997.

preserve of the exclusive rich. Hermippus, *Basket-Bearers* fr. 63 is a good example, listing many imports into the Piraeus in a mixture of grain imports and cushions and other sympotic equipment.[25] Certain fancy refinements in materials and foodstuffs are identified and mocked, but not ritual distinctive to the wealthy. The class-levelling god Dionysus presided over rituals in wealthy homes and in communal drinking festivals alike.

Everybody drank wine mixed with water, neat wine being reserved for libations to the gods, special rituals, and non-Greek outsiders. Drinking by women of status who did not attend male symposia is not well attested, not because it did not happen, but because textual codes prescribed silence about women of status. As for many details of food consumption, comedy is our best source, since it focuses on the minor details of life and does tell us something of what women ate and drank and of the diet of the poor. The details are useful, but are always encased in the social order, which takes male civic behaviour as the criterion for all practice, albeit adapted to comic preoccupations. Thus comic men and women both have big appetites for wine and sex; comedy will tell us too about the complex meals of the rich, eager to display their wealth, but the descriptions are mainly of myriad fish dishes and meat and game, and the list rather takes over from a credible reflection of reality. Some people did eat with massive displays, but who and what is not really in the record, any more than truly credible evidence of the specialist cooks that people might have hired for a day's special feasting.

The symposium might be taken to excessive lengths in descriptions of the Hellenistic kings who followed Alexander. An elaborate description by Callixenus, quoted by Athenaeus of Naucratis in the *Deipnosophistae* in the second-century CE, gives much sympotic detail of a celebratory procession by Ptolemy Philadelphus in Alexandria. Large numbers of followers played out sympotic scenes in a kind of moving carnival that brought the *andron* into the streets, mixed with exotic Asian animals such as panthers that were traditionally associated with the god Dionysus.[26] Here we see sympotic elements combined with festive elements to emphasise royal prestige in the public space, a phenomenon discussed further below (p. 179). The element of scale and display has expanded a widespread but small-scale practice of citizens drinking together in ritual patterns during a civic festival.[27]

Comedy – that is civic drama for the massed ranks of citizens in their thousands – had many ways of asserting communal values, and

[25] Wilkins 2000, 156–62.   [26] Ath. 5.197c–203b.   [27] Parker 2005, 155–78.

drinking ritual was one of them, often reserved for a final flourish of drinking together by protagonist and chorus, such as in Aristophanes' *Peace* (421), or in fourth-century comedy as a Dionysiac revel between scenes, such as in Menander's *Dyscolus*.[28] In contrasting scenes of comic disapproval, self-serving politicians who took bribes might be vilified for their enormous appetites for fish and other foods; citizens who toadied to the rich in an undignified need for food handouts were a big comic feature, first in the early fifth century in the Sicilian comedy of Epicharmus;[29] and those who sold their independence for food were caricatured, most frequently as 'flatterers' and 'parasites'. This latter term, once honorific for priests who 'feasted with' the gods, was in comedy debased to those whose belly drove their life choices. The parasite, along with the greedy sex worker, the clever slave, and the boastful chef, were comic creations who may represent a parody of characters about town in the fourth century; but a much more import-ant function of these low-life characters, as Fisher has shown, is to exemplify troubling interstices in the fabric of society between the hard-working poor and the leisured classes of the wealthy elite.[30] Individuals may find ways to move across the divide of work and leisure by offering sexual and other services in return for food and patronage. The stability of the city might be destabilised by such transactions based on desire and fluid status among social pariahs. Here we see the normative role of the civic drama, used to ridicule deviant consumption.

Distinction

If ritual constrained citizens into approved behaviours of consumption through principles of equality at the sacrifice and symposium, other mechanisms allowed the rich and powerful to display distinctions. Greek texts express unease at luxurious developments from the late fifth century onwards, diverting concerns from foreign excess, especially among Persians, to domestic examples. Herodotus charts Eastern devel-opments, while Xenophon and others develop the vocabulary of 'pleas-ant experience' (*hedypatheia*), and Plato the discourse of luxury in the city state at both individual and political levels in his *Republic*. The first of these luxurious developments was to amass a large group of supporters, who might benefit the largesse of the powerful individual. In a form of wealth distribution, the rich man might feed as many people as possible.

---

[28] Wilkins 2000. [29] Fragments 34–5 Kaibel. [30] Fisher 2000.

The *Flatterers* of the comic poet Eupolis treats this subject, in an attack on the wealthy Callias.[31] Opponents would characterise this as the feeding of parasites, and the lack of equality experienced by the hangers-on might be mocked. Social constraints might thus be brought to bear on such food dependency and lack of independent spirit.

The rich man might approach such feeding of others in a more acceptable way; instead of boosting his private power base, he might sponsor public feasting or drinking. Voluntary public donations in a system known as euergetism are a major feature of the Hellenistic and Roman periods and a form of wealth redistribution that fits well into the patterns of monarchy presided over by the successors of Alexander, as well as in the Greek world under the Roman empire. Schmitt Pantel has drawn on the abundant inscriptional record to show that such public benefactions might take the form of subsidies for dining in public spaces, of having subsidised wine-drinking (*geusis* or 'tasting'), and of many variations to produce public consumption at private expense.[32] What had been a communal obligation and form of taxation in an independent city was now a voluntary system of benefaction, with accompanying civic recognition publicly displayed on stone by the donor. On a royal scale, an enormous festival might be staged, as that for Ptolemy Philadelphus mentioned above (p. 179), or that of Antiochus IV also recorded by Athenaeus in the *Deipnosophistae*.[33] Similarly, Plutarch describes Mark Antony received as a new Dionysus in his journey through the Greek cities of Asia Minor to the new love of his life, Cleopatra, in Egypt.[34] These were all adaptations of the connection between Dionysiac civic ritual and royal display. These distinctively Greek forms contrast with the ultimate example of royal display, the Persian court in the sixth and fifth centuries, which many Greek authors held up as the contrast to their restrained and civic ways. Unlike Greek civic ritual, the Persian king brought all the products of his vast territories to the royal cities such as Susa and Ecbatana, where he ate alone to emphasise his separateness and proximity to the divine. What was in fact a centralising system of wealth, which brought together agricultural wealth and redistributed it back through the nobility and social classes, was seen by the Greeks as monarchical and luxurious, the antithesis to the small city state. Persian excess was further evidenced in a system of sacrifice which consumed the animal 'whole' rather than butchered into equal chunks and distributed to all citizens and their

---

[31] Fisher 2000.   [32] Schmitt Pantel 1992.   [33] Ath. 5.194, 10.439; cf. Polyb. 30.25–6.
[34] Plut. *Ant.* 49.

families. Monarchy always remained foreign and suspect in the Greek mind, but nevertheless gradually took over the Greek world. In the archaic period, 'tyrants' ruled some cities until they were expelled; in the fifth and fourth centuries, the agricultural riches of Sicily maintained wealthy tyrannical courts which promoted special eating and luxurious forms of cooking (including Europe's earliest cookery book by Archestratus of Gela, which extols luxury and appetite, in clever sympotic verse parodying the archaic didacticism of Hesiod);[35] and the Macedonian kings of northern Greece increased their influence over the Greek world during the fourth century, leading to Alexander's annexation of Greece and the Persian empire in the 320s. Thereafter, the Successor kings such as the Ptolemies and Seleucids ruled over vast territories and formerly free cities, until their Roman annexation and rule by a Roman emperor from 30 onwards. These dramatic political changes were reflected in city life, with dining clubs, euergetism, and some display of wealth grafted on to what had been cities and hinterland. Greek and Roman interactions brought a cultural fusion in dining and civic consumption.

Distinction might also be marked in dining ware, especially if it was of silver; less expensively in fine painted pottery; and in furniture and dining apparatus. From the archaic period, reclining on couches at dinner and symposium was favoured by international elites from the eastern Mediterranean to the Etruscans and peoples further west.[36] As indicated above (p. 178), everyone might participate in symposia, but the rich could add style to form: Lissarrague has shown the sophistication of images on vases, a contrasting approach to the connoisseurship of Beazley and others, based on painters and styles.[37] Corner has brought out wonderfully poetic elaborations within drinking ritual.[38] Verse might reflect shared male values in the archaic city; images were more often mythical or dramatic paradigms than everyday scenes: the symposium offered a special world which at the same time reflected shared values. While quite modest homes had sympotic parts of the house for the purpose, display and refinement was always a possibility, even in the democratic city.

Foodstuffs themselves also played an important part in display and distinction. That the rich ate more and better is the best summary. More refined bread (most of the population ate barley porridges wet or dry);

---

[35] For gastronomic and zoological detail, see Wilkins and Hill [1994] 2011 and Olson and Sens 2000.
[36] Murray 1990.   [37] Lissarrague 1990; Beazley 1956.   [38] Corner 2015.

more meat; more varied fish than cheap shoaling fish such as anchovies and sardines.[39] They could also eat complex dishes. This is picked up from the fifth century onwards in that great collector of food details, Athenaeus (see above, p. 179), who more than any other records the ways of luxury. Imported foods such as pepper and ginger are part of it; but much more important are strange prepared dishes, *abyrtake* and *kandaulos*. These appear to originate in the wealthy cities of the Ionian coast and involve rich mixtures of cheese and meat stock. This is the most complex that ancient cooking seems to have got, and it is censured by comic poets, philosophers, and medical works alike (see below, p. 184, on the medical understanding of rich foods).

Graeco-Roman Synthesis

Foods had come into the Mediterranean from Asia since the earliest times, whether the olive, cereals, and the vine with agricultural technology; the chicken (not really established as *the* eating fowl until well into the Roman period); or eating on couches, adapted from the pastoralist practices of the Assyrians and Persians to become formal dining and drinking, and becoming so widespread that Jesus, for example, dined thus with his contemporaries in the first century CE. Fruits continued to arrive from the East, such as the peach and apricot, and spices such as ginger and pepper. The latter are little known before Theophrastus (author of 'On Plants', *Historia Plantarum*) in the fourth century, but were widely used by the first century CE. Greek and Roman foodways interacted in multiple ways in the wealthy cities of Anatolia, as Mitchell has magisterially shown.[40] Foods distinctive to the Greek (and Roman) palate include the giant fennels *silphium* and *asaphoetida*;[41] oily fish fermented in concrete tanks from the Black Sea to the Spanish and Portuguese coasts (an extensive industry),[42] and many varieties of wine. No matter what the city, wine was the main drink, mixed with water, and drunk in the presence of Dionysus; cereals were consumed under the auspices of Demeter and Persephone; and olive oil produced with the help of Athena, the latter used so extensively that in many ways external applications exceeded internal. Athenaeus of Naucratis remains the most comprehensive guide.

---

[39] von Reden 2007a.   [40] Mitchell 2015.
[41] Significantly, the first was produced in a Mediterranean context, Cyrenaica, while the latter was an exotic import from what is now Afghanistan.
[42] Curtis 1991.

Galen is our much more theoretical guide for variation in foods within the eastern Roman empire of the second century CE; on how food works in the body; and on the process of consumption. Rich sauces and other luxuries are not recommended;[43] nor are unusual parts of fish.[44] Rather, the food that the body needs is what is familiar – that is produced in the climate and region inhabited by the consumer – and what is closest in nature to the body of the consumer so that minimal assimilation from food into blood is possible. The red mullet, Galen tells us, while a fish prized by discriminating consumers, is nevertheless a fish excellent for health, since its flesh is closest to that of human beings and best able to undergo digestion into blood.[45] Its economic value is second to its nutritional suitability, provided, like all fish, that it has grown in sea water which is clean and unpolluted. Galen dismisses those who pay ridiculous prices for the liver of mullet, since the rarity value is not mirrored in the health benefits. The suitability of mullet flesh to the human body is equalled only by that of pigs, which is so close to the nature of human flesh that it is easily digested and very nutritious.[46] Galen claims in a dubious aside that similarity in nature is exploited by dishonest innkeepers who serve human flesh as pork. But that claim aside, Galen's point is that the consumer will most benefit from nourishing food that is raised in the land and seas close to the consumer: foods from the local environment best suit the human body, because it too is a natural creature in its own environment. Rarities and exotica remain, in contrast, symbols of wealth which are only incidental to health.

Galen is invaluable to us since he combines an understanding of consumption beyond the structures of elite display – how much energy does a manual worker need is a key medical question he addresses[47] – with a detailed understanding of how the human body assimilates food. And all the time Galen operates this perspective within the texts and writing traditions of the Greek educated elite, as had the Hippocratic author 800 years earlier who declared how the human body evolved from eating wild plants like animals to its high state of cooked foods suitable for consumption (see above, p. 173). This medical overview rests on a scientific basis to one side of sacrificial ritual and patterns of commensality, while putting cooking (in the form of digestion) at the heart of Greek culture.

---

[43] Gal. *alim. fac.* 2.51.
[44] The liver of red mullet is dismissed as a pointless luxury; cock's testicles and goose's wings are good, but birds' intestines inedible: *alim. fac.* 3.20 and 3.26.
[45] Gal. *alim. fac.* 3.26.   [46] Gal. *alim. fac.* 3.1.   [47] Gal. *alim. fac.* 1.7.

Conclusion and Future Research

The archaeological study of bones and botanical remains reveals much about the ancient diet. Current work on Herculaneum, Pompeii, Carthage, and Athens helps to show the cultural synthesis across the Graeco-Roman world.[48] Literary and technical studies of texts, especially medical texts, will show further cultural patterns, such as balance and diversity, lying behind ancient thought and practice and will sharpen understanding of the moralistic codes of consumption directing Greek literature and philosophy. Further integration of textual, inscriptional, and archaeological evidence will reveal social practice beyond the vocal elite 5 per cent, to really focus on the 95 per cent of the population. Pitts and Griffin, for example, a study in Dorset in the UK, showed that Roman teeth were chemically more healthy than British teeth.[49] More too is needed on gender, new methods and new questions to reveal evidence for the female half of the population, to extend what Garnsey and others have started.[50]

Further Reading

Wilkins and Hill 2006 give an overview of ancient food consumption and nutrition, as does Garnsey 1999. Wilkins, Harvey, and Dobson 1995 and Wilkins and Nadeau 2015 give a multi-authored approach to many foods with regional and temporal perspectives, the latter from Homer to the Middle Ages, with a full bibliography. Dalby 2003 provides an accessible alphabetical survey, with good notes on sources. On wine, Murray 1990 and Murray and Teçusan 1995 are excellent.

---

[48] Bisel and Bisel 2002; Lazer 2009; Papathanasiou, Richards, and Fox 2015; Lagia 2015a and 2015b.

[49] Pitts and Griffin 2012.   [50] Garnsey 1999.

13: THE AGRICULTURAL ECONOMY

Daniel Jew

INTRODUCTION

Agriculture formed the subsistence base of the Greek economies: 'the ancient Greek world was massively and unalterably rural'.[1] Even the estimated 10–50 per cent of urban population would often have farmed surrounding fields.[2] Most Greek communities were relatively small: 60 per cent of cities with known territory were smaller than ca. 10 km by 10 km.[3] Against this backdrop of small, predominantly rural city-states, many Greek farmers must have aimed to meet their own needs, to diversify to reduce risk, and to generate a normal surplus. However, evidence for networks and exchange suggest some coexisting degree of market-oriented production.[4]

CLIMATE AND TOPOGRAPHY

Climate conditions in the early twentieth century were likely similar to those of the classical period.[5] Most of the ancient Greek world lay within the subtropical high climate zone, encompassing several main climate types.[6] Southern Greece, Ionia, the Aegean, and most of Asia Minor have a 'Mediterranean' climate (Köppen-Geiger type Csa). Rainfall is low and concentrated in mild winters; drought is frequent in summer. Areas of mainland Greece close to the Pindus mountains receive ca. 800 mm or more of rain per year; those further east receive less. Southern Attica, where Athens lies, receives a mere ca. 400 mm per year, with high risk of crop failure.[7] Macedonia, Thrace, Thessaly, and parts of the Black Sea coast have a temperate climate more similar to that of continental Europe (Köppen-Geiger Cfa/Cfb). Highland regions experience alpine conditions, with

---

[1] Cartledge 2002, 20.
[2] Estimates: Horden and Purcell 2000, 92; Hansen 2006b, 18–19. Fields: Jameson 1992, 141.
[3] Hansen 2006b, 18. [4] Cartledge 2002, 12–16. [5] Jew forthcoming.
[6] Lionello 2012a, xxii. [7] Garnsey 1988, 10.

winter snow. More than half of mainland Greece is mountain; habitation is concentrated in the coastal plains and valleys. In 1929, less than a fifth of Greek land was reported as cultivable.[8] Soils were mainly limestone-based and poor in the key nutrients of nitrogen and phosphorus.[9]

CROPS AND ANIMALS

The 'Mediterranean triad' of grain, olives, and vines predominated in ancient times. Leguminous pulses are sometimes added, forming a quartet.[10] Main annual crops were cultivated in a winter-sown, rain-fed dry farming regime; irrigation was reserved mainly for garden plots (*kepoi*). Naked (free-threshing) wheats and hulled barley were the norm.[11] Wheat was a higher-status food, but barley was more able to withstand drought. *Alphita* (barley-meal) was a typical staple (Thuc. 4.16.1; 7.87.2). Lentils, broad beans, and chickpeas were common pulses (Theophr. *Hist. pl.* 8.1.1–4). Perennial crops like the olive were well adapted to survive summer drought. Cattle, mules, donkeys, pigs, goats, and sheep were kept, either as work animals or to provide milk, cheese, and other products.

EVIDENCE

Literary Texts and Forensic Speeches

The *Iliad* and *Odyssey* make scattered references to agriculture and husbandry in Dark Age Greece. Two significant passages are the description of ploughing on the shield of Achilles (*Il.* 18.540–60) and that of Laertes' farm (*Od.* 24.205–31, 245–6, 336–44). Hesiod's moralistic poem, the *Works and Days* (ca. 700), is set in a small community in Boeotia and provides details of the working of a modest-sized farm. Xenophon's *Oeconomicus* (ca. 362) outlines how a rich landowner should best manage his estate.[12] Both the *Works and Days* and *Oeconomicus* are biased toward the agricultural and pastoral norms of the relatively wealthy.[13] Theophrastus' botanical treatises, the *Causes of Plants* and *Inquiry into Plants* (fourth century), give evidence for crops in Greece. Aristotle's *Historia animalium* and *Constitution of Athens* (7.3–4),

---

[8] National Statistical Service of Greece, *Agriculture and Livestock Census of Greece 1929* (Frontmatter), iii.
[9] Caldis 1947, 135.   [10] Sarpaki 1992.
[11] Sallares 1991, 326–32; Garnsey 1999, 14–15; Lister and Jones 2013, 442–4 and fig. 3.
[12] Pomeroy 1994.   [13] Hodkinson 1988, 36–7.

both fourth century, furnish information about domesticated animals and the Solonic property classes at Athens.[14] Surviving forensic speeches at Athens (early to mid-fourth century) give details about farms and estates. These include the estates of Phainippus and Hagnias (Dem. 42, 43; Isae. 11) and what may be a rural farm (Dem. 47).[15]

Inscriptions

Leases of sacred and public land, for cultivation or pasture, were common across the Greek world.[16] The Attic *stelai* list the possessions of fifty or so rich Athenians (the *hermokopidai*) who had property confiscated in 414/13 for mutilating the herms. These lists provide detailed but incomplete information about landed estates, agricultural equipment, and slaves.[17] The Attic *horoi* were inscribed boundary stones giving notice that a piece of land was encumbered by debt, as such providing information about mortgages and the potential location of farm residences in the countryside.[18] Finally, the *Rationes Centesimarum* recorded a 1 per cent tax on the sale of land and houses in fourth-century Athens, providing possible evidence for farmhouses or other structures.[19]

Archaeological Evidence

Various rural structures across Greece have been interpreted as farmhouses or storage towers.[20] These include the Vari and Dema houses in Attica.[21] From the 1980s, intensive survey – pedestrian teams traversing a landscape to record visible structural remains and pottery scatter – gained popularity.[22] Survey has vastly improved the record of sites and settlement. Other specialised methods include simulation of least-cost path routes and chemical analysis of palaeobotanical remains.[23]

Comparative and Ethnographical Data

Traditional pre-mechanised Greek agriculture from 1860 to 1950 is often used as a base of comparison to ancient farming, as it is in this

---

[14] de Ste Croix 2004, ch. 1.
[15] Burford Cooper 1977, 164. For further discussion of this type of evidence, see Jones 2004, ch. 1 and McHugh 2017, 13–17.
[16] Osborne 1988; Papazarkadas 2011.   [17] *IG* I^3 421–30; Pritchett 1953.   [18] Finley 1951.
[19] Lambert 1997, 226.   [20] McHugh 2017, chs. 1 and 3.
[21] Jones, Sackett, and Graham 1962; Jones, Graham, and Sackett 1973.
[22] Alcock and Cherry 2004.   [23] McHugh 2017, ch. 4; Sarpaki 1992.

chapter. It is particularly useful, since this is the only period for which we have any numerical data for crop yields and land use.[24] Ethnography provides insights into agricultural practices during this period, adding further context to the data.[25]

THE ANCIENT GREEK AGRICULTURAL YEAR

The rhythms of the agricultural year are known from Hesiod, the calendar of festivals at Athens, and modern Greek ethnography.[26] Hesiod instructs listeners to begin sowing cereals when the Pleaides set in November and to harvest when they rise in early May (*Op.* 383). The year's vintage also had to be gathered and pressed in September and October, and olives were pruned, pricked, and crushed on a biennial cycle from October to December. Exact timings varied by regional climate, the year's weather, and farmers' decisions. Grain-sowing and harvest nevertheless ordered much of ancient Greek life. The off seasons in spring and late summer were used for other key dimensions of life: to discharge civic duties, to hold the Panhellenic games and civic festivals, for monumental building, and to go to war.[27]

Sowing

Oxen plough yoked to a wooden ard in the *Works and Days* (427–41); vases, coins, and statuettes also similarly depict ploughing oxen.[28] Mules are used instead in one instance in Homer (*Il.* 10.351), and an equine is shown ploughing on an Attic drinking cup. The Hesiodic ard was still in use in the early twentieth century. It scratched a furrow in the soil, breaking up weeds and tilling topsoil, but unlike the modern steel plough did not turn over the soil. Sowing was achieved by broadcasting (scattering by hand) after the plough.

Digging

Hand cultivation was necessary on small plots or sloped land, for maintaining and manuring olives and other fruit trees, and for weeding

---

[24] Garnsey 1988, 8–14; Gallant 1991, 77–8; Jew forthcoming.   [25] Forbes 2007; Halstead 2014.
[26] Osborne 1987, 13–16; Isager and Skydsgaard 1995, ch. 11; Foxhall 2007, 127.
[27] Osborne 1987, 13–14; Osborne 2010, 100.
[28] This section owes a large debt to Isager and Skydsgaard 1995, ch. 3.

and intensification. Hoes are attested on vases and in the literature (*Il.* 21.257–9; Theophr. *Caus. pl.* 3.20.8; Xen. *Oec.* 17.15). Hesiod recommends that a slave follow the ploughing-and-sowing team with a hoe (*makele*; *Op.* 470), a practice observed in modern times with women and children of the household.[29] Dibbling or row sowing (dropping seeds into small holes or furrows) require less seed than broadcasting but are more labour-intensive.

Harvest

Field crops require reaping, binding, threshing, and winnowing during harvest (Xen. *Oec.* 18.1–9). The hand sickle (*drepanon, depane, arpe*) was used for reaping (Hes. *Op.* 473). Reaping and binding are described on the shield of Achilles (*Il.* 18.550–5). Homer alludes to winnowing on the threshing floor (*aloe*; *Il.* 5.499–504); a number of ancient stone circles identified as such have been discovered.[30] Demosthenes mentions two large threshing-floors, ca. 30 m in diameter, on Phainippus' estate (42.6). From ethnographic evidence, animals tethered to a rotating bar trod on crops to thresh the edible portion from the straw and chaff (husks, pods, ears). A fork (*ptyon*) and basket (*liknon*) were used for winnowing, which required a gentle breeze. Crops were vulnerable to weather and marauding livestock until stored.[31]

Transportation and Post-Harvest Processing

Hesiod describes wooden carts and wagons in detail (*Op.* 423ff), and Demosthenes mentions 'ass-drivers' (42.7). Bound sheaves required transportation from field to threshing floor, and processed grain from floor to storage. Grain had to be further hand-milled before cooking. Food preparation, together with spinning, likely took up much of women's time (*Od.* 20.105–19, cf. Thuc. 2.78.3).[32]

Processing Vines and Olives

Grapes were gathered in large wickerwork baskets and pressed with feet and knees on wooden or stone pressing boards (or in stone vats). The juice flowed into a large ceramic collection pot (*hypolenion*). Olives were

---

[29] Halstead 2014, 17–18. [30] Young 1956. [31] Halstead 2014, 133.
[32] Jameson 1977–8, 138.

beaten or shaken from trees with poles or picked directly from branches by climbers or with ladders.[33] Olives were crushed with a hand mortar, rotary mill (*trapetum*), or large-scale lever press to produce olive oil.

Irrigation

In 1929, less than 10 per cent of cultivated land in Greece was irrigated. Modern pumps greatly increased the level of irrigation after World War II.[34] Dry farming was likely the norm in ancient Greece; watering was probably restricted to smaller garden plots close to residences (*kepoi*).[35]

EXTENSIVE VS INTENSIVE AGRICULTURE

The agricultural calendar, crops, tools and implements, and technology outlined above are all uncontroversial. Other, heavily debated aspects of Greek agriculture include the balance between subsistence and market, degree of biennial fallow, settlement (nucleated or dispersed), livestock (whether kept via transhumance or mixed farming), and the extent of slavery in agriculture. These unknowns cluster to form two contrasting models (Fig. 13.1): the 'traditional model' (extensive cultivation) still held up widely in classical scholarship and the 'new model' (intensive cultivation), though no longer really 'new'.

Extensive Cultivation

Under the traditional model, agriculture is generally 'extensive': wheat or barley are grown in a two- or three-field rotation system. One of these fields is left unsown each year (cultivated, bare short fallow) so that soil nutrients and ca. 20 per cent of rainwater are retained for the next crop.[36] The fallow field is ploughed during the spring off season to remove weeds. The process was ideally repeated in summer and autumn, giving rise to the *tripolos* (thrice-ploughed field) of Hesiod and Homer (Hes. *Op.* 462–4; Hom. *Il.* 18.542; *Od.* 5.127). Extensive agriculture emphasises the use of draft animals, with stall-feeding costs a drain on output.[37]

---

[33] Foxhall 2007, 124–81.
[34] National Statistical Service of Greece, *Agriculture and Livestock Census of Greece 1929* (Frontmatter), 7; Sallares 1991, 303.
[35] Burford 1993, 136.   [36] Sallares 1991, 385. *Pace* Halstead 2014, 201.   [37] Halstead 1987, 84.

Traditional Model (Isager and Skydsgaard 1995)

- Extensive
- Cultivated bare short fallow (2-year cycle)
- Nucleated settlement
- Transhumance
- More animal-powered
- Low labour and manure inputs

New Model (Halstead 1987, Hodkinson 1988)

- Intensive
- Annual cropping (pulse/fodder—grain rotation)
- Dispersed settlement
- Mixed farming
- More human-powered
- High labour and manure inputs *(impacts slavery)*

13.1 Traditional and new models of Greek agriculture

Extensive agriculture was the normal pattern in early twentieth-century Greece due to two main factors: fragmentation of holdings and nucleated settlement. Farmers lived in central villages, often several hours' walk to fields.[38] The Greek system of partible inheritance led to ownership of several small strips rather than consolidated holdings. Intensification (manuring and weeding) was reserved for vineyards, orchards, and smaller patches of vegetables closer to homes.[39] The system as a whole produced lower yields but was an economically rational calculus of the cost of labour inputs in relation to outputs.

The modern Greek practice of transhumance also divorced stock-keeping from farming.[40] Large flocks and herds grazed on marginal lowland in the winter. They were moved to upland pastures watered by snowmelt in the summer by semi-nomadic pastoralists, such as the *Sarakatsani* and *Vlachs*.[41] Manure, the main source of fertiliser before the widespread use of chemicals from the 1930s, was unavailable for half the year.[42] In turn, the preference for cultivated bare fallow over a fodder crop (or uncultivated weeds) meant that livestock had insufficient grazing in the lowlands. The shepherds playing a role in a tragedy of the fifth-century Athenian poet Sophocles (*OT* 1132–9), and statuette dedications by herdsmen in Arcadia, provide examples of ancient

---

[38] Five kilometres is a notional limit: Burford 1993, 57.   [39] Halstead 1987, 82.
[40] See overview of debate at Howe 2008, 13–25.   [41] Hodkinson 1988, 51–8.
[42] Chemicals: Jew forthcoming.

pastoralists. Aristotle strongly implies that at least some cities had specialised pastoralists (*Pol.* 1319a19–33; cf. *Hist. an.* 610b30–611a9.).[43]

Intensive Cultivation

The new model suggests that large-scale pastoralism was limited, since
ancient Greece was divided into relatively small political territories.[44]
Instead, small flocks and herds were kept in lowlands year-round (mixed
farming), providing the manure needed for annual cropping.[45] In turn,
uncultivated green fallow (allowing weeds to grow), or the cultivation
of a fodder crop in rotation with grain, provided material for grazing (cf.
Theophr. *Hist. pl.* 8.7.4, 8.11.9).[46] Annual cropping was known to
Xenophon and Theophrastus (Xen. *Oec.* 16.14–15; Theophr. *Caus. pl.*
4.8.1–3; *Hist. pl.* 8.2.9, 8.7.2, 9.1), and several leases either mandate
a fodder crop (*IG* II² 1241; 2493) or expressly forbid it (*IG* II² 2408).
Ethnography suggests that ancient small plots were often intensively
cultivated.[47] From 1911 to 1938, only about a third of cultivable land in
Greece was left fallow in any given year, suggesting that some land was
cropped annually or on a three-field rotation. On the whole, intensification implies the calculated decision to increase labour inputs for
diminishing marginal outputs.[48]

LAND USE AND LAND TENURE

In 1961, land in Greece was reported as cropland (30 per cent), pasture
(41 per cent), forest (21 per cent), or 'other' (7 per cent; including roads,
built areas, and water bodies).[49] According to the FAO (Food and
Agriculture Organization of the United Nations), cropland in ancient
Greece would notionally include land under annual and forage crops (e.g.
grain), land under long-term crops (vines, olives, and other fruit), and
fallow.[50] Pasture and grazing land was marginal: poor, rocky, sloped,

---

[43] Skydsgaard 1988, 75; Hodkinson 1988, 36; Isager and Skydsgaard 1995, 99–101; and above all
Howe 2008.
[44] Hodkinson 1988, 52–8.
[45] Jameson 1977–8, 127–9; Halstead 1987, 82–5; Hodkinson 1988, 38–51.
[46] Multi-cropping i.e. planting a summer crop is also possible: see Gallant 1991, 54–6; cf. Theophr.
Hist. pl. 8.4.6.
[47] Halstead 2014, 202–3.   [48] Jameson 1977–8, 127; Halstead 1987, 82.
[49] National Statistical Service of Greece, *Distribution of the Country's Area by Basic Categories of Land
Use* 1961, 1, table 1.1.
[50] As used in the 2020 World Census of Agriculture (Food and Agriculture Organization of the
United Nations 2017, 68).

marshy, or too distant from residences to conveniently farm. Such *eschatiai* nevertheless formed a buffer that could potentially be exploited for grazing, or for agriculture via stone-clearing, terracing or drainage.[51]

Land could be owned by the gods (via religious sanctuaries e.g. at Delos), the polis, demes, or private individuals.[52] Some public land was subject to grazing rights (usually to citizens of the polis and those with grants of *epinomia*). Public, sacred, and deme land was leased for cultivation or grazing, often for periods of ten or more years.[53] Leasing seemed to carry a sense both of privilege and fulfilment of duty to deme, city, and gods, and as such lessees were often well-to-do, respected members of the community.[54] Private leases seem on the whole to have been shorter (e.g. Lys. 7.9–11).

Private land was typically owned by citizens of the polis. The ideal self-sufficiency of a citizen household (*oikos*) was tied to the idea of the ownership of an ancestral portion (*kleros*) of the city's land.[55] It is this landownership which provided the ideological basis for the equality of the 'middling' (*metrios*) citizen-farmer-hoplite of the archaic and classical periods.[56] The ideal *kleros* was a family farm perhaps around forty to sixty *plethra* in size (ca. 3.6–5.5 ha); in 167, the city of Pharsalus made sixty-*plethtra* grants of *kleroi* to new citizens (*DGE* 567).[57] Comparative evidence shows that ca. 3 ha (ca. thirty-five *plethra*) are required to feed a household of five, with peasant farms of ca. 4–6 ha a norm in many pre-modern societies.[58] In practice, however, the size of a family's holdings changed according to fortune. The Greek system of partible inheritance tended to fragment holdings (Dem. 43.19); scattered ownership was likely the norm at Athens (Lys. 7.24; Dem. 42.4–5).[59]

TYPES OF CULTIVATORS

Advocates of both the extensive and intensive cultivation models agree that, in practice, farmers adopted a range of choices according to circumstance.[60] Halstead has emphasised that, in making such choices, 'the farmer is aiming at a moving target with a weapon of gradually

---

[51] Jameson 1977–8, 128; Burford Cooper 1977, 172.   [52] Osborne 1988; Papazarkadas 2011.
[53] Burford 1993, 20–7; Howe 2008, 89–93.   [54] McHugh 2017, 39–40.
[55] Burford 1993, 34.
[56] Burford Cooper 1977, 163, 168–9; Hanson 1999, 106–24; Morris 2000, 111–13.
[57] See Burford Cooper 1977, 168–9, with critique at Foxhall 1992, 156.
[58] Gallant 1991, 82–6 and fig. 4.7.
[59] Burford Cooper 1977, 164–5; Burford 1993, 56, 58, 119; McHugh 2017, 18–19. Larger tracts of plain-land in northern Greece may have been an exception: Burford 1993, 72.
[60] Isager and Skydsgaard 1995, 112–14; cf. McHugh 2017, 42–3.

shifting calibre' i.e. changing household needs versus available labour.[61] Plot size, wealth, and distance to fields represent other key variables. Three analytic types of ancient farmers can arguably be discerned from the evidence.

Middling Farmers: ca. Four to Ten Hectares

These 'hoplite', 'middling', or 'yeoman' farmers correspond to the Solonic *zeugitai* at Athens (Arist. [*Ath. Pol.*] 7.3–4). Hesiod's farm falls into this type.[62] Comparative evidence suggests that ca. five hectares of land is the threshold for keeping draft animals, and that ca. eight hectares of land are required to sustain a typical household with biennial fallow.[63] Middling farmers would have farmed the land themselves, perhaps utilising one or more slaves. They could practise extensive agriculture but could also intensify if needed: bringing marginal land under cultivation, increasing labour inputs (soil preparation, manuring, weeding), and practising mixed farming.[64] Livestock would be kept in smaller flocks, of ca. fifty animals or fewer.[65] The *autourgos* (self-employed) farmer in the sources seems to encompass this type, and those poorer (Pl. *Rep.* 8.565a; Eur. *Or.* 918–20; Xen. *Oec.* 5.3–4; Men. *Dys.* 369–70).[66]

Large Landowners: ca. Ten Hectares and Above

Foxhall suggests that each of the thousand wealthiest Athenians owned twenty to fifty hectares of land, and the next thousand ten to twenty hectares.[67] These roughly correspond to the top two Solonic classes, the *pentakosiomedimnoi* (five-hundred-measure-men) and *hippeis* (cavalrymen). The largest known single plot at Athens belonged to Phainippus (forty-five hectares); other large tracts belonged to Timesius (ca. sixteen hectares) and Lysimachus (ca. nine hectares).[68] Ischomachus's large farm in the *Oeconomicus* is of this type. Ischomachus has a slave workforce under the direction of a bailiff (Xen. *Oec.* 12.2, 13.1–4), and Adeimantus' farm in Thasos was farmed *in absentia* in this manner (*IG* I[3] 436.44). However, free labour could be added during peaks. Large

---

[61] Halstead 1987, 85.   [62] Burford 1993, 87; Hanson 1999, 101–6.
[63] Jameson 1977–8, 131; Halstead 1987, 84; Hodkinson 1988, 39; Osborne 2010, 95.
[64] See Jameson 1977–8, 128–9; see McHugh 2017, 25–7 for literature on terracing.
[65] Hodkinson 1988, 62.   [66] Burford 1993, 168–72.   [67] Foxhall 1992, 156–7.
[68] Burford 1993, 69.

landowners farmed for profit as well as their own needs, storing and selling grain, olive oil, firewood, and other produce.[69] Pericles' man of business sold surplus on the market (Plut. *Per.* 16.3–5), and Hagnias' estate held over 1,000 olive trees, far above household needs (Dem. 43.69). The rich were also more likely to have large flocks and herds under the care of herdsmen, moving to uplands annually. One Euboulus from third-century Orchomenus had 220 large and 1,000 small livestock (*SEG* 29.439). The *Oeconomicus* implies that large landowners normatively practised extensive agriculture (Xen. *Oec.* 16.10–15). Intensification was however still possible, particularly if slave labour was housed close to fields.

Poorer Households: ca. One to Three Hectares

Pliny famously quotes Manius Curtius' saying in the Roman period, that 'anyone for whom seven *iugera* is insufficient is a dangerous citizen' (*HN* 18.4; equal to ca. twenty *plethra* or 1.8 ha). It has been suggested that ca. two hectares can support an average household 'if worked by hand'.[70] Comparative data suggests that ca. 2.5 to 3 ha is the threshold for subsistence, and that those with less survive by borrowing and taking on external work.[71] With small plots and mouths to feed, struggling farmers would naturally desire to intensify. Other options include resource-sharing (labour or animal exchanges; Hes. *Op.* 451) or hiring out as day labour (Xen. *Hier.* 6.10; Dem. 18.51; Ar. *Vesp.* 711–12).[72] Smallholders could also seek to rent or lease additional land. Any animals kept were likely to have been grazed on nearby fallow or scrubland, providing manure, milk, and cheese year-round.[73]

DIVERSIFICATION, STORAGE, AND MARKETS

To some degree, local microclimates encouraged specialisation. Attica, with meagre rain, favoured barley over wheat (Theophr. *Hist. pl.* 8.8.2; *IG* II² 1672). Ionia and the coast of Asia Minor are well suited for vines.[74] However, subsistence farmers would arguably have aimed to diversify, to reduce vulnerability to endemic crop failure caused by high climate variability.[75] Diversification additionally exploited the fact that tasks

---

[69] Osborne 2010, ch. 6; Foxhall 2007, 38–42, 183.   [70] Halstead 1987, 84.
[71] Gallant 1991, 82–6.   [72] See McHugh 2017, 38–9 with literature.
[73] Hodkinson 1988, 48–51.   [74] Burford 1993, 75.   [75] Garnsey 1988, 8–17.

relating to viticulture and oleiculture are spread more evenly across the year.[76] The aim of producing a 'normal surplus', and the storage of at least a year's reserve, may have been a household norm (Arist. [*Oec.*] 1348b15–22).[77] Large man-sized jars for long-term storage (*pithoi*) found at a range of sites, holding ca. 800–900 litres of produce, seem to support this notion.[78]

Even poorer households must have participated in the market to obtain everyday items (Arist. *Pol.* 1257a5–35).[79] Roads with wheel ruts for carts provided connectivity at the local level.[80] Many cities had a fixed marketplace in the civic centre (the agora) and, at Athens, in the outlying villages (demes) as well.[81] Temporary stalls at regular religious festivals provided further opportunities for sale. Merchants (*emporioi*) specialised in long-distance trade, though the sale of grain was often regulated. Sicily and the Black Sea were known for cereals; the northern climate zone in turn could not grow olives. Wine amphorae from Chios, the Chalcidice, Lesbos, Thasos, and Samos have been found in shipwrecks and settlements across the Greek world, indicating the popularity of those vintages.[82] The state itself could be an important source of demand: the Greater Panathenaia festival at Athens required over 2,000 large amphorae of oil (ca. 80,000 litres) every four years.[83]

NUCLEATED OR DISPERSED SETTLEMENT?

In pre-war modern Greece, farmers lived in centralised hamlets or villages rather than on isolated farms. Nucleated settlement precludes 'the possibility of widespread cereal/pulse rotation', one of the keys to intensification.[84] By the archaic period, both first-order sites (urban centres) and second-order sites (villages and hamlets) had emerged across Greece, forming the various poleis (city-states).[85] At Athens, the polis and deme centres were key to civic life.[86] The debate over settlement thus revolves around the question of whether third-order sites – isolated towers, buildings, and other structures scattered across the

---

[76] Jameson 1977–8, 129, 139.   [77] Gallant 1991, 94–8; Garnsey 1999, 24–8.
[78] See McHugh 2017, 58, table 3.1; Gallant 1991, 96.   [79] Lewis 2018b, 189–91.
[80] Pikoulas 2007, 86; McHugh 2017, 144–6.   [81] Bresson 2016b, 236–8.
[82] Möller 2007, 364; Bresson 2016b, 126–7.   [83] von Reden 2007a, 405–6; Shear 2003, 102–3.
[84] Halstead 1987, 82.
[85] Snodgrass 1981, 33–40; Jameson, Runnels, and van Andel 1994, 254, 374–5; Mee and Forbes 1997, 60, 66–7.
[86] Osborne 1985; Jones 2004.

landscape – were occupied seasonally or permanently, if at all.[87] In Osborne's words: 'is it a farm?'[88]

The epigraphic evidence is inconclusive. At Athens, the *horoi* and *Rationes Centesimarum* both contain the term *chorion kai oikia* (land and house), implying farmland with an associated house or structure.[89] The Attic *stelai* list *oikiai* amongst farm property of the *hermokopidai*.[90] Additionally, a number of leases identify *oikiai* on rural land.[91] These evidence, however, cannot prove that such buildings were inhabited, since they may indicate field structures used to process and store produce and equipment.[92]

Rural sites potentially associated with farming include large buildings with attached towers, courtyard, storerooms, oil presses, cisterns, and threshing floors; smaller single towers or buildings with two or more rooms; and more rudimentary structures (shacks).[93] Large sites often follow the pattern of *oikia, pyrgos, aule* (living quarters, tower, and courtyard) given in Demosthenes' description of the farm raided by Euergus and Mnesiboulus (Dem. 47.56). The Vari house follows this pattern.[94] Domestic ceramic assemblages at large sites can include cooking ware, fine tableware (such as salt cellars and drinking cups), transport and storage ware, and other items such as coins, agricultural tools, and loom weights.[95] These finds indicate the sites were actively occupied, and potentially inhabited at least seasonally. Single towers with associated agricultural buildings and equipment, and other free-standing towers, have been found in southern Attica, the Argolid, and elsewhere.[96] Such towers may have had defensive and agricultural functions and housed slaves.

Estimates based on field survey in the southern Argolid, Keos, Methana, and Boeotia suggest that between two-thirds and three-quarters of the populations of those regions lived in nucleated settlements in the classical to Hellenistic periods.[97] However, in smaller poleis such habitation may still lie relatively close to fields. Ultimately, despite ample evidence for activity at and occupation of third-order sites, the degree to which they were inhabited remains an open question.

---

[87] Osborne 1987, 56–62; Jameson 1994; McHugh 2017, ch. 3.   [88] Osborne 2010, ch. 7.
[89] Jones 2004, 24; Lambert 1997, 226.   [90] Pritchett 1953; Pritchett and Pippin 1956, 261–9.
[91] Jones 2004, 30; McHugh 2017, 49.   [92] Mendoni 1994, 150.   [93] Mendoni 1994, 156.
[94] Jones, Graham, and Sackett 1973.   [95] McHugh 2017, 57–60, 69–70, with references.
[96] Young 1956; Jameson, Runnels, and van Andel 1994, 248–50, appendix A; Lohmann 1992; Morris and Papadopoulos 2005; McHugh 2017, 60–73.
[97] McHugh 2017, 32–3, with references.

AGRICULTURAL LABOUR

Who farmed the land? Agricultural labour can be analysed on a scale of dependency, ranging from slaves and slave-like dependent populations such as the Spartan helots, to free hired labour and members of the citizen household.[98] Scholars debate about the degree to which Greek agriculture – particularly at Athens – relied upon chattel slaves.[99] Jameson and Lewis suggest that middling farmers would regularly have been slaveowners, and Osborne that even those less fortunate would 'rarely have had no slave at all'.[100] Wood argues for a more egalitarian Athens with fewer slaves amongst the hoplite and poorer classes. Hanson's position is somewhat in between.[101]

The Attic orators assume that all citizen jurors, rich and poor, own slaves (Dem. 45.86; Lys. 5.5). Even the poor man of Lysias' speech *On the State Dole to the Invalid* suggests that it would not be unreasonable for him to own a slave 'if able' (Lys. 24.6). These statements may however be merely rhetorical. Some of the *hermo-kopidai* (wealthy Athenians accused to have been involved in the mutilation of the Hermes in 415) had at least one to sixteen slaves each, and Diogenes Laertius claims that various philosophers each owned eight to thirteen slaves (Diog. Laert. 5.11–16, 51–74). Slaveholding characters in Aristophanes' plays own two to eight, or more, slaves each.[102] Ninety-five slaveowners can be identified in the lists of Athenian ship crews from the late Peloponnesian war (*IG* I[3] 1032). Up to seven owned at least three slaves, up to twelve at least two, and the remainder at least one.[103] On the whole, 'the trend wherein slave ownership dwindles as we descend farther down the wealth spectrum is tolerably clear'.[104]

Greek agriculture never seems to have developed the chained slave-gangs of the Roman *latifundia* (large estates), even in contexts such as large-scale absentee farming by slaves at Rheneia in the third century.[105] However, an increase in slave use from the fifth and fourth centuries may indicate intensification at Chios and elsewhere (Thuc. 8.40.2). Morris and Papadopoulos have argued that towers were used for intensification, with slaves quartered and locked overnight together with equipment and produce.[106]

---

[98] Jameson 1992.   [99] See useful summaries at Fisher 2001, 39–47; Lewis 2018b, 180–3.
[100] Osborne 2010, 89; Jameson 1977–8, 132–41; Lewis 2018b, 183–93.
[101] Wood 1988, 50–80; Hanson 1999, 63–70.   [102] Lewis 2018b, 185.
[103] Osborne 2010, 88–9; Garlan 1988, 166; Lewis 2018b, 171–2.   [104] Lewis 2018b: 172.
[105] Osborne 1987, 71.   [106] Morris and Papadopoulos 2005, 184–200.

Sparta, Thessaly, Crete, Argos, and other cities had dependent classes, who were 'between free men and slaves' (Poll. 3.83). Of these, the Spartan helots are the best known. In the early archaic period, the helots were reduced to a serf-like form of intercommunal servitude. The helots surrendered a 'long-established rent' (*apophora*; Plut. *Mor.* 239e) to their Spartan masters; Tyrtaeus implies this was 'full half the fruit their ploughed land produced' (West, *IE²* fr. 6). Historically, 50 per cent sharecropping has been a common tenancy arrangement, and Hodkinson suggests that this is the best way to understand the helot–Spartiate relationship.[107]

Finally, free labour was available via seasonal day labour, exchanges with neighbours, or from one's own household (cf. Hes. *Op.* 349–51, 453–4).[108] Ethnography strongly suggests that women of sub-elite households worked alongside menfolk during agricultural peaks, particularly during reaping and winnowing.[109]

ANIMAL HUSBANDRY

Domesticated animals filled several needs in the Greek world. Horses, cattle, and flocks formed the traditional means for Greek elites to display wealth, power, and status.[110] Horses, requiring valuable grassland, were a luxury.[111] Alcibiades openly argues that his lavish entry of seven chariot teams in the Olympic games should give him the right of command (Thuc. 6.16.1–4). The second-richest Solonic class in Athens, the *hippeis*, each maintained a horse for cavalry service (Xen. *Oec.* 3.10). Sparta and Thessaly were known for horse- and cattle-breeding (Pl. *Alc.* 1.122d–e; Xen. *Lac.* 6.3; Hom. *Il.* 18.573–6) and Arcadia, Pan's homeland of legend, for sheep (Pind. *Ol.* 6.100, 169).

Draft animals – oxen, mules, and donkeys – were more widely owned and used for ploughing and transport. Despite Aristotle's assertion that 'the ox is the poor man's slave' (Arist. *Pol.* 1252b12), draft animals required fodder and the right type of land to be viable. Sheep and goats could provide wool, milk, and cheese, and (if slaughtered) meat and hide (Dem. 47; Isae. 6.33; Athen. 402b–e).[112] Goats are particularly suited to Greek ecology, able to survive on the ubiquitous sloped scrubland and on waste agricultural products (cf. Ael. *NA* 16.32).

---

[107] Hodkinson 1992.   [108] Jameson 1977–8, 131–2.
[109] Jameson 1977–8, 137–8; Halstead 2014, ch. 3.   [110] Howe 2008, 29–31.
[111] Hodkinson 1988, 64; Burford 1993, 72–4; Howe 2008, 32–3, 108–18.
[112] Howe 2008, 51–2.

Larger flocks of fifty or more were more likely to have been transhumant.[113] The need for pasture could lead to border grazing conflicts which sometimes escalated into full-blown war.[114]

CONCLUSION

The agricultural economy remains fundamental for understanding ancient Greek society. Debates over the character of Greek agriculture look set to continue, particularly around three loci: market/subsistence orientation, intensive/extensive practices, and slave/free labour. In general, the view of greater intensification from the fifth century, with increased specialisation and market participation, a greater degree of mixed farming, and stronger rural occupation has gained traction in the last decades, with the 'peasant subsistence' model fighting a rearguard action. The longevity of these debates reflects Cartledge's assertion that they are merely two sides of a coin: a 70 per cent subsistence economy and 30 per cent market-oriented one (my figures are purely notional and indicative, though significantly changed from Cartledge's).[115] Above all, local Greek agriculturalists adapted strategically according to their needs, environment, and resources. Fresh evidence would help invigorate these debates; possible future directions include further aggregation and comparison of survey data and further critical use of ethnography and comparative data to model labour-hours, yields, and productivity.

Further Reading

On agriculture in general, see Sallares 1991, Burford 1993, and Isager and Skydsgaard 1995. On olives, see Foxhall 2007. For risk and the household life cycle, see Gallant 1991. On slavery, see Jameson 1977–8, 1992; Fisher 2001; Osborne 2010, ch. 5, and Lewis 2018b. On settlement, see Osborne 2010, ch. 7 and McHugh 2017. For animal husbandry, Hodkinson 1988 and Howe 2008. On Sparta, see Hodkinson 2000. For ethnography, see Halstead 2014. On modelling grain production, see Garnsey 1988, ch. 6 and Jew forthcoming.

---

[113] Hodkinson 1988, 55–60.   [114] Howe 2008, ch. 4; Burford Cooper 1977, 172–3.
[115] Cartledge 2002, 13–14.

14: THE NON-AGRICULTURAL ECONOMY: ARTISANS, TRADERS, WOMEN, AND SLAVES

Daniel Jew

INTRODUCTION

Agriculture was the primary means of making a living in ancient Greece. However, the 'good life' within the polis also required a range of artisanal work such as building, weaving, and shoemaking (Pl. *Rep.* 369a–371e; Arist. *Pol.* 1252a10–35, 1256b30). Scholars debate the scale of the non-agricultural economy, which included primary extraction, secondary craft production, and the tertiary sector of trade, goods, and services.

Two central questions help diagnose conditions within the non-agricultural economy, even if neither can be answered conclusively from current evidence. The first, foundational question is that of the total size of the market economy. Agricultural produce and basic crafts such as textiles and ceramics could be internally consumed by households or sold at market. The older view, advocated most strongly by Moses Finley, envisioned an autarchic, subsistence-based peasant society dominated by agriculture (Chapter 1, this volume).[1] Trade and market exchange, mainly in luxury goods, formed a thin veneer, driven by a status-conscious elite for whom exchange was 'embedded' in social relations. This view has come under sustained challenge in the last twenty years, with a number of new studies emphasising the potential size of market exchange and its permeation across society (Chapters 8 and 15, this volume).[2]

A second, related question is that of the structure, organisation, and composition of craft, services, and trade. What proportion of the urban population made their primary living outside of agriculture, as

---

[1] Finley [1973] 1999; Cartledge 2002, 12–16; Launaro 2016.
[2] See Harris and Lewis 2016; Bresson 2016b.

opposed to simply living in the city whilst farming surrounding fields? And what civic statuses did business owners, operators, and workers hold? The fact that non-citizens, women, and slaves feature prominently within the non-agricultural workforce raises the significance of this aspect of the economy, in the sense that it encompasses the 'history from below' of often difficult-to-locate underclasses. This is in contrast to the study of agriculture, an activity which met the ideal of the male citizen elite.

EVIDENCE AND PROBLEMS

The evidence for crafts and trade is diffuse and potentially supports both the subsistence and market visions of the Greek economy, though there is an overall picture of increasing market connectivity by the end of the Hellenistic period (Chapter 5, this volume). Philosophical writing, law-court speeches, and Attic comedy provide some evidence for crafts. Key works include Plato's *Republic* (ca. 380 BCE), Aristotle's *Politics* (late fourth century), and Xenophon's treatise on household management, the *Oeconomicus* (ca. 362). A speech of Demosthenes describes the operation of slave workshops in some detail (Dem. 29). Additionally, Aristophanes' plays (425–388) portray a wide variety of trades and products.

Inscriptions and epigraphy form a second major group of sources. Relevant public records include laws and decrees, building accounts, public leases, and records of public financial transactions. Private curse tablets and votive dedications sometimes provide occupations.[3] Three sets of inscriptions deserve special mention. The first are the Attic Stelai.[4] The second are the detailed building accounts of religious sanctuaries, particularly the Parthenon (447–433) and the Erechtheion (409 to post-394), which at times list workers' names, tasks, demotics, payment, and status.[5] The third are the *phialai* inscriptions or 'Attic manumissions' (ca. 330–310).[6] These list the dedications of 413 metics or ex-slaves (freedmen); their exact status and dedicatory purpose are disputed.[7] Of these, 160 individuals (64 of whom are women) have listed occupations.

[3] Epitaphs, votives: Burford 1972, 170–2, 176–9. Curse tablets: Acton 2014, 9.
[4] See Chapter 13, this volume.
[5] *IG* i³ 436–51 (Parthenon); *IG* i³ 474–9 (Erechtheion). See Feyel 2006 on these, plus accounts at Eleusis, Delos, and Delphi.
[6] *IG* ii² 1553–78; Lewis 1959, 1968.
[7] Rosivach 1989; Cohen 2000, 152–3; Meyer 2010; Kennedy 2014, 126.

Archaeological finds form the final source for non-agricultural occupations. Surviving artisanal work from the classical world can range from entire monumental buildings and large cult statues to small tools and objects. Evidence for production includes pottery kilns, loom weights and spindle whorls for textiles, and casting pits for statues.[8] Finework is sometimes signed, allowing individual craftsmen to be identified.[9] Many objects, such as the Berlin Foundry Cup, depict craftsmen at work.[10]

Despite this seeming wealth, the surviving evidence is biased, with Athens heavily over-represented. Archaeological discoveries are impacted by dig locations and factors such as the low survival of wooden objects and textiles. From the fifth century, Athens became increasingly distinct from the rest of Greece due to its size, population, naval empire, silver mines, and strategic port. The fact that Lucius Mummius' legions sacked Corinth in 146, destroying vast numbers of civic inscriptions, compounds our over-reliance on an unrepresentative and exceptional Athens.

ELITE ATTITUDES TO CRAFT

No writings of Greek artisans survive, other than short dedications, signatures, epitaphs, and the rare epigram.[11] Elite male attitudes towards craft have thus tended to dominate modern views. The ideal Greek citizen worked his own family farm, also serving as a hoplite (Xen. *Oec.* 5.1, 7–8). In some cities, failure to own sufficient land might disqualify one from citizenship altogether (Arist. *Pol.* 1278a20–4). Xenophon contrasts the ideal citizen-hoplite-farmer with 'the so-called "banausic" occupations': those who live by such means are deemed effeminate and poor defenders of the city (*Oec.* 4.2–3). Similarly, Aristotle attributes a 'natural banausic-ness' to both slaves and barbarians, predisposing them to manual work (*Pol.* 1252a5–13). Conversely, 'the best-ordered city will not make the manual labourer (*banausos*) a citizen' (*Pol.* 1278a5). The Spartiates allegedly did not engage in craft at all (Plut. *Ages.* 26.4–5; Xen. *Lac.* 7.2). The attitude against craft was said to be least strong in Corinth (Hdt. 2.167). However, philosophical writers also admit, at least tacitly, that craftsmen were a necessity for the Greek way of life (Pl. *Rep.* 371e; Xen. *Lac.* 7.2, *Mem.* 2.7.6). Socrates himself may have been raised as a stonemason.[12]

---

[8] Acton 2014, 13, 15.   [9] Sapirstein 2013; Acton 2014, 14–15.

[10] Burford 1972, 71, 169; Acton 2014, 126, 137.

[11] Epigrams of Parrhasius: Ath. 12.62; Xen. *Mem.* 10.1–6. The *Canon* of Polyclitus is known from Galen and Euclid.

[12] This tradition depends on a late source: Diog. Laert. 2.19 (third century CE).

Occupations and Trades

Harris and Lewis have provided a partial catalogue of attested occupations in Athens. Harris lists 170 occupations from literary and epigraphic sources (500–250 BCE), which exclude public offices.[13] Lewis lists commodities given in Old Comedy, with 140 related occupations, such as 'potter' (*kerameus*) for the various ceramic trades.[14] The compilation of trades from Harris and Lewis, and a number of other sources, is shown in Tables 14.1 and 14.2.

The extant references to craft, trade, and service occupations are often informal and descriptive. 'Above all we must guard against the nominalist fallacy when counting occupations, that is, to make the mistake of assuming that each name must refer to a separate and distinct occupation' (E. M. Harris).[15] For instance, the terms 'leather-seller' (*byrsopoles*, Ar. *Eq.* 44), 'hide-tanner' (*skylodepses*, *IG* I³ 146), and 'leatherworker' (*skytotomos*, Aeschin. 1.97, also translatable as 'shoemaker') could all potentially have been used of the same person in antiquity. Other uses are clearly

Table 14.1 *Count of terms for roles and occupations in classical Athens, by sector*[a]

Agriculture and animal husbandry (29 terms): e.g. *ampelourgos* (vine-dresser), *georgos* (farmer), *keporos* (gardener), *skapheus* (ditch-digger), *aipolos* (goatherd), *onokomos* (ass-keeper), *polodamnes* (horse-breaker)

Primary extraction (8 terms): e.g. *hylotomos* (woodcutter), *metalleutes* (miner), *misthotos* (manual labourer)

Craft (106 terms): e.g. *khalkeus* (smith), *daktyliogluphos* (gem-engraver), *kerameus* (potter), *lithourgos* (stoneworker), *naupegos* (shipbuilder), *skylodepses* (hide-tanner), *skytotomos* (leatherworker or shoemaker), *xylourgos* (carpenter)

Retail and trade (77 terms): e.g. *elaipoles* (olives), *emporos* (merchant), *kreopoles* (butcher), *lykhnopoles* (lamps), *mageiros* (cook), *oinopoles* (wine), *pharmakopoles* (drugs and medicines), *sitopoles* (grain), *tarichopoles* (salt-fish)

Services (46 terms): e.g. *hypokrites* (reciter/actor), *didaskalos* (teacher), *porthmeus* (ferryman), *rhaptes* (clothes-mender), *trapezites* (banker)

[a] N of attested terms = 260. Some terms are listed under more than one sector; compiled from Brock 1994; Harris 2002b; 2014; Harris and Lewis 2016, 24 n. 123; Meyer 2010; Acton 2014, 277 n. 77; with references therein. Masculines/feminines of the same have been counted as a single term. Includes slave roles which would involve cash exchange if performed by a free person.

---

[13] Harris 2002b, 68.   [14] Harris and Lewis 2016, 24 n.123; Lewis 2016.
[15] Harris 2002b, 68; cf. Feyel 2006, 392–4.

Table 14.2 *Count of terms for attested womens' roles in the non-agricultural economy in classical Athens, by sector*[a]

Primary extraction (1): *phuganistria* (wood-gatherer)

Craft, textiles (6): *amorgantinos/erithos* (wool-worker), *akestria* (garment-sewer), *baptria* (dyer), *gnapheus* (fuller), *talasiourgos* (wool-weaver, or generic term for housewife)

Craft, other (5): *khrysotria* (gilder), ?*grapheus* (vase-painter), *murepsos* (perfume-maker), ?*lophopoie* (helmet-crest-maker), *skytotome* (shoemaker)

Retail, primary products (16): *alphitopoleteria* (barley-meal), *artopolis* (bread), *arouraia/lakhanopoletria* (vegetables), *gelgopolis* (garlic), *halopolis* (salt), *iskhadopolis* (dried figs), *kalamides* (reeds), *kodome/kodomeutria* (toasted grain), *lekithos* (gruel), *melitopolis* (honey), *myropolis* (perfume), *ospriopolis* (pulses), *sesamopolis* (sesame), *skandika* (herbs), *spermatopolis* (seed)

Retail, simple secondary products (2): *stephaneplokousia/stephanopolis* (garlands/wreaths), *tainiopolis* (ribbons)

Retail, complex secondary products (5): *kharitopolis* (charms), *demiourge* (confectioner), *himatiopolis* (clothes or cloaks), *libanotopolis* (incense), ?*pilopolis* (felt caps)

Retail, other (1): *kapelis* (generic term for vendor, or innkeeper)

Services (16): *aleiptria* (masseuse), *auletris* (flute-player), *balaneutria* (bath-manager), *hetaira/porne* (courtesan/prostitute), ?*iatria* (physician), *kitharistria/kitharodos* (kithara-player), *kommotria* (lady's maid), *maia* (midwife), *orkhestris* (dancer), *pandokeutria* (innkeeper), *plyntria* (clothes-washer), *psaltria* (harpist), *tamia* (housekeeper), *therapaina* (maidservant), *titthe* (wet-nurse), *trophos* (dry-nurse)

---

[a] N of attested terms = 53; conjectural feminine terms are indicated '?'

synonymous: the *skylodepses* and *byrsodepses* given in the inscription of *IG* II² 1576.5–6 are both simply tanners. Conversely, a 'jack of all trades' such as one Nicodamus at Delphi may be listed several times, under disparate roles.[16] The given roles are not necessarily full-time occupations; the woman portrayed in the *Lysistrata* (Ar. *Lys.* 735) did her wool-spinning within the household.

ECONOMIC SECTORS AND SPECIALISATION

The occupations attested can be analysed using the typology of primary, secondary, and tertiary sectors within economies, developed by Fisher, Clark, and Kuznets.[17] Agriculture, animal husbandry and fishing, and the

---

[16] See Feyel 2006, 333–5.

[17] Kuznets 1965. I use 'sector' here in a different sense from Harris 2002b, who uses 'sector' in the sense that Kuznets uses for different 'industries' (such as metalworking) within broad sectors.

raw extraction of natural resources can be considered primary occupations. Craft manufacture – in what we would term today cottage or artisanal trades – is secondary. Finally, retail and long-distance trade – the sale of both primary and manufactured products, and services where no actual goods are exchanged (such as dry-nursing) – form the tertiary sector.

A high level of specialisation within artisanal trades is evident from the sources, suggesting that larger, well-connected cities could support a heterogeneous tier of craftsmen. For instance, Demosthenes' knife-makers (*machairopoioi*, Dem 27.9. cf. Ar. *Av.* 442) were not just smiths, but ones who apparently specialised in making knives or swords. Harris argues that trades at Athens demonstrate a strong 'horizontal' specialisation, that is a strong diversity of roles within certain trades (cf. Xen. *Cyr.* 8.2.5).[18] On the other hand, there appears to have been little vertical specialisation – the hierarchical levels of management within a firm commonly seen in the modern world. One tier of supervision, by a slave foreman, seems to have been the structural limit (below, p. 217–8). The degree of possible local specialisation was ultimately driven by total market demand, including any external demand for exported goods.[19] Bulk or long-distance trade – the province of *kapeloi* (retailers), *emporoi* (traders), and *naukleroi* (shippers) – seems to have dealt primarily in agricultural goods, raw materials, textiles, and ceramics and higher-value luxury products such as dyes and perfumes.[20]

Barriers to Entry: Low- and High-Skilled Products

High skill requirements acted as barriers to entry for new producers and enabled differentiation of products within markets, including export markets.[21] Some trades, such as ceramics, produced valuable fineware requiring highly skilled (and potentially highly paid) artisans. But the same industry also produced coarser everyday commodities – the kind of basic clay pots that anyone could make. In the same vein, Aristotle contrasts disenfranchised and presumably low-skilled 'hired labourers' (*thetes*) within oligarchies, from wealthy, and thus enfranchised, 'artisans' (*technitai*, those with *techne* or artisanal skill; *Pol.* 1278a22–5).

The retail and trade sector can be similarly analysed: sale of primary produce, sale of simple secondary products that almost anyone could make, and sale of more complex crafted items. Plato distinguishes 'selling one's own products' (*autopolike* – implied to be more virtuous)

[18] Harris 2002b.   [19] Bresson 2016b, 343–7.
[20] On trade and networks, see ibid., chs. 13–14.   [21] Acton 2014, 41–3.

from 'selling others' produce' (*metabletike* – less so), with the latter called 'retailing' (*kapelike*) in the city (*Soph.* 223 c–d).[22] Plato's attitude likely reflects citizens' slant toward primary production, but the *autopolike/metabletike* distinction still provides a useful analytic, particularly in the case of women's attested retailing (below, p. 214–7).

THE THEORY OF THE FIRM: WORKSHOP SIZE AND THE HOUSEHOLD

Why did small workshops dominate the Greek world, despite the large number of occupations and high level of specialisation evident at Athens? One key reason must surely lie with the fact that the ancient Greek workshop was not a separate business entity. Instead, the household (*oikos*) formed the basic socio-economic unit of Greek society, organising labour towards both agricultural and non-agricultural ends (Xen. *Oec.* 7.33–42). Slaves and family members likely made textiles, pottery, and other objects in their spare time to meet household needs. Some workshops (*ergasteria*) were either based within or near the home, for example, in a side-shed. Most trades required only a spare room or courtyard, simple tools, and readily constructed kilns or furnaces.[23] Two workshops of Philocrates in 342/1 lay adjacent to his house in Athens but were listed separately in the confiscation register from which they are known.[24] Nevertheless, such workshops were still extensions of the household. There was no legal distinction between an owner and his business, similar in this respect to a modern-day sole proprietorship. The items listed in Demosthenes' inheritance intermingle workshop inventory (e.g. raw materials) with possessions of the household proper.[25]

Even workshops physically separate from the household seem often to have been occupied by a sole artisan and a handful of slave assistants or apprentices.[26] During the construction of the Erechtheion, the fluting of each eastern column was subcontracted to different teams. Most teams consisted of four to seven individuals: a citizen, his slaves, and any additional members.[27] It seems likely that each team was a pre-existing business concern at Athens, perhaps with ad hoc additions.[28] This pattern of small teams permeates the building accounts at Athens

[22] Millett 1990, 185.   [23] Acton 2014, 14.   [24] Osborne 1985, 52–3.
[25] Cohen 1992, 65; Harris 2002b, 82–3.
[26] Bresson 2016b, 188. Apprenticing: Burford 1972, 88–90.
[27] *IG* I³ 476; Feyel 2006, 31–53, 324.   [28] Acton 2014, 211–12.

and elsewhere. The largest known workshop at Athens is that of Lysias and Polemarchus, who claimed to have had 700 shields and 120 slaves confiscated by the Thirty Tyrants in 404 (Lys. 12.8, 19). Pasion owned a shield workshop with an estimated sixty slaves (ca. 360–80), and the father of the orator Demosthenes owned two workshops with fifty-two or fifty-three slaves (Dem. 36.4, 27.9). But these are the very largest we hear of.[29] Outside of major cities like Athens, Corinth, Syracuse, Alexandria, and Hellenistic Antioch, average workshops must have been much smaller.

Coase's modern theory of the firm suggests that business concerns will expand when it is cheaper to internalise a transaction, rather than securing it externally via the market.[30] The fact that most Greek workshops were limited to a size of two to six members thus strongly suggests that it was not efficient to expand, through vertical integration, to reach the larger sizes common after the industrial revolution (Chapter 8, this volume). For instance, a certain Artemis, a gilder, worked alongside her husband Dionysius, the helmet-maker (*Syll.*[3] 1177 = *IG* III[3] 69.4); their business could evidently sustain both at once. However, occupations such as glue-boiler (*kollepsos*; *IG* II[2] 1558.10–13) suggest that specialised functions were often best outsourced. It may have been more feasible for a woodworking operation to buy glue on the market rather than to expand to support another full-time member. Another potential limitation was the labour market, since only poorer citizens, metics, or slaves would occupy certain craft and trade roles (see below, p. 214–8).

NOTABLE TRADES

The following brief survey helps to provide a sense of the major clusters of trades and markets. These clusters potentially indicate levels of market demand and networks of trade at the local and regional level, which permitted a degree of specialisation, particularly within the cities indicated.

Mining

The Laurium district in south-east Attica produced an estimated twenty tons of silver per year in the fifth and parts of the fourth century, with

---

[29] Davies 2007a, 347–8; Acton 2014, 28, 269; Lewis 2018b, 171, 177–8.
[30] See related analysis of Roman manufacture in Hawkins 2012.

a workforce of 10,000 to 30,000.[31] The mines were operated though leases to private individuals. Silver was minted into the famous Athenian owl tetradrachms by public slaves (Ar. *Vesp.* 1007 schol.), at a rate of over a million coins per year.[32] Similarly, in the Hellenistic period, much of Macedonia's world-beating wealth came from the gold and silver mines of Mount Pangaeum.

Public Building

Monumental building was one of the largest-scale and most expensive craft undertakings in the ancient Greek world, underwritten and organised by the polis. Public projects and sanctuaries often had civic commissions for construction and maintenance (the *epistatai* and *teichopoioi* at Athens), with detailed accounts.[33] Work was subcontracted out to independent teams by a chief architect.

Quarrying

Vast quantities of marble were required for monumental building. The Parthenon required an estimated 100,000 tons of stone.[34] Quarrying was likely performed by slave teams, but it was semi-skilled or even skilled work. Blocks, columns, and statuary were often trimmed to rough shape at the quarry.[35] Transportation of blocks for public building at Athens was contracted out to small teams of private oxen-and-wagon owners, representing spare capacity after harvest.[36]

Marble and Bronze Statuary

Large marble or bronze statues were commissioned by the city (e.g. *IG* II² 555), often dedicated to gods or goddesses (*IG* II² 3109) or as honorific statues. Private statuary, such as grave monuments, also survives. Famous sculptors include Phidias, Polyclitus, Myron, and Praxiteles.[37] There is strong evidence that districts near the Athenian agora housed smithies, marble workshops, and other related trades.[38]

---

[31] Acton 2014, 117; see also below, on slaves. This section owes a large debt to Acton.
[32] Ibid., 133.   [33] Ibid., 205–15; Feyel 2006.   [34] Acton 2014, 205–6.
[35] Burford 1972, 76; on slaves, Acton 2014, 206 and Harris 2002b.
[36] See references at Acton 2014, 207.   [37] Ibid., 218–19.   [38] Young 1951; Mattusch 1977.

Pottery and Ceramics

Greek ceramics were ubiquitous and ranged from commissioned fine-ware by celebrity painters such as Euthymides to undifferentiated every-day coarseware.[39] Products include wine cups, cooking pots, storage jars, chamber pots, terracotta lamps, and roof tiles. The use of maker's stamps and signatures have allowed art historians and archaeologists to trace workshops, painters, and schools.[40] Athens had a *kerameikos* (ceramics) quarter north-west of the agora – the name survives to this day.[41] Corinth similarly had an active ceramics district from the seventh to third centuries.[42] A typical workshop may have had four to six workers operating a single kiln.

Leatherwork

Animal hide yielded a surprisingly wide range of everyday implements, including shoes and sandals, wineskins, sword sheaths, oar-port covers, and leather leads.[43] Tanning was smelly, unpleasant work; as such the tanning district often lay outside the city (e.g. the Cydathon district at Athens: *IG* I^3 227).

Metalwork

Metal items ranged from ship's rams and anchors (Diod. Sic. 20.9; *IG* II^2 1609.114) to weapons, armour, agricultural implements, household utensils, ornaments, and jewellery.[44] At Athens, metalsmiths seem to have specialised in one type of ore, such as gold, silver, iron, or bronze. The state was a potential source of business: Dionysius of Syracuse was said to have stockpiled 140,000 shields and 14,000 hoplite cuirasses (Diod. Sic. 14.43.2), and Athens provided a shield and spear to all youths in military service (Arist. [*Ath. Pol.*] 32.4).

Woodwork and Shipbuilding

Wood was a primary material with a wide range of uses. Crafted items include furniture, tools, and musical instruments, with a wide range of

---

[39] Acton 2014, ch. 3.   [40] Sapirstein 2013.
[41] Bresson 2016b, 190. Workshops relocated south in the fourth century.   [42] Stillwell 1948.
[43] Acton 2014, 166–8.   [44] See ibid., 126–45 and table 4.1.

related specialisations. Athens also had a large shipbuilding industry, with 340 triremes built by 354 and 57 different naval architects (chief shipbuilders) listed from 360–320 (*IG* II² 1612–32).[45] Corinth, Corcyra, Syracuse, and other major cities also had shipbuilding programmes.

Textiles

Wool was the most common textile material in Greece.[46] Cities along the wool route from Asia Minor to Greece, such as Cyprus, Megara, and Corinth, became known for their textiles.[47] Milesian wool was particularly famous (Ar. *Lys.* 729) and concentrated finds of looms, weights, and spindles at Olynthus may indicate market-oriented production.[48] Clothesmaking involved scouring wool, carding, spinning into thread, weaving, fulling, and, if desired, dyeing. The first and last few steps were perhaps done outside the home by commercial enterprises (cf. dyer, *bapheus*; Pl. *Rep.* 429d; Lys. 32.20), but the vast majority of other textile work was done by women in the household.

CITIZENS, RESIDENT ALIENS, AND THE NON-AGRICULTURAL ECONOMY

Elite and sub-elite citizens, and resident aliens, played contrasting structural roles within the non-agricultural economy. Elite citizens might own business concerns and invest in maritime trade; poorer citizens were more likely to be directly involved. Resident aliens probably made up the bulk of those involved in craft and trade in most cities; some were ex-slaves (freedmen) originally purchased as labour.

Elite Citizens

Greek social attitudes towards banausic work and self-sufficiency constrained the ways in which citizens could conduct, or associate themselves with, wage labour, crafts, and trade. Rich citizens could however still own productive slaves and *ergasteria*. Attic comedy and forensic speeches reveal that a favourite form of invective was the insinuation that the opponent was a common, banausic tradesman. Cleon is thus accused of being a tanner, and Cleophon a lyre-maker (Ar. *Eq.* 129–35;

---

[45] Burford 1972, 64. [46] Acton 2014, 147–62. [47] Bresson 2016b, 353–8; Acton 2014, 150.
[48] Cahill 2002.

Andoc. 1.46). Despite allegedly owning 1,000 mining slaves, Nicias is never attacked in this manner but is instead depicted as one of the *kaloi kagathoi* (leading gentlemen). Scholars suggest that this distinction lay with the fact that Cleon and Cleophon (or their fathers) were at some point directly involved in their workshops.[49] Nicias, on the other hand, earned a form of passive income, not dissimilar to renting out land, by leasing out his slaves (Xen. *Vect.* 4.14). Similarly, Demosthenes Senior had 7,000 dr. passively invested in maritime loans (Dem. 27.11), but at least twelve other Athenians, perhaps of less elite status, are known to have been more directly involved in maritime trade.[50]

Middling and Poorer Citizens

Many less-fortunate citizens must have made their living from craft and trade. In Xenophon's *Memorabilia*, Socrates states that the Athenian citizens' assembly is made up of fullers, shoemakers, builders, smiths, farmers, merchants, and 'traffickers in the marketplace who think of nothing but buying cheap and selling dear' (3.7.6). The building accounts of the Erechtheion and at Eleusis show twenty-two and twenty-nine citizen artisans respectively, comprising 23 per cent and 34 per cent of those with identifiable statuses.[51] In 403 BCE, 5,000 Athenian citizens out of an estimated 30,000 owned no land at all (Dion. Hal. 34). Since the long-term employment of one citizen by another was seen as disreputably close to slavery (Isae. 5.39; Isoc. 14.48; Xen. *Mem.* 2.8.3–4), such citizens had limited work options. The main possibilities were renting farmland, seasonal day labour, or engaging in craft or trade.[52]

Resident Aliens

Many cities had a sizeable number of non-citizen residents, both Greek and non-Greek. These residents were called *synoikoi, paroikoi, metoikoi* (metics, the term used at Athens), and various other names.[53] Such non-resident statuses are attested in at least seventy classical and Hellenistic cities.[54] Metics and freedmen formed the natural mercantile class of the polis, filling craft and trade occupations. It also seems natural that

---

[49] Burford 1972, 156–7. [50] Reed 2003, 27–8. [51] Feyel 2006, 320–8.
[52] At Athens, public payments could provide supplementary income.
[53] Whitehead 1984; Akrigg 2015. [54] Whitehead 1984, 47.

freedmen, trained in a skilled trade as a slave, would continue to earn their living through the same after manumission. This was the case with the banker Phormio (Dem. 45.71–2).[55] We know of no Greek city where non-citizens had the usual right to own land; this fact alone implies that most resident aliens made their living from craft and trade. Some artisans involved in public building at Delos were given a monthly or annual food-and-clothing allowance in 282–279, and others tax exemptions. These allowances, together with the system of fines for incomplete work at Delphi, suggest that there was a mobile force of itinerant craftsmen in Greece who plied their trade wherever needed.[56]

Athens is estimated to have had a total of 20,000 adult male metics in the fourth century. Foreigners could apply for metic status after one month's residence by enrolling in an Attic deme. This process required the patronage of a citizen protector (*prostates*); failure to enrol could lead to prosecution and sale into slavery. Manumitted slaves (freedmen) were often granted metic status at Athens, with the former master as *prostates*. Freedmen retained some obligations to their ex-masters and at Athens could be prosecuted, and re-enslaved, for failing to adhere to these.[57] Such obligations seem to have become increasing common across Greece in the Hellenistic period.[58] At Athens, metics were subject to a poll tax of 12 dr. per year (the *metoikon*; 6 dr. for women) and the war tax (*eisphora*, Chapter 18, this volume). Metics were also liable to provide liturgies and military service according to wealth (Thuc. 2.31.2, 7.63; Xen. *Vect.* 2.1).

WOMEN AND THE NON-AGRICULTURAL ECONOMY

Women of various statuses inhabited the Greek polis, ranging from the family members of adult male citizens to metics and slaves. All three groups were invariably bound to the non-agricultural economy, either through the imperative for home textile production or through retail and services. Within these roles, women constituted a significant part of the non-agricultural workforce, but they are often only intermittently visible in the literary and archaeological sources.

Table 14.2 lists, to my knowledge, all extant non-agricultural roles of women attested for classical Athens. Like Table 14.1 it is not a count of total source-mentions of each term (for which *talasiourgos*, wool-weaver would win handily) but is rather a count of discrete terms. The

---

[55] Cohen 2000, 137.   [56] Feyel 2006, 336–8.
[57] The *dike apostasiou* procedure: Zelnick-Abramovitz 2005, 274–92.
[58] The *paramone* agreements: Garlan 1988, 81–2; Fisher 2001, 68.

distribution is somewhat random: for instance, women must have sold many types of produce apart from those which have survived in the sources. Even so, a number of trends are apparent: the majority of craft roles attested are textile-related; retail skews toward primary and simple products; and service roles tend to be household- or entertainment-related.

In Demosthenes 57, Euxitheus' opponent is able to cast aspersions on his citizenship simply by revealing that his mother had worked as a wet-nurse (*titthe*, 57.35). For citizen women, 'paid work ... [was seen as] degrading, embarrassing and only acceptable as a temporary expedient under the compulsion of poverty'.[59] The respectable woman of the house was expected to 'remain indoors' and 'toil constantly' to manage its labour, economic outputs, food, and stores (Xen. *Oec.* 7.29–37; cf. Lys. 4.7–9, Pl. *Leg.* 7.805e). However, women lower on the social scale must have had a much closer relationship to the agora.[60]

Penelope's weaving work in the *Odyssey* exemplifies her womanly virtue (19.137–50; cf. Xen. *Mem.* 3.9.11, Pl. *Alc.* 1.126e). Spinning and weaving for the household must have occupied much of the time of women of all statuses. Textiles were an excellent store of wealth (Arist. [*Oec.*] 9.3.6; Aeschin. 1.97 schol.), and the *Oeconomicus* suggests that teaching women slaves how to spin will double their value (Xen. *Oec.* 7.41, cf. 9.8–9). In the *phialai* inscriptions, fifty-one out of sixty-four women are described as wool-workers (*talasiourgoi*).[61] This characterisation may arise from a conventional formula for names and simply denote that they were housewives.[62] If true, this reinforces the idea that the two roles were virtually synonymous. On the whole, the magnitude of women's contribution to the economy through textiles went underrecognised in scholarship until relatively recently.[63]

A few pieces of evidence indicate a minority of women artisans; such women most likely practised in the context of household businesses.[64] Artemis the gilder has been mentioned above (p. 209).[65] We also know of two women shoemakers (*IG* ii² 1578.5, *IG* iii 12.2) and a perfume-maker, perhaps a slave (*IG* ii² 11688). The Caputi Hydria contains the only extant depiction of a woman vase-painter in the classical period, though another piece

[59] Brock 1994, 336.   [60] Harris 2014, 200.   [61] *IG* ii² 1553–78. See Kennedy 2014, ch. 5.
[62] Rosivach 1989, 369–70. See Acton 2014, 277; Wrenhaven 2009 and Kennedy 2014, 131–2 for other interpretations, particularly on *talasiourgos* as euphemism for 'prostitute'.
[63] Pomeroy 1994, 61–5.   [64] Acton 2014, 276–8; Venit 1988.
[65] The dating of the inscription for Artemis and Dionysius may be Hellenistic.

shows a female helmet-crester.[66] Pliny mentions three women wall-painters in the Hellenistic period (*NH* 35.147). Overall, the evidence indicates that men dominated artisanal trades.

Gathering flora and engaging in crafts such as making floral wreaths and garlands, would have provided a ready route to income for the needy (Ar. *Thesm.* 446–58). In 329/8, one Artemis of Piraeus was contracted to supply reed baskets worth 70 dr. at Eleusis. Another Thettale supplied felt caps (*IG* II² 1672.1.64, 70–1). Euxitheus and his mother sold ribbons (Dem. 57.31). The accounts at Epidaurus and inscriptions at Delos similarly mention a handful of women involve in handmade crafts.[67] Of the twenty-four retail roles of women in Table 14.2 all but six (75 per cent) are of primary produce or simple crafts.

The services listed in Table 14.2 tend to fall into two categories, relating either to the household or to entertainment. Domestically, both wet- and dry-nurses are well-attested roles often held by slaves.[68] Grave inscriptions of nurses and evidence for manumissions indicate close relationships with former charges.[69] The housekeeper (*tamia*, Xen. *Oec.* 9.10–11), maidservant (*therapaina*, Andoc. 1.64), and lady's maid (*kommotria*, Pl. *Rep.* 373c) represent slave roles within the household.

Midwifery was a respected profession, practised by Socrates' mother Phainarete, a citizen woman (Pl. *Tht.* 149a).[70] The grave inscription of 'Phanostrate, midwife and physician' (*iatros*), from mid-fourth-century Athens (*IG* II² 6873), is the only reliable attestation of a classical woman physician.[71] However, the notion that some midwives acted as physicians is supported by Plato (*Rep.* 454d), who gives the hypothetical example of a woman skilled in the physician's art (*iatrike*). Such expertise would naturally flow from midwives' work within the *gynaikeion* (household women's quarters).

Musical entertainers hired for the *symposion* (the men's post-dinner drinking party) are often associated with prostitution. This tie is particularly strong for dancers, flutists, and kithara-players (Metagenes fr. 4; Aeschin. 1.41; Ar. *Nub.* 996).[72] Both male and female prostitution were prevalent in Greece (Dem. 59; Xen. *Symp.* 2.2–3). However, the scholarly aspersion that practically all musicians were prostitutes has come under recent challenge.[73] It nevertheless seems safe to assume

---

[66] *ARV²* 571.73, 1659; *ARV²* 658.29.   [67] Feyel 2006, 331.   [68] Taylor 2017, 135–40.
[69] See Brock 1994, 336 n. 4. Manumission: *IG* II² 1559.60; Dem. 47.55–6; Men. *Sam.* 236–8.
[70] Taylor 2017, 140–6.   [71] Brock 1994, 340; Taylor 2017, 142–5.
[72] Kapparis 2018, 275–84.   [73] Kennedy 2014, 127–30.

that slaves and ex-slaves often filled these less reputable roles (cf. Ar. *Eccl.* 719–20).

SLAVES AND THE NON-AGRICULTURAL ECONOMY

Slaves and freedmen played key structural roles in the non-agricultural economy. Aristotle's statement that 'in ancient times the artisan class in some city-states consisted of slaves or foreigners, owing to which the great mass of them are so even now' (*Pol.* 1278a5) was less a guide to the past than a statement of contemporaneous truth. Finley opines that 'one stimulus for chattel slavery came from the growth of urban production'.[74] In general, slaves had greater autonomy, and chance to buy their freedom, the further removed they were from the primary sector. It is perhaps this factor that led Plato and the author of the *Constitution of the Athenians* to observe that one could not distinguish slaves and the free poor at Athens from dress or public behaviour (*Rep.* 563b; Ps.-Xen. 10.10–12). Unlike citizens, slaves had no political or military obligations on their time. It was thus advantageous to use slaves in crafts and services, since such obligations would otherwise imply a loss of income.[75]

Household servants appear under a wide variety of terms (e.g. *diakonos*, servant; *doulos/oiketes*, slave; or *pais*, literally boy).[76] Masters with few slaves probably used them for all purposes: in fields during the agricultural season; within the household; and, for hoplites, as armour-bearers while on campaign (Thuc. 3.17.4; Hdt. 9.29). Richer house-holds could perhaps afford greater specialisation, deploying house slaves as doorkeepers, housekeepers, cooks, and butlers, or as personal attend-ants or *paidogogoi* (slave tutors for a male child; Pl. *Alc.* 1.122b).

The Attic orator Hypereides suggests that there were over 150,000 slaves at Athens in ca. 338 (Hyp. fr. 18 Blass). This figure is in the top range of modern estimates; Hypereides may have been merely guessing, exaggerating, or both.[77] Nevertheless, his speech indicates that Athenians thought there were a large number of slaves deployed to primary extraction at Athens. Scholars think there were ca. 10,000–20,000 mining slaves in the fifth and fourth centuries, rising to ca. 30,000 at peak activity.[78] The structures in the Laurium district interpreted as watchtowers suggest that this concentration of slaves was seen as a security risk.[79] In the *Poroi*, published in 355, Xenophon claims that

[74] Finley [1973] 1999, 70. [75] Osborne 2010, 96. [76] See the list at Lewis 2018b, 298.
[77] Osborne 2010, 86. [78] Garlan 1988, 65–7. [79] Fisher 2001, 50.

Nicias owned 1,000 mining slaves, Hipponicus 600, and Philemonides 300 (4.14–15). Nicias' slaves were let out to Sosias the Thracian at the rate of an obol a day per man. In a remarkable fourth-century epitaph, a slave miner, Atotas of Paphlagonia, claims descent from the Homeric hero Pylaimenes (*IG* II² 10051). The fact that Atotas had a memorial at all indicates that he was a relatively elite slave, perhaps akin to Sosias, but even so the following line from his epitaph hints at a hard life: '[I am now buried in] a distant land, in which my body has rested from toils.'

Most scholars think that some slaves (so-called *choris oikountes*) lived and worked independently, often under the watchful eye of a supervisor (himself a slave).[80] In Aeschines, a foreman (*hegemon ergasteriou*) of nine or ten leatherworkers paid a fixed daily sum (*apophora*) of three obols for himself, and two for each of the others, to his owner (1.97). The foreman probably ran the business independently, paying wages to the other slaves and keeping any profit. Post-330, three slaves *choris oikountes* operated a perfume-making workshop (Hyp. *Ath.* 9.23–4).[81] This pattern had several mutual advantages for both slaves and masters. The slaves gained a measure of practical independence and could potentially save to purchase their freedom, while the master gained a fixed return with low risk and little effort.

Perhaps the most fortunate slaves were bankers and business agents.[82] At Athens, slaves could own property de facto with their master's consent (Diog. Laert. 5.14; Men. *Her.* 27–36). Athenian slaves were however technically unable to enter contracts or testify in court, except under torture. Despite these obstacles, some slaves were able to act as banking agents (Dem. 36) and perhaps also engage in long-distance trade (Dem. 32.4–9, 34.5–10). In these cases, 'legal adaptation surmounted such incapacity';[83] owners and law courts were able to adopt workarounds, sometimes allowing slaves to testify (such as in maritime cases, the *dikai emporikai*) and at other times using legal fictions (such as Pasion's use of a citizen as his front: Isoc. 17.33).

Finally, slaves were themselves bought and sold.[84] Slaves in classical Athens seem to have cost an average of ca. 150–200 dr. (Xen. *Mem.* 2.5.2; Attic Stelai, above, p. 203), with prices as high as two slaves for half a talent (Dem. 59.29).[85] The notional annual earnings of a skilled

---

[80] Garlan 1988, 71; Cohen 2000, 135, 163; Acton 2014, 287–8.
[81] See also the charcoal-maker in Menander (*Epit.* 378–80). If the *phialai* inscriptions are interpreted as manumissions, then any ex-slave listed as living in a different deme from their master could potentially have been *choris oikountes*.
[82] Cohen 1992, 90–101; Acton 2014, 286–7. [83] Cohen 2017, 132.
[84] See Garlan 1988, 45–55. [85] Ibid., 54–5; Acton 2014, 283; Lewis 2018b, 170–1.

craftsman was 300 dr.[86] By the Hellenistic period, the price of conditional manumissions at Delphi (likely indicating slave prices) had risen to ca. 400–450 dr., perhaps due to a fall in supply.[87] Thrace, Scythia, and Phrygia – the modern-day Balkans, Black Sea coast, and Turkey – were common sources of slaves.[88] Major cities along trade routes, such as Chios, Corinth, Aegina, and Athens, all trafficked in slaves. Toward the end of the Hellenistic period, Delos was particularly famed as a slave market. Strabo characterises it as receiving and dispatching tens of thousands (literal myriads) of slaves per day, though this may be a rhetorical exaggeration (14.5.2).

CONCLUSION

The surviving evidence tells us much about the structure and nature of the non-agricultural economy in ancient Greece, even if we can make only basic estimates with regard to total scale. Landless citizens, women, metics, freedmen, and slaves were heavily involved in the provision of the goods, services, and leisure which enabled a hegemonic minority of adult male farmer-hoplite-citizens to meet the Greek ideal for living. These workers often did so as extensions of the *oikos* in various forms, within structural conditions that frequently discouraged separate concerns from exceeding labour sizes of two to six, with the limit of a single manager at most. At the same time, at least in the large, interconnected cities, aggregate demand for goods and services was sufficient to permit a high degree of horizontal specialisation.

    The attitudes of the elite minority also bias the evidence. The non-agricultural economy and its workers can thus be said to represent part of the history of subalterns, or E. P. Thompson's history from below. Compared to agriculture, the non-agricultural economy is relatively under-researched, perhaps mirroring the bias in evidence toward citizens. Part of the challenge of writing such a history is that the relevant evidence is scattered across literature, epigraphy, and various archaeological finds. It is thus a Herculean task to create a catalogue of all occupations and trade goods given across the sources for even just Athens, building in this respect on the labours of Harris and Lewis. Such work would greatly benefit from the establishment of a common scholarly database. Parametric models such as Acton's provide another possible way forward towards analysing structure and scale.[89]

---

[86] Earnings based on 300 days' work at one drachm per day.   [87] Garlan 1988, 81.
[88] Ibid., 46–7, 53–4; Fisher 2001, 37.   [89] Acton 2014, appendix.

Further Reading

On the role of non-agricultural labour in the wider economy, see Davies 2007a and Bresson 2016b. On craft and trade, Burford 1972, Harris 2002b, and Acton 2014. On maritime trade, Reed 2003. On the application of the theory of the firm to the Roman economy, Hawkins 2012. On work and workers in the building accounts, Feyel 2006. On metics and freedmen, Whitehead 1984, Zelnick-Abramovitz 2005, and Akrigg 2015. On women, Brock 1994, Harris 2014, Kennedy 2014, and Taylor 2017. On slaves, Garlan 1988, Cohen 2000, Fisher 2001, Osborne 2010, ch. 5, and Lewis 2018b.[90]

[90] With thanks to Jacqueline Yu and Sarah Suah for able research assistantship, and Sitta von Reden for very helpful editorial feedback.

15: MARKETS

Alain Bresson

INTRODUCTION

The market in ancient Greece should be understood as a specific institutional construct, which among other things created the conditions for an unusually advanced division of labour. Each city was a market space of its own, with its own rules and logic. But the network of hundreds of Greek city-states also created the conditions for the development of an original form of international market.[1]

THE MARKET, DIVISION OF LABOUR, AND PROPERTY RIGHTS

The Market and the City

The market experienced a distinct form of development in ancient Greece within the framework of the city-state. Its very existence is linked to the development of the specific political institutions of the world of the cities. The end of the second millennium saw the collapse of the large Bronze Age kingdoms of the eastern Mediterranean. After a while, most large kingdoms rebuilt themselves on a similar basis, with a powerful ruler at their head exacting a heavy tribute and monopolizing the available surplus, alongside large sanctuaries controlling vast tracts of land and their resources. In Greece, after the collapse of the Mycenaean kingdoms, no big states were recreated. The Greek world experienced a form of development that was profoundly original (Chapter 2, this volume). It was now split up into hundreds of micro-states. In parallel, social and economic life was under community control, not under the authority of a king monopolizing state power or extraordinarily rich 'temples' (in Greece from the late archaic and classical period onwards, the sacred tended to come under the control of the community). The

---

[1] For a historiographical approach to the question of the market in antiquity, see Morley 2013.

level of taxation was comparatively low (see below p. 234 on this point), and an unusually high proportion of individual output could potentially be put on the market.

Greek cities were ruled by law, which protected property rights. Against this view, Emily Mackil insists on the limitations of property rights in ancient Greece, pointing to the frequent civil wars, to the conflicts and rivalries in the domestic political landscape, and to the poorly regulated seizures of the cargoes of foreign merchants.[2] Admittedly, the ancient Greek world was not a stable, modern capitalist state. But this should not obscure the existence of secure property rights in Greece, acknowledged in a political structure where all citizens were equal before the law. One aspect illustrating the existence of this legal framework – and one of the main reasons why the situation of slaves was so harsh in Greece – is the fact that they were the absolute possession of their masters.

This makes a significant contrast with other societies of the ancient world, where, at every level of the social ladder, property rights were less clearly defined. In Egypt before Alexander, the complexity of the status of land property (land of the king, of the temples, and of grandees, in connection with the traditional rights of the local peasant communities) could give rise to specific conflicts. At the local level, property rights were based on social networks. In the Third Intermediate period, if conflicts occurred, they could be solved by resorting to oracular consultations and by the judgements of local courts, and, in the Saite and Persian periods, on arbitration by agents of the king.[3] Obtaining justice meant seemingly first of all securing the support of a powerful patron positioned higher in the social or administrative hierarchy.

Moreover, sometimes unrestrained violence could be unleashed by members of the elite to establish new property rights to their benefit. From Egypt under Achaemenid control comes a document that illustrates the real balance of power between the members of the Persian administration and the local population, which provided the conditions for the forced recruitment of a labour force. In the second half of the fifth century, the satrap Aršama writes from Mesopotamia to his subordinate Nakhthor in Egypt and reminds him of his previous orders: 'You are to be diligent. Guard [my] personnel and goods forcefully, so that there shall not be a[n]y loss from my estate. Also, from elsewhere, personnel of artisans of every kind, seek (in) sufficient (numbers), and bring (them) into my courtyard, and mark (them) with my brand, and

---

[2] Mackil 2018.   [3] Muhs 2016, 145–8 and 178–81, respectively.

make (them) over to my estate, just as the [pre]vious officials were doing.'[4] In Mesopotamia, our sources show that all manner of contracts were concluded for labour or trade.[5] But legal guarantees were limited by the fact that a superior authority could always decide to use all means to achieve its goals.[6] Seeking and obtaining justice through legal means was thus comparatively more difficult than in Greece.

The Market, Self-Provision, and Division of Labour

The market is not the only way by which goods may change hands. Other means include individual gifts, social transfers, taxes, and tribute. Although very different in nature, these four means of transfer share among them the common characteristic that, when performed, they are unidirectional, that is, there is no direct reciprocal transfer of goods in the other direction for a value deemed socially equivalent, which conversely is the definition of market exchange. The respective role of the market and other forms of the allocation of goods in ancient societies has been long debated. Individual gifts of all kinds were a common social practice. Also, states (cities and kingdoms) exacted taxes in large amounts, and they had the monopoly to do so. They could also transfer goods for the benefit of their 'nationals', although most often their expenditure corresponded to reimbursement for services rendered, such as serving in the army. Besides, in traditional societies with a comparatively low productivity level, a large majority of the production (of food but also of all other products) is intended for self-consumption, and only a limited fraction of the output can be put on the market by the independent producers. As for the rents potentially extracted by large landowners or the revenue from taxes collected by the state, the problem is determining the share put on the market versus that supplied under the form of transfers or rations to specific users (such as the army for the state or the workers occupied in building construction).

For most Greek cities, the majority of the population lived in the countryside, and even if there was a sizeable urban population, according to the model of the agro-town, landowners, even if they lived in a city, were supplied directly from the estates they possessed in the

---

[4] *ALBL* 2, TAD A6.10 ll. 5–8. Date: see *ALBL* 1, 38–44, and the commentary in *ALBL* 3, 76, 80–4.

[5] Jursa 2009.

[6] See Ma 2020 for the above-mentioned intervention of Aršama in Egypt and for the fate of the Murašu firm in Nippur, which long operated for Aršama but was finally taken over by him.

countryside.[7] This background of self-provision and consumption does not seem to create the conditions for an extensive market. But the characteristic feature of the economy of the Greek world is precisely that, thanks to a comparatively high level of both domestic and international division of labour, satisfying the needs of an unusually high proportion of the population was achieved through the market, and no longer only through self-provision or allocation of rations. There existed in Greece, both for the classical and the Hellenistic periods (for the latter with a shift of prosperity towards the eastern Aegean), an unprecedented population level living off goods purchased on the market. This situation was also due to the existence of a comparatively high level of urban population. In classical (Aegean) Greece, Josiah Ober estimates the urban population at 32 per cent of the overall population. The ratio of the urban population in western Europe during the early modern period was in the range of 10 to 12 per cent, before Holland reached 45 per cent in the seventeenth century, and England and Wales approximately 30 per cent around 1800.[8] In most large cities, the majority of the urban population was disconnected from food production in the countryside and lived off other activities, such as craftsmanship, trade, or other services (Chapter 14, this volume). The high level of division of labour within the city presupposed that one could resort to the market for acquiring all the items necessary for life, from food to shoes to ceramics. The rural population was not severed from the agora for the simple reason that individual producers regularly visited the market to sell their own products, which provided them the opportunity to acquire goods necessary for the household but not home-produced.

Nuance should be introduced, both geographically and chronologically. While, in the fourth century, Athens had already migrated to the advanced market model, the sizeable city of Olynthus in northern Greece still presented a mixed profile. Some of the city districts with houses containing large storage facilities correspond to the model of the agro-town.[9] But other city districts (interestingly, closer to the agora) do not present the same large-scale storage capacity but are oriented

---

[7] For the model of the agro-town (and its considerable literature), characteristic of Mediterranean Europe, especially of southern Italy and Spain, see Curtis 2013.

[8] Ober 2015a, 87–8. For the estimates of urban population in ancient Greece, the 'shotgun method' proposed by Mogens H. Hansen (2006b) has provoked a large debate. Whatever the exact number (which changed over time and fluctuated regionally), it should not be doubted that the proportion of urban population was comparatively higher in Greece than in the other regions of the ancient world.

[9] See the case of Olynthus analysed by Cahill 2002, 225–36.

towards craftsmanship activity and have a large space devoted to shops.[10] In a more general approach, a clear evolution can be observed through the archaic, classical, and Hellenistic periods. From a society where, in the early archaic period, production for self-consumption was the rule and resorting to the market the exception for the majority of the population, in the late Hellenistic period, resorting to the market to satisfy one's needs was the norm for urban populations. Now people purchased their flour and even their bread on the market, and women no longer processed grain at home, which was still common in the classical period.[11] More broadly, the activities and cityscapes of the towns were deeply transformed, as can be observed by a comparison between Olynthus (destroyed in 348) and Pompeii (destroyed in 79 CE).[12] Even if, in aggregate terms, given the weight of the rural population, production for self-consumption was still overwhelmingly present in the Greek countryside (Chapter 12, this volume), and even if the model of the agro-town was never completely eliminated for the smaller and even middle-sized cities like Pompeii in Roman Italy, the market – as a means of transferring goods and a social dynamic reaching well beyond the urban population – played an unprecedented role in Greek society before the transformation which took place in Europe in the late medieval and early modern period.

Property Rights

The existence of the market presupposes the existence of partners who can make their own decisions for the destination of the goods they possess. In other words, the existence of the market is preconditioned upon the existence of a regime of private property, where numerous partners are able to enter and exit the market of their own free will, with goods that are socially acknowledged as their own. In ancient Greece, it was the city that provided the framework for private property. Citizenship meant having full property rights within each city (and probably to some extent in the other cities in the framework of a *koinon*).[13] By extension, or so to speak by delegation, the property rights of

---

[10] Cahill 2002, 236–65, 281–8.
[11] Bresson 2016b, 195–8, 208–11, with the introduction of new technologies (hopper-rubber and the rotary mill, and then the watermill) in the background.
[12] Mayer 2012, 16–17, 25–41. It is legitimate to use the case of Pompeii since the characteristics of this city were obviously similar to those of the Greek East in the late Hellenistic period. The city was destroyed in 79 CE, but by and large most of the characteristics of its city life were already present in the late Republican period.
[13] For property rights in the framework of a *koinon*, see Mackil 2013, 259–62.

foreigners could be guaranteed by the city, but they were strictly limited; thus, except by special privilege, foreigners had no right to landed property.

For Hernando de Soto, followed by Edward Harris, providing legal protection for the rights of ownership is a key factor for economic development.[14] Greek cities fulfilled this role in an effective way. Thus, in Athens, the records of *poletai* (state auctioneers) recorded the public property sales. Engaging in private transactions in the agora was the best way to uphold one's property rights. Witnesses could be summoned if necessary, and for transactions of a certain amount written contracts were drafted, which would allow buyers to prove their right of ownership and to benefit from the legal guarantee offered by the city, its magistrates, and its courts. These contracts could be recorded by trusted individuals playing the role of notaries, but as early as the classical period, and more systematically in the Hellenistic period, the contracts could be kept in city archives or in temples.[15] In the eastern Mediterranean during the Imperial period, we have numerous references in funerary inscriptions to city archives, proving that it was perfectly common for any city to have such archives.[16]

A fundamental characteristic of the world of Greek cities is also the active role of the city institutions in maintaining property rights. The city magistrates accomplished their tasks under the strict control of the community. The risks of bribery of the magistrates were offset by the fact that they were normally renewed every year, that they acted in panels (and thus could monitor one another), and that they had to render accounts before specific officials who exercised control over them.[17] Freely concluded contracts were legally binding. A crucial point was that if a partner felt he was abused and if no arbitration agreement could be concluded, he could take legal action before a civic court to seek redress (Chapter 17, this volume). Judges – sorted by lot (in democratic regimes) from among large panels of candidates – offered the best chance of providing impartial justice. Finally, it should be emphasized that these services were offered

---

[14] Harris 2016. This is certainly right in the short term, with two important provisos: (1) the definition of what an object of property can be, and (2) the level of social inequality. In the ancient world, the existence of slavery, and the extreme inequality that developed after the destruction of the traditional de jure egalitarian model of the Greek city by Rome, became obstacles to growth; see Bresson 2016b, 207, 217–22.

[15] Faraguna 2013b. See the case of the city of Pella in Macedon, destroyed in the early first century; Akamatis 2012, 55–6. See also Game 2009 for the recording of deeds of land sales on stone.

[16] Harter-Uibopuu 2013.

[17] For market magistrates, see the series of cases from various cities in Fröhlich 2004, index p. 600 s.v. 'agoranomes' and p. 608 s.v. 'épimélètes' (for the *emporion* of Delos).

at minimal cost, for market taxes were low and, if going before a court implied advancing legal fees, only the losing party bore the cost of the legal action in the end.

Putting the emphasis on institutions and the law as a constituent framework of ancient Greek cities does not mean adopting an abstract and transcendent view of the role of law. Far from it: with Zinon Papakonstantinou (who focused on the archaic period), one should rather insist on the 'negotiable and contestable' character of the laws in the ancient Greek cities.[18] They were an object of discussion and conflict. But the familiarity of the citizens with their laws proves also the central role they played in the life of the community.

THE DOMESTIC MARKET

The Agora

As we see from Homer, and even though by then it already had a commercial function, the agora was originally the assembly of the citizens and the place where they met. With the ever-more egalitarian social relations that developed in the archaic period, the agora, or domestic market (as opposed to the *emporion*, or market for import–export), also became the main location where people exchanged their goods. Self-consumption and acquisition through exchange in a micro-network never disappeared but were now included within a broader exchange network encompassing the whole territory of the city.

The place for exchange (the market) was the main public square, the agora.[19] It was originally only an open space in the centre of the city, with a very limited number of buildings, such as temples and a small storeroom where the magistrates of the market could deposit the equipment they needed to perform their office. Petty traders performed their operations under stalls or tents. Over time, the meeting place of the assembly commonly moved to a specific location (such as the hill of the Pnyx at Athens). But the agora kept a political function and there was no separation between the political and economic use of this public space other than a specific timing for each activity. Beginning in the classical period and systematized in the Hellenistic and Imperial periods, a monumental transformation occurred. On the various sides of the

---

[18] Papakonstantinou 2008, 131 for the quotation, and more broadly 71–126.
[19] On the institutions of the domestic market, see Bresson 2016b, 225–59 and Harris 2019.

squares, stoas (porticos) were built, where artisans could permanently install their workshops and where merchants could store their goods in locked rooms. In some cases, stone pavements were installed. Later on, sometimes, as in the case of Athens, daily trade was even transferred to a place distinct from the old agora, which then completely lost its commercial function.[20] Mostly, although not exclusively, in the rural areas, periodic fairs (*panegyreis* linked to the presence of sanctuaries and festivals) were the general rule in every period.[21]

Information Asymmetry and the Rule of Law

The fundamental challenge to any exchange operation is the existence of asymmetric information between the seller, who knows all of the characteristics of his goods, and the buyer, who does not. The city aimed at limiting this asymmetry and establishing trust between partners by providing a strict legal framework for these activities. To start with, the opening and closing times of the market, which could be marked by the sound of a bell, were defined by the city. Initially, as we saw, the space was not typically bounded by monumental structures, but from a religious and legal perspective it was always well defined, which could require no more than simply boundary stones.[22] The agora was under the protection of specific gods: Hermes, the god of traders, the Charites (the Graces), the goddesses of harmonious exchange, and Aphrodite. The presence of these gods was supposed to establish an atmosphere of trust in commercial activity. But beyond the gods and the oaths that could be taken in their names, there (apparently) existed in each city a specific legal corpus, the *agoranomikos nomos*, which governed the transactions performed in the agora, under the authority of specific magistrates, the *agoranomoi*.[23]

These laws aimed at guaranteeing that both partners would not be harmed in a transaction. They had to protect the sellers, lest they be mistreated by rogue customers, but more importantly they had to make sure that the interests of the buyers would be respected. For this reason, laws specified that no adulterated product could be sold in the agora. Thus, it was forbidden to add water to wine or to milk, to sell flour mixed with bran, or to mix cheaper barley flour with more-expensive wheat flour. The laws also forbade fraud with regard to the quantity of

---

[20] Dickenson 2017, 236–52.   [21] De Ligt 1993; Chandezon 2000a; Holleran 2012, 181–92.
[22] See Erdas 2012 and Bresson 2016b, 240; *pace* Dickenson 2017, 3–5.
[23] See in general the papers collected in the volume Capdetrey and Hasenohr 2012.

goods that were sold. This implied a strict control of the weights and measures used by the merchants. The city established official standards of weights and measures, carefully kept in sanctuaries or public buildings. It also produced large numbers of weights and measures bearing the seal of the state, which the merchants could use directly or as standards against which they could check the conformity of their own weights and measures. Standards also existed for objects produced in large quantities, such as tiles. The carrying capacity of amphoras also corresponded to standards which were specific to the cities where these amphoras were produced.[24]

The instrument of payment, which typically took the form of coinage (usually in silver, but also in gold for high-value payments, and from the end of the fifth century overwhelmingly in bronze for small payments), was also under the control of the state (Chapter 16, this volume). In the Greek world, kingdoms and cities could adopt different policies. Some imposed the usage of their own coins, if indeed they minted their own coinage. Others, even if they minted coins, preferred to also accept the circulation of foreign coinages. Many small cities that had no precious metal coinage (and even no bronze coinage for the smallest of them) gave legal-tender status to specific series of foreign coinages. For small change, locally minted bronze coins were also mass-produced. Counterfeits raised a problem. In some cases, as with the law of Athens of 375/4, the city also allowed trading partners to have the silver coins offered in payment tested by a controller. In the early fourth century, the coins of Athens had been widely imitated, and the flow of money coming back to Athens could include some of these imitations. According to the likeliest interpretation of this law, the controller, who first eliminated counterfeit coins, determined which coins were authentic Attic coinage (which no one would be allowed to refuse) and which, although of good silver, were not (which one was free to accept or not).[25]

In the model of the ideal city he offers in the *Laws* (11.915e), Plato proposes that no one selling merchandise for an amount higher than fifty drachms should be allowed to leave the city, so that they might be held accountable if any conflict concerning the sale arises. The protection provided by law especially applied to slave sales (and that of animals; indeed, slaves were treated as animals from a legal viewpoint). Thus, if the seller had concealed that the slave suffers from a serious disease like phthisis or strangury, Plato (*Leg.* 11.916a–c) recommends that the

---

[24] Bresson 2016b, 172, 243.   [25] Ober 2008, 211–40.

ordinary buyer should have a right of restitution for the defective slave for six months, with an extension to one year for epilepsy. The case would be judged before a committee of three doctors, and the fine for the losing party would be twice the amount of the sale if the seller is a professional slave trader, and simply the full amount if both parties are ordinary people. These and similar legal provisions aimed at compensating for the asymmetric information between seller and buyer by deterring the seller from committing fraud.

Transactions in the agora presupposed the paying of taxes. The *eponion* was a tax generally of a small amount, in the order of 1 to 5 per cent, that was paid by the buyer. Other taxes of the same type might be enforced, like the *kerykeia*, or auction tax, that was paid for auction sales, or the *xenika* paid in Athens by the foreigners wanting to trade in the agora.[26] Transacting in the agora was in the best interest of both sellers and buyers. The stalls selling similar produce (ceramics, metal, fish, meat, etc.) were grouped together. Thus, customers knew immediately where to go to find what they needed. They saved time and could easily compare the goods that were being offered. They could also compare the prices, which was to their advantage. As for the sellers, they knew that the customers would quickly find the place where they sold their goods. The display of goods also had a dark side. Some special goods were sold at auctions, and this was the case for slaves. They were sold in the framework of special installations, the 'circles' (*kykloi*), where the slaves were exposed before the eyes of potential customers.[27] Living the traumatizing experience of being paraded before the customers in these installations was seemingly a common nightmare.[28]

As for the domestic market, the agora played a central role. If small cities had only one agora, large cities like Athens had several – two main ones in Athens and Piraeus, and a series of local ones in the countryside.[29] The agora was par excellence the place of retail trade. Its attraction is archaeologically well attested by the heavy concentration of coins found on its sites, almost exclusively in bronze, the coinage of retail trade from the fourth century onwards.[30] But beyond retail trade, all kinds of other transactions could also be performed in the agora.

---

[26] *Kerykeia*: Migeotte 2014, 265–7, 513–14, and Fawcett 2016, 166–9, 171–3; *xenika*: Dem. 57.31 and 57.34, with Migeotte 2014, 514 n. 402.
[27] See for Delos Moretti, Fincker, and Chankowski 2012.
[28] Men. *Ephesian* fr. 150 in *PCG* (with Harp., s.v. κύκλοι (Dindorf, p. 186) for the explanation of the type of sale).
[29] See Kakavogianni and Anetakis 2012 for some of the local agoras in Attica.
[30] The best case is provided by the Athenian agora: see Kroll 1993, 24–112, 322–9.

The civic territory was thus conceived of as an integrated economic space, under the authority of the city and to the benefit of its citizens, the guarantee being extended to visiting foreigners for either a short or long period of time, provided they respected the laws. For this reason, although the general principle was that sellers were free to set the prices they wished for the goods they offered for sale, the city could impose its own rules in a certain number of cases.[31] The idea was to maintain the prices of basic goods, primarily grain (wheat and barley) or flour, at a reasonable level.[32] Wholesale prices were ordinarily determined by supply and demand on the international market, but the city could impose maximum margins on retailers (e.g. Lys. 22.8: for grain in Athens, one obol per drachm). For some goods, like fish or tripe products, it could set maximum prices. Other strategies included price interventions over the course of the same day (if the prices were originally set too high by a trader and his competitors set lower ones, he was not able to sell his goods) and forcing wholesale dealers to turn into retailers.[33]

MARKETS AND INTERNATIONAL NETWORKS

Trade in the Ancient Greek World

In the ancient world, be it for production or for trade, the operators were not large firms, which is the scenario corresponding to the huge accumulations of capital and know-how that are characteristic of modern capitalism (Chapters 8 and 14, this volume).[34] This is clearly because (in the case of production) large workforce concentrations and (in the case of trade) grand-scale organizations, with permanent bureaus and large numbers of employees operating in various branches around the Mediterranean, would have been altogether unprofitable given the structure of the market. On an ordinary basis, demand was both seasonal and irregular, with boosts in demand linked to army or navy mobilizations or to building enterprises (in the case of temples or city walls).[35] The many political or social shocks (wars, epidemics, episodes of poor crops) created additional uncertainty. Limiting the business operation to a well-circumscribed period and strictly with the minimum capital and workforce necessary was the best way to minimize risk.

---

[31] See Bresson 2016b, 255–9.   [32] Eich 2006, 218–19.   [33] Bresson 2016b, 257–9.
[34] See Bresson 2014, 57–8 and von Reden 2019b.
[35] For seasonal boosts in demand in Rome linked to the demand of the upper classes, see Hawkins 2016.

Launching a trading operation commonly meant finding business partners, often recruited on the basis of family or ethnic solidarities, that is people on and with whom one had both information and social links that would limit the risk of fraud.[36] The structures of property, which included the right to own slaves, meant that it was common to resort to slaves for many lower-rank operations. Freedmen, who although officially free also had to remain frequently under the overlordship of their former masters, often ran business operations, investing capital in the venture from both their former masters and their own holdings. Potential traders could also borrow money from moneylenders, for whom this was a means of investing their money for profit. Until they reimbursed the capital and interest, they were linked by a liability (*symbolaion*) to the moneylenders.[37]

The Logic of International Trade and the International Division of Labour

Ancient Greek cities developed two types of attitudes towards international exchange: closed market and open trade. Some, like Sparta, remained stubbornly closed to foreign exchange until they were wiped off the political stage and lost any significance.[38] Others, like classical Athens, were opened to foreign trade, and their economies were even fully dependent on it. The implementation of a system of international division of labour and the logic of cost saving by resorting to the international market gave cities that chose this option a considerable comparative advantage. The Roman conquest of the Mediterranean lowered the barriers to trade and created new opportunities. The late Hellenistic period (which for Rome corresponds to that of the end of the Republic) also saw an unprecedented increase in the volume of goods exchanged, as testified by the rising curve of shipwrecks found in the Mediterranean.[39] However, if the end point is the same, the starting point is not, and as far as the logic of foreign exchange is concerned, there also exist significant differences between the ancient and modern worlds.

Modern policies are mainly built on the view that capital, labour, and know-how are essentially 'fungible' goods, which is to say that they are essentially interchangeable in performing their tasks. Only a few states escape this logic, those that can live off their exports of raw products (in

---

[36] Bresson 2018a.   [37] Harris 2015.   [38] Bresson 2021.   [39] Parker 1992; Wilson 2011.

particular, oil and gas), which for them constitute economic rents. In the ancient world, the situation was different in that, among the factors of production, natural advantages prevailed over technology and labour (which does not mean that the aggregate value of artisanal production was negligible, Chapter 13, this volume). In value, production was mainly dependent on the availability of natural resources, and value-creation processes like craftsmanship or trading, which were not directly linked to the possession of natural resources, represented only a minor share of global output. Just like today, the role of exports was to get the cash that would permit one to import the goods needed by the local population, whatever their purpose (as consumer goods or as production goods). But in a global economic landscape which, given the means of production available, was characterized not by supply overflow but by scarcity and uncertainty (because of the ups and downs of agricultural production), the most common solution for producing goods for export was to use one's natural advantages. This meant exploiting the resources of one's territory that were non-existent or comparatively rare elsewhere. This was the way to maximize the use of the local workforce and capital. The logic of an international division of labour was primarily based on the logic of unequal distribution of natural endowments. Profits from trade were derived mainly from transfers from one region to the other according to this logic, as, for instance, between the regions producing grain and those producing wine and oil.[40] This included all kinds of micro-specializations, such as the production of charcoal, condiments, and plants used for medical purposes like oregano, or murex, the shell that would be used to produce purple dye.[41]

It was widely acknowledged by the Greeks themselves that, given the unequal distribution of natural endowments, no city could be self-sufficient but that each had to get from abroad all sorts of goods that were necessary for the life of its inhabitants. Just as a citizen had to live in a city to become *autarkes*, the cities had to cooperate on the international market to achieve *autarkeia*, the real self-sufficiency, which should not be confused with modern autarky.[42] If Sparta was able to drastically limit the volume of its foreign exchange (and the presence of foreign traders on its soil), it was because it possessed an exceptionally large territory in the classical period (the largest of all Greek cities with ca. 8,500 square kilometres at the end of the archaic period) and because this territory was itself very diverse.

---

[40] On this model, see Bresson 2016b, 348–52.   [41] See Bresson 2016b, 339–414.
[42] Bresson 2016a.

All cities had to export and import, even those that were very traditional and mostly oriented toward self-consumption. They literally had to invent a form of specialization that would allow them to be part of the flow of international exchange. This was true of the smallest, like Hermione on the coast of the Peloponnese, which was famous abroad for its purple dye. But the rule also applied to the biggest, like Athens, where, beyond marble, honey, and ceramics, and no doubt many other objects of craftsmanship that have left no archaeological trace, the silver from the Laurium mines was the main export good (Xen. *Vect.* 4.1–12). Some cities even specialized in craftsmanship production, especially textiles and leather, and, as becomes ever clearer in the Roman period, they drew the bulk of their revenues from these products.[43]

Obviously, directly or indirectly, most Greek cities were connected to the international market, both for small-scale exchange at a regional level, in the style of the connectivity advocated by Horden and Purcell, and for long-distance trade.[44]

An International Trade Network

The fundamental principle governing the relations between cities was that their ports were open to traders of any provenance (except of course for those with whom they were at war). The most common tax rate between city-states seems to have been a 2 per cent duty (*pentekoste*) that was collected in the harbours on all imports and exports.[45] This was comparatively a very low rate, which per se was a strong encouragement for foreign exchange. The hundreds of Greek cities were forced to cooperate. Their relatively small size meant that they could not envisage raising high customs duties, under threat of being by-passed by traders and soon finding themselves in extreme hardship.

By comparison, the level of customs duties in the world of the kingdoms was much higher. A customs document from Egypt from 475 shows how heavy the duties levied were when entering the country (they were significantly lower when leaving it). For the Greek traders coming to Achaemenid Egypt, an in-kind tax of roughly one-fifth of their cargo was levied, plus a heavy flat tax in gold and silver.[46] As for the level of customs duties, they were, interestingly, of the same order (namely, very high) in the (Greek-dominated) Hellenistic kingdoms.[47]

[43] Benda-Weber 2013 (textiles) and Bresson 2018b (leather).   [44] Horden and Purcell 2000.
[45] Bresson 2016b, 308.   [46] For the detail, see Yardeni 1994 and Briant and Descat 1998, 73–9.
[47] Bresson 2012.

Trade Policies and State Interventions

The open-market policy existing between cities does not mean that there was no control over the goods that came in and out: for tax or security reasons such controls were inevitable. The customs officer was certainly the character who best defined the legal environment of a Greek port. Above all, the open-market policy does not mean that all goods were available for export or import. Thus, any city could permanently or temporarily ban some exports or imports. For exports, this was often the case with grain, for cities where there was a permanent imbalance, or a temporary risk thereof, between grain production and population level. Thus, while respecting the principle of an open-market economy, it was perfectly allowable for a city to define its own import and export policy.

The real anguish for the people of any city was not to be able to feed themselves if the grain supplies on which they usually relied had unexpectedly dropped. For the cities usually relying on their domestic grain production, this could occur because of local crop failure precipitated by poor weather. For those usually relying on the international market, it could be because of widespread climate issues or because of the consequences of international political crisis or war. One way to deal proactively with these situations was to conclude trade agreements with partners that would guarantee a right of pre-emption for a certain amount (and other privileges like lower tax rates). In a crisis situation, this would allow the city to receive a minimal quota of import, while others that would not benefit from these privileges would simply starve. Another common form of direct intervention, of which we have many examples, is the city sending abroad 'grain buyers' (*sitonai*), who would buy grain with state funds in other markets. More broadly, the city could accumulate grain reserves in state granaries.[48] State intervention was thus clearly a way to overcome a market deficiency, when the 'free hand of the market' per se proved unable to meet the needs of all the partners involved in domestic and international trade.

CONCLUSION AND FUTURE RESEARCH

In ancient Greece, each city was a closed unit unto itself, which meant that there were as many local situations as there were cities for the

---

[48] Bresson 2016b, 332–6 and Reger 1993 for the case of Delos (Hellenistic period). For the creation of regional bonds of economic solidarity in the framework of regional *koina* (confederations), see Mackil 2013, 237–325.

realization of market legislation and price levels. But these legal frameworks were very similar to one another, which allowed any Greek visiting another city to find a legal environment with which he was immediately familiar. As for prices, beyond local economic circumstances and the ratio of each city's home production to consumption, the main drivers for overall changes in price were in the short term the quantities of goods brought onto the market, which depended on supplies produced both locally as well as internationally, and in the long term the money supply, which was characteristically international in nature. The evolutions of local prices were the resonant signal echoing the connection of domestic markets with the international one.

While the analyses on ancient Greek markets have made decisive progress in the last two decades, much remains to explore in detail. But the most promising approach now seems to compare the main features of the markets of ancient Greece with forms of market structures and organizations of other societies before capitalism. This should be the main target of future research.

Further Reading

The chapters in Scheidel, Morris, and Saller 2007 remain essential for market development in the Graeco-Roman world. J. G. Manning 2018 offers an important long-term perspective on markets and trade in the Near Eastern/Mediterranean region.

16: MONEY, CREDIT, AND BANKING

David M. Schaps

INTRODUCTION

Coinage was invented in Lydia in the late seventh century, in India and China probably afterward but independently.[1] Money, on the other hand, appears in all societies at a certain level of complexity.[2] It is a *medium of exchange* that can buy anything; a *measure of value* that compares incommensurate items; a *store of value* for perishable items or services; and a *medium of payment* to atone for crimes, damages, or insults. Before coinage, these four functions were not usually performed by the same item.[3] The Linear B tablets show no evidence of money.[4] In Homer, oxen measure value, and bronze utensils, particularly tripods, store it. Trade is barter, with no intermediary; insults are atoned with items appropriate to the offense and relative rank of the parties.[5] In archaic Crete, bronze utensils were a medium of payment, and perhaps of trade.[6] In the Near East, silver, weighed but rarely stamped and only roughly standardized, had all the functions of money,[7] and Greeks must have conformed to this at least in international trade.[8] But once invented, only coins meant money to Greeks,[9] despite economic realities that allowed the same coins to serve for more than one transaction at a time.

If wealth was "plenty of coin" (Arist. *Pol.* 1.9 1257b9) and there was "no limit to wealth for mortals" (Solon fr. 13.71 West, *IE²*), more was always better. The Greeks called making money from money *chrematistike*; we call it finance. One method was to lend it at interest; another, in the fragmented Greek world, was to exchange one city's coin or one denomination for another, or to charge a commission for ascertaining a coin's authenticity. Making money from other people's money was

---

[1] Schaps 2007.   [2] Pryor 1977, 149–83.
[3] Polanyi 1957, 264, 266; Einzig 1966, 428–30, but cf. Melitz 1970.
[4] Killen 2008, 174 n. 38; cf. Luján 2011.   [5] Schaps 2004, 65–9.   [6] Guarducci 1944–5.
[7] Schaps 2004, 34–56, 222–35, revising Balmuth 1967, who considered coinage a continuation of Near Eastern technological developments.
[8] On internal use of bullion, see Kroll 2001; 2008b; *contra* Schaps 2001a, 96–100.
[9] Schaps 2008.

practiced in credit, monetary exchange, and banking, all discussed in this chapter.

COINAGE

The earliest coins were made of electrum, an alloy of gold and silver;[10] its composition could be, but was not always, carefully controlled.[11] Why someone first made it into thousands of small disks with identical images is unattested, but suggestions abound. The ancients hypothesized that coins were invented for international commerce (Arist. *Pol.* 1.9 1257a31–41) or retail trade (Paul. *Dig.* 18.1.1); modern theories suggest mercenaries' pay,[12] tokens for payments to the state,[13] prestigious gifts,[14] exploitation[15], standardization[16] of electrum's imprecise value, or making plunder useful to ordinary soldiers.[17]

Herodotus (1.94.1) credits the Lydians – probably Croesus – with gold and silver coinages; silver, refined to extreme purity,[18] became standard throughout almost all of Greece. A vast number of Greek polities minted coins;[19] many others did not. A few, notably Cyzicus,[20] continued to coin electrum. On the edges of Greek culture, bronze, either as weighed lumps (*aes rude* in early Italy) or in more developed forms (*aes signatum* and *aes grave* in Italy,[21] arrowhead- and dolphin-coins in the Black Sea area[22]), served a monetary or quasi-monetary function. In Greece itself, bronze coins[23] eventually replaced very small silver ones for small change.[24]

The Persian kings continued the Lydian bimetallic coinage until Darius replaced it with golden *darics* and silver *sigloi*. The former served chiefly for hoarding or bribery, the latter for trade – but only in Asia Minor, where coinage predated the Persian conquest.[25] The Levant and Mesopotamia continued to weigh *Hacksilber*, chopped-up jewelry or bullion evaluated by weight; the first coins – sometimes imitation Athenian owls – appear in the mid-fifth century.[26]

Greek coins were an intaglio pattern struck on a silver disk. The basic unit was the stater (being worth two, three, or four drachms), subdivided into obols (with six obols to a drachm), and forming larger

---

[10] Cowell and Hyne 2000; Keyser and Clark 2001. [11] Cook 1958. [12] Kraay 1964, 89.
[13] Price 1983. [14] Bolin 1958, 11–45. [15] Wallace 1987, 392–3.
[16] See van Alfen and Wartenberg 2020 for he latest discussion of the early electrum coinage.
[17] Schaps 2007, 313–18. [18] Lenormant 1878, 187–92. [19] Schaps 2004, 104–10.
[20] Mildenberg 1993–4. [21] Vecchi 2013. [22] Anokhin 1986; Karyškovskij 1988.
[23] Psoma 2013. [24] Kim 2002, revising Kraay 1964. [25] Le Rider 2001, 165–205.
[26] Elayi and Elayi 2014, 92–9.

units, not minted into coins, such as the mna (originally a Near Eastern unit of weight weighing 60 or 100 drachms) and the talent (60 mnai). Indian punch-marked silver coins and Chinese cast-bronze coins may be somewhat later, but the different technologies suggest that they were independently invented. Beginning with Alexander's conquest, Indian punch-marked coins were eventually replaced by Greek-style struck disks; Chinese cast-bronze coins persisted until 1912.[27]

Most coinages circulated only locally,[28] but a few – first Aeginetan "turtles", then definitively Athenian "owls" – were distributed widely throughout Greece and beyond. The gold *daric* was universally prized, and the electrum Cyzicene stater universally accepted, particularly in the Black Sea region. The *philippeioi* of Philip and Alexander the Great replaced *darics*, remaining the gold coin of choice well into the Roman period.

Coins are a silver commodity whose device guarantees weight and fineness; they are also tokens, valued because they can be traded. Tokens need not be valuable, but coins that traders will not accept are worthless. Greek coins were generally of high quality, because no Panhellenic authority could enforce their acceptability; in an emergency, coins of base metal might be issued (Ar. *Ran.* 718–37). In Ptolemaic Egypt, where the internal need for coins far surpassed their external use, powerful kings imposed lighter coins throughout the realm, increasing the volume of coinage and profiting from its reminting; even so, the shortage of silver led to an extensive copper issue, whose value eventually could not be artificially maintained.[29]

Greek poleis chose among a few systems of weights. The Corinthian stater weighed 8.60 grams, the Aeginetan 12.47, the Lydian (Milesian) 14.3; the Attic or Euboean drachm weighed 4.36 grams; the Persian gold *daric* weighed 8.4 grams, the silver *siglos* 5.6.[30] There were other standards, and authorities might change them; but Greece never had, like medieval Europe, hundreds of independent and incommensurate systems in a small space.

Since every polis used its own device, recognizing a coin required expertise, and counterfeiting was a problem. A touchstone could compare a coin's color to that of pure gold; a chisel cut would expose base metal under a silver wash. More professional fakes required more sophistication, and fourth-century Athens had public slaves in the banking district and the Piraeus to distinguish authentic coins from counterfeits.[31]

---

[27] Schaps 2007.   [28] Kraay 1964.   [29] von Reden 2007b, 43–8, 58–78.   [30] Mittag 2016, 13.
[31] Stroud 1974.

Coins were small but brought the little they could say into every house and shop. They announced who was boss: in classical Greece, a few letters and/or a symbol identified the polis, but from Philip of Macedon onwards royal coinage had the ruler's portrait – "heads," to this day. Subject cities might mint, but this declined under Roman influence.[32] Details communicated subtler messages: Alexander seated as Zeus-Ammon advertised his conquest of Egypt, Alexander in elephant-helmet did the same for India. The word *king* publicized each successor's self-assumed title. A divine image implied the deity's protection; a thunderbolt boasted, or warned, of the king's power. Greek dynasts, unlike Roman emperors, did not regularly advertise victories by issuing coins, but the idea was not unknown (Plut. *Vit. Alex.* 4.9).

A few polities insisted on the exclusive use of their coinage. An Athenian law decreed the use of Athenian coins, weights, and measures throughout the empire (*ATL* ii D.14 = *SEG* 26.72); Olbia required Olbian silver and bronze coinage (*IKalchedon* 16 = *Syll.*[3] 218); and only Ptolemaic coins circulated in Egypt.[33] Various motives have been suggested: assertion of control, encouragement of monetization, profits from reminting,[34] imposition of otherwise unpopular coinage. None can be proven, nor was the rationale necessarily always the same.

Although markets can exist without coins, it was coinage that spurred the transformation of the *agora* from a place of assembly into a commercial market.[35] International trade, which Greeks had long pursued for profit, was also facilitated by the Athenian owls that served as intermediaries between export and import cargos throughout the eastern Mediterranean.

MONEY AND GREEK STATES

Money and Government

The Greeks were acutely aware of the power of money. Pisistratus amassed wealth in silver-rich southern Thrace to regain his twice-lost tyranny; Cimon's wealth curried favor with the populace, and Pericles' public works allegedly had a similar intention.[36] In the fourth century, Eubulus and Lycurgus built political careers on successful financial management.

[32] Martin 1985; Meadows 2001.   [33] von Reden 2007b, 43–8.   [34] Rostovtzeff 1941, 402–4.
[35] Schaps 1997.   [36] Schaps 2004, 124–37.

Power could also be used to gain money. The promise of wealth could attract and control dependents and supporters – and that made money a danger to democracy. Athens subjected all outgoing office-holders to *euthynai*, a scrutiny of their financial management, and the practice was imitated elsewhere. Accusations of bribery were not uncommon. For many public functions – building projects, naval management, and temple administration, among others – accounting inscriptions are our best source of information.

If money went out, money had to come in; but taxation varied greatly. Direct taxation of citizens was a touchy subject. Fifth-century Athens could support herself from tribute, and Hellenistic monarchies could rent royal lands and tax non-Greek subjects, although in Egypt this required monetization of an entire economy previously conducted in kind.[37] Seigniorage, the profit from minting money, could add to the coffers, and poleis, too, could rent public property and tax noncitizens. Liturgies, the imposition of major projects on wealthy Athenians, blossomed into Hellenistic euergetism, whereby the wealthy endowed civic institutions and projects in return for honor.[38] But finance was always a problem, and Greek lore abounded with stratagems to raise money (Arist. [*Oec.*] 2).

Money and Warfare

Greeks knew only too well how decisive money could be in war. Themistocles saved Greece with triremes built with Laurium silver; afterward, the alliance was perpetuated not by a united army but by a united treasury, with money as welcome as troops. When the Peloponnesian War began, Pericles encouraged the Athenians by reciting their assets (Thuc. 2.13.–5); by its end, the combatants competed for Persian money to keep their navies afloat. In urging the Athenians to resist Philip of Macedon, Demosthenes did not neglect proper funding (Dem. 1.19–20). Money kept the Hellenistic kingdoms' mercenary armies in the field,[39] though soldiers' pay was poor and irregular, and their hope for fortune was enemy plunder.[40] Misuse of money could be as catastrophic as its lack, as Thucydides made clear.[41] Money was not, and is not, the only determinant of military success, but its importance was enormous at all periods.

---

[37] von Reden 2007b, 79–110; see also Chapter 17, this volume.   [38] Veyne 1976.
[39] See Pritchard 2019, 169–79.   [40] Pritchett 1971, 3–29.   [41] Kallet-Marx 1993; Kallet 2001.

Money and Cult

Almost every aspect of religion – building and maintaining temples, sacrificing animals, staging processions and competitions – required money. It might come from individuals or states desiring the gods' good will, from the sale or rental of religious honors and sacred property, or from a war, whose victor customarily dedicated a tithe of the booty.[42] The temples of Greece were great storehouses of silver and gold,[43] requiring careful management strictly overseen; the managers' inscriptions preserve precious information on prices and wages.

Temples could be pillaged. A non-Greek might have no compunctions about plundering the defeated god, nor were Greeks themselves always above such behavior. Not only enemies looted temples: tyrants and poleis might take or borrow treasure, with repayment a pious intention. The continued willingness to deposit wealth in temples suggests that these violations were never the rule.[44]

An entire sacred economy coexisted with the general economy: demand for foodstuffs, building materials, and other ritual appurtenances depended on festivals and sacred places.[45] Considerable sums went from the temples' treasuries to cattlemen, farmers, builders, and other workmen and suppliers.

Money and Labor

In Homer, as commonly in agricultural societies, a person might work for nothing more than food and perhaps clothing; but in classical times, work was purchased for money. Buying a slave was the most direct way, but only practical for a permanent need; a slave who worked occasionally still had to be fed constantly. Slaves could be used to make money, either by renting them out or by having them ply a trade, with a share – presumably a large one – for the owner.

Hired free laborers might be paid by the day, by the prytany, or by the job (*IG* I^3 435 *passim*); a slave's wages were no lower but went to his master. Wages depended on the work done, the time, and the place.[46] The job determined length of employment; many workers would show up – not necessarily every morning – in the *agora* hoping to be hired.[47] Artisans, generally paid by piecework,[48] might be attached to

---

[42] Pritchett 1971, 93–100.   [43] Seaford 2004, 68–87.   [44] Pritchett 1991, 160–8.
[45] McInerney 2010 146–72; Gallant 1991, 126–7.   [46] Loomis 1998, 232–50.   [47] Fuks 1951.
[48] Feyel 2006, 416–22.

a workshop. A few official positions offered a monthly or annual salary. For large or small projects contractors were hired; major projects could be lucrative enough to attract professionals from all over Greece.[49]

Most farmers produced for their families and sold only the surplus, but money had its effect. There was production for sale and even for export, and those who rented farms from temples and poleis must have expected a profit. In Attica, the success of Solon's prohibition of debt-bondage was probably helped by the possibility of selling one's land and supporting oneself in the city's monetized economy.[50]

In Hellenistic times, farming seems to have become more precarious, partly, perhaps, because monetary taxes exposed farmers yet more to indebtedness and its concomitant dangers of subjection, expropriation, and penury.[51] But the slave-worked *latifundia* of Rome and the wide feudal estates of medieval Europe never became the rule in ancient Greece.

CREDIT

Credit is more fundamental than money to community and economy: loans from the richer or more fortunate keep the needier from ruin or starvation, and start-up capital (*aphorme*) enables projects – planting, buying merchandise, commercial voyages – for future profit. Credit can exist without money: a favor generally expects a return when needed, and such debts can be calculated with crushing accuracy. Greeks calculated debts – loans, dowries, mortgages, fines, taxes, tribute – in monetary terms, but credit took many forms, sometimes for profit and sometimes from communal responsibility.

Some people borrow in the hope of generating a profit after repayment, with interest if necessary. Others borrow for an urgent need – dowries, fines, or simply food and drink – that will not enrich them. It has been claimed that credit in Athens was overwhelmingly nonproductive,[52] but commercial, "productive" credit was widely available, as were nonproductive loans, both from individual professional moneylenders and from banks.[53] We cannot measure their relative importance. Few loans' purpose is attested, but lending, large and small, financed much of Athens' extensive commerce, building, and manufacture.

---

[49] Schaps 1996.   [50] Schaps 2004, 163–7.   [51] Gallant 1991, 182–96.
[52] Bogaert 1968, 356–7; Millett 1991, 59–74.   [53] Cohen 1992, 32–6; Schaps 2004, 241–6.

Agriculture is inherently risky, dependent upon conditions that can be neither predicted nor controlled. Farmers often need the help of others. Seeds, tools, wagons, and storage facilities are all required, and not everyone owns enough of them;[54] labor for planting and harvesting may also require funds that can only be repaid when the crop is sold.[55] Land itself may be a credit mechanism, rented to farmers for a share in the produce.[56] Tenant farmers in particular might require credit to sow and work the land, and in Ptolemaic Egypt. seed loans and "labor" loans (*eis katerga*) are well attested.[57] There was mutual self-help among neighbors and patronage by the wealthy to the poor;[58] but neighbors, who needed the same items, might refuse, and generosity could beget crippling debt, dependency, and serfdom.[59]

Modern lenders rarely lend without interest. In Athens, though interest-free loans were a good deal more available than they are today, interest was common, and the rates often quite high; the law explicitly permitted any rate the lender wished (Lys. 10.18). Ordinary ("landed") loans bore interest according to the time until repayment; maritime loans paid a certain percentage at the safe return, no matter how long it had taken (see below, p. 246).[60]

Modern suppliers regularly extend credit: payment is expected within an agreed period from the sale of the merchandise. This was not the practice in Athens, and it has been doubted whether Greek law recognized a sale without immediate payment.[61] Such sales certainly took place, and various legal explanations were devised; but an impecunious person generally needed someone to lend him coins before he could accumulate merchandise to sell.

Sources of Credit

Friends, neighbors, or relatives might be expected, or prevailed upon, to lend without interest from friendship or duty. Such transactions might be informal, or drawn up with documents and even interest; they were part of *xenia*, help that people were expected to give to those close to them.[62] But business relations, too, were often – indeed, were expected to be – relationships of friendship and trust, so that a loan may equally be a matter of friendship, or business, or both.[63]

---

[54] Gallant 1991, 155–8.   [55] Gallant 1991, 164–5.   [56] Gallant 1991, 163–4.
[57] von Reden 2007b, 204–10.   [58] Gallant 1991, 143–69; von Reden 2007b, 227–52.
[59] V. D. Hanson 1999, 134–42; van Wees 1999.
[60] Millett 1991, 91–108, 127–217; Cohen 1992, 44–60.
[61] Pringsheim 1950; *contra* Todd 1993, 255–7, 264–8; Carawan 2006.
[62] Millett 1991, 109–53; Herman 1987, 92–4.   [63] Shipton 1997, 411–12.

Where one loan is insufficient, a modern borrower goes from lender to lender, collecting something from each; but in Athens, a friend or relative might take it upon himself to organize a loan from a number of contributors, to be repaid in installments. This was an *eranos*, once a term for a meal to which each guest contributed (Hom. *Od.* 1.226), but later a loan for friendship or business. There is some disagreement as to whether an *eranos* might bear interest.[64] The meager evidence we can squeeze from the *horoi* (boundary stones marking mortgaged land) suggests, but can hardly prove, that individuals' loans could be as large as *eranoi* from an entire group of wealthy contributors.[65]

The smallest sums were lent by so-called *obolostatai*, who would lend a tradesman a small amount when the day began to be repaid with interest at its end. Their interest, as a percentage, was exorbitant, and they were regarded with opprobrium; but there must have been a high rate of default, and *obolostatai* surely made retail trade possible for people whose capital was meager – the very people for whom retail trade was a desirable option.

Money was lent against real security at all periods, but we are best informed where we have inscriptions or papyri. In Attica, *horoi* sometimes speak of "revocable sale" (*prasis epi lysei*), sometimes "security" (*hypotheke*), and sometimes "mortgaged property" (*apotimema*). There is disagreement as to whether this reflects a legal difference, and if so, what it was: whether the mortgage was substitutive (foreclosure canceled the entire loan) or collateral (foreclosure canceled only its value), and whether the creditor could take the land if the debtor wanted to pay.[66] We also find "revocable sale," though not usually so called, in Ptolemaic Egypt,[67] and some fragments of land registers are preserved on stone. Farmland, houses, and workshops might all be mortgaged. The purpose is inscribed only for dowries, where money will not have changed hands: the bride's father, unable or unwilling to provide cash, mortgaged land to the groom, who would take it if the dowry was not paid (or, perhaps more likely, at the father's death).

The temples of Greece, as mentioned above (p. 246), held great amounts of treasure, which they could lend out for a profit. These loans were carefully managed, with a standard contract, guarantors, and fixed interest. Few cities of Greece lent as the temples did, but many advanced money to contractors. This, though not a loan – the contractor was expected to execute the project, not to return the money – carried the usual danger of default, against which the state defended itself by requiring guarantors and severe penalties for default.

---

[64] Vondeling 1961, 27–76; Millett 1991, 153–9; Cohen 1992, 207–15.
[65] Shipton 2000, 59–60.   [66] Fine 1951; Finley 1951; Harris 2013a.   [67] Pestman 1985.

Greek cities also figure as borrowers: not, like modern states, as regular financial policy, but for special needs – war or famine relief or (increasingly in the Hellenistic period, when war was no longer a municipal affair) public works (Chapter 5, this volume). The lenders might be wealthy "benefactors" – euergetism again, augmenting the lender's status in return for his generosity. Public subscriptions, with each individual lending a small sum, were another method.[68]

Maritime Loans

Maritime commerce was risky, with opportunities for large profit. It was financed by a special kind of loan, similar to what the English later called a bottomry loan, to be repaid, with substantial fixed interest, upon successful completion of the voyage; if the ship sank, the loan was canceled.[69] Being both loan and insurance, this left room for abuse; [Dem.] 32 alleges that the borrower sank the ship intentionally to avoid repayment, and though the ship in [Dem.] 35 came in, the unsuccessful borrowers did not repay the loan.[70]

Athenian law courts adjudicated disagreements, but no state mechanism enforced their decision, and collection was generally a matter of self-help. If a debt was not paid, the creditor could bring community pressure, even organizing friends and neighbors to collect by force.[71] Usually this will have been either unnecessary or unavailing; anyone likely to borrow again was well advised to pay his debts, and if he could not – or if, like Demosthenes' guardian Aphobos, he hid his assets successfully – no force could collect money that was not there. Perhaps stronger community pressure could be exerted by *eranos*-creditors acting together; the reciprocity institutionalized in *xenia* also had a moral force, at least in Athens.[72] Elsewhere, there is little evidence about private law enforcement, but Ptolemaic Egypt did have police with considerable local autonomy, concerned with enforcing royal decrees but also available to private citizens.[73] It is not clear whether this made collection any easier.

BANKING

Banking in its modern sense, "getting risky income from other people's money" (Dem. 36.11), first occurs in ancient Greece. In ancient

[68] Migeotte 1984.   [69] Cohen 1992, 52–8.   [70] Schaps 2001b.   [71] Hunter 1994, 129–43.
[72] Herman 1987, 92–4.   [73] Bauschatz 2013.

Mesopotamia, the royal palace, temples, and private merchants granted loans and accepted deposits but did not lend the money deposited with them.[74] It was the "table" (*trapeza*) of the Greek moneychanger that developed into a bank, but one different from modern banks in both essentials and details.

A *trapezites* accepted deposits and made loans, providing liquidity to borrowers and increasing the supply of money generally available. He also changed money, a much more important matter in the fragmented Greek world than in the Near Eastern empires; others (*argyramoiboi*) could do this, but for large transactions, few commanded a banker's resources. Through foreign connections, he could arrange payment abroad, saving his customer the risk and expense of transporting a large volume of coin. By accepting deposits of money and valuables, he performed another important function: hiding a person's wealth from thieves who might steal it, creditors who might collect it, or officials who might tax it. For this reason, banks regularly performed transactions without witnesses, despite the legal risk involved. Money deposited was available for the banker's use, subject to the requirement to return it to the depositor; whether the depositor received any additional return seems to have been negotiable.[75]

Athenian banks lent large and small, though never trifling, sums,[76] and might even cooperate in a loan too large for one of them.[77] It was not, as has been claimed,[78] particularly outsiders who might borrow from banks;[79] but alternative credit sources sufficed to keep them from dominating the economy as modern banks do. Many of these alternatives have modern parallels – family loans, pawnbrokers, credit unions, government loans – and modern banks may restrict their ability to compete.

Bankers might be citizens or noncitizens, but the bank was a family enterprise, operated not by citizen employees but by the banker's wife and slaves, who participated fully, even entering into agreements that could obligate the banker himself. Some banks were leased, with the owner receiving a fixed return from a manager, free or slave, who took the profit. Legal restrictions on capacity were relaxed or circumvented. A noncitizen banker might be represented by a citizen; a slave's testimony, otherwise inadmissible except under torture, may have been admissible in banking cases. In the famous case of Pasio, the slave himself

---

[74] Bogaert 1966.   [75] Cohen 1992, 18–22, 111–21, 191–207.   [76] Cohen 1992, 22–5.
[77] Cohen 1992, 128–9, 142.   [78] Millett 1991, 206–17.
[79] Cohen 1992, 121–50; Shipton 1997, 401–12, 417–21.

was manumitted, took over the bank, was eventually granted citizenship, and left it to his own slave Phormio (Davies, *APF* 11672).[80]

The Banks of Ptolemaic Egypt

The Ptolemies established royal banks probably in the reign of Ptolemy I (322–283), whose chief function was to manage royal revenue; but this involved them directly in the local economy, since salaries, grain purchases, cult activities, and virtually all local administrative functions required access to the bank's reservoir of cash. The branches had considerable autonomy to use their revenues locally, and their ability to lend to third parties enabled them, not unlike the Athenian bankers, to finance business activities – though unlike the Athenians, they were always subject to the rules of the higher authority: their regulatory functions meant more to the economy than their lending and borrowing.[81] A development particular to Egypt was the transfer of funds from one account to another (usually to or from the treasury) without any coins changing hands.[82] This became so routine that where the Bible has Haman speak of "weighing" (*eshqol*) money into the king's treasury, the Septuagint has him promise to "write it over" (*diagrapso*: Esther 3:9).

There were also licenced banks in Egypt that changed money and offered loans, as well as pawnbrokers (*tokistai*) who lent money against tangible security; these latter, having received an item for security, will have been able to serve a wider population than the licenced bankers, who relied on their personal acquaintance with the lender.[83]

CONCLUSION

The invention of coinage brought about a widespread monetization of Greece. Market transactions and wage payments were exclusively mediated by coin; state functions, including warfare, were heavily dependent on money, and new ways of raising it – not only new taxes, but liturgies and euergetism – were devised. Greek religion depended on money, and the great temples were storehouses of treasure. Agriculture, though less thoroughly monetized, was not unaffected, and the cultural effects, though undoubtedly real, are sometimes hard to define – perhaps because we ourselves remain captive to them.

---

[80] Cohen 1992, 61–110.   [81] von Reden 2007b, 253–95.   [82] Preisigke 1910.
[83] von Reden 2007b, 111, 162–71.

Credit might be extended informally among friends, but the Greeks had many more structured forms of credit, both with and without interest. Mortgages and *eranoi* often financed dowries and other private expenses; "business loans," from the small sums of the *obolostates* to the large maritime loans that financed overseas trade, greased the wheels of commerce; and temples lent money, while cities, for special needs, might lend or borrow. But the greatest innovation of Greek finance was the bank, where depositors' funds were both safeguarded and reinvested.

For all the similarities, much of modern banking – even ignoring the recent revolution of instant electronic communication – did not exist in antiquity. With no limited liability, an Athenian bank was legally indistinguishable from its owner, who was personally liable for all debts, so that the bank's failure – a not uncommon occurrence[84] – meant the banker's total ruin. The situation was probably similar for the independent banks of Egypt.

With no paper money, the sense lingered, though often violated, that a coin's real value was its worth as bullion. This limited considerably the liquidity that banks could provide: although they could effect book transfers, execute remote payments, and effectively create money by lending against deposits, they were restricted by the necessity of having actual coin readily available. To spend in one year, as the USA did in 2018, thirteen times the value of its precious metal,[85] was unimaginable. There were no checks, and leverage – borrowing with only enough security to cover any likely loss – would not have been acceptable to lenders. Banks provided much-needed credit, liability, and trustworthiness; but tied to the concept of the coin, their activities were much more circumscribed, and their failures much less dangerous.

Further Reading

For greater detail, see Schaps 2004. On banking and credit, Bogaert 1968, Cohen 1992, and Millett 1991, best read in conjunction; on the *eranos* Vondeling 1961; for Hellenistic Egypt von Reden 2007b; on euergetism Veyne 1976; on mortgages, Fine 1951, Finley 1951, and Harris's 2013a retrospective view; on cultural aspects, Kurke 1991; 1999, von Reden 2003, and Seaford 2004.

---

[84] Cohen 1992, 215–24.
[85] Gold reserves $310.5 billion, expenditures $4.094 trillion: figures from US Department of the Treasury.

17: DISPUTE RESOLUTION

Kaja Harter-Uíbopuu

INTRODUCTION

Throughout the history of Greek poleis, the state or its numerous subdivisions exerted influence on economic actors by establishing norms or formal regulations. These can be found both in private and in public law, and at an intrastate and interstate level. There was thus an institutional and legal framework within which transactions could take place safely and which supported economic development and growth.[1] Within this general framework, the following chapter will concentrate on one important aspect: forms of dispute resolution. Wherever humans interact, there is the possibility of conflict. This holds true especially when they deal with each other in economic matters. Ownership of land and its products, transactions of goods and labour (commerce), and the collection of levies and taxes were the most likely reasons for controversies. Greek city-states provided the judicial structures and thus the necessary – sometimes mandatory – help for the (re-)establishment of non-aggressive personal relationships. Legal regulations that have survived in literary, epigraphic, and papyrological sources refer in the majority of cases to prescriptions and sanctions related to the conduct of people and to the possible dispute resolution based thereon, rather than dealing with matters of legal principle and definitions of substance. Their main concern was to establish not so much what was the law but how a person could obtain justice. There were in principle two ways to achieve this: whoever had been wronged (be it a private person or a community) could either seek redress and obtain material compensation or have the offender punished. While these two options were available in any legal dispute, it is important to ask whether litigation in economic affairs was different from that of other cases.

---

[1] Bresson 2016b, 225–34; Harris and Lewis 2016, 28–31; van Wees 2009, 460–4 on the archaic polis.

Aiming at Good Order: The Archaic Polis

In early archaic times, justice within communities seems to have been administered mainly by *basileis* (rulers),[2] as is shown in Homer and Hesiod.[3] Homer does not mention economic disputes specifically, since trade, one of the main reason for such disputes, does not seem to have been regarded as a suitable occupation for the noble heroes.[4] In Hesiod, a suit against his brother Perses had developed from a controversy over inheritance. The dispute was decided by the *basileis*, but in ways that the poet found most unjust: by taking bribes they were persuaded to side with his brother (Hes. *Op.* 34–9). Hesiod also alludes to disputes in the agora (*Op.* 27–32), which might have been commercial disputes, although we cannot be sure.

Many reforms attributed to the Athenian lawgiver Solon in 594/3 can be linked to economic problems. The abolishment of enslavement for debt (so-called debt bondage) formed the basis of a new social system based on a free citizen body no longer of landowners alone.[5] He also dealt with questions of inheritance, especially the introduction of wills, the suppression of excessive luxury, and the regulation of interests between owners of adjoining properties. Most important for the Athenian economy was his prohibition of export with the exception of olive oil. Any offence against the law was to be punished with a curse that the *archon* (magistrate) administered on the delinquent, and he was threatened himself if he failed to chastise the offender (Plut. *Vit. Sol.* 24.1). A curse was tantamount to capital punishment, as it prevented the delinquent from further participation in the political and religious activities of the polis. In practice, it meant exile. A close parallel to this new form of state interference can be found in the city of Teos (Asia Minor), where citizens interfering with the grain trade were also cursed.[6] It is evident that the polis as a community was harmed by the trespasser and therefore demanded punishment rather than mere compensation for damage. Punishment had a double purpose: it expelled the offender from the community and prevented other members of the community from committing the same crime. Solon also introduced general procedural reforms pertaining to economic matters. For

---

[2] No single translation of the term *basileus* can be accurate, as holds true for all other Greek terms used in this chapter.
[3] Duran 1999, 27–30; on the long-standing dispute over the origins of procedural law, see Thür 1996 versus Gagarin 2008, 19–33.
[4] See the reproaches of Euryalus to Odysseus, when he refused the invitation to a competition, accusing him of being a merchant and huckster (Hom. *Od.* 8.159–64). Cf. Osborne 2007, 295–7 on the literary representation of the economy in Homer.
[5] Bresson 2016b, 106–7.   [6] Youni 2011. Teos: Osborne and Rhodes 2017, no 102.

example, by introducing proper trials for every case, he restricted arbitrary force, as would be found in neighbouring tyrannies (F39 in Ruschenbusch 2014). In the fourth century, the *Constitution of the Athenians* regarded Solon's prohibition of loans secured upon a person (debt bondage), the introduction of the possibility for anyone to indict offenders, and the right of appeal to jury courts as those measures which supported the *demos* most (*Ath. Pol.* 9.1). All these changes were part of a new 'good order' (*eunomia*) in times of social crises and a development towards greater equality for all citizens before the law.

Dispute Resolution in the Market of the Classical and Hellenistic Polis

The importance of the market increased when larger parts of the population of Greek poleis were disconnected from their own food production and engaged in urban occupations (Chapter 15, this volume).[7] Although this change did not take place in all poleis at the same, it is to be seen as the common background that affected the development of the legal enactments providing the institutional framework for the safe transfer of goods and labour. Such a safe transfer was not only the basis for economic growth and wealth but also for conflict resolution between private persons or between individuals and the state. Thus, dispute resolution plays an important role in matters of family and succession as well as of property and its transferral.[8] Offering impartial and unprejudiced ways of resolving conflicts both by extrajudicial practice and by a court system was one of the most important purposes of the ancient state. Three main types of proceedings can be distinguished according to the parties involved: disputes (a) between two private persons concerning contracts or other liabilities, (b) between a private person and the state, again stemming from both contracts or offences, and (c) over the behaviour of representatives of the state (i.e. magistrates) dealing with economic matters.

Disputes between Private Parties

Whatever was owned by a private person could be alienated by contract, which imposed obligations on both sides. In a sale, on the one hand,

---

[7] For the distinction between the 'landed' market (*agora*) and the 'maritime' markets (*emporion*), see Cohen 2005, 290–2.

[8] Mackil 2018 convincingly stresses the imperfection of Greek states in protecting private property rights (regarding land and houses); see Chapter 23, this volume.

unrestricted ownership was to be transferred for the payment of a price by the seller to the buyer. On the other hand, use without the actual transfer of ownership could be made possible by the lessor for the tenant in a lease. In both cases, the first difficulty envisaged was that the transferor did not actually have the right to dispose of the object. Once challenged, the buyer had three options: first, to turn to the seller, return the object, be reimbursed, and let him pursue the dispute; secondly, to engage in the conflict himself and prove his ownership; or thirdly, to hand the object over to the person who challenged him and then demand the price and damages from the seller.[9] By providing the procedural means to protect the interests of the buyer as well as the actual owner (if they were indeed different persons), the state was able to reduce the disadvantages of the asymmetric knowledge prevailing in the ancient market (Chapter 15, this volume).[10] Thus, regulations for procedures in these cases of *bebaiosis* (legal warranty) are mentioned in literary sources as well as in epigraphic texts.[11] Another important form of support for private parties regarding the transfer of goods was to provide for records of these transactions. Written contracts were not only regularly attested to by witnesses, as the vast papyrological evidence from Ptolemaic Egypt shows, but also kept either by private persons trusted by the parties or in official archives. Regarding the sale of land, this registration seems to have become mandatory in many poleis (Arist. *Pol.* 1321b, 34–7).[12]

Regulations for the warranty against eviction are also the core of the *bebaiosis* clause (warranty clause) to be found in private contracts both of sale and of lease, which have come to us in the Ptolemaic papyri.[13] The vendor or lessor has to guarantee unrestricted use by the buyer or lessee; in many cases, he is threatened with a harsh contractual penalty. This shows the tendency to adapt the contracts between private individuals with foresight of possible sources for conflicts and to ensure that neither party to the agreement risked being cheated. Still, even these clauses were only useful when they could be enforced in a *dikasterion* (law court).

---

[9] Kaser 1944, 151–8; Harrison 1968, 206–14; Pringsheim 1950, 431–6.

[10] See Chapter 14, this volume; Harris 2016, 121.

[11] Plat. *Leg.* 916a; Pollux 8.34–5; Theophr. *Frg.* 97, 23–5; *FD iii* 1,486 (treaty between Delphi and Pellana, 285–280); *IC* IV 161 (treaty between Miletus and Gortyn, mid-third century).

[12] Faraguna 2015; Harris 2016, 127–33.

[13] E.g. *P.Köln* I 50, ll. 28–9, 99 BCE (sale) and *BGU* VI 1267 ll. 16–20, third century (lease), the latter with a contractual penalty of 500 dr. for eviction. Although the papyrological evidence from Egypt provides a large body of evidence for dispute resolution, the influence of Greek and Demotic (indigenous) Egyptian law is open to debate; see Keenan, Manning, and Yiftach-Firanko 2014, 17–19 for discussion and further literature.

Another possible source for disputes in economic matters was the quality of the object. The evidence for these concerns mainly the sale of slaves, since the risks for the buyer were especially high in this form of trade. Again, it seems that he was to be protected against any loss based on misinformation. Already Hypereides states that an Athenian law stipulated that the seller had to inform the buyer of any vices (Hyp. *Ath.* 15). The sanction seems to have been the possible return of the slave and the reimbursement of the buyer.[14] An inscription from Abdera (Thrace, ca. 350) not only shows that the obligation to give correct information in this polis probably pertained to livestock as well but also hints at deadlines, arguably necessary for filing complaints in case of neglect of the regulation.[15] The Graeco-Egyptian deeds of the early Roman period provide two different types of sale: a slave could either be bought 'as he is', without the possibility of returning him except for the case of epilepsy and leprosy (*P.Stras.* 79); or alternatively, the buyer could guarantee different qualities in the slave, usually by including a penalty for the breach of the contract (*BGU* IV 1059). The basis of this development still has to be seen in the judicial frame the state supplies: whenever the clauses agreed upon by two private persons in a deed actually offer them the possibility of entering into organized dispute resolution before mediators, arbitrators, and judges, and whenever the sanctions envisaged in the contract are not only a threat but can be enforced, the risks and uncertainties of the exchange of goods are reduced.

How could a decision be reached and what was to be expected from it? Again, the law of Athens will have to be taken as an example, since it is for this polis that most sources have survived. Still, the basic principles can be assumed to have been adopted in other poleis as well.[16] Whenever a citizen felt wronged, he could prosecute his opponent with a private lawsuit (*dike*). This involved private initiative on his side: after determining to which magistracy to turn, he had to hand in the written indictment and challenge the defendant to meet him on a certain date. If the magistrate accepted the plea, he set the date for the pre-trial at which both parties presented their arguments, witnesses, and proofs and would answer to certain questions or challenges posed by their opponent. The role of the magistrate was, on the one hand, to guarantee the orderly

---

[14] Jakab 1997, 96 and (on Hypereides' speech) 86–8. On the close connections of this speech to Attic comedy, see Horváth 2007.

[15] *IThracAeg.* 3. Jakab 1997, 90–3.

[16] For the question of whether Greek poleis developed different legal systems independently or shared some basic principles, Gagarin 2005 with further literature.

conduct of the meeting and, on the other, to try to mediate an agreement. Most of the private cases had to be brought before the Forty, that is, the jurors who decided lesser cases themselves and forwarded the others to arbitrators, from where they could go on to the courts. Others were presented according to their jurisdiction to different boards of magistrates, who had the same tasks.[17] In deep distrust of decisions taken by single judges, the Athenians developed an elaborate system of assembling large boards of jurors who would be sorted out of the group of volunteers present at the court buildings on any day suitable for trials. These juries then heard the arguments of both parties and decided immediately afterwards whether to support the claim of the plaintiff or reject it and protect the defendant. After the verdict, which was by any means irreversible, private initiative was required once more: the successful plaintiff had was entitled to exact the monetary fine from his opponent. The necessary acts of seizing items of the defendant's property had to be performed by the plaintiff and were controlled by public officials.[18] Several principles of this rule of law – not only in Athens – provided the necessary legal certainty that formed the legal framework for economic relations between the citizens of the polis: the separation of the two parts of the procedure (magistrate and jury), the decision reached by a large jury that would either support the plaintiff and grant access to the property of the defendant or defend the latter, the orality of the proceedings, the immediacy guaranteed by the presence of the parties, the publicity of the trial, and the procedural economy and concentration on one day in court.[19]

Yet it was not only the possible judgement by a (democratic) court of jurors that created the trust necessary in the market but also the – sometimes mandatory – procedural steps leading towards it. Again, most of the information relates to Athens, but the epigraphic evidence shows that similar principles are likely to have been practised by many poleis.[20] First, all private cases (*dikai idiai*, private lawsuits) could be brought before private arbitrators, with the consent of the parties involved. This consent was the basis of the enforcement of the sentence of the arbitrators, which had the same impact as a court verdict. Secondly, the engagement of a public arbitrator was compulsory in all cases involving

[17] On the competences of the magistrates, see Arist. [*Ath. Pol.*] 43–62.
[18] Bers and Lanni 2003; Thür 2000, 31–5; in detail, Harrison 1971. On the exaction, Harrison 1971, 185–90.
[19] Thür 2000, 36–9. Herakleides Kritikos (*BNJ* 369A = *FGrH* 2022 F.1.15–16) presents the conditions in Boeotian Thebes, where no system of justice seems to have protected the citizens (Bresson 2016b, 317–18).
[20] Steinwenter 1971.

more than ten drachms in dispute. Thus, the element of negotiation and compromise did not only play a role in the initial elaboration of a contract but also in the possible solution of conflicts arising from it.

A special class of cases in Athens seem to have concerned merchants travelling by sea. Lysias refers to a board of judges called *nautodikai* (judges of trials involving seafarers).[21] These seem to have been in charge of trials involving merchants, maybe granting certain privileges of time and place to them. From the middle of the fourth century onwards, *dikai emporikai* (maritime commercial lawsuits) were introduced as a special class of suits. Brought before the *thesmothetai* (magistrates), they had to be decided within one month. There were other particularities connected with this procedural protection of trade as well, as described by Demosthenes (33.1–2 and 34.3–35.42): the relevant law allowed merchants and shipowners to go to court if they suffered any wrong in the port or when sailing from or to Athens. The basis seems to have been a written agreement (*syngraphe*, covenant). Moreover, the actions that could only be brought in winter (Dem. 33.23) were open to metics (resident foreigners) and foreigners as well, thus extending the protection of the law to two groups important for the economic welfare of the city. On the other hand, the speaker against Apatourios in Demosthenes' speech 33 explains that imprisonment had been specified as a sanction for offenders in order to deter wrongdoing towards any of the merchants. This might hint at the fact that foreigners not only were plaintiffs but also often enough defendants, and that precautions were taken against their leaving the city without meeting their duties after the verdict.[22]

Disputes between Private Persons and the State

Two possible scenarios can be envisaged for controversies between private individuals and the polis. On the one hand, the polis frequently entered into contracts with its citizens or even with foreigners. These cases would therefore have a contractual basis. On the other hand, private persons transgressing the regulations of the state would be opposed to the community or its representatives in litigation arising from their offences.

---

[21] Lys. 17.5.

[22] Harris 2015, 12–17 on a new interpretation of the term *symbolaion* and a reassessment of the sources on the *dikai emporikai*. Cf. also in more detail Cohen 1973; Cohen 2005, 300–2; Lanni 2006, 149–74; Bresson 2016b, 322–4.

A typical example for the first category are labour contracts as they occurred, for instance, in a city's building projects. Numerous inscriptions ranging from the general regulation of public building enterprises in Tegea (*IG* v 2, 6A) to architectural specifications of the work (*IOropos* 292) or financial accounts of the progress (e.g. in Epidaurus *IG* IV I² 103–16) present different aspects thereof.[23] Through public announcements, the contracts were auctioned off to builders or craftsmen (*ergonai*, contractors) who promised to execute the project at the lowest cost.[24] The details in the contract concern their obligations and responsibilities as well as the remuneration in several instalments and envisaged high fines for late delivery or bad quality of their work. The polis as a party to the contract was represented by a commission of men in charge of not only finding potential contractors but also controlling their work.[25] It was their task to follow progress at the construction site closely, to monitor the quality of the material as well as its installation which sometimes was specified in the contract (*IG* VII 3073, Lebadeia). The *syngraphos* (covenant) from Tegea (*IG* v 2, 6A) shows the commissioners (*esdoteres*) of the polis in different roles when dealing with disputes and their resolution. They were to act as magistrates with the power to impose summary fines when it came to persons who would disturb the auction, cause damage at the construction site, or hinder the *ergonai* in any way.[26] If the potential offenders objected to the punishment, the *esdoteres* had to bring the case to the local court and act as plaintiffs in the trial. They were also allowed to discipline any disobedient worker or to exclude constructors in certain cases.

Moreover, the *esdoteres* were also in charge of enforcing the penalties agreed upon for the breach of the contract, especially when it came to late delivery or bad quality of the work.[27] In these cases, they represented the polis as a party to the agreement and were to make sure that the *ergonai* would fulfil every single obligation they had entered. Interestingly, there seem to have been only a few clauses regarding the obligations of the polis vis-à-vis the contractor. In Delos, the representatives of the polis, the *hieropoioi* (supervisors of the temple) and the *epistatai* (overseers) were held liable for any payment they did not hand over. They were to be punished in the same way as the contractor, but

---

[23] Although the inscriptions record very different legal deeds, they are often to be found named collectively as 'building inscriptions'. The last decade has seen new approaches towards these sources: Prignitz 2018, 37–8; Pitt 2016, 194–5.

[24] For comparable but possibly slightly different forms of labour contracts for construction work in Ptolemaic Egpyt, von Reden 2014.

[25] Prignitz 2018, 42–4; Pitt 2016, 198–201.   [26] Rubinstein 2018, 123–4.

[27] Thür and Taeuber 1994, 32–4

the case seemed to be a question of the control of these magistrates rather than of a breach of contract by the polis.[28] Since the inscriptions containing decrees and laws regarding public building were in most cases published in order to promote the reputation of the city, the texts did not bring up any misdemeanours on the city's side.

Apart from litigation arising from contracts, many disputes between cities and private persons arose out of the transgression of rules and regulations of conduct valid both for citizens and foreigners. Due to the lack of official prosecutors, private initiative was necessary in these public trials just as in private litigation. Still, the interests of the community had to be protected, even if no damage had been inflicted on any of its citizens directly. Therefore, either magistrates or private persons taking an interest in the business of their hometown could act on behalf of the polis and thus stand against the defendant. In what follows, the regulations of local markets will be taken as examples to explain different forms of dispute resolution and the provisions for guaranteeing security for all participants in order to maintain well-organized and functioning markets (Chapter 15, this volume).

The magistrates in charge were usually the *agoranomoi* (overseers of the market), who seem to have had remarkable powers when dealing with transgressors of the regulations of the polis.[29] On the one hand, they were able to impose summary fines, that is to punish without the formal verdict of a *dikasterion*. On the other hand, they were obliged to pursue offences by bringing the perpetrators to court. Epigraphic sources presenting the procedures often do not allow us to distinguish clearly between these two acts;[30] therefore, both have to be considered. The law on the celebration of the mysteries in Andania provides a good example, as it regulates certain specifications of the market and introduces the civic magistrate, the *agoranomos*, and his competences (*IG* V 1, 1390, Andania, first century). The *hieroi*[31] forming the organizing committee of the festival were to determine a marketplace for the transactions. In this market, the *agoranomoi* had to ensure the quality of the products, the regularity of weights and measures, and the proper behaviour of all

---

[28] Thür 1984, 509–10.

[29] In order to keep up orderly behaviour under their supervision, they were at times equipped with a rod and able to inflict corporal punishment on slaves. Cf. Roubineau 2012, 48–51; Harter-Uibopuu 2003, 154–6 and Jakab 1997, 80–2.

[30] Rubinstein 2018, 107–13; cf. Harris 2007, 162–4 on the power of magistrates in the context of the Athenian markets.

[31] The *hieroi* (sacred men) were members of a religious association in charge of the festivities of the mysteries in Andania.

participants.[32] For any transgression, the *agoranomos* had the right to impose a fine of twenty drachms on free persons or a whipping in the case of slaves. These regulations correspond to epigraphic records from Erythrai, where the *agoranomoi* were in charge of exacting a monetary fine in the case of cheating and treachery in wool trading, or from Delos concerning the sale of wood.[33] They represented the polis in exercising their coercive power. In none of these cases is any institution mentioned that would determine the question of whether the supposed transgressor was actually guilty or not. The text from Andania just hints at another prerequisite: the final decision on the fine was to be taken by the *hieroi*. Thus, formal control of magistrates was possible by means of appeal. The initiative probably lay with the person who was fined; he had to object and ask for a trial, in which case he would have the role of the plaintiff and the magistrate of the defendant.[34] In this way, the summary fines were an appropriate measure to regulate the behaviour of the participants in local markets by punishing transgressors swiftly. At the same time, the legal constraints restricting the absolute power of a magistrate created trust in the city's judicial system.

On Thasos in the fifth century, any private volunteer was invited to take part in the process of litigation concerning the large-scale trade of wine.[35] If successful, he could expect a reward amounting to half of the fine that had to be paid, but he also risked losing a preliminary deposit. All *politai* (citizens) were thus involved in helping to uphold good order by denouncing and pursuing culprits.[36] An inscription from Delos shows the intervention of the city to try to avert the increase of the price of wood and charcoal with rigid prohibitions of sale.[37] Any transgressor of these prohibitions risked high fines, with the legal process including both a volunteer and the *agoranomoi*. The volunteer was asked to report the offence to the *agoranomoi*, who would then refer the case to the *dikasterion*. At the trial, it was again the duty of the volunteer to stand up as plaintiff and secure a conviction of the accused. If he was successful, he was to receive two-thirds of the sum exacted from the defendant. Interestingly, the money was to be exacted by the *agoranomoi* and not the private citizen. The example suggests the possibly close collaboration between the magistrates under whose competences the cases were to be

---

[32] *IG* v 1, 1390, ll. 100–3.
[33] *IErythrai und Klazomenai* 15 (fourth century); *IDélos* 509 (235–200).
[34] Harter-Uibopuu 2002, 154–6. For comparable regulations from other poleis, see Rubinstein 2018, 112–21 and Wörrle 1988, 202–7.
[35] *SEG* 36, 790 and 792; *IG* xii Suppl. 347. Bresson 2016b, 171–3 on the sale of wine.
[36] On the system of volunteer prosecution, its backgrounds and advantages cf. Rubinstein 2003.
[37] *IDélos* 509 (235–200) with Bresson 2016b, 327–31.

subsumed and the citizens of the polis who were to make sure that the necessary regulations were respected in all circumstances. The regulation of the export of ruddle in Keos (*IG* II^2 1128) extends the call for reports not only to free men but also to slaves, who were to receive their freedom in exchange. However, the role of the volunteer was limited to a mere denunciator.[38]

The Control of Magistrates Dealing with Economic Matters

As has been shown, the powers of representatives of the polis responsible for markets or involved in other economic matters were quite extensive. Therefore, steps to enable all citizens to control them were envisaged in laws and decrees of the poleis from the beginning of written law onwards, or even before. This proved especially necessary where they were to impose summary fines, in order to protect the participants in the markets from unjust sentencing. Control was also needed when magistrates intervened actively and performed duties regulated by laws and decrees. If they failed to do so, penalties were inflicted.

An example for the first category is to be found in a decree concerning the renting of four *kapeleia* (shops) in the Heraion of Samos (*IG* XII 6, 1, 169, ca. 245/4 BCE). The *neopoiai* (wardens of the temple) were in control of all affairs concerning small trade within the sanctuary and were both able to impose summary fines (ll. 32 and 15) and preside over a court (ll. 27–8). Still, in the first instance, the magistrates themselves were subject to judicial control, exercised by the *dikasterion* of the polis either on the initiative of the punished, or on their own initiative, if the culprit did not pay the fine.[39] From the island of Thasos comes an example of controlling *agoranomoi* who did not comply with their task of overseeing the lease of the garden of Herakles (*IG* XII 8, 265, fourth century). The text states that not only were the *agoranomos* and the priest of Asklepios, who was to act together with him, to owe a daily fine dedicated to Asklepios, but that even the *apologoi*, who had the duty of prosecuting them, risked payment if they failed to do so.[40]

---

[38] Lytle 2013 explains the economic background of this interesting decree.

[39] Thür and Taeuber 1978, 222–3; Thür and Taeuber 1994, 38–9; and Rubinstein 2018, 112–17 on the imposition of summary fines and the constraint of the magistrate's power by the possibility of contradiction. Bresson 2016b, 246–50 concentrates on the authority of the *agoranomoi* when bringing a case to court.

[40] Rubinstein 2003, 96–8.

INTERSTATE REGULATIONS

In a system where citizenship provided the basis for the ownership of land, legitimate marriage, and thus the transfer of property to one's children – as well as access to the city's court system in order to protect the entitlements – any exchange crossing borders had to be regulated. Trade with neighbouring poleis or communities from farther away, be it small-scale or involving large quantities of goods, would only be successful if both parties were able to trust that they were protected by the law of each polis and were given the possibility of resolving their disputes on a common basis of neutral jurisdiction.[41] The practice of reprisal (*sylan*, to seize) – used frequently by the Greeks to target any fellow citizen of a presumed offender – threatened voyages and trade. Thus, agreements to exclude such seizure either within specified places like sanctuaries (Chapter 19, this volume) or the whole polis in which a foreigner traded proved extremely beneficial for the functioning of a well-organized system of the legal protection of economic exchange.[42]

There were two other ways of overcoming the politically limited access to legal protection in Greek poleis: first, foreigners could be represented by citizens in court and thus be granted indirect access to the judiciary. By asking citizens to represent members of a foreign state as *proxenoi* (patrons) – usually chosen for their personal relations with the state – an institutionalized network connecting the city-states and their inhabitants was established in the sixth century and lasted until the early imperial period.[43] Still, granting access to the local magistrates and courts to foreigners, especially those who lived in a polis more or less permanently, was regarded as more promising. Thus, secondly, a polis could establish rules for non-citizens living on its territory in order to provide them with certain civic rights. As *metoikoi*, *epoikoi*, or *paroikoi* (all three terms denoting non-citizen residents in Greek poleis), they formed a distinct group for whom the acquisition of land was usually forbidden. Therefore, they worked as craftsmen, traders, and bankers, thus influencing the economic life in the city-state and often enough reaching considerable social status. In Athens, down to the fourth century, *metoikoi* still

---

[41] Bresson 2016b, 317–22; Harter-Uibopuu 2021.

[42] Above all Bravo 1980, cf. Gauthier 1972, 210–19. Cf. now also Mackil 2018, 334–6 on the consequences of the possibility of seizure for the question of property security.

[43] Mack 2015; Marek 1984. Aesch. *Supp.* 910–29 with Gauthier 1972, 54–7 and *IG* XII 5, 528, ll. 6–10 (Keos, fourth century) with Mack 2015, 20–1.

needed the representation of a personal *prostates* (Chapter 14, this volume), but they were given the privilege of being allowed to address the *archon polemarchos* (magistrate) with their claims.[44]

Alternatively, the polis could enter into a bilateral agreement with another polis regulating any litigation that might arise between their citizens. The *symbola* (covenant) between Chalaeum and Oeantheia (ca. 450) is a good example, as it combines the prohibition of *sylan* with provisions for jurisdiction. While there was a complicated system of *xenodikai* (judges for foreigners) for cases arising out of the inhibited reprisal, whoever lived in the partner city for more than one month was allowed to use local law and local courts in order to proceed; but they then also had to stand trial there.[45] Sometimes special courts were established in order to hear cases involving citizens of different states. The most elaborate text of this phenomenon is the *synbola* dating to 302–300 between the Peloponnesian cities of Stymphalus and Sicyon.[46] A *dikasterion* for foreigners was to be set up regularly, with jurors of both cities deciding cases that had been prepared and brought before them. Moreover, there were possibilities for addressing the local courts in special affairs as well as direct decisions of magistrates in minor questions. The guidelines seem to have been established to provide for independent and neutral instances that were satisfactory both for the plaintiffs and defendants, for comprehensive and yet obligatory procedures, and for a swift resolution of disputes that would facilitate regular and sometimes intensive economic exchange across the borders.

CONCLUSIONS

While not all dispute resolution had economic problems as its background, it was vital for the functioning of interpersonal economic transactions and markets as well. A transparent judicial system, open to all participants of a community, formed its basis. Supervision over institutions and markets was performed by magistrates, who were equipped with powers to act swiftly, on the spot, and efficiently. Moreover, the system of volunteers provided a means of detecting failures of the state and official transgressions of regulations. It was also

[44] Fisher 2006. Regarding procedural regulations for *metoikoi* in Athens, see Harrison 1968, 187–99.
[45] *IG* IX 1² 717, ll. 5–8. Bravo 1980, 890–911; cf. Gauthier 1972.
[46] *Synbola*: *IG* V 2, 357 with Thür and Taeuber 1994, no. 17, and Thür 1995. For a similar regulation in the Hellenic League of Antigonos I and Demetrios Poliorketes, see *IG* IV 1² 68 with Harter-Uibopuu 2003.

deemed necessary to control the power of the magistrates by allowing appeal against their decisions. Parties involved in litigation could be both private persons and the polis and its magistrates. The attempt to specify precisely their role during the preparation of a trial or in court proceedings often explains the complicated regulations preserved in literary, epigraphic, and papyrological sources. Yet well-considered possibilities for obtaining justice did not only enhance trust in the legal system but also in the economy and exchange with the polis.

Further Reading

For the responsibilities and constraints of magistrates, see Bresson 2016b, Rubinstein 2018 and 2003 and Capdetrey and Hasenohr 2012 (on the *agoranomoi*). Lanni 2006 and Harris 2007 provide thoughtful insight into the system of jurisdiction in Athens. A discussion of the regulations of different kinds of markets can be found in Cohen 2005; for landed property, see Harris 2016 and Mackil 2018. General aspects of the status of non-citizen residents are discussed in Mack 2015 and Fisher 2006.

18: Taxation and Tribute

Andrew Monson

Introduction

Taxation and tribute intersect in critical ways with the wider economy. The modern tax state is a mutually dependent relationship between government and capital.[1] Any state interested in maximizing revenue has an interest in fostering capital accumulation and investment while reducing the economic friction of transaction costs (Chapter 23, this volume). On the other hand, there are always strong temptations on the side of the ruler and on the side of the taxpayers to "free-ride," which political institutions must prevent. An autocratic state profits directly from overtaxing its subjects, sharing only a fraction of the damage.[2] Where governments rule by the consent of citizens who bear the brunt of taxation, as in many Greek city-states, they are in a better position to credibly commit to a fiscal regime that is predictable and calibrated to respond to state needs without putting too much pressure on trade and production.[3] Premodern tax states emerged only in extraordinary circumstances and reverted easily to tributary forms of extraction, with predatory demands on taxpayers and low net revenues per capita.

Compared with taxation, tribute is a blunt instrument of state finance. It implies levies on communities without detailed knowledge of the people, resources, and transactions by which those levies are funded. A warlord, emperor, or polis who sets tribute must either err on the side of caution by keeping tributary demands low or risk decimating economic production. The upshot for students of the Greek economy is that tribute too easily becomes either a crushing burden or a mere token subservience that allows local elites to capture revenue. Although tributary empires sometimes overlay complex local tax structures, the rulers lack the capability or willingness to impose their own administrative apparatus, especially when they rule over large and diverse territories. The Macedonian kings ruling over the eastern

---

[1] Schumpeter [1918] 1991.   [2] North, Wallis, and Weingast 2009.   [3] Ober 2015a.

Mediterranean, Asia, and Egypt in the Hellenistic period recognized the extraordinary fiscal capacities of city-states and sought to protect or imitate their institutions. To varying degrees, however, they and even the city-states themselves also developed weapons of coercion and tributary extraction antithetical to consent-based governance.

TRIBUTARY REGIMES

Tribute consists of payments from subjected political communities to their overlord and often serves to pass the costs of government, especially warfare, onto groups beyond those on whom the state depends for legitimacy. Latin *tributum* was originally an extraordinary property tax on Roman citizens (like the Greek *eisphora* discussed below, p. 271), which fell into disuse after 167, and came to be associated with direct taxes in the provinces. Greek *phoros* from *pherein* "to pay, contribute" could refer to plunder or to lump-sum payments by conquered cities or satrapies, as well as taxes paid by individuals. Strabo (11.8.3) writes that the plain-dwellers of Hyrcania, Nesaea, and Parthia agreed to pay Central Asian nomads tribute (*phoros*), which consisted of the right to plunder their territory at appointed times each year; if they plundered on more than those occasions, then the inhabitants would go to war. Such tributary relations could acquire ritualized forms and even resemble voluntary gifts or contributions to allies. Skythian nomads regularly came to collect their gifts (*dora*) from the Greek citizens of Olbia on the Black Sea, which ensured the partially unwalled city's protection; when the treasury was empty, their benefactor Protogenes advanced them hundreds of gold pieces to appease the Skythian chief (*Syll.*[3] 495; Austin 2006, no. 115).

A similar phenomenon may be observed in the incipient formation of agrarian states. In the Homeric epics, for example, plunder was one of the essential means for kings to reward their military entourage and attract men for military service. Agamemnon is called the "lord of many islands," and if the Achaeans succeeded at sacking Troy, it was imagined that the Trojans and their descendants would pay tribute (*phoros*) to the Argives (Hom. *Il.* 2.69–144). Hoping to win over Achilles, Agamemnon offered him his daughter in marriage and a dowry of seven cities, which "will honor him with gifts as though he were a god, and beneath his scepter will bring his ordinances to prosperous fulfillment" (*Il.* 9.149–56, 291–8). Menelaus was confident about receiving gifts from cities when traveling in the Peloponnese (*Od.* 15.80–5). On a smaller scale, such relationships are analogous to the formation of hegemonic or imperial states that struggle to integrate subjected communities and where the line between consensual gifts and coercive tribute is porous.

In fifth-century Greece, the Delian League adopted the term *phoros* for what was initially a voluntary payment. Aristides was praised for his assessment (Plut. *Vit. Arist.* 24), but fiscal pressure in the Peloponnesian War prompted Athens to ratchet up the tribute. One-sixtieth went to the treasury of Athena, recorded on a series of inscriptions that survive from 454/3 to 406/5.[4] Athens' increasing monopoly on violence and lack of institutional constraints ultimately tempted it to limit or transgress its allies' sovereignty. The term *phoros* became tainted by the experience of the fifth-century empire, so when Athens formed a new confederacy in 378/7, the charter explicitly forbade it. The league's council (*synedrion*) had to consent to contributions (*syntaxeis*) to the common treasury and was normally responsible for assessing them.[5] Even then, the line between coercion and consent, just as gift and tribute, was fluid, so Athens' commitment to the rules could be tested in crises such as the events leading to allied revolt in the Social War of 357–355 (Diod. Sic. 16.7.21–2).[6] Though probably a rhetorical exaggeration, a contemporary Athenian politician could claim, "they called tribute payments (*phoroi*) contributions (*syntaxeis*) because the Greeks were loath to pay them by the name of tribute payments."[7]

According to Herodotus (1.6), Croesus had been the first to demand tribute (*phoros*) from the Greeks of Asia Minor. When Cyrus conquered his kingdom, tribute fell to the Persians, and Darius I was allegedly responsible for reforming the tributary system from ad hoc demands of "gifts" into standardized payments from each satrapy.[8] Herodotus was unaware of the complexity of Achaemenid taxation in Babylonia, but his account is perhaps basically accurate for the western empire or at least the Greek cities of Asia Minor.[9] In 493/2, after the Ionian revolt, the Persian governor Artaphernes fixed the *phoroi* of each city according to new measurements of their land (Hdt. 6.42; Diod. Sic. 10.25.4).[10] This one-time survey provided a point of reference, but the rates remained fixed thereafter because the satrap, much less the king, had little knowledge of local economic realities. Those who did have

[4] *ATL*; Meiggs, *AE* 234–54; Samons 2000.
[5] Rhodes and Osborne 2003, no. 22 with comm. 101–2, cf. no. 72.   [6] Cargill 1981, 124–7.
[7] *FGrH* 115 F 98; cf. Plut. *Vit. Sol.* 15.
[8] Hdt. 3.90–4; Plutarch, *Mor.* 172; Polyaenus, *Strat.* 7.11.3.   [9] Jursa 2011.
[10] Aperghis 2004, 139–42.

that knowledge could use it to siphon away tax revenue from the central government. It was a tributary regime that depended on the mediation of local elites, who possessed considerable autonomy from the state.

At the top of the pyramid, the satrap was assessed a fixed tribute to the king. Under the satrap, there were districts called chiliarchies, as well as Greek cities that would be liable for fixed payments to the satrap. They in turn would have collected the fixed amounts assessed on villages and agricultural estates as well as other royal taxes.[11] These were usually designated with the plural form of *phoros* or *dasmos*; the latter was perhaps the older Greek term for Achaemenid tribute.[12] The estate of Mnesimachus in the Hellenistic period must originally have been allocated by an Achaemenid king or satrap because the assessment of taxes (*phoroi*) paid to the chiliarchy implies subdivisions of the gold *daric* (Chapter 16, this volume), which was no longer used after Alexander's conquest; the rate was one-twelfth of the value of the estate.[13] When cities were allocated to individuals, as when Cyrus the Younger gave several Greek cities to the Spartan Lysander (Xen. *Hell.* 2.1.11, 2.1.14; Plut. *Vit. Lys.* 9.2; Diod. Sic. 13.104.4), they became beneficiaries of the royal taxes. Cities or their local governors could exempt individuals from city taxes and royal taxes arising from the tribute levied on the community but not necessarily from all royal taxes, which implies some penetration of local economies already in the Achaemenid period (*Syll.*[3] 311; *ILabraunda* 42).

Tribute obligations enabled Greek city-states to justify direct taxes. To put it differently, an empire's protection allowed local rulers, such as the tyrants and oligarchs on whom the Persians relied, to extract taxes from the population without their consent. Athens probably based its own fifth-century tributary system on the Achaemenid one in Asia Minor.[14] However, it is likely that Athens' allies in the fifth century passed much of the cost onto the wealthy as property taxes (*eisphorai*).[15] Democratic factions could count on Athens' military support in the event of strife. That does not exclude the possibility that revenue derived through indirect taxes was also factored into the tribute assessment.[16] However, the Athenians' contribution (*syntaxis*) to its own fourth-century confederacy was raised primarily through the *eisphora* on elite property.[17] There was an element of consent on the part of allies, as already noted, which resembles the assessment of federal

---

[11] Debord 1999, 41–4.   [12] Xen. *Oec.* 4.9–11; Murray 1966.
[13] Descat 1985; Aperghis 2004, 137–9; Thonemann 2009.   [14] Raaflaub 2009.
[15] Samons 2000, 91 n. 37, 182, 236 n. 88, 252; cf. Chankowski 2007.
[16] Figueira 1998, 52, 58, 106, 298–9; cf. ibid., 514 n. 47.   [17] Brun 1983, 29, 41.

contributions of other Greek leagues.[18] Similarly, the supreme magistrate (*tagos*) of Thessaly was entitled to tribute and manpower from the cities and surrounding communities (*perioikoi*), which were levied at fixed amounts and passed down to individuals.[19]

Alexander the Great announced at Ephesus in 334 that the Greeks in Asia were to be free, autonomous, and *aphorologetos* or exempt from royal taxation (Diod. Sic. 17.24.1). Most cities were still expected to make collective contributions (*syntaxeis*) to his campaign, but these were not the same as *phoroi*, which also refer to the taxes on individuals. He clarified his decree's applicability to Greeks of Naulochon, an ethnically mixed settlement within Prienean territory, giving them the same status as Prienean citizens, who would be charged taxes (*phoroi*) only on landholdings within two villages that he claimed as his own. He added that Priene would be exempt from the *syntaxis*.[20] The Greek city of Aspendos initially agreed to pay a contribution of silver and horses previously given to the Persian king as tribute, a payment that exemplifies the *syntaxis*. When the city reneged on its promise, Alexander forced it to obey the satrapal administration and to pay taxes (*phoroi*) to the Macedonians (Arr. *Anab.* 1.26.3, 1.27.4). Alexander appointed several financial officials alongside or above the satraps, who were tasked with the assessment of taxes (*phoroi*) in cities such as Aspendos and other subjected territories that did not benefit from his decree (Arr. *Anab.* 1.17.7, 3.5.4, 3.6.4, 3.16.4).

FROM TRIBUTE TO TAXATION

Whereas tribute is a mediated form of extraction, largely divorced from economic processes, taxation requires local knowledge about property, population, productivity, and flows of goods. With administrative and monetary reforms, royal officials in the Hellenistic kingdoms increasingly penetrated below intermediate levels of tributary extraction to maximize what James C. Scott calls a society's legibility.[21] The second book of the Aristotelian *Oikonomika* encourages overseers of the satrapal and city financial administration to learn as much as possible about local taxes. It cites the land tax (*ekphorion* or *dekate*) as the most important one but also mentions various poll taxes, tolls and market taxes, taxes on trades and professions, and others. While these taxes existed in the

---

[18] Mackil 2013, 295–304.
[19] Xen. *Hell.* 6.1.9, 12, 19; *IG* IX 2, 257 with van Wees 2013, 154–5 n. 33.
[20] *IPriene* 1, Thonemann 2013a.   [21] Scott 1998.

Achaemenid empire, specialized officials were now being exhorted to develop comprehensive systems drawing on Greek expertise and anecdotes. It is a unique specimen of a fiscal handbook, which parallels other technical treatises (cf. Polyaenus, *Strat.*) produced in the Hellenistic period.

The foundation of cities was one of the most effective ways by which the kings reshaped the political landscape to assert greater fiscal control over land and trade (Chapters 4, 5, and 9, this volume). Tribute on Greek cities as an annual lump sum appears to have become the exception rather than the rule.[22] The case of Amlada in Pisidia, where Eumenes II demanded an annual tribute of two talents of silver (*RC* 17) is unusual. Instead, the royal economy permeated the city's economic fabric. Whether the city or king had sovereignty (*kyreia*) over particular revenues was always up for negotiation, and there were typically separate royal (*to basilikon*) and city (*to politikon*) treasuries in each city (e.g. *IMylasa* 1.201, ll. 8–11). The visibility of tax exemption (*ateleia*) granted to cities by the kings in Asia Minor testifies to its exceptionality; they needed to be set in stone, and even that was not enough. Attalid rule in Asia Minor after 188 was exceptional for the degree of autonomy that cities obtained and for the dynasty's willingness to alienate royal land to cities' territory. To the extent that the cities were more adept at achieving fiscal legibility than a central bureaucracy, this was not necessarily a less-profitable solution.[23] On the other hand, the Attalids at that time were arguably more comfortable than either the Ptolemies or the Seleucids with conceding a large share of the agricultural surplus to urban elites.

Hellenistic Egypt provides the best example of an increasingly thick state (even by ancient Egyptian standards) that closely monitored and enforced tax collection to maximize revenue (see also Chapter 9, this volume). Land had been surveyed and taxed in Egypt for millennia, but nothing compares to the elaborate procedures adopted in the third century.[24] Detailed census registers were used to levy a salt tax on virtually all men and women, including Greeks. The rates were low, but it had to be paid in coin, so it helped accelerate the process of monetization that is visible throughout the Hellenistic world. Much higher capitation taxes are attested in the late Ptolemaic period, but only men were charged, and the rates varied.[25] Poll taxes existed within the royal territories of other Hellenistic monarchies too. Antiochus III exempted temple personnel in Jerusalem from a poll tax.[26] In the

---

[22] Schuler 2007; Capdetrey 2007; Kaye 2015.   [23] Thonemann 2013b.
[24] Armoni 2012, 172–228.   [25] Monson 2014.   [26] Joseph. *AJ* 12.142.

Attalid kingdom, inhabitants of a Carian village next to the city of Telmessus but on royal land had to pay a poll tax in coin (Maier 1959, no. 76, Austin 2006, no. 238). In Greek city-states, by contrast, regular capitation taxes such as the *metoikion* (metics' tax) in Athens normally fell only on non-citizen residents. However, they could be incorporated into emergency tax levies (*eisphora*) on citizens.[27]

The once-dominant theory of absolute royal ownership, which is akin to the discredited theory of oriental despotism and the Marxist Asiatic mode of production, has been subject to withering critique. Hellenistic kings were sovereign over their land with robust claims on its surplus but recognized entrenched social and legal conventions.[28] In Hellenistic Egypt, a new papyrus from the second century reveals that most of the land in one southern province was classed as private land (*idioktetos ge*), which could be bought and sold, and was subject to royal taxes (*en phorologiai*). The average rate of tax was 5⅓ *artabas* per *aroura* (*P. Haun.* IV 70). That was about one-quarter to one-half of the harvest, comparable to the rates paid by cultivators of other royal land, who lacked property rights. It was obviously effective in some regions to privatize royal land without the king surrendering his fiscal claims.

The layers of mediation between Hellenistic kings and the economy are well illustrated in Coele Syria. Royal taxes and tribute were guaranteed by a pyramidal regime of large-scale tax farmers and local rulers. Josephus (*AJ* 12.4) relates that the Jewish high priest Onias withheld tribute of twenty talents. His nephew Joseph traveled to the Ptolemaic king in Alexandria, just as tax farmers were arriving from Syria-Phoenicia in the southern Levant. Joseph convinced him that they were colluding with low bids and obtained the farm for the entire province. Later, Antiochus III granted Ptolemy V a share of the province's total revenue as a dowry for Cleopatra I through a tax-farming scheme.[29] Fiscal pressure after 188 prompted the Seleucids to maximize revenue by cutting into the profits and autonomy of cities and local elites. Antiochus IV sold the Jewish high priesthood to whomever offered the highest tribute, and a Seleucid governor contemplated an annual sale (2 Macc. 4.7–10, 11.1–3). At one point the inhabitants were required to pay taxes to the king, including one-third of the harvest, without a high priest as intermediary (Joseph. *AJ* 13.2.3; 1 Macc. 10–11). These Seleucid innovations for fiscal legibility foundered on fierce Jewish resistance.[30]

---

[27] See below, p. 271; Gauthier 1991, 60–4; Migeotte 2014, 244–8, 507–8.
[28] J. G. Manning 2010, 55–72.   [29] Kaye and Amitay 2015.
[30] Mittwoch 1955; Aperghis 2004, 169–71; Honigman 2014; Monson 2016.

CONSENT AND COERCION

Apart from Athens' fifth-century empire, there were few Greek city-states that could finance themselves primarily from tribute, so they had to raise revenue internally. The power of citizens in the polis encouraged city officials to search for alternative sources of revenue such as indirect taxes and mineral resources or to pass the burden onto resident aliens and foreign subjects. However, cities could and frequently did resort to taxing their citizens. Athenians who obtained allotments of land on the islands of Imbros, Lemnos, and Skyros had to contribute to Athens' grain supply.[31] Herodotus (6.46) implies that citizens of Thasos regularly paid taxes on agricultural yields until their mining revenue was sufficient to abolish them. Mende ceased to tax land and houses in the fourth century thanks to the proceeds of its indirect taxes but kept a register of land and houses for emergencies.[32] Extraordinary levies, known as *eisphorai*, typically fell on either property or produce (cf. Pl. *Leg.* 955de) and were a common feature of the Greeks' fiscal repertoire. The same term was used for periodic levies of federal taxes by Greek federations on member states.[33] It connotes a measure of consent and legitimacy for the public fund, which was vital for compliance.

Some Greek cities, especially in Asia Minor and Crete, ruled over subject populations who enjoyed customary land tenure for paying direct taxes (*phoroi*) to the city treasury.[34] Sparta went even further, enslaving the Messenians and Laconians instead of collecting state taxes from them (Paus. 4.14.4–5). The polis collectively owned these helots, but they worked land belonging to individual citizens. Consequently, Sparta's fiscal capacity lagged far behind its military strength. In the fourth century, Aristotle (*Pol.* 1271b, 11–15) claims, "The public finance of Sparta is badly organized, for when compelled to wage large-scale wars there is nothing in the state treasury, and the Spartans pay extraordinary levies (*eisphorai*) badly because most of the land is owned by them so they do not scrutinize one another's contributions."[35] Having a thin state enabled Sparta's landowning oligarchy to keep the helots' surplus in private hands and to devote themselves fully to military exercise by which to oppress them and wage war. They abhorred the redistribution of land or public revenue by state officials, whether kings, generals, or political reformers, whose ambitions threatened to undermine their celebrated mixed constitution.

---

[31] Stroud 1998; Magnetto, Erdas, and Carusi 2010.
[32] Arist. [*Oec.*] 2.2.21a; Migeotte 2014, 237.   [33] Mackil 2013, 295–304.   [34] Migeotte 2014.
[35] Cf. Loomis 1992, 82–3.

Sparta's system contrasts with Athenian public finance, but both can be traced back to patterns observable in the Homeric epics of the early archaic period. When the Phaeacian king Alcinous wished to provide Odysseus with a ship, he had to ask the other *basileis* at an assembly to contribute towards the public fund and told them to recover their expenses from the *demos* (Hom. *Od.* 13.10–15). We have, in other words, a protostate with an assembly of aristocratic warriors, which consents to pay an extraordinary tax and also legitimizes its extortion from the people. Unlike Sparta, archaic Athens had no helot population to oppress, so elites were tied more by kinship and patronage to the agricultural producers. For public expenses such as sacrifices, religious events, and above all warfare, the Athenians organized their territory into forty-eight districts called *naukrariai*, each controlled by one local notable (*naukraros*). His title hints at an original duty to provide a ship, but his contributions also included horsemen for the cavalry and other resources for the treasury; they were empowered to levy taxes (*eisphorai*) within their home district.[36]

The classical Athenian *eisphora* evolved out of these archaic institutions. Solon's classes were linked to political rights, so the wealthy had an incentive to report their agricultural income, which facilitated taxation. The tithe of agricultural income levied by Pisistratus (Arist. [*Ath. Pol.*] 16.4), at the rate of one-twentieth under Hippias (Thuc. 6.54.5), would have been more feasible to levy as a percentage of one's declared income bracket than as a real percentage of the harvest. Hippias introduced several other measures to enhance Athens' fiscal capacity as well, including the trierarchy (Arist. [*Oec.*] 2.2.4), which was one of the most onerous public liturgies that the wealthy had to perform in the classical period.[37] The trireme revolutionized naval warfare in the late sixth century and dramatically increased its costs, necessitating further reforms by Cleisthenes (Arist. [*Oec.*] 21.5) and the democratic government, which created the more progressive *eisphora* described by Pollux.[38]

Imperial tribute, mining revenue, and a busy harbor allowed Athens to avoid regular *eisphora* levies, but when the empire collapsed at the end of the fifth century, the Athenians had to innovate again. In 378/7, when the Second Confederacy was founded, they made a new assessment of elite property, a percentage of which was to be paid for each *eisphora* (Polyb. 2.62.6; Dem. 27).[39] At the same time, Athens developed a more centralized system of budgeting and allocating its

---

[36] Arist. [*Ath. Pol.*] 8.3; van Wees 2013, 44–61.   [37] Gabrielsen 1994a.
[38] van Wees 2013, 85–91.   [39] Brun 1983; Migeotte 2014, 518–24.

revenue to keep up with the cost of warfare. This "planification" of public revenue was typical of Greek city-states in the fourth and third centuries.[40] Although wealthy taxpayers scorned property levies and confiscations, which Aristotle (*Pol.* 1320a; cf. Dem. 22.51) attributes to democracies generally, polis institutions protected their property rights. The fiscal burden of the wealthy, including liturgies, as well as their voluntary contributions and loans to the state, gave them a powerful rhetorical defense and in some cases control of the fiscal administration itself. This grand bargain, forged in an era of costly interstate warfare, contributed to Athens' high per capita revenue and expenditure, which reached a scale virtually unmatched until the rise of modern tax states.[41]

Kings recognized the fiscal advantages of Greek city-state institutions. Arrian (*Anab.* 1.16.5) tells us that Alexander exempted the families of Macedonians who perished at Granicus in 334 from property taxes (*eisphorai kata tas kteseis hekaston*). The Macedonian kings in Egypt likewise adopted extraordinary levies on property modeled on those of Greek city-states. Ptolemy IV Philopator required his subjects to declare the value of their houses and pay a special tax on them.[42] Ptolemy VI Philometor turned to his Graeco-Macedonian settlers (*katoikoi*) in Egypt for an *eisphora* of a lump sum of wheat, which was apportioned among them as a land tax (*P.Lips.* II 124; *P.Tebt.* I 99). Cleopatra VII later instituted this type of wheat levy on the *katoikoi*, again coupled with the crown tax (*stephanos*); they are described as an *eisphora* levied periodically in extraordinary circumstances (*C.Ord. Ptol.* 75–6; *BGU* 8.1760).[43] The Attalid king Eumenes II likewise imposed an *eisphora* on some of the military settlers (*katoikountes*) in Apollonioucharax in Asia Minor, perhaps only the wealthy.[44]

It was common for such levies to take the form of capitation taxes, especially when they fell on citizens without property or when property assessment was unfeasible. To raise money for war in the fourth century, the Athenians of Potidaea assessed property values and, for citizens without property, fixed the value of each person (*soma*) at two minas (Ath. [*Oec.*] 2.2.5); for an *eisphora* of one-twentieth, for example, one would pay ten drachms. When the Athenian mercenary commander Chabrias offered King Taos of Egypt advice for his war with Persia, he too proposed taxes on the value of one's house or one's person (*soma*) (Arist. [*Oec.*] 2.2.25a). Benefactors of Priene and two Carian cities in the

[40] Gabrielsen 1994a; Leppin 1995; Rhodes 2013; Migeotte 2014, 58–69, 444–9.
[41] van Wees 2013, 1; Fawcett 2016, 90–2.   [42] Armoni 2012, 215 n. 153.
[43] Monson 2012, 176–84.   [44] Thonemann 2011, 24.

Hellenistic period were honored with an exemption for their person (*ateleia tou somatos*). To be free from more onerous public liturgies in Priene such as the trierarchy and the duty of paying the *eisphora* in advance required even greater benefactions (*IPriene* 174). Perhaps the *eisphora* in Priene was not on property, at least not solely. The city of Amyzon in Caria, for example, partitioned its *eisphora* among adult citizens on their person at the same five-drachm rate. Xanthos in Lycia distinguishes the *eisphora* of the richest citizens (on property?) from the *epibole* or impost of all citizens (on persons?), which the assembly was forbidden by its own decree from levying for nine years.[45]

Property taxes have historically succeeded at tapping elite wealth in premodern societies only when the state enjoys legitimacy based on the taxpayers' consent as well as the coercive power to execute its authority. One witnesses these obstacles in the texts from Ptolemaic Egypt cited above: the house tax was followed by a major revolt and was never repeated. The accounts for the *eisphora* of Ptolemy VI indicate that military settlers refused to pay, and by 118 it had been abolished. When Cleopatra VII revived it, her finance minister issued threats to her overseers of revenue, holding them liable for arrears, and Alexandrian landowners were still able to carve out an exemption. Compliance varied in Greek city-states, as Aristotle's remark about Sparta illustrates, but scaling up quasi-consensual taxation to larger polities was even more difficult. In medieval England, for example, it took horrendous wars, the Magna Carta, and the birth of Parliament for Plantagenet kings (the ruling dynasty in England from 1154 to 1399) to impose periodic taxes as a percentage of property values on the model of Italian city communes.

TAXATION AND THE ECONOMY

A wide range of indirect taxes were levied in the Greek city-states, including various sales taxes, fees, tolls, and the like, but customs and harbor taxes stand out as particularly important.[46] The customs law of the Roman province of Asia provides details about procedures, most of which date back to the Hellenistic period.[47] Nicholas Purcell links their significance to the connectivity of seaborne trade, but politics must have been a factor too.[48] Bronze Age palatial societies in the Aegean relied more on agricultural levies of livestock and cereals. After those fiscal

[45] Gauthier 1991, 61–8; Amyzon: Robert and Robert 1983, 217–26 no. 28; Xanthos: Bousquet 1988b, 15, ll. 53–7.

[46] Migeotte 2014, 248–76.   [47] Cottier et al. 2008.   [48] Purcell 2005.

institutions collapsed, Dark Age chiefdoms and the archaic polis depended on aristocratic cooperation for collective action. It was never easy to get people to pay taxes voluntarily, and in the absence of a coercive bureaucracy, there was often no choice but to find alternative sources of revenue if the kings or governing officials wished to pursue their goals autonomously from the ruling class.

All it took was control over key nodes of exchange such as harbors, bridges, passes, city gates, and markets to acquire a protection monopoly and levy taxes. There is virtually no state in antiquity that did not do so, but few profited from and depended on them as much as the Greek city-states. The volume of trade was a key factor, which maritime connectivity facilitated, but that depended on other factors, some endogenous to the fiscal regime. Many small Greek cities could not rely on indirect taxes and had to make levies on people and their property.[49] Besides a high volume of trade, states needed to absorb the volatility and unpredictability inherent in such revenues. One of the pitfalls of relying on indirect taxes is that they tend to dry up precipitously precisely when they are needed most, in times of war and economic instability. Greek city-states were able to rely so heavily on indirect taxes because they were capable of making credible commitments to protect the interests of traders, of regulating tax farms (see below, p. 276) that ensured the fiscal legibility necessary for planning expenditure, and of contracting public debt to weather deficits.

An ancestor of customs duties are gifts such as the mixing bowl that Phoenicians gave to Thoas upon landing in his harbor (Hom. *Il.* 23.741– 5). Such prestige items might help fortify the ruler's position amidst his aristocratic competitors. Yet early Greek trade was still a violent affair, hardly distinguishable from piracy, and without a strong state a ruler's goodwill was worth little. The Isthmus of Corinth was an exceptional geographical choke point, where the Bacchiadae dynasty established power by controlling trade (Strab. 8.6.20). A port such as Ephesus could demand large sums of gold, silver, and wood as early as 600 or 550 (*IEphesos* 1 1). One may compare it with the payments attested in the Aramaic customs-duty papyrus from Egypt (Porten and Yardeni 1993, C3.7, ca. 475), which shows a 10 percent *ad valorem* duty on imports by Greek and Phoenician ships through the *emporion* of Thonis/Naucratis. The rates in Egypt and the Near East were generally higher than in Greece and display greater variability, even arbitrariness. In Ptolemaic Egypt, customs duties on goods

---

[49] Cf. Gauthier 1991, 65–6.

imported through Alexandria were as high as 50 percent on some com-modities (*P.Cair.Zen.* 1 59012). Taxes this high were possible because the rulers regulated access to large, rich markets in the manner of stationary bandits, who profited directly from taxes while suffering only indirectly from harming the traders and consumers, who lacked political influence.[50]

In the city-states of classical and Hellenistic Greece the most common rate for import and export duties (*exagogia* and *eisagogia*) was a mere 2 percent. It was sometimes called the *ellimenion* or "harbor duty," though the same term could also apply narrowly to the fee for using the harbor or to both simultaneously.[51] Rates probably had to be kept low because there was more competition between Aegean sea-ports, which worked in the traders' favor, and because the cost of taxation would be passed onto citizens who exerted control over the government. The city-states used tax exemptions to stimulate trade, to rebuild after wars or famines, and to reward benefactions. In 413, the Athenians introduced a 5 percent duty on all goods transported by sea in place of tribute (Thuc. 7.28.3–4). This short-lived experiment shows how far Athens was moving away from a tributary empire towards a thicker pan-Hellenic state under Athenian domination. If the switch from tribute to indirect tax had been permanent, it might have aligned Athens' interests even more tightly with the facilitation of trade. Early Hellenistic Rhodes kept the seas free from piracy thanks to its harbor revenue, farmed out at 1,000,000 drachms annually or roughly a quarter of Athens' imperial tribute in 425 (Thuc. 2.13.2), until Rome turned Delos into a rival tax-free port in 167 (Polyb. 30.31.10–12).

Tax farming (that is, the purchase by auction (and thus usually prepayment) of the entire estimated volume of a certain indirect tax by private entrepreneurs for one year) is historically common among premodern states, as it improved legibility and mitigated the risk of indirect taxes, but Greek institutions are distinctive. First, there was relatively open access to tax-farm auctions. In the Neo-Babylonian and Achaemenid empires, the business was dominated by a few powerful dynasties of politically connected and capital-rich entrepreneurs similar to those of Hellenistic Syria-Phoenicia noted above (p. 270). This was Macedonia's problem in the 370s, when the Athenian politician Callistratus advised the king how to double his revenue by lowering surety requirements, which allowed wealthy bidders to exclude

---

[50] Olson 2000 on the stationary-bandit state model that has been found useful to understand a ruler's choice to share some benefits with other parties and the development of legal rights to secure property and facilitate trade; see e.g., Monson 2012, 24–5, 249–55; and Monson 2015.
[51] Cararra 2014.

competitors (Arist. [*Oec.*] 2.2.22). Second, by almost any premodern comparison, the legal constraints on tax farmers in the Greek city-states were considerable. They had little autonomy and slim profit margins, preventing the degree of extortion witnessed by Rome's *publicani* in the later Hellenistic period or the notorious Ottoman *mültezim*.[52]

CONCLUSION

The element of consent that made Greek property taxes yield potentially high revenue in the classical period also made them contingent and irregular. When tributary exploitation or mining and other income sources were viable strategies of easing the citizens' tax burden, many Greek city-states made use of them. In his treatise on Athenian public finance, Xenophon condemned tribute as an unjust source of revenue but wanted to relieve the city's dependence on the property taxes of wealthy citizens. He urged Athenians to attract more taxpaying resident aliens, to encourage trade, and to invest in harbor facilities and especially silver mines (Xen. *Vect.* 2.1–3.13). They obviously implemented many of his suggestions, liberalizing conditions for foreigners, introducing overseers to ensure the purity of coinage and lower transaction costs on the market, and streamlining the commercial laws, so traders could get swift justice in Athenian courts.[53] Athenian revenue and expenditure in the fourth century rose to per capita levels that were probably not matched before early modern European tax states.

Athens is a special case, but the Greeks undoubtedly shared a common fiscal repertoire, where innovations spread quickly through social networks and peer-polity competition. Tributary states, by contrast, typically extract revenue from subjected communities without much intervention in their economic organization. While they may offer protection, it is often no better than that of organized criminals, as described by St. Augustine (*De civ. D.* 4.4). When the government is not accountable to law, it loses the trust and legitimacy that enhance taxpayer compliance and encourage productivity and trade. Athens' own fifth-century empire testifies to the irresistible temptation to exploit its allies' resources. That was also a dilemma for Hellenistic kings, who valued the legibility and legitimation of cities and federations, imitating their fiscal and legal institutions, but were too rich and powerful to credibly commit to constitutional monarchy.

[52] Tan 2017, 40–67.   [53] Ober 2015a, 244–6.

Further Reading

The most important recent work on the Greek city-states is Migeotte 2014, which focuses on the classical and Hellenistic period; for general surveys see also Gabrielsen 1994a and Mackil 2015b. For the archaic period, especially Athens, see van Wees 2013. Classical Athens is the subject of several outstanding survey articles, including Rhodes 2013, Ober 2015a, and Fawcett 2016; for the Athenian tribute, see Samons 2000. Achaemenid tribute was the topic of Briant and Herrenschmidt 1989, but for new Babylonian perspectives, see Kleber 2015. Kaye 2015 surveys taxation and tribute in the Hellenistic east with a focus on Asia Minor, while Capdetrey 2007 analyzes the Seleucid empire and Huss 2011 assembles material from Ptolemaic Egypt. Klinkott, Kubisch, and Müller-Wollermann 2007 and Monson and Scheidel 2015 provide studies of fiscal institutions in the Greek world and comparable societies.

PART IV

NETWORKS

19: RELIGIOUS NETWORKS

Véronique Chankowski

INTRODUCTION

In the Greek city, religious and economic activity were intimately bound up with the civic framework. While many economic connections can be observed within the religious sphere, their links are not straightforward. Max Weber's suggestion of connections between Protestant ethics and capitalism does not carry over to antiquity, since for Weber ancient capitalism was mainly agrarian, while 'banking capitalism' was typical of Catholic countries and 'corporate capitalism' of Protestant traditions.[1] The Judeo-Christian tradition in general tends to emphasize a conflict between religious practice and the market, an opposition perpetuated in medieval scholastic thought and its theories of 'just price', which aimed to moderate financial practices thought to be driven by an excessive desire for profit.[2] The moral stance of such politics immediately raises the question of the effects that religious norms have on economic performance: did the connections between religion and the economy in the ancient world affect the economy positively, or did they lock exchange into principles that discredited profit and thus impeded growth? As the civic framework was so important for both religious and economic practices in ancient Greece, we need to ask in what ways the Greek city, the guarantor of the proper functioning of cults, affected the particular relationship between religion and the economy.

The concept of networks has been used relatively rarely for answering these questions. While network and connectivity approaches have become essential for the study of monetary circulation and exchange (Chapter 20, this volume), they have only recently been applied to religious networks with the assumption that these were also networks of exchange.[3] The question that needs to be tackled is to determine the exact articulation of economic relationships within cult

[1] Mommsen 2005.   [2] De Roover 1958; Chankowski, Lenoble, and Maucourant 2019.
[3] See for instance Kowalzig 2018.

and other religious activities. Did economic relationships follow pre-existing religious networks, or did cults accompany economic activities just as they accompanied other areas of social life? Insofar as religious activity concerns several levels of society – individuals, the state, civic subdivisions, associations, and various forms of solidarity groups – the question arises of whether the same codes of conduct applied to religious and economic interaction, or whether religious and economic network relationships were competing or conflicting. Were economic activities in religious contexts embedded in politics, or did particular religious norms support them? What kinds of economic power structures were generated through religious networks? Sanctuaries were privileged places for the honorary decrees which form our best evidence for elite networks between cities.[4]

CULTS AND THE FLOW OF TRADE

Religious practices surrounded all commercial activities in the Greek world. Cults and rituals accompanied the travels of merchants and sailors.[5] Several deities were involved in the protection of seafarers asking for safe travel. Prayers often invoked Poseidon and Aphrodite, as well as Zeus *Soter*, Athena *Soteira*, Athena or Aphrodite *Pontie*, Dionysus, the maritime Nymphai, and *Euploia* as the divinized abstraction of good navigation, as can be seen in several literary and epigraphic testimonies.[6] A regulation from Cos prescribed that sailors should sacrifice to Aphrodite *Pontie* in the appropriate sanctuary when they stayed there or passed through.[7]

Anchors made of wood, stone, or lead were frequently dedicated to saviour deities, possibly in commemoration of perils encountered by the navigator reaching port safely.[8] Aphrodite *Epilimenia*, who received votive anchors in her sanctuary in Aegina, is also mentioned in the dedication of a Chian bowl found in Naucratis, from the sailor

---

[4] See for instance Étienne 2018 on the sanctuary of Apollo on Delos.

[5] Wachsmuth 1967; Lindenlauf 2003; Fenet 2016.

[6] Dionysus is celebrated as a god who brings all the goods of the world by sea in Hermippus (Ath. 1.27e: 'Muses, who live in Olympus, tell me about all the goods Dionysus has provided to humans since his travels by sea on a black ship'); votive inscriptions to Euploia after a safe maritime journey: *IG* XII 5, 712, 25–30 (Syros); *IG* XII 8, 581–86 (Thasos); the Coryphaios ends the *Philoctetes* with this injunction: 'Let us all go together and pray to the Marine Nymphs to protect our return' (Soph. *Phil.* 1469–71).

[7] *IG* XII 4, 319, l. 6.

[8] Delos: Deonna 1938, 198. Aegina: *IG* IV² 2, 1005 (anchor from the fifth century dedicated to Aphrodite Epilimenia).

Sostratus.[9] If this Sostratus was an Aeginetan trader from the same family as mentioned by Herodotus (4.152), it would be a clear testimony of the spread of worship through sailors, who prayed at home to the same goddess Aphrodite for a safe journey and thanked her upon their arrival at the foreign port for heeding their prayer.[10]

On board, several artefacts found in shipwrecks were intended to protect the crew and to make the gods favourable for the sea crossing: portable altars, statuettes, lead horns, and *louteria* for ritual ablutions.[11] Athenaeus (15.676a), quoting Polycharmus of Naucratis, reports that sailors were saved from shipwreck during a violent storm after they prayed to a statuette of Aphrodite from Cyprus. The ship was thus not just a cargo platform for the transport of goods but also a communication platform between men and gods, in the form of ritual acts, sacrifices, and libations.

Cults and rituals were also part of the life of traders and retailers working in shops and markets. Next to their stalls and *skenai* (tents), which were provided for itinerant merchants, gods and heroes were present in the form of sanctuaries, altars, and statues. There was a functional connection between cults and the market, expressed by the epithet *agoraios* for deities such as Zeus and Hermes. Merchants, moreover, often used oaths – and perjuries in some cases – invoking gods in order to assure their customers of their honesty. Sometimes oaths were even substituted for written contracts in commercial transactions.[12] In the description of his ideal city, Plato condemns oaths that accompanied fraud and lies in the agora (*Leg.* 11.917c). *Kapeloi* (retail traders) were also known to use curses (*katadesmoi*) by invoking underground deities such as Hermes, Demeter, Persephone, or Hekate against their commercial competitors. Extant tablets (*defixiones*) tell of hopes for divine vengeance against opponents who ruined *kapeleia*.[13] Several deities were invoked by both sailors and merchants of the agora, without very clear indications of what shaped this pantheon. Eventually, it was the epithet added to the name of a god or goddess that constituted the pantheon, and the network of divinities specific to the sea and the market protected the success of commercial activities.

---

[9] Williams 1983, but doubts are expressed by Möller 2000, 56–7.

[10] Polinskaya 2013, 197–202.

[11] These artefacts, which are generally found at the stern of the ship, are clearly distinct from the ship's cargo.

[12] Dover 1994, 249; Burkert 1985, 250–4; Silver 1995, 10–18 with Near East parallels; Rauh 1993, 129–50.

[13] See for instance a recently published *defixio* found in Piraeus by Lamont 2015. See also Sinn 2005.

At the level of civic communities, it can be observed from the earliest phases of colonization in the archaic period (Chapter 3, this volume) that religion travelled with people, taking root in the load-breaking points that constituted the nodes of commercial networks. When the Phocaeans left their city, threatened by the Achaemenid expansion during the middle of the sixth century, they organized the whole community to flee westwards, taking with them 'the statues of the gods from the sanctuaries and other offerings' (Hdt. 1.167). In the account of Massalia's foundation, the Phocaeans are said to have founded the cult of Ephesian Artemis, as advised in a dream: 'Aristarche, one of the most-esteemed women in this city, saw in a dream the goddess standing before her and ordering her to embark with the Phocaeans, taking with her a model of the sanctuary' (Strab. 4.1.4). There is a close connection between sanctuaries and *emporia*: the great *emporia* of the archaic period such as Gravisca, Pyrgi, and Naucratis were all organized around important sanctuaries.[14]

Cult places and cult networks related to local or regional trade[15] should not make us forget long-distance maritime networks. Usually, Greeks moving to foreign cities within the Hellenic world did not need to build their own sanctuaries, since all Greeks shared a common pantheon, and access to sanctuaries was not restricted to the citizens of a city. Foreigners (whether Greeks or non-Greeks) could dedicate and even make sacrifices there. The situation was different once Greeks left the Greek cultural framework and had to seek permission from local authorities to raise sanctuaries for their gods.

Greek traders travelling to Egypt benefited from agreements with the pharaonic authorities since archaic times, as Herodotus tells us:

> Being a friend of the Greeks, Amasis gave some of them signs
> of his benevolence; in particular, to those who came to
> Egypt, he offered to live in the city of Naucratis; to those
> who did not want to live there, but who were brought there
> by navigation, he granted sites to build altars and sanctuaries
> to their gods. The largest of these sanctuaries, the most
> famous and visited, called *Hellenion*, was founded in com-
> mon by the following cities: the Ionian cities of Chios, Teos,
> Phocaea, and Clazomenae; the Dorian cities of Rhodes,
> Cnidus, Halicarnassus, Phaselis; and a single Aeolian city,
> that of Mytilene. These are the cities to which the sanctuary

[14] Bresson and Rouillard 1993; Krämer 2016.   [15] Kowalzig 2018.

belongs, those that also provide the market prefects; all the other cities that claim to be part of it claim to be part of it without any rights. Apart from this sanctuary, the Aeginetans in particular founded a sanctuary of Zeus; the Samians, another of Hera; the Milesians, one of Apollo.[16]

According to Herodotus, the establishment of Greek sanctuaries in a place bounded and authorized by Egyptian authority was mainly addressed to transient traders who were not residents of Naucratis. In the case of mobile merchants, religious sites were granted. The installation of sanctuaries, the largest of which being the *Hellenion*, made it possible to build and organize governance of Naucratis, since the founding cities were those that controlled the port and organized the collection of taxes (Chapter 18, this volume). These Greek cities, with Chios in a dominating role, formed a club providing privileged access to commercial partners and institutions in Egypt. Rival cities, such as Miletus and Aegina, also used the establishment of sanctuaries to occupy this coveted land.

Recent studies have shown that Herodotus' story is better understood alongside Egyptian institutional contexts rather than in the light of Greek practices. In the Egyptian world, the pharaoh's donation of land was always in favour of an institution, that is, in the vast majority of cases a temple. Such transactions allowed property belonging in the king's domain to be attached to the domain of a god.[17] The Egyptian authorities showed that they were willing to establish commercial partnerships with the Greeks, but at the same time they limited their influence to a well-defined area within Egyptian territory, which also served to control commercial operations and tax revenue that could be derived from them. This concession of space corresponded to the articulation of 'the port domain' for Naucratis, as revealed by a decree of the Saïte period.[18] It was therefore Amasis who gave a legal framework for the Greek presence in Naucratis, even though relations with Greek merchants preceded his

---

[16] Hdt. 2.178.
[17] Yoyotte 1991/2, 1993/4, 1994/5; Agut-Labordère 2012; Möller 2000, 94–118. On recent excavations and research on Naucratis, see the Naucratis Project conducted by the British Museum https://ics.sas.ac.uk/research/research-projects/naukratis-project. The Hellenion has been explored since 2012 in a new program of excavation (R. Thomas, J. Johnston, and A. Masson).
[18] The decree of Nektanebo is known through the Naucratis Stele and by another stone recently discovered by F. Goddio in Heracleion-Thonis (Goddio, Fabre, and Gerick 2006, 218); Agut-Labordère 2012, 355–7.

reign, as shown by pottery finds at the site. It was only in the fourth century, when the Greek cities involved in the *emporion* fell under Persian domination, that the Saïte empire of Egypt, in the hope of guarding its independence, put an end to the concessions and transformed Naucratis into a city, opening the port to all merchants and contributing to its 'Egyptianization'.

The case of Naucratis has parallels in fourth-century Athens, where foreign traders who did not share the cult practices of the Greeks requested permission to establish their own cults. An Athenian decree of the late fourth century has preserved the decision of the Athenian people to authorize the merchants of Citium (Cyprus) to establish their own cult of Aphrodite in Athens – Aphrodite here most likely being the Greek translation for the Phoenician goddess Astarte.[19] Again, trade with Cyprus was much older than the decree that granted the Citians the right to build a sanctuary for their own worship. The decree explicitly says that it was part of a series of such concessions, since it refers to Egyptians who had also received the right to worship Isis:

> With regard to the lawful request made by the merchants (*emporoi*) of Citium, in asking the people for the right of ownership (*enktesis*) of land on which to establish an Aphrodite sanctuary, the people are pleased to grant the merchants of Citium the right of ownership of land on which to establish an Aphrodite sanctuary, as the Egyptians have established an Isis sanctuary.[20]

Among the community of Citians in Athens, there were probably both resident foreigners acting as trade intermediaries and Cypriot merchants passing through. The Athenian decree also shows that the request to pursue a native cult was part of the procedures that welcomed foreign traders. The Citians asked for the right to own land, but the purpose of the land was specifically noted, suggesting that the establishment of foreigners and their cults was a particular concern of the city.

No less than thirty-one cults have been identified in the Piraeus, including fifteen foreign cults originating from Greek, Thracian, and eastern areas between the fifth and second centuries.[21] In many cases, the ethnic origin of the devotees suggests that these cults belonged to trading communities (Egyptians, Cypriots, Levantines, etc.). In addition, many religious associations (so-called *thiasotai* or *orgeones*) that

---

[19] Baslez and Briquel-Chatonnet 1991.   [20] *IG* II 2, 337.   [21] Garland 1987, 109.

included citizens and foreigners flourished in the Piraeus (Chapter 21, this volume), suggesting close relations between the two groups. Several cults were located in the urban centre of Piraeus, while some of them were closer to the *emporion*.

The expansion of the Greek world after Alexander's conquests gave rise to greater religious interaction. Yet the same phenomenon of sites being assigned to cults for commercial communities persisted. Delos provides good examples for religious associations that brought together merchants of the same city: the *Poseidoniastai* ('Poseidon worshippers') of Berytos and the *Hermaistai* ('Hermes worshippers') of Tyre, as well as the Italian *Kompetaliastai* (worshippers of the *lares Compitales*), can serve as examples.[22] A dedication of the *Poseidonistai* from Berytos specifies that they were *emporoi*, *naukleroi*, and *ekdocheis* (importers, shippers, and warehouse keepers) networked by their professional activities, their cult practices, and their ethnicity. Foreign cults, or those perceived as such, established in Greek cultural landscapes gave rise to gradual assimilation, as was the case with the Egyptian gods in Delos when Athens took over the responsibility of managing their sanctuaries in the second century.[23]

From the archaic period onwards, *emporia* and port cities were cosmopolitan environments in which different rituals and cults coexisted. As vectors of cultural identity, they hosted many sanctuaries serving not only as sacred spaces but also as protected places: *asylia* or the right of asylum in cases of legal prosecution or any other form of persecution, applied to all Greek sanctuaries and is the strongest expression of the protective role of sanctuaries. But sanctuaries, whether hosting Greek or foreign cults, also responded to an institutional mode that relied on the city.

SANCTUARIES AT THE CENTRE OF ECONOMIC ACTIVITY

In the Greek world, sanctuaries were economic centres under the authority of cities. The gods had the status of a legal person capable of owning property. They lived in their temple, were adorned with the offerings of the pilgrims, and could own immovable and movable property, including cash.[24] The origin of their property (consecrations, confiscations, or even purchases) was as diverse as the particular history

---

[22] *IDélos* 1730–2.   [23] Bruneau 1970, 621–38; Rauh 1993; Trümper 2006.
[24] Davies 2001b; Chankowski 2011.

of each sanctuary. In addition to offerings, which often constituted a cache of precious metal, gods owned land and movable property consecrated by the city. These possessions were the starting point of the inherited duty of the cities to take care of the temple property and to make it grow.

Indeed, there was no clergy in the Greek world. Priests and priestesses were in charge of the organization of the cult, but the management of the god's property was the responsibility of the entire city collectively. The latter appointed magistrates, usually in a college and with an annual rotation of responsibilities, who assumed the administrative tasks related to the property of the gods. These magistrates reported their activities to the appropriate commission, like all other civic magistrates.[25] The property of the gods thus acquired the status of a public reserve, protected both by the divinity and by the city. Efficient managerial practices were intended to increase the resources of the sacred patrimony.

The business of temples becomes particularly visible from the late fourth century onwards, when many cities developed the 'epigraphic habit' of engraving on stone the annual accounts of their sanctuaries, or at least some record of the financial operations during a specific period of time. While offering important insights into the finances of a temple, the accounts and reports do not offer easy access to the total income and outgoings of these temples. The habit of inscribing records on stone could be quite independent of the regular archive-keeping on non-durable materials that have not survived. This imbalance in the evidence is difficult to control and makes it problematic to quantify sacred wealth with any degree of certainty. Even so, we still have plenty of evidence for the nature and politics of temple economies.

Temples as Business Units

Athens was probably the first city in the Greek world to develop extensive financial and administrative strategies in order to integrate the property of the gods into imperial politics.[26] From the fifth century onwards, we have evidence for the financial management of the gods' property in sanctuaries both of larger influence, such as the temple of Athena (the Parthenon) on the Acropolis of Athens, Demeter and Core's temple in Eleusis, and Apollo's sanctuary on Delos (where the

---

[25] Fröhlich 2004.   [26] Samons 2000; Chankowski 2008.

treasury of the Delian League was kept until 454), and small sanctuaries in the demes (local communities in Attica) or sanctuaries belonging to associations. Land-leasing contracts demonstrate the diffusion of administrative practices.[27] An epigraphic document from the very modest and shattered sanctuary of the hero Egretes in the Attic deme of Melite shows that the *temenos* (sacred precinct and land belonging to the sanctuary) was rented to a private individual, who cultivated the land and used the buildings while leaving the sanctuary to the local worshippers during their annual celebration (*IG* II[2] 2499). The contract stipulates that the tenant was responsible for the maintenance of all buildings belonging to the sanctuary. The income derived from the lease was used to finance the organization of the annual festival and the sacrifice, making this small sanctuary economically self-sufficient.

The sanctuary of Delphi owned a considerable amount of precious metal stored as a reserve to be used sparingly. For the construction of the sixth-century temple, it had been necessary to collect 300 talents (1.8 million drachms), for which the Delphians and the amphictyony (a group of associated poleis) had organized a vast collection (Hdt. 2.180; Arist. [*Ath. Pol.*] 19.4). In addition to the funds collected by the city of Delphi, the aristocratic family of the Alcmeonids of Athens contributed so generously that it was still remembered in the fifth century. The reconstruction of the Apollo temple after an earthquake in the fourth century was made possible by the financial contributions of the cities and, after the third Sacred War (356–346), by the fines paid by the Phocians, imposed on them for their looting of the sanctuary.[28] Diodorus (16.56.6) mentions that the Phocians stole 10,000 talents in order to pay mercenaries, an estimate which was probably exaggerated.[29] The sanctuary of Apollo on Delos had about forty talents in precious offerings and about twenty talents in bullion circulating in loans and other investments at the end of the third century. Its wealth, again, was accumulated in the form of silver *phialai* (drinking cups), but they were accounted for in monetary terms based on the Attic coin standard.[30]

The wealth of large sanctuaries competed with that of the wealthiest individuals. The property of the Apollo temple of Delos just mentioned far exceeded the fortune of Demosthenes' super-rich father,

---

[27] Pernin 2014.   [28] Bousquet 1988a, 155–65.

[29] Davies 2007b, 76–92. Diodorus also suggests that the stolen items of gold were worth 4,000 talents of silver (Diod. Sic. 16.28.2, 16.30.1, 16.37.2, 16.56.5), the rest probably being in silver, but undoubtedly also not coined.

[30] Chankowski 2019; see also Marcellesi 2004 for Miletus and Didyma.

owner of various large manufacturing workshops, which according to his son amounted to some fourteen talents (Dem. 27.4 and 9–11). However, it was less than the seventy talents and more reported to have belonged to the banker Pasion, who also ran a thriving business in Athens during the fourth century (Dem. 36.5–6). Such comparisons are important to make in order to understand the role of temples in the ancient economy. Compared to the spending capacity of Hellenistic kings, their treasures were rather more limited: Kallias of Sphettos in 270/69 received for the city of Athens from Ptolemy II fifty talents of silver and 20,000 *medimnoi* of wheat (about 1.12 million litres and worth about sixteen talents).[31]

A sanctuary was usually under permanent construction. The maintenance and repair of often-old buildings, the construction of new buildings for religious purpose, and the expansion of the sanctuary led cities to seek financing (through public borrowing, the use of benefactors, and the use of their own resources) and to implement major construction projects. Organized in a rigorous administrative form involving architects, supervisory boards, preliminary estimates, and financial reports, these sites attracted craftsmen and companies from an entire regional basin and sometimes beyond. The building records of the major construction projects carried out in the sanctuaries in Epidaurus, Delphi, and Delos show that the administrators recruited free men, both citizens and foreigners, including some women, but also freedmen and sometimes slaves. According to the accounts of these sanctuaries, the workforce seems extremely mobile. A small number of workers remained employed in small recurring jobs for many years, but most were temporary workers.[32] Knowing that they could not count on any stable labour pool, the administrators of the sanctuaries did not hesitate to recruit foreigners from far away. While the Epidaurus site retained a regional dimension in the Peloponnese and adjacent territories during the fourth century, the Delphi accounts of the same period show recruitment throughout Greece.[33] This may be due to a greater attractiveness of this sanctuary, or to a greater ability of its building administrators (the city and the amphictyony) to advertise their job offers.

Whether for new buildings or for regular cult activities, shrines created very particular kinds of demand not only on the labour market but also on markets for other goods.[34] They were consumers of

---

[31] Shear 1978, ll. 50–5; Robert and Robert 1981, no. 230.
[32] Feyel 2006, 332–40; Prignitz 2014 for Epidaurus.   [33] Feyel 2006, 348–68.
[34] von Reden 2012.

sacrificial animals – sometimes at a gigantic scale – as well as of wood for altars, oil for the preparation of banquets, and many tools: keys, locks, tableware, furniture, and much more. The elasticity of a temple's demand, with great peaks at the time of festivals, contributed to the creation of a network of suppliers with whom the administrators of the sacred treasury had to negotiate the best price. Part of the attractiveness of sanctuaries lay in their monetary reserves, which generated trust and ensured that the craftsmen received payment in accordance with the contracts negotiated at the time of the auction.

Another well-documented economic activity of sanctuaries was the leasing of sacred land and sacred buildings, as well as the tax awards that could be generated from sacred property.[35] They found in the sanctuary's land and real-estate assets the possibility of expanding their agricultural, artisanal, or commercial activities without having to invest into land or houses. For non-citizen residents (metics), there was the additional advantage that, given they were prevented from owning land and houses in the polis, they could participate in the well-respected pursuit of agrarian activity. The annual accounts of the administration of the sanctuary of Apollo on Delos show that competition between tenants was fierce when the land was put up for auction at the end of a lease period. Some of them lost land they had been cultivating for several generations.[36] The beneficiaries of contracts were usually local people who provided a local network gravitating towards the sanctuary.

Other people, or sometimes those same farmers, benefited from interest-bearing loans from the sacred funds.[37] The lending activities of the sanctuaries varied according to the capital they owned. In the sanctuary of Rhamnous, for example, the loan of modest sums corresponding to the purchase price of a ploughing ox or a slave (about 150 drachms) shows that the sanctuary supported a local clientele. The same type of local network can be observed in the lending activities of the sanctuary of Apollo on Delos. In this case, however, lending sometimes expanded into a regional financial network, with loans being made to the Cycladic cities.[38] The evidence of the sanctuary of Artemis at Ephesus in Asia Minor demonstrates that access to the sacred funds was easy for anybody needing financial support.[39] Sacred funds were usually lent out from accumulated money, but sometimes it was provided by endowments made to sanctuaries or specific festivals. By doing

---

[35] Rousset 2013.   [36] Prêtre 2002, 262–3; Vial 1984, 317–37.   [37] Chankowski 2011, 149–59.
[38] Chankowski 2008, 359–75; Gabrielsen 2005.
[39] Xen. An. 5.7–13; Aristid. Or. 23.24; Walser 2008.

this, the benefactor increased his own and his family's popularity by donating money or land to a sanctuary. As with a modern endowment, the donation consisted of a sum of money or any other asset that had to remain untouched for ever, while the proceeds of its profitable use (in loans or leases) were dedicated to a particular purpose. The administration of the endowment was subject to strict rules monitored by civic institutions and the public, while the administrators of the sanctuary invested it according to the usual rules of interest-bearing loans (or leases), whose proceeds each year financed a sacrifice, a festival, or a banquet in the donor's honour.[40] Shrines thus played an attractive role in distributing credit in a highly accessible way, even if local citizens were privileged for reasons of security, as it was always necessary to offer guarantees that the sacred funds would be repaid.

Temples thus made the property of their gods grow through profitable business. Renting sacred land, levying taxes and fees on the use of sacred spaces, and extending interest-bearing loans from the sacred monetary assets were the typical activities that made sanctuaries work as economic units. These activities made them important nodes of business networks. The extent of the business varied according to the influence of the sanctuary, but there were common elements. Often, when a city had several sanctuaries, financial affairs tended to be concentrated in the main sanctuary: Artemis in Ephesus, Apollo in Delos, Artemis in Magnesia on the Meander, and so on.[41] The wealth of temples, either stored as reserves or integrated into financial circulation, contributed to their being nodes of complex networks of economic interests; they were a collective resource for the entire region and for both individuals and cities. These networks were also more wide-ranging than the much-more-restricted networks of local bankers and businessmen. Depending on the region, not everyone had the same access to money in a world where the lack of liquidity created fierce competition between players.

It was above all the money of the sanctuary that attracted a wide range of local people: farmers, tenants looking to set up a business, people looking for capital, craftsmen, and entrepreneurs looking for employment or loans. Within the city, an attractive sanctuary functioned as a large company that created not just employment but also economic and financial opportunities. This had consequences for the civic community. An inscription from Cyzicus shows the concern of the civic authorities when major works in the city created an influx of

---

[40] Chankowski 2019 for the case of Delos.   [41] Ibid.

craftsmen shopping in the market, thus driving up food prices (*Syll.*[3] 799, ll. 20–1).

Festivals and Markets

Sanctuaries often brought together large numbers of people during religious festivals. There were craftsmen who sold their votive objects, shopkeepers who fed the crowds, and tavern-keepers who housed them, all benefiting from the affluence of the religious festival. The sanctuaries in turn benefited from the festivals and the commercial activities that took place in their course. They received precious-metal offerings or monetary donations from the pilgrims that increased the god's patrimony. The inventories of the sanctuary of Apollo on Delos between the fifth and the first centuries show a remarkable variety of geographic and social origins of the donors: small offerings of local pilgrims were dedicated alongside sumptuous offerings of kings and courtiers, while several wealthy individuals also increased their visibility by offering to the sanctuary libation vases and statuettes bearing their names.[42] In some cases, local farmers offered living animals as a tithe to thank the god for their prosperity. The animal was not supposed to be sacrificed, but it replaced a monetized offering, probably because these donors had little or no access to cash.[43] The administrators sold the animal in the market and donated a precious-metal offering corresponding to the weight of the silver obtained.

Pausanias suggests other important functions of festivals and the fairs (*panegyreis*) accompanying them. He describes in detail the festival for Isis at Tithorea, an extra-urban sanctuary north-east of Delphi on the other side of Mount Parnassus (10.32.8–15). The fair took place on the third day and was housed in a kind of camp with temporary shelter. There were all kinds of goods on offer, but above all slaves and livestock. *Panegyreis* thus not only supplied the festival but had important economic effects in the rural world around the sanctuary. Farmers came together and bought their goods, bringing the countryside closer to the market. In Asia Minor, many such examples are known from the epigraphic record of the Hellenistic and Roman imperial periods.[44]

---

[42] Hamilton 1999.

[43] *IG* XI 2, 224, B, l. 27; *IG* XII 2, 287, B, l. 90; *IDélos* 298, A, l. 108–12. See Chankowski 2019 for the interpretation of the passage.

[44] Debord 1982; Dignas 2002. For instance, Strab. 12.3 (Comana); *RC*, no. 47 (a local *panegyris* in a sanctuary between Pergamon and Thyateira).

It was not accidental that most of the major eastern sanctuaries were located on the Achaemenid road leading right across Anatolia.[45]

THE POLITICS OF RELIGIOUS AND ECONOMIC NETWORKS

Commercial networks contributed to the spread of worship through the movements of people. In turn, sanctuaries facilitated the development of commercial activities thanks to their financial capacity. As sites of regular building work, places of worship, and occasions of temporary fairs, they were places where people met and made contracts. Their frequent connection with *emporia* outside the Greek world facilitated the development of relations between Greek and non-Greek populations, as they provided a protected space where common codes of behaviour applied to all participants.

The recognition of the *asylia* of a *temenos* was part of the negotiations that a city conducted with external political powers. The Aetolians, for example, received many requests for *asylia* from several cities in the Greek world, as the region was particularly threatened by piracy in the Hellenistic period.[46] The city of Ephesus, moreover, continuously sought to expand its territory into parts that were included in the sanctuary's *asylia*.[47] The fact that sanctuaries were safe places increased trust in exchange and stimulated their frequency. Part of the success of the free port of Delos, which attracted unusual numbers of bankers, warehouse keepers, and traders, must be attributed, together with the political choice of Rome and the monetary policy of Athens, to the fact that it was a place protected by its sacred character.

The greatest beneficiary of a large sanctuary was the civic community in charge of its management. A passage in Athenaeus describes the Delians as 'parasites', capturing well the economic interdependence of the Delian people and the sanctuary (4.173b–c).[48] Characteristically, the decrees of Delos always invoked the benefits for the city when mentioning the sanctuary's activities. The network of relationships that cities entertained were often linked with the relationships of their sanctuaries, especially when international relations were concerned. Thus, the honorary decrees of the great sanctuaries of Delphi and Delos often reflect the grants of honours to political figures who at the same time were important interlocutors of the Delphian amphictyony

---

[45] Debord 1982, 10–11.   [46] Rigsby 1996.   [47] Walser 2008.   [48] Constantakopoulou 2017.

or of the League of the Islanders (founded in 314). The latter even used these sanctuaries as their headquarters.

This is why other cities also sought to use the influence of their sanctuaries to expand their networks. In 208, the city of Magnesia on the Meander established new games named *Leucophryenia* after Artemis Leucophryena, their tutelary divinity. The initiative was based on an apparition of the goddess and an oracle that stated: 'The situation is much better for those who honour Pythian Apollo and Artemis Leucophryena and who recognize the city and territory of the Magnetai as sacred and inviolable' (*IMagn.* 16, ll. 4–8). In order to make the new games known throughout the Greek world and to give them the status of being Panhellenic, the city sent messengers to as far as Sicily in the west and Iran in the east. The decree institutionalizing the games describes the circumstances as follows:

> all those to whom they had sent embassies, in the category of
> peoples and in the category of cities, have decided by vote to
> honour Artemis Leucophryena and to consider the city and
> territory of the Magnetai as inviolable, because of the
> exhortation of the god and the existence of bonds of
> friendship towards them all as well as family ties dating back
> to the Magnetai's ancestors.[49]

In Magnesia, the process extended over many years and was linked to the development of the cult of Artemis as well as the growth of the city. At around the same time, the city invested in the construction of a new temple, using the services of a famous architect, Hermogenes. The Panhellenic recognition of the new games in honour of Artemis were in a way the return on an investment designed to increase Magnesia's attractiveness as a node of a religious and economic network. The Magnesians received some hundred responses from the requested states and had them engraved on the walls surrounding their agora. These walls were the formal expression of their wide public relationships and international policy.[50]

Myths and cult connections also supported the initiatives of the cities to build networks. The best example is the widespread practice of constructing legendary kinship ties based on local histories and mythologies, often going back to the founding hero of the cities. Sometimes these cities were very distant from each other. In the expanded Greek world of the Hellenistic period, mythologies served to create links and

---

[49] *IMagn.* 16, ll. 32–5.   [50] Slater and Summa 2006.

to make distant locations more familiar. These networking activities frequently involved economic interests.[51] For example, Cytinium, a small city in the Doris, at the end of the third century solicited help from several bigger cities by referring to shared mythologies and kinship ties. Hit by an earthquake and war destruction, the Cytinians asked the city of Xanthos to provide financial assistance for rebuilding their city walls. Xanthos' response, echoing the Cytinians' rhetoric, shows that the embassy's request was based on a long genealogical argument proving the common origin of the two peoples through their mythical founders and ancestors. The Cytinians also argued that they had powerful network ties already, which probably made them more attractive partners. Their legendary relationships included the Aetolians and the Ptolemaic king who was 'related to the Dorians by the Argive kings descended from Herakles'.[52] Worship of the same gods and heroes was a common source from which communities drew in order to strengthen their network relationships. The fact that Greek mythology was not codified made it very suitable for this kind of diplomacy. Homonymy between mythical heroes and modifications of legends created kinship ties where mythologies in principle had no points of contact.[53]

CONCLUSION

Religious networks were complementary to other relationships that united cities with each other, as well as individuals within the cities. Cults were part of a civic heritage that communities built in order to create connections and acquire power and attractiveness in networks, just as they used the potential of their territory, their specific forms of production, and other economic capacities to increase their influence. The politics of civic outreach were part of the Greek agonistic culture combined with a general spirit of emulation that was typical for relationships between cities. They were by no means free from the desire of domination, as is shown by imperialism based on religious justifications. Individuals used religious networks for their own economic benefit and also to increase their connections. Greek polytheism, conceived as a network of divinities with a host of connections and rivalries, was the basis of the profoundly relational nature of the Greek economy. It also formed the basis of the social contract that united individuals with their civic communities.

---

[51] Curty 1995. [52] Bousquet 1988b; Rousset 1989. [53] Curty 1995, 242–58.

Further Reading

There are so far no studies specifically devoted to the interdependence of religious and commercial networks. Malkin 2011 uses network theory to analyse colonial relationships across the Mediterranean, which often included commercial relationships. Kowalzig 2018 is the first attempt to relate trade to religious connectivity; a more comprehensive study is in preparation by the same author. Bresson 2016b, J. G. Manning 2018, and Terpstra 2019 provide general background for the issues discussed in this chapter.

20: MONETARY NETWORKS

Peter van Alfen

INTRODUCTION

The temporal and spatial patterns we observe in amassed numismatic evidence such as data from hoards and die studies allow us to make inferences about the production and consumption of ancient Greek coins.[1] In trying to grasp the way in which these patterns relate to people, power, and places, we frequently use the terms "zone," "system," or "network."[2] The term "zone" generally implies a bounded, mappable geographic space within which monetary production and use was tightly controlled by a political power; the term "system," while less geographically imbedded, suggests a deliberately structured framework within which monetary use, if not production, was regulated to a large extent by political powers.[3] The term "network," on the other hand, has broader connotations, being used to describe both formal and informal connections, generally at the international level, between those producing coins, those using them, or both. In one recent study, for example, Sitta von Reden explores how the use of similar weight standards among some Greek coin producers offers "a reflection of monetary networks," which, she suggests, were sometimes established by political elites for the purpose of facilitating trade.[4] While her study describes in general terms the spatial and functional aspects of the observed production-oriented networks, it is not entirely clear in all the cases she cites what the nodes (or vertices) of the networks should be (political elites? traders? poleis?), what the links (or edges) represent (formal treaties?), or how the observed networks (d)evolved over time. Lack of specificity of this sort, however, is not uncommon in

---

[1] My focus here is on monetary networks associated with the use of coins rather than other monetary instruments or money more broadly. For the distinctions, see van Alfen 2018a.
[2] van Alfen 2018b.   [3] Thonemann 2015b, ch. 6.
[4] von Reden 2010, ch. 3 ("Monetary Networks"); the quote is from p. 65.

our descriptions of ancient monetary networks, as is the case when the concept of networks is invoked as a heuristic tool or metaphor for connectivity within ancient studies more generally.[5] This is something we shall return to in a moment.

Within the last decade, formal network analysis has been increasingly recognized within some branches of ancient studies as a potentially useful tool for describing and understanding observed connections not just between people but also between people and material culture.[6] Only recently have a handful of scholars begun to apply this type of analysis to numismatic data sets; their results have yet to be published, but this foray promises to open a new avenue of investigation for the evidence we have at hand.[7] Even so, the use of network analysis for exploring material culture evidence from the ancient world has its limitations. Tom Brughmans and Carl Knappett in particular have shown this to be the case as they have sought to develop methodologies for network analysis tailored to ancient material culture, based in part on the existing analytical tools of Social Network Analysis (SNA) and Actor Network Theory (ANT), both of which have seen extended use and development within the social and hard sciences.[8] SNA provides a means for studying social networks where the individuals and their ties to one another are known; ANT is better suited to the analysis of nonsocial relationships, such as those between archaeological artifacts per se, or artifacts and people in sociomaterial interactions. For the study of ancient material culture, both SNA and ANT have their drawbacks, including the ways in which physical (geographic) space rather than relational space, and change over time rather than snapshot views of a network, can be incorporated into the analyses. While highlighting these problems, Brughmans and Knappett have identified additional issues with the ways in which networks, whether as a metaphor for connectivity or as a tool for formal analysis, are often described and presented in the study of material culture. These include, among other things, a lack of specificity in what the nodes and links represent, problems of scale, and the processes of change within a network. With numismatics now on the cusp of adopting network analysis as a methodological approach, giving some attention to these problems

[5] See, for example, Malkin, Constantakopoulou, and Panagopoulou 2007a; Malkin 2011 (esp. ch. 1); Bresson 2015, ch. 13; Taylor and Vlassopoulos 2015. Cf. Knappett 2013, 3–4, 13; Brughmans 2010, 285–6.
[6] E.g. Ruffini 2008; Kistler et al. 2015.
[7] I am aware of studies in preparation by Alain Bresson, Ryan Horne, and Katerina Panagopoulou, who apply formal network analysis to ancient Greek numismatic evidence.
[8] Brughmans 2010; Knappett 2011; 2013; cf. Leidwanger and Knappett 2018.

and how they might relate to ancient monetary networks, from both methodological and descriptive perspectives, seems worthwhile. Thus, I address here four aspects of Greek monetary networks, those that relate to coinage, that require greater explication. These are: (1) monetary object biography; (2) network agents; (3) network process; and (4) network scale.

MONETARY OBJECT BIOGRAPHY

Any man-made object, including ancient coins, follows a trajectory from production to distribution to consumption, three separate yet interconnected stages in its life, which have themselves been the focus of a great deal of theorizing not just by economists but by anthropologists and archaeologists as well.[9] Their concern has been to try to understand the ways in which the interactions with objects that people have either as individuals or as social groups evolve as these objects move through time and space. The way in which an ancient mint worker perceived and interacted with the coin he struck, for example, was arguably quite different from that of the government accountant who received it, which in turn was quite different from that of a person spending the coin, or that of a modern curator viewing the same coin in a museum tray centuries later. Here, we will not dwell on this theoretical work, which tends not to focus on monetary objects, which have their own complications, except to note that it is useful for our purposes for a couple of reasons. It draws attention to each of the life stages of a coin and how each of these might operate independently of the others; and it draws attention to the evolution of the perception and function of a coin across time and space.[10]

We can expect to find networks of different sizes and qualities at each stage of a coin's life. At the production stage, for example, these would include not just those associated with the physical production of a coin, linking magistrates, managers, mint workers, and metal suppliers, but perhaps more importantly, those associated with the highest political and social processes of making the final decisions about coin production, such as what types of coins to produce, how many, and what designs to put on them. The social and political networks within any polis's governing body were sure to have an impact on the decisions about coin production in terms of the personal or collective preferences for

---

[9] Appadurai 1986; Hoskins 1998.   [10] Krmnicek 2009.

striking certain types of coins over others and the perceived benefits to be derived from the production of specific types of coins. We learn from an inscription from second-century Sestus, for example, that the *demos* (the governing populace) made the collective decision to strike a new bronze coinage for the sake of both prestige and profit; a magistrate named Menas was singled out for his diligence in overseeing this act.[11] This inscription presents the result of a process of policy deliberation, with some obviously pushing for adoption and some possibly resisting, with Menas, and those within his network, perhaps playing a key role in the decision-making.

After a coin was struck, it then entered the distribution stage, which for our purposes here I consider to be the movement of coins while under control of the state. We really have no idea what happened to coins in the immediate aftermath of production, particularly the amount of time that have might passed after they left the anvil to the moment they were paid out to the first recipients, or how far they might have traveled before that occurred. We can assume that many coins were paid out within the general area of where they were struck and within a comparatively short period of time afterward, but we do not know what agents were responsible for this or how coins were transferred from the production facility to state coffers.[12] At the same time, however, we know that some coins were transported beyond polis boundaries while still under state control, before being used to meet state debts, which might have included, for example, payments to other states as tribute or indemnities.[13] States also received their own coins back, at times along with foreign coinage as part of tribute, tax, or other payments; some portion of these older coins were probably added to state coffers along with newly struck coins and so reentered distribution networks.[14] In any case, these distribution networks probably were not large or overly complex, involving comparatively few individuals or institutions, which could nevertheless be dispersed geographically.

The final stage of a coin's life, that of consumption, began at the moment it left state control and was paid out to the first recipient. This is the most difficult stage to grasp, due to the potential for tremendous

---

[11] *OGIS* 339. For a translation and discussion of the relevant parts of the inscription, see Martin 1985, 238–42; Thonemann 2015b, 130–1.

[12] Lockyear 2007, ch. 3 offers a model of late Roman Republican coin distribution and circulation; no such general model yet exists for the distribution and circulation of Greek coinage.

[13] de Callataÿ 2006a provides examples of such payments in a discussion of the evidence for the transportation of (Greek) coins *en masse* by state agents and others.

[14] See Figueira 1998, ch. 10 for the recirculation of coinage within the fifth-century Athenian empire.

transactional and social complexities spread across great expanses of time and space. Each of the coins we recover in hoards and in excavations may have passed through dozens, if not hundreds or thousands of hands, pairwise exchanges that took place not just between private individuals but also between those acting on behalf of larger or smaller organizations, including states. The links between them may have been characterized by stronger or weaker social, political, or economic ties, irrespective of the physical distance in between, with the coins themselves serving as media of exchange, gifts or dedications, ornaments, collectibles, or any of these or other functions in turn or repetitively. Any momentary or permanent shift in the function or perspective of a coin in this last stage was sure to have an impact on the networks it could be associated with. We might expect, for example, that the networks a coin was associated with while being used as a medium of exchange would be different from those in which a coin was being traded as a collectible or given as a gift.[15]

The list of hypothetical networks that a coin could be associated with over the course of its lifetime might then be quite lengthy. Recognizing the distinct stages of its life and the possibly shifting functions and perceptions of a coin might help to isolate some of these networks from others and to gauge their comparative sizes and qualities. We might, for example, expect to find a limited number of smaller-sized networks, in terms of the number of nodes, linking political elites or institutions within the production stage. In the distribution stage, again we might expect a limited number of smaller-sized, but possibly spatially expansive, networks linking politically or institutionally tied individuals or organizations. In the consumption stage, the number and type of networks and their scale in terms of their spatial and temporal extent and the magnitude of the linked entities could vary considerably. Thus, over the course of its life, a single coin could be associated with just a handful of networks, or dozens, irrespective of how other similar coins were handled *en masse*. This tension between singular objects and assemblages with coinage is a particular problem; despite the fact that coins were mass-produced, and often traveled *en masse* together through networks, nevertheless individual coins could, and often did, travel through atypical networks and so might have different but still important stories to tell.[16]

---

[15] See Gitler and Kahanov 2002 for possible evidence of coin collecting in the ancient Greek world.

[16] Picard 2011, 83, for example, suggests that the atypical assemblage of coins in the late sixth-century hoard found in Taranto, Italy (*IGCH* 1174) came about from the actions of a Greek

NETWORK AGENTS

A number of individuals, or agents, played key roles in forming and maintaining the networks, including, for example, political authorities at the highest levels of government and midlevel magistrates overseeing production or soldiers spending their pay on entertainment. Here we focus on only two sets of agents: those involved in the decisions to strike coins within Greek poleis and those involved in the monetary circulation of the coins.

While it is not clear what exactly its role was in the production of the earliest coins, the polis *qua* state had by the end of the sixth century acquired a near monopoly over the issuance of coinage, effectively banning the private production of monetary instruments.[17] Located within the governing structure of poleis, often closely associated with the sovereign power, were those individuals, whether a single ruler, a council, or the *demos* at large, who had the power to make the final decisions about coin production, including whether or not to mint, in which metals and denominations, and what designs and inscriptions to place on the obverse and reverse. Generally, we do not possess enough evidence to determine who precisely these individuals were at any given moment, or the reasons they had for making the decision to strike coins in every instance, although state (military) payments and external trade are typically suggested as reasons.[18] To a surprisingly large extent, however, many of the decisions they made appear to have deliberately aligned the production of their own coinage with that of other states whether on a formal or informal basis, creating links between coin producers.

Aside from the coinages issued jointly by poleis within the larger collective political structures of *koina* (leagues), such as those in Hellenistic Lycia and Achaea, we know of many instances in which decision-makers appear to have entered into formal agreements with others to issue coins cooperatively.[19] Notable examples include the late fifth-century so-called ΣΥΝ coinage issued by a number of poleis in Asia Minor and the *cistophoroi* coinages issued by a number of the same poleis in the second century.[20] Again, the reasons for these cooperative

---

pirate. Cf. Knappett 2011, 7–8 on the problems of single objects versus assemblages in network analysis.

[17] van Alfen 2020.

[18] Cf. n. 11 above. De Callataÿ 2000 marshals modern analogies, a statistical analysis of the relevant passages in ps.-Aristotle's *Oeconomica*, and numismatic data to argue that military payments were the primary reason for Greek coin production.

[19] Mackil and van Alfen 2006; Mackil 2013, 247–55; Thonemann 2015b, ch. 4.

[20] For the ΣΥΝ coinage, see Meadows 2011, 287–92; for the *cistophoroi*, see Meadows 2013; Thonemann 2015b, 77–82.

arrangements are not always clear, but we can presume that they were structured along the lines of preexisting ties between the decision-makers in the individual poleis, which might have included, among other things, military alliances, long-standing trade partnerships, or cultural or political bonds. As the example of the cooperative electrum coinage issued by Mytilene and Phocaea in the fifth and fourth centuries illustrates, many of these bi- and multilateral arrangements were probably formalized by contracts specifying the obligations of the participating poleis.[21]

Perhaps more common, however, were informal coordinated efforts or unilateral actions to strike coins that could potentially circulate alongside those produced by other poleis, probably for reasons related to trade or other cross-border payments. Already in the archaic period, for example, a number of poleis in the Greek mainland, in the islands, and in Asia Minor struck coins on the Aeginetan weight standard, with little indication that there were formal monetary arrangements between the decision-makers.[22] Similarly, over the course of the fourth century in western Asia Minor, numerous poleis struck coins on the Chian weight standard.[23] Throughout the Hellenistic period, still more examples can be added, notably with the posthumous coinages produced in the names of rulers like Alexander the Great and Lysimachus and with the so-called *stephanephoroi* coinages.[24]

In all such cases, we can be certain the decisions taken by the agents were intended to create new formal monetary networks based on preexisting ties, or to join in existing monetary networks through the back door as it were. In either case, the decisions and actions taken were premeditated. The same cannot necessarily be said for those responsible for circulating coins as monetary instruments. Once a coin left state possession, having been paid out to the first recipient, then moving on to the second, the third, and so on, the speed and extent to which a coin moved from hand to hand depended on a host of factors, including its desirability and functionality within certain types of transactions, as well as any superimposed restrictions on its mobility. For example, generally, although not always, smaller-denomination coins made of nonprecious metals tended to circulate close to where they were produced, since

---

[21] A late fifth-century inscription (*IG* XII 2,1) details some of the obligations that those in Mytilene and Phocaea agreed to; for a translation and commentary, see Mackil and van Alfen 2006, 210–14.

[22] Sheedy 2006; 2012.   [23] Meadows 2011.

[24] Thonemann 2015, ch. 1 and 57–60 on the *stephanephoroi* (wreathed) coinages; van Alfen 2018b; Meadows 2013; de Callataÿ 2013.

their desirability, which might have been a function of state-imposed valuations on the coins, tended to decrease the farther away from home the coin traveled.[25] Conversely, larger denomination precious-metal coins tended to maintain desirability over greater distances due to the commodity value of the metal being close to the denominated value of the coin. Nevertheless, a precious-metal coin's desirability at greater distances could also be affected by the coinage's reputation, whether good or bad, and by other factors like its weight standard.[26] Transactions involving coinage could then take place quickly and without difficulty, if the coins offered were desirable and appropriate for the transaction from the seller's viewpoint, or require further negotiation to determine the terms of acceptability, or might fail completely, if the coins were not desirable.[27] Despite evidence that the state wielded some power to impose the acceptability of coins, and thus shape the networks through which coins circulated, the power of individuals within markets was as great as the state's, if not more so.[28] Ultimately, no matter the injunctions of the state, individual agents within a transaction had the final say in whether to accept or reject coins for any number of reasons and by doing so could influence the behavior of others.[29] The collective actions of large numbers of like-minded individuals might thus give shape to localized or cross-border networks in which certain types of coins for certain types of transactions were accepted on a regular basis.

From our hoard data, it is possible to observe the rough outlines of some networks, but it is unlikely that we can acquire the detailed information needed to identify any of the individual agents involved (the nodes) or the specific transactions (the links) that moved the coins through these consumption networks.[30] Because of the prominence in the historical and epigraphic record of named political and economic elites, who often served in decision-making positions within polis and other governments, there is a greater possibility that we can identify

[25] de Callataÿ 2006b.
[26] On currency desirability and competition see Cohen 1998 and 2015. By the late fifth century, the Athenian "owl" coinage had become so highly desirable in many parts of the Near East that it was widely imitated; see van Alfen 2012.
[27] Problems with currency acceptability in transactions in Athenian markets required new legislation to be enacted in 375 to provide safeguards and assurances; see Ober 2008, 220–40; Psoma 2011b. People, it seems, could be rather fickle about which coins were acceptable, as one of Theophrastus' characters (no. 4, "The Boor") illustrates.
[28] van Alfen 2018b.
[29] For these and other aspects of ancient market behavior, see Johnstone 2011, ch. 2.
[30] One exception can be found in Demosthenes 35 (*Against Lacritus*), where it is implied that two brothers from Phaselis, Artemon and Apollodorus, transported a significant number of coins (ca. 1,500 owl tetradrachms?) from Athens to Mende to purchase a cargo of wine there some time around 350.

some decision-making agents involved in production networks, if not their reasons for creating monetary links with others elsewhere.[31]

NETWORK PROCESS

Ancient monetary networks were inherently unstable and thus were dynamic and changed over time. Production and distribution networks were, among other things, subject within poleis to changes in political regimes and externally to changes in political alignments and alliances; some of this international entropy could be overcome by occasional recommitments and renewals of the terms, as seems to have been the case in the long-lasting agreement between Mytliene and Phocaea to produce a cooperative coinage, for example.[32] In consumption networks, a litany of factors could affect the composition, shape, and extent of a network, including sociopolitical disruptions like war, the supply of desirable coins, shifts in their desirability or fashion, and so on.[33]

How then did ancient monetary networks come into being, evolve, and collapse? For production networks based on formal political or economic alliances, the answer seems more straightforward than for other types of networks (Chapters 19 and 21, this volume). Preexisting political and economic ties between the producers provided the basis for establishing a monetary network, modifying it if necessary, and deliberately shutting it down or letting it wither once it had served its purpose.[34] For informal production networks, the process would presumably be less regularized. The decision-making agents in poleis could take unilateral steps to align the production of their coins with those produced by others, expecting that their coins would be acceptable within existing networks; this could be done by changing weight standards, alloys, denominations, or types to align with foreign coinages.[35] It is also possible that production networks established by formal means could evolve into an informal network, as seems to have been the case in the fourth century with the widespread adoption of the Chian weight standard for coinage by producers in Asia Minor.[36]

---

[31] Cf. n. 11 above.   [32] Cf. n. 21 above.

[33] See Meadows 2001, 56 for the notion of "fashion" coinages in the Hellenistic period.

[34] As for example with the ΣΥΝ coinage; see n. 20 above.

[35] For the incentives to change weight standards, see Schmitz 1986; Psoma 2016. Cahn 1970, 178–92 discusses the interoperability of many of the coinages produced in archaic- and classical-period Asia Minor. The widespread phenomenon of imitative coinages seems to have been driven in part by a desire on the part of producers to participate in existing networks; see van Alfen 2005.

[36] Meadows 2011.

Hegemonic powers also played an important role in establishing monetary networks. Within Asia Minor, for example, a number of poleis in the fifth and fourth centuries appear to have struck Persian-weight coins more or less simultaneously, either in lieu of or alongside their own indigenous-weight coinage, presumably at the behest of Persian authorities to support their military activities in the region.[37] It has also been argued that many of the coinages produced in the northern Aegean in the final decades of the sixth century were struck in some sort of coordinated way in order to pay tribute to the Persians.[38] Perhaps the best-known example by an imperial power creating a monetary network was that of the Athenians in the last quarter of the fifth century. Their so-called Standards Decree directed its dozens of tributary allies to use only Athenian weights, measures, and coinage.[39] As noted above (p. 305), attempts by the state to legislate consumption probably met with mixed success, since agents within transactions might not comply with the state's wishes; indeed, the policy promulgated in the Standards Decree appears to have been short-lived and unsuccessful.

Even if we concede that states had some ability to control the use of their coins, and thus to create and shape monetary networks, at least within the territories they controlled, consumption networks in general were probably regulated not by legislation but rather by social forces like reputation and perceptions of trustworthiness, which, if positive, could elevate demand, not just locally but abroad as well.[40] Throughout the course of the fifth century, for example, the Athenian owl coinage became the most highly desirable coinage throughout the Levant, in Egypt, and in Arabia, based presumably not just on their availability but also on their reputation for quality.[41] Demand for the owls was substantial enough that both private and state producers struck large quantities of owl imitations, some of which made their way back to Athens, causing transactional problems in the markets there.[42] Similarly, throughout the course of the third century, coins of the type first struck by Alexander the Great ("Alexanders") were effectively imitated by dozens of civic and royal mints across the eastern Mediterranean for over a century after the conqueror had died (posthumous Alexander-type coins, Chapters 4 and 5, this volume).[43] How demand for owls and

---

[37] Ellis-Evans and van Alfen 2018.   [38] Picard 2011; 2012; Tzamalis 2011.

[39] *IG* i³ 1453. The bibliography on the Decree is vast; for a recent, but controversial full-length study see Figueira 1998; see also von Reden 2010, 76–8; Hatzopoulos 2013–14.

[40] von Reden 2007b, ch. 2, for example, discusses the tension between the Ptolemaic state attempting to impose bronze coinage on those within Egypt and the pushback from users due to problems with the valuation of the coins.

[41] van Alfen 2012.   [42] Cf. n. 27 above.   [43] Meadows 2001.

then Alexanders was first established and ultimately cascaded across trade and other networks is a problem that has not yet received much attention.[44] Newly introduced coins faced reputational barriers that would have to be overcome in each transaction using the coins for the first time; the greater the distance from the source of the coins, the higher the potential barriers. Modeling how coins moved through these barriers and then across different types of (social) networks ever outward could help to explain how some coins became all but universally accepted, while others did not.

NETWORK SCALE

Much of the way in which we study Greek coins is in relationship to physical space. Distribution patterns allow us to speak of coin circulation within and across smaller and larger spaces, like poleis and regions. Similarly, we might identify multiple poleis within a region, like southern Italy in the later sixth century, participating in the production of the same or similar coinages for shared purposes.[45] Within ancient monetary studies, we are accustomed to imagining networks operating at a particularly large scale and associating them closely with physical space, for example, linking poleis across regions. The nodes of these networks tend therefore to be at the level of an entire polis – for example, Athens – or something even larger – for example, Egypt – while the links between them span great distances. One way to think about scale and networks then is in geographic terms: How much territory does the network encompass? How long are the links?

Implied within these vast geographic networks, however, are the relationships between actual individuals or organizations. It is, after all, not the cities themselves that formed the links, but the people within them. As people, like traders and elites, came and went between cities, the physical distance between people might have changed, while the relationship between them remained unchanged. These two aspects of the networks we seek to identify, the geographic/physical and the relational, have implications regarding their scale.

In his work on networks and archaeology, Carl Knappett draws attention to the problem of scale and network analysis, noting distinctions between macro-, meso-, and microscale networks.[46] It is possible to identify Greek monetary networks of these three general scales as well

---

[44] van Alfen 2018b.   [45] See Mackil and van Alfen 2006, 208–10.
[46] Knappett 2011, chs. 4–6.

if we think of macroscale networks as being interregional, mesoscale networks as being regional, and microscale networks as being sub-regional, that is at or below the level of the polis.

As noted above in the case of fifth- and fourth-century Athenian owls and fourth- and third-century Alexander-types, these coinages achieved great popularity and demand across a broad, interregional swath of the eastern Mediterranean and Near Eastern worlds, suggesting that some of the networks within which they moved were geographically extensive. The basis or function of such far-reaching networks with a marked preference for single types of coins is not known, although trade and mercenaries on the move have often been suggested.[47] Hoard evidence from archaic Egypt, by contrast, is also indicative of long-distance networks, but perhaps of a different sort. The many different types of coinages from all parts of the Aegean found in these hoards, particularly those under Persian control, is suggestive of transfers of coinage received as tribute payments in one part of the empire and moved to another part.[48] Thus the interregional networks involved were functioning essentially as distribution networks for the sake of the Persian imperial administration. Other evidence for interregional distribution networks is difficult to identify securely, although we can surmise such networks existed.[49]

Many cooperative coinages appear to have been produced for use within regional rather than interregional networks. In some cases, an attempt seems to have been made to create a closed currency zone containing the networks within which only the coins produced by the cooperating cities would circulate. Several cooperative coinages were struck on reduced weight standards, suggesting that mandatory exchange at par of full-weight coinages for the zone's underweight coinage took place at the border. Since traders and other users would have little interest in exporting the underweight coinage from the zone, a restricted circulation and benefit to the issuers could be enforced. Evidence for such a closed system is readily forthcoming from Ptolemaic Egypt;[50] similar closed systems but at a regional level have been suggested for southern Italy in the latter part of the sixth century and for

---

[47] Trade: van Alfen 2012. Mercenaries: Thonemann 2015b, 14, 27, 30.   [48] Picard 2012.

[49] Duyrat 2016, 374–9, for example, argues that the so-called wreathed tetradrachms (*stephane-phoroi*) produced by a handful of poleis in Attalid-controlled Asia Minor in the second century and found in significant numbers in Syria were struck specifically for Alexander I Balas' attempt to overthrow power in Seleucid Syria.

[50] Le Rider and de Callataÿ 2006, 130–69; von Reden 2007b, 42–8.

Asia Minor under the Lydians in the sixth century and then under the Attalids in the second century (Chapters 4, 5, and 8, this volume).[51]

More common perhaps were regional monetary networks that developed from the bottom up, as it were, as the result of persistent interaction and lasting connections between those inhabiting the poleis within a region. We find, for example, a widespread adoption of the Aeginetan weight standard and style of striking coins in the archaic Cyclades; a shared weight standard and denominational system in the archaic- and early classical-period Troad; and the pervasive adoption of the Chian weight standard in fourth-century Asia Minor. The regional alignment of weight standards and denominations in all these examples appears to have been less a matter of deliberate cooperation than informal coordination based, presumably, on the needs of those engaged in region-wide trade and other activities.[52]

As noted, hoards and excavated coins finds show generally that smaller denominations, especially those in base metals, tended not to travel far beyond the polis where the coins were struck, probably due to the overvaluation of such coins.[53] Their limited circulation probably also reflects networks using the coins that differed from those involved in regional and interregional activities. Not all coin users buying their daily bread, for example, were necessarily involved in overseas commerce. Some of these subpolis networks might have been confined to certain parts of a polis, developing and evolving through the daily interactions of groups of families, neighbors, and shopkeepers. The ability of the polis to offer a continuous supply of small change for their daily needs may have been strained at times, requiring innovative and unofficial solutions arising within these networks.[54]

We know of at least one case, however, of a microscale network that was created *ab novo* for a special purpose. While besieging Olynthus in 364–362, the Athenian general Timotheus lacked the silver coins he needed to pay his troops so they could buy their provisions and so struck his own bronze coins. In order to convince the surrounding merchants to accept these, Timotheus concluded a separate deal with them, promising future conversions into silver. The solution appears to have been

---

[51] Lydia: Le Rider 2001, 96–100; Italy: Le Rider 1989; Attalid: Meadows 2013 (who argues a closed system did not exist in the Attalid kingdom).

[52] Cyclades: Sheedy 2006; 2012; Troad: Ellis-Evans and van Alfen 2018; Asia Minor: Meadows 2011.

[53] Cf. n. 25 above.

[54] Such might have been the case in Athens with the *kollyboi* (small bronze tokens), although the matter is disputed; see Figueira 1998, 504–8, 520–1; Kroll 2015. Cf. Sheedy 2015.

acceptable and this highly localized network operated for the duration.[55]

If we can identify monetary networks of different scales, what then was the relationship, if any, between these networks? It is of course conceivable that the same individuals involved in a local micronetwork were also involved in regional or interregional networks, but whether this means there was much crossover between the networks is open to question, in part because of the specialized coinages that were used in each of the networks.[56] Thus, we should perhaps picture monetary networks of different scales overlapping in some locations, and perhaps using some of the same nodes (vertices), but not necessarily otherwise interacting.

CONCLUSION

Money is an amazingly complex phenomenon, born of social, political, and economic needs, that defies easy explanation or definition.[57] Because of this inherent complexity, ancient monetary instruments like coins were associated with networks that differed in significant ways from those associated with other types of material culture. The transactional function of coinage in general and of certain types of coins in particular meant that coins came to be and then moved across time and space and among institutions and people in ways that other things, like amphoras and cups, did not. These differences are important to keep in mind as we seek new ways, such as formal network analyses, to identify and study ancient monetary networks.

Further Reading

To date there have been no formal network analyses of ancient Greek numismatics and monetary systems published. Less-formal presentations of Greek numismatic and monetary networks can be found in a number of studies including von Reden 2010. Lockyear 2007 offers one of the most sophisticated analyses of networks and ancient coin movement available, but one that does not utilize formal network analysis per se. An accessible introduction to the

---

[55] Ps.-Arist. *Oec.* 2.2.23 (1350a); Sheedy 2015.   [56] Cf. Marcellesi 2000.   [57] van Alfen 2018a.

application of formal network analysis to ancient material culture can be found in Knappett 2011; the volume edited by Knappett and Leidwanger 2018 provides illustrations of the application of network analysis to interregional trade in a way that could be useful to the future study of ancient monetary networks.

21: SOCIAL NETWORKS, ASSOCIATIONS AND TRADE

Vincent Gabrielsen

INTRODUCTION

If social networks and trade are nowadays considered to be closely linked, in the economy of Greek antiquity they were inseparable.[1] This was mostly due to the character of ancient trade: an immensely complex social activity which, although it often yielded great economic gains, also made traders face severe obstacles, catalysts of risk and loss. Their parameters included the ability of existing technology to increase speed, lessen physical distance and move bulk; the level of the financial sector; communications and timely access to reliable information; governmental regulation (including economic favouritism, e.g. taxation versus tax exemption); and the right to seek justice for contract enforcement.[2]

None of them, however, could match the challenges issuing from a different quarter. While ancient and later societies insisted on maintaining a sharp divide between public and private economic activity, their actual stand towards that divide remained a supremely ambiguous one and the cause of a clash. The unrestrained freedom which traders deemed the most profitable way of pursuing their *private* economic interests clashed with the restrictions that states were prone to impose (in the form of laws and moral value sets) in order to protect or further public/communal interests; uncontrolled profit-making, some argued, was harmful for the community. Yet, at the same time, the profits from privately conducted trade were thought to be just as indispensable to states as many of the legal regulations of states were to traders. This quandary of the divide in question has exercised many a theoretician. For instance, no sooner did Max Weber (1864–1920) posit the strict separation of private and public, and the subordination of the former to the later, than he conceded that the public – represented by his impartial, law-acting state bureaucracy, and the rationalistic spirit behind it – had become an 'iron cage' that enslaved

[1] Rauch 2001.   [2] See Lawall and van Alfen 2011.

humanity.[3] Weber, a sociologist of hierarchy, not of networks, thus noted the quandary but did not attempt to solve it.

Only recently has a solution begun to emerge from various directions. Arguably, the theoretical framework of the New Institutional Economics owes its popularity among ancient historians to its ambition to lessen the divide mentioned above by emphasising the role of state institutions in private economic activity (Chapter 23, this volume).[4] Similar in effect, though different in approach, seems to be Mark Granovetter's demonstration of the impact of social relationships on economic activity, the factor connecting private and public here being the social network.[5] Granovetter and others, moreover, have taken up the challenge of questioning another important divide, that expressed by the bedrock neoclassical distinction between 'personalised exchange' – the network – and 'arms-length exchange' – the so-called anonymous market, where interaction between participants is mediated by competitively determined prices.[6] Thus, while it certainly seems premature to replace *The Wealth of Nations* with *The Wealth of Networks*,[7] many now recognise the network as a primary means through which institutional and market structures are conceptualised.[8]

Ancient networks were by design constraint-fighters, bridge-builders and distance-shortening devices, social distance included. These traits made them an integral part of the market, not a competitor to it, and that circumstance seriously discredits the sharp dichotomy traditionally said to exist between market-driven (or private) trade and state-influenced trade. Moreover, the contribution of social networks to the economic integration of large parts of the ancient world, it will be argued here, was far greater than the conventional view attributes to them by seeing them as merely mechanisms of supply and distribution. Providing commercial transactions, especially those over long distances, with an organisational framework, networks became the engines of both *particularised* and *generalised* trust; the first refers to trust shared by network members only, the second to that shared by a larger circle of outsiders. Additionally, networks were incomparable transmitters of top-quality information.

Not all networks, of course, possessed these characteristics to an equal degree, since they differed markedly from each other in several respects. Above all, they differed in their level of organisation, their

---

[3] Weber [1920] 2003, 181; on the separation of private and public, see esp. Weber [1922] 1978, 957.
[4] North 1990; 2005; Marinescu 2014.   [5] Granovetter 1985.   [6] Rauch and Casella 2001.
[7] Proposed by Benkler 2006; see Berry 2008.
[8] Rauch and Hamilton 2001, esp. 21; Terpstra 2019.

intended duration and the degree of bonding among their members. For example, consortia or syndicates such as those formed for the purpose of farming the right to collect a tax[9] or the right to enjoy monopoly over the sale of a commodity[10] (which for a Greek-speaking person also belong to the broader category of *koinoniai/koina*)[11] scored low in all three of the aspects just mentioned: they had only a most rudimentary organisation, if any; and members were bonded by virtue of a legal contract, at the expiry of which (typically after a year) the network dissolved. Radically different from these was the kind of network that will be discussed in this chapter: it featured a developed organisation; it was intended to last indefinitely; *nomoi* ('laws and regulations'), not a business contract, governed its existence; and finally, the bonding between members, rather than being contractual, rested on a prime personal relationship, namely, friendship (*philia*).

All these are the characteristics of the private association, which in Greek is also termed *koinon*. From the fourth century onwards, this kind of network became the preferred organisational home of traders, especially traders' diasporas, and of other professionals. More importantly, after ca. 300 it rapidly multiplied and spread across the Mediterranean ports and commercial centres, all the while enhancing its collective leverage and avowed membership advantages; and it did this to such a degree as to be attractive to nearly all social strata and groupings, businessmen and power-holders in particular. Becoming the hallmark of such collectives, these advantages, however, impacted on the economy also when the members did not explicitly identify themselves to outsiders as traders or other professionals. This, in short, is the network in the guise of the associational phenomenon. Contrary to how kindred networks are said to have achieved their effectiveness, that is on account of their *weak* ties,[12] the strength of this one lay in its fostering *strong* ties.

RELIGIOUS AND POLITICAL COMMUNITIES

Professing a trade as a member of an association remained an advisable practice for centuries. 'Concerning the Ordering and Regulation of Associations of the Crafts Called N' is the title of a document found in

---

[9] E.g. Andoc. 1.133–4 (Athens, 402/1).
[10] E.g. *P.Mich.* v 245, Inv. 657 (Tebtynis, Egypt, 47 CE), with Gabrielsen 2016b, 92–5.
[11] *Koinonia*: Arist. *Eth. Nic.* 8.9.5 (1160a) and Arist. *Eth. Eud.* 7.9.3 (1241b); see also Justinian's *Dig.* 47.2.4, allegedly preserving a law ascribed to Solon. *Koinon: P.Mich.* v 245, Inv. 657, l. 25.
[12] Granovetter 1983.

the late-ninth-century CE collection of materials by Gabriel, the bishop of Basra in Iraq. Written in Syriac, this extraordinary document preserves the rules and regulations of a specific association, but in an anonymised form, so as to be used as a prototype by anyone wishing to establish an association.[13] Strikingly, despite its titular emphasis on a common profession, the document's thirty-two regulations are mostly concerned with ethical conduct and religious practice (it is taken for granted that all members are of the Christian faith). Modern commentators are therefore correct to recognise here many of the features of the ancient 'cult' or 'religious' association; particularly, they find close similarities to the epigraphically preserved 'law' of a known association, the *Iobachoi* of second-century CE Athens.[14] The notion to which this Syriac document pays heed seems quite clear: formalised networks constitute the most appropriate organisational edifice for the triad of communal life, worship, and vocational occupation.

Our earliest evidence for adherence to that notion dates from the 330s. In 334/3, traders from Citium on Cyprus took steps to formalise their settlement and communal existence in Piraeus. Their first corporate act was to present themselves to outsiders as a community of professionals (traders, *emporoi*) and as a community of worshippers. Having collectively obtained the Athenian government's permission to own land, they built a sanctuary to be their base on Attic soil; their avowed religious focus was the cult of Aphrodite, here probably the Greek version of the Levantine Astarte.[15] Shortly before, a group of immigrant merchants from Egypt had done precisely the same thing, making their own sanctuary of Isis their locus of communal life. Such new arrivals in Piraeus not only added to the existing trading communities, such as, for instance, 'the merchants and shippers', an association with manifest links to Phoenician Sidon.[16] More significantly, they presaged a phenomenon that spread like wildfire almost everywhere in Hellenistic and Roman times.

Vocational occupation and religiosity thus became increasingly the insignia of proliferating merchants' 'colonies' in Athens, Alexandria, Ephesus, Ostia and many other places.[17] Most lucid is the evidence from

---

[13] Text in English transl.: Brock 2009.

[14] The association's proper name is the Baccheion: *IG* II[2] 1368; *LSCG* 51 (164/5 CE); *CAPInv.* 339 (I. Arnaoutoglou).

[15] *IG* II[2] 333.

[16] The association was instrumental in the Athenian people's voting of honorary awards (including the titles of *proxenos* and *euergetes*) to Apollonides son of Demetrios from Sidon: *IG* II[3] 379 (Piraeus, 320(?)). Cf. *CAPInv.* 292 (I. Arnaoutoglou).

[17] The copious evidence is discussed in Rauh 1993; van Nijf 1997; Dittmann-Schöne 2010; Gibbs 2011 and 2015; Rohde 2012; Terpstra 2013.

Delos, where associations of easterners rubbed shoulders with associations formed by westerners. Some easterners originated from Berytus (the *Poseidoniastai emporoi* (merchants), *naukleroi* (shippers) *and ekdocheis* (warehouse-keepers)); others originated from Tyre (the *Herakleistai* merchants and shippers).[18] The associations of their western partners were formed by communities of Italians who called themselves *Apolloniastai*, or *Hermaistai*, or *Poseidoniastai* or, finally *Kompetaliastai*.[19] Archaeologically, Delos also provides so far the best attestation for associational space, which is represented by the magnificent House of the Berytian Poseidoniastai;[20] and for commercial space, which is represented by the extensive merchandise storage facilities within the city.[21] Likewise, in near-contemporary Lindos on Rhodes a community of 'foreign residents' (*katoikeuntes xenoi*), besides identifying themselves as a union of farmers (*georgeuntes*) and shippers (*nauklareuntes*), acted as ardent devotees of Lindian Athana.[22] From the first century on, westerners' associational diasporas named *Rhomaioi hoi katoikountes/Italici qui negotiantur* (or *naukleroi/navicularii* and *pragmateuomenoi/negotiatores*) mushroomed in mainland Greece, the Aegean islands, Alexandria and especially coastal and inland Asia Minor.[23]

The bilingualism that several of these communities are seen to be practising implies both integration and preservation of links to the place of origin.[24] As the principal language of its honorary decree, the Piraeus-based Association (*koinon*) of the Sidonians used Phoenician; and its membership identified themselves as worshippers of the god Ba'al of Sidon. But the decree itself shows them to be fully conversant with the vocabulary and procedures of Greek political institutions.[25] Similarly, the letter sent by the Tyrians residing in Campanian Puteoli to the political authorities of their 'supreme fatherland', and published in an inscription of 174 CE, is in Greek.[26] This community consisted of traders and shippers who, using a rented building as their 'station' (*he station*),

---

[18] *IDélos* 1772 (Berytians) and 1519 (Tyrians), cf. *CAPInv.* 9 and 12 (A. Cazemier). See Baslez 2013.
[19] E.g. *IDélos* 1730–1. On all these associations Flambard 1982, 68, 71; Rauh 1993, 110; see also Chapter 19 this volume.
[20] Hasenohr 2001; Trümper 2006 and 2011; Zarmakoupi 2015b; on religious associations on Delos, see Chapter 19, this volume.
[21] Karvonis 2008; Karvonis and Malmary 2018.
[22] *SEG* 14, 511 (improved text of *ILindos* II 384b, ll. 15–17).
[23] Rohde 2012, 367–77; Terpstra 2013, 171–221; Rice 2016, 104–6. Cf. also van Andringa 2003; Corsten 2018.
[24] Adams, Janse, and Swain 2002, esp. ch. 5.
[25] *IG* II² 2946, from the second half of third century: Teixidor 1980; Ameling 1990 (*SEG* 40, 187), *contra* the less likely date of 320/19: Baslez and Briquel-Chatonet 1991.
[26] *IG* XIV 830, with Sosin 1999 and Terpstra 2013, 51–94.

were equally occupied on the one hand with the worship of their 'paternal gods' (it so turns out that the cult statue of their 'God of Sarepta' had been shipped from Tyre to Puteoli);[27] and on the other with the celebration of 'the sacred days of the supreme [Roman] emperor'; they thus straddled two cult spheres and two cultural spheres, a local one and a universal one. In contrast to an allegedly thriving branch community formed by compatriots in Rome, however, the prosperity of this one is said to have dwindled, which is the reason why its members, through their letter, petitioned the authorities of their *patris* for continued financial support in order to pay the rent for their *station*. Tyre responded positively to the request for financial help. Here, as in other cases (the Citian and Egyptian diasporas in Piraeus, among others), establishment of cult-centred commercial hubs abroad – whether state-subsidised or not – meant as a rule the branching out of an existing trading network into new and promising commercial zones, not the wholesale emigration of such a network from a poverty-stricken homeland.

So far, we have been considering entities whose preoccupation with trade is evident from their name. However, with the Tyrians in Puteoli things are different: only by chance do we get to know of their profession as shippers and merchants, the association's full name being *hoi Tyrioi stationarioi stationos Tyriakes tes en koloniai Sebastei Potiolois.* Their case is representative of a much-larger number of instances in which, though the membership actually possessed a certain professional profile, the association's name does not disclose that profile but publicises instead other concerns, predominantly religious ones. This circumstance alone suffices to dismiss as invalid the time-honoured habit of identifying associations according to the Name–Kind–Purpose formula and classifying them as 'professional' or 'religious'.[28] Cult worship was common to practically all of them, and, as we shall see, for a good reason. In fact, the associations' addiction to religious observance – administered by specially appointed personnel (*hiereis, hieropoioi*, etc.) and taking place within their own precincts or those of others – is one of the best-documented aspects of their activities. It is also the feature that lays bare the associations' proficiency in the art of institutional homomorphism, that is their ability to become indistinguishable from entities usually known by their own designation, in this case, the religious community. Conglomerations of astute profit-seekers thus transmuted into formalised congregations of worshippers.

---

[27] *OGIS* 594, with Torrey 1949 and Tran Tam Tinh 1972, 136–7.
[28] See e.g. de Cenival 1972; Egelhaaf-Gaiser and Schäfer 2002; Dittmann-Schöne 2010.

Equally well, if not better, attested is the association's other capacity, to metamorphose into a political community. Whether the collective in question was one of the Attic *koina* of *thiasotai* and *eranistai* of about 300;[29] or the third-century Association (*koinon*) of Phrygians on the tiny island of Astypalaia;[30] or the Berytian *Poseidoniastai* Merchants, Shippers and Warehouse-Keepers in second-century Delos; or the *Synodos* of Landowners (*geouchoi*) in second-/first-century Psenamosis, Egypt;[31] or the Tyrians in 174 CE Puteoli – in all instances, the model for collective organisation, articulation of ideas and action unfailingly remained one and the same: the Greek polis and its institutions.[32] Officials, law sets, membership assemblies, collective decision-making and publication of decisions on inscriptions were their main organisational trappings, and nearly all of them betray adherence to a broadly democratic mindset. From Sicily through to the north Black Sea littoral and to Arabia, communities that were created in private show themselves adequately versed in the technicalities, procedures and phraseology of public/polis language, especially the language of the democratic decree.[33] Around 150, the limits of institutional homomorphism were being pushed even farther when the Teos-based association of the Dionysiac *technitai* (i.e the Ionian-Hellespontine branch of this extensive associational network) began issuing its own coinage, from which a tetradrachm survives.[34] The state, it would seem, now shared its own apparel with a private lookalike.

Organisational sameness, attended by homogeneity of religious practice, was thereby being diffused over a large expanse, with the altar, the dedicatory monument and the inscribed (honorary) decree as high-standing emblems of its peculiar orientation. The first (the altar) broadcast 'piety' (*eusebeia*), which is the manifestation of faith and of faith's secular counterpart, 'faith in other people'. The other two (the inscribed decree and the dedication) broadcast 'good order' (*eunomia*), 'impeccable moral habitus' (*arete*) and readiness to recompense benefactors.

---

[29] Arnaoutoglou 2003; Thomsen 2015; Gabrielsen 2016a, 129–34.
[30] *IdI* 88, cf. *CAPInv.* 154 (S. Skaltsa).   [31] *IProse* 40, cf. *CAPInv.* 38 (M. Paganini).
[32] Gabrielsen 2009.
[33] Sicily (Halaisa): *to koinon tōn hiereōn tou Apollonos* (*SEG* 59, 1100), probably end of the first century, cf. *CAPInv.* 1314 (J. Prag). Black Sea (Kallatis): *bakchikos thiasos* (*I.Kallatis* 35, 36, 42–6), cf. *CAPInv.* 1186 (A. Avram). Arabia (Gerasa): *hiera synodos* (*IGerasa* 192), ca. 114 CE, cf. *CAPInv.* 599 (B. Eckhardt).
[34] Full name: *to koinon tōn peri ton Dionyson technitōn tōn en Ionia kai Hellesponti kai tōn peri ton Kathegemona Dionyson*: Aneziri 2003, D 11a ll. 2–4. Cf. *CAPInv.* 1801 (B. Eckhardt). Tetradrachm: Lorber and Hoover 2003.

Demonstrable possession of these qualities confirmed possession of a further one, 'trust' (*pistis*). Nowhere is the proclivity of *eunomia* and *arete* to produce trust (*pistis*) and 'good repute' (*eukleia*) expressed more succinctly than in the preserved fragments of the work of an anonymous thinker from ca. 400.[35]

Thus, from around the mid-fourth century onwards, traders, as members of ethnically homogeneous or ethnically mixed associations, joined the larger conglomeration of like-minded 'brotherhoods' that shared a common way of governance, action articulation and self-presentation to outsiders. Within this associational world, business partners from near and far became sharers of a market-oriented culture. Attending such cultural integration was the significant economic effect of an increased market integration. This phenomenon – at least the organisational part of it – seems to have stretched far beyond the limits of the Mediterranean world. Supply and demand for specific commodities traded between the Mediterranean world and the Indian Ocean world, it is now shown, was channelled through organisations which, though physically worlds apart, were similarly built and economically interactive. These were the Graeco-Roman associations of craftsmen and traders, on the one hand, and their Indian counterparts (termed *shreni* and *nigama*) on the other.[36]

Formalised networks, in brief, helped trade to break out of its insular, localised, lone-peddler mode and to amalgamate with a far-reaching organisational *koine* geared to promote market integration, battle constraints to trade and reduce transactional costs. Associational space, whose geographical expanse had by the turn of the third century grown considerably, translated directly into economic space. This invites us to consider concretely how religious communities-*cum*-small republics metamorphosed into a segment of a third institution, the market.

ASSOCIATIONS AND THE MARKET

States and private networks complemented each other in providing traders with a platform of competitive advantage by lowering transaction costs. Those joining that platform prospered. The economic efflorescence, or growth,[37] that seems to have occurred in the Greek and Hellenistic world from the fourth century owed much to this

---

[35] *Anonymous Iamblichi* fr. 2 (96.20 Pistelli = DK 89 B2): *arete, pistis* and *eukleia*; fr. 17 (101.17–104.14 Pistelli = DK 89 B7): *eunomia* and *pistis*. Cf. Faraguna 2012.
[36] Evers 2017, esp. chs. 1 and 8.
[37] For references, see the overview in J. G. Manning 2018, ch. 8.

complementarity. Providing economic actors with a platform of competitive advantage need not necessarily cancel out 'arms-length exchange', for interaction between participants that is mediated by competitively determined prices is accepted to be a prime feature of the market.

Tax revenue and the supply of vital commodities were the main reasons behind the active support of states to trade. Various initiatives were launched. For instance, using their own networking mechanisms (interstate relations and the institution of *proxenia*),[38] states secured cost-reducing privileges abroad for all merchants, foreign and native, who used their ports as operational bases. Among these 'group privileges' was tax exemption (*ateleia*) in designated foreign ports/markets (though rarely at one's home port) and the right to be the first to procure a specific commodity, an advantage of immense importance whenever supply was limited.[39] In all likelihood, we will never be able to estimate the per cargo cost-reduction accruing, for instance, from the tax exemption enjoyed by Rhodes-based merchants in all the ports of the Seleucid kingdom, in the east, and in Syracuse, in the west.[40] The same can be said of Antiochus IV's grant to the city of Miletus ca. 165 BCE of tax freedom for the importation of goods from Milesian territory into his kingdom – the king's expressed intent being 'the growth (*epauxesin*) of the revenues of the polis of Miletus and those of each private individual'.[41] Yet, even a rough, impressionistic reckoning suffices to appreciate what it meant to be a part of the platform of competitive advantage.

Risk reduction, which also means cost reduction, was a further initiative. Ancient states, acting as the first insurance firms, used their military arm to protect merchants from predators, especially those at sea; the 'protection route' thus became the privileged sibling of the trade route.[42] Access to relatively cheap credit, finally, was a further component that states added to the trader's platform of competitive advantage. Especially after ca. 300, polities – through a purpose-created institution, the State Bank, or through the treasuries of their sanctuaries or, again, through public loans of private cash – became vibrant actors in moneylending.[43]

However, while these and similar state-institutional initiatives (laws, access to law-courts, etc.) definitely furthered private economic

---

[38] Particularly proxenies: Mack 2015 and the online database Proxeny Networks in the Ancient Greek World (PNAW): http://proxenies.csad.ox.ac.uk/evidence.
[39] Gabrielsen 2011.
[40] Seleucid kingdom: Polyb. 5.89.9; 21.43.17. Syracuse: Polyb. 5.88.7; Diod. 26.8.
[41] *Milet* 6.3, no. 1039 II/III.   [42] Gabrielsen 2013.   [43] Gabrielsen 2005.

interests, they did so only to a certain degree. Public influence on, or stimulus to, economic activity clearly had its limits. First of all, because states remained states: that is, their field of action towards easing private moneymaking was constrained, partly by some of their own institutions and moral prescripts (as is exemplified by the maintenance of a distinction between citizen and foreigner); partly by their commitment to protecting communal interests against the supposedly harmful effects of unrestricted private moneymaking. And secondly, because the transactional relationship into which states entered with the trader (infrastructural services in return for taxes) was regulated by its own supply-and-demand mechanisms. Thus, where the state stopped short, its lookalike, the association, stepped in to do the job, a complementary relationship. Private economic actors, now forming empowered collectives clad as political and religious communities, became the bridges connecting 'personalised exchange' and 'arms-length exchange'.

The modalities are illustrated nicely by the grain-trade network headed by Cleomenes of Naucratis, Alexander's governor in Egypt. Even though, as far as we know, it never developed into an association proper, its set-up and operational logic had much in common with what by then (ca. 330) had emerged as a relatively novel way of conducting trade, namely, by syndication.[44] United by a common interest, namely to remove constraints to their private enrichment, Cleomenes, a powerholder, and an assortment of private actors had joined forces to create a web of commercial nodes dispersed at key *emporia* in the eastern Mediterranean, Athens and Rhodes amongst them. Soon Cleomenes' thrifty network drew to itself more associates: at about the same time as merchants from Citium and Egypt were establishing a corporate existence at Athens (see above, p. 316), two Athens-based trade partners decided to join Cleomenes' network. Even though they were contractually obliged to transport grain from Egypt to Athens, the two trade partners allegedly breached their contract, making Rhodes their base of operations. There, besides trading in Egyptian grain, they entered the banking business, supplying others with maritime loans. Obviously, like other professionals, these two erstwhile 'lone-peddlers' had realised what lucrative economic advantages were to be had from doing business as members of a private collective.

Still, the most interesting observations regarding Cleomenes' network seem to be the following two. First, its successful operation, and

---

[44] This and the following is based on [Dem.] 56, esp. 7–8; and Arist. [*Oec.*] II, 33a (1352a 16–23), 33b (1352b 15–19). Novel way of conducting trade: Gabrielsen 2013, 78–9.

hence the profits of its members, depended just as much on impersonal supply/demand mechanisms as it did on the platform of competitive advantage that its power-holding leader and his associates had constructed for themselves. By this I mean that, indeed, the level of prices at different places decided the direction of their shipments; but at the same time these local prices were themselves influenced by the network's activities, primarily their withholding of Egyptian grain until demand for it rose to higher levels. Second, the network's well-coordinated economic action certainly did rely on speedily disseminated and reliable information about grain prices, risk-reducing trust and the quick shipment of grain to whatever destinations where prices were currently reported to be high. Its paramount strength, however (one which, as we shall see, it shared with the association proper), consisted of the functional complementarity it professed via the coordinated action of its various subsections: moneylenders, informants, purveyors of grain (i.e. shippers, *naukleroi*, or 'merchants sailing with the cargo', *epipleontes emporoi*), receivers of the commodity, who may have doubled as managers of storage facilities, and redistributors – in short, the network's syndication of discrete business assignments that in aggregate covered an extended geographical area. It is this complementarity that, besides other advantages, bridged 'personal exchange' and the market. In some associations, it is this very functional complementarity, too, which can be read directly from the professions making up their name.

When mapping the distribution patterns of ceramics and other artefacts, we tend to connect the dots from A (place of origin/production) to B (place of consumption/ find spot) by drawing a straight line between the two, the assumption being that the direct route was also the economically most advantageous route. The way in which the subsections of Cleomenes' network cooperated falsifies that assumption, as does also the concept of transit trade. Functional complementarity – its exact geographical spread and pattern on the ground being determined mostly by demand and price considerations – often necessitated the involvement of more than two dots; hence, to link A and B in such cases, we must draw sometimes up to several indirect or bent lines. This is because it was the specific configuration of the network and its degree of organisational cohesion, rather than the physical distance which the merchandise had to travel as such, that decided the amount of risk-reducing trust, the quality of information attending transactions and so ultimately the overall cost of transacting. Our understanding of the concept of transit trade has been considerably advanced by studies documenting the contribution of state or religious institutions to the development of famed commercial centres (Delos, Rhodes, Alexandria, Apamea in Phrygia, etc.).[45] The same is true of works on the physical infrastructure of commerce, that is harbours and particularly storage facilities, private or public.[46] What remains to be more fully appreciated, however, is the substantial contribution of the formalised private network – the association – to the creation of the entrepôt. Cleomenes' network is not the sole example supporting this.

Further support comes from a papyrus of about 258 from the Zenon archive. It informs us that goods sent from Sidon to Apollonius the *dioiketes* and his people have arrived in Egypt, not via the direct route along the Phoenician and Palestinian coast, but via Rhodes. The dispatcher of the goods from Sidon to Rhodes is one Abdemoun, who describes Zenon, the redistributing agent on Rhodes, as 'my brother' (*ho adelphos emou*). Customs and other duties (*tele*) were paid at the final destination (Pelusium in Alexandria) by one Aristeus on behalf of the final recipient, Apollonius. Probably, what we are witnessing here is one subsection of a business syndicate at work. If, as seems plausible, on arrival the goods had already been pre-paid, while the 'customer' himself was responsible for payment of import dues,[47] then the whole affair can be characterised as an order placed with, and executed by, a syndicate operating pretty much like a 'firm' – the execution of its final duty (import of the goods to Egypt) being unburdened by taxes. 'Brother', in the papyrus text, might indicate a real family relationship, despite the difference in ethnicity indicated by the personal names Zenon and Abdemoun. There is, however, an alternative and more likely view: since 'brother', describing now a fictive family relationship, was also a designation frequently used amongst members of (particularly 'eastern') associations,[48] it is likely that in this instance Apollonius was serviced by an associational network of merchants who used Rhodes as an entrepôt; 'my brother' – as the dispatcher's additional description of the redistributor on Rhodes – would only have meant one thing: 'good faith'.

Thus, what was drawing up the lines of trade routes, besides the goods traded, was network-created trust. Demand and prices, in turn, were drawing up the geographical layout of networks. Here we may have a likely – market-driven and market-influencing – blueprint

[45] Capdetrey and Hasenohr 2012; Bresson 2016b.
[46] Harbours: Ladstätter, Pirson, and Schmidts 2015; Preiser-Kapeller and Daim 2015. Storage facilities: Chankowski, Lafon, and Virlouvet 2018; esp. Chankowski 2018. See also the project database Entrepôts et lieux de stockage du monde gréco-romaine antique: www.entrepots-anr.efa.gr.
[47] Gabrielsen 2013, 79–81. [48] Harland 2005.

behind the branching out of associations of traders' diasporas mentioned earlier (p. 318).

Functional complementarity bridged also the realm of the private with that of the public. Though privately created, most associations maintained a pronounced public profile – public meaning here both 'communal' and 'of the state'. With their capacity as 'political communities' to grant honours, they attracted benefactors from inside as well as outside their membership. In 149/8, the 'Poseidoniastai Merchants, Shippers and Warehouse-Keepers from Berytus' on Delos thanked their benefactor, the wealthy banker Marcus Minatius, through awards of splendid honours.[49] On Delos, too, the 'Synodos of the Eldest Warehouse-Keepers (presbyteroi egdocheis) Who Are Based in Alexandria' thanked Krokos, the Ptolemaic governor of Cyprus (in ca. 127–116), for his goodwill (eunoia) and justice (dikaiosyne) towards their association and towards other foreigners; this they did through a dedication of statues to Apollo, Artemis and Leto;[50] the 'Warehouse-Keepers and Shippers Who Are Based in Phoenician Laodikeia', another group active on Delos, dedicated (ca. 178) a statue of Heliodorus, the syntrophos of Seleucus IV, as thanks for his benefactions to the association.[51] Incidentally, the latter two associations – one based in Alexandria, the other in Laodicea, but both being active on Delos – may provide further evidence for the process of branching out. The recipient of exquisite honours awarded in 112/11 by the 'Shippers and Merchants Who Carry the Synodos of Zeus Xeneios' in Athens was a public official, the superintendent of the harbour of Piraeus, who, additionally, had been designated by the association as its proxenos – another telling illustration of how the networking institutions of the polis were being appropriated by these private republics.[52] In second-century CE Histria, in the Black Sea, Ada the daughter of Hekataius, a member of the city's foremost families, was performing benefactions towards private associations and civic units.[53] A benefactor and a benefactress were the recipients of honours from the Association of Leatherworkers (technitai skyteis) in imperial Termessus, in Pisidia.[54]

[49] IDélos 1520, cf. CAPInv. 9 (A. Cazemier).
[50] IDélos 1528, ll. 7–9, 12; IDélos 1529, ll. 5–6, 8: Synodos tōn en Alexandreiai presbyterōn egdocheōn – presbyteroi probably implying the existence of another such association of a more recent date: Poland 1909, 108, 171–2. At Oxyrynchus, to koinon tōn ekdocheōn is attested in 338(?) CE: P. Oxy. LIV 3772. On both of these koina: CAPInv. 894 (A. Cazemier) and 1450 (M. Gibbs and Ph. Venticinque). Discussion of the evidence for warehouses and warehouse-keepers (including their associations) in Chankowski 2018, 27–32.
[51] IG XI 4 1114.   [52] IG II² 1012.   [53] IHistria 57, cf. van Nijf 1997, 149–50.
[54] TAM III.1 4, 62, 114 (second to third century CE).

These are only a few, chronologically and geographically dispersed examples from the larger assemblage of evidence attesting to the close links that associations were prone to forge with local economies and elites. Rhodes provides the richest evidence both for multiple associational membership and for the habit of local notabilities to become the founders of up to several associations each: in the early first century, no fewer than ten such units simultaneously honoured a politically prominent individual, two of which bear his name.[55] Multiple membership also enabled resourceful foreigners – attested as benefactors, founders and presidents of *koina* – to climb up the social ladder and as 'corporate barons' to carve for themselves a place within the local associational aristocracy: Dionysodorus from Alexandria, lifelong president of two prestigious Rhodian associations, and a profusely honoured member of further ones, exemplifies this trend.[56] A related assemblage of evidence, commencing with our record on fourth-century Athenian *eranistai*, shows the associations as competitive players in the supply of credit, a task which they entrusted to specially designated officials (*hierotamiai*, *ekdaneistai*, etc.) and which often ensued from their obligation to put the money of foundations under their care to work.[57] Associational treasuries, too, spearheaded active participation in local activities, sacred or secular, via frequent involvement in public munificence and fundraising schemes. In these and further instances, 'private' and 'public' were so bridged as to create the corporate society.[58]

All this repudiates the view that associations, supposedly like the medieval guilds, remained closed-ended cells of little import for the economy, keeping, as it were, their collective benefits reserved for their members only. According to this view, associations and guilds are monopoly-like entities running on particularised trust, whereas the real fertiliser of the economy is generalised and uniform trust, the product of effective states.[59] Nothing could be farther from the truth. The examples cited above show the ancient associations to have been permeable organisations with strong interactions among themselves and with their social environment.[60] As ceaseless engines of honorific awards, they only ranked second to states; indeed, they often stood close to people who ran states. Their self-presentation as political-*cum*-religious

---

[55] Maiuri, *NSER* 18.   [56] *IG* XII 1 155 (second century), cf. Gabrielsen 1994b.
[57] On groups of *eranistai*, see now Thomsen 2015. See also e.g. *Clara Rhodos* 2 (1932) 175, no. 4, l. 7 (*hierotamias*); *IG* XII 3 330 (third century), l. 150 and *IG* XII 3 329 (third to second century), ll. 12–14 (*ekdaneistai* in each of two associations).
[58] Thomsen 2020.   [59] Ogilvie 2005; 2008.   [60] See also van Nijf 1997, 73–146.

communities, finally, turned them into a prime source of both generalised and particularised trust.

CONCLUSION

The proliferation and spread of trading communities owed much to the economic attractions of commercial centres. These attractions were the combined outcome of state initiative and market mechanisms, mostly of a burgeoning demand, including that for manpower. Soon, the associational networks themselves became part of the attractions and hence a segment of the economy of manpower. Not only did they lure entrepreneurial and skilled human resource to come to a given polity, more importantly, they also provided a good measure of the bonding which was needed in order to ensure that this valuable resource changed its habitual mobility with fixity: more and more transient businessmen were choosing to become 'residents' (*katoikoi*) – on Delos, in the early second century, in Ephesus in the first, on Rhodes, Alexandria and Athens even earlier. The foreigners who manned associations exerted an immensely fertilising influence on their local environment. Using associative life as their 'middle ground', a politically underprivileged but economically potent population segment became able to interact directly – that is, uninhibited by legal or ideological constraints – with the local citizenry and to penetrate into societal areas which were traditionally off limits.[61] Procurement and bonding of industrious human resource, in short, was itself an economic transaction of the first order. In this area, too, the associational network is seen to be taking over where the state, deeply committed to its own ideology, stopped short.

Further Reading

A lucid and stimulating account of ancient trade networks is offered by Terpstra 2019, to be supplemented by Terpstra 2013. A good introduction to network theory is Granovetter 1983; Rauch and Cassela 2001 give an overview of the theoretical debate about market versus network. The ancient Greek associations are discussed in Arnaoutoglou 2003 and Gabrielsen 2009; the economic aspects of ancient associations are treated by van Nijf 1997; Gabrielsen 2001; 2009. On the role of religion in trade and associational life, see Rauh 1993 and Gabrielsen 2016b.

---

[61] Gabrielsen 2001.

PART V

PERFORMANCE

THEORETICAL APPROACHES

22: POLITICAL ECONOMY AND THE GROWTH OF MARKETS AND CAPITAL

Armin Eich

INTRODUCTION

The ancients lacked a word for what we call economy. The Greek term *oikonomia*, from which 'economy' is etymologically derived, essentially meant 'the art of running a household'. Part of this art (and only part) was the ability to keep private finances in order. This original sense of the word 'economy' was still understood in the days of Adam Smith (1723–90) and some decades on. In this time, the adjective 'political' was used in combination with 'economy' to convey to the reader that the writer was concerned with economic problems transcending the household level, in other words with questions of a national or even an international dimension.

In the eighteenth century, 'political economy' meant approximately the same as the contemporary term 'national economics' (translated by Rousseau as *économie générale*). It is by no means to be confused with the concept of 'economic policies'. The science of political economy, rather, undertook to identify the forces and factors which exerted some kind of impact (economic or other) on economic processes, and to specify the nature of this impact. This was sometimes done in a systematic way, as was the case in the *Tableau Économique* by François Quesnay (1758), and sometimes with a preference for stylistic vividness, the most pertinent example being Adam Smith's *Wealth of Nations* (1776). However, apart from differences in style, it was a common aim of this literature to explain the mechanisms through which value was created and increased. In this respect, traditional political economy has some affinities with the contemporary school of New Institutional Economics (NIE; Chapter 23, this volume), which, however, focuses on historical institutions from the single perspective of whether or not they have been (or are still) conducive to economic growth. Political economy, in contrast, is less well grounded in a methodological system (or some may say, has no commonly agreed methodology at all) but is more open to integrating new perspectives or aspects. Thus, the current edition of the *Palgrave Handbook of Contemporary International Political Economy* includes, for example, climate change and mass migration among the factors which are influencing economic processes.[1] Factors of this type, not being 'institutions' in a sociological sense, are of no interest to NIE.

DEBATING POLITICAL ECONOMY

Political economy has gone through an era of 'critique' which led to important adjustments and extensions of scope. The most widely known of the critics is Karl Marx (1818–83), who endeavoured to write a fundamental 'Critique of Political Economy', the phrase forming the subtitle of his (unfinished) main work *Das Kapital* (*Capital*). In this context, political economy came to mean the whole set of beliefs, theoretic foundations and economic theories which explain and legitimize the capitalist mode of production. When the revolutionary appeal of this line of thought made itself felt in academic circles, a whole range of concepts and idioms[2] used by the classic writers of political economy (and also by Marx and his followers) tended to be avoided by established scholars henceforth. The concept of political economy itself was replaced by (National) Economics. Therefore, the term political economy today includes some kind of 'going back to the roots' or 'remaining in touch with the classical tradition'. Additionally, it may imply (but does not necessarily do so) taking into account Marxian or other criticism of the classic positions.

Irrespective of whether one espouses the critical way of reading the classic texts or not, it has to be borne in mind that in the days of Adam Smith the industrial revolution had just set in. Large factories, the acceleration of travelling speed and sophisticated financial instruments were yet to develop. Many economic processes took place in ways that were structurally closer to antiquity than to modern times. For instance, governments in the days of Adam Smith were with respect to the grain supply confronted with problems similar to the ones ancient Athens or

---

[1] Shaw et al. (2019).
[2] Compare, for instance, the vivid descriptions of class conflict in Smith's *Wealth of Nation* (1,8) or in Ricardo's *Principles of Political Economy and Taxation*: 'I am convinced, that the substitution of machinery for human labour, is often very injurious to the interests of the class of labourers.' (p. 380, ed. R. M. Hartwell, 1971).

Corinth faced, albeit in larger dimensions. Nor did the means these problems were dealt with vary very much from those applied in proto-industrial Europe. Although lacking the theoretical sophistication and mathematical precision of current approaches, classical political economy had the advantage of being closer in touch with the realities of pre-industrial economic life than we are in the twenty-first century.

Under these conditions, for Adam Smith, growth was not yet an abstract phenomenon assessed in quantitative terms and mathematical formulae, but a perceptible process taking place before one's eyes. As Adam Smith put it, 'When we compare, therefore, the state of a nation at two different periods, and find ... that its lands are better cultivated, its manufactures more numerous and more flourishing, and its trade more extensive, we may be assured that its capital must have increased during the interval between those two periods' (*Wealth of Nations* 2.3).[3] From this point of view, growth manifested itself, among other factors, in the soil providing larger crop yields, manufactures becoming more numerous, trade expanding, and so on. To be sure, in everyday speech 'growth' is even nowadays associated with phenomena like those just mentioned. But in a more technical language, 'growth' has become a virtually invisible reality. A landscape before one's eyes may grow richer in agricultural terms, but if the resulting harvests cause prices to fall and profits go down measurably, the economy is regarded as shrinking.

Most students of the economy of classical Greece use the term 'growth' in the way Adam Smith used it: as 'increase' in the quoted passage. Our sources allow us to observe, for example, an increase of valuable objects such as coins, domestic animals, furniture and so on. Also, an increase in the average size of certain objects such as houses is frequently understood as an indicator of growth (see below, p. 336). Things become more complicate, however, when the Smithian concept of growth, that is an increase of wealth as a visible reality, is conflated with the more recent meaning of growth as a mathematically measurable process.

In the following, it is necessary, first, to briefly recapitulate the argument of those researchers who held, or hold, that significant growth did not exist in the ancient Greek world ('Stagnation versus Growth'). In 'Indicators of Growth', recent research that strongly advocates in favour of ancient growth is presented. In 'Economic Growth in Ancient Greece', attention will be drawn to some theoretical problems regarding

---

[3] Cf. D. Ricardo, *Principles of Political Economy and Taxation* (p. 101, ed. R. M. Hartwell, 1971).

the optimistic view of growth in antiquity. In 'Geo-Economic Driving Forces in the Process of Growth', some frequently overlooked factors which are relevant to the understanding of ancient growth are discussed.

STAGNATION VERSUS GROWTH

During the nineteenth and through many decades of the twentieth century, most historians of antiquity took it for granted (without paying much attention to the issue) that the ancient economies were structurally not very different from early modern ones. In 1973, Moses Finley challenged this assumption in *The Ancient Economy*, which, for the first time, made use of a wide spectrum of ancient sources to show that Graeco-Roman antiquity was a socio-economic formation *sui generis*, with characteristic attitudes towards markets, labour and wealth.[4] The social world which Finley put before our eyes was mainly composed of a huge part of the population living at or near subsistence level and a small wealthy elite which indulged in politics, war and other elite hobbies without showing the least interest in technical innovation, profit maximizing or increasing agricultural yields. Finley's position allowed for some exceptions and variations, but he draws an overall picture of a social system which rendered any question regarding growth, whether in the Smithian or modern sense, obsolete. Some thirty years after the publication of *The Ancient Economy*, as voices raising doubts as to the applicability of the Finleyan model became more numerous, Paul Millett, emphasizing the usefulness of Finley's approach, proposed that in classical antiquity, except for the first two centuries CE, growth rates were so low and progress so slow 'that it is hard to imagine any underlying secular improvements in living conditions being apparent to contemporaries'.[5] Moreover, according to Millett, the 'small economies' of ancient Greece were extremely vulnerable to exogenous shocks, exposing whatever little progress had been made to the constant risk of being swamped in less than a moment, for instance through the effects of warfare or natural disaster. While acknowledging that there might have been, albeit regionally limited, some increase in wealth even in the centuries before the *pax Romana* (the first two centuries CE, regarded by Millet as a special era for which actual growth of wealth is undeniable), Millett doubted whether the evidence indicates a rise of wealth per capita ('everybody' owning more

---

[4] Finley [1973] 1999 for the third edition; see also Finley 1965.   [5] Millett 2001, 36.

goods) or rather reflects a growth of population, causing an absolute growth of goods produced as additional mouths needed to be fed. Furthermore, expanding the areas of land under cultivation to produce the food surplus required by demographic growth meant that increasingly land of poor soil was put to agricultural use, which implies that productivity per agricultural unit in the total account declined. Millett concedes that, during the classical era in some states, large sums of money were spent on the construction of monumental buildings, but this meant only, according to Millett, that capital was removed from the productive cycle and was 'locked up' in durable consumer goods and stripped of its potential to create growth.

Contrary to this line of thought, several important studies have been published recently aiming to prove that there was considerable and sustained economic growth in ancient Greece at least from the ninth century. The proponents of this view have collected a huge wealth of data, the analysis of which led to the reconstruction of basic trends in the Greek economy that will be outlined in the next section.

INDICATORS OF GROWTH

The least problematic development (in terms of empirical traceability) is the sustained demographic upward trend, acknowledged by Millett as well as by his critics, which started at the end of the Dark Ages and reached its climax in the fourth century. A major step towards the comprehensive understanding of this phenomenon was achieved by a paper published by John Bintliff in 1997, which included the evaluation of archaeological surveys of thirty Greek regions, predominantly in mainland Greece but also in the Aegean.[6] Bintliff considered the numbers of settlements on a region-by-region basis and the increase or decrease of these numbers through time, as well as changes in size of the individual settlements. It emerged that every region under consideration was affected by demographic growth, which was, however, unevenly spread across time, the core region of Greece around the Isthmus of Corinth (Attica, Boeotia, Corinth, Argolis) being the first to experience a major upward trend (from the ninth century onwards).

The movement of the 'Second Colonisation' (eighth to sixth centuries), affecting *inter alia* southern Italy and France, Sicily and the Black Sea coasts, expanded the scope of demographic growth as well as

[6] Bintliff 1997.

the number of local markets. According to a recent estimate, the Greek population of the Aegean and western Mediterranean rose from well under 500,000 in the ninth to ca. 4,000,000 in the fourth century[7] or even, taking all poleis into account, up to 'a total between 7.5 and 10 million'.[8] Correspondingly, the number of private dwelling houses increased massively in the same span of time. More importantly, houses became significantly more spacious. To give but one current estimate, whereas the living space on the ground floor of a typical ninth-century house was in the order of magnitude of some 80 m^2, residential space on the ground floor of a median dwelling house (often – as opposed to houses of the Early Iron Age – equipped with an upper storey) in the fourth century was 360 m^2.[9]

A further indicator of growth is usually seen in the increasing degree of specialization and division of labour,[10] a natural corollary of the growth of cities and the numerical increase of permanent city-dwellers. It has been estimated that during the classical period about a quarter of the overall Greek population lived in rather large poleis (with a median population of 17,000 individuals) and nearly 40 per cent in large cities with a median population of 35,000 city-dwellers or more.[11] These agglomerations were centres of additional demand for agricultural products, for the purchase of which the urban population needed money. They thus had to produce or offer equivalent value in the form of craft products or services. Even agricultural tools and implements were in the classical period to a significant degree produced by specialized artisans, who according to Xenophon at least in part were city-dwellers (see Chapters 13 and 14 in this volume).[12] Hence, the total amount of transactions is likely to have risen.

Scheidel assumes that the fact that the population(s) of Hellas grew sustainably over centuries was partly 'due to ongoing technolo-gical innovation', high population size and density providing favour-able conditions for the development of 'markets of information about technology'.[13] Additionally, the decentralized structure of the city-state civilization in connection with its competitive ideology and practice has been characterized as being conducive to institutional innovation (for instance, in the fields of contractual and procedural law (Chapter 17, this volume), money management or trade), thus enhancing a favourable environment for the lowering of transaction

---

[7] Morris 2004, 727.   [8] Hansen 2006b, 28.   [9] Ober 2015a, 82.
[10] Amply documented (for Athens) by Acton 2014.   [11] Ober 2015a, 86.
[12] Xen. *Cyr.* 8.2.5; Amouretti 2000.   [13] Scheidel 2007, 43 (quote), but cp. 52.

costs and the spurring of economic activity.[14] The coastal lines of many littoral regions of the Mediterranean and the Black Sea were, from the age of the archaic colonization (Chapter 3, this volume), dotted with attractive seaports often maintaining privileged relations to cities and tribes further inland, thus bringing about a high degree of what has influentially been called connectivity.[15] Great trading harbours like the Piraeus, Syracuse, Rhodes, Aegina, Thasos or Cnidus, rising to prominence during the fifth or fourth century, functioned as centres of attraction for the flow of commodities and capital as well as transit points focused on the needs of long-distance trade. Not surprisingly, it is – according to the numbers of dated shipwrecks per century – very probable that the aggregate number of journeys of merchant ships dramatically rose from the archaic to the classical period.[16]

The quantity of money in circulation appears to have multiplied between the sixth and the fourth century, coin hoards of the fourth century containing on average roughly four times as many coins as sixth-century hoards (the median is twice as much), while the number of known coin hoards is approximately two-and-a-half times higher for the fourth in comparison to the fifth century.[17] Obviously, not only the small wealthy elite but also the (in terms of historical comparison) rather well-off middle classes and, to a certain extent, the poor increasingly participated in the monetized economy. It is commonly asserted that wages (calculated on the basis of wheat equivalents) in classical Greece were by comparison with other historical societies rather high and, what is more, rose during the fourth century.[18]

As one drachm (documented in public records of the fifth and fourth centuries as a fairly common daily wage, when governments acted as employers) bought, according to the calculation of Kron, ca. 9.5 litres of wheat, the grain price level is understood to be rather low for the relatively well-off middle classes, whose spare money thus could create additional demand for goods other than the essentials.[19] Furthermore, it can be shown that the total amount of paid working hours in Attica rose dramatically during the second half of the fifth century. The most impressive example is John Salmon's calculation of working time con-sumed on construction sites by finishing the surfaces of blocks before fitting them into their position. This type of work is singled out by Salmon as a uniform activity, allowing the amounts of work performed

---

[14] Ober 2015a, 101–22.   [15] Horden and Purcell 2000, 123–72.   [16] Bresson 2014, 48–50.
[17] Ober 2015a, 83. See p. 341–2 below, however, for a note of caution regarding the wage growth of the fourth century.
[18] Ober 2015a, 93–5.   [19] Kron 2011, 132 n. 25.

at different times and places to be compared quantitatively. Particularly striking are the results for Periclean Athens (ca. 461–429): 'In twenty-five years it (sc. this generation) built three times what the Corinthians achieved in two and a half centuries.'[20]

ECONOMIC GROWTH IN ANCIENT GREECE: SOME OPEN QUESTIONS

The abundance of data recently collected leaves no doubt that the material wealth of Greek societies significantly increased in the time from the ninth to the fourth century. The validity of this statement is not impaired by the fact that the starting level of the development in the ninth century was very low and that a long process was necessary to merely reach the prosperity level of the late Bronze Age again, a level which, after all, appears to have been significantly surpassed in the classical period.[21] Nevertheless, some problems concerning the nature of growth remain.

Using archaeological finds and data to reconstruct economic growth (or contraction) implies that the actual findings will be of a 'Smithian' type as described above (p. 333): if there was growth, then it is traceable as a visible increase of the numbers of people, cities, commodities and so on. But things become different when one turns to the more recent concept of growth laid out above (p. 333), that is to say growth as a mathematically analysable process. In this case, the material evidence uncovered by archaeological research can only be used as proxy data, because robust statistical material on economic growth, which is an indispensable prerequisite for quantifying growth mathematically, did not exist in antiquity.

Nevertheless, scholars have used archaeological data to calculate ancient growth rates mathematically, for instance growth rates per year (related sometimes to per capita production of goods or, more often, to per capita or aggregate consumption). Ian Morris, for instance, estimates that 'typical consumption' growth rates (per capita) from the eighth to the third century were 'at an annual rate of 0.6–0.9 percent' or at least (taking as a basis somewhat less-optimistic rates of demographic growth) 0.3–0.5 per cent per annum.[22] Josiah Ober states that 'the actual rate of Greek per capita growth 800–300 B.C.E. was probably 0.15 per cent',[23] whereas Walter Scheidel assumes 0.16 per cent per year to be the correct figure.[24]

---

[20] Salmon 2001, 198.   [21] Morris 2004, 729.   [22] Morris 2004, 727.   [23] Ober 2015a, 82.
[24] Scheidel 2007, 44.

Without precise statistical data about (all) monetary transactions carried out in an economy in a defined period of time, growth rates expressed in percentage terms cannot be established in a methodologically tenable way. In today's capitalist economies, every transaction is, or should be, recorded and can be quantified in terms of value by a general unit of account: monetary value. Hence, it is possible to determine that the consumption in an economy grew in the course of a year by, for example, 2.5 per cent as measured in monetary value, regardless of what has been consumed, whether books, apples or houses. Such a general unit of evaluation is usually not available when we are dealing with ancient data. For instance, people in the Argolis obviously consumed no small quantities of beef in the eleventh century; later on, when beef became scarce, people ate more goats and sheep.[25] How would one quantify this change in figures of percentage? Greek houses can be shown to have usually had six rooms in the classical period instead of one or two at the end of the Early Iron Age.[26] The average age at death (for women) rose from ca. thirty-one years on average in the Early Iron Age to some thirty-seven years in the classical period.[27] Each single process, taken in isolation, can be appropriately or at least plausibly quantified. But, taken together, these inhomogeneous data cannot be translated into statistical terms reflecting a linear process of growth. The point is that modern statistics covering growth are related to the exchange (or market) value of commodities, whereas the archaeological material from antiquity provides information mainly on utility values and the development of standards of living in general, variables that do not fit easily into a common mathematical framework.

But things are even more complicated than that. Although the term 'growth' is understood by contemporary researchers in many ways,[28] the term usually refers, when used without any further specification, to the aggregate output of economies expressed in monetary value, giving the total amount of prices obtained by goods and services produced in the economies under consideration. The whole process of collecting and using the relevant data is fraught with organizational and theoretical difficulties, but these problems need not detain us here. It is nonetheless useful to recall that using monetary value for measuring growth is suitable for achieving precise and verifiable results, which provide important information on economic performance, but have the disadvantage of masking very different economic and social realities. To

---

[25] Morris 2004, 719. [26] Morris 2004, 720–2. [27] Morris 2009b, 114.
[28] See e.g. Abramovitz 1989, 3–79.

repeat the example given above, a bumper crop may lead to falling prices, thus bringing about economic decline in the agrarian sector. On the other hand, crop failures can lead to supply shortages in specific markets, with the effect of prices going up. If customers can afford to pay the higher prices, there will be economic growth, although the quantity of goods in circulation is decreasing. Moreover, growth as a function of GDP is compatible with downward trends of other economically important indicators, for instance profitability of investments.[29] The same is possible for other indicators, such as real wages or the overall quantity of goods: they may be declining, while GDP is growing.

These problems, inherent in the modern standard concept of economic growth, are partly relevant also for classical and Hellenistic Greece, since its economy appears to have fulfilled some prerequisites to make the application of the contemporary guiding concept of growth theoretically viable. To begin with, the Greek economy of the fifth and fourth centuries was almost completely monetarized. As the many currencies of the Greek city states were convertible against each other,[30] the economic activity of a given period – for example, a year – could (from a purely theoretical point of view) be represented by the aggregate amount of all payment transactions carried out in that period, expressed in terms of a leading currency such as the Athenian drachm. If the aggregate sum of the year under consideration rose in comparison to the previous year, we might speak of growth in the same way as modern economists do. Unfortunately, the Greeks did not (and could not) collect the relevant data. Nevertheless, even if no effort to document all transfers of money was made, the transfers did take place, so that their total value corresponded to something like a Gross National Product that could contract, remain stable, or increase from year to year.

Is it possible to determine whether the late archaic and classical Greek economy (the preceding centuries, lacking a uniform measure of value, being per definitionem not relevant here) contracted, stagnated or grew in this modern sense of the term 'growth'? The increasing quantity of coinage in circulation seems to support the argument that a growing number of transactions took place in the period between the sixth and the fourth century. This would appear to confirm that there had been growth – that is, a net increase of monetary profits – at least as an overall trend. If this is correct, it remains to be asked, as growth of profits could mask different realities, what the economic and social realities behind this kind of statistical growth in classical Greece might have been.

---

[29] Brenner 2006, 99–121.   [30] Bresson 2017b, 271–3.

Unfortunately, this question is not easy to answer with our present state of knowledge. The archaeological data outlined above appear to confirm that rising growth rates and the increase in amounts of goods progressed at an approximately equal pace. Thus, one might imagine a hypothetical graph representing the development of aggregate profits as going slightly but continuously upwards. But some caveats are in order.

First, it should be noted that, as outlined above (p. 333), an increase of the 'national product' in terms of monetary value does not necessarily mean that goods became correspondingly more plentiful, let alone that the quality of life generally improved. If, for instance, fewer merchant ships called at the port of Athens, the total quantity of imported commodities would decrease, implying from the viewpoint of consumers a shrinking process. But scarcity of vital goods would drive prices up, thus multiplying the profits of traders, as, for instance, a tripling of grain prices could easily result in a six-fold increase of the merchants' profit.[31] This increase in profit would be recorded as growth by common modern standards, even though the availability of consumer goods decreased; and vice versa, since an oversupply of vital foodstuffs could lead to declining growth in terms of monetary profits. The – in most cases – relatively short periods in which growth in terms of growing profits of merchants prevailed could bring about considerable stress for the poorer consumers. It is, therefore, necessary to ask in every single case what exactly is implied in economic and social terms when an economy is said to be growing, as the mere concept of growth covers various realities.

Wages are frequently used as an indicator for growth and are supposed to have risen sustainably during the fourth century. However, it must be said that virtually no explicit evidence for wages paid in the free labour market exists. The quite plentiful evidence on pay levels applies only to public wages, which could – as Vincent Rosivach has demonstrated[32] – fulfil the function of wartime relief payments, as did for instance the unusually high wages paid for labour in the Athenian construction business during the last years of the Peloponnesian War. These public wages are, therefore, likely to have been somewhat higher than free-market pay levels. The one-and-a-half drachm, however, attested twice as a daily wage rate for unskilled workers in an account of the Eleusinian *epistatai* (overseers of construction work) in 328 (*IG* II² 1672, ll. 33 and 45), is a quite unique figure in our sources[33] and should

---

[31] Bresson 2003, 148–9. [32] Rosivach 2011.

[33] Clinton 2008, 185–8. Compare, however, the *per diem* allowance of 1.5 drachms paid to the participants of some assemblies in late fourth-century Athens (Arist. *Ath. Pol.* 62.2).

not, as is often done, be treated as a basis for calculating the long-term development of ancient Greek wage rates.[34] More to the point are the rates of soldiers' pay, which amounted during the classic and Hellenistic period to three or four obols a day or, when war chests were well filled, to one drachm.[35] The generals who contracted mercenaries competed with demand for civilian labour, so that it is rather improbable that they paid less than their competitors on a regular basis. Hence, it appears to be unlikely that in the course of the fourth century wages rose to a level two or three times higher than military pay rates. Moreover, it is useful to remember that ancient wage labourers as a rule had no regular income but were paid for specific tasks, such as the transport of a certain amount of wood, or were hired on a daily basis. It is far from certain whether their working power was continuously in demand. Furthermore, the accounts of the Apollo sanctuary on Delos show that only a small proportion of the workers hired by the administrators of the sanctuary took on two or more tasks in the course of a year. Out of 669 attested artisans, 419 were content with one job in a year.[36] Annual income, therefore, would have been significantly less than a day's pay multiplied by the number of working days per year. In the light of these considerations, the assumption that wage levels in Classical Greece were extraordinarily high (p. 337, n. 17) seems to be rather optimistic.

In addition, some qualifying remarks regarding the immense increase of working hours in the second half of the fifth century, forcefully illustrated by John Salmon (see p. 338, n. 20), are in order. It is beyond doubt that the number of working hours performed in total (not per capita) increased in the period from the archaic to the classical period. But it needs to be taken into consideration that, while in Athens input was surely on the rise, it might have been declining in other places. As for instance John Cook noted long ago, there is no single major building project recorded in the Ionian cities of Asia Minor for the first half of the fifth century after large-scale building activity in the sixth century, especially in Samos, Ephesus and Didyma.[37] Local production levels and trade activity between the Ionian cities appear to have been low during these decades.[38] Similarly, it has recently been shown[39] that finds and features indicating transregional trade of Cretan poleis became rare or disappeared after the foundation of the Delian League (478/7). These findings appear to reflect the overwhelming competitive

---

[34] Ober 2015a, 95 (with references).   [35] Pritchett 1971, 3–29; Loomis 1998, 32–61.
[36] Feyel 2007.   [37] Cook 1961. Compare the qualifying remarks by Osborne 2008, 215–16.
[38] Lawall 2013, 109.   [39] Erickson 2013.

advantage of the Athenian marketplace and the migration of workers from their hometowns to Athens (and perhaps to other places with attractive labour markets). It must be recognized, however, that the downtrend in economic activity at the margins of the Delian League took place one or two generations before labour demand in Athens increased dramatically. Nevertheless, it might be asked whether the striking growth of labour demand in Attica was partly due to a process of economic concentration, in the course of which a considerable part of the overall Greek work force migrated from the periphery of the Aegean world to the centre. In the fourth century, the trend reversed: the population of Attica is estimated to have formed 6 per cent of the whole Greek population in the fifth century, but declined to less than 4 per cent in the fourth, whereas the population in some parts of Greece rose by 10 or 20 per cent.[40] As a consequence, the total amount of work performed certainly became geographically more evenly distributed in the fourth and third centuries than in the fifth, but it did not necessarily grow.

Turning to technological innovation, it is striking that for the centuries of rapid demographic growth, no major innovation or sustained improvement of agricultural techniques is recorded. In the tabular overviews of 'technical improvements and innovations in agriculture and the processing of food, wine and oil' and of the 'technical development of the watermill' compiled by Kenneth D. White, the so-called hopper-rubber-mill is the only item which is unambiguously assigned to a time before the third century.[41] The vast majority of ancient inventions enhancing agricultural productivity date to Roman times, and some of the more spectacular kinds to late antiquity only. It may be significant that it is an author of the fourth-century CE who underscored the saving of working time and therefore manpower as a major advantage of using machines (in this case a mechanical harvester).[42] This lends support to the argument that it was the decline and not the growth of population that provided decisive incentives to substitute manpower with mechanical power.

It may have been rather unspectacular innovations which set the preconditions for demographic growth in the classical period, as for instance a more systematic use of manuring, terracing and other traditional agricultural techniques. The extension of the fertile years of women, depending on improved nutrition, entailed a rising number

---

[40] Morris 2009b, 115.   [41] White 1984, 195–201.
[42] Pall. *op. agr.* 7.2: *et ita per paucos itus et reditus brevi horarum spatio tota messis inpletur.*

of children born. When population size reached a critical level in a sizable number of poleis, more and bigger merchant ships were built to cope with the large quantities of grain needed to feed the increasing population. The use of tenons and mortise joints made possible the construction of ships with greater carrying capacity (from ca. thirty tons in the archaic period to sixty to a hundred tons in late classical times).[43] Other inventions may have left no traces. Nevertheless, it would be exaggeration to conclude that growth in the classical period was due to technological innovation. Basically, the phenomenon of technologically driven growth is associated with modern market economies, under the parameters of which growth is normally generated when owners of capital increase the amount of capital invested into producer goods like machinery and into technological improvement. This may happen either by borrowing additional money (so-called productive loans) or by spending a higher proportion of income on productive purposes, or by a combination of both. Technological progress is thus applied to lower production costs and, consequently, to an increase of returns. If innovations implemented by one producer turn out to be successful, competitors are compelled to adopt similar improvements. Thus, innovation is structurally embedded in the economic process itself (Chapter 26, this volume). Ancient Greek economic innovation, by contrast, was characterized by randomness, because it was not structurally grounded in a competitive economic process (contrast Chapter 27, this volume). It can be concluded, therefore, that on the whole Moses Finley's ideas were far from being misleading and are still waiting to be reconciled with more recent approaches to economic performance.

Geo-Economic Driving Forces in the Process of Growth: Some Conclusions

The basic intention of political economy is, as was argued in the introduction to this chapter, to identify and evaluate various factors impacting on economic processes. Some of the factors which are deemed relevant by current research have been discussed in the preceding sections. In this concluding section, I would like to call attention to several causes of economic growth (in the Smithian sense) which are sometimes overlooked but were essential contributions to the nature of the classical economic system.

---

[43] Bresson 2014, 64.

Arguably, the economic system of the classical period depended to a large degree on a geo-economic framework brought about by government action.[44] This is not to say that there existed any preconceived plan of how to build a prosperous economy. Rather, it was the free interplay of sharply competing political forces which helped to bring about the socio-economic system called 'wealthy Greece' in current literature (Chapter 27, this volume). Particularly important was the establishing of (relatively) extensive pacified areas, where commodities and information could move freely. Because of the severe competition between the numerous city states, this could not be accomplished by concerted action but was attempted, and sometimes achieved, by militarily dominant cities driven by imperial ambition. The most important examples are the Athenian confederacies in the fifth and fourth centuries, but also Syracuse in the fifth or Rhodes in the third and second centuries. Under these circumstances, the construction of an appropriate infrastructure – such as ports, ship arsenals, stores, marketplaces, interventions in the price-formation process and a massive fiscally driven demand for, among other things, military goods and services maintained by the dominant poleis – played their part in bringing about a multi-layered system of intensified (and partly unequal) exchange. Encouraging grain imports by using military and diplomatic power helped sustain a large population in Attica, which in terms of density by far exceeded the carrying capacity of the land and furthered demand for goods and services. Attica developed into a central area of attraction for commodities and immigrants, on the one hand, and became the home of a highly diversified manufacturing industry producing exportable goods, on the other (Chapters 8, 13 and 14, this volume).[45]

The area of empire where the *hegemon* (superior power) obtained direct control (mainly the Aegean islands and the northern and eastern coastal zones of that sea) consisted of formerly relatively self-sufficient regions which, in the course of the fifth century, merged into a supra-regional trade zone characterized by a free flow of communication and comparatively safe trade routes. This zone comprised, apart from the imperial territory as such, trading routes reaching as far as Egypt and the corridor to the Bosporan kingdom. There followed an outer layer formed by what I have called 'small empires' on the periphery of the Greek world, as for instance the north-western coastal zone of the Black Sea, controlled by Olbia, or the region of dominant Sinopean influence in the south-eastern zone of the same sea (see also Chapter 7, this

---

[44] See Eich 2006, esp. chs. 2 and 6.   [45] Acton 2014.

volume).[46] The inhabitants of the peripheral zones functioned as agents mediating trade contacts with their 'barbarian' hinterland, like Olbia which maintained contacts reaching deep into Scythian territories and beyond, or Massilia brokering trade connections between the Mediterranean and the neighbouring Celtic peoples. The outermost layer consisted of the non-Greek people who lived beyond the fringe of the Greek small empires and practised trade with the peripheral *emporia* of these small empires.

The politically created system of the core–periphery type offered a great number of profitable opportunities for enterprising people, for instance by benefiting from the advantages of asymmetrical trade with the 'barbarian fringes' or by profiting from open sea routes and access to crucial market information such as prevailing prices or crop failure. Many of the system's characteristics survived the demise of the Athenian empire at the end of the fifth century, albeit in modified form. Looked upon from this angle, the economic prosperity of classical and Hellenistic Greece can be understood as a by-product of two main political developments in the archaic and early classical period: colonization and empire building.

Further Reading

Although most arguments of Finley [1973] 1999 are today deemed to be refuted, it still remains essential reading, as new approaches can only be understood against this background. Also time-honoured, but by no means outdated, is Isager and Hansen 1975. Designed as a commentary on some important fourth-century forensic speeches treating business matters, this book is the most vivid introduction to Greek economic institutions and practices. Bresson 2016b provides a comprehensive introduction to the ancient Greek economy, inspired by New Institutional Economics without being dogmatic. Ober 2015a is most instructive for major economic trends of ancient Greece, even if some of its methodological procedures may be debatable.

---

[46] Eich 2006, 137–41.

23: New Institutional Economics, Economic Growth, and Institutional Change

Sitta von Reden and Barbara Kowalzig

Introduction

Over the last twenty years, New Institutional Economics (NIE) has been a highly influential model in the study of the Greek and Roman economy. Although both its assumptions and methods are controversial, NIE approaches have changed the agenda of ancient economic history. NIE has sidestepped the long-standing conflict between 'primitivist' arguments of economic stagnation and 'modernist' views of market development and replaced it with a shared focus on the complex mechanisms of economic processes relative to local institutional arrangements (Chapter 1, this volume). Crucial for this turn has been its focus on institutions, that is, above all, social norms and legal frameworks. Through its emphasis on institutions thus defined, NIE includes within its frame of analysis certain social and political contexts, which for historians is paramount for understanding pre-capitalist economic behaviour.[1]

The overall goal of New Institutional economic history is to explain economic development, and notably growth, in line with a much-quoted phrase by the Nobel Prize-winning economist Douglass North (1920–2015): it is 'the task of economic history to explain the structure and performance of economies through time'.[2] NIE approaches and methods have therefore inspired quite specific research directions in ancient economic history. First, historians have developed a stronger sense of the

---

[1] The following is a very brief survey foregrounding some issues and leaving aside others; more detailed discussions can be found in Frier and Kehoe 2007; Bresson 2016b, 19–27; and J. G. Manning 2018. Critical reviews of the approach's broader implications for the study of the ancient world include e.g. Hobson 2014 (11–13 on how NIE tends to make (neo-)primitivists and modernists subscribe to the same presuppositions) and Verboven 2015. Both Verboven and Lewis 2018a see greater potential in North's later interest in behavioural theory (North 2005).

[2] North 1981, 3; cf. programmatically Morris, Saller, and Scheidel 2007.

importance of particular legal and political contexts for economic development.[3] Secondly, as quantification is the major methodological tool for NIE, it has stimulated research into identifying new, quantifiable kinds of evidence that would allow measuring economic growth more accurately.[4] Even if we are still far away from having robust data, we now have a better understanding of the orders of magnitude of income and output in particular economic sectors.[5] Thirdly, as NIE approaches are grounded in the social sciences, they have encouraged comparative research.[6] This has led to severe criticism by some historians, as the language and simplification necessary to communicate ancient evidence across disciplines seem to flatten the uniqueness and diversity of this evidence.[7] Such criticism can be countered, however, if two very different aims and interests of NIE are separated from each other. For some scholars, NIE offers an analytical model by which certain outcomes may be predicted, such as economic growth or the rise of democracy.[8] Others pursue the more moderate aim of asking in what ways institutions and state structures affected ancient economic performance.[9] NIE models have been applied more and less strictly, and findings have both confirmed and questioned the original methodology. Some NIE scholars, moreover, are more confident in the rigour of their data, and it is important to distinguish between the quantifying methodologies that NIE demands and the theoretical framework it provides.

We suggest that NIE offers a fruitful conceptual matrix for asking new questions – with or without the answers necessarily staying within the NIE model. By contrast, the aim of the NIE method to predict and quantify outcomes and the broader implications of the approach are far more difficult to accept and defend. Particularly problematic is its commitment to certain kinds of growth as the desirable outcome and litmus of economic development, together with the assumption of the universal benefits of that growth, with its end point and gold standard explicitly or implicitly based on successful economies of the West.[10] It is also important to remember that NIE played a pivotal role in shaping a particular brand of development

---

[3] J. G. Manning 2005; Frier and Kehoe 2007; Bresson 2016b; Mackil 2018; Terpstra 2019.
[4] J. G. Manning 2018; Weaverdyck 2019 for a survey of quantifiable data.
[5] de Callataÿ 2014.
[6] Ober 2015a; Kron 2015 and forthcoming; Morris 2002; Manning and Morris 2005 for the distinction between traditional humanistic methods of interpretation and social-science methods of explanation and prediction.
[7] Boldizzoni 2011.   [8] E.g. Ober 2012; 2015a; Lyttkens 2013; Carugati 2019.
[9] E.g. Morris, Saller, and Scheidel 2007; Monson 2012; Mackil 2018; Bresson 2016b; J. G. Manning 2018; Terpstra 2019.
[10] E.g. Faundez 2016 for a discussion of the Western bias of NIE; Hobson 2014 problematizing it for ancient history.

economics referred to as the 'Washington Consensus', which became deeply associated with neoliberal agendas, including very clear ideas of what beneficial outcomes should be and what sorts of institutions might be required to produce them – ideas that in the meantime have proven highly troublesome and morally questionable.[11] Similarly controversial therefore is a certain sort of universalism, whereby categories of analysis originally developed for understanding the rise of Western capitalism are transferred to other historical periods and societies.[12]

NEW INSTITUTIONAL ECONOMICS: SOME PARADIGMS

NIE entered ancient history in the particular version of Douglass North and was developed by him in a series of books and articles that show a continuous adaptation of his approach.[13] North retained the neoclassical commitment to price-setting markets as the most effective mechanism of distribution. He also held on to methodological individualism, rational choice theory, and the self-interested, maximizing actor, so central to neoclassical economic theory. But he strongly emphasized social and historical factors influencing individual economic behaviour.[14]

In assuming stable preferences and perfect information on the part of the individual actor, neoclassical economics in North's view was ill equipped to explain change over time; it took institutions structuring social behaviour for granted, whereas they are arguably an important variable in determining individuals' choices. Institutions, in North's definition, are 'the rules of the game in a society . . . the humanly devised constraints that shape human interaction'; they can be both formal, including laws, property rights, and constitutions, and informal, that is social conventions, codes of behaviour, cultural values, and religious beliefs. 'The major role of institutions in a society,' he continues, 'is to

---

[11] Escobar 1995; Harvey 2005. Kleinfeld 2012, 86–7 points to a simplistic adoption of Northian ideas of institutions on the part of international financial agencies; see also Williamson 2000.

[12] Hobson 2014.

[13] North 1981; 1990; 2005; 2009 (with Wallis and Weingast). For assessments of North's contribution to NIE see, from the economist's perspective, Ménard and Shirley 2005b; cf. Faundez 2016. For an analysis from the angle of the philosophy of economics and economic anthropology, see Krul 2018. What follows is necessarily compressed and simplifying.

[14] On the contradictions arising in North's theory from adopting the principle of methodological individualism, i.e. the idea that choice is driven by individual motivations rather than class or group dynamics, see Krul 2018, 117–25; ibid., 125–32 on rationality; some observations also in Faundez 2016, 386, 389, 402–3.

reduce uncertainty by establishing a stable (though not necessarily efficient) structure to human interaction.'[15] Institutions are thus conceived as the result of a form of social cooperation; they come into being in order to offset the unpredictability of social and by extension economic life. In other words, institutions emerge from an effort to lower what economists call transaction costs, the costs involved in exchanging information.

The term and theory of transaction costs go back to two other well-known economists, Ronald Coase (1910–2013) and his pupil Oliver Williamson (1932–2020). Coase argued that, contrary to the assumptions of conventional market economics, participation in markets incurs costs that rational agents had to, and did, calculate.[16] These costs arise from various uncertainties; among these are search costs, referring to the costs of finding adequate partners for transactions and suitable contractual agreements for exchanges. Other costs are uncertainty costs relating to assessing the quality of the goods or the honesty of the transacting partner in an anonymous market; and they include regulation costs, that is, how much the state interferes with the market in its own interest, such as by taxing away large amounts of private income or seizing commodities without warning. Because of these uncertainty costs, many transactions are more advantageous when they are settled within 'organizations': face-to-face corporations that are usually governed by social hierarchies and dependency structures. Though coming with social costs, they are not as anonymous, competitive, and unpredictable as markets are.[17] Oliver Williamson extended these lines of thought by developing a broader range of costs that occur before, during, and after transactions.[18]

Institutional frameworks that societies construct for themselves strive to minimize transaction costs (Chapter 27, this volume). Rational actors will always look for the forms of transaction that incur the least cost, shifting the emphasis from maximizing profits to minimizing costs. Economic history in this model must identify and question the institutional conditions of economic behaviour with a view to market development and economic growth. The ability of institutions to change economic processes is pivotal. A successful institutional framework reacts and adapts to changing circumstances by providing incentives from within to innovate in a sort of evolutionary process termed 'adaptive efficiency', the ability to be sufficiently flexible to

---

[15] North 1990, 1, 6.   [16] Coase 1937.   [17] North 1981, 33–41.
[18] Williamson 1975; see also Williamson 2005.

improve.[19] It is also in this context that North applied the concept of path dependence to institutional orders, which describes an endogenous dynamic structure that determines their development.[20]

According to North, transactions are constrained not only by institutions but also by state power. Only an effective state is able to enforce formal rules. The protection of private property rights takes pride of place here. Secure property rights allow economic actors to transact their assets without third-party encroachment and to invest them safely for the sake of material benefits in the future.[21] An effective state, moreover, has to demonstrate what North and Weingast call a 'creditable commitment' to its own rules, including the use, and guarantee of a stable value, of money and monetary instruments.[22] For state authority can potentially be abused, so that, rather than encouraging investment and economic development, it prevents them by its own predatory practices.[23]

The services that states provide create their own costs, such as monitoring and enforcing rules, or the costs of delegating power to agents who might deviate or follow their own interests.[24] Another kind of cost emerges from the state's obligation to protect its members and territory from external violence. North suggests that, as the costs of military protection and the fiscal regime are intimately linked, the size of states and that of military costs grow in tandem. For example, in order to protect the borders of an archaic polis, triremes would not have been economically efficient or politically viable. Accordingly, hoplite warfare was the most effective means of defending a landscape cultivated by a moderately well-off peasantry.[25] As states grew in size, and warfare came to be based more regularly on paid mercenaries, state investment in warfare financed by tribute gained a comparative advantage over hoplite warfare. However, even if states showed a certain commitment to their own institutions and rules, state revenue was not always used for

---

[19] North 1990, 80–1; North 2005, 70, with Krul 2018, 137–93 on North's theory of cultural evolution more broadly.

[20] North 1990, esp. 73–104.

[21] The degree to which property rights are never complete but should be approached as a larger or smaller bundle of rights will be discussed below, p. 355–7; see Monson 2012; Mackil 2018.

[22] North and Weingast 1989.

[23] In the context of this chapter, we will not discuss the degree to which North's classical liberalism favoured states ideally protecting strong private property rights, furthering free markets, and minimally interfering in trade (see Krul 2018, 85–6; Faundez 2016, 385), nor the role of private actors versus state institutions in economic growth; in relation to the Roman economy, see Erdkamp's 2014 comments on Temin 2012; for a famous debate on the medieval 'Law Merchant', see Milgrom, North, and Weingast 1990 versus Edwards and Ogilvie 2012.

[24] North 1981, 24–6.

[25] Conversely, the need to field such armies sustained such an agrarian regime in the long term: Davies 2007a, and below.

the benefit of their subjects, and high tax rates and extortionate tribute often covered not just regulation or protection costs. North put it in the form of a paradox: the existence of the state was essential for lowering transaction costs, but it was also the main source of exploitation, and thus of economic failure.[26]

Therefore, while the NIE theoretical programme focuses on social norms, legal structures, and state development as related factors guiding actors' choices, it also helps to problematize their interdependence. The problematizing aspects of NIE theory, and instances of institutional failure, deserve greater attention in ancient economic history than they have received in the initial euphoria over NIE's potential to explain growth scenarios. While we cannot undertake that here, what follows illustrates some of the ways in which NIE has been brought into the study of ancient Greek economic history to show its uses and limitations for the field.

New Institutional Economic History and the Ancient Economy

Economic Growth

New Institutional approaches to the ancient economy were pioneered by a group of scholars at the Universities of Stanford and Chicago. Already in 1992, Ian Morris observed that the debate over the ancient economy had become unproductive.[27] In subsequent publications, he proposed new directions of research in order to straddle the boundary between interpretative historical methods and quantifying and comparative methods typical of the social sciences.[28] Morris provided examples of his methodology by adopting more reliably quantifiable data in order to demonstrate the scale of economic growth in ancient Greece, while turning to methods guided by New Institutional models for explanation. In an influential paper, he analysed two kinds of archaeological evidence – skeleton remains and house sizes – in order to establish that between 800 and 300, standards of living improved significantly in comparison with the 300-year periods before and after this phase.[29] To judge from bone and teeth material, both women's and men's diets improved, while house sizes, measured in terms of roofed

---

[26] North 1981, 26; see also Mackil 2018, and below.   [27] Morris 1994.
[28] Morris 2002; Morris and Manning 2005.
[29] Morris 2004; for discussion of the problems related to the sample, see also Chapter 22, this volume.

areas in ground-floor plans, increased between 650 and 450 and then jumped significantly in the fourth century. These findings led to the conclusion that the capacity of an individual Greek to consume beyond subsistence grew by a factor of three, five, or possibly even ten, depending on the consumption regime assumed. Even more startling was the increase of aggregate consumption. In the Aegean and the western Greek colonies, populations increased by a factor of about ten, leading to an estimated fifteen- to twenty-fold increase of aggregate (total) consumption. This represented an average growth rate of 0.6 to 0.9 per cent per year, which compared favourably with that of Holland between 1580 and 1820 (0.5 per cent) and Britain in a period of continued industrialization between 1820 and 1929 (2.5 per cent).

Morris's figures have been central to NIE arguments in ancient history ever since. Ober adopted them together with other parameters (such as urbanization and coin volumes) in order to show that Greece was not as poor as had been suggested by previous scholars (see also Chapter 27, this volume).[30] Kron discussed them with a distinctly comparative perspective (alongside urbanization and population growth), suggesting that classical Greek economic growth was equal to that of Holland and England in the eighteenth and nineteenth centuries.[31] Bresson went so far as to call the exceptional economic growth of Greece the real hero of the Greek polis.[32] Morris himself put it in more provocative terms: rather than assuming that some sort of 'Greek miracle' of the sixth and fifth centuries brought about new forms of philosophy, historiography, drama, art, and democratic politics despite technological stagnation, an underlying 'economic miracle' might have played its role in bringing about classical Greek culture.[33]

While this is an intriguing perspective on the cultural achievements of ancient Greece, as it is, the model has its limitations. Changes in the size of houses do represent long-term trends in Greek history that saw significant political and institutional transformation, in terms both of formal law and informal social norms and of practical politics. But while citizenship rights, democratic participation in government institutions, the introduction of coinage, banks, and maritime law courts fall into this period of growth, direct correlations between particular institutional changes and economic performance are difficult to demonstrate.[34] Morris himself suggests that, alongside male egalitarianism and property rights, the geopolitical location of Greece, and its ever-intensifying

---

[30] Ober 2010b; id. 2015a, 71–89.   [31] Kron forthcoming.   [32] Bresson 2016b, xxi.
[33] Morris 2004, 728, 734.   [34] Bresson 2016b, 225–60 for a discussion of these changes.

connections with the exchange networks of the Afro-Asian empires through Greek migration, must have spurred on economic development as well (see also Chapter 22, this volume). In conclusion, he concedes that 'the details of institutions and ideologies may have mattered less than Greece's geographic position, which was well suited to acting as a trading middleman in times of high population density'.[35]

Furthermore, there is no evidence that Greek economies declined after the heyday of classical democracy and the conquests of Alexander the Great. Kron has gathered data on house sizes from Hellenistic Olynthus and Priene, arguing that, although there was a slight downward trend of median sizes, this was hardly significant. Hellenistic cities boasted a middling class just as prosperous as classical cities (see also Chapter 5, this volume).[36] Mackil (2013) and Bresson (2016b) have shown that Hellenistic poleis flourished under changing institutional and political conditions, most likely because they managed to devise cooperative institutions like common coinages and joint citizenship rights in order to meet their financial needs. But a lack of long-term figures for economic development that also include the new imperial economies of Egypt and Asia makes it hard to compare economic growth in the classical era with that of subsequent centuries. Not only are assessments of growth rates in the Hellenistic period far more complicated than in previous periods (Chapter 5, this volume), but the nature of state structures and the effect of rich imperial peripheries, among them areas of limited statehood, also create problems for explaining economic change in the framework of NIE approaches.

Entitlement and Incentive Structures

The desire to make a profit lies at the heart of neoclassical concepts of market development. The maximizing individual drives both supply and demand, thus stimulating markets and economic growth. While NIE does not call into question these basic assumptions, the institutional conditions for income to become secure and morally accepted are vital for its explanatory framework. Osborne has pointed out the concern of early Greek poetry with fair distribution (who deserves the profit of warfare, land, gift-giving, etc.?) and entitlement structures, castigating those who take more than their fair share.[37] For example, in Hesiod's *Works and Days* (early seventh century), problems of entitlement to a family's land are central to

[35] Morris 2004, 736. [36] Kron forthcoming. [37] Osborne 2009b for the following.

the conflict between two brothers, as is the question of who has the authority to arbitrate their conflict. Both Homer and Hesiod raise the problem of the social and political legitimacy of profit and private property-holding, and of the associated legal practices. They express a need for institutionalized forms of income distribution, adjudication of justice, and the protection of rightfully acquired property.

In the course of the long process by which both legitimate claims to income and state-protected property rights were negotiated, the reforms attributed to Solon brought about new institutional solutions.[38] The abolition of debt bondage led to the foundation of a free male citizen body, whose poorer members were no longer to be enslaved. The Solonian property classes distributed the rights of participating in the political process, creating a stronger sense of the importance of property rights for acquiring political status. Scholars largely agree that the Solonian reforms were the response to agricultural crises that followed population growth and an increase in commercial exchange between Greece, the western Mediterranean, and the Near East.[39] For a relatively small but entrepreneurial part of the population, the expanding economic environment offered new opportunities for profiting from growing levels of supply and demand.[40] At the same time, the new property qualifications that clearly defined the entitlement to political office created incentives for individuals to increase their income in order to further their access to political power. It is difficult to quantify the effects that institutional and political change created for the economy of Athens. The surge in the production of ceramics and sculpture in circulation as well as monumental architecture point to aggregate economic growth that was publicly visible.[41]

Property Rights and Their Limits

NIE makes well-defined private property rights a key condition for effective exchange, investment, and economic growth. If it is clear who owns what, what kind of rights ownership encompasses, and how it can be exercised, property rights lower transaction costs and increase incentives to invest in assets, all leading to more efficient use of these

---

[38] Morris 2002 for this interpretation.
[39] E.g. Morris 2002, 38; Bresson 2016b, 106–7. For the theoretical connection between population growth, scarcity of land, and the development of greater bundles of property rights in the context of Roman Egypt, see Monson 2012, 20–1.
[40] Morris 2002.   [41] Osborne 2009b.

assets and to economic development.[42] Yet the establishment of property rights and the costs of their enforcement are a double-edged sword in the cost calculation of NIE theory. For one thing, establishing property rights vis-à-vis others incurs costs for both the state and individuals. As the conflicts of the archaic period show, it fuels social tensions and competing interests between the state and its subjects or citizens. The combined social, political, and economic crises of the seventh century expressed in Hesiod's poetry do not seem to have been resolved by the end of the century.[43] Marginal and peripheral lands, furthermore, such as deserts, seashores, or forests, are difficult to attribute to either the local owners of the land or to those who enjoy the common right to their resources.

By the time of the classical period, Greek poleis had firm notions of private ownership, which, according to Aristotle, was defined as being safe, alienable, inheritable, and useful.[44] There were public procedures and magistrates who arbitrated and tried to prevent property disputes.[45] There were actions for eviction that owners could use against those who occupied their property illegally.[46] The Athenian *poletai* ran land registers for several monitoring purposes but also in order to make it easier to resolve disputes. Further procedures, such as the notification of sale to safeguard against the sale of encumbered property, reduced the costs of asymmetrical information between buyer and seller.[47] However, property rights are rarely fully exclusive. They remain encumbered with obligations and duties to third parties and the state. As we know from classical Athens, the collective citizen body guaranteed itself secure property rights over land and freed itself from regular taxation, but it did not assign these privileges to the large numbers of resident aliens who formed the greater part of the population active in markets and trade (Chapters 11 and 13, this volume).

J. G. Manning has emphasized the interdependence of a gradual development of private property rights, formal rule enforcement, state development, and economic growth in Ptolemaic Egypt.[48] Yet it is questionable to what extent state procedures for conflict settlement were designed with private and commercial interests in mind.[49] When the link between state development, property rights, and incentive

---

[42] Frier and Kehoe 2007, 134–5; Mackil 2018, 317–18.   [43] Morris 2002.
[44] Arist. *Rh.* 1361a; for discussion, see Maffi 2005; Bresson 2016b, 225–30; Harris 2016.
[45] Bresson 2016b, 227.   [46] Harris 2016, 118.   [47] Mackil 2018.
[48] J. G. Manning 2003; 2005; 2010; 2015b; 2018. For a more pessimistic assessment of Egyptian capacity for growth, Kron forthcoming.
[49] Athenian maritime courts clearly did so (Cohen 2005), but Bauschatz 2013, 7–8, 160–218 observes that the Ptolemaic police were called to action mainly in cases of fiscal conflicts.

structures is made key to explaining economic performance, it is important to ask under what circumstances states enforced which rules, and whether they transgressed those rules for their own benefit. The largely unquestioned right of states to seize cargoes of foreign merchant ships, or their willingness not to pursue such seizure on behalf of individuals without a legal claim, are examples of the limited willingness of ancient states to enforce property rights.[50] Similarly, confiscation of private property as a penalty for treason, overturning the laws, embezzlement of funds, and debts to the state were other ways by which states asserted ultimate authority over private property rights. Even in democratic Athens with its comparatively robust legal system, property security was subordinated to the political and fiscal interests of the state and the hazards of interpersonal conflicts, calling for a more nuanced consideration of the interdependence of secure property rights and economic growth.[51]

Terpstra (2019), moreover, has questioned the role of the Ptolemaic state as a major rule enforcer, especially where foreign trade and commercial relationships in distant lands were concerned. Drawing on some key texts in the Zenon archive (Chapter 9, this volume), he shows how a royal appointee, despite doing business in an official capacity, could not rely on public institutions when suffering from fraud or ill treatment. Much more effective than state protection were social trust networks to which business agents and merchants turned in the attempt to secure their legal rights (Chapter 21, this volume). While the Ptolemies introduced enhanced institutions that encouraged economic enterprise (coinage, banks, contractual law, a police force, and so on), such enterprises likewise relied on private social mechanisms in order to be mobilized and economically effective.

CONCLUSIONS

Recent research emphasizes that, in the course of 500 years, formal institutions in Greek polities changed considerably in tandem with the development of state structures. One might be tempted to see the expressions of uncertainty over fair distribution of income and entitlements to economic profit in Homer and Hesiod and the development of firm notions of property rights in Aristotle's time as marking two stages of a process of ongoing institutional changes that stimulated long-term

---

[50] De Souza 1999, 43–96, emphasizing the intersection between piracy and mercenary warfare.
[51] Mackil 2018.

economic growth in the Greek world. Various studies have discussed the details of this development in order to demonstrate how institutional change lowered the costs of transactions and thus contributed to increasing economic performance in the Greek world. Yet as research has improved our data and modes of explanation, studies more sensitive to the complexity of ancient institutional development have appeared, showing not only that, for example, property rights were less secure and well defined than one might think but also that Greek economic development cannot be reduced to a simple correlation between state-guaranteed property rights, public rule enforcement, and economic growth.[52] As Douglass North himself emphasized, property rights and enforcement structures are deeply entangled with political interests, social hierarchies, and ideologies that are slow to change and might impede economic change at the same pace as political and demographic change. Moreover, it begins to emerge that a simple opposition between public authority and private economic behaviour is hard to sustain, given the fundamental importance of social trust networks and private organizations; these did not operate separately from, or as alternatives to, markets but were crucial to the development of trust networks within them. They provided self-help, information, and financial support structures, as well as opportunities for communication with public institutions in economic environments that were insufficiently protected by public law.[53] One might further add that research in ancient history in the mould of NIE has so far typically focused on formal institutions and has been less concerned with that other tantalizing set of 'rules of the game', informal constraints, such as social codes, cultural values, and religious beliefs.[54] Even though he dedicated much of his late oeuvre to trying to pinpoint the interaction of social norms and formal institutions on the one hand and the role of cultural values (including religious beliefs) in causing, slowing down, or limiting political and economic change on the other, North did not fully work out a theory on this issue.[55] In conclusion, while New Institutional approaches offer powerful tools for investigating the conditions that may have furthered economic development in the ancient world, they should not turn into an ideology of market power spuriously projected

---

[52] Mackil 2018; Terpstra 2019.   [53] See also n. 24 above.

[54] See however Padilla Peralta 2020.

[55] North used cognitive science to develop his idea of 'mental models' underlying cultural values (North 2005, 23–37, 48). While preoccupied with cultural learning (North 2005, e.g. 15, 68–74, 136; North, Wallis, and Weingast 2009, 27–9) and singling out the 'unique evolution' of western Europe (North 2005, 127–45), he refrained from directly stipulating a change of collective belief systems as a precondition for institutional development (North 2005, esp. 155–65, cf. 48–80).

onto antiquity on the basis of a selective use of NIE's theoretical assumptions.

Further Reading

NIE is best approached through the writings of Douglass North himself (esp. North 1990). Krul 2018 critically discusses North's work from the perspective of economic anthropology and the philosophy of economics, including North's engagement with the institutionalism of Karl Polanyi. Greif 2006 has caused much controversy in applying NIE methods to understanding the differences in agency relations among the medieval merchant communities of the Maghribi Jews and the Genovese traders. Bresson 2016b, esp. 225–54, and J. G. Manning 2005 are most instructive for NIE approaches to economic growth in the Greek and Hellenistic world. Mackil 2018 sets the agenda for a more differentiated view on property rights in ancient Greek cities. Manning and Morris 2005 is a very insightful discussion of social science versus humanistic approaches to the ancient economy and includes comparative material from other ancient societies.

24: REGIONALISM, FEDERALISM, AND MEDITERRANEAN CONNECTIVITY

Emily Mackil

INTRODUCTION

Modern political scientists and economists agree that federal institutions promote economic efficiency and economic growth. I have argued elsewhere that the ancient Greek states most frequently known as *koina* (sing. *koinon*), which shared many features identified with federal states in the modern world, brought significant and distinctive economic advantages to their citizens.[1] Is it, however, possible to demonstrate a correlation between the establishment of federal institutions and an increased rate of economic growth? This chapter will introduce the theoretical and empirical arguments for this correlation in the early modern and modern periods, outline the ways in which such arguments both do and do not apply to the Greek *koina*, and suggest several alternative pathways for economic growth resulting from federal institutions. Given that during the classical period around 40 percent of the poleis of mainland Greece and the Peloponnese were participants, at one time or another, in a *koinon*, and that the figure would likely be higher for the Hellenistic period if we had the data to calculate it, it seems plausible to suggest that federalism may have contributed significantly to the overall trajectory of extensive economic growth during the period ca. 800 to 300.[2]

FEDERALISM AND ECONOMIC PERFORMANCE: MODERN ARGUMENTS

There are three main strands in what is known loosely as fiscal federalism, the modern argument that federalism enhances economic performance.

---

[1] Mackil 2013, 237–325; Mackil 2015a. For an introduction to the *koinon* as an ancient state, see Mackil 2012 as well as Beck and Funke 2015, 1–29.

[2] Number of poleis participating in a *koinon*: Mackil 2012, 305–6.

The first is the claim that the decentralization of decision-making in general leads also to decentralized economic policy decisions, which have a salutary effect on local economies. The second is that federal states in general are effective at redistributing resources. The third – and perhaps the most interesting – is the so-called fiscal interest model, which suggests that decentralized fiscal policy, a characteristic of federal states, tends to yield an investment of state revenues in market-enhancing public goods. I shall briefly discuss each claim in turn.

The idea that federalism enhances economic performance in general flows from two claims related to the structuring of incentives. The first is that by allowing local governments to establish their own fiscal policies within a framework of open borders and mobility within the larger federation, federal states enable an interjurisdictional competition wherein citizens may choose their residence based on the economic (and other) incentives presented by each member state.[3] Low-tax states that attract high numbers of residents might encourage other states to follow suit in order to maintain (or regain) their population. The second is that the decentralization of fiscal policy-making creates incentives for both central and local governments to adhere to their commitments rather than shirking or engaging in corruption.[4]

The redistributive capacity of federalism is theoretically high. Federal states tend to govern large territories with diverse and unevenly distributed resources; centralized fiscal decision-making enables the redistribution of these resources. Some scholars argue that the adoption of such redistributive practices, properly structured, can ameliorate interregional conflicts over highly localized and valuable resources, while others insist that redistributive efforts only exacerbate conflicts and suppose that decentralized fiscal decision-making enhances political coherence by "reassuring rich regions that their wealth will not be expropriated by poor regions."[5] Recent empirical research also suggests, however, that a rejection of such potential redistributive functions – a strong commitment to decentralized fiscal policy-making – lends federalism a powerful advantage in attempts to move from dictatorship to democracy, insofar as decentralized decision-making can protect "the economic interests . . . of the once-ruling elite."[6]

The third strand of fiscal federalism further explains why decentralized fiscal policy-making should be good for the economy. All

---

[3] Tiebout 1956; Oates 1972.   [4] Weingast 1995.
[5] Redistribution to ameliorate conflicts: Boix 2003, 168–9. Decentralized fiscal practices to enhance coherence: Rodden 2006, 365.
[6] Inman 2008, 29.

governments require revenue to pursue their goals, but within a federal state there is an institutional choice as to whether local governments will generate their own revenue or simply receive it from the federal government. The receipt of funds from the federal government tends to encourage corruption, whereas local governments that raise their own revenue more often invest it in public goods that enhance market activity and thereby stimulate the local economy. It is thus argued that governments that work toward their own fiscal interest will promote local economic growth. Insofar as this occurs across the federation, extensive and widespread growth is expected to occur.[7]

PROBLEMS OF EVIDENCE AND ANALYSIS

Intensive and extensive economic growth in the Greek world, across the period from ca. 800 to ca. 300, has been detected on the basis of increased house sizes, greater bodily stature and increased life expectancy, increased monetization, and rising per capita consumption among a population that was itself growing rapidly and settled in a proliferating number of increasingly densely populated urban centers.[8] For a growing population to have not just maintained but even improved its quality of life over a significant period of time is a sure sign that the volume of goods and services available per person were increasing, assuming a relatively equitable distribution of these gains. This, in a nutshell, is economic growth. And this remarkable trajectory of growth in the Greek world has been explained as a function of the heavy reliance on slave labor and of both technological and institutional innovations that reduced transaction costs and encouraged investment in human capital, spurred on by a "competitive ecology of city-states."[9]

Into this existing framework for thinking about economic growth it might be possible to categorize the economic policies that developed within the Greek federal states as an institutional innovation with beneficial effects on economic performance. There are, however, two challenges at the outset to making this assertion. The first is that the data upon which this general picture of growth has been built are proxies that

---

[7] Weingast 2005.

[8] Archaeological indicia: Morris 2004; 2005. Monetization: Ober 2010b, 252 and Ober 2015a, 83–4. Demographic growth: Scheidel 2003. Urbanization: Hansen 2006b. Consumption: Morris 2004; von Reden 2007a; Ober 2010b, 250–1; see also Chapters 21, 22, and 27, this volume.

[9] Bresson 2016b, 214, 222 (slave labor); ibid., 208–19 (innovation); Ober 2010b; 2015 for an institutional explanation. On transaction-cost analysis among other tenets of New Institutional Economics, Chapter 23, this volume.

track changes in living standards, which are certainly correlated to growth in an environment of demographic expansion but should not be mistaken for direct metrics of growth. As was already argued in the previous two chapters, the data are neither fine-grained nor comprehensive, and the limited nature of our evidence dictates a necessarily scattershot approach. This means that we can neither analyze growth over smaller periods of time than several centuries nor analyze growth over time within any given region of the Greek world with any confidence.[10] The second challenge arises from the first one. Given our lack of any data series on production and income over time and across space in antiquity, it is impossible to prove, via quantitative methods, that the adoption of federal institutions in a given region, which is in most cases a fairly precisely dated event, can be correlated with economic growth in that region. Given that federation occurred entirely within a period (ca. 800–300) already marked by growth that has been explained by other factors, it seems impossible to disaggregate any growth that might have occurred as a result of federation from the broader pattern of growth in the Greek world. One would thus need somehow to measure economic growth in all regions and for each of the centuries in question, and then look for a rate of growth in federated regions (e.g. Boeotia, Phocis, Thessaly, Aetolia, Achaea) that outstripped the rate of growth in regions where *koina* never developed. This is simply impossible.

A few specific examples may be useful. Archaeologists have determined that the city of Olynthus, the largest settlement in the *koinon* of the Chalcideis, grew steadily from 403 to 348, a period that coincides with the state's most robust federal institutions. Yet it is impossible to attribute the growth to those federal institutions, for it represents only a continuation of a trajectory of urban expansion that began with the synoikism of surrounding poleis into Olynthus in 432 and continued largely unabated to the end of the fifth century, a period during which Olynthus was an independent, autonomous polis.[11] Thespiae, a midsized Boeotian polis, has been intensively surveyed by archaeologists. Thespiae had a history of opposition to Thebes and its leadership of the Boeotian *koinon* in the fifth and fourth centuries; in 424 the Thebans destroyed the city walls of Thespiae, and in 371 they attacked the city and expelled its

---

[10] On the coarse-grained chronological nature of the analysis, see Ober 2010b, 249 n. 13.

[11] Hoepfner and Schwandner 1994, 71, 92–3, 103; Cahill 2002, 35–45. Zahrnt 2015 offers a concise account of the history of the *koinon* of the Chalcideis.

inhabitants.[12] Thespians participated in Alexander's sack of Thebes in 335 but joined the refounded Boeotian *koinon* in the very late fourth or early third century. The city remained a member of the Hellenistic federal state until its dismemberment under Roman pressure in 172/1. We might expect, a priori, to see a marked drop in occupation density from 424, or at least 371, to perhaps 335, followed by a steady increase. Yet recent research has suggested that the maximum extent of the built-up area of Thespiae was reached in the classical and early Hellenistic periods and that it had a population size that was roughly equivalent in the early fourth century and in the Hellenistic period.[13] The urban history of Thespiae as deduced from archaeological survey is thus at odds with the ancient reports of catastrophic events and institutional shifts; one explanation may be a rhetorical overstatement among ancient authors critical of Thebes of the calamities Thespiae suffered.[14] These two cities within a *koinon*, one excavated and one surveyed, exemplify the limits of archaeological data to inform us about the relationship between institutional change and economic growth.

Despite these challenges, it is possible to think about how the institutional innovation of the *koinon* could have fostered economic growth. The modern theoretical and empirical literature just surveyed offers some possibilities, and hints in the ancient evidence offer others.

INSTITUTIONS AND ECONOMIC GROWTH IN GREEK FEDERAL STATES

Decentralized fiscal decision-making, highlighted in modern studies of fiscal federalism, is indeed a hallmark of Greek federal states, where we have sufficient evidence to discern such arrangements. Some *koina* collected taxes from the harbors within their territory as well as direct taxes from member poleis, while leaving the collection of other tax revenues to member poleis to fund their own public needs. Thus the *koinon* of the Chalcideis in northern Greece collected export and transit taxes on timber exchanged with the Macedonian king Amyntas in the early fourth century, rather than leaving those poleis through which the trade was conducted to impose their own levies.[15] The Thessalian

---

[12] City walls destroyed in 424: Thuc. 4.133.1. City attacked in 371: Xen. *Hell.* 06.3.1, 5; Diod. Sic. 15.46.6, 15.51.3; Isocr. 6.27; Dem. 16.4, 25, 28; Tuplin 1986.

[13] Bintliff et al. 2017, 100–1.   [14] Bintliff et al. 2017, 102; Snodgrass 2016.

[15] Rhodes and Osborne 2003, no. 12, ll. 15–17; Mackil 2015a, 495–6.

koinon appears to have done the same in the mid-fourth century, and we have incontrovertible evidence that the *koinon*, rather than any of its member poleis, imposed a 5 percent tax on imports and exports throughout the state's territory in the second century.[16] And in Lykia in the first and second centuries CE, it was likewise the *koinon* that levied duties on goods imported to and exported from the region, while taxes were also imposed on the transport of goods across polis boundaries within the *koinon*.[17]

Direct taxes paid by member states to a federal government were styled "contributions" (*eisphorai*) and were intended to fund the activities of the federal state, probably military activity above all. In early fourth-century Boeotia, much care was taken to ensure that the contributions demanded from each cluster of poleis, which formed an administrative district, were directly proportional to the size of their population and territory.[18] In Hellenistic Achaea, likewise, member cities were obligated to make contributions to the federal government.[19]

With the exception of these two federal taxes, it appears to have been left to each member polis to determine and enforce its own fiscal policies. We catch glimpses here and there, afforded by the rich epigraphic record of Hellenistic Boeotia in particular. Here, a federal law on military training imposed on all member poleis the obligation to train their youths but left it up to each polis to make its own arrangements with a suitable trainer and to provide him with a salary.[20] Anthedon, a small polis on the Boeotian coast of the Euboean strait, distinguished by the maritime orientation of its economy, appears to have imposed duties on the catches of fishermen who brought their goods to the port for sale during the period when it was a member of the Boeotian *koinon*.[21] As far as we can tell, it was the polis of Anthedon that imposed and collected these duties, thus setting the Boeotian *koinon* apart from federal states – such as those of the Chalcidice and Thessaly in the fourth century and Lykia in the Roman imperial period – that placed harbor dues throughout the region in the hands of the federal government. And it was therefore the polis of Anthedon that decided how to use the revenues it derived from these harbor dues.

---

[16] Fourth century: Just. *Epit.* 11.3.1–2 with Dem. 1.22. Second century: Helly 2008, 91–6 (*SEG* 58.525).

[17] *IKaunos* no. 35 (Caunus); *SEG* 35.1439 (Myra); Takmer 2007 with *SEG* 57.1666 (Andriake).

[18] *Hell. Oxy.* 16.4 (Bartoletti) with Mackil 2013, 296–8.

[19] Polyb. 4.60 with Mackil 2013, 299–300.   [20] *SEG* 32.496; Mackil 2013, 441–2 (T27).

[21] Anthedon's maritime economy: Herakleides Kritikos, *BNJ* 369A 23–4 with Bresson 2015. Tax on fish imports: *SEG* 60.495 with Lytle 2010.

The most striking evidence for decentralized fiscal policy in Greek federal states also exposes fiscal shortfalls among the poleis. When member poleis experienced this, they were evidently unable to turn to the *koinon* for a bailout. Instead they resorted to borrowing money from other poleis as well as from private lenders. The inscriptions that record their debts also reveal the freedom with which member poleis allocated their landed resources to such creditors as a form of repayment or compensation for delayed payment.[22] The ability of member poleis to access credit from other member poleis, from poleis outside the *koinon*, and from private creditors means, however, that the *koinon*'s refusal to engage in a top-down redistribution of resources does not amount to the imposition of a "hard budget constraint" on member states, a key characteristic of fiscal federalism.[23] What is more, although most *koina* produced a federal coinage with a regional badge and legend, these coins were often produced cooperatively by multiple polis mints within the region or were supplemented by smaller-denomination coins produced exclusively by member poleis. In modern terms, then, the federal government did not have an exclusive power to mint money, nor did it place any restrictions on the credit to which member states might gain access.

The third strand of the theory of fiscal federalism claims that decentralized fiscal authority creates among member states an incentive to foster market activity locally by investing the revenue they raise directly in market-enhancing public goods. Investment in these public goods is economically beneficial not only to individuals engaged in local trade but also to the member state itself, insofar as increased market activity yields an increased tax base. It seems a priori likely that this could have been true in the Greek world, where transaction taxes bulked large in the fiscal portfolio of every polis.[24]

In the world of small poleis that comprised the member states of Greek *koina*, we rarely have any evidence of how local tax revenue was invested, but a few clues suggest that it was at least sometimes beneficial to the local economy in the sense that political scientists would predict. The tax on fish brought into the harbor of Anthedon for sale, briefly discussed above (p. 365), is one such example. The document from which that levy has been inferred is a peculiar list of saltwater and freshwater fish with their maximum prices. It was found at the inland Boeotian polis Akraiphia and issued by the local *agonarchs*, known

---

[22] Migeotte 1984, nos. 11, 12, 16A–B with Mackil 2013, 443–8 (T29, 30, 32).
[23] Weingast 1995, 4.   [24] Purcell 2005.

elsewhere as *agoranomoi* or market officials.[25] Ephraim Lytle has argued that the list of saltwater fish with their maximum prices was adapted from an alphabetized list of saltwater fish subject to import duties at a coastal polis, most likely Anthedon.[26] In this case, then, although we do not know what Anthedon did with the revenue derived from this tax, it did create a basic infrastructure for the sale of fish within the region, however unwittingly or accidentally. For the alphabetized list, which would have facilitated the work of customs officials at Anthedon, created a basis for other rules regarding the sale of fish in other markets within the *koinon*. It seems likely that the measure of the *agonarchs* at Akraiphia, fixing maximum prices for the fish they expected to appear in the market, would have encouraged both sellers and buyers to participate; it thus qualifies as a market-enhancing strategy, indirectly associated with the local tax regime at a fellow member polis of the Boeotian *koinon*. If the Akraiphians also collected a tax on the sales, which is totally undocumented but not at all unlikely, it would be plausible to suggest that this practice increased the revenue base of the polis. This would point toward economic growth emerging out of the decentralized fiscal policy-making regime of the Boeotian federal state.

An episode from Hellenistic Achaea exposes a rather different dynamic, wherein the failure of the *koinon* to invest the revenue it collected from member states in the most fundamental market-enhancing public good – defense – provoked outrage among those member states. During the Social War in the late third century, three western Achaean member poleis (Dymae, Tritaia, and Pharai) sent a request for military assistance to the *koinon* following an Aetolian invasion, in which their territory was ravaged and an important fortification seized. The request was denied for lack of funds. The cities, vulnerable because they were perched on the western flank of the territory of the Achaean *koinon*, responded to this rejection by refusing to pay their "shared contributions" (*koinas eisphoras*) to the *koinon* and used the funds instead to hire their own mercenary force for the defense of their territory.[27] Following this rupture, the western cities appear to have negotiated with the *koinon* and quickly returned to full-fledged membership. It is striking to see not the member states but the federal government being accused by its constituents of free-riding, and the case provides a fine illustration of self-enforcing federal institutions, in which the various participants in the federal bargain hold one another to

---

[25] See Mackil 2013, 268–9 with no. 109.   [26] Lytle 2010, 274–5, 277–80.
[27] Polyb. 4.59–60; Plut. *Vit. Arat.* 37 with Grandjean 2000, 318–19; Mackil 2013, 299–300.

account for violations of its terms, a dynamic that modern political scientists suggest is critical to the stability of the fragile federal bargain.[28] In the case of Hellenistic Achaea, then, the norm appears to have been that the federal government would invest its revenue in public goods, and occasional failure to do so was met with prompt and stiff resistance.

In sum, our evidence suggests that federal institutions in the Greek world aligned in some ways with the modern theory that federalism promotes economic growth. As a general rule, fiscal decision-making was decentralized: the *koinon* demanded contributions from its member states, which directly funded public goods, above all defense and related expenses. This was not, then rent-seeking behavior, and in at least one case a challenge from member poleis prevented the *koinon* from slipping into it. Poleis levied and collected their own taxes and appear to have decided how to use the resulting revenue; there is evidence that they learned from one another and that some of these fiscal policies had what might be termed market-enhancing effects. On the other hand, we cannot conclude that *koina* imposed hard budget constraints on member poleis, insofar as they had some capacity to mint money locally and no centrally imposed restrictions on borrowing.

FRAGMENTATION, CONNECTIVITY, AND FEDERALISM: ANCIENT PRACTICES AND ECONOMIC PERFORMANCE

However, a more open look at the ancient evidence, unconstrained by a search for patterns that conform to contemporary models, suggests a different economic logic to federalism, which offers potential alternative pathways to economic growth. A speech put in the mouth of one Kleigenes of Akanthus, addressing the Spartan assembly in an appeal for help against the growing power of the Chalcidian *koinon* in northern Greece in 382, emphasizes several economic advantages that flowed to its citizens from that state's federal institutions. These are the pooling of diverse and complementary resources and rights of intermarriage (*epigamia*) and real property ownership (*enktesis*) throughout the *koinon*.[29] These two benefits go hand in hand. In the geologically and

---

[28] Riker 1964; Weingast 2005, 160–4.

[29] Xen. *Hell.* 5.2.16–19. For full discussion of this speech, see Bearzot 2004, 47–52; see also Mackil 2013, 264–89 with a discussion of the evidence for resource complementarity achieved by *koina* in the Chalcidice, Boeotia, Achaea, and Aetolia.

ecologically fragmented Mediterranean environment, access to a diverse array of resources was severely challenged by the political fragmentation of the classical Greek world, a mosaic of more than a thousand poleis, each of which as a rule preserved land ownership as a privilege for its own citizens and frequently disincentivized exogamy with laws on citizenship and inheritance.[30] When *koina* extended the rights of *epigamia* and *enktesis* throughout the territory of the *koinon* to all citizens, regardless of their primary polis citizenship, they made it possible for them to acquire, and to keep in their family, land with resources quite different from those available within their own polis. These institutions made it possible for citizens to pursue economic activities predicated on the integration of coast and hinterland, of mountain and sea, of pastureland and agricultural land.

The extension of property rights by the *koinon* to citizens of all member poleis might be taken to imply a commitment on the part of the state to the protection of citizen property. Indeed, the provision of property security has been taken to be a primary function of the state since the first century, and contemporary theorists working in the New Institutional Economics (NIE) regard property security as a fundamental condition for economic growth, along with the enforceability of contracts (Chapter 23, this volume).[31] It is clear that Greek states in general took steps to protect the property rights of their citizens, providing laws that governed purchase, sale, and bequest.[32] There is evidence that a few also kept registers of the real property holdings of their citizens, an important legal mechanism to forestall disputes and facilitate both sales and the extension of credit on security of property.[33] Direct evidence for such registers is entirely lacking for the *koina* of the Greek world, but records of real-estate transactions in the fourth-century Chalcidice may point to the *koinon*'s commitment to the preservation of such information.[34]

Simply by aggregating member poleis into a united military force, *koina* dramatically increased their military capacity, which meant stronger offensive and defensive abilities, the protection of independence, and more victories that sometimes produced significant hauls of plunder.[35] It also certainly contributed to improved diplomatic clout. Thus, for example, the

---

[30] Fragmentation: Horden and Purcell 2000. More than a thousand poleis: *IACP*.

[31] Cic. *Off.* 1.20–1, II.78–9. Property security as a foundation for economic growth in NIE: Furubotn and Richter 2005, 79–133.

[32] Lyttkens 2013, 123–6; Bresson 2016b, 225–230.   [33] Harris 2016.

[34] Game 2008, nos. 13–28 (Olynthus), 29–33 (Stolus), 34–5 (Polichne), 38 (Torone). See Mackil 2013, 257–8.

[35] Increased military capacity: *Hell. Oxy.* 16.4 reports that the Boeotian *koinon* had a paper strength of 11,000 citizen hoplites at the turn of the fourth century. When troop numbers for Boeotian

Achaean *koinon* received direct financial support from the Ptolemaic kingdom to support its ongoing opposition to the Antigonids from 251 to 226.[36] And Xenophon makes the explicit claim that when the Theban statesman Pelopidas went to Susa in 367, he "had a great advantage with the king" among other reasons because of the Thebans' recent victories against Sparta.[37]

That embassy resulted in a decree sent by the Persian king with several political ultimatums favorable to the Thebans and their friends and threatening to the Athenians and Spartans. It has been suggested that it also resulted in a supply of gold from Persia to Boeotia.[38] There is no explicit evidence to support that hypothesis, but it has recently been proposed that a rare series of electrum and gold coins issued by the Thebans belongs to the mid-360s, rather than to the 390s, and is to be associated with a program of Boeotian naval expansion undertaken in that period. The implication of the date is to tentatively confirm the old hypothesis that the Persian king's envoys brought the gold to Thebes in the wake of Pelopidas' embassy.[39]

The peculiar electrum and gold coinages issued by Thebes in the fourth century point to a final form of resource pooling among the poleis of a *koinon* that may have promoted economic growth. Greek federal states normally began to produce some form of cooperative coinage from the inception of those institutions, and sometimes even prior to it. Arrangements varied across time and place, but the most common pattern was the production of higher-value silver coins with a type and legend that designated them products of the federal state, alongside the production of smaller-denomination silver and bronze coins by the member poleis that were nonetheless marked, usually by obverse type, as belonging to the regional coinage. The economic advantages are obvious: coins produced on a single weight standard with a type that was recognizable across the region were certainly more readily acceptable in local and regional markets than a proliferation of local types potentially produced on different weight standards and of questionable or significantly variable metal content. We should therefore expect that they had the effect of reducing transaction costs.

---

forces are recorded, they hover around 7,000: Delium, 424 (Thuc. 4.93.3–4); liberation of Theban Cadmea, 379 (Diod. Sic. 15.2–4); Leuctra, 371 (Diod. Sic. 15.52.2). By contrast, at the battle of Plataea, the lone Boeotian polis of Plataea fielded 600 men (Hdt. 9.28.6). Improved military outcome is well illustrated by the success of the Boeotian military under Theban leadership from 379–362: Mackil 2013, 69–75, 78–82. Plunder: Polyb. 5.94.9 (Achaea).

[36] Plut. *Vit. Arat.* 12–13; Polyb. 2.51.2.   [37] Xen. *Hell.* 7.1.34–5.

[38] Buckler 1980, 155–6, 160–1.   [39] Gartland 2013.

Most *koina* in mainland Greece, including the Achaean, Arcadian, Boeotian, Phocian, Locrian, Aetolian, and Thessalian, minted on the Aeginetan weight standard, while those to the northwest – the Epirote, Illyrian, and Acarnanian – minted on the Corcyraean standard (Chapter 16, this volume, on weight standards). These coinages tended to circulate predominantly within the region in which they were minted and quite widely also in other regions using the same standard.[40] They are rarely found in hoards in regions utilizing a different standard, which suggests that they were not widely accepted or desirable as a trade currency. It is thus likely that federal coinage, like instances of nonfederal cooperative minting arrangements, was intended to promote regional exchange and meet federal expenses.[41] The extent to which it actually did so is regrettably not demonstrable given the current state of our evidence.

CONCLUSION

The modern theory of fiscal federalism predicts that federal institutions should enhance economic efficiency and thus produce greater economic growth than would be achieved in the same region without federal institutions. The key feature responsible for this advantage is taken to be decentralized fiscal decision-making. Evidence from the best-attested Greek federal states confirms that fiscal decision-making was largely but not entirely decentralized. *Koina* imposed contribution requirements on their member poleis but left it to them to decide how to raise those and other revenues. In some cases, however, it is clear that federal governments prohibited the imposition of taxes across polis boundaries within the territory of a *koinon,* thus placing an important limit on the freedom of subunits to determine their own fiscal policies. Greek federal states adopted other strategies to enhance their economies that stem from the particular ecology of the ancient Mediterranean and its institutions. Monetary production was coordinated, and in some cases centralized, facilitating the movement of goods regionally and reducing transaction costs. And more broadly, *koina* facilitated the pooling of diverse and complementary resources, which historians expect to have had salutary effects on the regional economy. It is, however, impossible to prove that these federal institutions and practices

---

[40] Psoma and Tsangari 2003.   [41] Mackil and van Alfen 2006; see also Chapter 19, this volume.

were responsible for economic growth in any of these states, despite our expectations that they should have done so.

Further Reading

Mackil 2012 as well as Beck and Funke 2015, 1–29 offer complementary, concise overviews of Greek federal states. Mackil 2013, 237–325 first made the case for the economic aspects of ancient federalism with respect to the central Greek *koina* of Boeotia, Achaea, and Aetolia. Mackil 2015a explores the applicability of that model to other *koina*. Weingast 1995 is fundamental for understanding the theory of fiscal federalism and is a good guide to the political science literature on that topic.

EMPIRICAL APPROACHES

25: CLIMATE, ENVIRONMENT, AND RESOURCES

Sturt W. Manning

INTRODUCTION

The general supposition in scholarly writing about ancient Greece is to assume, since the mid-Holocene shift to the drier conditions now typical of the Mediterranean climate region, that the climate and environment (and natural resources: flora and fauna) of the classical period were broadly similar to those observed in the premodern, premechanized, preurbanized nineteenth and twentieth centuries CE. Thus, we assume a traditional past similar to that recorded as antiquarians, archaeologists, and historians created the modern field of ancient history.[1] A few suggestions that climate change and in particular drought were historically important in the classical period have been made, notably Camp's thesis of a multidecade drought in the later fourth century,[2] but the evidence employed has usually been argued to be inappropriate or contradicted when examined critically.[3] Thus, although Sallares ends a discussion of the topic stating "the question of secular changes in the climate in classical antiquity and their possible causes and effects remains an interesting field for future research,"[4] a *plus ça change , plus c'est la même chose* approach ("the more it changes, the more it stays the same") has largely dominated approaches in the field. As discussed below, some reassessment is now necessary.

At the same time, the pioneering syntheses of Greek climate highlighted the very different and diverse local regimes within Greece, with a general decline of precipitation from west to east

---

[1] E.g. Mariolopoulos 1925; Philippson 1948; for a recent review, see Bintliff 2012, 9–20.
[2] Camp 1982.   [3] Sallares 1991, 392–3.   [4] Ibid., 395.

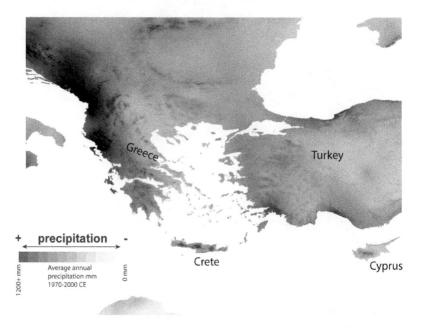

25.1 Average annual precipitation 1970–2000 CE for the Aegean region. Darker grey = wetter, lighter grey = drier. Data from WorldClim Version 2 (http://worldclim.org/).

(allowing for elevation) (Fig. 25.1) and average temperature rising north to south, but again largely determined by elevation.[5] They also lead us to observe that Athens, focus of so much of the attention of ancient historians and source of much of our text record, is located in an unusually dry region and thus is atypical of Greece as a whole (see Fig. 25.2); there is, for example, ample evidence from ancient sources of malaria associated with water and wetlands in both Greece and Italy.[6] Indeed, the very variety and intersections of a multitude of microenvironmental niches within the (not-so-homogenous) Mediterranean is a major theme of the iconoclastic volume of Horden and Purcell (2000), as is a dismissal of any simple association of ecology or climate with historical causation. Purcell thus characterizes Mediterranean history in terms of the very local, centered on the "primary producer's constant struggle to outmaneuver very local regimes of environmental risk," paired with the opportunities and risks

---

[5] As evident in recent climate syntheses, e.g. Gofa et al. 2019; Mamara et al. 2017.
[6] Sallares 1991, 271–81; Sallares 2002.

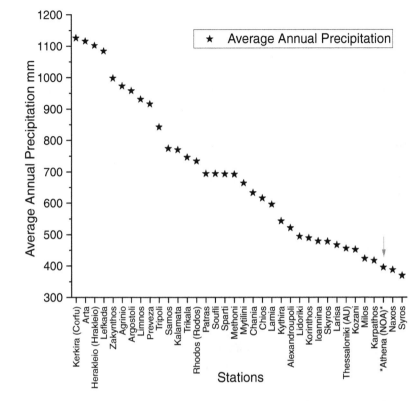

25.2 Average values for annual rainfall (in mm) for the recorded periods (which vary) for the thirty-six Greek meteorological stations discussed in Pnevmatikos and Katsoulis 2006, table 3. Athens – at 395 mm per annum (indicated by the arrow) – is well below the average for twentieth-century Greece as a whole of 620 mm per year (Pnevmatikos and Katsoulis 2006, 334). Actual annual rainfall for Athens in turn varies markedly around this average value: see Figure 25.3. The average value for Thessaloniki is 456 mm, and the average for Kalamata is 770 mm.

through external "relations" with different areas and potentials via "connectivities."[7] The articulation and outcome of such intersections in the human sphere are increasingly evident from both text and archaeological records, especially survey evidence for the wider landscape. Recent studies unsurprisingly identify a settlement peak in Greece in the classical/Hellenistic era.[8] The question is whether and how climate played a role in this florescence.

---

[7] Purcell 2014, 62.   [8] Bintliff 2012; Ober 2015a; Weiberg et al. 2019, fig. 5.

LOCAL AND REGIONAL CLIMATE REGIMES

At the local to regional level, the *plus ça change* model has focused on the general characteristics of the typical Mediterranean climate regime, with its relatively wet winters and long dry summers. Typically, for many lower-elevation areas this means overall a modest annual rainfall total. Since any average value in fact means variations up and down on an interannual basis, and variations downward in the case of a modest rainfall potentially indicate too little available water for viable subsistence crops and so drought, there has been, especially since the impact of the work of Garnsey (1988), a focus on the interannual variations that in turn affect the productivity of staple crops like cereals. Of course, drought is not the only threat; indeed, even if we restrict ourselves to precipitation, far too much rainfall and in too short a period can be equally destructive of crops and stored resources and so potentially of relevance to history as more than a very temporary "blip" (and so historically forcing) – an occurrence noted from Diodorus Siculus (12.58.3–4) regarding Athens and central Greece in 431[9] – and argued as relevant for historical cases elsewhere at other times.[10] Such variations have direct, but also indirect, effects – for example, creating or limiting potential threats from various agricultural pests and pathogens. As part of a focus on "pronounced local irregularity"[11] as characteristic of the Mediterranean, this leads us to reconsider any ability to make casual generalizing assessments across regions.

Figure 25.3 shows the recorded rainfall (precipitation) for Athens, Kalamata, and Thessaloniki in the recent past as an indication of such interannual variability. For Athens, thirty-one years (19 percent) show annual precipitation below the approximate 300 mm level required for a viable wheat harvest,[12] creating a local-source food supply challenge. Seven years (4 percent) see a second such year in a row when we might anticipate severe crisis, as usual "one-bad-year" coping mechanisms (diversification, storage, social strategies)[13] will have already been stretched or exhausted. There were three years with less than 300 mm precipitation in four from 1890–3 and four of five such years from 1898–1902, indicating occasional periods (the respective second years in these groupings, or 2 percent of years in the record) of likely real stress/crisis. But Thessaloniki, still in one of the drier regions of Greece, seventh driest

---

[9] Sallares 1991, 97–8.
[10] E.g. Cook et al. 2015, 3; Büntgen and Di Cosmo 2016; but cf. Pinke et al. 2017.
[11] Horden and Purcell 2000, 13.   [12] Garnsey 1988, 10.
[13] E.g. Forbes 1989, 93–4; Halstead 2014, 162; S. W. Manning 2018, 281.

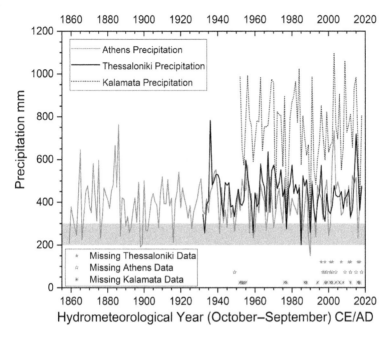

25.3 Recorded precipitation (mm) for Athens, Kalamata, and Thessaloniki, Greece, by hydrometeorological year (treated as October to September following the standard observation that the rainy season in Greece "begins in October and ends in April (Karapiperis & Katsoulis 1969)" (Pnevmatikos and Katsoulis 2006: 336), with the year assigned to the "growing" season year; thus the post-December annual year is plotted). The gray box indicates 300–200 mm of precipitation – the approximate threshold for viable dryland farming of cereals in the absence of irrigation, etc. (e.g. Wilkinson 2004; Garnsey 1988). Stars indicate years where one or more monthly values are missing or problematic (in all 1.2 percent of values for Athens, 5 percent of values for Kalamata, and 1.1 percent of values for Thessaloniki) – such months given zero value in the figure, so real precipitation numbers for these years are likely at least slightly higher than shown. Data from KNMI Climate Explorer (https://climexp.knmi.nl/start.cgi), which employs information from the Global Historical Climatology Network-Monthly (GHCN-M) datasets (see www.ncdc.noaa.gov/ghcnm/), both accessed January 2019.

of thirty-six meteorological stations in Fig. 25.2, with a stated annual average precipitation of 456 mm, saw in contrast just five years with less than 300 mm of precipitation (6 percent) and no instances of two such years in a row in the recorded period. This highlights the extremely marginal status of Athens (and some other areas) in terms of precipitation.

This is important, as it is reasonable to assume that local Attic subsistence production was central to its economy in the peak fifth century, until the point in the Peloponnesian War when the Spartans occupied Decelea (413), and Thucydides comments on the major change.[14] In complete contrast, if the meteorological station at Kalamata (annual average precipitation 770 mm, Fig. 25.3) is considered as a proxy for some of the area controlled by classical Sparta, then, across the sixty-eight years represented, the annual rainfall was never less than 326 mm and under 400 mm only in four years. Adding missing monthly values, the totals were in fact higher for twenty years, including for three of the four under 400 mm years. Thus, the crop-failure risk due to the threat of drought was very substantially less here when compared to Athens, and agricultural productivity likely much greater. At the same time, we may note that there were alternative strategies available. In particular, the olive offered a key economic resource,[15] especially suited to the lower elevation and drier areas of Greece,[16] including Attica. The conventional attempts of the Spartans at agricultural ravaging, including of olive trees, in Attica in the earlier years of the Peloponnesian War very much highlight the cultural and economic importance of this resource.[17]

Such regional and interannual variations are of central importance to economic models and have been much commented on in existing literature. They are central to now long-standing views on the nature of social adaptation in the semiarid and more marginal areas of Greece and other parts of the world.[18] They form a local regime.

MACROCLIMATE REGIMES

The other regime for consideration here is the wider, "macro," greater region of connectivities. The marked change in just the past decade or so for this topic is the information available in terms of larger-scale climate history. In 1962, observation of a mere couple of pieces (*empolia*) of cypress (*Cupressus* sp.) wood from inside columns of the Parthenon formed the basis of a claim to recognize similar growth patterns in that period – the 200 years leading up to the construction of the Parthenon in the second half of the fifth century – as in recent

---

[14] Thuc. 7.27.3–28.1, with Garnsey 1988 and Sallares 1991, 97–8.
[15] Horden and Purcell 2000, 209–13; Foxhall 2007.
[16] Renfrew 1972, fig. 18.12; reproduced in Bintliff 2012, fig. 1.1.
[17] Although agricultural devastation associated with ancient warfare is often exaggerated and truly destroying crops like olives and vines, etc. is more difficult than it seems; see Hanson 1998.
[18] Garnsey 1988; Halstead and O'Shea 1989; Wilkinson 2004.

times.[19] Today, this is clearly an inadequate evidential basis for many reasons. A large set of records from a number of sources, in particular pollen, lake/maritime cores, speleothems, dendrochronology, geomorphology, vegetation histories, corals, sea level variations, and many others, now exist, which variously indicate aspects of climate and environmental history as relevant to Greece and its wider region over various premodern periods.[20] The increasing availability of a range of long time series starts to open up the potential of considering wider climate trends (low-frequency changes) as well as instances of single- to a few-year perturbations (high-frequency changes) and of exploring the relations between factors like disease history and climate trends/forcing beyond the level of general hypothesis.[21] Only a few of the climate records as yet reaching back to the classical era are truly high-resolution (that is, close to annual scale).[22] But, increasingly, we have the potential now to consider both the local and macro at a resolution capable of bringing the two worldviews into potential and even productive dialogue. We start to see the big picture, even if much detail will only come from future work. These data suggest one very important change to the *plus ça change* view. In broad macroterms, current syntheses of Holocene-era palaeoclimate for the Balkan region (including Greece) observe the following:[23]

(i) a driest point around the beginning of the third millennium (4900 BP [Before Present], measuring from 1950 CE),

(ii) continuing dry conditions through the mid-sixth century (2500 BP) (with a driest east Mediterranean period as a whole around the beginning of the first millennium ±300 years),

(iii) then a wetter interval from the mid-sixth century to the mid-first century CE (1900 BP), before

(iv) a return to a general dry trend through to the present.

Observation (iii) is important: a wetter interval during the classical and Hellenistic to early Roman periods. Nonetheless, it must be admitted that as yet we are still faced with a need for more and finer-resolution data sets if we are successfully to articulate the relationships between climate and history. Specifics in terms of timing and connections are

---

[19] Mariolopoulos 1962.
[20] Finné et al. 2011; Finné et al. 2019; Luterbacher et al. 2012; McCormick et al. 2012; Cook et al. 2015; Izdebski et al. 2016b; Weiberg et al. 2019. Increasing detail and analytical potential is already available for the last millennium for the eastern Mediterranean, e.g. Xoplaki et al. 2018.
[21] Sallares 2014 for disease histories.   [22] Finné et al. 2011; Finné et al. 2019.
[23] Finné et al. 2019.

necessary, as illustrated in a critique of the American Southwest case.[24] The conclusions proposed to date from the available fairly coarse time series – such as "it appears that the most extensive use of the landscape in Classical and Hellenistic times had the benefit of wetter conditions"[25] – are rather less than overwhelming or specific.

CAPITAL, CLIMATE, AND ENVIRONMENT

Garnsey's research in 1988 recalibrated considerations of subsistence and its social and political dimensions. In particular, he demonstrated the importance of agricultural resources and land around Athens for provision of the city. All this was timely and important, but, as Horden and Purcell note, an overemphasis just on peasants and subsistence is too narrow and obscures other possible potentials and issues.[26] Apart from olives and the vine – two of the "Mediterranean triad" of olives, the vine, and grain – pastoralism has to be considered in addition as important, widespread, and in-built for ancient Greece, offering a means to buffer against marginal years or circumstances.[27] Similarly, Horden and Purcell highlight that water management was likely more important than often appreciated in the ancient world, although there is a relative dearth of evidence for technological inno-vation in this or related areas, or substantial infrastructure (like water mills) for classical Greece.[28] But analogy with recent ethnographic observation in another Mediterranean semiarid area offers one further direction for thought, where climate and "the marginal" offer a different perspective and potential.

Wilkinson's (2004) study of the region around the archaeological site of Tell Sweyat in the west of the Djezireh of northern Syria, a largely marginal landscape with average rainfall less than Athens, combining eth-noarchaeology with geoarchaeology, indicates – in addition to pastoralism – a potentially important aspect of use of marginal land. Wilkinson observes that the exploitation of particularly marginal land – where the risk is beyond that plausible for the independent risk-averse subsistence farmer – is none-theless possible in situations where large (i.e. wealthy) landowners with capital expand into these areas. These individuals or families can afford "to

---

[24] Kintigh and Ingram 2018.   [25] Weiberg et al. 2019.
[26] Horden and Purcell 2000, 263–8, 592.
[27] Renfrew 1972 on the Mediterranean triad; Forbes 1995 on pastoralism in Greece; on buffering and agricultural practices, see Halstead and O'Shea 1989; Halstead 2014.
[28] Horden and Purcell 2000, 244–7.

absorb some of the risk of crop failure in order to recoup a profit during wet years. This risk is unacceptable to subsistence farmers in a traditional economy who must minimize risk by guaranteeing a certain minimal yield each year."[29] This situation is potentially relevant even when we consider the more-marginal areas of Attica or other marginal loci in Greece. We should not necessarily just assume that it is the unfortunate and poorest subsistence farmers who are left occupying the most marginal of land and who are therefore in effect unable to succeed and exploit its occasional potential because of immediate subsistence needs and a lack of capital. Instead, in situations where there is proximate or accessible (a key point!) marginal land, such as that not too far from a village or city, that could be exploited if labor could be provided and where loss is regularly expected – but in occasional good years the profit made will more than exceed the net overall losses (i.e. investment waiting for such a return) – there is a mechanism for wealth generation, employment, and building loyalty/debt and followers, as well as additional agricultural production for consumption or sale. Athens and Attica may offer such a dynamic situation in the postaristocratic, post-Solon and post-Cleisthenes, context (with old regional/aristocratic land control and protection-racket models ended) and particularly in periods of wider economic growth (e.g. the fifth century). While marginal on average, and some areas therefore submarginal, the land could provide substantial profits for those with capital and the ability to invest long-term, who were able to support free or slave labor on the most marginal land outside usual subsistence risk. The climate variability, if we take the recent period as an approximate guide, would indicate reasonable to good years for wheat (a valued, superior cereal crop) with reasonable frequency. If we arbitrarily consider annual rainfall of about 120+ percent of the average as likely to promote an unusually good harvest in Attica, then such a "good" year occurs almost 21 percent of years, or just over one year in five (Fig. 25.3).[30] Much too infrequent for an "on-the-margin" subsistence farmer, but regularly enough to reward patient investment for return for those capable of undertaking this step.

---

[29] Wilkinson 2004, 41.

[30] Of course, there are further relevant factors, such as the time of year the rain falls, but the overall rainfall correlates well in general with productivity. The assumption behind this discussion is *not* of a static, traditional Attic countryside under the control of regional and aristocratic leaders extracting protection/rent from those (e.g. the *hektemoroi*) in their orbit, but instead of a landscape – after the reforms of Solon and Cleisthenes that ended such a system (see Harris 1997) – where new dynamic economic opportunities existed for investors with capital (and the available evidence suggests there was, then, change and new, wider exploitation of the countryside: Harris 2002a, 426–7).

Climate and Historical Change?

A common historian's response at this point in such a discussion is to express concern, if not dismay, that the aim of the exercise, apparently to explain history by reference to climate, is misconceived. It is of course true that all too often articles on climate records in scientific journals make sweeping claims that climate equals something (major), usually the collapse of civilization. These studies typically are simplistic and in need of much greater investigation and nuance.[31] Climate episodes and decades, if not century-scale periods, are elided too easily with complicated historical trajectories, although increasingly there has been a move towards a "consilient", or better relational, position trying to integrate or relate science and humanities approaches.[32] Detailed papers and books have begun to appear in the last decade attempting to develop interwoven narratives.[33] The challenge works both ways. Scientific data are relevant only as they relate to and can inform historical and thus social, economic, and political analysis. But equally, attempting to ignore relatively obvious consensus assessments from replicated scientific sources through rhetorical strategies, inappropriate statistics, and obfuscation[34] is a largely nonproductive dead-end.

An example of the major shift in recent years is the claimed recognition of a "Late Antique Little Ice Age" (LALIA), running from the mid-sixth to mid-seventh centuries CE, or similarly but slightly differently dated, a "Dark Age Cold Period" (DACP).[35] Unusual conditions and perhaps very large volcanic eruption(s) had been proposed for several decades previously for the mid-sixth century CE.[36] The major solar minimum in the later seventh century CE was also noted,[37] but now they were tied together into a longer colder period that, it is argued, explains a series of historical changes across Eurasia.[38] Even more intriguing is where this leaves the "Younger Fill." This distinct, relatively recent sediment layer, sometimes associated with archaeological material suggesting a post-Roman date, was recognized around the Mediterranean region and originally associated with climatic origins in

---

[31] For such criticism, see e.g. Butzer 2012; Butzer and Endfield 2012; Knapp and Manning 2016; Haldon et al. 2018; Mordechai et al. 2019; Sessa 2019.

[32] McCormick et al. 2012; Izdebski et al. 2016a; Haldon et al. 2018.

[33] E.g. White 2011; Xoplaki et al. 2016; Harper 2017 – but cf. Sessa 2019.

[34] E.g. Kelly and Ó Gráda 2014a; Kelly and Ó Gráda 2014b; cf. Büntgen and Hellman 2014; White 2014.

[35] Büntgen et al. 2016 for the LALIA; for the DACP, dated to the fifth to eighth century CE, Helama, Jones, and Briffa 2017.

[36] Discussions and references in McCormick et al. 2012.   [37] S. W. Manning 2013.

[38] Büntgen et al. 2016; Helama, Jones, and Briffa 2017.

pioneering work by Vita-Finzi (1969) – although much subsequent scholarship argued instead for primarily anthropogenic causes. However, although the initial characterization and chronology of the Younger Fill has become more complicated, as reviewed by Bintliff (2002), it increasingly appears that Vita-Finzi was at least partly correct to identify as important a marked change in precipitation patterns and erosion around this same time (post-Roman era).[39] Thus, although the focus recently has been on temperature and cooling, which is generally agreed upon while the particular unusual extent within the more limited LALIA interval is disputed, this systemic change could in fact prove equally or more relevant to changes in the agricultural support base, taxation systems, and other economic changes across the late antique world. The analysis and synthesis of Büntgen et al. (2016) of the extensive tree-ring data acting as a temperature proxy, as well as other data from sixty-five records comprising ice cores, speleothems, lake sediments, marine sediments, glaciers, and historical documents, in addition to tree rings in a supplementary table, are impressive, although none are from the Mediterranean.[40] Less clear is exactly how the circumstances observed caused or forced history.[41] As usual in this genre, Büntgen et al. largely regard apparent temporal approximations as sufficient arguments. For example, the combination of major volcanic eruptions and the impact of their aerosols[42] and a decade or more of unusually cooler temperatures from the 530s to 540s CE does immediately precede or correlate with the Justinian plague (first attested in 541 CE) and various other problems noted in the historical record. But the strict temporal and causal associations of most of the other historical episodes of change noted by Büntgen et al. are less clear. For example, of the ten change/collapse events listed by Büntgen et al., only four actually correlate with the marked very cold intervals in either the European tree-ring records or those of the Altai mountains/Central Asia, and two fall more or less in between cold intervals. A rather perfunctory penultimate paragraph addresses the issue of historical linkage. It starts by stating that "although any hypothesis of a causal nexus between the volcanic-induced sixth-century unprecedented thermal shock and subsequent plague outbreaks, rising and falling empires, human migrations, and political upheaval *requires caution* [my italics],"

---

[39] For critique of the original climate hypothesis (and of aspects of the chronology and observations involved with the Younger Fill work by Vita-Finzi and Bintliff), see Wagstaff 1981. For the view that, nonetheless, with recent information, part of the original Vita-Finzi climate hypothesis may be relevant, see e.g. Constante et al. 2011.

[40] Büntgen et al. 2016.   [41] Haldon 2016.   [42] Helama et al. 2018.

before, however, noting that "to overcome reductionist approaches, the use of palaeoclimatic evidence in historical arguments has to be combined with multifactor analyses and non-deterministic explanations." This is just what is lacking in the short space of such a journal article.

Without doubt, specific sharp, dramatic climate change that undermines subsistence or substantially changes environmental parameters can affect the local world.[43] If such climate change affects the wider region, then this could make it break apart or impact on connectivities and larger systems, too. There are two obvious complications rarely addressed in studies like the one by Büntgen et al. (2016).[44] First, there is the very variegated nature of the greater Mediterranean and its countless microclimates and contexts, and the tendency for there to be opposite processes occurring in the west versus east Mediterranean – as indeed is evident in the same late Roman/late antique period just discussed, where there are very contrasting trajectories in the northwestern and southeastern Mediterranean especially.[45] Second, and more fundamental: human systems are remarkably resilient and capable of adapting to meet most challenges, given a little time, from years to much longer intervals.[46] What they cannot cope with so successfully is sudden substantial change outside all expectation, preparation, and experience, which lasts long enough to overwhelm all and any coping strategies that a society has in place or could reasonably try, or which brings entirely new threats. Given what we know of most ancient Mediterranean "bad-year" economic strategies, two or more consecutive bad or worse years of failed harvests, for example, is the real danger in terms of subsistence threat. The rule of thumb was storage and other strategies to be able to ride out one bad, or even disastrous, year. Two such calamitous years in a row would likely be too much to cope with and could be historically forcing, and even more so if there are other bad years within another one or two years.[47] Migration, socioeconomic and political collapse, starvation, and disease can be anticipated in such circumstances. In a given marginal location, such as Athens, two bad years in a row, usually caused by a lack of necessary rainfall in such a semiarid zone, are not infrequent (see above, p. 376), although two years in a row that

---

[43] Although, as Halstead 2014 argues, subsistence farmers have a large range of strategies to try to mitigate such problems.

[44] See also Büntgen et al. 2011 trying to explain the decline of the Roman empire.

[45] Horden and Purcell 2000 on the heterogeneity of the Mediterranean region; Roberts et al. 2012 on opposite processes in the western and eastern Mediterranean (also Finné et al. 2019); McCormick et al. 2012; S. W. Manning 2013 on the late antique period.

[46] Halstead and O'Shea 1989; Halstead 2014; Horden and Purcell 2000; Brooke 2014.

[47] S. W. Manning 2018.

defeat even a hardship to "starvation" diet of barley are in fact rare.[48] In wider terms, two really bad years in a row are typically very rare when we consider available long-term climate records from the Aegean region.[49]

Beyond subsistence, disease and especially historically transformative threats like plague are sometimes associated with climate change,[50] though identifying the exact connection is often less than clear.[51] Büntgen et al. and Helama et al. suggest a possible association of the volcanic cooling in the later 530s to early 540s CE with the outbreak of plague under Justinian.[52] This is based on the coincidence of dates that then becomes a statement that "volcanic forcing triggering the climatic cooling *arguably* [my italics] provoked the first impulse to the plague in CE 541 ... *possibly* ... *it is hypothesized* [my italics] ... the cool weather of CE 541 was beneficial to rat survival and flea reproduction."[53] A review of plagues in premodern Europe identifies an association with outbreaks following cold and dry periods.[54] But one might predict that this could vary locally by microenvironment/climate zone. If we consider some of the available indicators from a variety of proxy records for the period around 541 CE, we see a mixed picture across Europe to the Mediterranean. The Old World Drought Atlas (OWDA), offering an estimated June–July–August (JJA) Palmer Drought Series Index (PDSI) reconstruction for summer moisture availability as derived from the analysis of a network of tree-ring data sets,[55] does not include the region of Constantinople for 535–541 CE, but, while northwestern Europe was relatively dry in those six years, except in 537 CE, which saw moderate moisture levels widely across Europe, the available reconstructions for the closest areas to Constantinople of central to southeastern Europe show relatively moist conditions in the years 535, 536, and 541 CE, becoming wetter in 537–540 CE. Figure 25.4 shows the composite 535–541 JJA PDSI reconstruction from the OWDA. Southeastern

[48] Garnsey 1988.   [49] S. W. Manning 2018.   [50] E.g. McMichael 2012; Schmid et al. 2015.

[51] Yue and Lee 2018a. The actual macroscale effects of the Justinian plague receive critique and should be reduced from a maximalist "catastrophe" perspective according to the study of Mordechai et al. 2019.

[52] Büntgen et al. 2016; Helama et al. 2018. See the critical review of the topic by Luterbacher et al. 2020 – approximate temporal correlation alone is not necessarily a causal association.

[53] With reference to the putative scenario outlined by McMichael 2012, 4734–5.

[54] Yue and Lee 2018b.

[55] Cook et al. 2015. The wider continental European picture suggests cooler and wetter conditions in the years immediately leading up to 541 (Luterbacher et al. 2020, fig. 4). However, as Luterbacher et al. (2020, 7) comment looking at plague occurrences over the past 2,500 years: "any simple correlation between plague reemergence and European summer temperatures ... or continental European summer precipitation is unapparent."

Reconstructed JJA PDSI

535 – 541

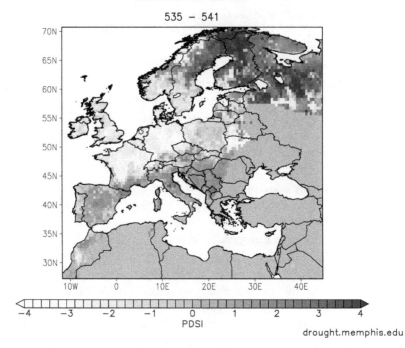

drought.memphis.edu

25.4 Reconstructed June–July–August (JJA) self-calibrating Palmer Drought Severity. Index values composite for the years 535–541 CE from a network of tree-ring time series from the Old World Drought Atlas (OWDA) (Cook et al. 2015). More negative values (lighter gray) are drier, more positive values (darker gray) are wetter. There are no data available in this reconstruction for Greece and Turkey (and the other areas without data tiles). Data from http://drought.memphis.edu/OWDA/Default.aspx.

Europe is relatively moist. Analysis of the stable isotope variations in the Sofular Cave speleothem, which offers a relatively proximate Black Sea-oriented record, also indicates moister conditions in the fifth and sixth centuries CE,[56] as does data from the Levant.[57] The Büntgen et al. (2011) reconstructions indicate cooler conditions from their Alpine tree-ring temperature data set and identify drier conditions from their north-western to central Europe record in the fifth and sixth centuries CE. The Spannagel Cave speleothem from the Austrian Alps also indicates cooling.[58] Hence, the evidence suggests conditions that are cooler and

---

[56] Fleitmann et al. 2009.   [57] See the synthesis by Rambeau and Black 2011.
[58] S. W. Manning 2013, fig. 17, fig. 18b, fig. 21; see also Figure 25.6 below.

if anything wetter in the region of Constantinople, and thus not entirely consistent with the plague initiation association suggested above.[59] This example illustrates the almost-inevitable complexities of any specific circumstance. While the overall case clearly is more suggestive than conclusive (further work is necessary to resolve timing, context, and vectors), it is nonetheless intriguing and could offer an example of a short-term "shock" event with a climate association that connects local and wider worlds and is historically forcing.

If we then consider the classical era and Greece, it is salutary to note the very large volcanic forcings dated to 430 in the Antarctic ice record and 426 in the Greenland ice record and associated with cooling in the available northern-hemisphere tree-ring record for a few years to a conspicuous minimum growth (cold year) at 425.[60] The bristlecone pine and other tree-ring records exhibit evidence associated with cooling, and thus likely often major volcanic eruption impacts, in several years between 425 and 417.[61] If one considers the records of solar irradiance determined from the solar proxies of radiocarbon (^{14}C) and beryllium-10 (^{10}Be),[62] there is a notable reduction in solar irradiance starting a little before or around 430, with a minimum around or a little after 400, and the overall "package" of associations – see Figure 25.5 – is similar to the mid-530s to 540s CE case.[63] There is nothing similar within several hundred years. The potential coincidence with the so-called plague at Athens breaking out in 430 (Thuc. 2.48.3), having originated, according to Thucydides, in North Africa before spreading to the Persian empire and Athens, is tantalizingly close.[64]

---

[59] However, cooler and wetter conditions could also be argued as relevant to a plague-initiation scenario in the Aegean, illustrating the contradictory nature of making sweeping hypotheses. For example, "cooler" and "wetter" in the lowland east Mediterranean (main cereal regions) likely will have led to increased harvests and so net positive conditions for increased rodent populations (and associated fleas) and for their connectivities with urban centers through increases in grain storage. In addition, since they are ectothermic, a reduction in high summer heat/dry conditions removes what is otherwise a limiting factor for flea survival and efficiency as a vector. Specific triggering circumstances in adjacent or connected regions may also be relevant, as raised as a possibility worth investigation regarding the southern Arabian Peninsula and the Horn of Africa for the Justinian plague (Luterbacher et al. 2020, 7).

[60] Sigl et al. 2015, fig. 2, fig. 3. They regard the dating accuracy of the ice-core evidence as less than five years. Based on comparisons with other cases, they conclude the relevant volcanic eruption was in the tropical region.

[61] Salzer and Hughes 2007, tables 2 and 6.

[62] Vieira et al. 2011; Steinhilber, Beer, and Fröhlich 2009; see also Roth and Joos 2013.

[63] Büntgen et al. 2016; Helama et al. 2018.

[64] Cohn 2018, 7–11. Nonetheless, as Luterbacher et al. (2020) highlight, no simple and straightforward pattern of correlation appears evident. Not all episodes of major volcanism link with plague and vice versa. Generally, we as yet lack sufficient high-resolution data to achieve clarity.

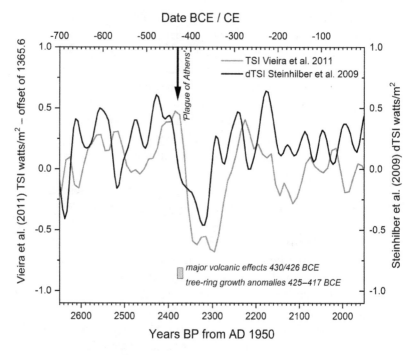

25.5 A comparison of the Total Solar Irradiance (TSI) reconstructions of Vieira et al. 2011, derived from the northern hemisphere ^{14}C record versus Steinhilber et al. 2009, derived from the Greenland [10]Be record. Data for the Vieira et al. 2011 TSI reconstruction available from www.mps.mpg.de/projects/sun-climate/data/t si_hol.txt; data for the Steinhilber et al. 2009 dTSI reconstruction available from ftp://ftp.ncdc.noaa.gov/pub/data/paleo/climate_forcing/solar_variability/stein hilber2009tsi.txt. The "plague of Athens" dates 430–429 BCE with a recurrence 427 BCE (Cohn 2018, 7–11). The major volcanic eruption(s) dated 430 BCE in the Antarctic record and 426 BCE in the Greenland record come from Sigl et al. 2015, figs. 2, 3. Three ring-growth anomaly dates linked with cooling and volcanic impacts come from Sigl et al. 2015, fig. 3, and Salzer and Hughes 2007, tables 2, 6.

Figure 25.6 shows four climate proxies relevant for the Northern Hemisphere (NH), to Europe, and to the Black Sea, which include (at least part of) the classical era. The very general NH Greenland ice-core temperature reconstruction (A in Figure 25.6) suggests general warming from ca. 600 to the Roman era, with a cooler blip in the fourth century.[65] The Austrian Alpine summer temperature record from tree rings (B in Figure 25.6) suggests generally cooling in the fifth to fourth

---

[65] Alley 2000; Cuffey and Clow 1997.

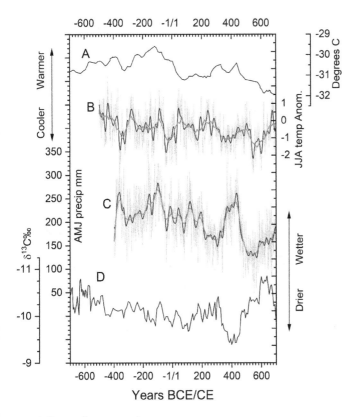

25.6 Some climate proxies 700 BCE to 700 CE.

A. Central Greenland temperature reconstruction (degrees C) from the GISP2 ice core based on stable isotope analysis and ice accumulation data (Alley 2000; Cuffey et al. 1997). Date from: ftp://ftp.ncdc.noaa.gov/pub/data/paleo/icecore/green land/summit/gisp2/isotopes/gisp2_temp_accum_alley2000.txt.

B. Reconstructed summer (June–July–August = JJA) temperature anomalies (degrees C) with respect to the instrumental 1901–2000 CE period record from the Büntgen et al. 2011 study for central Europe from tree-rings (Austrian Alps). Light gray = annual values, black = ten-year FFT smoothing, dark gray = sixty-year adjacent average smoothing.

C. Reconstructed precipitation (April–May–June = AMJ) in mm with respect to the instrumental 1901–2000 CE period record from the Büntgen et al. 2011 study for north-west–central Europe from tree rings. Light gray = annual values, black = ten-year FFT smoothing, dark gray = sixty-year adjacent average smoothing. Data for B and C from: ftp://ftp.ncdc.noaa.gov/pub/data/paleo/treering/reconstructions/ europe/buentgen2011europe.txt.

D. Sofular Cave δ^{13}C speleothem record indicative of moisture (Fleitmann et al. 2009). Data from: ftp://ftp.ncdc.noaa.gov/pub/data/paleo/speleothem/asia/tur key/sofular2009.txt.

centuries, before warming and a long, relatively stable period through the third century CE.[66] The northwestern and central Europe spring-precipitation reconstruction from tree rings (C in Figure 25.6) only begins at the start of the fourth century, when relatively moist before a decline; conditions are then increasingly moist through the second century before becoming drier but stable until the end of the second century CE.[67] It is then drier in the third century CE before becoming wetter and cooler in the fourth century, and then much drier during the fifth into the sixth centuries CE. The carbon-13 record from the Sofular Cave speleothem from northwestern Anatolia, which is a moisture proxy (D in Figure 25.6), shows fairly stable conditions for most of the classical era.[68] There is something of a minor decline in the sixth to fourth centuries, before stable conditions to the fourth century CE, when there is a change to much drier conditions to the start of the fifth century CE. It is then increasingly wetter from the mid-fifth century through to the start of the seventh century CE. With reference to Figure 25.5, we can also note that solar irradiance was relatively stable through most of the classical period. This is the period from after a grand solar minimum in the eighth century through to the grand solar minimum in the seventh century CE, with the exceptions of a solar maximum in the mid-fifth century and the solar minimum episode in the earlier fourth century.[69] No especial climate driver is evident across much of the main classical period from ca. 600 BCE to 200 CE, other than relatively stable and benign conditions that permit largely uninterrupted social and economic developments until a set of various changes in the third to seventh centuries CE. While apparently unremarkable, such circumstances are in fact uncommon over the longer durée. They distinguish the Bronze Age and the classical period when considering the entire span of the Holocene.[70]

Conclusion

We are only just beginning to resolve long-term climate history, and its complications, in serious detail. The subsequent challenge will be how (and whether and when) to associate such records with history as cause

[66] Büntgen et al. 2011. [67] Ibid. [68] Fleitmann et al. 2009.
[69] Usoskin, Solanki, and Kovaltsov 2007.
[70] Finné et al. 2011; Finné et al. 2019; McCormick et al. 2012; S. W. Manning 2013; Weiberg et al. 2019.

(primary or associated) and, progressively through the Holocene as humans started to shape their environment in a substantive and sustained way, effect(s) leading to the now much-discussed Anthropocene. The Greek florescence from the classical to the Hellenistic periods appears associated with a relatively stable/benign and likely wetter interval in general climate history for the region. These conditions will have aided growth. But they do not by themselves explain agency and historical contingencies.

Further Reading

For an up-to-date summary of Mediterranean environment, palaeoclimate, and human demography, see the special edition of *The Holocene* 29 (5), 703–937, May 29, 2019. On climate and long-term history, Brooke 2014. On the Mediterranean landscape and connectivities, Horden and Purcell 2000 and Purcell 2014. On Mediterranean subsistence farming, Halstead 2014.

26: TECHNOLOGICAL PROGRESS

Serafina Cuomo

INTRODUCTION

This chapter will consider Greek perspectives on technological progress: what it was, whether it was happening, and whether it was a good thing. While necessarily selective, I shall strive to remain resolutely emic throughout.[1] I shall therefore not discuss whether there was technological progress in the ancient Greek world as seen from our modern perspective. Nor will I discuss, even though counterfactuals can be fun,[2] why the ancient Greeks did not direct technology towards productivity and economic growth more systematically and vigorously than they seem to have done. Today, technology and 'the economy' tend to come as a pair. Views about a technology, its inception and development, its validity or uselessness, often stem from its perceived potential to save labour or increase profit.[3] It was not always so, not least because the ancient Greek economy, as will become clear to the readers of this volume, was profoundly dissimilar from many economies of today.

The Greek term *techne* was defined as a knowledge activity, or knowledge practice, aimed at producing an effect or an object in the real world. Things we would not necessarily classify as technology (e.g. medicine, rhetoric, or divination) were ascribed to the same category, in the same way as things that we do classify as technology (e.g. carpentry, sculpture, architecture, or metal-working). Many ancient Greeks would have agreed that mathematics, at least in some of its forms, was a *techne*, and Plato debated at length whether philosophy was a *techne*.[4]

---

[1] Emic is a term used in the social sciences for views that are those of a society's members themselves.
[2] See e.g. Morley 2000.   [3] See Schatzberg 2018.
[4] A good synthesis in Nussbaum 1986, 94–9; cf. also Cuomo 2007, ch. 1 with further references; Angiers 2012, ch. 1–2.

Did the ancient Greeks have an idea of progress? Yes, they did, but as we shall see, not in the sense of a collective march towards an incrementally positive future.[5] There are relatively few technological advances that can be seen to constitute 'objective' or 'unlimited' progress – even today in a time when almost everything once hailed as progress for humankind has exhibited a darker side. Too many cars pollute the atmosphere. Too many antibiotics make us more exposed to infections. Intensive agriculture depletes the soil, and so on. The Greeks gave us technological inception myths like those of Prometheus, Hephaestus, and Pandora, so they did know that *technai* can change the world. However, they were also deeply aware of both the positive and negative consequences of that change. Unqualified, triumphant technological progress was not something that the Greeks appear to have ever envisaged, or even hoped for. Thus, Edelstein argued in 1967 that 'progress meant enlightenment more than material progress . . . control of the environment was not of primary concern. Advance was not measured by statistics of export and import or industrial production in general', and according to den Boer (1977), progress was 'a continuous, inevitable, and never-ending progression towards improvement in a community', but not an emic concept to the Greeks.[6]

THE MODERN HISTORIOGRAPHY OF ANCIENT GREEK PROGRESS

In the first half of the twentieth century, Pierre-Maxime Schuhl and Alexandre Koyré explored the question of why Graeco-Roman technology had not progressed further than it did. The perceived genius of some ancient philosophers and scientists seemed at odds with the failure to revolutionize the world around them. This perceived lack of innovation – the state of being 'stuck' (*blocage*) in primitive ways of doing things – was characterized in terms of ideas and attitudes and set in contrast to the mindset that produced the Scientific Revolution.[7] In an influential 1965 article, however, Moses Finley forged an explicit and tenacious link between lack of technological innovation and a stagnant ancient economy. Epoch-making inventions were overall scarce in Graeco-Roman antiquity, and textual evidence such as Suetonius' report that the emperor Vespasian dismissed a labour-saving device on account of the Roman plebs needing work (Suet. *Vesp.* 18), demonstrated in Finley's view that

---

[5] Blundell 1986, ch. 7, is useful on this point.   [6] Edelstein 1967, 49; den Boer 1977, 11.
[7] Schuhl 1938; for Koyré, see Chimisso 2008, esp. ch. 5.

Greek and Roman political institutions stifled technical creativity. Exceptions, such as military technology and the entertaining yet ultimately futile crafting of *automata*, were few.[8] The presence of slavery negated the necessity of developing ideas that saved labour and increased productivity. Finley also pointed to 'the clear, almost total divorce between science and practice'.[9] He thus grafted the lack of technological progress to a well-established and coherent picture of the ancient economy, society, and culture.[10]

At the end of the 1960s, however, the two publications by Ludwig Edelstein, already mentioned, and Eric R. Dodds inaugurated a new historiographical turn in the study of progress in the ancient Greek world.[11] Despite Edelstein's occasional over-enthusiasm,[12] both surveys eschewed monolithic depictions and acknowledged the diversity of ancient views. While Edelstein linked the progressivism of the fourth century to its 'refined and modernized' economy,[13] thus moving away from Finley's more static picture, Dodds charted the rise of a new philosophical nostalgia for the Golden Age against the decline of the traditional polis model and the advent of the Hellenistic kingdoms.[14] Again, in the late 1980s, Sue Blundell explored the question of the origins of humankind in Greek and Latin literature and similarly concluded that there was an idea of progress, albeit not the exponential progress found in modern times, and, secondly, that ideas of progress ebbed and flowed throughout antiquity.[15]

Recent historiography has, on the one hand, attempted to produce models of the ancient economy that eschew excessive generalizations and allow for greater fine-tuning than Finley's picture; on the other hand, scholars have increasingly questioned both the teleological character of the term 'progress' and the excessive emphasis on innovation at the expense of other aspects in the life of a technology, such as the use, maintenance, and distribution of technological knowledge. In 2000, Kevin Greene painted a very different picture from Finley's, drawing on archaeological evidence to show that neither technology nor the economy had been as stagnant as they might have appeared through the lens of just ancient texts. Greene also tempered the

---

[8] Finley 1965, 42–3. [9] Finley 1965, 32. [10] Cf. mainly Finley [1973] 1999.
[11] Edelstein 1967, published posthumously; Dodds 1973, based on a lecture originally given in 1969.
[12] E.g. Edelstein 1967, ch. 1, on Xenophanes. *DK* 21 B 18, ends with the words: 'The period of enlightenment had begun' (ibid., 19); *contra* den Boer 1977, 11–12. See also Edelstein's 'declaration of independence' anticipating modern times, Edelstein 1967, 40.
[13] Edelstein 1967, 81 and Dodds 1973, 2–4, 20. [14] Dodds 1973, 14–15, 17.
[15] Blundell 1986, 103–7.

uniformity of the previous picture by tracing distinctions between different places, periods, institutional contexts, and different branches of technology.[16]

ANCIENT GREEK VIEWS OF TECHNOLOGICAL PROGRESS

While, as Greene has demonstrated, there may be evidence of techno-logical change applied to the economy in the archaeological record, most of the evidence we have about how technology and change were viewed by the ancient Greeks themselves, up to and including the Hellenistic period, comes from literary texts. Inscriptions, as well as the material culture of technology, are fundamental to our understand-ing of how practitioners lived, worked, and viewed themselves, yet, arguably, those sources cannot be made to talk directly to the theme of how progress, that is, technological change over time, was conceptualized.[17]

Anthropologies of Technai

The idea of *technai*, with or without divine intervention, bringing major changes to the human condition is found in classical Greek tragedy. The protagonist of *Prometheus Bound*, attributed to the tragic poet Aeschylus and put on stage before 430, is harshly punished by Zeus for stealing fire and giving it to humankind. In a powerful monologue, the titan defi-antly defends his decision to alleviate human suffering through the gifts of housebuilding and wood-working, weather-reading, numbers, let-ters, husbandry, sailing, medicine, divination, and metal-mining. Relief from hard work is mentioned alongside the invention of the yoke. All *technai* come from him, Prometheus says; they have taken humankind from infancy, a state where life was like a muddled dream, to a mindful condition, where people not only subsist but move forward towards further discoveries, beyond necessity.[18]

Similarly in Sophocles' *Antigone* (ca. 441), in the midst of Kreon's prohibition of the burial of the bodies of his enemies and Antigone's

---

[16] Greene 2000; more recently Greene 2009 and Raepsaet 2008.
[17] I will have to be selective in my choice of sources; the reader is referred to Edelstein 1967 for a fuller survey of the available literary evidence.
[18] [Aesch.] *PV* 436–506, cf. also 249–54. Cf. Edelstein 1967, 43 and n. 46; Dodds 1973, 5–7; Podlecki 2005, 25–6, with further references; Ruffell 2012.

rebellious decision to bury her brother after all, a chorus of old Theban men sing of the wondrous-yet-terrible things achieved by humankind: sailing, agriculture, hunting and fishing, husbandry, house-building, medicine, as well as words, thoughts, and politics.[19] No benign divinity is mentioned; it is humankind's own contriving – the term *mechane* figures repeatedly – that has led to their use of *technai*. Almost by contrast, the Hippocratic treatise *On Ancient Medicine* grounds the progress of humankind from a brutish, animal-like state to the present in a specific technical domain: the preparation of food. The author writes: 'From wheat, by moistening, winnowing, grinding, sifting, kneading, and baking it they made bread, and from barley they made barley cake.'[20] Thus, medicine itself, which originated from cooking, has made significant discoveries over a long period of time and is going to make more discoveries in the future. While the language itself is not gendered, we know that at the time preparing food was predominantly women's work. Might the Hippocratic author be implicating women in technological progress?[21]

Philosophical authors also put forward the proposition that *technai* contributed to the development of humankind from an inferior initial state to its present condition. Both Plato's *Republic* and *Laws* depict technology as inextricably linked to civilization.[22] His *Protagoras* also provides a version of the birth of technology myth, according to which Prometheus stole and gave humankind both fire and *sophia* to compensate for his brother Epimetheus having used up all divine gifts in equipping animals for survival. Protagoras, the narrator, adds that, while wisdom in the other arts is unequally distributed, the gods made sure that everybody possesses the *techne* of politics.[23]

Later on, Diodorus steps out at the beginning of his comprehensive history to describe origins. Early men are animal-like and disordered and seem hardly able to survive. While no divine agent is involved, Diodorus' account, whatever his sources, features abstract elements to the human condition as agents of change: fear (*phobos*)

---

[19] Soph. *Ant.* 332–75, cf. Cairns 2016, 59–66, with further references. Theseus in Eur. *Supp.* 195–218 also mentions a god who rescued us from our previous brutish state through the gift of speech, agriculture, building, seafaring, and divination.

[20] [Hippoc.], *VM* 3.5 (tr. M. Schiefsky); see also Rosen 2016. Cf. the account, attributed to Theophrastus, of the gradual development of agriculture and, almost in parallel, the change from vegetarian to animal sacrifice, in Porph. *Abst.* 2.5–9.1.

[21] A Greek epigram describing the introduction of the watermill (possibly first century CE) also mentions the labour of women: see Bresson 2016b, 197.

[22] Pl. *Resp.* 369c–373d, Pl. *Leg.* 678–9, 889c–890a.

[23] Pl. *Prt.* 320d–323a; cf. Dodds 1973, 9–10; Sihvola 1989, part 2; Yona 2015 with further references.

drove early humans together, precipitating the invention of language; experience (*peira*) taught them to shelter in caves and store food; necessity (*chreia*) instructed them, leading to the discovery of *technai*.[24] While the narratives we have sketched above all differ in genre and emphasis, they share a view of pre-technology humankind as, essentially, nasty, brutish, and short, closer to infancy, or to animals, than to the present state of things. Certainly, some Greek authors hanker for an imagined, technology-less Golden Age of yore. For others, however, technology, for good or bad, is seen as a feature of what it means to be human.[25]

Techne *in Practice: The Case of Catapults*

Military technology provides a straightforward story of technological progress on emic terms.[26] We have a discovery story in (again) Diodorus, according to whom Dionysius, tyrant of Syracuse, fostered such a concentration of human and material resources in 399, in preparation for war with Carthage, that 'the catapult was invented at this time in Syracuse, since the ablest skilled workmen had been gathered from everywhere into one place'.[27]

We also have developmental accounts. Philo of Byzantium (third century) charts the history of the progress in catapult technology, starting from a situation where devices that were built to be identical produced in fact very different results, through trial-and-error experiments, to a situation, in the present, where the technician can, within some margins of error and reasonable expectation, control the relationship between the size of the machine, the size of the projectile, and the range of the catapult. Philo describes this transition from chance to regularity in terms of repeated and cumulative experience, leading eventually to a mathematical formulation. A couple of points deserve mention. First of all, Philo frames progress in chronological terms, from the past to the present, the old to the new. He recognizes that previous practitioners set the path for the future: they first conceived of the catapult[28] and then identified what they needed to look for next.[29]

---

[24] Diod. Sic. 1.8.
[25] Edelstein 1967, 34; Sihvola 1989, 100–1; Asper 2013, 414–18. An interesting version of *technophilia* and love of innovation as constituents of Athenian identity at Thuc. 1.71.2–3.
[26] See e.g. Edelstein 1967, 82; Cuomo 2007, ch. 2.
[27] Diod. Sic. 14.42.1 (tr. C. H. Oldfather); the whole episode at Diod. Sic. 14.41–3; cf. Dodds 1973, 10–11; Dalley and Oleson 2003.
[28] Philo of Byzantium *Belopoeica* 58.30–5, cf. Edelstein 1967, 142; Schiefsky 2015.
[29] Philo of Byzantium *Belopoeica* 50.20–1.

Nonetheless, he explicitly presents himself as improving on old designs.[30] He also lists systematically the criteria for what constitutes better technology in the case of catapults: range, strength, ease of construction, appearance, and cost.[31] Technology is seen as a collective effort towards further improvement, and thus as both a social and an epistemic enterprise. The refinement of knowledge about catapults, which in Philo's account becomes more and more mathematized, is described also as a refinement in methodology. Whereas early practitioners had to experiment with range and building almost from scratch, the accumulation of knowledge over the years allowed later practitioners to take some things for granted and rely on 'formulas' or 'recipes', that is, sets of machine specifications that were already known to work.

The first point to note is that progress is identified with a knowledge community which is able to transmit and accumulate knowledge across time and space. Secondly, and in line with Diodorus' invention story, Philo openly attributes a key role in achieving progress to institutional support and patronage. He mentions Rhodes but singles out Alexandria as a hotbed of technological achievement, because the Ptolemaic kings, he says, were lovers both of good reputation, or fame, and of the *technai*.[32] Institutional support, at least in the case of catapults, is seen as crucial to the success of the knowledge community, and thus of progress. And yet, with the exception of the consideration of cost, which comes last on Philo's list of criteria for a good catapult, what we would call the economy does not enter the picture at all, even when technology was part of the economy.[33]

Hero of Alexandria's *Belopoeica*[34] is another, later, treatise which also traces the development from simple, relatively small catapults, to larger, more powerful, and more complex ones. Like Philo, Hero frames progress in terms of the joint efforts over time of both earlier and more recent technicians and presents a trajectory from empirical knowledge towards greater regularity and reliability, again sanctioned by the application of mathematical procedures.[35] Hero also advocates for the crucial role that technology, in the shape of better and better

---

[30] Ibid., 67.28–32.   [31] Ibid., 59–62.

[32] Ibid., 50.24–9; cf. also Xen. *Hier.* 9.9–10. Alexandria was a 'super-hub' in terms of network theory: Archibald 2011, 59.

[33] Catapults certainly fit Chaniotis 2011 concerning the economic impact of war on Hellenistic poleis.

[34] Or, according to Rihll 2007, *Ctesibius*.   [35] Heron *bel.* 112–13.

catapults, can play in the security of the community and the happiness of the people living in it.[36]

It would appear, then, that catapult construction is a real-life case of technological progress in antiquity: it looks like it *actually* followed an upward trajectory. It ticks the boxes of institutional support, visibility, meeting a strong societal demand, and of science and technology working together to produce better results. The interest in innovation in military technology did not abate – *pace* Frontinus (35–103 CE): reliefs on the Column of Trajan may depict new types of catapult to those we find in Philo's or Hero's *Belopoeica*,[37] and new war engines were devised, on paper, well into late antiquity.[38] At the same time, we must note that, first, the available archaeological evidence, supplemented by reconstruction archaeology and textual evidence from other sources, collectively paints a picture where local variants of the technology, and old and new catapults, appear to have coexisted, and where technological choices were not inevitably in favour of the more recent, or the better technology.[39] Secondly, we are in a position to trace a trajectory only because practitioners and users from within the field of catapult construction participated in a literary culture which made it significant for them to write about their technology, and because they conceptualized epistemic, social, and technological changes in terms of progress, according to explicit criteria, and precipitated by human ingenuity and collaboration. Progress in catapult construction is visible to us, and is visible on emic terms, because there was a knowledge community, or a succession of knowledge communities, with the necessary resources and motivation to reflect on the status of their knowledge.

We do not need to emphasize that this was not the case for many other forms of knowledge, or knowledge communities, in antiquity. Most ancient Greek and Roman technologies fit Zosia Archibald's model, which links innovation to mobility. She points out that "expertise, which in the ancient world effectively required person to person contacts, diffuses along social networks'.[40] Personal knowledge is almost by definition tacit knowledge,[41] and again almost by definition is not susceptible of being written down or being fully expressed into words. Much of the expertise in Philo's or Hero's treatises on building catapults

---

[36] Heron *bel.* 71–4. Take a small step forward in time, and a different perspective is found in Sextus Julius Frontinus' *Stratagems*. The Roman general comments on how, at the time of writing (between the first and second century CE), military technology seems to have reached its peak, with no expectation of further improvement (Frontin. *Str.* 3.1.)

[37] See J. Coulston's website *Trajan's Column* at https://arts.st-andrews.ac.uk/trajans-column/.

[38] Cf. the anonymous *De rebus bellicis*.   [39] See Rihll 2007; Campbell 2011.

[40] Archibald 2011, 59.   [41] See e.g. Cuomo 2016; Roby 2016.

was tacit, but enough of it was made explicit and written down for the meta-phenomenon of technological progress to be constituted and eventually made visible to us.

THE MORALITY OF TECHNOLOGICAL PROGRESS

Technology is morally ambiguous: is Prometheus' punishment just? Is Zeus a tyrant, or a regulator of the excesses of human control of the natural world? The praise of *technai* in *Antigone* is profoundly ambivalent, concluding with a warning, in its turn echoed by a reflection on human fragility and god-sanctioned destruction.[42] In our texts, the moral ambiguity of technology can be cast as a religious problem, or a problem of 'going against nature'. But the gods also stand in for political authority, particularly of an aristocratic kind, and nature also signifies traditional or ideal societal structures, as 'the way things are'. Therefore, the moral ambiguity is also about what technology can do to power and politics, and how it can affect social hierarchies. The economy, in the sense of money, wealth, growth, productivity, is, in the ancient sources' representation, almost epiphenomenal to this.

Thus, the moral question regarding technological progress is not independent of its political and social contexts, and those contexts vary. There is a sense in which, by virtue of being teachable and not in-born, *technai*, both socially and epistemologically, are a democratic, 'open-access' form of knowledge and practice. Edelstein, for instance, indirectly read this feature into Xenophanes' pronouncements on progress, while pointing out the strong current within Platonic thought which subordinates any *techne* to an ulterior goal, the good, about which philosophy is the ultimate arbiter.[43] By the same token, then, Plato's epistemic subordination of *techne* to other forms of knowledge plays out in social and political terms, and its limitations can be read as indictments of the contribution that technology and its practitioners can really make to the polis. Plato's Protagoras does not think that the *technai* in their raw state, as it were, are sufficient for a good life: they have to exist in the social and political context of justice and shame, and they have to be taught and learnt.[44] In Blundell's words on *Prometheus Bound*, 'technology brings with it inevitable suffering, and ensures that our existence, though better than that endured by animals, can never encompass the freedom from pain and anxiety which is characteristic of the divine'.[45]

---

[42] Soph. *Ant.* 582–625; cf. Nussbaum 1986, 72–5; Cairns 2016, 59–66.
[43] Edelstein 1967, 15–16, 112.   [44] See Sihvola 1989, part 2, ch. 7.   [45] Blundell 1986, 173.

Discourses about the excitement and danger of technological progress are also about questioning and confirming human hierarchies.

Martha Nussbaum summarizes the dilemma in different but equally useful terms, as a contrast between *techne*, which offers some degree of control, and *tyche* – 'chance' or uncertainty.[46] This certainly fits very well the examples we have considered, including our case study of catapult construction, in that better technology is explicitly presented as something that minimizes the element of chance in loading and shooting a catapult. In other words, technology improves our lives by reducing the risk that we might starve, or be killed, because of inclement weather, an unlucky encounter with a more powerful opponent, or indeed our natural weaknesses in comparison to other animals. Technology reduces fear and alleviates necessity. On the other hand, technology does not seem to reduce labour to any significant degree. The self-moving maidens of Hephaestus are the high-tech versions of slaves. Even then, Hephaestus sweats and labours; he does not seem to have aimed his technological genius at the reduction of his own labour.[47] There are few ancient Greek scenarios where human labour is alleviated or in fact eliminated: the notably *techne*-less golden age, or the epigram about the invention of the water-wheel mentioned before (n. 21). In those scenarios, the saving of labour is represented less as achieved by technology than by a cooperative and motherly nature.

Thus, the gifts of Prometheus are not about improving productivity – rather, they make it easier to guarantee that labour will reap some fruit, that our efforts will not fall victim to chance and be in vain, that our life will be ameliorated, even if it comes at the cost of work and struggle. That cost is the inevitable corollary of the morally ambiguous and hybrid nature of technology.

CONCLUSION

There was indeed a notion of technological development in the Greek world. Various *technai*, whether discovered by humans or gifted by a god, were seen as having effected a change which had lifted humankind from a helpless, child-like or brutish, animal-like state to its current position. It is important to note that, while such developments are

---

[46] Nussbaum 1986, 94–5.
[47] Hom. *Il.* 18.416–21; cf. Arist. *Pol.* 1253b 33–5, where Aristotle regards it as particularly detrimental to the social fabric of a household (and thus the polis) if slaves are replaced by *automata*.

seemingly cataclysmic and often presented as disruptive, the idea that technology proceeds slowly and cautiously is a common motif in many of our sources. Philo cites the sculptor Polycleitus to the effect that 'the good is produced little by little through many numbers'.[48] The advent of *technai* can also be seen, alternatively, as marking the end of a golden age, where tasks presently performed by technology had taken place without it, for example, land producing crops without agriculture.[49] Either way, *technai* were seen as an essential component of the current human condition and a factor in its development over time, whether towards a better, or a worse, outcome. Thus, there was what we could call an anthropology of technological progress.[50]

More specifically, there are examples of technologies – here, catapult construction – whose path towards greater dissemination, firmer knowledge basis, and improved performance was seen as a progressive history by the ancients themselves. Both political rulers and practitioners, past and present, are depicted as playing an important role in such histories. Thus, there was what we could call a historiography of technological progress.

The ethical ramifications of technological development could be seen as potentially dangerous, as ultimately precipitating disorder and subversion of traditionally accepted authority. This threat can also be seen as a catalyst for the social anxiety of our (mostly elite) sources towards the practitioners of *technai*, who in Greek society, largely speaking, were not members of the elite and could in fact be slaves. On the other hand, technical treatises are careful to indicate not only that technology is good but also that their authors, who often identify as practitioners, possess the moral qualities necessary to manage and control the power and consequences of their expert knowledge.[51] Thus, there was an ethics of technological progress. In fact, there was, in my view, a diverse and controversial ethics of technological progress. The ethics of technological progress was, in a wide sense of the word, political.

---

[48] Philo of Byzantium *Belopoeica* 50.5–6; Cf. Arist. *Poet.* 1449a 13–15: tragedy changing *kata mikron* until it achieved its own nature; Arist. *Soph. el.* 183b 29–31: the progress of the *techne* of rhetoric; Diod. Sic. 1.8: changes in the lifestyle of early humans take place *kat'oligon* (3), *kata mikron* (8).

[49] On these themes in Hesiod, see e.g. Sihvola 1989.

[50] Sihvola 1989, 98 about Plato's Protagoras myth: it is 'first and foremost an analytical means of presenting the essential elements of a general theory of human nature and the necessary characteristic of human society, and not a historical account of the gradual development of this society'.

[51] On this, see e.g. Vernant 2006a, 269–70 and 2006b.

Finally, the economic impact or significance of technological progress is not at the fore in our extant Greek sources, even in the case of *technai* and technical practitioners with a manifest economic role, such as agriculture or metallurgy. This could be due to the fact that what was meant in Greek and Roman antiquity by 'economy', 'technological', and 'progress' is significantly different from our views of those concepts today. When Plato's Protagoras, before narrating his version of Prometheus' myth, introduces himself as a teacher of 'good management of the household', which is as close as it gets in ancient Greek to 'the economy', such a skill is paired with proper political participation, not with wealth acquisition.[52] Thus, there was, in my view, no 'economy' of technological progress on its own, because, to state the obvious, economies, ancient and modern, are always embedded (Chapter 22, this volume).[53] Managing technological progress meant, first and foremost, being able to harness and regulate its social and moral power.

Further Reading

Most aspects treated in this chapter are discussed at greater length in the contributions to the *Oxford Handbook of Technology* edited by Oleson 2009; Humphrey, Oleson, and Sherwood 1998 is a valuable collection of sources in translation; Rihll 2013 offers a short introduction to technology and its social contexts in the Greek and Roman worlds. Mayor 2018 on ancient robotics is a fascinating discussion of a theme not yet much discussed among ancient historians.

---

[52] Pl. *Prt.* 318e.   [53] See Foxhall 2007.

27: INEQUALITY

Josiah Ober and Walter Scheidel

INTRODUCTION

How unequally were wealth and income distributed among the residents of a classical Greek city-state? The extent of material inequality and its relationship to economic development are central questions for historians of all periods. In recent decades, historians of ancient Greece have sought to provide the basis for answering those questions by attempting to estimate the distribution of wealth and income in Athens (and to a lesser degree in other Greek poleis) by reference to statements in ancient texts, proxy data, and simple models. While there remains much room for debate on specifics, we suggest that, for certain periods of Athenian history, very rough, but nonetheless suggestive, estimates can be offered of the distribution of wealth across the citizen population and the distribution of income across the entire population.

This chapter proceeds as follows: Following a very brief sketch of ancient Greek economic performance ("Economic Development"), the second section ("Inequality") discusses material inequality in Greece, with special reference to Athens, and in comparison with other reasonably well-studied premodern economies. Next, "A Theory of Economic Growth with Low Inequality" sets out a hypothesis for explaining how Greek political institutions and competition among individuals and states drove comparatively high levels of growth, while inequality remained comparatively low. The final section tests this hypothesis against some more and less familiar facts about Greek history.

ECONOMIC DEVELOPMENT

Compared to most other ancient societies, we have a relatively rich body of evidence for ancient Greek economic development from the archaic through the classical eras, and for wealth and income distribution in the age of Plato and Aristotle (fourth century). The emerging picture is one of high (by premodern standards) levels of extensive and intensive economic growth.[1] Indeed, a substantial and growing body of data points to the ancient Greek world as a likely outlier in premodern economic history. The years from ca. 800 to 300 appear to have been a sustained period of economic efflorescence (the term is that of Goldstone 2002), that is, a delimited era of sharply increased levels of material affluence and high culture.

The population of the Greek world expanded dramatically from its post-Bronze Age nadir. So did median per capita consumption, perhaps roughly doubling over the period 800 to 300. By the late fourth century, average per capita consumption for the Greek world was probably in the range of three times bare subsistence – and substantially higher in Athens (and perhaps other advanced poleis). The per capita growth rate from 800 to 300 was perhaps 0.15 percent per annum, with an aggregate annual growth rate for "core Greece" (in its nineteenth-century borders) of somewhere around 0.6 to 0.9 percent. While meager by modern standards, this is high when compared to some other premodern economies and compares favorably with the most dynamic European economies of the early modern period, England and Holland.

Urbanization, commonly employed by economic historians of premodernity as a proxy for economic growth, likewise rose to very high levels: based on plausible assumptions about population density in intramural settlements, Hansen has suggested that about half of the population of late fourth-century Greece lived in intramural "urban" centers, and perhaps a third in towns of 5,000 persons or more, the standard for "urban" that is employed by many demographers studying premodernity.[2]

Unlike in later historical periods, urban growth did not noticeably coincide with a deterioration in health and welfare. While the data on change over time in the health of Greek populations are difficult to interpret, it appears from studies of human bones found in excavations that the average life span of Greek men and women reaching adulthood increased substantially from the end of the Dark Age to the fourth century: the ages at death of individuals surviving childhood seems to have increased by about ten years for both men and women over this period: from about twenty-six to thirty-six for women, and from under

---

[1] Ober (2010b and 2015a) discusses the evidence for and literature on Greek economic growth. Key growth proxies were developed by Morris 2004. For real incomes, see Scheidel 2010.
[2] Hansen 2006b, 26–9.

thirty to about forty for men.[3] The most recent isotopic analysis by Anna Lagia (2015a) of skeletal remains from three cemeteries with classical, as well as Hellenistic and Roman, burials confirms that classical-level adult Athenian nutrition (measured by protein levels) was good and better than in the subsequent eras.

In sum, by the late classical period, Hellas was precociously densely populated and urbanized. The number of Greeks who lived in urban areas was remarkably high by premodern standards. They lived in much bigger houses (Morris 2004) and in substantially healthier conditions than could have been dreamed of either by their own distant ancestors, by Greeks in subsequent eras before the twentieth century, or by most people through human history.

INEQUALITY

Political and economic development is frequently associated with growing inequality. This raises the question of how to reconcile the Greek record of strong economic performance with relatively moderate disparities in income and wealth. The evidence for relatively high levels of *political* equality among native males in many (although not all) Greek city-states is well-enough known, and we will not rehearse it here. Political equality among native males was especially strongly associated with democracy and is by far best documented for classical Athens. As one of us has argued in detail (Ober 2008), Athens was in some ways exceptional as a polis (very big, very high-performing, with robust institutions that proved robust to exogenous shock) – but in other ways, Athens is exemplary of the "citizen-centered" and prosperous Greek city-states. This is important, insofar as our evidence for wealth and income distribution is heavily concentrated in Athens; based on admittedly limited evidence, rough estimates of inequality can be offered for the distribution of land among citizen households, total wealth among citizen households, and income among all residents of Attica.

Independent studies by Osborne (1992) and Foxhall (1997, 2002) concluded that, based on the numbers offered in the historical tradition of the Solonian reforms, about 7.5 to 9 percent of citizens owned about 30 to 35 percent of the land of Attica; some 20 percent owned little or no land. Excluding those at the top and bottom of the

---

[3] Greek life expectancy: Morris 2004, 714–20; Kron 2005; von Reden 2007a, 388–90. Improved life expectancy for those surviving childhood: Morris 2004, 715, fig. 2.

distribution, we are left with roughly 60 to 65 percent of the land being owned by about 70 to 75 percent of the citizen population. Using these figures we may calculate a Gini coefficient of inequality. The Gini coefficient is an index (from 0 to 1) of inequality in a given population. The lower the Gini coefficient, the more equitably the good in question is distributed across the population (0.1 is very equal; 0.9 very unequal). The Gini coefficient may also be displayed visually by a Lorenz curve; the further the curve falls below a line describing a 45-degree angle (perfect equality), the greater the level of inequality (see Figure 27.1). The calculated Gini coefficient for Solonian Athens land distribution comes to 0.48. Julián Gallego (2016) has calculated landholding inequality in late classical Athens (using eight rather than three wealth classes) at 0.441. Although the baseline Athenian figures do not tell us anything about some relevant factors affecting the value of land, such as the distribution of especially productive land or financial encumbrances on landholdings, Morris concludes that, when compared to other premodern societies, with substantially higher Gini coefficients, "the basic point is clear: landholding among citizens was unusually egalitarian in classical Athens."[4]

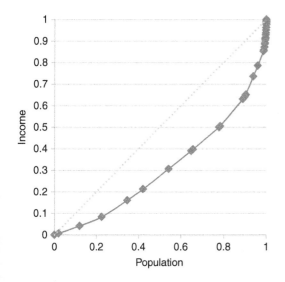

27.1 Athenian income distribution (based on the model in Ober 2017). Lorenz curve; Gini = 0.38.

---

[4] Morris 1998, 235–6. Quote, ibid., 236. As Claire Taylor has pointed out to us, Morris misreported the Gini coefficient as 0.382–0.386, whereas it is actually ca. 0.48 (taking the figure of 9 percent owning 35 percent of the land); but Morris's general point remains valid.

Kron has attempted to calculate total wealth distribution among citizen families in late fourth-century Athens. Kron calculates that the richest 1 percent of the citizen population owned about 30 percent of all private wealth, while the top 10 percent owned about 60 percent of the wealth. This yields a Gini coefficient of 0.708. Kron compares this figure to the Gini wealth coefficients for several modern societies. The late-classical Athenian level of total-wealth inequality is roughly comparable to that of the USA in 1953–4 (0.71), after the great compression of the 1930s and 40s. It is less equal than Canada in 1998 (0.69), but more equal than Florence in 1427 (0.788) or the USA in 1998 (0.794). It is much more equal than the USA or England in the early twentieth century (0.93 and 0.95 respectively).[5]

Economists typically assess material inequality by measuring income. Although it is not possible to calculate an income Gini for all Hellas, on the basis of a model of wealth distribution for later fourth-century Athens (Ober 2017), we estimate the income Gini for the whole of Athenian society (including slaves and resident foreigners) in the later fourth century to be 0.38.[6] This is lower than the Gini estimate of 0.42 to 0.44 suggested by Walter Scheidel and Steven Friesen (2009) for the high Roman empire. The Athenian curve is illustrated in Figure 27.1. The difference arises from the substantially larger Athenian population of persons who fall in the middle range, between the richest and poorest. The estimated Athenian income Gini is also substantially lower than relatively high-performing early modern European economies.[7] Furthermore, the income distribution model is based on documentary evidence for Athens in the fourth century that suggests that pay rates for unskilled labor, measured in liters of wheat per day, were very substantially (3.7 to 4.6 times) above the level of bare subsistence. These Athenian pay rates are comparable to pay rates in early modern Holland and much higher than other known ancient and medieval societies.[8]

The estimated income-distribution model for Athens allows us to calculate estimated consumption as a multiple of subsistence for the

---

[5] Kron forthcoming. The overall Gini wealth index for Athenian society as a whole, including slaves and metics, would surely be substantially higher – we cannot say how much higher because there is no way to calculate wealth of metics or slaves. Wealth inequality, as measured by the Gini coefficient, is typically much higher than income inequality, considered below, p. 409.

[6] Ober 2017. It attempts to nuance the model offered in Ober 2015a, table 4.8. The "optimistic" model developed there yielded an income Gini of 0.40.

[7] Scheidel and Friesen 2009, 84–5. By way of early modern comparisons, Milanovic, Lindert, and Williamson 2011, table 2 report the income Gini for Tuscany in 1427 = 0.46; Holland in 1561 = 0.56; England and Wales in 1688 = 0.45; France in 1788 = 0.56.

[8] Ober 2015a, esp. ch. 4.

entire population of Athens. Athenian mean per capita income is estimated at 0.032 talents per year, which, when translated (as above) into a multiple of bare subsistence, means that a median family consumed at about 4.5 times subsistence (4.5S). This in turn allows us to measure inequality in Athens in a way that is in some respects more useful than the simple Gini coefficient.

The economist Branko Milanovic and his collaborators have developed an "Inequality Extraction Ratio" (IER), which measures the percentage of actual extraction of surplus (above the subsistence minimum) income within a given society by that society's elite as a percentage of maximum feasible inequality. Extraction beyond that level would leave some without the necessary means of survival. As Milanovic, Lindert, and Williamson (2011) demonstrate, relatively high levels of inequality and close approaches to the possibility frontier are common in premodern societies (as in the Gini inequality coefficient, a lower score means less inequality). The median of the Milanovic, Lindert, and Williamson study group is an IER of about 75 percent (see Table 27.1). Based on the Athens income/population model, Athens' IER is about 49 percent, a comparatively long way from the possibility frontier. Because Athens combined relatively high rates of consumption above subsistence with relatively low income inequality measured by the Gini coefficient, it is a low outlier among premodern societies in terms of the IER – lower than England and Wales in 1688, and very much lower than most other societies measured in Milanovic, Lindert, and Williamson's collection of case studies.

Table 27.1 *Income inequality extraction ratio (% of maximum feasible inequality)*

Preindustrial average	77
Athens late 4th c. BCE	49
Roman Empire 14 CE	75
Holland 1561	76
France 1788	76
England and Wales 1688	57

Note: Source for all but Athens: Milanovic, Lindert, and Williamson 2011.

This result is consistent with the evidence for relatively low wealth and landholding inequality, cited above (p. 407), and with Lagia's (2015a) isotopic analysis of the classical-era remains of (presumably) elite and nonelite individuals in three ancient cemeteries in Attica. Lagia found not only that nutrition in the classical era was very good overall but also that the level of nutrition (measured by protein intake) did not vary significantly among elite Athenians, ordinary urban residents, and a very small sample of presumed slaves buried in the mining district in south Attica. By contrast, as Lagia points out, analysis of Bronze Age and medieval human burials show stark differences in elite and nonelite nutrition.

As noted above (p. 406), Athens was in some ways exceptional in the world of the city-states, but there is some reason to believe that Athens was not a strong outlier in the Greek world in respect to its relatively egalitarian distribution of wealth and income. House sizes can be employed as an indirect proxy of both consumption and inequality. Morris (2004) has demonstrated that, based on the archaeological evidence, archaic/classical Greek settlements were not characterized by a few mansions and many huts. Rather, across the entire half-millennium from 800 to 300, the distribution of Greek houses tends to cluster around the median house size. The size of larger houses (the top quartile in floor plan) failed to diverge markedly from that of smaller houses (the bottom quartile). The size of larger and smaller houses grew more or less in lockstep across the period: by 300, houses in the 75th percentile of the distribution were only about one-fifth again (roughly 50 m^2) as large as those at the 25th percentile.[9]

A comparative survey of house sizes at Olynthus and other well-preserved Greek urban areas by Geoffrey Kron confirms this general picture: unlike (e.g.) nineteenth-century England, the distribution of house sizes at mid-fourth-century Olynthus follows a bell curve: most houses fall in the middle, rather than on the far left (tiny house) side, of the distribution. Overall inequality among house sizes at Olynthus was low. In later periods of antiquity, from the Hellenistic through Roman eras, house sizes diverged (i.e. the Gini coefficient of inequality increased); by the late Roman period, the difference in size between great villas and ordinary houses is immense.[10]

In terms of inequality, as in terms of growth, Hellas appears to be something of an outlier in premodern history. By contrast, in two other

---

[9] Morris 2004, 722–3.
[10] Kron 2014 and forthcoming. For Olynthus houses, Kron 2014, 129, table 2 estimates the Gini coefficient of inequality at 0.14, considerably lower than later Hellenistic and Roman-era Greek cities. Cf. Bintliff 2012, ch. 13.

well-documented cases of substantial ancient economic growth that have been recently and carefully studied – Babylon in the sixth century and the Roman empire in the first century through second century CE – growth appears to correlate with high and increasing wealth and income inequality.[11]

A THEORY OF ECONOMIC GROWTH WITH LOW INEQUALITY

The following hypothesis purports to explain how and why a particular set of political institutions typical of the classical Greek world (especially, but not uniquely, manifest in democratic Athens) provided Greeks with good reasons to make choices that resulted in the Greek city-states growing relatively wealthy while inequality remained relatively low: fair rules and fierce competition within a market-like ecology of states incentivized social and human capital investment and rewarded innovation, while lowering transaction costs.

The macro-level phenomenon of Hellas' wealth arose from micro-level behavior: more or less rational (expected utility-maximizing) choices made by many social, interdependent, justice-seeking individuals.[12] Efflorescence was not a result of central planning, nor did any Greek have the conceptual means to measure or to explain the phenomenon. That phenomenon was shaped by social-evolutionary processes that tended to select functionally efficient rules in a competitive environment. Rules were made self-consciously by legislators, individual and collective, in many individual poleis. But the process by which rules were selected and distributed across the ecology was outside the control of any individual agent. The "wealthy Hellas" effect arose from uncounted individual and collective choices but was not readily predicted by them. The political economy of the Greek polis ecology was, that is to say, an emergent phenomenon.[13]

Greek rule egalitarianism (i.e. relatively open and equal access to institutions)[14] meant in practice that many adult males (and in some

---

[11] Rome: Scheidel and Friesen 2009. Babylon: Jursa 2010, with Scheidel 2017, 48.

[12] List and Spiekermann 2013 demonstrate that a methodological focus on individuals as choice-making agents (in the form of "supervenience individualism") is compatible with some forms of causal-explanatory "holism" in respect to considering institutions as collective actors.

[13] Emergence and the relationship between micro-level and high-level phenomena: Petitot 2010.

[14] The neologistic phrase "rule egalitarianism" (conceptually similar to what North, Wallis, and Weingast 2009 call "impersonality") is modeled on the term "rule consequentialism," commonly used by ethicists. The rule consequentialist focuses on social rules (as opposed to

poleis, by the late fourth century, some noncitizens), rather than just a few elites, had equal high standing in respect to major institutions: to property, law, and personal security (Chapter 17, this volume). They had more or less equal access to information relevant to the effective use of those institutions and to the information produced by institutions (laws, public policy). They were treated as equals by the public officials responsible for enforcing institutional rules. In sum, they expected to be treated fairly, and their expectations were, on the whole, met. In an ideal rule-egalitarian society, all persons subject to the rules would be treated as equals. In the Greek world, those enjoying equal high standing were, in the first instance, the adult male citizens – although, in some poleis, including Athens, equal standing in respect to certain social and legal institutions was eventually extended beyond the citizen body.

Rule egalitarianism drove economic growth, first by creating incentives for investment in the development of social and human capital, and next by lowering transaction costs. A rule-egalitarian regime produces rules that respect individual equality of standing, as opposed to establishing a strictly equal distribution of goods. Yet rule egalitarianism has substantial distributional effects: equality in respect to rules pushes back against extremes of inequality in the distribution of wealth and income. Rule egalitarianism may best be thought of as a limited form of opportunity egalitarianism. It is limited because equality of access and treatment is in respect to institutions and public information, not to all valuable goods. The key points are, first, that it is possible for a society to be committed to equality for citizens in respect to rules governing standing without being committed to complete equality of outcomes or all social opportunities, and, next, that more-equal rules tend to moderate extremes of wealth and income inequality through progressive taxation and limiting opportunities for rent-seeking by the powerful.

Rule egalitarianism is a major factor in lowering transaction costs (and thus in increasing the value of social cooperation) because inequality, in respect to access to information relevant to a transaction, or in respect to access to and fair treatment within the institutions potentially affecting a transaction, drives up transaction costs. Relevant sorts of information include, for example, the laws governing market exchanges; weights, measures, and quality standards; and the reliability

individual acts) that will maximize aggregate welfare (or alternatively, aggregate preference satisfaction).

of the currency in circulation. Institutions relevant to transaction costs include property rights, contracts, and dispute-resolution procedures.[15]

Social norms and rules that treat individuals as equals can have substantial effects on economic growth by building human capital – that is, by increasing both median individual skill levels, and by increasing the aggregate societal stock of knowledge. Relative equality in respect to access to institutions (e.g. law and property rights) and the expectation of fair treatment by officials within institutions encourages investments by individuals in learning new skills and increases net social returns to the employment of diverse skills. It does so because norms and rules that protect personal security, property rights, and individuals' dignity lessen fear of the powerful.

Rationally chosen individual investment in human capital development can, in the aggregate, have powerfully positive economic effects through increasing societal levels of specialization and productivity. Individuals who choose to invest in acquiring skills, who have freedom to seek out different domains, and who have specific natural capacities (e.g. high intelligence, manual dexterity) have reason to seek out those domains in which their capacities can be more effectively exercised. Societal productivity increases because greater specialization of economic function produces more diverse goods more efficiently, and because workers in each specialized domain, having invested in gaining expertise, are individually more productive. If information about the quality of goods is widely shared, then better goods will be produced and exchanged at a lower cost, enabling more people to consume a diverse range of goods at a higher level.

Competition among individuals, to create more high-value goods and services, and to provide more valued public goods (and to be compensated accordingly with pay and honors), is promoted by the (relatively) even playing field created by (relatively) fair rules equalizing access to institutions and information. Meanwhile, competition between states within a decentralized ecology of states creates incentives for cooperation among many individuals with shared identities and interests (as citizens or, e.g. "Athenians"). Competition also promotes innovation in institutions facilitating interpersonal and interstate cooperation (alliances, trade agreements, federations). Innovation and cooperation, in the context of low transaction costs, encourage interstate learning and borrowing of institutional best practices. As these practices are shared across an extensive ecology of states, each with high

---

[15] See, recently, Kehoe, Ratzan, and Yiftach-Firanko 2015.

incentives for identification of comparative advantage, specialization, and exchange, there is a greater aggregate return to social cooperation. Competition drives growth, when the competitors believe that the background rules governing their interactions are reasonably fair.

State institutions that insure citizens against potentially cata-strophic losses enable individuals and families to invest more capital in enterprises with the potential for raising individual and aggregate wel-fare. Such policies raise the specter of moral hazard – that is, privatizing the gains of risk-seeking by distributing profits to the risk-taker, while socializing losses by requiring others to pay for gambles that fail. But if a risk-limiting insurance institution is properly designed (i.e. part of the loss is borne by the risk-taker), it serves an equalizing function that may have the effect of increasing aggregate welfare and lowering inequality. Aggregate welfare is promoted because the state, unlike a single family, can spread risk of famine, accident, or death in war across a large pool. If the design challenge is met, the playing field is leveled, because the stakes of embarking on a path of attempted self-improvement are lowered from potential disaster to survivable loss. And so the relatively poor man can reasonably afford to take a risk that would otherwise have been open only to a much-wealthier man.

If high-benefit enterprises are available and the chances of success are better than even, and if the cost of risk insurance is underwritten in part by progressive taxation, the right policies will, over time, lead to more people advancing from relative poverty to middling status and thus to lower inequality. The net effect is positive for overall economic growth.[16]

GREEK HISTORY

The Greeks were not strangers to the idea of incentives and pursuit of rational self-interest, and they certainly understood the correlation between ambition, achievement, and equality of standing. When Herodotus sought to explain the break-out of Athenian military cap-acity after the democratic revolution of 508, he argued that "while [the Athenians] were oppressed, they were, as men working for a master,

---

[16] Gallant 1991 assumes high levels of risk aversion on the part of ancient Greek subsistence farmers and suggests possible family risk-buffering strategies, based in part on evidence from subsistence farming in early modern Greece. But, if the arguments presented here are correct, the classical Greek economy was not predicated on the risk aversion of families of subsistence farmers. Public insurance and risk: Burke 2005; Möller 2007, 375–83; Ober 2008, 254–8. Mackil 2004 shows how a somewhat similar risk-insurance mechanism operated in some interpolis relations.

cowardly, but when they were freed, each one was eager to achieve for himself."[17] If we are to judge by their literature, ancient Greeks had a solid "folk" understanding of how individuals make choices in light of strategic calculations of interests centered on expected utility and anticipation of others' behavior. Although the Greeks lacked a general theory of prices and markets, the aggregate of rules protecting individuals from exploitation, and of many subsequent individual choices to invest in human and social capital, led to the emergence of a comparatively vibrant, at least partially market-based, economy, and the basic mechanisms were understood by Greek theorists.[18]

No Greek community was ever rule egalitarian "all the way down" – women, foreigners, and slaves were never treated as true equals. But among native males, the level of equality was remarkable when compared to other premodern (indeed pre-twentieth-century CE) societies. A turn to relatively stronger forms of egalitarianism in Greece began in the eighth century, and the general trend continued (although not without interruption) through the classical era.[19] In many classical Greek poleis, rule egalitarianism among native men was codified as citizen government. In focusing on the citizen, Spartan-style citizen aristocracy and Athenian-style participatory democracy may be regarded as different versions of the same general regime type. Some Greek communities were, in George Orwell's memorable phrase, more equal than others. But even Greek oligarchies were strikingly egalitarian by the standards of other premodern societies. The constitutional development of individual polis communities was certainly not uniformly in the direction of greater equality of access and fair treatment for natives. Yet, with the increasing prevalence of democracy, the median Greek polis was *more* rule egalitarian in the later fourth century, at the height of the classical efflorescence, than it had been 500, 300, or even 100 years previously.[20]

Along with providing citizens, and at least certain noncitizens, with institutionalized security against arbitrary expropriation, some Greek states encouraged investment by citizens in learning skills relevant to the provision of valuable public goods, notably security and public services, which benefited all citizens. Greek "public insurance"

---

[17] Hdt. 5.78 with Ober 2015a, ch. 7.
[18] Ober 2009. Cf. North, Wallis, and Weingast 2009, who emphasize the behavioral implications of individuals being treated impersonally in institutional contexts. See further Ober 2012.
[19] Morris 1987; and Ober 2015a, ch. 6.
[20] Morris 1996; Raaflaub 1996; Cartledge 1996. See also Runciman 1990; Foxhall 2002, 218 regards "substantial inequalities in landholding" as a "paradox".

institutions (best documented for Athens, but not unique to it) included grain price stabilization and subsidization (reducing the risk of famine), welfare provisions for invalids (reducing the risk of loss of work capacity [Chapter 15, this volume]), and state-supported upbringing of war orphans (reducing the risk of military service by heads of families). Taxes that supported risk insurance and provided other public goods (security and infrastructure improvement) were divided between indirect taxes on exchange and direct taxes on wealth. Wealth taxes at Athens (where, as usual, our documentation is best) fell on the elite. Redistributive wealth taxes were high enough to reduce inequality, but low enough to avoid dangerous levels of elite defection in the form of widespread tax avoidance or revolutionary agitation. Overall, Athenian state spending seems to have been in the range of 10 to 15 percent of Gross Domestic Income. This is not high by the standards of modern states, but it is very high by premodern standards of comparison.[21]

Examples of economically valuable individual human-capital investments in the Greek (and a fortiori Athenian) world that could plausibly have been promoted by rule equality include literacy, numeracy, and mastery of banking and credit instruments. Other, perhaps less-obvious investments in human capital included military training, mastering various aspects of polis governance (e.g. rhetoric and public speaking, public finance, civil and criminal law), and individual efforts to build bridges across localized and inward-looking social networks.[22]

Fair-rule regimes ought to be more economically productive than rule-inegalitarian regimes. Moreover, the transaction cost benefit ought to increase if access is made more equal over time. In fact, Greek weights and measures were standardized in several widely adopted systems in the archaic and classical periods (Chapters 16 and 20, this volume). In the case of democratic Athens, access to information and institutions did become somewhat more open and equal, as the laws were increasingly standardized (e.g. in the legal reforms of 410 to 400), better publicized (e.g. by being displayed epigraphically), and more efficiently archived. The Athenian state provided traders with free access to market officials and specialists in detecting fraudulent coins. Parties to certain commercial transactions were put on a more equal footing with the introduction

---

[21] Ober 2015a, 243–52; 2015b. Fawcett 2016 for Athenian taxation. Other premodern fiscal regimes: Monson and Scheidel 2015.

[22] Numeracy: Netz 2002; banking and credit instruments: Cohen 1992; rhetoric etc. and social networks: Ober 2008, ch. 4.

of the special "maritime cases," in which resident foreigners, visitors, and probably even slaves had full legal standing.[23]

Continuous innovation is a primary driver of sustainable economic growth. Today, we often think of economically productive innovations as technological; improved energy capture (use of fossil fuels) was, for example, a major driver of the historically remarkable rates of economic growth enjoyed by some relatively highly developed countries in the nineteenth and twentieth centuries. Although the classical Greek world unquestionably benefited from a range of technological advances, technological development does not seem likely, on the face of it, to account adequately for the intensity and duration of the classical efflorescence.[24]

Technology is, however, only one domain in which continuous growth-positive innovation is possible. The Greek world was arguably a standout in its development of new public institutions that served to increase the level and value of social cooperation without resort to top-down command and control. Valuable institutional innovations were spurred by high levels of local and interstate competition and spread by the circulation of information and learning. Democracy and federalism are just two, well-known and well-documented, examples of institutional innovation that spread across the Greek world in the classical era and that are plausibly associated with higher levels of productive social cooperation and thus with economic growth (Chapter 24, this volume).[25]

Competition among Greek communities could be a high-stakes affair, potentially ending in the loss of independence, loss of important material and psychic assets, or even annihilation. The high level of competition between rivals placed a premium on finding effective means, institutional and cultural, to build and to sustain intracommunity cooperation. One of the basic lessons that the fifth-century Greek historian and political theorist Thucydides offers his readers (positively in Pericles' Funeral Oration in book 2, negatively in the Corcyra civil-war narrative in book 3) is that communities capable of coordinating the actions of an extensive membership had a better chance to do well in high-stakes intercommunity competitions.[26]

---

[23] These developments are detailed in Ober 2015a, chs. 6–9.

[24] Energy capture and growth: Morris 2010. Technology in the Greek world: Greene 2000; Schneider 2007; Oleson 2009. Agriculture: Sallares 1991; industrial production: Acton 2014; mining and hydraulics: van Liefferinge et al. 2013.

[25] Federalism: Mackil 2013; Beck and Funke 2015; spread of democracy: Teegarden 2014.

[26] High stakes of interstate conflict: Ober 2008, 80–4. Thucydides on Corcyra's civil war: Ober 2000; Thucydides on rational cooperation and competitive advantage: Ober 2010a. Scheidel

Social institutions can provide both incentives for cooperation and mechanisms for facilitating coordination, and classical Greeks were well aware of this potential.[27] One result of endemic Greek intercommunity competition was, therefore, a proclivity to value cooperation- and coordination-promoting institutional innovations: a state that succeeded in developing a more-effective way to capture the benefits of cooperation across its population gained a corresponding competitive advantage vis à vis its local rivals. Notably, as has recently been demonstrated in detail, in the classical era many Greeks (and a fortiori the Athenians) had freed themselves from "the grip of the past," in that they were quite willing to embrace the positive value of novelty in many domains.[28]

Greek communities readily learned from one another. Every new institutional innovation was tested in the competitive environment of the city-state ecology. There were, of course, many reasons for polis B *not* to imitate polis A's performance-positive institution. Most obviously, the new institution might be disruptive to polis B's existing social equilibrium, a disruption that would, among other undesired outcomes, result in a net loss of cooperative capacity. Classical Sparta was a case in point. The Spartan social system was overall resistant to disruptive innovation, which proved a disadvantage in the early phases of the Peloponnesian War, and over the long run drove up domestic inequality.[29] Yet in other cases, the perceived chance to improve polis B's performance, and thus do better relative to its rivals, would be a sufficient incentive to adopt polis A's innovation. Even the Spartans eventually recognized the need to adapt. Some innovations, such as the federal leagues of central Greece (Chapter 24, this volume), were widely adopted across certain regions. Other highly successful innovations were adopted across the polis ecology. Widely (although never universally) adopted institutional innovations included coinage, euergetism, the "epigraphic habit" of inscribing public documents on stone, diplomatic arrangements, theater, and cult.

Of course not all Greeks, and not all Greek communities, were equally innovative or equally willing to emulate successful innovations developed elsewhere. But the Greek world overall saw what appears to be a strikingly high level of institutional innovation and emulation across

2017, 188–99 stresses the importance of competitive military mobilization as a constraint on inequality within Greek polities.

[27] Institutions and coordination: Weingast 1997; Greek awareness: Ober 2009; 2012.

[28] Greek embrace of novelty: D'Angour 2011, arguing against, especially, van Groningen 1953.

[29] Ober 2010b and 2015a, ch. 8. Spartan inequality: Hodkinson 2000, 399–445.

the ecology of states over the 500 years from the beginning of an age of expansion in about 800 to the classical peak in the late fourth century. Major domains of institutional innovation include citizenship, warfare, law, and federalism. In the domain of state governance, both democracy and oligarchy were especially hot areas of institutional innovation and interstate learning. And, ominously for the continued independence of the leading Greek poleis, interstate learning readily jumped from city-states to potentially predatory central-authority states, through the medium of highly mobile Greek experts. Several such states were developing quickly on the frontiers of the Greek world in the fourth century, an era in which expert mobility seems to have reached new peaks.[30]

CONCLUSION

Overall, the extended city-state environment thus operated as something approaching an open market for institutions. Opportunities for imitation were facilitated – transaction costs lowered – by the ease of communication across polis borders, which was in turn facilitated by the shared culture of the Greek world. Because this "market in institutions" favored the development and dissemination of more effective modes of social cooperation, Hellas grew wealthier.[31] The "fair rules and fierce competition hypothesis," when tested against Greek history, helps to explain how and why Hellas grew wealthy, while sustaining relatively low levels of inequality. Many (but certainly not all) Greeks and Greek communities benefited from higher levels of economic specialization and higher-value exchanges of goods and services in the context of relatively low inequality. The chance to gain greater payoffs – fame and honor as well as wealth – drove incremental improvements in existing domains and led innovators to pioneer new domains, while innovations spread readily across the ecology. The same hypothesis helps explain the efflorescence of high culture in the archaic and classical periods, which included new forms of art and architecture, literature, visual and per-formance art, and scientific advances – as well as the emergence and spectacular flourishing of moral and political philosophy concerned (inter alia) with the relationship between equality and democracy.

---

[30] Interstate learning among democracies: Teegarden 2014. Among oligarchies: Simonton 2017. Institutional borrowing by non-Greek authoritarian states, especially in the fourth century, and role of mobile experts: Ober 2015a, ch. 10; Pyzyk 2015.

[31] Innovative adaptations of the institution of coined money are a good case in point; for some particularly interesting innovations in this domain, see Mackil and van Alfen 2006.

Further Reading

Many of the themes raised in this chapter are discussed more fully in Ober 2018 and 2015a, especially chapters 4 and 5. For aspects of inequality in Athens, see also Ober 2017. Scheidel 2017 provides the most comprehensive survey of the history of economic inequality. For economic growth in the Greek world, see in particular Acton 2014; Bresson 2016b; Harris, Lewis, and Woolmer 2016. Taylor 2017 discusses poverty and well-being.

REFERENCES

Abraham, K. (2004) *Business and Politics under the Persian Empire: The Financial Dealings of Marduk-nāṣir-apli of the House of Egibi (521–487 B.C.E.)*. Bethesda, MD.

Abramovitz, M. (1989) *Thinking about Growth and Other Essays on Economic Growth and Welfare*. Cambridge.

Acton, P. H. (2014) *Poiesis: Manufacturing in Classical Athens*. Oxford.

Adams, J. N., Janse, M., and Swain, S. (eds.) (2002) *Bilingualism in Ancient Society. Language Contact and the Written Text*. Oxford.

Adams, R. M. (1981) *Heartland of Cities: Survey of Ancient Settlement and Land Use in the Central Floodplain of the Euphrates*. Chicago.

Adiego, I. J., Tiverios, M., Manakidou, E., and Tsiafakis, D. (2012) "Two Carian inscriptions from Karabournaki/Thessaloniki, Greece," in *Stephanèphoros. De l'économie antique à l'Asie Mineure: Hommages à Raymond Descat*, ed. K. Konuk. Bordeaux, 195–202.

Agut-Labordère, D. (2012) "Le statut égyptien de Naucratis," in *Communautés locales et pouvoir central dans l'Orient hellénistique et romain*, ed. C. Feyel. Nancy, 353–73.

Akamatis, I. M. (2012) "L'agora de Pella," in Chankowski and Karvonis 2012, 49–59.

Akrigg, B. (2007) "The nature and implications of Athens' changed social structure and economy," in *Debating the Athenian Cultural Revolution: Art, Literature, Philosophy, and Politics 430–380 BC*, ed. R. Osborne. Cambridge, 27–43.

Akrigg, B. (2015) "Metics in Athens," in Taylor and Vlassopoulos 2015, 155–76.

Akrigg, B. (2019) *Population and Economy in Classical Athens*. Cambridge.

Alcock, S. (1993) *Graecia Capta: The Landscapes of Roman Greece*. Cambridge.

Alcock, S. (1994) "Breaking up the Greek world: survey and society," in *Classical Greece: Ancient Histories and Modern Ideologies*, ed. I. Morris. Cambridge, 171–237.

Alcock, S. (2007) "The eastern Mediterranean," in Scheidel, Morris, and Saller 2007, 671–98.

Alcock, S. and Cherry, J. F. (eds.) (2004) *Side-by-Side Survey: Comparative Regional Studies in the Mediterranean World*. Oxford.

Alexandridou, A. (2017) "'Sacred' or profane? Interpreting Late Geometric edifices in proximity to burials in Attica," in *Constructing Social Identities in Early Iron Age and Archaic Greece*, ed. A. Tsingarida and I. S. Lemos. Brussels, 43–72.

Allamani-Souri, V. (2012) "Archaic pottery groups from the Souroti cemetery in the prefecture of Thessaloniki and selected vases from the Toumba settlement in Thessaloniki," in Tiverios, Misaïlidou-Despotidou, Manakidou, and Arvanitaki 2012, 283–96.

Alley, R. B. (2000) "The Younger Dryas cold interval as viewed from central Greenland," *Quaternary Science Reviews* 19, 213–26.

Alram-Stern, E. and Deger-Jalkotzy, S. (eds.) (2006) *Aigeira I, die mykenische Akropolis, Part 3: Vormykenische Keramik, Kleinfunde, archäozoologische und archäobotanische Hinterlassenschaften, naturwissenschaftliche Datierung.* Vienna.

Alram, M. (2012) "The coinage of the Persian empire," in Metcalf 2012, 61–87.

Ameling, W. (1990) "Κοινὸν τῶν Σιδωνίων," *Zeitschrift für Papyrologie und Epigraphik* 8, 188–99.

Amouretti, M.-C. (1986) *Le pain et l'huile dans la Grèce antique: de l'araire au moulin.* Paris.

Amouretti, M.-C. (2000) "L'artisanat indispensable au fonctionnement de l'agriculture," in *L'artisanat en Grèce ancienne: Les productions, les diffusions,* ed. F. Blondé and A. Muller. Villeneuve-d'Ascq, 147–64.

Andreau, J., Briant, P., and Descat, R. (eds.) (1997) *Économie antique: Prix et formation des prix dans les économies antiques.* Saint-Bertrand-de-Comminges.

Andreau, J., Briant, P., and Descat, R. (eds.) (2000) *Économie antique: La guerre dans les économies antiques.* Saint-Bertrand-de-Comminges.

Aneziri, S. (2003) *Die Vereine der dionysischen Techniten im Kontext der hellenistischen Gesellschaft. Untersuchungen zur Geschichte, Organisation und Wirkung der hellenistischen Technitenvereine.* Stuttgart.

Angiers, T. (2012) *Techne in Aristotle's Ethics. Crafting the Moral Life.* London.

Anokhin, V. A. (1986) "Monety-strelki," in *Ol'vija i ee okruga: sbornik naučnych trudov,* ed. A. S. Rusjaeva. Kiev, 68–89.

Aperghis, G. G. (2004) *The Seleukid Royal Economy: The Finances and Financial Administration of the Seleukid Empire.* Cambridge.

Appadurai, A. (ed.) (1986) *The Social Life of Things: Commodities in Cultural Perspective.* Cambridge.

Archibald, Z. H. (2000) "Space, hierarchy, and community in archaic and classical Macedonia, Thessaly, and Thrace," in *Alternatives to Athens: Varieties of Political Organization and Community in Ancient Greece,* ed. R. Brock and S. Hodkinson. Oxford, 212–32.

Archibald, Z. H. (2000–1) "The Odrysian river port near Vetren, Bulgaria, and the Pistiros inscription," *Talanta* 32/33, 253–75.

Archibald, Z. H. (2006) "The central and north Balkan peninsula," in Kinzl 2006, 115–36.

Archibald, Z. H. (2011) "Mobility and innovation in Hellenistic economies: the causes and consequences of human traffic," in Archibald, Davies, and Gabrielsen 2011, 42–65.

Archibald, Z. H. (2013a) *Ancient Economies of the Northern Aegean, Fifth to First Centuries* BC. Oxford.

Archibald, Z. H. (2013b) "Joining up the dots: making economic sense of pottery distributions in the Aegean and beyond," in Tsingarida and Viviers 2013, 135–57.

Archibald, Z. H. (2015) "Social life of Thrace," in Valeva, Nankov, and Graninger 2015, 385–98.

Archibald, Z. H. (2016) "Moving upcountry: ancient travel from coastal ports to inland harbours," in Höghammer, Alroth, and Lindgren 2016, 37–64.

Archibald, Z. H. (2019) "Tegeas from Torone and some truths about ancient markets," in *The Power of Individual and Community in Ancient Athens and Beyond: Essays in Honour of John K. Davies,* ed. Z. H. Archibald and J. Haywood. Swansea, 177–211.

Archibald, Z. H., Davies, J. K., and Gabrielsen, V. (eds.) (2005) *Making, Moving and Managing: The New World of Ancient Economies, 323–31* BC. Oxford.

Archibald, Z. H, Davies, J. K., and Gabrielsen, V. (eds.) (2011) *The Economies of Hellenistic Societies, Third to First Centuries* BC. Oxford.

Archibald, Z. H., Davies, J. K., Gabrielsen, V., and Oliver, G. (eds.) (2001) *Hellenistic Economies*. London.

Armoni, C. A. (2012) *Studien zur Verwaltung des Ptolemäischen Ägypten: Das Amt des Basilikos Grammateus*. Paderborn.

Arnaoutoglou, I. (2003) *Thusias heneka kai synousias. Private Religious Associations in Hellenstic Athens*. Athens.

Ashton, R. (2012) "The Hellenistic world: the cities of mainland Greece," in Metcalf 2012, 191–210.

Asper, M. (2013) "Making up progress – in ancient Greek science writing," in *Writing Science: Medical and Mathematical Authorship in Ancient Greece*, ed. M. Asper. Berlin, 411–30.

Austin, M. M. (1986) "Hellenistic kings, war and the economy," *Classical Quarterly* 36, 450–66.

Austin, M. M. (2006) *The Hellenistic World from Alexander to the Roman Conquest: A Selection of Ancient Sources in Translation*. Cambridge.

Avram, A. (2014) "La mer Noire et la Méditerrannée: quelques aspects concernant la mobilité des personnes," in *Interconnectivity in the Mediterranean and Pontic World during the Hellenistic and Roman Periods*, ed. V. Cojocaru, A. Coşkun, and M. Dana. Cluj-Napoca, 99–132.

Avram, A., Hind, J., and Tsetskhladze, G. (2004) "The Black Sea area," in Hansen and Nielsen 2004, 924–73.

Badoud, N. (2018) "Bolli Rodii a Siracusa, Taranto e nell'area adriatica: sul commercio del vino et del grano in età ellenistica," in *Realtà medioadriatiche a confronto: contatti e scambi tra le due sponde*, ed. G. de Benedittis. Campobasso, 121–34.

Bagnall, R. S. (1976) *The Administration of the Ptolemaic Possessions Outside Egypt*. Leiden.

Bagnall, R. S. and Derow, P. (2004) *The Hellenistic Period: Historical Sources in Translation*. Oxford.

Balandier, C. (2004) "L'importance de la production du miel dans l'économie gréco-romaine," *Pallas* 64, 183–96.

Balmuth, M. S. (1967) "The monetary forerunners of coinage in Phoenicia and Palestine," in *The Patterns of Monetary Development in Phoenicia and Palestine in Antiquity*, ed. A. Kindler. Tel Aviv, 25–32.

Balmuth, M. S. (ed.) (2001) *Hacksilber to Coinage: New Insights into the Monetary History of the Near East and Greece*. New York.

Baralis, A. (2015) "Le statut de la main-d'oeuvre à Héraclée du Pont et en Mer Noire," in *La main-d'oeuvre agricole en Méditerranée archaïque*, ed. J. Zurbach. Bordeaux, 197–234.

Baslez, M.-F. (2013) "Les associations à Délos: depuis les débuts de l'indépendance (fin du IVe siècle) à la période de la colonie athénienne (milieu du IIe siècle)," in *Groupes et associations dans les cités grecques (IIIe siècle av. J.-C.–IIe siècle apr. J.-C.)*, ed. P. Fröhlich and P. Hamon. Geneva, 227–49.

Baslez, M.-F. and Briquel-Chatonet, F. (1991) "Un exemple d'integration phénicienne au monde grec: les Sidoniens au Pirée à la fin du IVe siècle," in *Atti del II congresso internazionale di studi fenici e punici, Roma 9–7 Novembre 1987*, ed. E. Acquaro. Rome, 229–40.

Bauschatz, J. (2013) *Law and Enforcement in Ptolemaic Egypt*. Cambridge.

Bearzot, C. (2004) *Federalismo e autonomia nelle Elleniche di Senofonte*. Milan.

Beaulieu, P.-A. (2000) "A finger in every pie: the institutional connections of a family of entrepreneurs in neo-Babylonian Larsa," in Bongenaar 2000, 43–72.

Beazley, J. D. (1956) *Attic Black-Figure Vase-Painters*. Oxford.

Beck, H. and Funke, P. (eds.) (2015) *Federalism in Greek Antiquity*. Cambridge.

Beloch, K. J. (1886) *Die Bevölkerung der griechisch-römischen Welt*. Leipzig.

Benda-Weber, I. (2013) "Textile production centres, products and merchants in the Roman province of Asia," in *Making Textiles in Pre-Roman and Roman Times: People, Places, Identities*, ed. M. Gleba and J. Pásztókai-Szeőke. Oxford, 171–91.

Benkler, Y. (2006) *The Wealth of Networks: How Social Production Transforms Markets and Freedom*. New Haven, CT.

Bennet, J. (2007) "The Aegean Bronze Age," in Scheidel, Morris, and Saller 2007, 175–210.

Berktold, M. M. (2005) "Die Astronomischen Tagebücher – eine Quelle zur Frage von Kontinuität oder Wandel in Kult und Wirtschaft des achaimenidischen Babylon," in *Von Sumer bis Homer: Festschrift für Manfred Schretter zum 60. Geburtstag am 25. Februar 2004*, ed. R. Robert. Münster, 105–52.

Berlin, A. M. (1997) "Archaeological sources for the history of Hellenistic Palestine. Between large forces: Palestine in the Hellenistic period," *Biblical Archaeology* 60, 3–51.

Berry, D. M. (2008) "The poverty of networks," *Theory, Culture, and Society* 25, 364–72.

Bers, V. and Lanni, A. (2003) "An introduction to the Athenian legal system," in *Athenian Law in its Democratic Context*, ed. A. Lanni. www.stoa.org/demos/intro_legal_system.pdf.

Besios, M. and Noulas, K. (2012) "Archaic pottery from the acropolis of ancient Methone" in Tiverios, Misaïlidou-Despotidou, Manakidou, and Arvanitaki 2012, 399–407.

Besios, M., Tzifopoulos, G. Z., and Kotsonas, A. (eds.) (2012) Μεθώνη Πιερίας: Επιγραφές, Χαραγματα και εμπορικά σύμβολα στη γεωμετρική και αρχαϊκή κεραμική από το Ὑπόγειο της Μεθώνης Πιερίας στη Μακεδονία. Thessaloniki.

Bingen, J. (1978) *Le Papyrus Revenue Laws – Tradition grecque et adaptation hellénistique*. Opladen.

Bingen, J. (2007) *Hellenistic Egypt: Monarchy, Society, Economy, Culture*. Berkeley, CA.

Bintliff, J. (1997) "Regional survey, demography, and the rise of complex societies in the ancient Aegean: Core-periphery, Neo-Malthusian, and other interpretive models," *Journal of Field Archaeology* 24.1, 1–38.

Bintliff, J. (2002) "Time, process and catastrophism in the study of Mediterranean alluvial history: a review," *World Archaeology* 33, 417–35.

Bintliff, J. (2012) *The Complete Archaeology of Greece: From Hunter-Gatherers to the 20th Century* AD. Chichester.

Bintliff, J., Farinetti, E., Slapšak, B., and Snodgrass, A. (2017) *Boeotia Project, Vol. II: The City of Thespiai. Survey at a Complex Urban Site*. Cambridge.

Bisel, S. C. and Bisel, J. F. (2002) "Health and nutrition at Herculaneum: an examination of human skeletal remains," in *The Natural History of Pompeii*, ed. W. F. Jashemski and F. G. Meyer. Cambridge, 451–75.

Blundell, S. (1986) *The Origins of Civilization in Greek and Roman Thought*. London.

Boehm, R. (2018) *City and Empire in the Age of the Successors: Urbanization and Social Response in the Making of the Hellenistic Kingdoms*. Berkeley, CA.

Boffo, L. (2001) "Lo statuto di terre, insediamenti e persone nell'Anatolia ellenistica: documenti recenti e problemi antichi," *Dike* 4, 233–55.

Bogaert, R. (1966) *Les origines antiques de la banque de dépôt: une mise au point accompagnée d'une esquisse des opérations de banque en Mésopotamie*. Leiden.

Bogaert, R. (1968) *Banques et banquiers dans les cités grecques*. Leiden.

Bogaert, R. (1994) *Trapezitica Aegyptiaca: recueil de recherches sur la banque en Egypte gréco-romaine*. Florence.

Bogaert, R. (1998) "Liste géographique des banques et des banquiers de l'Égypte ptolémaïque," *Zeitschrift für Papyrologie und Epigraphik* 120, 165–202.

Boix, C. (2003) *Democracy and Redistribution*. Cambridge.

Boiy, T. (2004) *Late Achaemenid and Hellenistic Babylon*. Leuven.

Boiy, T. (2007) *Between High and Low: A Chronology of the Early Hellenistic Period*. Frankfurt am Main.

Boiy, T. (2010a) "Temple building in Hellenistic Babylonia," in *From the Foundations to the Crenellations: Essays on Temple Building in the Ancient Near East Hebrew Bible*, ed. M. J. Boda and J. R. Novotny. Münster, 211–20.

Boiy, T. (2010b) "Royal and satrapal armies in Babylonia during the Second Diadoch War: the 'Chronicle of the Successors' on the events during the seventh year of Philip Arrhidaeus (= 317/316 BC)," *Journal of Hellenic Studies* 130, 1–13.

Boiy, T. and Mittag, P. F. (2011) "Die lokalen Eliten in Babylonien" in Dreyer and Mittag 2011, 105–31.

Boldizzoni, F. (2011) *The Poverty of Clio: Resurrecting Economic History*. Princeton, NJ.

Bolin, S. (1958) *State and Currency in the Roman Empire to 300 A.D.* Stockholm.

Bongenaar, A. C. V. M. (1999) "Money in the Neo-Babylonian Institutions," in *Trade and Finance in Ancient Mesopotamia (MOS Studies 1): Proceedings of the First MOS Sympaosium, Leiden 1997*, ed. J. G. Dercksen. Istanbul, 159–74.

Bongenaar, A. C. V. M. (ed.) (2000) *Interdependency of Institutions and Private Entrepreneurs*. Istanbul.

Boserup, E. (1965) *The Conditions of Agricultural Growth: The Economics of Agrarian Change Under Population Pressure*. London.

Bousquet, J. (1988a) *Etudes sur les comptes de Delphes*. Paris.

Bousquet, J. (1988b) "La stèle des Kyténiens au Letôon de Xanthos," *Revue des Études Grecques* 101, 12–53.

Braund, D. (2007) "Black Sea grain for Athens? From Herodotus to Demosthenes," in Gabrielsen and Lund 2007, 39–68.

Bravo, B. (1980) "*Sulân*. Représailles et justice privée contre des étrangers dans les cités grecques," *Annali della Scuola Normale Superiore di Pisa* ser. III vol. 10, 675–987.

Brenner, R. (2006) *The Economics of Global Turbulence: The Advanced Capitalist Economies from Long Boom to Long Downturn, 1945–2005*. London.

Bresson, A. (2003) "Merchants and politics in ancient Greece: social and economic aspects," in *Mercanti e politica nel mondo antico*, ed. C. Zaccagnini. Rome, 139–63.

Bresson, A. (2007) "La construction d'un espace d'approvisionnement: les cités égéennes et le grain de mer noire," in Bresson, Ivantchik, and Ferrary 2007, 49–68.

Bresson, A. (2011) "Grain from Cyrene," in Archibald, Davies, and Gabrielsen 2011, 66–95.

Bresson, A. (2012) "Wine, oil and delicacies at the Pelousion customs," in *Das imperiale Rom und der hellenistische Osten: Festschrift für Jürgen Deininger zum 75. Geburtstag*, ed. L.-M. Günther and V. Grieb. Stuttgart, 69–88.

Bresson, A. (2014) "Capitalism and the ancient Greek economy," in *The Cambridge History of Capitalism, Vol. 1: The Rise of Capitalism: From Ancient Origins to 1848*, ed. L. Neal and J. G. Williamson. Cambridge, 43–74.

Bresson, A. (2015) "Red fishermen from Anthedon," in *Menschen und Orte der Antike: Festschrift für Helmut Halfmann zum 65. Geburtstag*, ed. S. Panzram, W. Riess, and C. Schäfer. Rahden, 69–84.

Bresson, A. (2016a) "Aristotle and foreign trade," in Harris, Lewis, and Woolmer 2016, 41–65.

Bresson, A. (2016b) *The Making of the Ancient Greek Economy: Institutions, Markets, and Growth in the City-States*. Princeton, NJ.

Bresson, A. (2017a) "Anthropogenic pollution in Greece and Rome," in *Pollution and the Environment in Ancient Life and Thought*, ed. O. D. Cordovana and G. F. Chiai. Stuttgart, 179–202.

Bresson, A. (2017b) "Money exchange and the economics of inequality in the ancient Greek and Roman world," in Derron 2017, 271–316.

Bresson, A. (2018a) "Flexible interfaces of the ancient Mediterranean world," in *The Emporion in the Ancient Western Mediterranean*, ed. É. Gailledrat, M. Dietler, and R. Plana-Mallart. Montpellier, 35–46.

Bresson, A. (2018b) "The cobblers of Kelainai-Apameia Kibotos," in *Munus Laetitiae. Studi miscellanei offerti a Maria Letizia Lazzarini*, vol. 1, ed. F. Camia, L. Del Monaco, and M. Nocita. Rome, 337–50.

Bresson, A. (2019) "The Athenian money supply in the late archaic and early classical period," *Journal of Ancient Civilizations* 34.2, 135–53.

Bresson, A. (2021) "Closed economy, debt and the Spartan crisis," in *Luxury and Wealth in Sparta and the Peloponnese*, ed. S. Hodkinson and C. Gallou. Swansea, 77–96.

Bresson, A., Ivantchik, A., and Ferrary, J.-L. (eds.) (2007) *Une Koinè Pontique: Cités grecques, sociétés indigènes, et empires mondiaux sur le littoral nord de la mer Noire (VIIe s. a. C.–IIIe s. p.C.)*. Bordeaux.

Bresson, A. and Rouillard, P. (eds.) (1993) *L'emporion*. Paris.

Briant, P. (2002) *From Cyrus to Alexander: A History of the Persian Empire*. Winona Lake, IN.

Briant, P. and Descat, R. (1998) "Un registre douanier de la satrapie d'Égypte à l'époque achéménide," *Bulletin d'Égyptologie* 121, 59–104.

Briant, P. and Herrenschmidt, C. (eds.) (1989) *Le tribut dans l'Empire perse*. Leuven.

Brock, R. (1994) "The labour of women in classical Athens," *Classical Quarterly* 44, 336–46.

Brock, S. (2009) "Regulations for an association of artisans from the late Sasanian or early Arab period," in *Transformations of Late Antiquity: Essays for Peter Brown*, ed. P. Rousseau and M. Papoutsakis. Farnham, 51–61.

Broodbank, C. (2013) *The Making of the Middle Sea: A History of the Mediterranean from the Beginning to the Emergence of the Classical World*. London.

Brooke, J. L. (2014) *Climate Change and the Course of Global History: A Rough Journey*. Cambridge.

Brosseder, U. (2015) "Complexity of interaction and exchange in Late Iron Age Eurasia," in *Complexity and Interaction along the Eurasian Steppe Zone in the First Millennium* CE, ed. J. Bemmann and M. Schmauder. Bonn, 199–333.

Broughton, T. R. S. (1938) "Roman Asia Minor," in *An Economic Survey of Ancient Rome, Vol. 4: Africa, Syria, Greece, Asia Minor*, ed. T. Frank. Baltimore, MD, 499–918.

Brughmans, T. (2010) "Connecting the dots: towards archaeological network analysis," *Oxford Journal of Archaeology* 29.3, 277–303.

Brun, P. (1983) *Eisphora. Syntaxis. Stratiotika: Recherches sur les finances militaires d'Athènes au IVe siècle av. J.-C.* Paris.

Bruneau, Ph. (1970) *Recherches sur les cultes de Délos à l'époque hellénistique et à l'époque impériale.* Paris.

Buckler, J. (1980) *The Theban Hegemony, 371–362* BC. Cambridge.

Bugh, G. R. (2006a) "Hellenistic military developments," in Bugh 2006b, 265–95.

Bugh, G. R. (ed.) (2006b) *The Cambridge Companion to the Hellenistic World.* Cambridge.

Büntgen, U. and Di Cosmo, N. (2016) "Climatic and environmental aspects of the Mongol withdrawal from Hungary in 1242 CE," *Scientific Reports* 6, 25606. DOI: https://doi.org/10.1038/srep25606.

Büntgen, U. and Hellman, L. (2014) "The Little Ice Age in scientific perspective: cold spells and caveats," *Journal of Interdisciplinary History* 44, 353–68.

Büntgen, U. et al. (2011) "2500 years of European climate variability and human susceptibility," *Science* 331, 578–82.

Büntgen, U. et al. (2016) "Cooling and societal change during the Late Antique Little Ice Age from 536 to around 660 AD," *Nature Geoscience* 9, 231–6.

Burford, A. (1972) *Craftsmen in Greek and Roman Society.* Ithaca, NY.

Burford, A. (1993) *Land and Labour in the Greek World.* Baltimore, MD.

Burford Cooper, A. (1977) "The family farm in Greece," *The Classical Journal* 73, 162–75.

Burke, E. M. (2005) "The habit of subsidization in classical Athens: toward a thetic ideology," *Classica et Mediaevalia* 56, 5–47.

Burkert, W. (1985) *Greek Religion.* Cambridge, MA.

Burkhardt, J., Oexle, O., andSpahn, P. (1992) "Wirtschaft," in *Geschichtliche Grundbegriffe: Historisches Lexikon zur politisch-sozialen Sprache in Deutschland*, vol. 7, ed. O. Brunner, W. Conze, and R. Koselleck. Stuttgart, 511–94.

Burrer, F. and Müller, H. (eds.) (2008) *Kriegskosten und Kriegsfinanzierung in der Antike.* Darmstadt.

Butzer, K. W. (2012) "Collapse, environment, and society," *Proceedings of the National Academy of Sciences of the United States of America* 109, 3632–9.

Butzer, K. W. and Endfield, G. H. (2012) "Critical perspectives on historical collapse," *Proceedings of the National Academy of Sciences of the United States of America* 109, 3628–31.

Cahill, N. (2002) *Household and City Organization at Olynthus.* New Haven, CT.

Cahn, H. A. (1970) *Knidos: Die Münzen des sechsten und des fünften Jahrhunderts v. Chr.* Berlin.

Cairns, D. (2016) *Sophocles: Antigone.* London.

Caldis, P. D. (1947) "Appendix D: Soil fertility," in *Report of the FAO Mission for Greece*, ed. Food and Agriculture Organization of the United Nations. Washington DC, 134–40.

Camp, J. McK. (1982) "Drought and famine in the 4th century B.C.," *Hesperia Supplements* 20, 9–17.

Campbell, D. B. (2011) "Ancient catapults: some hypotheses re-examined," *Hesperia* 80, 677–700.

Canevaro, M., Erskine, A., Gray, B. D., and Ober, J. (eds.) (2018) *Ancient Greek History and Contemporary Social Science.* Edinburgh.

Capdetrey, L. (2007) *Le pouvoir séleucide: Territoire, administration, finances d'un royaume hellénistique (312–129 avant J.-C.).* Rennes.

Capdetrey, L. and Hasenohr, C. (eds.) (2012) *Agoranomes et édiles: Institutions des marchés antiques.* Bordeaux.

Cararra, A. (2014) "Tax and trade in ancient Greece: about the *Ellimenion* and the harbour duties," *Revue des Études Anciennes* 116, 441–64.

Carawan, E. (2006) "The Athenian law of agreement," *Greek, Roman, and Byzantine Studies* 46, 339–74.

Cardete, M. C. (2019) "Long and short-distance transhumance in ancient Greece: the case of Arkadia," *Oxford Journal of Archaeology* 38.1, 105–21.

Cargill, J. (1981) *The Second Athenian League: Empire or Free Alliance?* Berkeley, CA.

Carlier, P. (1984) *La royauté en Grèce avant Alexandre.* Strasbourg.

Carlson, D. (2013) "A view from the sea: the archaeology of maritime trade in the 5th century BC Aegean," in Slawisch 2013, 1–24.

Cartledge, P. (1996) "Comparatively equal," in Ober and Hedrick 1996, 175–86.

Cartledge, P. (2002) "The economy (economies) of ancient Greece," in *The Ancient Economy*, ed. W. Scheidel and S. von Reden. New York, 11–32.

Cartledge, P., Cohen, E. E., and Foxhall, L. (eds.) (2002) *Money, Labour and Land: Approaches to the Economies of Ancient Greece.* London.

Carugati, F. (2019) *Creating a Constitution: Law, Democracy, and Growth in Ancient Athens.* Princeton, NJ.

Chandezon, C. (1998) "Paysage et économie rurale en Asie Mineure à l'époque hellénistique: à partir de quelques baux de Mylasa (IIe–Ier siècle avant J.-C.)," *Histoire et sociétés rurales* 9, 33–56.

Chandezon, C. (2000a) "Foires et panégyries dans le monde grec classique et hellénistique," *Revue des études grecques* 113, 70–100.

Chandezon, C. (2000b) "Guerre, agriculture et crises d'après les inscriptions hellénistiques," in Andreau, Briant, and Descat 2000, 231–52.

Chandezon, C. (2003a) *L'élevage en Grèce (fin Ve–fin Ier s. a.C.): L'apport des sources épigraphiques.* Bordeaux.

Chandezon, C. (2003b) "Les campagnes de l'Ouest de l'Asie Mineure à l'époque hellénistique," *Pallas* 62, 193–217.

Chandezon, C. (2011) "Some aspects of large estate management in the Greek world during classical and Hellenistic times," in Archibald, Davies, and Gabrielsen 2011, 96–121.

Chaniotis, A. (2005) *War in the Hellenistic World.* London.

Chaniotis, A. (2008) Review of E. Feyel, *Les artisans dans les sanctuaires grecs aux époques classique et hellénistique à travers la documentation financière en Grèce*, Athens 2006, *Classical Review* 58, 196–7.

Chaniotis, A. (2011) "The impact of war on the economy of Hellenistic poleis: demand creation, short-term influences, long-term impacts," in Archibald, Davies, and Gabrielsen 2011, 122–41.

Chaniotis, A. (2017) "Political culture in the cities of the Northern Black Sea regions in the 'Long Hellenistic Age' (the epigraphic evidence)," in Kozlovskaya 2017, 141–66.

Chaniotis, A. (2018) *Age of Conquest: The Greek World from Alexander to Hadrian.* London.

Chankowski, V. (2007) "Les catégories du vocabulaire de la fiscalité dans les cités grecques," in *Vocabulaire et expression de l'économie dans le monde antique*, ed. J. Andreau and V. Chankowski. Pessac, 299–331.

Chankowski, V. (2008) *Athènes et Délos à l'époque classique: Recherches sur l'administration du sanctuaire d'Apollon délien*. Paris.

Chankowski, V. (2011) "Divine financiers: cults as consumers and generators of value," in Archibald, Davies, and Gabrielsen 2011, 142–65.

Chankowski, V. (2018) "Stockage et distribution: en enjeu dans les circuits économiques du monde grec," in Chankowski, Lafon, and Virlouvet 2018, 15–42.

Chankowski, V. (2019) *Parasites du dieu: Comptables, financiers et commerçants dans la Délos hellénistique*. Athens.

Chankowski, V. and Karvonis, P. (eds.) (2012) *Tout vendre, tout acheter: Structures et équipements des marchés antiques*. Bordeaux.

Chankowski, V., Lafon, X., and Virlouvet, C. (eds.) (2018) *Entrepôts et circuits de distribution en Méditerranée antique*. Athens.

Chankowski, V., Lenoble, C., and Maucourant, J. (eds.) (2019) *Les infortunes du juste prix*. Rennes.

Chankowski-Sablé, V. (1997) "Le sanctuaire d'Apollon et le marché délien," in Andreau, Briant, and Descat 1997, 73–89.

Chatzidimitriou, A. (2010) "Transport of goods in the Mediterranean from the geometric to the classical periods. Images and meaning," *Bollettino di archeologia on line* 1 2010. https://bollettinodiarcheologiaonline.beniculturali.it/wp-content/uploads/2019/01/1_CHATZIDIMITRIOU.pdf.

Cherry, J. F. and Davis, J. L. (1991) "The Ptolemaic base at Koressos on Keos," *The Annual of the British School at Athens* 86, 9–28.

Chimisso, C. (2008) *Writing the History of the Mind: Philosophy and Science in France, 1900 to 1960s*. London.

Clarysse, W. (1979) "Egyptian estate-holders in the Ptolemaic period," in *State and Temple Economy in the Ancient Near East*, ed. E. Lipinski. Leuven, 731–43.

Clarysse, W. and Thompson, D. J. (2006) *Counting the People in Hellenistic Egypt*. Cambridge.

Clay, J. S., Malkin, I., and Tzifopoulos, Y. Z. (eds.) (2017) *Panhellenes at Methone: Graphê in Late Geometric and Protoarchaic Methone, Macedonia (ca. 700 BC)*. Berlin.

Clinton, K. (2008) *Eleusis: The Inscriptions on Stone: Documents of the Sanctuary of the Two Goddesses and Public Documents of the Deme, Vol. 2: Commentary*. Athens.

Coase, R. (1937) "The nature of the firm," *Economica* 4, 386–405.

Cohen, B. J. (1998) *The Geography of Money*. Ithaca, NY.

Cohen, B. J. (2015) *Currency Power: Understanding Monetary Rivalry*. Princeton, NJ.

Cohen, E. E. (1973) *Ancient Athenian Maritime Courts*. Princeton, NJ.

Cohen, E. E. (1992) *Athenian Economy and Society: A Banking Perspective*. Princeton, NJ.

Cohen, E. E. (2000) *The Athenian Nation*. Princeton, NJ.

Cohen, E. E. (2005) "Commercial law," in Gagarin and Cohen 2005, 290–302.

Cohen, E. E. (2017) "Overcoming legal incapacities at Athens: juridical adaptations facilitating the business activity of slaves," in *Ancient Guardianship: Legal Incapacities in the Ancient World*, ed. U. Yiftach. Trieste, 127–43.

Cohen, G. M. (1995) *The Hellenistic Settlements in Europe, the Islands, and Asia Minor*. Berkeley, CA.

Cohen, G. M. (2013) *The Hellenistic Settlements in the East from Armenia and Mesopotamia to Bactria and India*. Berkeley, CA.

Cohn, S. K. (2018) *Epidemics: Hate and Compassion from the Plague of Athens to AIDS*. Oxford.

Coldstream, N. (1988) "Early Greek pottery in Tyre and Cyprus: some preliminary comparisons," *Report of the Department of Antiquities Cyprus* 1988.2, 35–44.

Constantakopoulou, C. (2010) *The Dance of the Islands: Insularity, Networks, the Athenian Empire and the Aegean World.* Oxford.

Constantakopoulou, C. (2017) *Aegean Interactions: Delos and Its Networks in the Third Century.* Oxford.

Constante, A., Peña, J. L., Muñoz, A., and Picazo, J. (2011) "Climate and anthropogenic factors affecting alluvial fan development during the late Holocene in the central Ebro valley, northeast Spain," *The Holocene* 21, 275–86.

Cook, E. R. et al. (2015) "Old World megadroughts and pluvials during the Common Era," *Science Advances* 1, e1500561.

Cook, J. M. (1961) "The problem of classical Ionia," *The Cambridge Classical Journal* 7, 9–18.

Cook, R. M. (1958) "Speculations on the origins of coinage," *Historia* 7, 257–62.

Corner, S. (2015) "Symposium," in Wilkins and Nadeau 2015, 234–42.

Corsten, T. (2018) "*Negotiatores* und lokale Märkte in Kleinasien. Überlegungen zu einer Rekonstruktion ländlicher Handelsnetzwerke," in *Infrastructure and Distribution in Ancient Economies*, ed. B. Woytek. Vienna, 381–92.

Cottier, M., Crawford, M. H., Crowther, C. V., Ferrary, J. L., Levick, B. M., Salomies, O., and Wörrle, M. (2008) *The Customs Law of Asia.* Oxford.

Coulton, J. J. (1993) "The Toumba building: description and analysis of the architecture," in *Lefkandi, Vol. 2: The Protogeometric Building at Toumba, Part 2: The Excavation, Architecture and Finds*, ed. M. R. Popham, L. H. Sackett, and P. G. Calligas. London, 30–70.

Cowell, M. R. and Hyne, K. (2000) "Scientific examination of the Lydian precious metal coinages," in *King Croesus' Gold: Excavations at Sardis and the History of Gold Refining*, ed. A. Ramage and P. T. Craddock. Cambridge, MA, 169–74.

Crawford, D. (1973) "The opium poppy: a study in Ptolemaic agriculture," in *Problèmes de la terre en Grèce ancienne*, ed. M. I. Finley. Paris, 223–51.

Crawford, D. (1978) "The good official of Ptolemaic Egypt," in *Das ptolemäische Ägypten*, ed. H. Maehler and V. M. Strocka. Mainz, 195–202.

Crielaard, J. P. (2009) "Cities," in *A Companion to Archaic Greece*, ed. K. Raaflaub and H. van Wees. Malden, MA, 347–72.

Criscuolo, L. (2011) "Observations on the economy in kind in Ptolemaic Egypt," in Archibald, Davies, and Gabrielsen 2011, 166–76.

Cuffey, K. M. and Clow, G. D. (1997) "Temperature, accumulation, and ice sheet elevation in central Greenland through the last deglacial transition," *Journal of Geophysical Research* 102, 26383–96.

Cuomo, S. (2007) *Technology and Culture in Greek and Roman Antiquity.* Cambridge.

Cuomo, S. (2016) "Tacit knowledge in Vitruvius," *Arethusa* 49, 125–43.

Curtis, D. (2013) "Is there an 'agro-town' model for southern Italy? Exploring the diverse roots and development of the agro-town structure through a comparative case study in Apulia," *Continuity and Change* 28, 377–419.

Curtis, R. I. (1991) *Garum and Salsamenta: Production and Commerce in Materia Medica.* Leiden.

Curty, O. (1995) *Les parentés légendaires entre cités grecques.* Geneva.

D'Angour, A. (2011) *The Greeks and the New: Novelty in Ancient Greek Imagination and Experience.* Cambridge.

Dakoronia, F. (2015) "Ceramic technology in Kynos," in Αρχαιολογικό Έργο Θεσσαλίας και Στερεάς Ελλάδας 4: Πρακτικά επιστημονικής συνάντησης, Βόλος 15.3–18.3.2012, ed. A. Mazarakis Ainian. Volos, 841–8.

Dalby, A. (1996) Siren Feasts. A History of Food and Gastronomy in Greece. London.

Dalby, A. (2003) Food in the Ancient World from A to Z. London.

Dalley, S. and Oleson, J. P. (2003) "Sennacherib, Archimedes, and the water screw," Technology and Culture 44, 1–26.

Dana, D. (2014) Onomasticon Thracicum: Répertoire des noms indigènes de Thrace, Macédoine orientale, Mésies, Dacie et Bithynie. Athens.

Dana, D. (2015) "Inscriptions," in Valeva, Nankov, and Graninger 2015, 243–64.

Dana, M. (2007) "Lettres grecques, dialectes nord-pontiques," Revue des Études Anciennes 109, 67–97.

Daubner, F. (2011) "Seleukidische und attalidische Gründungen in Westkleinasien – Datierung, Funktion und Status," in Militärsiedlungen und Territorialherrschaft in der Antike, ed. F. Daubner. Berlin, 41–63.

Davidson, J. N. (1997) Courtesans and Fishcakes: The Consuming Passions of Classical Athens. London.

Davies, J. K. (1984) "Cultural, social and economic features of the Hellenistic world," in The Cambridge Ancient History. Vol. 7.1: The Hellenistic World, ed. F. W. Walbank, A. E. Astin, M. W. Frederiksen, and R. M. Ogilvie. 2nd ed. Cambridge, 257–320.

Davies, J. K. (2001a) "Hellenistic economies in the post-Finley era," in Archibald, Davies, Gabrielsen, and Oliver 2001, 11–62.

Davies, J. K. (2001b) "Temples, credit and the circulation of money," in Meadows and Shipton 2001, 117–28.

Davies, J. K. (2006) "Hellenistic economies," in Bugh 2006b, 73–92.

Davies, J. K. (2007a) "Classical Greece: production," in Scheidel, Morris, and Saller 2007, 333–61.

Davies, J. K. (2007b) "The Phokian hierosylia at Delphi: quantities and consequences," in Corolla Cosma Rodewald, ed. N. Sekunda. Gdańsk, 75–96.

Davies, J. K. (2011) "The well-balanced polis: Ephesos," in Archibald, Davies, and Gabrielsen 2011, 177–206.

Davies, J. K. (2013) "Corridors, cleruchies, commodities, and coins: the pre-history of the Athenian empire," in Slawisch 2013, 43–66.

Day, L. P. (2016) "History of Vronda and society of the LM IIIC settlement," in Gesell and Day 2016, 195–232.

Day, L. P. (2017) "Identifying family structures in Early Iron Age Crete," in Huebner and Nathan 2017, 29–43.

De Callataÿ, F. (1989) "Des trésor royaux achéménides aux monnayages d'Alexandre: espèces immobiliées et espèces circulantes," Revue des études anciennes 91, 25–74.

De Callataÿ, F. (2000) "Guerres et monnayages à l'époque hellénistique: essai de mise en perspective suivi d'une annexe sur le monnayage de Mithridate VI Eupator," in Andreau, Briant, and Descat 2000, 337–64.

De Callataÿ, F. (2005a) "A quantitative survey of Hellenistic coinages: recent achievements," in Archibald, Davies, and Gabrielsen 2005, 73–91.

De Callataÿ, F. (2005b) "L'instauration par Ptolémée Ier Sôter d'une économie monétaire fermée," in L'exception égyptienne? Production et échanges monétaires en Égypte hellénistique et romaine, ed. F. Duyrat and O. Picard. Cairo, 117–34.

De Callataÿ, F. (2006a) "Le transport des monnaies dans le monde grec," *Revue velge de numismatique et sigillographie* 152, 5–14.

De Callataÿ, F. (2006b) "Greek coins from archaeological excavations: a conspectus of conspectuses and a call for chronological tables," in van Alfen 2006, 177–200.

De Callataÿ, F. (2012) "Royal Hellenistic coinages: from Alexander to Mithradates," in Metcalf 2012, 175–90.

De Callataÿ, F. (2013) "The coinages of the Attalids and their neighbours: a quantified overview," in Thonemann 2013b, 207–44.

De Callataÿ, F. (ed.) (2014) *Quantifying the Greco-Roman Economy and Beyond.* Bari.

De Cenival, F. (1972) *Les associations religieuses en Égypte d'après les documents démotiques.* Cairo.

De Ligt, L. (1993) *Fairs and Markets in the Roman Empire: Economic and Social Aspects of Periodic Trade in a Preindustrial Society.* Amsterdam.

De Roover, R. (1958) "The concept of the just price: theory and economic policy," *Journal of Economic History* 18, 418–34.

De Souza, P. (1999) *Piracy in the Greek and Roman Worlds.* Cambridge.

De Ste Croix, G. E. M. (1981) *The Class Struggle in the Ancient Greek World.* London.

De Ste Croix, G. E. M. (2004) *Athenian Democratic Origins and Other Essays,* ed. D. Harvey and R. Parker. Oxford.

Debord, P. (1982) *Aspects sociaux et économiques de la vie religieuse dans l'Anatolie gréco-romaine.* Leiden.

Debord, P. (1999) *L'Asie mineure au IVe siècle (412–323 a.C.). Pouvoirs et jeux politiques.* Bordeaux.

Decourt, J.-Cl., Nielsen, Th. H., and Helly, B. (2004) "Thessalia and adjacent regions," in Hansen and Nielsen 2004, 676–731.

Deger-Jalkotzy, S. (1998) "The Aegean islands and the breakdown of the Mycenaean palaces around 1200 B.C.," in *Eastern Mediterranean: Cyprus, Dodecanese, Crete: 16th–6th Cent. B.C.,* ed. V. Karageorghis and N. Stampolidis. Athens, 105–20.

Demetriou, D. (2012) *Negotiating Identity in the Ancient Mediterranean: The Archaic and Classical Greek Multiethnic Emporia.* Cambridge.

Den Boer, W. (1977) *Progress in the Greece of Thucydides.* Amsterdam.

Deonna, W. (1938) *Le mobilier délien.* Athens.

Derron, P. (ed.) (2017) *Économie et inégalité: Ressources, échanges et pouvoir dans l'Antiquité classique.* Vandœuvres.

Descamps-Lequime, S. (ed.) (2011) *Au royaume d'Alexandre le Grand: La Macédoine antique.* Paris.

Descat, R. (1985) "Mnésimachos, Hérodote et le système tributaire achéménide," *Revues des études anciennes* 87, 97–112.

Descat, R. (2001) "La loi délienne sur les bois et charbons et le rôle de Délos comme marché," *Revues des études anciennes* 103, 125–30.

Descoeudres, J.-P. (2008) "Central Greece on the eve of the colonisation movement," in *Greek Colonisation: An Account of Greek Colonies and Other Settlements Overseas,* ed. G. Tsetskhladze. Leiden, 289–382.

Descoeudres, J.-P. and Paspalas, S. A. (eds.) (2015) *Zagora in Context: Settlements and Intercommunal Links in the Geometric Period (900–700 BC).* Sydney.

Detienne, M. (1993) *The Gardens of Adonis: Spices in Greek Mythology.* Princeton, NJ.

Dibble, W. F. (2017) "Politika zoa: animals and social change in ancient Greece (1600–300 B.C.)." Unpublished DPhil thesis, University of Cincinnati.

Dickenson, C. P. (2017) *On the Agora: The Evolution of a Public Space in Hellenistic and Roman Greece (c. 323 BC–267 AD)*. Leiden.

Dickinson, O. (2006) *The Aegean from Bronze Age to Iron Age: Continuity and Change Between the Twelfth and the Eighth Centuries BC*. London.

Dignas, B. (2002) *Economy of the Sacred in Hellenistic and Roman Asia Minor*. Oxford.

Dimitrova, N. M. (2008) *Theoroi and Initiates in Samothrace: The Epigraphic Evidence*. Princeton, NJ.

Dittmann-Schöne, I. (2010) *Die Berufsvereine in den Städten des kaiserzeitlichen Kleinasiens*. Regensburg.

Dodds, E. R. (1973) "The ancient concept of progress," in *The Ancient Concept of Progress and Other Essays on Greek Literature and Belief*, ed. E. R. Dodds. Oxford, 1–25.

Dogaer, N. (2021) "Markets and Monopolies: The Role of the State in Industry and Trade in Ptolemaic Egypt." Unpublished dissertation, Katholieke Universiteit Leuven.

Domaradzka, L. (2005) "Graeco-Thracian relations in the upper Maritsa valley (5th–4th Centuries BC) (based on epigraphic evidence)," in *The Culture of Thracians and Their Neighbours*, ed. J. Bouzek and L. Domaradzka. Oxford, 19–26.

Domaradzki, M. (1987) "Les données numismatiques et les études de la culture thrace du second Age du Fer," *Numizmatika* 21.4, 4–18.

Domingo Gygax, M. (2005) "Change and continuity in the administration of Ptolemaic Lycia: a note on P. Tebt. I 8," *Bulletin of the American Society of Papyrologists* 42, 45–50.

Donlan, W. (1982) "Reciprocities in Homer," *Classical World* 75, 137–75.

Donlan, W. (1997) "The Homeric economy," in *A New Companion to Homer*, ed. I. Morris and B. Powell. Leiden, 649–67.

Doukellis, P. N. and Mendoni, L. G. (eds.) (1994) *Structures rurales et sociétés antiques*. Paris.

Dover, J. K. (1994) *Greek Popular Morality in the Time of Plato and Aristotle*. Indianapolis.

Drake, B. L. (2012) "The influence of climatic change on the Late Bronze Age collapse and the Greek Dark Ages," *Journal of Archaeological Science* 39.6, 1862–70.

Dreyer, B. and Mittag, P. F. (eds.) (2011) *Lokale Eliten und hellenistische Könige: Zwischen Kooperation und Konfrontation*. Berlin.

Dubois, L. (1996) *Inscriptions grecques dialectales d'Olbia du Pont*. Geneva.

Ducat, J. (1990) *Les hilotes*. Paris.

Ducat, J. (2015) "Les hilotes à l'époque archaïque," in *La main-d'œuvre agricole en Méditerranée archaïque*, ed. J. Zurbach. Bordeaux, 165–95.

Dupont, P. (2007) "Le Pont Euxin archaïque: lac milésien ou lac nord-ionien? Un point de vue de céramologue," in Bresson, Ivantchik, and Ferrary 2007, 29–36.

Duran, M. (1999) "Oaths and settlement of disputes in Hesiod Op 27–41," *Zeitschrift der Savigny-Stiftung für Rechtsgeschichte. Romanistische Abteilung* 116, 25–48.

Durand, X. (1997) *Des Grecs en Palestine au IIIe siècle avant Jésus Christ: Le dossier syrien des archives de Zénon de Caunos (261–252)*. Paris.

Duyrat, F. (2016) *Wealth and Warfare: The Archaeology of Money in Ancient Syria*. New York.

Duyrat, F. and Grandjean, C. (eds.) (2016) *Les monnaies de fouille du monde grec, VIe–Ier s. a.C. Apports, Approches, et Méthodes*. Bordeaux.

Earle, T. K. (1977) "A reappraisal of redistribution: complex Hawaiian chiefdoms," in *Exchange Systems in Prehistory*, ed. T. K. Earle and J. E. Ericson. New York, 213–29.

Edelstein, L. (1967) *The Idea of Progress in Classical Antiquity*. Baltimore, MD.

Eder, B. (2006) "The world of Telemachus: western Greece 1200–700 BC," in *Ancient Greece: From the Mycenaean Palaces to the Age of Homer*, ed. S. Deger-Jalkotzy and I. S. Lemos. Edinburgh, 549–80.

Eder, B. (2015) "Die Kontinuität bronzener Ringhenkeldreifüße im sozialen Kontext der Transformation der mykenischen Welt zwischen 1200 und 700," in *ΠΟΛΥΜΑΘΕΙΑ: Festschrift für Hartmut Matthäus anläßlich seines 65. Geburtstages*, ed. S. Nawracala und R. Nawracala. Aachen, 115–33.

Eder, B. and Jung, R. (2005) "On the character of social relations between Greece and Italy in the 12th/11th c. B.C.," in *Emporia: Aegeans in the Central and Eastern Mediterranean*, vol. 2, ed. R. Laffineur and E. Greco. Liège, 485–95.

Eder, B. and Lemos, I. S. (2020) "From the collapse of the Mycenaean palaces to the emergence of Early Iron Age communities," in Lemos and Kotsonas 2020, vol. 1, 133–60.

Edson, Ch. (1970) "Early Macedonia," *Archaia Makedonia* 1, 17–44.

Edwards, J. and Ogilvie, S. (2012) "What lessons for economic development can we draw from the Champagne fairs?," *Explorations in Economic History* 49, 131–48.

Egelhaaf-Gaiser, U. and Schäfer, A. (eds.) (2002) *Religiöse Vereine in der römischen Antike: Untersuchungen zu Organisation, Ritual und Raumordnung*. Tübingen.

Eich, A. (2006) *Die politische Ökonomie des antiken Griechenland: 6.–3. Jahrhundert v. Chr.* Cologne.

Einzig, P. (1966) *Primitive Money: In Its Ethnological, Historical, and Economic Aspects*. 2nd ed. Oxford.

Elayi, J. and Elayi, A. G. (2014) *A Monetary and Political History of the Phoenician City of Byblos in the Fifth–Fourth Centuries B.C.E.* Winona Lake, IN.

Ellis-Evans, A. (2019) *The Kingdom of Priam: Lesbos and the Troad between Anatolia and the Aegean*. Oxford.

Ellis-Evans, A. and van Alfen, P. G. (2018) "Preliminary observations on the archaic silver coinage of Lampsakos in its regional context," in *Second International Congress on the History of Money and Numismatics in the Mediterranean World, 5–8 January 2017 Antalya: Proceedings*, ed. O. Tekin. Antalya, 41–52.

Engen, D. T. (2010) *Honor and Profit: Athenian Trade Policy and the Economy and Society of Greece, 415–307 BC*. Ann Arbor, MI.

Erdas, D. (2012) "Aspetti giuridici dell'agora greca," in *Agora greca, agorai di Sicilia*, ed. C. Ampolo. Pisa, 57–69.

Erdkamp, P. (2014) "How modern was the market economy of the Roman world?," *Oeconomia* 4, 225–35.

Erickson, B. (2013) "Island archaeologies and the economy of the Athenian empire," in Slawisch 2013, 67–83.

Escobar, A. (1995) *Encountering Development: The Making and Unmaking of the Third World*. Princeton, NJ.

Étienne, R. (ed.) (2018) *Le sanctuaire d'Apollon à Délos: Architecture, topographie, histoire*. Athens.

Evely, D. (ed.) (2006) *Lefkandi, Vol. 4: The Bronze Age: The Late Helladic IIIC Settlement at Xeropolis*. London.

Evers, K. G. (2017) *Worlds Apart Trading Together: The Organisation of Long-Distance Trade between Rome and India in Antiquity*. Oxford.

Fabian, L. (2019) "The Arsakid Empire," in *Handbook of Ancient Afro-Eurasian Economies*, vol. 1, ed. S. von Reden, Berlin and Boston, 205–40.

Fabre, D. and Goddio, F. (2010) "The development and operation of the Portus Magnus in Alexandria," in *Alexandria and the North-Western Delta*, ed. D. Robinson and A. Wilson. Oxford, 53–74.

Fachard, S. (2016) "Modelling the territories of Attic demes: a computational approach," in *The Archaeology of Greece and Rome: Studies in Honour of Anthony Snodgrass*, ed. J. Bintliff and K. Rutter. Edinburgh, 192–222.

Fachard, S. (2017) "The resources of the borderlands: control, inequality, and exchange on the Attic–Boeotian borders," in Derron 2017, 19–73.

Fachard, S. and Pirisino, D. (2015) "Routes out of Attica," in *Autopsy in Athens: Recent Archaeological Research on Athens and Attica*, ed. M. M. Miles. Oxford, 139–53.

Faraguna, M. (2012) "*Pistis* and *Apistia*: aspects of the development of social and economic relations in classical Greece," *Mediterraneo antico* 15, 355–74.

Faraguna, M. (ed.) (2013a) *Archives and Archival Documents in Ancient Societies*. Trieste.

Faraguna, M. (2013b) "Archives in classical Greece: some observations," in Faraguna 2013a, 163–71.

Faraguna, M. (2015) "Archives, documents, and legal practices in the Greek polis," in *The Oxford Handbook of Ancient Greek Law*, ed. E. M. Harris and M. Canevaro. DOI: 10.1093/oxfordhb/9780199599257.013.14.

Fasolo, M. (2005) *La Via Egnatia. I: Da Apollonia e Dyrrachium ad Herakleia Lynkestidos.* 2nd ed. Rome.

Faucher, T. (2018) "L'or des Ptolémées: l'exploitation de l'or dans le désert Oriental," in *Le désert oriental d'Égypte durant la période gréco-romaine: bilans archéologiques*, ed. J.-P. Brun, T. Faucher, B. Redon, and S. Sidebotham. Paris, 1–16.

Faucher, T. (ed.) (2020) *Money Rules! The Monetary Economy of Egypt, from Persians until the Beginning of Islam.* Cairo.

Faucher, T. and Redon, B. (2014) "Le prix de l'entrée au bain en Égypte hellénistique et romaine d'après les données textuelles et numismatiques," in *25 siècles de bain collectif en Orient Proche-Orient, Égypte et péninsule Arabique*, ed. M.-F. Boussac, S. Denoix, T. Fournet, and B. Redon. Cairo, 835–55.

Faucher, T., Marcellesi, M.-C., and Picard, O. (eds.) (2011) *Nomisma: La circulation monétaire dans le monde grec.* Athens.

Faulseit, E. K. (ed.) (2016) *Beyond Collapse: Archaeological Perspectives on Resilience, Revitalization, and Transformation in Complex Societies.* Carbondale, IL.

Faundez, J. (2016) "Douglass North's theory of institutions: lessons for law and development," *Hague Journal on the Rule of Law* 8, 373–419.

Fawcett, P. (2016) "'When I squeeze you with *eisphorai*: taxes and tax policy in classical Athens," *Hesperia* 85, 153–99.

Felsch, R. (1981) "Mykenischer Kult im Heiligtum bei Kalapodi?," in *Sanctuaries and Cults in the Aegean Bronze Age*, ed. R. Hägg and N. Marinatos. Stockholm, 81–8.

Fenet, A. (2016) *Les dieux olympiens et la mer: Espaces et pratiques cultuelles.* Rome.

Ferrary, J.-L. (2002) "La création de la province d'Asie et la présence italienne en Asie Mineure," in *Les Italiens dans le monde Grec, IIe siècle av. J.-C.–Ier siècle ap. J.-C.: Circulation, activités, intégration*, ed. C. Mueller and C. Hasenohr. Paris, 133–46.

Feyel, C. (2006) *Les artisans dans les sanctuaires grecs aux époques classique et hellénistique à travers la documentation financière en Grèce.* Athens.

Feyel, C. (2007) "Le monde du travail à travers les comptes de construction des grands sanctuaires grecs," *Pallas* 74, 77–92.

Figueira, T. J. (1981) *Aegina: Society and Politics.* New York.

Figueira, T. J. (1991) *Athens and Aigina in the Age of Imperial Colonization.* Baltimore, MD.

Figueira, T. J. (1998) *The Power of Money: Coinage and Politics in the Athenian Empire.* Philadelphia, PA.

Fine, J. V. A. (1951) *Horoi: Studies in Mortgage, Real Security and Land Tenure in Ancient Athens.* Athens.

Finkel, I. L., van der Spek, R. J., and Pirngruber, R. (eds.) (forthcoming) *Babylonian Chronographic Texts from the Hellenistic Period.*

Finley, M. I. (1951) *Studies in Land and Credit in Ancient Athens, 500–200 B.C.* New Brunswick, NJ.

Finley, M. I. (1965) "Technical innovation and economic progress in the ancient world," *Economic History Review* 18, 29–45.

Finley, M. I. (1978) *The World of Odysseus.* 2nd ed. New York.

Finley, M. I. [1973] (1999) *The Ancient Economy.* 3rd ed. Berkeley, CA.

Finné, M., Holmgren, K., Sundqvist, H. S., Weiberg, E., and Lindblom, M. (2011) "Climate in the eastern Mediterranean, and adjacent regions, during the past 6000 years – a review," *Journal of Archaeological Science* 38, 3153–73.

Finné, M., Woodbridge, J., Labuhn, I., and Roberts, C. N. (2019) "Holocene hydro-climatic variability in the Mediterranean: a synthetic multi-proxy reconstruction," *The Holocene* 29, 847–63.

Fischer-Bossert, W. (2018) "Electrum coinage of the seventh century BC," in *Second International Congress on the History of Money and Numismatics in the Mediterranean World, 5–8 Jan. 2017 Antalya: Proceedings,* ed. O. Tekin. Istanbul, 15–23.

Fischer-Bovet, C. (2011) "Counting the Greeks in Egypt: immigration in the first century of Ptolemaic rule," in *Demography in the Graeco-Roman World: New Insights and Approaches,* ed. C. Holeran and A. Pudsey. Cambridge, 135–54.

Fischer-Bovet, C. (2014) *Army and Society in Ptolemaic Egypt.* Cambridge.

Fisher, N. (2000) "Symposiasts, fish-eaters and flatterers: social mobility and moral concerns," in *The Rivals of Aristophanes: Studies in Athenian Old Comedy,* ed. D. Harvey and J. Wilkins. London, 355–96.

Fisher, N. (2006) "Citizens, foreigners and slaves in Greek society," in Kinzl 2006, 327–49.

Fisher, N. R. E. (2001) *Slavery in Classical Greece.* 2nd ed. London.

Flambard, J. M. (1982) "Observations sur la nature des *Magistri* italiens de Délos," *Opuscula Instituti Romani Finlandiae* 2, 67–77.

Flament, C. (2007) *Une économie monétarisée: Athènes à l'époque classique (440–338): Contribution à l'étude du phénomène monétaire en Grèce ancienne.* Louvain-la-Neuve.

Fleitmann, D. et al. (2009) "Timing and climatic impact of Greenland interstadials recorded in stalagmites from northern Turkey," *Geophysical Research Letters* 36, L19707.

Food and Agriculture Organization of the United Nations (2017) *World Programme for the Census of Agriculture 2020. Vol. 1: Programme, Concepts and Definitions.* Rome.

Forbes, H. (1989) "Of grandfathers and grand theories: the hierarchized ordering of responses to hazard in a Greek rural community," in Halstead and O'Shea 1989, 87–97.

Forbes, H. (1995) "The identification of pastoralist sites within the context of estate-based agriculture in ancient Greece: beyond the 'transhumance versus agro-pastoralism' debate," *Annual of the British School at Athens* 90, 325–38.

Forbes, H. (1996) "The uses of the uncultivated landscape in modern Greece: a pointer to the value of the wilderness in antiquity?," in *Human Landscapes in Classical Antiquity*, ed. G. Shipley and J. Salmon. London, 68–97.

Forbes, H. (2007) *Meaning and Identity in a Greek Landscape: An Archaeological Ethnography*. Cambridge.

Forbes, H. and Foxhall, L. (1982) "Sitometreia: the role of grain as a staple food in classical antiquity," *Chiron* 12, 41–90.

Forsdyke, S. (2006) "Land, labor and economy in Solonian Athens: breaking the impasse between history and archaeology," in *Solon of Athens*, ed. J. H. Blok and A. Lardinois. Leiden, 334–50.

Forsdyke, S. (2012) *Slaves Tell Tales: And Other Episodes in the Politics of Popular Culture in Ancient Greece*. Princeton, NJ.

Foxhall, L. (1992) "The control of the Attic landscape," in Wells 1992, 155–9.

Foxhall, L. (1997) "A view from the top: evaluating the Solonian property classes," in *The Development of the Polis in Archaic Greece*, ed. L. G. Mitchell and P. J. Rhodes. London, 113–36.

Foxhall, L. (2002) "Access to resources in classical Greece: the egalitarianism of the polis in practice," in Cartledge, Cohen, and Foxhall 2002, 209–20.

Foxhall, L. (2007) *Olive Cultivation in Ancient Greece: Seeking the Ancient Economy*. Oxford.

Foxhall, L. (2013) "Can we see the 'hoplite revolution' on the ground? Archaeological landscapes, material culture and social status in early Greece," in *Men of Bronze: Hoplite Warfare in Ancient Greece*, ed. D. Kagan and G. Viggiano. Princeton, NJ, 194–221.

Foxhall, L. (2014) "Households, hierarchies, territories and landscapes in Bronze Age and Iron Age Greece," in Knapp and van Dommelen 2014, 417–36.

Frier, B. W. and Kehoe, D. F. (2007) "Law and economic institutions," in Scheidel, Morris, and Saller 2007, 113–44.

Fröhlich, P. (2004) *Les cités grecques et le contrôle des magistrats (IVe–Ier siècle avant J.-C.)*. Geneva.

Fuks, A. (1951) "Κολωνὸς μίσθιος: labour exchange in classical Athens," *Eranos* 49, 171–3.

Furubotn, E. and Richter, R. (2005) *Institutions and Economic Theory: The Contribution of the New Institutional Economics*. 2nd ed. Ann Arbor, MI.

Gabrielsen, V. (1994a) *Financing the Athenian Fleet: Public Taxation and Social Relations*. Baltimore, MD.

Gabrielsen, V. (1994b) "The Rhodian associations honouring Dionysodoros from Alexandria," *Classica et Mediaevalia* 45, 137–60.

Gabrielsen, V. (1997) *The Naval Aristocracy of Hellenistic Rhodes*. Aarhus.

Gabrielsen, V. (2001) "The Rhodian associations and economic activity," in Archibald, Davies, Gabrielsen, and Oliver 2001, 215–44.

Gabrielsen, V. (2005) "Banking and credit operations in Hellenistic times," in Archibald, Davies, and Gabrielsen 2005, 136–64.

Gabrielsen, V. (2007) "Trade and tribute: Byzantion and the Black Sea straits," in Gabrielsen and Lund 2007, 287–324.

Gabrielsen, V. (2009) "Brotherhoods of faith and provident planning: the non-public associations of the Greek world," in Malkin, Constantakopoulou, and Panagopoulou 2009, 176–203.

Gabrielsen, V. (2011) "Profitable partnerships: monopolies, traders, kings and cities," in Archibald, Davies, and Gabrielsen 2011, 216–50.

Gabrielsen, V. (2013) "Rhodes and the Ptolemaic kingdom: the commercial infrastructures," in *The Ptolemies, the Sea, and the Nile: Studies in Waterborne Power*, ed. K. Buraselis and M. Stephanou. Cambridge, 66–81.

Gabrielsen, V. (2016a) "Associations, modernization and the return of the private network in Athens," in *Die athenische Demokratie im 4. Jahrhundert: Zwischen Modernisierung und Tradition*, ed. C. Tiersch. Stuttgart, 121–62.

Gabrielsen, V. (2016b) "Be faithful and prosper. Associations, trust and the economy of security," in *Antike Wirtschaft und ihre Kulturelle Prägung/The Cultural Shaping of the Ancient Economy*, ed. K. Droß-Krüpe, S. Föllinger, and K. Ruffing. Wiesbaden, 87–111.

Gabrielsen, V. and Lund, J. (eds.) (2007) *The Black Sea in Antiquity: Regional and Interregional Economic Exchanges*. Aarhus.

Gabrielsen, V. and Thomsen, C. A. (eds.) (2015) *Private Associations and the Public Sphere: Proceedings of a Symposium Held at the Royal Danish Academy of Sciences and Letters, 9–11 September 2010*. Copenhagen.

Gagarin, M. (2005) "The unity of Greek law," in Gagarin and Cohen 2005, 29–40.

Gagarin, M. (2008) *Writing Greek Law*. Cambridge.

Gagarin, M. and Cohen, D. (eds.) (2005) *The Cambridge Companion to Ancient Greek Law*. Cambridge.

Gaignerot-Driessen, F. (2016) *De l'occupation postpalatiale à la cité-état grecque: le cas du Miranbello (Crète)*. Leuven.

Galaty, M. and Parkinson, W. A. (eds.) (2007) *Rethinking Mycenaean Palaces* II. 2nd ed. Los Angeles.

Gallant, T. W. (1991) *Risk and Survival in Ancient Greece: Reconstructing the Rural Domestic Economy*. Stanford, CA.

Gallego, J. (2016) "El campesinado y la distribución de la tierra en la Atenas del siglo IV a.C.," *Gerión* 34, 43–75.

Game, J. (2008) *Actes de vente dans le monde grec: témoignages épigraphiques des ventes immobilières*. Lyon.

Garlan, Y. (1988) *Slavery in Ancient Greece*. 2nd ed. Ithaca, NY.

Garlan, Y. (1999) *Les timbres amphoriques de Thasos*. Vol. I: *Timbres protothasiens et thasiens anciens*. Athens.

Garland, R. (1987) *The Piraeus: From the Fifth to the First Century* BC. London.

Garland, R. (2014) *Wandering Greeks: The Ancient Greek Diaspora from the Age of Homer to the Death of Alexander the Great*. Princeton, NJ.

Garnsey, P. (1988) *Famine and Food Supply in the Graeco-Roman World: Responses to Risk and Crisis*. Cambridge.

Garnsey, P. (1999) *Food and Society in Classical Antiquity*. Cambridge.

Gartland, S. (2013) "The electrum coinage of Thebes," *The Numismatic Chronicle* 173, 1–10.

Gartland, S. (2016) *Boiotia in the Fourth Century BC*, Philadelphia, PA.

Gatzolis, C. A. and Psoma, S. E. (2016) "Olynthos and Stageira: Bronze coinage and political history," in Duyrat and Grandjean 2016, 83–96.

Gauthier, P. (1972) *Symbola: Les étrangers et la justice dans les cites grecques*. Nancy.

Gauthier, P. (1991) "Ἀτέλεια τοῦ σώματος," *Chiron* 21, 49–68.

Gesell, G. C. and Day, L. P. (eds.) (2016) *Kavousi IIC: The Late Minoan Settlement at Vronda: Specialist Reports and Analyses*. Philadelphia.

Gibbs, M. (2011) "Trade associations in Roman Egypt: their raison d'être," *Ancient Society* 41, 291–315.

Gibbs, M. (2015) "The trade associations of Ptolemaic Egypt," in Gabrielsen and Thomsen 2015, 241–69.

Gimatzidis, S. (2010) *Die Stadt Sindos: eine Siedlung von der späten Bronze- bis zur klassischen Zeit am Thermaischen Golf in Makedonien.* Rahden.

Gimatzidis, S. (2020) "The economy of early Greek colonisation in the northern Aegean," *Journal of Greek Archaeology* 5, 243–62.

Gitler, H. and Kahanov, Y. (2002) "A late Hellenistic coin hoard," *Coin Hoards* 9, 259–68.

Goddio, F., Fabre, D., and Gerick, C. (eds.) (2006) *Trésors engloutis d'Egypte. Catalogue de l'exposition.* Paris.

Gofa, F., Mamara, A., Anadranistakis, M., and Flocas, H. (2019) "Developing gridded climate data sets of precipitation for Greece based on homogenized time series," *Climate* 7.68. https://doi.org/10.3390/cli7050068.

Goldstone, J. A. (1991) *Revolution and Rebellion in the Early Modern World.* Berkeley, CA.

Goldstone, J. A. (2002) "Efflorescences and economic growth in world history: rethinking the 'Rise of the West' and the Industrial Revolution," *Journal of World History* 13, 323–89.

Gomme, A. W. (1933) *The Population of Athens in the Fifth and Fourth Centuries* B.C. Oxford.

González-Ruibal, A. and Ruiz-Gálvez, M. (2016) "House societies in the ancient Mediterranean (2000–500 BC)," *Journal of World Prehistory* 29.4, 383–437.

Gounaris, A. (2005) "Cult places in the Cyclades during the protogeometric and geometric periods: their contribution in interpreting the rise of the Cycladic poleis," in *Architecture and Archaeology in the Cyclades: Papers in Honour of J. J. Coulton*, ed. M. Yeroulanou and M. Stamatopoulou. Oxford, 13–68.

Grandjean, C. (1990) "Le monnayage d'argent et de bronze d'Hermioné, Argolide," *Revue numismatique* 32, 28–55.

Grandjean, C. (1998) "La valeur des monnaies de bronze du Péloponnèse à l'epoque classique et hellenistique," *Revue numismatique* 153, 31–40.

Grandjean, C. (2000) "Guerre et monnaie en Grèce ancienne: le cas du *koinon* achaïen" in Andreau, Briant, and Descat 2000, 315–36.

Granovetter, M. (1983) "The strength of weak ties: a network theory revisited," *Sociological Theory* 1, 203–33.

Granovetter, M. (1985) "Economic action and social structure: the problem of embeddedness," *American Journal of Sociology* 91, 481–510.

Granovetter, M. (2005) "Comment on Liviani and Bedford," in Manning and Morris 2005, 84–90.

Graslin-Thomé, L. (2016a) "Long-distance trade in Neo-Babylonian Mesopotamia: the effect of institutional changes," in Moreno García 2016, 167–86.

Graslin-Thomé, L. (2016b) "Imported textiles and dyes in first-millennium BCE Babylonia and the emergence of new consumption needs," in *Textiles, Trade and Theories: From the Ancient Near East to the Mediterranean*, ed. K. Droß-Krüpe and M.-L. Nosch. Münster, 63–77.

Graves, A. M. (2011) "The Greeks in western Asia Minor," in Steadman and McMahon 2011, 500–14.

Greene, K. (2000) "Technological innovation and economic progress in the ancient world: M. I. Finley reconsidered," *Economic History Review* 53, 29–59.

Greene, K. (2009) "Inventors, invention, and attitudes toward innovation," in Oleson 2009, 800–18.

Greif, A. (2006) *Institutions and the Path to the Modern Economy: Lessons from Medieval Trade*. Cambridge.

Guarducci, M. (1944–5) "Tripodi, lebeti, oboli," *Rivista di filologia classica (n.s.)* 22–3, 171–80.

Günther, L-M (ed.) (2012) *Migration und Bürgerrecht in der hellenistischen Welt*. Wiesbaden.

Hackl, J. and Pirngruber, R. (2015) "Prices and related data from northern Babylonia in the late Achaemenid and early Hellenistic periods, c. 480–300 BC," in van der Spek, van Leeuwen, and van Zanden 2015, 107–27.

Haggis, D. C. (2013) "Social organization and aggregated settlement structure in an archaic Greek city on Crete (ca. 600 BC)," in *From Prehistoric Villages to Cities: Settlement Aggregation and Community Transformation*, ed. J. Birch. New York, 63–86.

Haggis, D. C. (2015) "The archaeology of urbanization: research design and the excavation of an archaic Greek city on Crete," in Haggis and Antonaccio 2015, 219–58.

Haggis, D. C. and Antonaccio, C. M. (eds.) (2015) *Classical Archaeology in Context: Theory and Practice in Excavation in the Greek World*. Berlin.

Hailer, U. (2008) *Einzelgehöfte im Bergland von Yavu (Zentrallykien)*, 2 vols. Bonn.

Haldon, J. (2016) "Cooling and societal change," *Nature Geoscience* 9, 191–2.

Haldon, J. et al. (2018) "History meets palaeoscience: consilience and collaboration in studying past societal responses to environmental change," *Proceedings of the National Academy of Sciences of the United States of America* 115, 3210–18.

Haldon, J. F. (2021) "The political economy of empire: "imperial capital" and the formation of central and regional elites," in *The Oxford World History of Empires*, vol. 1, ed. P. F. Bang, C. A. Bayly, and W. Scheidel. Oxford, 179–202.

Hall, J. M. (2014) *A History of the Archaic Greek World, ca. 1200–479 BCE*. 2nd ed. Chichester.

Halstead, P. (1987) "Traditional and ancient rural economy in Mediterranean Europe: plus ça change?," *The Journal of Hellenic Studies* 107, 77–87.

Halstead, P. (2007) "Toward a model of Mycenaean palatial mobilization," in Galaty and Parkinson 2007, 66–73.

Halstead, P. (2011) "Redistribution in Aegean palatial societies: terminology, scale, and significance," *American Journal of Archaeology* 115.2, 229–35.

Halstead, P. (2014) *Two Oxen Ahead: Pre-Mechanized Farming in the Mediterranean*. Hoboken, NJ.

Halstead, P. and O'Shea, J. (eds.) (1989) *Bad Year Economics: Cultural Responses to Risk and Uncertainty*. Cambridge.

Hamilton, R. (1999) *Treasure Map: A Guide to the Delian Inventories*. Ann Arbor, MI.

Hammond, N. G. L. (1972) *A History of Macedonia I: Historical Geography and Prehistory*. Oxford.

Hansen, M. H. (1986). *Demography and Democracy: The Number of Athenian Citizens in the Fourth Century B.C.* Herning.

Hansen, M. H. (1988) *Three Studies in Athenian Demography*. Copenhagen.

Hansen, M. H. (2006a) *Studies in the Population of Aigina, Athens and Eretria*. Copenhagen.

Hansen, M. H. (2006b) *The Shotgun Method: The Demography of the Ancient Greek City-State Culture*. Columbia, MO.

Hansen, M. H. and Nielsen, T. H. (eds.) (2004) *An Inventory of Archaic and Classical Poleis*. Oxford.

Hanson, V. D. (1998) *Warfare and Agriculture in Classical Greece*. Rev. ed. Berkeley, CA.

Hanson, V. D. (1999) *The Other Greeks: The Family Farm and the Agrarian Roots of Western Civilization*. 2nd ed. Berkeley, CA.

Harl, K. W. (2011) "The Greeks in Anatolia: from the migrations to Alexander the Great," in Steadman and McMahon 2011, 752–74.

Harland, P. (2005) "Familial dimensions of group identity: 'brothers' (ΑΔΕΛΦΟΙ) in associations of the Greek East," *Journal of Biblical Literature* 124, 491–513.

Harper, K. (2017) *The Fate of Rome: Climate, Disease, and the End of an Empire*. Princeton, NJ.

Harper, K. and McCormick, M. (2018) "Reconstructing the Roman Climate," in *The Science of Roman History: Biology, Climate, and the Future of the Past*, ed. W. Scheidel. Princeton, NJ, 11–52.

Harris, E. M. (1997) "A new solution to the riddle of seischtheia," in *The Development of the Polis in the Archaic Period*, ed. L. Mitchell and P. J. Rhodes. Abingdon, 103–12.

Harris, E. M. (2002a) "Did Solon abolish debt-bondage," *Classical Quarterly* 52, 415–30.

Harris, E. M. (2002b) "Workshop, marketplace and household: the nature of technical specialization in classical Athens and its influence on economy and society," in Cartledge, Cohen, and Foxhall 2002, 67–99.

Harris, E. M. (2007) "Who enforced the law in Classical Athens?," in *Symposion 2005: Vorträge zur griechischen und hellenistischen Rechtsgeschichte. Salerno, 14.–18. September 2005*, ed. E. Cantarella. Vienna, 159–76.

Harris, E. M. (2012) "Homer, Hesiod, and the 'origins' of Greek slavery," *Revue des études anciennes* 114, 345–66.

Harris, E. M. (2013a) "Finley's *Studies in Land and Credit* sixty years later," *Dike* 16, 123–46.

Harris, E. M. (2013b) "Were there business agents in classical Greece? The evidence of some lead letters," in *Legal Documents in Ancient Societies (LDAS)* I, *The Letter: Law, State, Society and the Epistolary Format in the Ancient World*, ed. U. Yivtach-Firanko. Wiesbaden, 105–24.

Harris, E. M. (2014) "Wife, housewife and marketplace: the role of women in the economy of classical Athens," in *Donne che contano nella storia greca*, ed. U. Bultrighini and E. Dimauro. Lanciano, 183–207.

Harris, E. M. (2015) "The meaning of the legal term *symbolaion*, the law about *dikai emporikai* and the role of the *paragraphe* procedure," *Dike* 18, 7–36.

Harris, E. M. (2016) "The legal foundations of economic growth in ancient Greece: the role of property records," in Harris, Lewis, and Woolmer 2016, 116–46.

Harris, E. M. (2019) "Markets in the ancient Greek world: an overview," in *Weights and Marketplaces from the Bronze Age to the Early Modern Period*, ed. L. Rahmstorf and E. Stratford. Kiel, 255–74.

Harris, E. M. and Lewis, D. M. (2016) "Introduction: markets in classical and Hellenistic Greece," in Harris, Lewis, and Woolmer 2016, 1–37.

Harris, E. M., Lewis, D. M., and Woolmer, M. (2016) *The Ancient Greek Economy: Markets, Households and City-States*. Cambridge.

Harris, W. V. (2005) "The Mediterranean and ancient history," in *Rethinking the Mediterranean*, ed. W. V. Harris. Oxford, 1–42.

Harris, W. V. (ed.) (2008) *The Monetary Systems of the Greeks and Romans*. Oxford.

Harrison, A. R. W. (1968) *The Law of Athens* I: *The Family and Property*. Oxford.

Harrison, A. R. W. (1971) *The Law of Athens* II: *Procedure*. Oxford.

Harter-Uibopuu, K. (2002) "Strafklauseln und gerichtliche Kontrolle in der Mysterieninschrift von Andania (IG V I, 1390)," *Dike* 5, 135–59.

Harter-Uibopuu, K. (2003) "Der Hellenenbund des Antigonos I Monophthalmos und des Demetrios Poliorketes, 302/1 v. Chr." in *Symposion 1999: Akten der Gesellschaft für griechische und hellenistische Rechtsgeschichte 14*, ed. G. Thür and F. J. Nieto. Cologne, 315–37.

Harter-Uibopuu, K. (2013) "Epigraphische Quellen zum Archivwesen in den griechischen Poleis des ausgehenden Hellenismus und der Kaiserzeit," in Faraguna 2013a, 273–305.

Harter-Uibopuu, K. (2021) "Fremde vor Gerichten der griechischen Städte," in *Konfliktlösung in der Antike, Handbuch zur Geschichte der Konfliktlösung in Europa*, ed. N. Grotkamp and A. Seelentag. Berlin, 147–56.

Harvey, D. (2005) *A Brief History of Neoliberalism*. Oxford.

Hasenohr C. (2001) "Les monuments des collèges italiens sur l'Agora des Compétaliastes à Délos," in *Constructions publiques et programmes édilitaires en Grèce entre le IIe s. av. J.-C. et le Ier s. ap. J.-C.*, ed. J.-Y. Marc and J.-C. Moretti. Paris, 329–48.

Hatcher, J. and Bailey, M. (2001) *Modelling the Middle Ages: The History and Theory of England's Economic Development*. Oxford.

Hatzaki, E. and Kotsonas, A. (2020) "Knossos and northern central Crete," in Lemos and Kotsonas 2020, vol. 2, 1029–53.

Hatzopoulos, M. (2012) "Τὰ τῶν ἐμποριτῶν φιλάνθρωπα: observations on the Pistiros inscription (SEG XLIII 486)," in Martzavou and Papazarkadas 2012, 14–23.

Hatzopoulos, M. B. (2013–14) "The Athenian standards decree: the Aphytis fragments," *Τεκμήρια* 12, 235–69.

Hawkins, C. (2012) "Manufacturing," in *The Cambridge Companion to the Roman Economy*, ed. W. Scheidel. Cambridge, 175–94.

Hawkins, C. (2016) *Roman Artisans and the Urban Economy*. Cambridge.

Helama, S. et al. (2018) "Volcanic dust veils from sixth century tree-ring isotopes linked to reduced irradiance, primary production and human health," *Scientific Reports* 8, 1339.

Helama, S., Jones, P. D., and Briffa, K. R. (2017) "Dark Ages Cold Period: a literature review and directions for future research," *The Holocene* 27, 1600–6.

Heller, A. (2010) *Das Babylonien der Spätzeit (7.–4. Jh.) in den klassischen und keilschriftlichen Quellen*. Berlin.

Helly, B. (2008) "Encore le blé thessalien. Trois décrets de Larisa (*IG* IX 2, 506) accordant aux Athéniens licence d'exportation et réduction des droits de douane sur leurs achats de blé," *Studi ellenistici* 20, 25–108.

Henkelman, W. F. M. and Folmer, M. L. (2016) "'Your tally is full!' On wooden credit records in and after the Achaemenid empire," in *Silver, Money and Credit: A Tribute to Robartus J. van der Spek on the Occasion of his 65th Birthday, on 18th September 2014*, ed. K. Kleber and R. Pirngruber. Leiden, 133–239.

Herlihy, D. and Klapisch-Zuber, C. (1985) *Tuscans and Their Families: A Study of the Florentine Catasto of 1427*. New Haven, CT.

Herman, G. (1987) *Ritualised Friendship and the Greek City*. Cambridge.

Herrmann, J. (1999) "The exportation of dolomitic marble from Thasos. A short overview," in Koukouli-Chrysanthaki, Muller, and Papadopoulos 1999, 57–65.

Hin, S. (2013) *The Demography of Roman Italy: Population Dynamics in an Ancient Conquest Society, 201 BC–14 CE*. Cambridge.

Hin, S. (2016) "Revisiting urban graveyard theory: migrant flows in Hellenistic and Roman Athens," in *Migration and Mobility in the Early Roman Empire*, ed. L. de Ligt and L. E. Tacoma. Leiden, 234–63.

Hobson, M. S. (2014) "A historiography of the study of the Roman economy: economic growth, development, and neoliberalism," in *TRAC 2013: Proceedings of the Twenty-Third Annual Theoretical Roman Archaeology Conference, King's College, London 2013*, ed. H. Platts, J. Pearce, C. Barron, J. Lundock, and J. Yoo. Oxford, 11–26.

Hodkinson, S. (1988) "Animal husbandry in the Greek polis," in Whittaker 1988, 35–74.

Hodkinson, S. (1992) "Sharecropping and Sparta's economic exploitation of the helots," in *ΦΙΛΟΛΑΚΩΝ: Lakonian Studies in Honour of Hector Catling*, ed. J. M. Sanders. London, 123–34.

Hodkinson, S. (2000) *Property and Wealth in Classical Sparta*. Swansea.

Hoepfner, W. and Schwandner, E.-L. (1994) *Haus und Stadt im klassischen Griechenland*, 2 vols. Munich.

Höghammer, K. (2016) "International networks of an island port in the Hellenistic period – the case of Kos," in Höghammer, Alroth, and Lindgren 2016, 95–165.

Höghammer, K., Alroth, B., and Lindgren, A. (eds.) (2016) *Ancient Ports: The Geography of Connections*. Uppsala.

Holleran, C. (2012) *Shopping in Ancient Rome*. Oxford.

Holling, C. S. and Gunderson, L. H. (2002) "Resilience and adaptive cycles," in *Panarchy: Understanding Transformations in Human and Natural Systems*, ed. L. H. Gunderson and C. S. Holling. Washington DC, 25–62.

Holt, F. L. (2016) *The Treasures of Alexander the Great: How One Man's Wealth Shaped the World*. Oxford.

Honigman, S. (2014) *Tales of High Priests and Taxes: The Books of the Maccabees and the Judean Rebellion Against Antiochos IV*. Berkeley, CA.

Hopkins, K. (1980) "Taxes and trade in the Roman economy (200 BC–AD 200)," *Journal of Roman Studies* 70, 101–25.

Horden, P. and Kinoshita, S. (eds.) (2014) *A Companion to Mediterranean History*. Chichester.

Horden, P. and Purcell, N. (2000) *The Corrupting Sea: A Study of Mediterranean History*. Oxford.

Hornblower, S. (1991) *A Commentary on Thucydides, Vol. I, Books I–III*. Oxford.

Hornblower, S. (2011) *The Greek World, 479–323 BC*. 4th ed. London.

Horváth, L. (2007) "Hypereides' Rede gegen Athenogenes und die zeitgenössische Komödie," *Wiener Studien* 120, 25–34.

Hoskins, J. (1998) *Biographical Objects: How Things Tell the Stories of People's Lives*. London.

Howe, T. (2008) *Pastoral Politics: Animals, Agriculture and Society in Ancient Greece*. Claremont, CA.

Huebner, S. R. (2017) "A Mediterranean family? A comparative approach to the ancient world," in Huebner and Nathan 2017, 3–26.

Huebner, S. R. and Nathan, G. (eds.) (2017) *Mediterranean Families in Antiquity: Households, Extended Families, and Domestic Space*. Chichester.

Huijs, J., Pirngruber, R., and van Leeuwen, B. (2015) "Climate, war and economic development: the case of second century BC Babylon," in van der Spek, van Leeuwen, and van Zanden 2015, 128–48.

Humphrey, J. W., Oleson, J. P., and Sherwood, A. N. (eds.) (1998) *Greek and Roman Technology: A Sourcebook. Annotated Translations of Greek and Latin Texts and Documents.* London.

Hunter, V. J. (1994) *Policing Athens: Social Control in the Attic Lawsuits, 420–320 B.C.* Princeton, NJ.

Huss, W. (2011) *Die Verwaltung des ptolemaiischen Reiches.* Munich.

Huss, W. (2012) *Die Wirtschaft Ägyptens in Hellenistischer Zeit.* Munich.

Inman, R. P. (2008) "Federalism's values and the values of federalism," *National Bureau of Economic Research Working Paper* 13735. www.nber.org/papers/w13735.

Iossif, P. (2015) "Who's wealthier? An estimation of the annual coin production of the Seleucids and the Ptolemies," *Revue Belge de Numismatique* 161, 233–72.

Iossif, P. and Lorber, C. (2021) "Monetary policies, coin production and currency supply in the Seleucid and Ptolemaic Empires," in *Comparing the Ptolemaic and Seleucid Empires*, ed. C. Fischer-Bovet and S. von Reden. Cambridge, 191–232.

Isager, S. and Hansen, H. H. (1975) *Aspects of Athenian Society in the Fourth Century B.C.: A Historical Introduction to and Commentary on the Paragraphe-Speeches and the Speech Against Dionysodorus in the Corpus Demosthenicum (XXXII–XXXVIII and LVI).* Odense.

Isager, S. and Skydsgaard, J. E. (1995) *Ancient Greek Agriculture: An Introduction.* 2nd ed. London.

Ismaelli, T. and Scardozzi, G. (eds.) (2016) *Ancient Quarries and Building Sites in Asia Minor: Research on Hierapolis in Phrygia and Other Cities in South-Western Anatolia: Archaeology, Archaeometry, Conservation.* Rome.

Ivantchik, A. (2017) "The Greeks and the Black Sea: the earliest ideas about the region and the beginning of colonization," in Kozlovskaya 2017, 7–25.

Izdebski, A. et al. (2016a) "Realising consilience: how better communication between archaeologists, historians and natural scientists can transform the study of past climate change in the Mediterranean," *Quaternary Science Reviews* 136, 5–22.

Izdebski, A., Pickett, J., Roberts, N., and Waliszewski, T. (2016b) "The environmental, archaeological and historical evidence for regional climatic changes and their societal impacts in the eastern Mediterranean in late antiquity," *Quaternary Science Reviews* 136, 189–208.

Jakab, E. (1997) *Praedicere und cavere beim Marktkauf: Sachmängel im griechischen und römischen Recht.* Munich.

Jameson, M. H. (1977–8) "Agriculture and slavery in classical Athens," *The Classical Journal* 73, 122–45.

Jameson, M. H. (1988) "Sacrifice and animal husbandry in classical Greece," in Whittaker 1988, 87–119.

Jameson, M. H. (1992) "Agricultural labour in ancient Greece," in Wells 1992, 135–46.

Jameson, M. H. (1994) "Class in the ancient Greek countryside," in Doukellis and Mendoni 1994, 55–63.

Jameson, M. H., Runnels, C. N., and van Andel, T. H. (1994) *A Greek Countryside: The Southern Argolid from Prehistory to the Present Day.* Stanford, CA.

Jew, D. (forthcoming) *The Probable Past: Agriculture and Carrying Capacity in Ancient Greece.* Cambridge.

Joannès, F. (2000) "Relations entre intérêts privés et biens des sanctuaires à l'époque néo-babylonienne," in Bongenaar 2000, 25–41.

Johnston, A. W. (1972) "The rehabilitation of Sostratos," *Parola del Passato* 27, 416–23.

Johnstone, S. (2011) *A History of Trust in Ancient Greece.* Chicago.

Jones, J. E., Graham, A. J., and Sackett, L. H. (1973) "An Attic country house below the Cave of Pan at Vari," *The Annual of the British School at Athens* 68, 355–452.

Jones, J. E., Sackett, L. H., and Graham, A. J. (1962) "The Dema house in Attica," *The Annual of the British School at Athens* 57, 75–114.

Jones, N. F. (2004) *Rural Athens Under the Democracy.* Philadelphia.

Johstono, P. (2020) *The Army of Ptolemaic Egypt, 323-204 BC: An Institutional and Operational History.* Barnsley.

Jung, R. and Mehofer, M. (2013) "Mycenaean Greece and Bronze Age Italy: cooperation, trade or war?," *Archäologisches Korrespondenzblatt* 43.2, 175–93.

Jursa, M. (1998) *Der Tempelzehnt in Babylonien: Vom siebenten bis zum dritten Jahrhundert v. Chr.* Münster.

Jursa, M. (2004) "Grundzüge der Wirtschaftsformen Babyloniens im ersten Jahrtausend v. Chr.," in *Commerce and Monetary Systems in the Ancient World: Means of Transmission and Cultural Interaction,* ed. R. Rollinger and C. Ulf. Stuttgart, 115–36.

Jursa, M. (2009) "Business companies in Babylonia in the first millennium B.C.: structure, economic strategies, social setting," in *The Knowledge Economy and Technological Capabilities: Egypt, the Near East and the Mediterranean, 2nd Millennium B.C.–1st Millennium A.D.,* ed. M. Wissa. Sabadel, 53–68.

Jursa, M. (2010). *Aspects of the Economic History of Babylonia in the First Millennium BC: Economic Geography, Economic Mentalities, Agriculture, the Use of Money and the Problem of Economic Growth.* Münster.

Jursa, M. (2011) "Taxation and service obligations in Babylonia from Nebuchadnezzar to Darius and the evidence for Darius' tax reform," in *Herodot und das Persische Weltreich,* ed. R. Rollinger, B. Truschnegg, and R. Bichler. Wiesbaden, 431–48.

Jursa, M. (2014) "Factor markets from the late seventh to the third century BCE," *Journal of the Economic and Social History of the Orient* 57.2, 173–202.

Jursa, M. (2015) "Market performance and market integration in Babylonia in the 'long sixth century' BC," in van der Spek, van Leeuwen, and van Zanden 2015, 83–106.

Jursa, M. (2018) "Money, silver and trust in Mesopotamia: the first millennium BC," in *Money, Currency and Crisis: In Search of Trust, 2000 BC to AD 2000,* ed. R. J. van der Spek and B. van Leeuwen. London, 102–31.

Kakavogianni, O. and Anetakis, M. (2012) "Les agoras commerciales des dèmes antiques de la Mésogée et de la région du Laurion," in Chankowski and Karvonis 2012, 185–99.

Kallet, L. (2001) *Money and the Corrosion of Power in Thucydides: The Sicilian Expedition and its Aftermath.* Berkeley, CA.

Kallet-Marx, L. (1993) *Money, Expense, and Naval Power in Thucydides' History 1–5.24.* Berkeley, CA.

Kapparis, K. A. (2018) *Prostitution in the Ancient Greek World.* Berlin.

Karapiperis, L. and Katsoulis, B. (1969) "Contribution to the study of rainfall in some central and western parts of Greece," *Memoirs of the National Observatory Athens* 19, 1–27.

Karouzou, E. (2020) "Thessaly," in Lemos and Kotsonas 2020, vol. 2, 883–912.

Karvonis, P. (2008) "Les installations commerciales dans la ville de Délos à l'époque hellénistique," *Bulletin de correspondance hellénique* 132, 182–211.

Karvonis, P. and Malmary, J.-J. (2018) "Délos, entrepôt méditerranéen: le stockage dans les installations commerciales," in Chankowski, Lafon, and Virlouvet 2018, 169–94.

Karyškovskij, P. O. (1988) *Monety Ol'vii: Očerk denežnogo obraščenija Severo-Zapadnogo Pričernomor'ja v antičnuju ėpochu.* Kyiv.

Kaser, M. (1944) "Der altgriechische Eigentumsschutz," *Zeitschrift der Savigny-Stiftung für Rechtsgeschichte. Romanistische Abteilung* 64, 134–205.

Kasseri, A. (2012) "Phoenician trade amphorae from Methone," in *Kerameus Paides*, ed. E. Kephalidou and D. Tsiafaki. Thessaloniki, 299–308.

Kavonis, P. and Malmary, J.-J. (2018) "Le stockage dans les installations commerciales," in Chankowski, Lafon, and Virlouvet 2018, 169–94.

Kaye, N. (2015) "Taxation in the Greco-Roman world: the Hellenistic east," *Oxford Handbooks Online*. DOI: 10.1093/oxfordhb/9780199935390.013.36.

Kaye, N. and Amitay, O. (2015) "Kleopatra's dowry: taxation and sovereignty between Hellenistic kingdoms," *Historia* 64, 131–55.

Keenan, J. G., Manning, J. G., and Yiftach-Firanko, U. (eds.) (2014) *Law and Legal Practice in Egypt from Alexander to the Arab Conquest: A Selection of Papyrological Sources in Translation, with Introductions and Commentary*. Cambridge.

Kehoe, D. P., Ratzan, D., and Yiftach-Firanko, U. (eds.) (2015) *Law and Transaction Costs in Ancient History*. Ann Arbor, MI.

Kelly, M. and Ó Gráda, C. (2014a) "The waning of the Little Ice Age: climate change in early modern Europe," *Journal of Interdisciplinary History* 44, 301–25.

Kelly, M. and Ó Gráda, C. (2014b) "Debating the Little Ice Age," *Journal of Interdisciplinary History* 45, 57–68.

Kennedy, R. F. (2014) *Immigrant Women in Athens: Gender, Ethnicity, and Citizenship in the Classical City*. New York.

Keyser, P. T. and Clark, D. D. (2001) "Analyzing and interpreting the metallurgy of early electrum coins," in Balmuth 2001, 105–26.

Kiderlen, E., Bode, M., Hauptmann, A., and Bassiakos, Y. (2016) "Tripod cauldrons produced at Olympia give evidence for trade with copper from Faynan (Jordan) to south west Greece, c. 950–750 BCE," *Journal of Archaeological Science: Reports* 8, 303–13.

Kierstead, J. and Klapaukh, R. (2018) "The distribution of wealthy Athenians in the Attic demes," in Canevaro, Erskine, Gray, and Ober 2018, 376–402.

Kilian-Dirlmeyer, I. (1985) "Fremde Weihungen in Griechischen Heiligtümern vom 8. bis zum Beginn des 7. Jahrhunderts v. Chr.," *Jahrbuch des Römisch-Germanischen Zentralmuseums Mainz* 32, 215–54.

Killen, J. T. (2007) "Critique: a view from the tablets," in Galaty and Parkinson 2007, 114–17.

Killen, J. T. (2008) "The Mycenaean economy," in *A Companion to Linear B: Mycenaean Greek Texts and Their World*, vol. 1, ed. Y. Duhoux and A. Morpurgo Davies. Louvain-la-Neuve, 159–200.

Killen, S. (2017) *Parasema: Offizielle Symbole griechischer Poleis und Bundesstaaten*. Wiesbaden.

Kim, H. S. (2002) "Small change and the moneyed economy," in Cartledge, Cohen, and Foxhall 2002, 44–51.

Kim, H. S. and Kroll, J. H. (2008) "A hoard of archaic coins of Colophon and unminted silver (CH 1.3)," *American Journal of Numismatics* 20, 53–103.

Kintigh, K. W. and Ingram, S. E. (2018) "Was the drought really responsible? Assessing statistical relationships between climate extremes and cultural transitions," *Journal of Archaeological Science* 89, 25–31.

Kinzl, K. H. (ed.) (2006) *A Companion to the Classical Greek World*. Malden, MA.

Kistler, E., Öhlinger, B., Mohr, M., and Hoernes, M. (eds.) (2015) *Sanctuaries and the Power of Consumption: Networking and the Formation of Elites in the Archaic Western Mediterranean World*. Wiesbaden.

Kleber, K. (2015) "Taxation in the Achaemenid empire," *Oxford Handbooks Online.* DOI: 10.1093/oxfordhb/9780199935390.013.34.

Klein, N. L. and Glowacki, K. (2016) "The architecture of Vronda," in Gesell and Day 2016, 1–46.

Kleinfeld, R. (2012) *Advancing the Rule of Law Abroad: Next Generation Reform.* Washington DC.

Klinkott, H. (2005). *Der Satrap: Ein achaimenidischer Amtsträger und seine Handlungsspielräume.* Frankfurt am Main.

Klinkott, H., Kubisch, S., and Müller-Wollermann, R. (eds.) (2007) *Geschenke und Steuern, Zölle und Tribute: Antike Abgabenformen in Anspruch und Wirklichkeit.* Leiden.

Knapp, A. B. and Manning, S. W. (2016) "Crisis in context: the end of the Late Bronze Age in the eastern Mediterranean," *American Journal of Archaeology* 120, 99–149.

Knapp, A. B. and van Dommelen, P. (eds.) (2014) *The Cambridge Prehistory of the Bronze and Iron Age Mediterranean.* Cambridge.

Knappett, C. (2011) *An Archaeology of Interaction: Network Perspectives on Material Culture and Society.* Oxford.

Knappett, C. (2013) "Introduction: why networks?," in *Network Analysis in Archaeology: New Approaches to Regional Interaction,* ed. C. Knappet. Oxford, 3–15.

Kolb, F. (2008) "Terrassenkomplexe, Pressanlagen und Wirtschaftsgebäude im Yavu-Bergland," in *Lykische Studien, Vol. 8: Keramik, Münzen, Kirchen und Wirtschaftskomplexe des zentrallykischen Yavu-Berglandes (Gebiet von Kyaneai),* ed. F. Kolb. Bonn, 195–246.

Kolonas, L., Sarri, K., Margariti, C., Vanden Berghe, I., Skals, I., and Nosch, M.-L. (2017) "Heirs of the loom? Funerary textiles from Stamna (Aitolia, Greece): a preliminary analysis," in *ΕΣΠΕΡΟΣ/Hesperos: The Aegean Seen from the West,* ed. M. Fotiadis, R. Laffineur, Y. Lolos, and A. Vlachopoulos. Leuven, 533–42.

Konuk, K. (2012) "Asia Minor to the Ionian Revolt," in Metcalf 2012, 43–60.

Kosmin, P. (2014) *The Land of the Elephant Kings: Space, Territory, and Ideology in the Seleucid Kingdom.* Cambridge, MA.

Kostoglou, M. (forthcoming) "Iron in Iron Age Greece (1200–800 BC)," in *Cambridge Companion to the Greek Early Iron Age,* ed. C. Antonaccio and J. Carter. Cambridge.

Kotsakis, K. (2017) "Trenches, borders, and boundaries: prehistoric research in Greek Macedonia," in Shapland and Stefani 2017, 58–68.

Kotsonas, A. (2006) "'Wealth and status in Iron Age Knossos," *Oxford Journal of Archaeology* 25.2, 149–72.

Kotsonas, A. (2012) "Η ενεπίγραφη κεραμική του 'Υπογείου': προέλευση, τυπολογία, χρονολόγηση και ερμηνεία,"in *Μεθώνη Πιερίας I: Επιγραφές, χαράγματα και εμπορικά σύμβολα στη γεωμετρική και αρχαϊκή κεραμική από το 'Υπόγειο' της Μεθώνης Πιερίας στη Μακεδονία,* ed. M. Bessios, Y. Tzifopoulos, and A. Kotsonas. Thessaloniki, 113–303.

Kotsonas, A. (2016) "Politics of periodization and the archaeology of early Greece," *American Journal of Archaeology* 120.2, 239–70.

Kotsonas, A. and Mokrišová, J. (2020) "Mobility, migration and colonisation," in Lemos and Kotsonas 2020, vol. 1, 217–46.

Kotsonas, A. et al. (2017) "Transport amphorae from Methone: an interdisciplinary study of production and trade ca. 700 BCE," in Clay, Malkin, and Tzifopoulos 2017, 9–19.

Koukouli-Chrysanthaki, Ch., Muller, A., and Papadopoulos, S. (eds.) (1999) *Thasos: matières premières et technologie de la préhistoire à nos jours.* Athens.

Kouli, K. (2012) "Vegetation development and human activities in Attiki (SE Greece) during the last 5,000 years," *Vegetation History and Archaeobotany* 21, 267–78.

Kowalzig, B. (2018) "Cults, cabotage and connectivity: experimenting with religious and economic networks in the Greco-Roman Mediterranean," in Leidwanger and Knappett 2018, 83–131.

Kozlovskaya, V. (ed.) (2017) *The Northern Black Sea in Antiquity: Networks, Connectivity, and Cultural Interactions.* Cambridge.

Kraay, C. M. (1964) "Hoards, small change and the origin of coinage," *The Journal of Hellenic Studies* 84, 76–91.

Krämer, R. P. (2016) "Trading goods – trading gods: Greek sanctuaries in the Mediterranean and their role as emporia and 'ports of trade' (7th–6th century BCE)," *Distant Worlds Journal* 1, 75–98.

Kramer-Hajos, M. (2016) *Mycenaean Greece and the Aegean World: Palace and Province in the Late Bronze Age.* Cambridge.

Kremydi, S. and Chryssanthaki-Nagle, K. (2016) "Aigeai and Amphipolis: numismatic circulation in two major Macedonian cities," in Duyrat and Grandjean 2016, 157–76.

Krmnicek, S. (2009) "Das Konzept der Objektbiographie in der antiken Numismatik," in *Coins in Context* I: *New Perspectives for the Interpretation of Coin Finds*, ed. H.-M. von Kaenel and F. Kemmers. Mainz, 47–59.

Kroll, J. H. (1979) "A chronology of early Athenian bronze coinage, ca. 350–325 BC," in *Greek Numismatics and Archaeology: Essays in Honor of Margaret Thompson*, ed. O. Mørkholm and N. M. Waggoner. Wetteren, 139–54.

Kroll, J. H. (1993) *The Athenian Agora. Vol. 26. The Greek Coins.* Princeton, NJ.

Kroll, J. H. (1996) "The Piraeus 1902 hoard of plated drachms and tetradrachms (*IGCH* 46)," in *ΧΑΡΑΚΤΗΡ – Αφιέρωμα Στη Μάντω Οικονομίδου.* Athens, 139–46.

Kroll, J. H. (2001) "Observations on monetary instruments in pre-coinage Greece," in Balmuth 2001, 77–92.

Kroll, J. H. (2008a) "Early Iron Age balance weights at Lefkandi, Euboea," *Oxford Journal of Archaeology* 27.1, 37–48.

Kroll, J. H. (2008b) "The monetary use of weighed bullion in archaic Greece," in Harris 2008, 12–37.

Kroll, J. H. (2009) "What about coinage?," in Ma, Papazarkadas, and Parker 2009, 195–209.

Kroll, J. H. (2015) "Small bronze tokens from the Athenian Agora: symbola or kolly-boi?," in Wartenberg and Amandry 2015, 107–16.

Kron, G. (2005) "Anthropometry, physical anthropology, and the reconstruction of ancient health, nutrition, and living standards," *Historia* 54, 68–83.

Kron, G. (2011) "The distribution of wealth at Athens in comparative perspective," *Zeitschrift für Papyrologie und Epigraphik* 179, 129–38.

Kron, G. (2014) "Comparative evidence and the reconstruction of the ancient economy: Greco-Roman housing and the level and distribution of wealth and income," in de Callataÿ 2014, 123–46.

Kron, G. (2015) "Classical Athenian trade in comparative perspective: literary and archaeological evidence," in Harris, Lewis, and Woolmer 2016, 356–80.

Kron, G. (forthcoming) "Growth and decline. Forms of growth. Estimating growth in the Greek world," in *The Oxford Handbook of Economies in the Classical World*, ed. E. Lo Cascio, A. Bresson, and F. Velde. Oxford.

Krul, M. (2018) *The New Institutional Economic History of Douglass C. North: A Critical Interpretation*. New York.

Kuhrt, A. (1987) "Berossus' Babyloniaka and Seleucid rule in Babylonia," in Kuhrt and Sherwin-White 1987, 32–56.

Kuhrt, A. (1990) "Alexander and Babylon," in *Achaemenid History, Vol. 5: The Roots of European Tradition*, ed. H. Sancisi-Weerdenburg and J. W. Drijvers. Leiden, 121–30.

Kuhrt, A. and Sherwin-White, S. (eds.) (1987) *Hellenism in the East: The Interaction of Greek and Non-Greek Civilizations from Syria to Central Asia after Alexander*. London.

Kuhrt, A. and Sherwin-White, S. (1993) *From Samarkhand to Sardis: A New Approach to the Seleucid Empire*. London.

Kurke, L. (1991) *The Traffic in Praise: Pindar and the Poetics of Social Economy*. Ithaca, NY.

Kurke, L. (1999) *Coins, Bodies, Games, and Gold: The Politics of Meaning in Archaic Greece*. Princeton, NJ.

Kuznets, S. S. (1965) *Economic Growth and Structure: Selected Essays*. New York.

Ladstätter, S., Pirson, F., and Schmidts, T. (eds.) (2015) *Harbours and Harbour Cities in the Eastern Mediterranean from Antiquity to the Byzantine Period: Recent Discoveries and Current Approaches*. Istanbul.

Lagia, A. (2015a) "Diet and the polis: an isotopic study of diet in Athens and Laurion during the classical, Hellenistic and imperial Roman periods," in Papathanasiou, Richards, and Fox 2015, 119–45.

Lagia, A. (2015b) "The potential and limitations of bioarchaeological investigations in classical contexts in Greece: an example from the polis of Athens," in Haggis and Antonaccio 2015, 149–73.

Lambert, S. D. (1997) *Rationes Centesimarum: Sales of Public Land in Lykourgan Athens*. Amsterdam.

Lambrinoudakis, V. and Zaphiropoulou, P. (1985) "Ἀνασκαφή Νάξου: Πλατεία Μητροπόλεως," *Praktika tes en Athenais Archaiologikes Etaireias* 140, 162–7.

Lamont, J. L. (2015) "A new commercial curse tablet from classical Athens," *Zeitschrift für Papyrologie und Epigraphik* 196, 159–74.

Lang, F. (2005) *Archaische Siedlungen in Griechenland: Struktur und Entwicklung*. Berlin.

Lang, F. (2007) "House – community – settlement: the new concept of living in archaic Greece," in *Building Communities: House, Settlement and Society in the Aegean and Beyond*, ed. R. Westgate, N. Fisher, and J. Whitley. London, 183–93.

Langdon, M. K. (2015) "Herders' graffiti," in *Axon: Studies in Honor of Ronald S. Stroud*, ed. A. P. Matthaiou and N. Papazarkadas. Athens, 49–58.

Lanni, A. (2006) *Law and Justice in the Courts of Classical Athens*. Cambridge.

Larsen, C. S. (2015) *Bioarchaeology: Interpreting Behavior from the Human Skeleton*. 2nd ed. Cambridge.

Launaro, A. (2016) "Finley and the ancient economy," in *M. I. Finley: An Ancient Historian and His Impact*, ed. D. Jew, R. Osborne, and M. Scott. Cambridge, 227–49.

Lawall, M. (2011) "Greek amphoras in the archaeological record," in *Pottery in the Archaeological Record: Greece and Beyond*, ed. M. L. Lawall and J. Lund. Aarhus, 37–50.

Lawall, M. (2013) "Patterns in the production and distribution of transport amphoras in the 5th century BC: an archaeological perspective on economic change," in Slawisch 2013, 103–20.

Lawall, M. (2016) "Transport amphoras, markets, and changing practices in the economies of Greece, sixth to first centuries BCE," in Harris, Lewis, and Woolmer 2016, 254–73.

Lawall, M. and van Alfen, P. (eds.) (2011) *Caveat Emptor: A Collection of Papers on Limitations in Ancient Greco-Roman Commerce*. Rahden.

Lazer, E. (2009) *Resurrecting Pompeii*. London.

Le Rider, G. (1977) *Le monnayage d'argent et d'or de Philippe II frappé en Macédoine de 359 à 294*. Paris.

Le Rider, G. (1989) "À propos d'un passage des *Poroi* de Xénophon: la question du change et les monnaies incuses d'Italie du Sud," in *Kraay-Mørkholm Essays: Numismatic Studies in Memory of C. M. Kraay and O. Mørkholm*, ed. G. Le Rider, K. Jenkins, N. Waggoner, and U. Westermark. Louvain-la-Neuve, 159–72.

Le Rider, G. (2001) *La naissance de la monnaie: pratiques monétaires de l'Orient ancien*. Paris.

Le Rider, G. and de Callataÿ, F. (2006) *Les Séleucides et les Ptolémées: l'héritage monétaire et financier d'Alexandre le Grand*. Monaco.

Le Rider, G. and Verdan, S. (2002) "La trouvaille d'Érétrie: réserve d'un orfèvre ou dépôt monétaire?," *Antike Kunst* 45, 133–52.

Leidwanger, J. and Knappett, C. (eds.) (2018) *Maritime Networks in the Ancient Mediterranean World*. Cambridge.

Lemos, I. S. (2002) *The Protogeometric Aegean: The Archaeology of the Late Eleventh and Tenth Centuries* BC. Oxford.

Lemos, I. S. (2012) "Euboea and Central Greece in the postpalatial and early Greek periods," *Archaeological Reports* 58, 19–27.

Lemos, I. S. (2014) "Communities in transformation: an archaeological survey from the 12th to the 9th century BC," *Pharos* 20.1, 161–91.

Lemos, I. S. (2020) "The transition from the Late Bronze to the Early Iron Age in Euboea and the Euboean Gulf," in *Euboica II, Pithekoussai and Euboea between East and West: Proceedings of the Conference, Lacco Ameno (Ischia, Naples), 14–17 May 2018*, vol. 1, ed. T. E. Cinquantaquattro and M. D'Acunto. Naples, 37–54.

Lemos, I. S. and Kotsonas, A. (eds.) (2020) *A Companion to the Archaeology of Early Greece and the Mediterranean*, 2 vols. Hoboken, NJ.

Lenormant, F. (1878) *La monnaie dans l'antiquité: leçons professées dans la chaire d'archéologie près la Bibliothèque Nationale en 1875–1877*, vol. 1. Paris.

Leppin, H. (1995) "Zur Entwicklung der Verwaltung öffentlicher Gelder im Athen des 4. Jahrhunderts v. Chr.," in *Die athenische Demokratie im 4. Jahrhundert v. Chr.*, ed. W. Eder. Stuttgart, 557–71.

Lewis, D. M. (1959) "Attic manumissions," *Hesperia* 28, 208–38.

Lewis, D. M. (1968) "Dedications of *phialai* at Athens," *Hesperia* 37, 368–80.

Lewis, D. M. (2016) "Appendix: commodities in classical Athens: the evidence of old comedy," in Harris, Lewis, and Woolmer 2016, 381–98.

Lewis, D. M. (2018a) "Behavioural economics and the economics of behaviour," in Canevaro, Erskine, Gray, and Ober 2018, 15–46.

Lewis, D. M. (2018b) *Greek Slave Systems in the Eastern Mediterranean Context, c. 800–146* BC. Oxford.

Lindenlauf, A. (2003) "The sea as a place of no return in ancient Greece," *World Archaeology* 35, 416–33.

Lionello, P. (2012a) "Foreword," in Lionello 2012b, xxi–xxiii.

Lionello, P. (ed.) (2012b) *The Climate of the Mediterranean Region: From the Past to the Future*. Amsterdam.

Lis, B. and Rückl, Š. (2011) "Our storerooms are full: impressed pithoi from Late Bronze/Early Iron Age East Lokris and Phokis and their socio-economic significance," in *Our Cups Are Full: Pottery and Society in the Aegean Bronze Age: Papers Presented to Jeremy B. Rutter on the Occasion of His 65th Birthday*, ed. W. Gauß, M. Lindblom, R. A. K. Smith, and J. C. Wright. Oxford, 154–68.

Lissarrague, F. (1990) *The Aesthetics of the Greek Banquet: Images of Wine and Ritual*. Princeton, NJ.

List, C. and Spiekermann, K. (2013) "Methodological individualism and holism in political science: a reconciliation," *American Political Science Review* 107, 629–43.

Lister, D. L. and Jones, M. K. (2013) "Is naked barley an eastern or a western crop? The combined evidence of archaeobotany and genetics," *Vegetation History and Archaeobotany* 22, 439–46.

Liston, M. A. (2017) "Human skeletal remains," in *The Athenian Agora, Vol. 36: The Early Iron Age: The Cemeteries*, ed. J. K. Papadopoulos and E. L. Smithson. Princeton, NJ, 503–60.

Livarda, A. and Kotzamani, G. (2019) "An exploration of the social role of plants in rituals in prehistoric Aegean with reference to the site of Xeropolis, Lefkandi, Euboea," in *Beyond the Polis: Ritual, Rites, and Cults in Early and Archaic Greece (12th–6th Centuries* BC*)*, ed. I. S. Lemos and A. Tsingarida. Brussels, 289–302.

Livieratou, A. (2020) "East Locris and Phocis," in Lemos and Kotsonas 2020, vol. 2, 815–35.

Lockyear, K. (2007) *Patterns and Process in Late Roman Republican Coin Hoards, 157–2 BC*. Oxford.

Lohmann, H. (1992) "Agriculture and country life in classical Attica," in Wells 1992, 29–60.

Lohmann, H. (1993) *Atene: Forschungen zu Siedlungs- und Wirtschaftsstruktur des klassischen Attika*. Cologne.

Lohmann, H. (1995) "Die Chora Athens im 4. Jahrhundert v. Chr.: Festungswesen, Bergbau und Siedlungen," in Walter 1995, 515–53.

Lohmann, H. (2004) "Milet und die Milesia: Eine antike Großstadt und ihr Umland im Wandel der Zeit," in *Chora und Polis*, ed. F. Kolb. Munich, 325–60.

Loomis, W. T. (1992) *The Spartan War Fund: IG v 1, 1 and a New Fragment*. Stuttgart.

Loomis, W. T. (1998) *Wages, Welfare Costs and Inflation in Classical Athens*. Ann Arbor, MI.

Lorber, C. (2012) "The coinage of the Ptolemies," in Metcalf 2012, 211–34.

Lorber, C. (2013) "The Grand Mutation: Ptolemaic bronze currency in the second century B.C.," in *Egitto dai Faraoni agli Arabi. Atti del Convegno Egitto: Amministrazione, economia, società, cultura dai Faraoni agli Arabi*, ed. S. Bussi. Rome and Pisa, 135–47.

Lorber, C. (2018) *Catalogue of Ptolemaic Coins. Part 1: Ptolemy I to IV*. New York.

Lorber, C. and Fischer-Bovet, C. (2020) "Getting paid in Ptolemaic Egypt in the 2nd and 1st centuries BC," in Faucher 2020, 169–202.

Lorber, C. and Hoover, O. (2003) "An unpublished tetradrachm issued by the artists of Dionysus," *Numismatic Chronicle* 163, 59–68.

Low, P. (2018) "Hegemonic legitimacy (and its absence) in classical Greece," in Canevaro, Erskine, Gray, and Ober 2018, 433–54.

Luján, E. R. (2011) "Payment and trade terminology on linear B tablets," in *Barter, Money and Coinage in the Ancient Mediterranean (10th–1st Centuries* BC*)*, ed. M. Paz García-Bellido, L. Callegarin, and A. Jiménez Díaz. Madrid, 25–32.

Luke, J. (2003) *Ports of Trade, Al Mina and Geometric Greek Pottery in the Levant*. Oxford.

Lund, J. (2000) "Rhodian amphorae in Rhodes and Alexandria as evidence of trade," in *Hellenistic Rhodes: Politics, Culture and Society*, ed. P. Bilde, T. Engberg-Pedersen, V. Gabrielsen, L. Hannestad, and J. Zahle. Aarhus, 187–204.

Luraghi, N. (2006) "Traders, pirates, warriors: the proto-history of Greek mercenary soldiers in the Eastern Mediterranean," *Phoenix* 40, 21–47.

Luterbacher, J. et al. (2012) "A review of 2000 years of paleoclimatic evidence in the Mediterranean," in Lionello 2012b, 87–185.

Luterbacher, J. et al. (2020) "Past pandemics and climate variability across the Mediterranean," *Euro-Mediterranean Journal for Environmental Integration* 5, 46. DOI: https://doi.org/10.1007/s41207-020-00197-5.

Lytle, E. (2010) "Fish lists in the wilderness: the social and economic history of a Boiotian price decree," *Hesperia* 79, 253–303.

Lytle, E. (2013) "Farmers into sailors: ship maintenance, Greek agriculture and the Athenian monopoly on Kean ruddle (IG II^2 1128)," *Greek, Roman, and Byzantine Studies* 53, 520–50.

Lyttkens, C. H. (2013) *Economic Analysis of Institutional Change in Ancient Greece: Politics, Taxation, and Rational Behaviour*. London.

Ma, J. (2020) "Aršama the vampire," in *Aršāma and His World. The Bodleian Letters in Context* III: *Aršāma's World*, ed. C. Tuplin and J. Ma. Oxford, 187–208.

Ma, J., Papazarkadas, N., and Parker, R. (eds.) (2009) *Interpreting the Athenian Empire*. London.

Mac Sweeney, N. (2013) *Foundation Myths and Politics in Ancient Ionia*. Cambridge.

Mac Sweeney, N. (ed.) (2014) *Foundation Myths in Ancient Societies: Dialogues and Discourses*. Philadelphia.

Mack, W. (2015) *Proxeny and Polis: Institutional Networks in the Ancient World*. Oxford.

Mackil, E. (2004) "Wandering cities: alternatives to catastrophe in the Greek polis," *American Journal of Archaeology* 108, 493–516.

Mackil, E. (2012) "The Greek *koinon*," in *The Oxford Handbook of the State in the Ancient Near East and Mediterranean*, ed. P. Bang and W. Scheidel. Oxford, 304–23.

Mackil, E. (2013) *Creating a Common Polity: Religion, Economy, and Politics in the Making of the Greek Koinon*. Berkeley, CA.

Mackil, E. (2015a) "The economics of federation in ancient Greece," in Beck and Funke 2015, 487–502.

Mackil, E. (2015b) "The Greek polis and *koinon*," in Monson and Scheidel 2015, 469–91.

Mackil, E. (2018) "Property security and its limits in classical Greece," in Canevaro, Erskine, Gray, and Ober 2018, 315–43.

Mackil, E. and van Alfen, P. (2006) "Cooperative coinage," in van Alfen 2006, 201–46.

Maffi, A. (2005) "De la loi de Solon à la loi d'Ilion ou comment défendre la démocratie," in *La violence dans les mondes grec et romain*, ed. J.-M. Bertrand. Paris, 137–62.

Magnetto, A., Erdas, D., and Carusi, C. (eds.) (2010) *Nuove ricerche sulla legge granaria ateniese del 374/3 a.C.* Florence.

Maier, F. G. (1959) *Griechische Mauerbauinschriften*. Heidelberg.

Malama, P. (2012) "Archaic pottery from ancient Galepsos," in Tiverios, Misaïlidou-Despotidou, Manakidou, and Arvanitaki 2012, 349–57.

Malkin, I. (2011) *A Small Greek World: Networks in the Ancient Mediterranean*. Oxford.

Malkin, I., Constantakopoulou, C., and Panagopoulou, K. (eds.) (2007a) *Greek and Roman Networks in the Mediterranean: Mediterranean Historical Review Special Issue 22.1.* London.

Malkin, I., Constantakopoulou, C., and Panagopoulou, K. (2007b) "Preface: networks in the ancient Mediterranean," in Malkin, Constantakopoulou, and Panagopoulou 2007a, 1–9.

Malthus, T. R. (1803) *An Essay on the Principle of Population: Or, a View of its Past and Present Effects on Human Happiness: With an Inquiry into our Prospects Respecting the Future Removal or Mitigation of the Evils which it Occasions.* 2nd ed. London.

Mamara, A. et al. (2017) "High resolution air temperature climatology for Greece for the period 1971–2000," *Meteorological Applications* 24, 191–205.

Manakidou, E. (2012) "Imported archaic Cycladic, Corinthian, and Attic pottery in ancient Oisyme," in Tiverios, Misaïlidou-Despotidou, Manakidou, and Arvanitaki 2012, 359–70.

Manning, J. G. (2003) *Land and Power in Ptolemaic Egypt: The Structure of Land Tenure.* Cambridge.

Manning, J. G. (2005) "Texts, contexts, subtexts and interpretative frameworks: beyond the parochial and toward (dynamic) modelling of the Ptolemaic economy," *Bulletin of the American Society of Papyrologists* 42, 235–56.

Manning, J. G. (2007) "Ptolemaic Egypt," in Scheidel, Morris, and Saller 2007, 434–59.

Manning, J. G. (2010) *The Last Pharaohs. Egypt under the Ptolemies 305–30 BC.* Princeton, NJ.

Manning, J. G. (2011) "Networks, hierarchies, and markets in the Ptolemaic economy," in Archibald, Davies, and Gabrielsen 2011, 296–323.

Manning, J. G. (2015a) "Hellenistic traders," in *Traders in the Ancient Mediterranean,* ed. T. Howe. Chicago, 101–40.

Manning, J. G. (2015b) "Ptolemaic governance and transaction costs," in Kehoe, Ratzan, and Yiftach-Firanko 2015, 51–79.

Manning, J. G. (2018) *The Open Sea: The Economic Life of the Ancient Mediterranean World from the Iron Age to the Rise of Rome.* Princeton, NJ.

Manning, J. G. and Morris, I. (eds.) (2005) *The Ancient Economy: Evidence and Models.* Stanford, CA.

Manning, J. G., Ludlow, F., Stine, A. R., Boos, W. R., Sigl, M., and Marlon, J. R. (2017) "Volcanic suppression of Nile summer flooding triggers revolt and constrains interstate conflict in ancient Egypt," *Nature Communications* 8, 1–10.

Manning, S. W. (2013) "The Roman world and climate: context, relevance of climate change, and some issues," in *The Ancient Mediterranean Environment between Science and History,* ed. W. V. Harris. Leiden, 103–70.

Manning, S. W. (2018) "Some perspectives on the frequency of significant, historically forcing drought and subsistence crises in Anatolia and Region," in *Water and Power in Past Societies,* ed. E. Holt. Albany, NY, 279–95.

Maran, J. and Papadimitriou, A. (2006) "Forschungen im Stadtgebiet von Tiryns 1999–2002," *Archäologischer Anzeiger* 2006.1, 97–169.

Maran, J. and Papadimitriou, A. (2016) "Gegen den Strom der Geschichte. Die nördliche Unterstadt von Tiryns: ein gescheitertes Urbanisierungsprojeckt der mykenischen Nachpalastzeit," *Archäologischer Anzeiger* 2016.2, 19–118.

Marcellesi, M.-C. (2000) "Commerce, monnaies locales et monnaies communes dans les États hellénistiques," *Revue des études grecques* 113.2, 326–58.

Marcellesi, M.-C. (2004) *Milet des Hécatomnides à la domination romaine: pratiques monétaires et histoire de la cité du IVe au IIe siècle av. J.-C.* Mayence.

Marcellesi, M.-C. (2012), *Pergame de la fin du Ve au début du Ier siècle avant J.-C.: pratiques monétaires et histoire.* Pisa.

Marek, C. (1984) *Die Proxenie.* Frankfurt/Main.

Marek, C. (2016) *In the Land of a Thousand Gods: A History of Asia Minor in the Ancient World*. Princeton, NJ.

Maresch, K. (1996) *Bronze und Silber: Papyrologische Beiträge zur Geschichte der Währung im ptolemäischen und römischen Ägypten bis zum 2. Jahrhundert n. Chr.* Wiesbaden.

Maresch, K. (2012) *Ptolemäische Bankpapyri aus dem Herakleopolites (P.Herakl.Bank): Papyri der Sammlungen in Heidelberg, Köln und Wien*. Paderborn.

Margaritis, E. (2013) "Archaeobotanical analysis: seed assemblage from the refuse pit Fo221," in Verdan 2013, 267–70.

Marinescu, C. (2014) "Why institutions matter: from economic development to development economics," *European Review* 22, 469–90.

Mariolopoulos, E. G. (1925) *Étude sur le climat de la Grèce. Précipitation. Stabilité du climate depuis les temps historiques*. Paris.

Mariolopoulos, E. G. (1962) "Fluctuation of rainfall in Attica during the years of the erection of the Parthenon," *Geofisica pura e applicate* 51, 243–62.

Martzavou, A. and Papazarkadas, N. (eds.) (2012) *Epigraphical Approaches to the Post-Classical Polis: Fourth Century BC to Second Century AD*. Oxford.

Martin, T. R. (1985) *Sovereignty and Coinage in Classical Greece*. Princeton, NJ.

Martinez, J.-L., Baralis, A., Mathieux, N., Stoyanov, T., and Tonkova, M. (eds.) (2015) *L'Épopée des rois thraces, des guerres médiques aux invasions celtes, 479–278 av. J.-C.: découvertes archéologiques en Bulgarie*. Paris.

Marzano, A. (2013) *Harvesting the Sea: The Exploitation of Marine Resources in the Roman Mediterranean*. Oxford.

Massar, N. and Verbanck-Piérart, A. (2013) "Follow the scent . . . Marketing perfume vases in the Greek world," in Tsingarida and Viviers 2013, 273–98.

Mattingly, D. J. and Salmon, J. (eds.) (2001) *Economies beyond Agriculture in the Classical World*. London.

Mattusch, C. C. (1977) "Bronze- and ironworking in the area of the Athenian agora," *Hesperia* 46, 340–79.

Mayer, E. (2012) *The Ancient Middle Class*. Cambridge, MA.

Mayor, A. (2018) *Gods and Robots: Myths, Machines, and Ancient Dreams of Technology*. Princeton, NJ.

Mazarakis Ainian, A. (1997) *From Rulers' Dwellings to Temples: Architecture, Religion and Society in Early Iron Age Greece (1100–700 B.C.)*. Jonsered.

Mazarakis Ainian, A. (1998) "Oropos in the Early Iron Age," in *Euboica: l'Eubea e la presenza euboica in Calcidica e in Occidente*, ed. M. Bats and B. D'Agostino. Naples, 179–215.

Mazarakis Ainian, A. (ed.) (2011) *The "Dark Ages" Revisited: Acts of an International Symposium in Memory of W. D. E. Coulson. University of Thessaly, Volos, 14–17 June 2007*, 2 vols. Volos.

Mazarakis Ainian, A. (2015) "The domestic and sacred space of Zagora in the context of the south Euboean Gulf," in Descoeudres and Paspalas 2015, 119–36.

McAnany, P. A. and Yoffee, N. (eds.) (2010) *Questioning Collapse: Human Resilience, Ecological Vulnerability, and the Aftermath of Empire*. Cambridge.

McCormick, M. et al. (2012) "Climate change during and after the Roman empire: reconstructing the past from scientific and historical evidence," *Journal of Interdisciplinary History* 43, 169–220.

McDonald, W. A., Coulson, W. D. E., and Rosser, J. (1983) *Excavations at Nichoria in Southwest Greece, Vol. 3: Dark Age and Byzantine Occupation*. Minneapolis.

McGeorge, P. J. P. (2018) "Bioarchaeological approach to the human remains from Clauss," in *The Mycenaean Cemetery at Achaia Clauss near Patras: People, Material Remains and Culture in Context*, ed. C. Paschalidis. Oxford, 477–92.

McHugh, M. (2017) *The Ancient Greek Farmstead*. Oxford.

McInerney, J. (1999) *The Folds of Parnassos: Land and Ethnicity in Ancient Phokis*. Austin, TX.

McInerney, J. (2010) *The Cattle of the Sun: Cows and Culture in the World of the Ancient Greeks*. Princeton, NJ.

McLoughlin, B. (2011) "The pithos makers at Zagora: ceramic technology and function in an agricultural settlement context," in Mazarakis Ainian 2011, 913–28.

McMichael, A. J. (2012) "Insights from past millennia into climatic impacts on human health and survival," *Proceedings of the National Academy of Sciences of the United States of America* 109, 4730–7.

Meadows, A. (2001) "Money, freedom and empire in the Hellenistic world," in Meadows and Shipton 2001, 53–63.

Meadows, A. (2011) "The Chian revolution: changing patterns of hoarding in 4th-century BC western Asia Minor," in Faucher, Marcellesi, and Picard (eds.) 2011, 273–95.

Meadows, A. (2013) "The closed currency system of the Attalid kingdom," in Thonemann 2013, 149–206.

Meadows, A. and Shipton, K. (eds.) (2001) *Money and Its Uses in the Ancient Greek World*. Oxford.

Mee, C. and Forbes, H. A. (eds.) (1997) *A Rough and Rocky Place: The Landscape and Settlement History of the Methana Peninsula, Greece*. Liverpool.

Meiggs, R. (1982) *Trees and Timber in the Ancient Mediterranean World*. Oxford.

Melitz, J. (1970) "The Polanyi School of anthropology on money: an economist's view," *American Anthropologist* 72, 1020–40.

Ménard, C. and Shirley, M. M. (eds.) (2005a) *Handbook of New Institutional Economics*. New York.

Ménard, C. and Shirley, M. M. (2005b) "Introduction," in Ménard and Shirley 2005a, 1–20.

Mendoni, L. G. (1994) "The organisation of the countryside in Kea," in Doukellis and Mendoni 1994, 147–62.

Metcalf, W. E. (ed.) (2012) *The Oxford Handbook of Greek and Roman Coinage*. Oxford.

Meyer, E. A. (2010) *Metics and the Athenian Phialai-Inscriptions: A Study in Athenian Epigraphy and Law*. Stuttgart.

Migeotte, L. (1984) *L'emprunt public dans les cités grecques: recueil des documents et analyse critique*. Quebec.

Migeotte, L. (1991) "Le pain quotidien dans les cités héllenistiques: à propos des fonds permanents pour l'approvisionnement en grain," *Cahiers du Centre Gustave Glotz* 2, 19–41 (repr. and updated in Migeotte 2011, 305–29).

Migeotte, L. (2001) "Le traité entre Milet et Pidasa (*Delphinion* 149): les clauses financières," in *Les cités d'Asie Mineure Occidentale au IIe siècle a.C.*, ed. A. Bresson and R. Descat. Bordeaux, 129–35 (repr. in Migeotte 2011, 401–8).

Migeotte, L. (2011), *Économie et finances publiques des cités grecques, vol. 1: choix d'articles publiés de 1976 à 2001*. Lyon.

Migeotte, L. (2014) *Les finances des cités grecques: aux périodes classique et hellénistique*. Paris.

Milanovic, B., Lindert, P. H., and Williamson, J. G. (2011) "Pre-industrial inequality," *Economic Journal* 121, 255–72.

Mildenberg, L. (1993–4) "The Cyzicenes: a reappraisal," *American Journal of Numismatics* 5–6, 1–12.

Milgrom, P. R., North, D. C., and Weingast, B. R. (1990) "The role of institutions in the revival of trade: the medieval law merchant, private judges and the Champagne fairs," *Economics and Politics* 2, 1–23.

Millett, P. (1990) "Sale, credit and exchange in Athenian law and society," in *NOMOS: Essays in Athenian Law, Politics, and Society*, ed. P. Cartledge, P. Millett, and S. C. Todd. Cambridge, 167–94.

Millett, P. (1991) *Lending and Borrowing in Ancient Athens*. Cambridge.

Millett, P. (2001) "Productive to some purpose? The problem of ancient economic growth," in Mattingly and Salmon 2001, 17–48.

Misaïlidou-Despotidou, V. (2012) "Archaic pottery from the cemetery of ancient Aphytis," in Tiverios, Misaïlidou-Despotidou, Manakidou, and Arvanitaki 2012, 371–84.

Mitchell, S. (1993) *Anatolia: Land, Men, and Gods in Asia Minor, Vol. 1: The Celts and the Impact of Roman Rule*. Oxford.

Mitchell, S. (2015) "Food, culture, and environment in ancient Asia Minor," in Wilkins and Nadeau 2015, 285–95.

Mitchell, S. (2017) "The Greek impact in Asia Minor 400–250 BCE," in *Hellenism and the Local Communities of the Eastern Mediterranean: 400 BCE–250 CE*, ed. B. Chrubasik and D. King. Oxford, 13–28.

Mittag, P. F. (2016) *Griechische Numismatik: Eine Einführung*. Heidelberg.

Mittwoch, A. (1955) "Tribute and land-tax in Seleucid Judaea," *Biblica* 36, 352–62.

Möller, A. (2000) *Naukratis: Trade in Archaic Greece*. Oxford.

Möller, A. (2007) "Classical Greece: distribution," in Scheidel, Morris, and Saller 2007, 362–84.

Mommsen, W. J. (2005) "From agrarian capitalism to the 'spirit' of modern capitalism: Max Weber's approaches to the protestant ethic," *Max Weber Studies* 5, 185–203.

Monakhov, S. Ju. and Kuznetsova, E. V. (2017) "Overseas trade in the Black Sea region from the archaic to the Hellenistic period," in Kozlovskaya 2017, 59–99.

Monerie, J. (2018) *L'économie de la Babylonie à l'époque hellénistique*. Berlin and Boston.

Monroe, C. M. (2009) *Scales of Fate: Trade, Tradition, and Transformation in the Eastern Mediterranean ca. 1350–1175 BCE*. Münster.

Monson, A. (2012) *From the Ptolemies to the Romans: Political and Economic Change in Egypt*. Cambridge.

Monson, A. (2014) "Late Ptolemaic capitation taxes and the poll tax in Roman Egypt," *The Bulletin of the American Society of Papyrologists* 51, 127–60.

Monson, A. (2015) "Hellenistic empires," in Monson and Scheidel 2015, 169–207.

Monson, A. (2016) "The Jewish high priesthood for sale: farming out temples in the Hellenistic Near East," *Journal of Jewish Studies* 67, 15–35.

Monson, A. and Scheidel, W. (eds.) (2015) *Fiscal Regimes and Political Economy of Premodern States*. Cambridge.

Morakis, A. (2015) "The *gamoroi* and the history of archaic Syracuse: a new examination," *Studi di antichità* 13, 33–50.

Moreno García, J. C. (ed.) (2016) *Dynamics of Production in the Ancient Near East 1300–500 BC*. Oxford.

Mordechai, L., Eisenberg, M., Newfield, T. P., Izdebski, A., Kay, J. E., and Poinar, H. (2019) "The Justinianic Plague: an inconsequential pandemic?," *Proceedings of the National Academy of Sciences of the United States of America* 116, 25546–54.

Mordvintseva, V. I. (2017) "The aetiological myth of the Russian empire and the study in Russia of cultural changes in the North Pontic region from the 3rd century BC to the 3rd century AD (prior to the 1920s)," *Ancient Civilizations from Scythia to Siberia* 23.2, 225–49.

Moreno, A. (2007) *Feeding the Democracy: The Athenian Grain Supply in the Fifth and Fourth Centuries* B.C. Oxford.

Moreno, A. (2008) "Hieron. The Greek sanctuary at the mouth of the Black Sea," *Hesperia* 77, 655–709.

Moretti, J.-C., Fincker, M., and Chankowski, V. (2012) "Les cercles de Sôkratès: un édifice commercial sur l'agora de Théophrastos à Délos," in Chankowski and Karvonis 2012, 225–46.

Morgan, C. (2003) *Early Greek States Beyond the Polis*. London.

Morgan, C. (2009) "The Early Iron Age," in Raaflaub and van Wees 2009, 43–63.

Morgenstern, P. (2016) "Bericht zu den archäozoologischen Funden aus Tiryns Stadt-Nordwest," in Maran and Papadimitriou 2016, 86–96.

Morley, N. (2000) "Trajan's engines," *Greece & Rome* 47, 197–210.

Morley, N. (2013) "The market in classical antiquity," in *Kauf – Konsum und Märkte Wirtschaftswelten im Fokus: Von der römischen Antike bis zur Gegenwart*, ed. M. Frass. Wiesbaden, 103–22.

Morris, I. (1987) *Burial and Ancient Society: The Rise of the Greek City-State*. Cambridge.

Morris, I. (1994) Review: "The Athenian Economy twenty years after *The Ancient Economy*," *Classical Philology* 89, 351–66.

Morris, I. (1996) "The strong principle of equality and the archaic origins of Greek democracy," in Ober and Hedrick 1996, 19–49.

Morris, I. (1998) "Archaeology as a kind of anthropology (a response to David Small)," in *Democracy 2500? Questions and Challenges*, ed. I. Morris and K. A. Raaflaub. Dubuque, IA, 229–39.

Morris, I. (2000) *Archaeology as Cultural History: Words and Things in Iron Age Greece*. Oxford.

Morris, I. (2001) "The use and abuse of Homer," in *Oxford Readings in Homer's Iliad*, ed. D. L. Cairns. Oxford, 57–91.

Morris, I. (2002) "Hard surfaces," in Cartledge, Cohen, and Foxhall 2002, 8–43.

Morris, I. (2004) "Economic growth in ancient Greece," *Journal of Institutional and Theoretical Economics* 160, 708–42.

Morris, I. (2005) "Archaeology, standards of living, and Greek economic history," in Manning and Morris 2005, 91–126.

Morris, I. (2007) "Early Iron Age Greece," in Scheidel, Morris, and Saller 2007, 211–41.

Morris, I. (2009a) "The eighth-century revolution," in Raaflaub and van Wees 2009, 64–80.

Morris, I. (2009b) "The greater Athenian state," in *The Dynamics of Ancient Empires: State Power from Assyria to Byzantium*, ed. I. Morris and W. Scheidel. Oxford, 99–177.

Morris, I. (2010) *Why the West Rules – For Now: The Patterns of History and What They Reveal about the Future*. New York.

Morris, I. and Manning, J. G. (2005) "Introduction," in Manning and Morris 2005, 1–46.

Morris, I., Saller, R., and Scheidel, W. (2007) "Introduction," in Scheidel, Morris, and Saller 2007, 1–12.

Morris, L. (2019) "Central Asian Empires," in *Handbook of Ancient Afro-Eurasian Economies*, vol. 1, ed. S. von Reden, Berlin and Boston, 53–94.

Morris, S. P. and Papadopoulos, J. K. (2005) "Greek towers and slaves: an archaeology of exploitation," *American Journal of Archaeology* 109, 155–225.

Mueller, K. (2006) *Settlements of the Ptolemies: City Foundations and New Settlement in the Hellenistic World*. Leuven.

Muhs, B. (2005) *Tax Receipts, Taxpayers, and Taxes in Early Ptolemaic Thebes*. Chicago.

Muhs, B. (2016) *The Ancient Egyptian Economy, 3000–30 BCE*. Cambridge.

Mulhall, A. D. (2015) "Animals and socio-economy in Late Bronze to Early Iron Age Greece: a zooarchaeological perspective from Lefkandi, Euboea." Unpublished DPhil thesis, University College London.

Muller, A. (2010) "D'Odonis à Thasos. Thraces et Grecs (viiiᵉ–viᵉ s.): essai de bilan," in Tréziny 2010, 212–24.

Müller, C. (2010) *D'Olbia à Tanaïs. Territoires et réseaux dans la mer Noire septentrionale aux époques classique et hellénistique*. Bordeaux.

Müller, C. (2011) "Autopsy of a crisis: wealth, Protogenes, and the city of Olbia," in Archibald, Davies, and Gabrielsen 2011, 324–44.

Murray, O. (1966) "Ὁ ἈΡΧΑΙΟΣ ΔΑΣΜΟΣ," *Historia* 15, 142–56.

Murray, O. (ed.) (1990) *Sympotica: A Symposium on the Symposion*. Oxford.

Murray, O. and Price, S. (eds.) (1990) *The Greek City: From Homer to Alexander*. Oxford.

Murray, O. and Teçusan, M. (eds.) (1995) *In Vino Veritas*. London.

Murray, S. C. (2017) *The Collapse of the Mycenaean Economy: Imports, Trade, and Institutions 1300–700 BCE*. Cambridge.

Musti, D. (1984) "Syria and the East," in *The Cambridge Ancient History. Vol. 7.1: The Hellenistic World*, ed. F. W. Walbank, A. E. Astin, M. W. Frederiksen, and R. M. Ogilvie. 2nd ed. Cambridge, 175–220.

Nakassis, D. (2010) "Reevaluating staple and wealth finance at Mycenaean Pylos," in *Political Economies of the Aegean Bronze Age*, ed. D. J. Pullen. Oxford, 127–48.

Nakassis, D. (2020) "The economy," in Lemos and Kotsonas 2020, vol. 1, 271–91.

Nakassis, D., Parkinson, W. A., and Galaty, M. L. (2011) "Redistribution in Aegean palatial societies: redistributive economies from a theoretical and cross-cultural perspective," *American Journal of Archaeology* 115.2, 177–84.

Netz, R. (2002) "Counter culture: towards a history of Greek numeracy," *History of Science* 40, 321–52.

Nevett, L. C. et al. (2017) "Towards a multi-scalar, multidisciplinary approach to the classical Greek city: the Olynthos Project," *Annual of the British School at Athens* 112, 1–52.

North, D. C. (1981) *Structure and Change in Economic History*. New York.

North, D. C. (1990) *Institutions, Institutional Change and Economic Performance*. Cambridge.

North, D. C. (1991) "Institutions," *Journal of Economic Perspectives* 5.1, 97–112.

North, D. C. (2005) *Understanding the Process of Economic Change*. Princeton, NJ.

North, D. C. and Weingast, B. R. (1989) "Constitutions and commitment: the evolution of institutions governing public choice in seventeenth-century England," *Journal of Economics* 49, 803–33.

North, D. C., Wallis, J. J., and Weingast, B. R. (2009) *Violence and Social Orders: A Conceptual Framework for Interpreting Recorded Human History*. Cambridge.

Nowicki, K. (2000) *Defensible Sites in Crete: c. 1200–800 B.C. (LM IIIB/IIIC through Early Geometric)*. Liège.

Nussbaum, M. (1986) *The Fragility of Goodness: Luck and Ethics in Greek Tragedy and Philosophy*. Cambridge.

Nutton, V. (2013) *Ancient Medicine*. London.

Oates, W. (1972) *Fiscal Federalism*. New York NY.

Obbink, D. (2016) "The newest Sappho," in *The Newest Sappho (P. Sapph. Obbink and P. GC inv. 105, frs. 1–4): Studies in Archaic and Classical Greek Song*, vol. 2, ed. A. Bierl and A. Lardinois. Leiden, 13–33.

Ober, J. (2000) "Political conflicts, political debates, and political thought," in *The Shorter Oxford History of Europe 1: Classical Greece*, ed. R. Osborne. Oxford, 111–38.

Ober, J. (2008) *Democracy and Knowledge: Innovation and Learning in Classical Athens*. Princeton, NJ.

Ober, J. (2009) "Public action and rational choice in classical Greek political theory," in *A Companion to Ancient Political Thought*, ed. R. A. Balot. Oxford, 70–84.

Ober, J. (2010a) "Thucydides on Athens' democratic advantage in the Archidamian War," in *War, Democracy and Culture in Classical Athens*, ed. D. Pritchard. Cambridge, 65–87.

Ober, J. (2010b) "Wealthy Hellas," *Transactions of the American Philological Association* 140, 241–86.

Ober, J. (2012) "Democracy's dignity," *American Political Science Review* 106, 827–46.

Ober, J. (2015a) *The Rise and Fall of Classical Athens*. Princeton, NJ.

Ober, J. (2015b) "Classical Athens," in Monson and Scheidel 2015, 492–522.

Ober, J. (2017) "Inequality in late-classical democratic Athens: evidence and models," in *Democracy and an Open Economy World Order*, ed. G. C. Bitros and N. C. Kyriazis. Cham, 125–46.

Ober, J. (2018) "Institutions, growth, and inequality in ancient Greece," in *Democracy, Justice, and Equality in Ancient Greece: Historical and Philosophical Perspectives*, ed. G. Anagnostopoulos and G. Santas. Cham, 15–37.

Ober, J. and Hedrick, C. (eds.) (1996) *Dēmokratia: A Conversation on Democracies, Ancient and Modern*. Princeton, NJ.

Ogilvie, S. (2005) "The use and abuse of trust: social capital and its deployment by early modern guilds," *Jahrbuch für Wirtschaftsgeschichte* 46, 15–52.

Ogilvie, S. (2008) "Rehabilitating the guilds: a reply," *Economic History Review* 61, 175–82.

Oleson, J. (ed.) (2009) *The Oxford Handbook of Engineering and Technology in the Classical World*. Oxford

Oliver, G. J. (2007) *War, Food, and Politics in Early Hellenistic Athens*. Oxford.

Olson, D. and Sens, A. (2000) *Archestratus: Hedupatheia*. Oxford.

Olson, W. (2000) *Power and Prosperity: Outgrowing Communist and Capitalist Dictatorships*. New York.

Orfanou, S. (2015) "Early Iron Age Greek copper-based technology: votive offerings from Thessaly." Unpublished DPhil thesis, University College London.

Osborne, R. (1985) *Demos: The Discovery of Classical Attika*. Cambridge.

Osborne, R. (1987) *Classical Landscape with Figures: The Ancient Greek City and Its Countryside*. London.

Osborne, R. (1988) "Social and economic implications of the leasing of land and property in classical and Hellenistic Greece," *Chiron* 18, 279–323.

Osborne, R. (1992) "Is it a farm? The definition of agricultural sites and settlements in ancient Greece," in Wells 1992, 22–7.

Osborne, R. (1995) "The economics and politics of slavery at Athens," in *The Greek World*, ed. A. Powell. London, 27–43.

Osborne, R. (1996) "Pots, trade and the archaic Greek economy," *Antiquity* 70.267, 31–44.

Osborne, R. (1998) "Early Greek colonization? The nature of Greek settlement in the west," in *Archaic Greece: New Approaches and New Evidence*, ed. N. Fisher and H. van Wees. London, 251–69.

Osborne, R. (2004) *Greek History*. London.

Osborne, R. (2007) "Archaic Greece," in Scheidel, Morris, and Saller 2007, 277–301.

Osborne, R. (2008) "Archaeology and the Athenian empire," in *The Athenian Empire*, ed. P. Low. Edinburgh, 211–24.

Osborne, R. (2009a) *Greece in the Making, 1200–479 BC*. 2nd ed. London.

Osborne, R. (2009b) "The economics of growth. The politics of entitlement," *The Classical Journal* 55, 97–125.

Osborne, R. (2010) *Athens and Athenian Democracy*. Cambridge.

Osborne, R. and Rhodes, P. J. (2017) *Greek Historical Inscriptions 478–404 BC*. Oxford.

Owen, S. (2005) "Analogy, archaeology, and archaic Greek colonization," in *Ancient Colonizations: Analogy, Similarity, and Difference*, ed. H. Hurst and S. Owen. London, 5–22.

Padilla Peralta, D. (2020) "Gods of trust: ancient Delos and the modern economics of religion," in *Pilgrimage and Economy*, ed. A. Collar and T. Myrup Kristenen. Leiden and Boston, 329–56.

Papadopoulos, J. K. (2003) *Ceramicus Redivivus: The Early Iron Age Potters' Field in the Area of the Classical Athenian Agora*. Princeton, NJ.

Papadopoulos, J. K. (2014) "Greece in the Early Iron Age: mobility, commodities, polities, and literacy," in Knapp and van Dommelen 2014, 178–95.

Papadopoulos, J. K. (2016) "The early history of the Greek alphabet: the new evidence from Eretria and Methone," *Antiquity* 90, 1238–54.

Papakonstantinou, Z. (2008) *Lawmaking and Adjudication in Archaic Greece*. London.

Papapostolou, I. A. (2008) *Θέρμος: Το Μέγαρο Β καί τό Πρώϊμο Ἱερό. Ἡ Ἀνασκαφή 1992–2003*. Athens.

Papathanasiou, A., Richards, M. P., and Fox, S. C. (eds.) (2015) *Archaeodiet in the Greek World: Dietary Reconstruction from Stable Isotope Analysis*. Athens.

Papathanasiou, A., Panagiotopoulou, E., Beltsios, K., Papakonstantinou, M.-F., and Sipsi, M. (2013) "Inferences from the human skeletal material of the Early Iron Age cemetery at Agios Dimitrios, Fthiotis, Central Greece," *Journal of Archaeological Science* 40.7, 2924–33.

Papazarkadas, N. (2011) *Sacred and Public Land in Ancient Athens*. Oxford.

Papazoglou, F. (1997) *Laoi et Paroikoi: recherches sur le structure de la société hellenistique*. Belgrade.

Pappi, E. and Triantaphyllou, S. (2011) "Mortuary practices and the human remains: a preliminary study of the geometric graves in Argos, Argolid," in Mazarakis Ainian 2011, 717–32.

Parker, A. J. (1992) *Ancient Shipwrecks of the Mediterranean and the Roman Provinces*. Oxford.

Parker, R. (2005) *Polytheism and Society at Athens*. Oxford.

Parker, R. (2011) *On Greek Religion*. Ithaca, NY.

Parkinson, W. A., Nakassis, D., and Galaty, M. L. (2013) "Crafts, specialists, and markets in Mycenaean Greece: introduction," *American Journal of Archaeology* 117.3, 413–22.

Pernin, I. (2014) *Les baux ruraux en Grèce ancienne: corpus épigraphique et étude*. Lyon.

Pestman, P. W. (1985) "Ventes provisoires de biens pour sûreté de dettes: ὠναὶ ἐν πίστει à Pathyris et à Krokodilopolis," in *Textes et études de papyrologie grecque, démotique et copte*, ed. P. W. Pestman. Leiden, 45–59.

Petitot, J. (2010) "Reduction and emergence in complex systems," in *Questioning Nineteenth-Century Assumptions about Knowledge: Reductionism*, ed. R. F. Lee. Binghamton, NY, 107–59.

Pfeiffer, S. (2010) "Der eponyme Offizier Tubias: ein lokaler Vertreter der ptolemäischen Herrschaft in Transjordanien," *Archiv für Papyrusforschung* 56, 242–57.

Pfeiffer, S. (2011) "Die Familie des Tubias: Eine (trans-)lokale Elite in Transjordanien," in Dreyer and Mittag 2011, 191–215.

Philippson, A. (1948) *Das Klima Griechenlands*. Bonn.

Picard, O. (1989) "Innovations monétaires dans la Grèce du IVe siècle," *Comptes rendus des séances de l'Académie des Inscriptions et Belles-Lettres* 133, 673–87.

Picard, O. (2011) "La circulation monétaire dans le monde grec: le cas de Thasos," in Faucher, Marcellesi, and Picard 2011, 79–109.

Picard, O. (2012) "Le trésor d'Assiout, ou les leçons d'un trésor," *Revue numismatique* 168, 51–62.

Picard, O. (2015) "La monnaie entre Thraces et Grecs," in Martinez et al. 2015, 172–5.

Pikoulas, G. (2007) "Travelling by land in ancient Greece" in *Travel, Geography and Culture in Ancient Greece, Egypt and the Near East*, ed. C. Adams and J. Roy. Oxford, 78–87.

Pinke, Z. et al. (2017) "Climate of doubt: a re-evaluation of Büntgen and Di Cosmo's environmental hypothesis for the Mongol withdrawal from Hungary, 1242 CE," *Scientific Reports* 7, 12695.

Pirngruber, R. (2017) *The Economy of Late Achaemenid and Seleucid Babylonia*. Cambridge.

Pitt, R. (2016) "Inscribing construction: the financing and administration of public building in Greek sanctuaries," in *A Companion to Greek Architecture*, ed. M. M. Miles. Malden, MA, 194–205.

Pitts, M. and Griffin, R. (2012) "Exploring health and social well-being in late Roman Britain: an intercemetery approach," *American Journal of Archaeology* 116.2, 253–76.

Pnevmatikos, J. D. and Katsoulis, B. D. (2006) "The changing rainfall regime in Greece and its impact on climatological means," *Meteorological Applications* 13, 331–45.

Podlecki, A. J. (ed.) (2005) *Aeschylus: Prometheus Bound*. Oxford.

Poland, F. (1909) *Geschichte des griechischen Vereinswesens*. Leipzig.

Polanyi, K. (1957) "The economy as instituted process," in *Trade and Market in the Early Empires: Economies in History and Theory*, ed. K. Polanyi, C. M. Arensberg, and H. W. Pearson. Glencoe, IL, 243–70.

Polinskaya, I. (2013) *A Local History of Greek Polytheism: Gods, People and the Land of Aigina 800–400 BCE*. Leiden.

Pomeroy, S. B. (1994) *Xenophon, Oeconomicus: A Social and Historical Commentary*. Oxford.

Popham, M. R., Sackett, L. H., and Themelis, P. G. (1979–80) *Lefkandi, Vol. 1: The Iron Age: The Settlement, the Cemeteries*, 2 vols. London.

Porten, B. and Yardeni, A. (eds.) (1993) *Textbook of Aramaic Documents from Ancient Egypt. Vol. 3: Literature, Accounts, Lists*. Jerusalem.

Powell, O. (2003) *Galen: On the Properties of Foodstuffs (De alimentorum facultatibus): Introduction, Translation and Commentary*. Cambridge.

Pratt, C. E. (2015) "The 'SOS' amphora: an update," *Annual of the British School at Athens* 110, 213–45.

Préaux, C. (1939) *L'Économie royale des Lagides*. New York.

Preiser-Kapeller, J. and Daim, F. (eds.) (2015) *Harbours and Maritime Networks as Complex Adaptive Systems*. Mainz.

Preisigke, F. (1910) *Girowesen im griechischen Ägypten: enthaltend Korngiro, Geldgiro, Girobanknotariat mit Einschluss des Archivwesens: ein Beitrag zur Geschichte des Verwaltungsdienstes im Altertume*. Strasbourg.

Prêtre, C. (ed.) (2002) *Nouveau choix d'inscriptions de Délos: Lois, comptes et inventaires*. Athens.

Price, M. J. (1983) "Thoughts on the beginnings of coinage," in *Studies in Numismatic Method Presented to Philip Grierson*, ed. C. N. L. Brooke, B. H. I. H. Stewart, J. G. Pollard, and T. R. Volk. Cambridge, 1–10.

Price, M. J. (1991) *The Coinage in the Name of Alexander the Great and Philip Arrhidaeus: A British Museum Catalogue*. Zurich.

Price, M. J. and Waggoner, N. M. (1975) *Archaic Greek Coinage: The Asyut Hoard*. London.

Prignitz, S. (2014) *Bauurkunden und Bauprogramm von Epidauros (400–350)*. Munich.

Prignitz, S. (2018) "Die altgriechische Bauvergabeordnung aus Tegea," in *Groß Bauen. Großbaustellen als kulturgeschichtliches Phänomen*, ed. K. Rheidt and W. Lorenz. Berlin, 37–46.

Pringsheim, F. (1950) *The Greek Law of Sale*. Weimar.

Pritchard, D. M. (2015) *Public Spending and Democracy in Classical Athens*. Austin, TX.

Pritchard, D. M. (2019) *Athenian Democracy at War*. Cambridge.

Pritchett, W. K. (1953) "The Attic stelai: Part I," *Hesperia* 22, 225–99.

Pritchett, W. K. (1971) *The Greek State at War, Vol. 1: Ancient Greek Military Practices*. Berkeley, CA.

Pritchett, W. K. (1991) *The Greek State at War*, vol. 5. Berkeley, CA.

Pritchett, W. K. and Pippin, A. (1956) "The Attic stelai: Part II," *Hesperia* 25, 178–328.

Pryor, F. L. (1977) *The Origins of the Economy: A Comparative Study of Distribution on Primitive and Peasant Economies*. New York.

Psoma, S. (2001) *Olynthe et les Chalcidiens de Thrace: Études de numismatique et d'histoire*. Stuttgart.

Psoma, S. (2011a) "La circulation monétaire et la thésaurisation en Thrace au nord des Rhodopes," in Faucher, Marcellesi, and Picard 2011, 143–68.

Psoma, S. (2011b) "The law of Nicophon (*SEG* 26.72) and Athenian imitations," *Revue belge de numismatique et de sigillographie* 157, 27–36.

Psoma, S. (2013) "La monnaie de bronze: les débuts d'une institution," in *Aux origines de la monnaie fiduciaire: Traditions métallurgiques et innovations numismatiques*, ed. C. Grandjean and A. Moustaka. Bordeaux, 57–70.

Psoma, S. (2016) "Choosing and changing monetary standards in the Greek world during the archaic and classical periods," in Harris, Lewis, and Woolmer 2016, 90–115.

Psoma, S. and Tsangari, D. (2003) "Monnaie commune et états fédéraux: La circulation des monnayages frappés par les états fédéraux du monde grec," in *The Idea of European Community in History. Conference Proceedings, Volume II: Aspects of Connecting Poleis and Ethne in Ancient Greece*, ed. K. Buraselis and K. Zoumboulakis. Athens, 111–42.

Purcell, N. (1990) "Mobility and the polis," in Murray and Price 1990, 29–58.

Purcell, N. (2005) "The ancient Mediterranean: the view from the customs house," in *Rethinking the Mediterranean*, ed. W. Harris. Oxford, 200–28.

Purcell, N. (2014) "The ancient Mediterranean," in Horden and Kinoshita 2014, 59–76.

Pyzyk, M. (2015) "Economies of expertise: knowledge and skill transfer in classical Greece." Unpublished PhD thesis, Stanford University.

Raaflaub, K. (1996) "Equalities and inequalities in Athenian democracy," in Ober and Hedrick 1996, 139–74.

Raaflaub, K. (2009) "Learning from the enemy: Athenian and Persian 'Instruments of Empire'," in Ma, Papazarkadas, and Parker 2009, 89–124.

Raaflaub, K. A. and van Wees, H. (eds.) (2009) *A Companion to Archaic Greece.* Malden, MA.

Raepsaet, G. (2008) "Histoire économique et techniques productives. Un dialogue de sourds?," *L'Antiquité classique* 77, 257–87.

Rambeau, C. and Black, S. (2011) "Palaeoenvironments of the southern Levant 5,000 BP to present: linking the geological and archaeological records," in *Water, Life and Civilisation: Climate, Environment and Society in the Jordan Valley*, ed. S. Mithen and E. Black. Cambridge, 94–104.

Rathbone, D. (1990) "Villages, land and population in Graeco-Roman Egypt," *Proceedings of the Cambridge Philological Society* 36, 103–42.

Rathbone, D. (2014) "Mediterranean and Near Eastern grain prices: some preliminary conclusions," in *Documentary Sources in Ancient Near Eastern and Greco-Roman Economic History*, ed. H. Baker and M. Jursa. Oxford, 313–22.

Rathbone, D., and von Reden, S. (2015) "Mediterranean grain prices in classical antiquity," in van der Spek, van Leeuwen, and van Zanden 2015, 149–235.

Rauch, J. E. (2001) "Business and social networks in international trade," *Journal of Economic Literature* 39, 1177–203.

Rauch, J. E. and Casella, A. (eds.) (2001) *Networks and Markets.* New York.

Rauch, J. E. and Hamilton, G. E. (2001) "Networks and markets: concepts for bridging disciplines," in Rauch and Casella 2001, 1–29.

Rauh, N. (1993) *The Sacred Bonds of Commerce: Religion, Economy, and Trade Society at Hellenistic Roman Delos, 166–87* B.C. Amsterdam.

Reed, C. M. (2003) *Maritime Traders in the Ancient Greek World.* Cambridge.

Reger, G. (1993) "The public purchase of grain on independent Delos," *Classical Antiquity* 12, 300–34.

Reger, G. (1994) *Regionalism and Change in the Economy of Independent Delos, 314–167* B.C. Berkeley, CA.

Reger, G. (2003) "The economy," in *A Companion to the Hellenistic World*, ed. A. Erskine. Malden, MA, 331–53.

Reger, G. (2004) "*Sympoliteiai* in Hellenistic Asia Minor," in *The Greco-Roman East: Politics, Culture, Society*, ed. S. Colvin. Cambridge, 145–80.

Reger, G. (2007) "Hellenistic Greece and western Asia Minor," in Scheidel, Morris, and Saller 2007, 460–86.

Reger, G. (2011) "Interregional economies in the Aegean basin," in Archibald, Davies, and Gabrielsen 2011, 368–89.

Reger, G. (2013) "Economic regionalism in theory and practice," in Tsingarida and Viviers 2013, 99–111.

Renfrew, C. (1972) *The Emergence of Civilisation: The Cyclades and the Aegean in the Third Millennium* BC. London.

Rhodes, P. J. (2013) "The organization of Athenian public finance," *Greece & Rome* 60, 203–31.

Rhodes, P. J. and Osborne, R. (2003) *Greek Historical Inscriptions 404–323 BC*. Oxford.

Rice, C. (2016) "Mercantile specialization and trading communities: economic strategies in Roman maritime communities," in *Urban Craftsmen and Traders in the Roman World*, ed. A. Wilson and M. Flohr. Oxford, 97–114.

Rigsby, K. J. (1996) *Asylia: Territorial Inviolability in the Hellenistic World*. Berkeley, CA.

Rihll, T. E. (2001) "Making money in classical Athens," in Mattingly and Salmon 2001, 115–42.

Rihll, T. E. (2007) *The Catapult: A History*. Yardley, PA.

Rihll, T. E. (2013) *Technology and Society in the Ancient Greek and Roman Worlds*. Blacksburg, VA.

Riker, W. H. (1964) *Federalism: Origins, Operations, and Significance*. Boston, MA.

Robert, J. and Robert, L. (1981) "Bulletin épigraphique," *Revue des études grecques* 94, 362–485.

Robert, J. and Robert, L. (1983) *Fouilles d'Amyzon en Carie. Vol. 1: Exploration, histoire, monnaies et inscriptions*. Paris.

Robert, L. (1960) *Hellenica: Recueil d'épigraphie, de numismatique et d'antiquités grecques*, vols. 11–12. Paris.

Robert, L. and Robert, J. (1976) "Une inscription grecque de Téos en Ionie: l'union de Téos et de Kyrbissos," *Journal des Savants* 1976.3–4, 154–235 (repr. in L. Robert (1990) *Opera Minora Selecta*, vol. 7. Amsterdam, 297–379).

Roberts, N. et al. (2012) "Palaeolimnological evidence for an east–west climate see-saw in the Mediterranean since AD 900," *Global and Planetary Change* 84–5, 23–34.

Robinson, D. and Goddio, F. (eds.) (2015) *Thonis Heracleion in Context: The Maritime Economy of the Egyptian Late Period*. Oxford.

Robinson, M. and Rowan, E. (2015) "Roman food remains in archaeology and the contents of a Roman sewer at Herculaneum," in Wilkins and Nadeau 2015, 105–15.

Roby, C. (2016) *Technical Ekphrasis in Greek and Roman Science and Literature: The Written Machine between Alexandria and Rome*. Cambridge.

Rodden, J. (2006) "Federalism," in *The Oxford Handbook of Political Economy*, ed. B. Weingast and D. Wittman. Oxford, 357–70.

Rohde, D. (2012) *Zwischen Individuum und Stadtgemeine: Die Integration von Collegia in Hafenstädten*. Mainz.

Rollinger, R. (2001) "The ancient Greeks and the impact of the ancient Near East: textual evidence and historical perspective (ca. 750–650 B.C.)," in *Mythology and Mythologies: Methodological Approaches to Intercultural Influences*, ed. R. M. Whiting. Helsinki, 233–64.

Rollinger, R. (2006) "The eastern Mediterranean and beyond: the relations between the worlds of the 'Greek' and the 'non-Greek' civilizations," in Kinzl 2006, 197–226.

Rose, P. W. (2019) "Capitalism in 'Wealthy Hellas'?," *Arion* 26, 111–52.

Rosen, R. M. (2016) "Towards a Hippocratic anthropology: *On Ancient Medicine* and the origins of humans," in *Ancient Concepts of the Hippocratic*, ed. L. Dean-Jones and R. M. Rosen. Leiden, 238–57.

Rosivach, V. J. (1989) "*Talasiourgoi* and *paidia* in *IG* 22 1553–78: a note on Athenian social history," *Historia* 38, 365–70.

Rosivach, V. J. (2011) "State pay as war relief in Peloponnesian-War Athens," *Greece & Rome* 58.2, 176–83.

Rostovtzeff, M. (1922) *A Large Estate in Egypt in the Third Century* B.C.: *A Study in Economic History*. Madison, WI.

Rostovtzeff, M. (1941) *The Social and Economic History of the Hellenistic World*, 3 vols. Oxford.

Roth, R. and Joos, F. (2013) "A reconstruction of radiocarbon production and total solar irradiance from the Holocene 14^C and CO_2 records: implications of data and model reconstructions," *Climate of the Past* 9, 1879–1909. DOI: https://doi.org/10.5194/cp-9-1879-2013.

Roubineau, J. M. (2012) "La main cruelle de l'agoranome," in Capdetrey and Hasenohr 2012, 47–59.

Rousset, D. (1989) "Les Doriens de la Métropole. Étude de topographie et de géographie historique," *Bulletin de correspondance hellénique* 113, 199–239.

Rousset, D. (2010) *De Lycie en Cabalide: La convention entre les Lyciens et Termessos près d'Oinoanda*. Geneva.

Rousset, D. (2013) "Sacred property and public property in the Greek city," *The Journal of Hellenic Studies* 133, 113–33.

Rubinstein, L. (2003) "Volunteer prosecutors in the Greek world," *Dike* 6, 87–113.

Rubinstein, L. (2018) "Summary fines in Greek inscriptions and the question of Greek law," in *Ancient Greek Law in the 21st Century*, ed. P. Perlman. Austin, TX, 104–43.

Ruffell, I. (2012) *Aeschylus: Prometheus Bound*. Bristol.

Ruffing, K. (2014) "Der Reichtum Babyloniens," in *From Source to History: Studies on Ancient Near Eastern Worlds and Beyond: Dedicated to Giovanni Lanfranchi on the Occasion of his 65th Birthday on June 23, 2014*, ed. S Gaspa, A. Greco, D. Morandi Bonacossi, S. Ponicha, and R. Rollinger. Münster, 637–46.

Ruffini, G. (2008) *Social Networks in Byzantine Egypt*. Cambridge.

Runciman, W. G. (1990) "Doomed to extinction: the polis as an evolutionary dead-end," in Murray and Price 1990, 348–67.

Ruschenbusch, E. (2014) *Solon: Das Gesetzeswerk – Fragmente. Übersetzung und Kommentar*, ed. K. Bringmann. 2nd ed. Stuttgart.

Russell, T. (2017) *Byzantium and the Bosporus. A Historical Study, from the Seventh Century* BC *until the Foundation of Constantinople*. Oxford.

Rutter, N. K. (1997) *The Greek Coinages of Southern Italy and Sicily*. London.

Sallares, R. (1991) *The Ecology of the Ancient Greek World*. Ithaca, NY.

Sallares, R. (2002) *Malaria and Rome: A History of Malaria in Ancient Italy*. Oxford.

Sallares, R. (2009) "Environmental history," in *A Companion to Ancient History*, ed. A. Erskine. Chichester, 164–74.

Sallares, R. (2014) "Disease," in Horden and Kinoshita 2014, 250–62.

Saller, R. (2002) "Framing the debate over growth in the ancient economy," in *The Ancient Economy*, ed. W. Scheidel and S. von Reden. Edinburgh, 251–69.

Saller, R. (2007) "Household and gender," in Scheidel, Morris, and Saller 2007, 87–112.

Salles, J.-F. (1987) "The Arab-Persian Gulf under the Seleucids," in Kuhrt and Sherwin-White 1987, 75–109.

Salmon, J. (1984) *Wealthy Corinth: A History of the City to 338* BC. Oxford.

Salmon, J. (2001) "Temples the measures of men: public building in the Greek economy," in Mattingly and Salmon 2001, 195–208.

Salviat, F. (1993) "Le vin de Rhodes et les plantations du dème d'Amos," in *La production du vin et de l'huile en Méditerranée*, ed. M.-C. Amouretti and J.-P. Brun. Paris, 151–61.

Salzer, M. W. and Hughes, M. K. (2007) "Bristlecone pine tree rings and volcanic eruptions over the last 5000 yr.," *Quaternary Research* 67, 57–68.

Samons, L. J., II (2000) *Empire of the Owl: Athenian Imperial Finance.* Stuttgart.

Sänger, P. (2015) "Military immigration and the emergence of cultural or ethnic identities: the case of Ptolemaic Egypt," *The Journal of Juristic Papyrology* 45, 229–53.

Sapirstein, P. (2013) "Painters, potters, and the scale of the Attic vase-painting industry," *American Journal of Archaeology* 117, 493–510.

Sarkisjan, G. (1997) "Hellenismus in Babylonien," *Altorientalische Forschungen* 24.2, 242–50.

Sarpaki, A. (1992) "The palaeobotanical approach: the Mediterranean triad or is it a quartet?," in Wells 1992, 61–76.

Sartre, M. (1995) *L'Asie Mineure et l'Anatolie d'Alexandre à Dioclétien: IVe siècle av. J.-C. / IIIe siècle après J.-C.* Paris.

Sartre, M. (2001) *D'Alexandre à Zénobie: histoire du Levant antique: IVe siècle av. J.-C. – IIIe siècle ap. J.-C.* Paris.

Schäfer, C. (2015) "Inspiration and impact of Seleucid royal representation," in *Mesopotamia in the Ancient World: Impact, Continuities, Parallels*, ed. R. Rollinger and E. van Dongen. Münster, 631–41.

Schaps, D. M. (1996) "Builders, contractors and power: financing and administering building projects in ancient Greece," in *Classical Studies in Honor of David Sohlberg*, ed. R. Katzoff. Ramat Gan, 77–89.

Schaps, D. M. (1997) "The monetization of the marketplace in Athens," in Andreau, Briant, and Descat 1997, 91–104.

Schaps, D. M. (2001a) "The conceptual prehistory of money and its impact on the Greek economy," in Balmuth 2001, 93–103.

Schaps, D. M. (2001b) "[Demosthenes] 35: little brother strikes out on his own," *Laverna* 12, 67–85.

Schaps, D. M. (2004) *The Invention of Coinage and the Monetization of Ancient Greece.* Ann Arbor, MI.

Schaps, D. M. (2007) "The invention of coinage in Lydia, in India, and in China," *Bulletin du Cercle d'Études Numismatiques* 44.1, 281–300 and 44.2, 313–22.

Schaps, D. M. (2008) "What was money in ancient Greece?," in Harris 2008, 38–48.

Schatzberg, E. (2018) *Technology: Critical History of a Concept.* Chicago.

Scheidel, W. (1995) "The most silent women of Greece and Rome: rural labour and women's life in the ancient world (I)," *Greece & Rome* 42.2, 202–17.

Scheidel, W. (1996) "The most silent women of Greece and Rome: rural labour and women's life in the ancient world (II)," *Greece & Rome* 43.1, 1–10.

Scheidel, W. (2003) "The Greek demographic expansion: models and comparisons," *The Journal of Hellenic Studies* 103, 120–40.

Scheidel, W. (2007) "Demography," in Scheidel, Morris, and Saller 2007, 38–86.

Scheidel, W. (2010) "Real wages in early economies: evidence for living standards from 2000 BCE to 1300 CE," *Journal of the Economic and Social History of the Orient* 53, 425–62.

Scheidel, W. (2012) "Introduction," in *The Cambridge Companion to the Roman Economy*, ed. W. Scheidel. Cambridge, 1–21.

Scheidel, W. (2017) *The Great Leveller: Violence and the History of Inequality from the Stone Age to the Twenty-First Century.* Princeton, NJ.

Scheidel, W. (2019) *Escape from Rome: The Failure of Empire and the Road to Prosperity.* Princeton, NJ.

Scheidel, W. and Friesen, S. J. (2009) "The size of the economy and the distribution of income in the Roman Empire," *Journal of Roman Studies* 99, 61–91.

Scheidel, W. and von Reden, S. (2002) "Introduction," in *The Ancient Economy*, ed. W. Scheidel and S. von Reden. Edinburgh, 1–10.

Scheidel, W., Morris, I., and Saller, R. (eds.) (2007) *The Cambridge Economic History of the Greco-Roman World*. Cambridge.

Schepartz, L. A., Fox, S. C., and Bourbou,C. (eds.) (2009) *New Directions in the Skeletal Biology of Greece*. Princeton, NJ.

Scheuble-Reiter, S. (2012) *Die Katökenreiter im ptolemäischen Ägypten*. Munich.

Schiefsky, M. (2015) "Techne and method in ancient artillery construction: the *Belopoeica* of Philo of Byzantium," in *The Frontiers of Ancient Science*, ed. B. Holmes and K. D. Fischer. Berlin, 613–51.

Schmid, B.V. et al. (2015) "Climate-driven introduction of the Black Death and successive plague reintroductions into Europe," *Proceedings of the National Academy of the United States of America* 112, 3020–5. DOI: https://doi.org/10.1073/pnas.1412887112.

Schmitt Pantel, P. (1992) *La cité au banquet: histoire des repas publics dans les cités grecques*. Rome.

Schmitz, W. (1986) "Händler, Bürger und Soldaten: Die Bedeutung von Münzgewichtveränderungen in der griechischen Poliswelt im 5. und 4. Jahrhundert v. Chr.," *Münstersche Beiträge zur antiken Handelsgeschichte* 2, 59–88.

Schneider, H. (2007) "Technology," in Scheidel, Morris, and Saller 2007, 144–71.

Schuhl, P.-M. (1938) *Machinisme et Philosophie*. Paris.

Schuler, C. (1998) *Ländliche Siedlungen und Gemeinden im hellenistischen und römischen Kleinasien*. Munich.

Schuler, C. (2004) "Landwirtschaft und königliche Verwaltung im hellenistischen Kleinasien," in *Le roi et l'économie: autonomies locales et structures royales dans l'économie de l'empire séleucide*, ed. V. Chankowski and F. Duyrat. Lyon, 509–32.

Schuler, C. (2007) "Tribute und Steuern im hellenistischen Kleinasien," in Klinkott, Kubisch, and Müller-Wollermann 2007, 371–405.

Schuler, C. and Walser, A. V. (2015) "Sympolitien und Synoikismen: Gesellschaftliche und urbanistische Implikationen von Konzentrationsprozessen in hellenistischer Zeit," in *Urbane Strukturen und bürgerliche Identität im Hellenismus*, ed. A. Matthaei and M. Zimmermann. Heidelberg, 350–9.

Schumpeter, J. [1918] (1991) "The crisis of the tax state: an essay in fiscal sociology," in *The Economics and Sociology of Capitalism*, ed. R. Swedberg. Princeton, NJ, 99–140.

Scott, J. C. (1998) *Seeing Like a State*. New Haven, CT.

Seaford, R. (2004) *Money and the Early Greek Mind: Homer, Philosophy, Tragedy*. Cambridge.

Sessa, K. (2019) "The new environmental fall of Rome: a methodological consideration," *Journal of Late Antiquity* 12, 211–55.

Sekunda, N. and de Souza, P. (2007) "Military forces," in *The Cambridge History of Greek and Roman Warfare*, ed. P. Sabin, H. van Wees, and M. Whitby. Cambridge, 325–56.

Shapland, A. and Stefani, E. (eds.) (2017) *Archaeology behind the Battle Lines: the Macedonian Campaign (1915–19)*. London.

Shaw, T. M., Mahrenbach, L. C., Modi, R., and Xu, Y.-C. (eds.) (2019) *The Palgrave Handbook of Contemporary International Political Economy*. London.

Shear, J. L. (2003) "Prizes from Athens: the list of Panathenaic prizes and the sacred oil," *Zeitschrift für Papyrologie und Epigraphik* 142, 87–108.

Shear, T. L., Jr. (1978) *Kallias of Sphettos and the Revolt of Athens in 286* B.C. Princeton, NJ.

Sheedy, K. A. (2006) *The Archaic and Early Classical Coinages of the Cyclades*. London.

Sheedy, K. A. (2012) "Aegina, the Cyclades, and Crete," in Metcalf 2012, 105–27.

Sheedy, K. A. (2015) "The emergency coinage of Timotheus (364–362 B.C.)," in Wartenberg and Amandry 2015, 203–23.

Shepherd, G. (2009) "Greek 'colonisation' in Sicily and the West: some problems of evidence and interpretation twenty-five years on," *Pallas* 79, 15–25.

Sherratt, S. (1994) "Commerce, iron and ideology: metallurgical innovation in 12th–11th century Cyprus," in *Cyprus in the 11th Century* BC, ed. V. Karageorghis. Nicosia, 59–106.

Sherratt, S. (2010) "Greeks and Phoenicians: perceptions of trade and traders in the early first millennium BC," in *Trade as Social Interaction: New Archaeological Approaches*, ed. A. Bauer and A. Agbe-Davies. Walnut Creek, CA, 119–42.

Sherratt, S. (2016) "From 'institutional' to 'private': traders, routes and commerce from the Late Bronze Age to the Iron Age," in Moreno García 2016, 289–301.

Sherwin-White, S. (1987) "Seleucid Babylonia: a case-study for the installation and development of Greek rule," in Kuhrt and Sherwin-White 1987, 1–31.

Shipley, D. G. J. (2018) *The Early Hellenistic Peloponnese: Politics, Economics, Networks 338–197* BC. Cambridge.

Shipton, K. M. W. (1997) "The private banks in fourth-century B.C. Athens: a reappraisal," *Classical Quarterly* 47.2, 396–422.

Shipton, K. M. W. (2000) *Leasing and Lending: The Cash Economy in Fourth-Century* BC *Athens*. London.

Sidebotham, S. (2011) *Berenike and the Ancient Maritime Spice Route*. Berkeley, CA.

Sigl, M. et al. (2015) "Timing and climate forcing of volcanic eruptions for the past 2,500 years," *Nature* 523, 543–9.

Sihvola, J. (1989) *Decay, Progress, the Good Life? Hesiod and Protagoras on the Development of Culture*. Helsinki.

Silver, M. (1995) *Economic Structures of Antiquity*. London.

Simonton, M. (2017) *Classical Greek Oligarchy: A Political History*. Princeton, NJ.

Sinn, U. (2005) "*Kapeleion*," in *Thesaurus Cultus et Rituum Antiquorum*, vol. IV, ed. V. Lambrinoudakis, J. C. Balty, and M. Greenberg. Los Angeles, 50–1.

Skydsgaard, J. E. (1988) "Transhumance in ancient Greece," in Whittaker 1988, 75–86.

Slater, W. and Summa, D. (2006) "Crowns at Magnesia," *Greek, Roman, and Byzantine Studies* 46, 275–99.

Slawisch, A. (ed.) (2013) *Handels- und Finanzgebaren in der Ägäis im 5. Jh. v. Chr. / Trade and Finance in the 5th C.* BC *Aegean World*. Istanbul.

Snodgrass, A. (1981) *Archaic Greece: The Age of Experiment*. Berkley, CA.

Snodgrass, A. (2016) "Thespiai and the fourth-century climax in Boiotia," in Gartland 2016, 9–31.

Snyder, L. M. and Reese, D. S. (2016) "The faunal remains," in Gesell and Day 2016, 169–80.

Sosin, J. D. (1999) "Tyrian *stationarii* at Puteoli," *Tyche* 14, 275–84.

Souvatzi, S. G. (2008) *A Social Archaeology of Households in Neolithic Greece: An Anthropological Approach*. Cambridge.

Starr, C. G. (1977) *The Economic and Social Growth of Early Greece, 800–500* BC. New York.

Steadman, S. R. and McMahon, G. (eds.) (2011) *The Oxford Handbook of Ancient Anatolia (10,000–323* B.C.E.). Oxford.

Stefani, E. (2017) "National ideology and the management of antiquities in Macedonia (late nineteenth – early twentieth century)," in Shapland and Stefani 2017, 19–39.

Steinhilber, F., Beer, J., and Fröhlich, C. (2009) "Total solar irradiance during the Holocene," *Geophysical Research Letters* 36, L19704.

Steinwenter, A. (1971) *Die Streitbeendigung durch Urteil, Schiedsspruch und Vergleich nach griechischem Rechte.* 2nd ed. Munich.

Stevens, K. (2014) "The Antiochus cylinder, Babylonian scholarship and Seleucid imperial ideology," *The Journal of Hellenic Studies* 134, 66–88.

Stillwell, A. N. (1948) "The potters' quarter," *Corinth* 15, 3–138.

Stockhammer, P. W. (2011) "Household archaeology in LHIIIC Tiryns," in *Household Archaeology in Ancient Israel and Beyond*, ed. A. Yasur-Landau, J. R. Ebeling, and L. B. Mazow. Leiden, 207–36.

Stolper, M. W. (1985) *Entrepreneur and Empire: The Murašu Archive, the Murašu Firm, and Persian Rule in Babylonia.* Istanbul.

Stolper, M. W. (1993–7) "Militärkolonisten," in *Reallexikon der Assyriologie und Vorderasiatischen Archäologie*, vol. 8, ed. D. O. Edzard. Berlin, 205–7.

Strootmann, R. (2014) *Courts and Elites in the Hellenistic Empires: The Near East After the Achaemenids, c. 330 to 30 BCE.* Edinburgh.

Stroud, R. S. (1974) "An Athenian law on silver coinage," *Hesperia* 43.2, 157–88.

Stroud, R. S. (1998) *The Athenian Grain-Tax Law of 374/3 B.C.* Princeton, NJ.

Tacoma, L. E. (2016) *Moving Romans: Migration to Rome in the Principate.* Oxford.

Takmer, B. (2007) "*Lex portorii provinciae Lyciae*: Ein Vorbericht über die Zollinschrift aus Andriake aus neronischer Zeit," *Gephyra* 4, 165–88.

Tan, J. (2017) *Power and Public Finance at Rome, 264–49 BCE.* Oxford.

Tandy, D. W. (1997) *Warriors into Traders: The Power of the Market in Early Greece.* Berkeley, CA.

Tandy, D. W. (2018) "In Hesiod's world," in *The Oxford Handbook of Hesiod*, ed. A. C. Loney and S. Scully. Oxford, 43–60.

Tartaron, T. F. (2013) *Maritime Networks in the Mycenaean World.* Cambridge.

Taylor, C. (2017) *Poverty, Wealth, and Well-Being: Experiencing Penia in Democratic Athens.* Oxford.

Taylor, C. and Vlassopoulos, K. (eds.) (2015) *Communities and Networks in the Ancient Greek World.* Oxford.

Teegarden, D. (2014) *Death to Tyrants! Ancient Greek Democracy and the Struggle against Tyranny.* Princeton, NJ.

Teixidor, J. (1980) "Assemblée législative en Phénicie d'aprés les inscriptions," *Syria* 57, 457–60.

Televantou, C. A. (2015) "Hypsile on Andros: the Geometric phase," in Descoeudres and Paspalas 2015, 83–7.

Temin, P. (2012) *The Roman Market Economy.* Princeton, NJ.

Terpstra, T. (2013) *Trading Communities in the Roman World: A Micro-Economic and Institutional Perspective.* Leiden.

Terpstra, T. (2019) *Trade in the Ancient Mediterranean: Private Order and Public Institutions.* Princeton, NJ.

Thompson, D. J. (1999) "Irrigation and drainage in the early Ptolemaic Fayyum," in *Agriculture in Egypt: From Pharaonic to Modern Times*, ed. A. K. Bowman and E. L. Rogan. Oxford, 107–22.

Thompson, D. J. (2006) "The Hellenistic family," in Bugh 2006b, 93–112.

Thompson, D. J. (2012) *Memphis under the Ptolemies*. 2nd ed. Princeton, NJ.

Thomsen, C. A. (2015) "The *eranistai* of classical Athens," *Greek, Roman, and Byzantine Studies* 55, 154–75.

Thomsen, C. A. (2020) *The Politics of Association in Hellenistic Rhodes*. Edinburgh.

Thonemann, P. (2009) "Estates and the land in early Hellenistic Asia Minor: the estate of Krateuas," *Chiron* 39, 363–94.

Thonemann, P. (2011) "Eumenes II and Apollonioucharax," *Gephyra* 8, 1–12.

Thonemann, P. (2012) "Alexander, Priene, and Naulochon," in Martzavou and Papazarkadas 2012, 23–36.

Thonemann, P. (2013a) "The Attalid State, 188–133 BC," in Thonemann 2013b, 1–47.

Thonemann, P. (ed.) (2013b) *Attalid Asia Minor: Money, International Relations and the State*. Oxford.

Thonemann, P. (2015a) "Pessinous and the Attalids: a new royal letter," *Zeitschrift für Papyrologie und Epigraphik* 194, 117–28.

Thonemann, P. (2015b) *The Hellenistic World: Using Coins as Sources*. Cambridge.

Thür, G. (1984) "Bemerkungen zum altgriechischen Werkvertrag (Die Bauvergabeordnung aus Tegea, IG V/2, 6A)," in *Studi in onore di Arnaldo Biscardi*, vol. v, ed. F. Pastori. Milan, 471–514.

Thür, G. (1995) "Zu den Hintergründen des Rechtsgewährungsvertrags zwischen Stymphalos und Demetrias," in *Rom und der griechische Osten: Festschrift für Hatto H. Schmitt zum 65. Geburtstag*, ed. C. Schubert and K. Brodersen. Stuttgart, 268–72.

Thür, G. (1996) "Oaths and dispute settlement in ancient Greek law," in *Greek Law in Its Political Setting: Justification not Justice*, ed. L. Foxhall and A. Lewis. Oxford, 57–72.

Thür, G. (2000) "Das Gerichtswesen Athens im 4. Jahrhundert v. Chr.," in *Große Prozesse im antiken Athen*, ed. L. Burckhardt and J. von Ungern-Sternberg. Munich, 30–49.

Thür, G. and Taeuber, H. (1978) "Prozeßrechtlicher Kommentar zur 'Krämerinschrift' von Samos," *Anzeiger der Philosophisch-Historischen Klasse der Österreichische Akademie der Wissenschaften* 115, 205–25.

Thür, G. and Taeuber, H. (1994) *Prozessrechtliche Inschriften der Griechischen Poleis: Arkadien (IPArk)*. Vienna.

Tiebout, C. (1956) "A pure theory of local expenditures," *Journal of Political Economy* 64, 416–24.

Tiverios, M. (2012) "Luxury Attic pottery in Macedonia," in Tiverios, Misaïlidou-Despotidou, Manakidou, and Arvanitaki 2012, 39–52.

Tiverios, M., Misaïlidou-Despotidou, V., Manakidou, E., and Arvanitaki, A. (eds.) (2012) *Η κεραμική της αρχαϊκής εποχής στο βορειο Αιγαιο και την περιφερεια του (700–480 π.χ.) / Archaic Pottery of the Northern Aegean and Its Periphery (700–480 BC)*. Thessaloniki.

Todd, S. C. (1993) *The Shape of Athenian Law*. Oxford.

Torrey, C. C. (1949) "The exiled God of Sarepta," *Berytus* 9, 45–9.

Tran Tam Tinh, V. (1972) *Le culte des divinités orientales en Campanie*. Leiden.

Tréziny, H. (ed.) (2010) *Grecs et indigènes de la Catalogne à la Mer Noire*. Aix-en-Provence.

Triantaphyllou, S. (2001) *A Bioarchaeological Approach to Prehistoric Cemetery Populations from Central and Western Greek Macedonia*. Oxford.

Trümper, M. (2006) "Negotiating religious and ethnic identity: the case of clubhouses in late Hellenistic Delos," in *Zwischen Kult und Gesellschaft: Kosmopolitische Zentren des antiken Mittelmeerraums als Aktionsraum von Kultvereinen und Religionsgemeinschaften,* ed. I. Nielsen. Augsburg, 113–50.

Trümper, M. (2011) "Where the Non-Delians met in Delos: the meeting-places of foreign associations and ethnic communities in late Hellenistic Delos," in *Political Culture and the Greek City after the Classical Age,* ed. O. van Nijf and R. Alston. Leuven, 49–100.

Tsingarida, A. and Viviers, D. (eds.) (2013) *Pottery Markets in the Ancient Greek World (8th–1st Centuries B.C.).* Brussels.

Tuplin, C. J. (1986) "The fate of Thespiai during the Theban hegemony," *Athenaeum* 64, 321–41.

Turchin, P. and Nefedov, S. A. (2009) *Secular Cycles.* Princeton, NJ.

Tzamalis, A. R. A. (2011) "Monnaies 'thraco-macédoniennes': quelques observations sur les monnaies au centaure et à la nymphe," in Faucher, Marcellesi, and Picard 2011, 67–77.

Tzochev, Ch. (2016a) "Markets, amphora trade, and wine industry: the case of Thasos," in Harris, Lewis, and Woolmer 2016, 230–53.

Tzochev, Ch. (2016b) *Amphora Stamps from Thasos,* Athenian Agora, vol. 37. Princeton, NJ.

Usoskin, I. G., Solanki, S. K., and Kovaltsov, G. A. (2007) "Grand minima and maxima of solar activity: new observational constraints," *Astronomy & Astrophysics* 471, 301–9.

Vacek, A. (2012) "Greek and related pottery from Al Mina: a case study of production, consumption and distribution of greek pottery in the eastern Mediterranean from the 9th to the end of the 7th century BC." Unpublished DPhil thesis, University of Oxford.

Vachtina, M. Ju. (2007) "Greek archaic orientalizing pottery from the barbarian sites of the forest-steppe zone of the northern Black Sea coastal region," in Gabrielsen and Lund 2007, 23–37.

Valdes Guia, M. (2019) "War in archaic Athens: *polis,* elites and military power," *Historia* 68, 126–49.

Valeva, J., Nankov, E., and Graninger, D. (eds.) (2015) *A Companion to Ancient Thrace.* Malden, MA.

Van Alfen, P. G. (2005) "Problems in ancient imitative and counterfeit coinage," in Archibald, Davies, and Gabrielsen 2005, 322–54.

Van Alfen, P. G. (ed.) (2006) *Agoranomia: Studies in Money and Exchange Presented to John H. Kroll.* New York.

Van Alfen, P. G. (2012) "Xenophon *Poroi* 3.2 and Athenian 'owls' in Aegean–Near Eastern long distance trade," in *I ritrovamenti monetali e i processi storico-economici nel mondo antico,* ed. M. Asolati and G. Gorini. Padua, 11–32.

Van Alfen, P. G. (2016) "Aegean-Levantine trade, 600–300 BCE: commodities, consumers, and the problem of autarkeia," in Harris, Lewis, and Woolmer 2016, 277–98.

Van Alfen, P. G. (2018a) "Muddle wrestling: grappling for conceptual clarity in archaic Greek money," in Canevaro, Erskine, Gray, and Ober 2018, 485–511.

Van Alfen, P. G. (2018b) "The destruction and (re)creation of monetary zones in the wake of Alexander the Great," in *Alexander the Great: A Linked Open World,* ed. S. Glenn, F. Duyrat, and A. Meadows. Bordeaux, 181–94.

Van Alfen, P. G. (2020) "The role of 'the state' and early electrum coinage," in van Alfen and Wartenberg 2020, 547–67.

Van Alfen, P. G. and Wartenberg, U. (eds.) (2020) *White Gold: Studies in Early Electrum Coinage*. New York and Jerusalem.

Van Andringa, W. (2003) "Cités et communautés d'expatriés installées dans l'empire romain: le cas des *cives Romani consistentes*," in *Les communautés religieuses dans le monde gréco-romain: Essais de définition*, ed. N. Belayche and S. C. Mimouni. Turnhout, 49–60.

Van Beek, B. (2017) *The Archive of the Architektones Kleon and Theodoros (P. Petrie Kleon)*. Leuven.

Van de Moortel, A. and Langdon, M. K. (2017) "Archaic ship graffiti from southern Attica, Greece: typology and preliminary contextual analysis," *The International Journal of Nautical Archaeology* 46, 382–405.

Van de Moortel, A. and Zachou, E. (2011) "The Bronze Age–Iron Age transition at Mitrou in East Lokris: evidence for continuity and discontinuity," in Mazarakis Ainian 2011, 331–47.

Van der Horst, P. W. (2014) "Judaism in Asia Minor," in P. W. van der Horst, *Studies in Ancient Judaism and Early Christianity*. Leiden, 143–60.

Van der Spek, R. J. (1987) "The Babylonian city," in Kuhrt and Sherwin-White 1987, 57–74.

Van der Spek, R. J. (2000) "The Seleucid state and economy," in *Production and Public Powers in Classical Antiquity*, ed. E. Lo Cascio and D. W. Rathbone. Cambridge, 27–36.

Van der Spek, R. J. (2007) "The Hellenistic Near East," in Scheidel, Morris, and Saller 2007, 409–33.

Van der Spek, R. J. and van Leeuwen, B. (2014) "Quantifying the integration of the Babylonian economy in the Mediterranean world using a new corpus of price data, 400–50 BC," in de Callataÿ 2014, 79–101.

Van der Spek, R. J., van Leeuwen, B., and van Zanden, J. L. (eds.) (2015) *A History of Market Performance: From Babylonia to the Modern World*. London.

Van Driel, G. (2002) *Elusive Silver: In Search of a Role for a Market in an Agrarian Environment: Aspects of Mesopotamia's Society*. Istanbul.

Van Groningen, B. A. (1953) *In the Grip of the Past: Essay on an Aspect of Greek Thought*. Leiden.

Van Liefferinge, K. et al. (2013) "Reconsidering the role of Thorikos within the Laurion silver mining area (Attica, Greece) through hydrological analyses," *Journal of Archaeological Science* 41, 272–84.

Van Nijf, O. (1997) *The Civic World of Professional Associations in the Roman East*. Amsterdam.

Van Wees, H. (1995) "Princes at dinner: social event and social structure in Homer," in *Homeric Questions: Proceedings of a Colloquium Organised by the Netherlands Institute at Athens, Athens 1993*, ed. J.-P. Crielaard. Amsterdam, 147–82.

Van Wees, H. (1999) "The mafia of early Greece: violent exploitation in the seventh and sixth centuries BC," in *Organised Crime in Antiquity*, ed. K. Hopwood. London, 1–51.

Van Wees, H. (2000) "Megara's mafiosi: timocracy and violence in Theognis," in *Alternatives to Athens: Varieties of Political Organization and Community in Ancient Greece*, ed. R. Brock and S. Hodkinson. Oxford, 52–67.

Van Wees, H. (2002) "Greed, generosity and gift-exchange in early Greece and the western Pacific," in *After the Past: Essays in Ancient History in Honour of H. W. Pleket*, ed. W. Jongman and M. Kleijwegt. Leiden, 341–78.

Van Wees, H. (2006) "Mass and elite in Solon's Athens: the property classes revisited," in *Solon of Athens*, ed. J. H. Blok and A. Lardinois. Leiden, 351–89.

Van Wees, H. (2009) "The economy," in Raaflaub and van Wees 2009, 444–67.

Van Wees, H. (2013) *Ships and Silver, Taxes and Tribute: A Fiscal History of Archaic Athens*. London.

Van Wees, H. (2017a) "The Lelantine War, c. 700 or c. 540 BC," in *The Encyclopedia of Ancient Battles*, ed. M. Whitby and H. Sidebottom. Malden, MA, 153–6.

Van Wees, H. (2017b) "Early Greek wars, 750–450 BC," in *The Encyclopedia of Ancient Battles*, ed. M. Whitby and H. Sidebottom. Malden, MA, 163–98.

Van Wees, H. (2020) "Heroic benefactors? The limits of generosity in Homer," in *Benefactors and the Polis*, ed. M. Domingo Gygax and A. Zuiderhoek. Cambridge, 15–43.

Van Wees, H. (2021) "The first Greek soldiers in Egypt. Myths and realities," in *Brill's Companion to Greek Land Warfare beyond the Phalanx*, ed. R. Konijnendijk, C. Kucewicz, and M. Lloyd. Leiden and New York, 293–344.

Vandorpe, K. (2013) "A happiness index for antiquity? Hellenistic Egypt as a case-study," in *Egitto dai Faraoni agli Arabi: Atti del Convegno Egitto: Amministrazione, economia, società, cultura dai Faraoni agli Arabi*, ed. S. Bussi. Pisa, 91–104.

Vandorpe, K. (2015) "Selling private real estate in a new monarchical setting: sale and community in Hellenistic Egypt," in *Sale and Community Documents from the Ancient World: Individuals' Autonomy and State Interference in the Ancient World*, ed. E. Jakab. Trieste, 99–115.

Vecchi, I. (2013) *Italian Cast Coinage: A Descriptive Catalogue of the Cast Bronze Coinage and Its Struck Counterparts in Ancient Italy from the 7th to 3rd Centuries BC*. London.

Véïsse, A.-E. (2004) *Les "révoltes Égyptiennes": recherches sur les troubles intérieurs en Égypte du règne de Ptolémée III Évergète à la conquête romaine*. Leuven.

Venit, M. S. (1988) "The Caputi Hydria and working women in classical Athens," *Classical World* 81, 265–72.

Verboven, K. (2015) "The knights who say NIE. Can Neo-Institutional Economics live up to its expectations in ancient history research?," in *Structure and Performance in the Roman Economy: Models, Methods and Case Studies*, ed. P. Erdkamp and K. Verboven. Brussels, 33–58.

Verdan, S. (2013) *Le sanctuaire d'Apollon Daphnéphoros à l'époque géométrique*. Gollion.

Vernant, J.-P. (1989) "At man's table: Hesiod's foundation myth of sacrifice," in *The Cuisine of Sacrifice among the Greeks*, ed. M. Detienne and J.-P. Vernant. Chicago, 21–86.

Vernant, J.-P. (2006a) "Prometheus and the technological function," in J.-P. Vernant, *Myth and Thought Among the Greeks*. New York, 263–74.

Vernant, J.-P. (2006b) "Work and nature in ancient Greece," in J.-P. Vernant, *Myth and Thought Among the Greeks*. New York, 275–92.

Vetters, M. (2011) "A clay ball with a Cypro-Minoan inscription from Tiryns," *Archäologischer Anzeiger* 2011.2, 1–49.

Veyne, P. (1976) *Le pain et le cirque: Sociologie historique d'un pluralisme politique*. Paris.

Vial, C. (1984) *Délos Indépendante: Étude d'une communauté civique et de ses institutions*. Paris.

Vieira, L. E. A., Solanki, S. K., Krovova, N. A., and Usoskin, I. (2011) "Evolution of the solar irradiance during the Holocene," *Astronomy & Astrophysics* 531, A6. DOI: 10.1051/0004-6361/201015843.

Villing, A. (2017) "Greece and Egypt: reconsidering early contact and exchange," in *Regional Stories: Towards a New Perception of the Early Greek World*, ed. A. Mazarakis-Ainian, A. Alexandridou, and X. Charalambidou. Volos, 563–96.

Vita-Finzi, C. (1969) *The Mediterranean Valleys: Geological Changes in Historical Times.* Cambridge.

Viviers, D. (2011) "Une cité crétoise à l'épreuve d'une garnison lagide: l'exemple d'Itanos," in *Pratiques et identités culturelles des armées hellénistiques du monde méditerranéen*, ed. J.-C. Couvenhes, S. Crouzet, and S. Péré-Noguès. Bordeaux, 35–64.

Vlassopoulos, K. (2013) *Greeks and Barbarians.* Cambridge.

Von Reden, S. (2003) *Exchange in Ancient Greece.* 2nd ed. London.

Von Reden, S. (2007a) "Classical Greece: consumption," in Scheidel, Morris, and Saller 2007, 385–406.

Von Reden, S. (2007b) *Money in Ptolemaic Egypt: From the Macedonian Conquest to the End of the Third Century* BC. Cambridge.

Von Reden, S. (2007c) "Wirtschaftliches Wachstum und institutioneller Wandel," in *Kulturgeschichte des Hellenismus: Von Alexander dem Großen bis Kleopatra*, ed. G. Weber. Stuttgart, 177–201.

Von Reden, S. (2010) *Money in Classical Antiquity.* Cambridge.

Von Reden, S. (2011) "Demand creation, consumption and power in Ptolemaic Egypt," in Archibald, Davies, and Gabrielsen 2011, 421–40.

Von Reden, S. (2012) "The monetary economy in the Greek world," in *Thesaurus Cultus et Rituum Antiquorum*, vol. VIII, ed. A. Hermary. Los Angeles, 111–27.

Von Reden, S. (2014) "Labour contracts," in *Law and Society in Ptolemaic, Roman and Byzantine Egypt*, ed. J. G. Manning and U. Yiftach. Cambridge, 402–10.

Von Reden, S. (2015) *Antike Wirtschaft: Enzyklopädie der griechisch-römischen Antike.* Munich.

Von Reden, S. (ed.) (2019a) *Handbook of Ancient Afro-Eurasian Economies. Vol. 1: Contexts.* Berlin.

Von Reden, S. (2019b) "Interstate trade," in *The Oxford Handbook of Demosthenes*, ed. G. Martin. Oxford, 209–20.

Von Reden, S. (2019c) "The Hellenistic empires," in von Reden 2019a, 15–52.

Von Reden, S. (2019d) "Trade," in *A Cultural History of Western Empires*, ed. C. F. Noreña. London, 63–86.

Von Reden, S. and Speidel, M. (2019) "Economy, frontiers, and the Silk Road in western historiographies of Graeco-Roman antiquity," in von Reden 2019a, 693–728.

Vondeling, J. (1961) *Eranos.* Groningen.

Voutsaki, S. (2001) "Economic control, power and prestige in the Mycenaean world: the archaeological evidence," in Voutsaki and Killen 2001, 195–213.

Voutsaki, S. and Killen, J. T. (eds.) (2001) *Economy and Politics in the Mycenaean Palace States.* Cambridge.

Wachsmuth, D. (1967) *Untersuchung zu den Antiken Sakralhandlungen bei Seereisen.* Berlin.

Waerzeggers, C. and Seire, M. (eds.) (2018) *Xerxes and Babylonia: The Cuneiform Evidence.* Leuven.

Wagstaff, J. M. (1981) "Buried assumptions: some problems in the interpretation of the 'Younger Fill' raised by recent data from Greece," *Journal of Archaeological Science* 8, 247–64.

Wallace, R. B. (1987) "The origin of electrum coinage," *American Journal of Archaeology* 91.3, 385–97.

Wallace, S. (2005) "Last chance to see? Karfi (Crete) in the twenty-first century: presentation of new architectural data and their analysis in the current context of research," *Annual of the British School at Athens* 100, 215–74.

Wallace, S. (2010) *Ancient Crete: From Successful Collapse to Democracy's Alternatives, Twelfth to Fifth Centuries* BC. Cambridge.

Wallinga, H. (2005) *Xerxes' Greek Adventure: The Naval Perspective.* Leiden.

Walser, A. V. (2008) *Bauern und Zinsnehmer: Politik, Recht und Wirtschaft im frühhellenistischen Ephesos.* Munich.

Walser, A. V. (2009) "Sympolitien und Siedlungsentwicklung," in *Stadtbilder im Hellenismus,* ed. A. Matthaei and M. Zimmermann. Berlin, 135–55.

Walser, A. V. (2015) "The finances of the cities of Asia Minor," *Topoi* 20.2, 411–33.

Walter, E. (ed.) (1995) *Die athenische Demokratie im 4. Jahrhundert v. Chr.: Vollendung oder Verfall einer Verfassungsform?* Stuttgart.

Wartenberg, U. (2016) "Die Geburt der Münze: Elektron als Geldmittel: Neue Wege der Forschung," *Mitteilungen der Österreichischen Numismatischen Gesellschaft* 56.1, 30–49.

Wartenberg, U. and Amandry, M. (eds.) (2015) *ΚΑΙΡΟΣ: Contributions to Numismatics in Honor of Basil Demetriadi.* New York.

Weaverdyck, E. (2019) "Material evidence," in von Reden 2019a, 311–42.

Weber, G. (1997) "Interaktion, Repräsentation und Herrschaft: Der Königshof im Hellenismus," in *Zwischen "Haus" und "Staat": Antike Höfe im Vergleich,* ed. A. Winterling. Munich, 27–71.

Weber, M. [1920] (2003) *The Protestant Ethic and The Spirit of Capitalism and Economy and Society.* New York.

Weber, M. [1922] (1978) *Economy and Society: An Outline of Interpretive Sociology,* ed. G. Roth and C. Whittich. Berkley, CA.

Weiberg, E. (2012) "'What can resilience theory do for (Aegean) archaeology?,'" in *Matters of Scale: Processes and Courses of Events in the Past and the Present,* ed. N. M. Burström and F. Fahlander. Stockholm, 147–66.

Weiberg, E. et al. (2019) "Long-term trends of land use and demography in Greece: a comparative study," *The Holocene* 29, 742–60.

Weiberg, E., et. al. (2016) "The socio-environmental history of the Peloponnese during the Holocene: towards an integrated understanding of the past," *Quaternary Science Reviews* 136, 40–65.

Weingast, B. R. (1995) "The economic role of political institutions: market-preserving federalism and economic development," *Journal of Law, Economics and Organization* 11, 1–31.

Weingast, B. R. (1997) "The political foundations of democracy and the rule of law," *American Political Science Review* 91, 245–63.

Weingast, B. R. (2005) "The performance and stability of federalism: an institutional perspective," in Ménard and Shirley 2005a, 149–72.

Weiskopf, M. (1987) "Asia Minor," in *Encyclopaedia Iranica,* vol. 2.7, ed. E. Yarshater. London, 757–64.

Wells, B. (ed.) (1992) *Agriculture in Ancient Greece.* Stockholm.

Wells, H. B. (1978) "The arrow-money of Thrace and southern Russia: a review and discussion of eastern European and Soviet writing," *Journal of the Society of Ancient Numismatics* 9, 6–9, 12, 24–6, 31.

White, K. D. (1984) *Greek and Roman Technology.* Ithaca, NY.

White, S. (2011) *The Climate of Rebellion in the Early Modern Ottoman Empire.* New York.

White, S. (2014) "The real Little Ice Age," *Journal of Interdisciplinary History* 44, 327–52.

Whitehead, D. (1984) "Immigrant communities in the classical polis: some principles for a synoptic treatment," *L'Antiquité classique* 53, 47–59.

Whitelaw, T. (2001) "Reading between the tablets: assesing Mycenaean palatial involvement in ceramic production and consumption," in Voutsaki and Killen 2001, 51–79.

Whittaker, C. R. (ed.) (1988) *Pastoral Economies of the Ancient World.* Cambridge.

Wiemer, H.-U. (2002) *Krieg, Handel und Piraterie: Untersuchungen zur Geschichte des hellenistischen Rhodos.* Berlin.

Wiesehöfer, J. (1999) "Kontinuität oder Zäsur? Babylon unter den Achaimeniden," in *Babylon: Focus Mesopotamischer Geschichte, Wiege früher Gelehrsamkeit, Mythos in der Moderne.* Saarbrücken, 167–88.

Wiesehöfer, J. (2017) "Antiochos III. und die Persis," in *Antiochos III et l'Orient: Journées d'études franco-allemandes, Nancy, 6–8 juin 2016,* ed. C. Feyel and L. Graslin-Thomé. Nancy, 245–54. .

Wilkins, J. (2000) *The Boastful Chef: The Discourse of Food in Ancient Greek Comedy.* Oxford.

Wilkins, J. and Hill, S. [1994] (2011) *Archestratus: The Life of Luxury.* Totnes.

Wilkins, J. and Hill, S. (2006) *Food in the Ancient World.* Oxford.

Wilkins, J. and Nadeau, R. (eds.) (2015) *A Companion to Food in the Ancient World.* Chichester.

Wilkins, J., Harvey, D., and Dobson, M. (eds.) (1995) *Food in Antiquity.* Exeter.

Wilkinson, T. J. (2004) *On the Margin of the Euphrates: Settlement and Land Use at Tell es-Sweyhat and in the Upper Lake Assad Area, Syria.* Chicago.

Will, E. (1985) "Pour une 'anthropologie coloniale' du monde hellénistique," in *The Craft of the Ancient Historian: Essays in Honor of Chester G. Starr,* ed. J. W. Eadie and J. Ober. Lanham, MD, 273–301.

Williams, D. (1983) "Aegina, Aphaia-Tempel: the pottery from Chios," *Archäologischer Anzeiger* 1983, 155–86.

Williamson, J. (2000) "What should the World Bank think about the Washington Consensus?," *World Bank Research Observer* 15, 251–64.

Williamson, O. (1975) *Markets and Hierarchies: The Anti-Trust Implications.* New York.

Williamson, O. (2005) "Transaction costs economics," in Ménard and Shirley 2005a, 41–67.

Wilson, A. (2011) "Developments in Mediterranean shipping and maritime trade from the Hellenistic period to AD 1000," in *Maritime Archaeology and Ancient Trade in the Mediterranean,* ed. D. Robinson and A. Wilson. Oxford, 33–59.

Wood, E. M. (1988) *Peasant-Citizen and Slave: The Foundations of Athenian Democracy.* London.

Woolmer, M. (2016) "Forging links between regions: trade policy in classical Athens," in Harris, Lewis, and Woolmer 2016, 66–89.

Wörrle, M. (1988) *Stadt und Fest im kaiserzeitlichen Kleinasien.* Munich.

Wörrle, M. (2003) "Inschriften von Herakleia am Latmos 3: Der Synoikismos der Latmioi mit den Pidaseis," *Chiron* 33, 121–44.

Wrenhaven, K. L. (2009) "The identity of the 'wool-workers' in the Attic manumissions," *Hesperia* 78, 367–86.

Wyns, V. (2016) "The state ideology of the Ptolemies: origins and influences," *Chronique d'Egypte* 92, 137–74.

Xoplaki, E. et al. (2016) "The medieval climate anomaly and Byzantium: a review of the evidence on climatic fluctuations, economic performance and societal change," *Quaternary Science Reviews* 136, 229–52.

Xoplaki, E. et al. (2018) "Modelling climate and societal resilience in the Eastern Mediterranean in the last millennium," *Human Ecology* 46, 363–79.

Yalçın, Ü, Özbal, H., and Paşamehmetoğlu, A. G. (eds.) (2008) *Ancient Mining in Turkey and the Eastern Mediterranean.* Ankara.

Yardeni, A. (1994) "Maritime trade and royal accountancy in an erased customs account from 475 B.C.E. on the Ahiqar Scroll from Elephantine," *Bulletin of the American School of Oriental Research* 293, 67–78.

Yona, S. (2015) "What about Hermes? A reconsideration of the myth of Prometheus in Plato's *Protagoras*," *Classical World* 108, 359–83.

Young, J. H. (1956) "Studies in south Attica: country estates at Sounion," *Hesperia* 25, 122–46.

Young, R. S. (1951) "An industrial district of ancient Athens," *Hesperia* 20, 135–288.

Youni, M. S. (2011) "L'imprécation et la loi: châtiment divine et sanctions pénales dans la *polis* grecque," in *Vertiges du droit: Mélanges franco-héllénique à la mémoire de Jacques Phytilis*, ed. A. Helmis, N. Kálnoky, and S. Kerneis. Paris, 393–404.

Yoyotte, J. (1991–2) "Naucratis, ville égyptienne," *Annuaire du Collège de France* 92, 634–44.

Yoyotte, J. (1993–4) "Les contacts entre Égyptiens et Grecs (VIIe–IIe siècles avant J.-C.): Naucratis, ville égyptienne (1992–1993. 1993–1994)," *Annuaire du Collège de France* 94, 679–92.

Yoyotte, J. (1994–5) "Les contacts entre Égyptiens et Grecs," *Annuaire du Collège de France* 95, 669–82.

Yue, R. P. H. and Lee, H. F. (2018a) "Climate change and plague history in Europe," *Science China Earth Sciences* 61, 163–77.

Yue, R. P. H. and Lee, H. F. (2018b) "Pre-industrial plague transmission is mediated by the synergistic effect of temperature and aridity index," *BMC Infectious Diseases* 18, 134.

Zahrnt, M. (2015) "The Chalkidike and the Chalkidians," in Beck and Funke 2015, 341–57.

Zarmakoupi, M. (2015a) "Hellenistic & Roman Delos: the city & its *emporion*," *Archaeological Reports* 61, 115–32.

Zarmakoupi, M. (2015b) "Les maisons des négociants italiens à Délos: structuration de l'espace domestique dans une societé en mouvement," *Cahiers «Mondes Anciens»* 7. DOI: https://doi.org/10.4000/mondesanciens.1588.

Zarmakoupi, M. (2018) "Délos, entrepôt méditerranéen: le stockage dans les maisons," in Chankowski, Lafon, and Virlouvet 2018, 195–207.

Zelnick-Abramovitz, R. (2005) *Not Wholly Free: The Concept of Manumission and the Status of Manumitted Slaves in the Ancient Greek World.* Leiden.

Zurbach, J. (2017) *Les hommes, la terre et la dette en Grèce, c. 1400–c. 500 a.C.* Bordeaux.

INDEX

Achaea, 265, 303, 367–8, 370–1
Achaemenid empire, 56, 58, 63,
    139–40, 276
administration, 142–4, 289
  fiscal, 271–4
  of temples, 147–8
    agora, 117, 227–8, 230, 240
    agoranomos, 259
    agriculture, Chapter 13, 51, 112, 244
    extensive, 50, 191–3
    fallow, 191–3
    farm size, 194–6
    fertility, 50, 142
    in Asia Minor, 81–6
    innovation, 67–8
    intensive, 50, 145, 193
    productivity, 378
    subsistence, 48, 186, 201
    agro-towns, 223–5
    Alexander the Great, 56, 60, 90, 91,
        141, 165, 268
    Alexandria, 63, 72
    Andania, 258–9
    animal husbandry, 36, 85, 107,
        192–3, 200–1
    Aristotle, 46, 204, 217, 268
    associations, 320–7
    asylia, 143, 287, 294
    Athens
    city of, 106, 118, 164–7
    plague of, 162, 387
  auction, 230, 257, 276

Babylonia, Chapter 10, 64, 116
banking, 69, 132, 136, 246–8, 321
Bintliff, John, 335
bioarchaeology, 22

Boeck, August, 3
Boeotia, 52, 68, 172, 177, 365, 366–7,
    370–1
Bresson, Alain, 2, 17
Byzantium, Chapter 7, 54, 59, 87

cabotage, 26, 57, 60, 97, 100
Callatis, 96
catapult, 397–400
ceramics, 25, 57, 99, 120, 207, 211, 323
Chalcidice, 52, 56, 101, 121, 364–5, 369
charcoal, 113–14, 259
Chios, 107, 119, 164, 199, 219, 284–5
cistophoroi, 90
city-state, 2, 80, 197, 221, 250, 418–19
class, 34–5, 176–83, 200, 212–14
    middling class/farmers, 6, 34, 46–8,
        194–5, 199, 354
cleruchs, 62, 65, 68, 127, 129
climate, 126–7, 159–60, 186–7
    climate change, 16, 26, 163, 169, 373,
        384, 385
    climate proxy data, 388–90
    in Asia Minor, 77
    in the classical period, 106
    interannual variation, 376, 378
    Late Antique Little Ice Age, 382–4
    precipitation, 82, 106, 186, 196, 373–8;
    see also Thessaly; Thrace
Coase, Ronald, 350
coinage, 42, 46, 52–7, 69–71, 229,
    238–40, 309
    federal, 371
    in Asia Minor, 91
    in Babylonia, 143–4
    in northern Greece and the Black
        Sea, 105

in the Ptolemaic empire, Chapter 9,
132–3
mints, 55–6, 69, 90, 135, 143, 229, 307,
366, 371
colonization, 80–1, 99, 145, 160, 161,
284; *see also* migration; settlement
commensality, 176–80
comparative methodology, 170
construction, 51–2, 116, 128, 210, 231,
257–8, 290
contracts, 63, 70, 101–3, 134, 253, 257,
283, 304; *see also* law
copper, 24, 41, 239
crafts, Chapter 14, 40, 216
craftsmen, Chapter 14, 88, 111, 115
credible commitment, 275, 351
credit, Chapter 16, 57, 60, 243–6, 292,
366
interest rates, 244–5

decree, 66, 126, 132, 285–6, 294–5,
317–20
Standards Decree, 307
Delos, 64, 73, 114, 117–19, 121–2, 219,
257, 287, 294, 317
demand, 3, 47–52, 67–70, 166, 231, 290,
322–5
democracy, 2, 118, 167, 241, 354, 361,
406, 415, 417, 419
demography, Chapter 11, 72, 335–6; *see
also* population
Demosthenes, 96, 118, 190, 203, 207, 215,
241, 256
dikai emporikai, 256
dikasterion, 258, 259, 262; *See also* law court
Diodorus, 289, 376, 396–8
Dodds, Eric R., 394

economy
"bad year" economics, 384
economic space, 65, 78, 231, 320
geoeconomics, 344–6
household, 19–23, 27
impact of technology on, 403
palace, 15
political, 43, 130–4
predatory, 30–5
temple, 242, 245, 249, 288–93

Edelstein, Ludwig, 394
egalitarianism, 353, 411–13, 415
Egypt, Chapter 5, Chapter 9, 222, 234,
239–40, 245–8, 253–4, 273–4,
284–7, 322–4
elites, 33–4, 37, 38–9, 40, 48, 73,
212–13
emporion, 117, 227, 275, 286, 287
entitlements, 261, 354–5, 357
environment, Chapter 25, 82, 160, 172,
186–7, 369
pollution, 114
eponion, 230
eranos, 37, 245, 246
ethics, 402
euergetism, 66–7, 72, 181, 182, 241,
246, 248

fairs, 228, 293–4
feasting, 20, 36–7, 181
federalism, Chapter 24, 66, 271, 417, 419;
see also koinon
fertility, 155, 158–9
finance, 237, 246, 249, 264, 271, 272
Finley, Moses, 1–3, 10, 202, 334, 344,
393–5
fiscal interest model, 361
fishing, 87–8, 114, 206
foreigners in the polis, 108, 213–14,
284, 415
as association members, 326, 327
legal status of, 226, 231, 256, 258,
261–2, 417
religion, 286
taxation, 356
freedmen, 203, 212, 214, 217, 219,
232, 290

Galen, 173–4, 176, 184
gender, 179, 185, 200
women, 121, 159, 169, 174, 190,
214–17, 396, 415
gifts, 25, 36–7, 40, 135, 223,
266
grain, 35, 59, 107–9, 322
Granovetter, Mark, 314
growth, economic, definition of,
352–4

harbors, 118, 144, 276–7, 324, 337, 364, 365
health, 22, 114, 173–4, 405–6
helots, 34, 199, 200, 271
hemp, 51
Herodotus, 91, 96, 142, 180, 266–7, 271, 284–6, 414
Hesiod, 16, 30–1, 35–6, 39–41, 45, 172, 187, 189–91, 251, 354
Hippocrates, 173–4, 396
Homer, 16, 31, 36–8, 45, 187, 215, 242
honey, 40, 45, 107
Hopkins, Keith, 11

inequality, Chapter 27, 29, 44, 72, 166–7
information asymmetry, 228
innovation, 125, 142–4, 249, 277, 336, 343–4, 393
    military, 399
institutional change, 65–71, 73, 336, 362, 413, 417–19
iron, 25, 41, 58, 86, 211

jewelry, 23, 25, 58, 211
Justinian, 383, 385

Knappet, Carl, 308
koinon, 55, 225, 314–15
Kron, Geoffrey, 73
kurtaš, 139, 146

labor, 44, 242–3, 257, 290, 341–3, 401
    division of labor, 47, 88, 224, 232–3, 336
Laurium, see mining
law, 222–3; see also contracts
    "Revenue Laws" papyrus, 132
    bebaiosis (legal warranty), 253
    dispute resolution, Chapter 17
    law codes, 163–4
    law courts, 218, 222, 246, 252, 262, 277, 353
    property, 225–7
Lewis, David M., 164
Linear B, 15, 237

Lydia, 32, 39, 41, 91, 145, 237, 238
Lykia, 365

magistrates, 130, 226–8, 254–6, 257–63, 268, 288, 300, 356
    control of, 260
Manning, Joseph, 126, 356
marble, 87, 97, 112, 210
Marx, Karl, 270, 332
medicine, 58, 173, 174, 176, 233, 396
Methone, 40, 101, 104
metics, 111, 167, 203, 214, 219, 256, 261, 270, 291
migration, 72, 79, 124, 127, 155, 158, 316, 332, 354; see also colonization and settlement
    in the classical period, 165
    mobility, 62, 149, 157, 327, 361, 399
    mobility in the archaic period, 160–1
    mobility in the Hellenistic period, 168–9
Milanovic, Branko, 409
Millet, Paul, 334
mining, 54, 86, 113, 209–10
    Laurium mines, 52, 112–14, 117, 119–20, 209, 234
money, Chapter 16, 229, 240–3
    monetization, 52–7, 69–71, 132–3, 143–4, 241, 337
    wages, 116, 136–7, 242, 337, 341–2
mortality, 158–9, 161, 165, 174
Murašu archive, 140
myth, 173, 295, 393, 396

natron, 58
Naucratis, 41–2, 275, 284–6
nautodikai, 256
network analysis, 299–300
network mobility, 23–6
New Institutional Economics, Chapter 23, 30, 314
North, Douglass, 347–50, 358
Nussbaum, Martha, 401
nutrition, 87, 172–5, 176, 406
    in the classical period, 410

oath, 228, 283
Ober, Josiah, 1–3, 224

occupations, 209–12
oikonomia, 2, 331
oikos, 2, 219; See also economy, household
olive oil, 25, 40, 44, 57, 107, 109–10, 190
Olynthus, 73, 178, 212, 224–5, 354, 363, 410

perfume, 25, 40
Philip II of Macedon, 56, 118, 165
Philo of Byzantium, 397–8
plague, 385–7
Plato, 45, 177, 180, 207, 216–17, 229, 392, 396, 400, 403
Plutarch, 116, 118, 142, 181
population
    decline of, 16–19, 155
    estimation of, 17
    growth of, 49–50, 71, 155, 169, 362, 405
    in the Hellenistic period, 167–70
pottery, 16, 23, 39, 42, 44, 47, 99, 120, 182, 204, 208, 211
Préaux, Claire, 125
precious metals, 38, 53, 58, 132, 211, 237
price control, 228–31
property, 272–4, 366–8
property rights, 222, 225–7, 355–7, 369
proxenia, 261, 321
proxy data, 155–6
Ptolemy I, 70
Ptolemy II, 61, 63, 66, 68, 133, 135, 290
Ptolemy III, 125, 128, 133
Ptolemy IV, 65, 125, 133, 273

quantification, 154, 163–4, 166, 170, 348

Rhodes, 103, 107, 115, 118, 284, 324, 326
Rome, city of, 2, 64
Rostovtzeff, Michael, 100, 125
royal land, 82–3

sacrifice, 283
    in Persia, 181
    private, 31, 172, 177, 282
    public, 37, 148, 177, 223, 272, 289, 292

salt, 87, 269
seafarers, 256, 282
Seleucus I, 64, 141, 143, 144
Seleucus II, 147
Seleucus IV, 325
settlement, 5, 31, 54, 64, 124, 149, 160, 169, 192, 197–8, 335; see also colonization and migration
shipbuilding, 51–2, 87, 113, 212
shortage, 51, 54, 59, 110, 175, 235, 239, 340
slavery, 32–3, 50, 120, 135, 164, 199, 217–19, 229–30, 362
Smith, Adam, 2, 3, 332–3
Socrates, 177, 204, 213
Solon, 39, 44, 237, 251–2, 355
Sparta, 378, 415
    economy, 271–2
    expansion, 33, 43
    food consumption in, 175
    horse-breeding, 39, 200
    population of, 165
    resistance to innovation, 48, 232, 418
    specialization, 2, 47, 115, 196, 207, 217, 336
stelai, Attic, 188, 198, 203, 218
storage, 21, 122, 188, 196–7, 224, 317, 323–4, 384
Strabo, 219
sylan, 261–2
symposium, 178–80, 182, 216
Syria, 31, 39, 65, 145, 270, 316, 380

taxation, Chapter 18, 43, 66, 118–19, 241
    agora, 230
    customs duties, 58, 234, 324
    in Asia Minor, 92
    in the Ptolemaic empire, 130–2
    tithe, 131, 143, 147, 242, 272, 293
technology, Chapter 26, 162, 164, 172, 313, 336
    in the Iron Age, 24
    innovation, 50, 168, 334, 380
    military, 65
temples, 177, 222, 227, 242
    administration of, 287–93

temples (cont.)
  in Babylonia, 147–8
textiles, 23, 135, 208, 212
Thasos, 103, 259–60, 271
Thebes, 363–4, 370
Thessaly, 18, 20, 24, 34, 200, 268, 363–5
  climate of, 186
  resistance to innovation, 48
Thrace, 39, 58, 65, 96, 98, 104, 131,
    219, 240
  climate of, 186
Thucydides, 43, 65, 94, 96, 241, 417
timber, 49, 51, 57–8, 87, 97, 114, 126,
    211, 259
tin, 24, 58
tithe, 47
trade, 57–9, 207, 237, 275–6
  in Asia Minor, 88–9
  in Athens and the Aegean, 122
  in Babylonia, 146–7
  in the Ptolemaic empire, 135–6
  maritime, 41, 57–8, 95–8, 284,
    322–4
transaction costs, 277, 320, 337, 352, 355,
    362, 371, 412–17
  theory of, 350
transaction costs,
treaties, interstate, 261–2

tribute, 2, 11, 58, 91, 131, 221–3, 265–70,
    276–7, 351
trust, 9, 228, 244, 255, 261, 294, 314, 320,
    323, 324, 326

uncertainty, 349–50
urbanization, 64, 71, 80–1, 88, 144, 160–2,
    168, 405

war, 33, 43–4, 46, 65–7, 93, 168–9,
    241
  in Babylonia, 141
  in the Ptolemaic empire, 127–8
  spoils of, 31–2
wages, see money, wages
wealth distribution, 406–11
Weber, Max, 281, 313
Weiberg, Erica, 28
wine, 25, 35, 39, 45, 57–8, 85, 107, 110,
    178–9, 190, 197
women, see gender
wood, see timber
wool, 44, 58, 85–6, 107, 212, 259
workshops, 23, 24, 208–9

Xenophon, 82, 96, 114, 180, 187, 193,
    204, 213, 277, 336, 370
  Oeconomicus, 106, 195, 203

CAMBRIDGE COMPANIONS TO THE ANCIENT WORLD

Other Titles in the Series

The Cambridge Companion to the Age of Justinian
Edited by Michael Maas

The Cambridge Companion to Ancient Greek Law
Edited by Michael Gagarin and David Cohen

The Cambridge Companion to the Age of Augustus
Edited by Karl Galinsky

The Cambridge Companion to the Hellenistic World
Edited by Glenn R. Bugh

The Cambridge Companion to the Age of Pericles
Edited by Loren J. Samons II

The Cambridge Companion to Archaic Greece
Edited by H. A. Shapiro

The Cambridge Companion to Ancient Greek Political Thought
Edited by Stephen Salkever

The Cambridge Companion to the Age of Constantine, Second Edition
Edited by Noel Lenski

The Cambridge Companion to the Roman Economy
Edited by Walter Scheidel

The Cambridge Companion to Ancient Rome
Edited by Paul Erdkamp

The Cambridge Companion to the Roman Republic, Second Edition
Edited by Harriet I. Flower

The Cambridge Companion to the Age of Attila
Edited by Michael Maas

The Cambridge Companion to Roman Law
Edited by David Johnston

The Cambridge Companion to the Age of Nero
Edited by Shadi Bartsch, Kirk Freudenburg, and Cedric Littlewood

The Cambridge Companion to Ancient Athens
Edited by Jenifer Neils and Dylan Rogers

The Cambridge Companion to Constantinople
Edited by Sarah Bassett

The Cambridge Companion to the Ancient Greek Economy
Edited by Sitta von Reden

CPSIA information can be obtained
at www.ICGtesting.com
Printed in the USA
LVHW052037110723
752129LV00003B/26